Canciones entre el Alma y el Esposo of Juan de la Cruz

A Hermeneutical Interpretation

David Brian Perrin

CANCIONES ENTRE EL ALMA Y EL ESPOSO OF JUAN DE LA CRUZ

A HERMENEUTICAL INTERPRETATION

DAVID BRIAN PERRIN

Catholic Scholars Press
San Francisco - London - Bethesda
1996

Library of Congress Cataloging-in-Publication Data

Perrin, David Brian, 1956-
    Canciones entre el alma y el esposo of Juan de la Cruz : a
hermeneutical interpretation / David Brian Perrin.
        p. cm.
    Includes bibliographical references and index.
    ISBN 1-57309-095-6 (alk. paper) - ISBN 1-57309-094-8 (pbk. :
alk. paper)
    1. John of the Cross, Saint, 1542-1591. Cantico espiritual.
    2. Mystical union. I. Title.
    BV5080.J7755P47   1996
    248.2'2--dc20   96-26844
                                                     CIP

Editorial Inquiries:
International Scholars Publications
7831 Woodmont Avenue, #345
Bethesda, MD 20814

To order: (800) 55-PUBLISH

DEDICATION

To my dear Grandmother

Annie F. Perrin (McGinnis)
(1904-1990)

Woman of Faith

Pouring out a thousand graces,
She passed these groves in haste;
and having looked at them,
with her image alone,
she clothed them in beauty.

Now she has entered
the sweet garden of her desire,
and she rests in delight,
laying her neck
on the gentle arms of her Beloved.

Paraphrase, *CO* 5 and *CO* 27

TABLE OF CONTENTS

viii

FORWARD I

Throughout North American society, an incredible hunger for spirituality pervades our time. More and more we find articles, books and conferences being organized around the relationship of spirituality to various individuals and groups. The medical profession, which had very often looked down upon spiritual aspects affecting health issues, now begins to recognize the important role they play in maintenance of health or healing, not necessarily curing. Some medical professionals see how important it is to develop a spirituality within their own lives -- personal and professional; for they realize that this is an essential feature of dealing holistically with those who seek their advice for treatment. Both religious and non-religious schools of higher education establish programs of academic study of spirituality and students are enrolling in these programs with a great deal of enthusiasm. Bookstores stock a variety of items dealing with spirituality, while some actually specialize in the sale of books dealing with the issue. Within the subjects found are works which present spiritualities of various stages in human life, spiritualities of couples, gay spirituality, disease and spirituality, and many other topics related to it.

What most saw as the exclusive domain of religion now comes to be seen as relevant and important in a completely non-religious context. Day by day, people discover that the goals and dreams of our consumer society simply do not answer the questions about life, suffering and death which they experience. Consequently, they turn to questions of being rather than questions of possessing. Even religion seems to have failed to present them with the answers to the questions with which they grapple day after day. Leaders from a variety of lifestyles begin to offer writings and even establish groups for people who desire more in life than they are finding. And this very often outside the context of any kind of institutional religious practice.

In such a context, it may be surprising at first sight to discover that many people in all these groups of people turn to the writings of the great sixteenth-century Spanish mystic, Saint John of the Cross. His passion for life and his depth of experience with the Absolute attract them. His songs of love between the lover and the Beloved speak of a wholeness which they desire. His narration of the "Dark Night of the Spirit" strikes a chord in the very heart of their own experience of life. To find meaning in the face of crisis is something they desire and Juan's development of the notion of impasse in the dark night of life's struggles provides a kind of hope and way of seeing which enables them not simply to tolerate adversity, but actually to live it out and thus find what they are searching for. Moreover, they find within the journey through life which he narrates a depth of beauty and enjoyment which enhances the human person and creation as a whole. Yet, reading Juan de la Cruz is not an easy task for a person so far removed from the times in which he wrote.

It is not simply a question of reading and finding an objective meaning which is involved. Rather in such a text, the reader play a key role in interacting with the text itself. And that role opens up to the reader a whole new way of being in the world. Each of us comes to a text with our own story. Who we re is a composite of who we have been. Our actions, our relationships with others and with creation constitute an intimate part of our story. It is all of this that we bring to the text for discovery and it is this which filters the meaning for us. As we meet the text we begin to discover the Mystery of our very own being -- and not just what the writer had intended. In fact to understand the text, especially in the case of writings from persons such as Juan de la Cruz and other great classical spiritual writers, we need to be open to the reality which lies beyond the verbalization. Meeting that reality through the text at hand leads us to "understand" our own lives in the here and now. Yet, most of the studies done on Juan provide us with what he meant and he understood. While all that is important, it cannot provide us in and of itself with the discovery of the transforming potential which the "reality-encountered-by-me" contains.

Professor David B. Perrin's fine study provides us with the framework of a methodology which enables us to discover in Juan de la Cruz' writings the transforming meaning for which people search. He takes the reader through the various methodologies which a variety of scholars use to delve into the meaning of Juan's monumental contribution both to the Christian mystical tradition and indeed, to positive human development. While he affirms the importance of these methodologies, he also demonstrates how they fall short of the potential to be found in those very writings they attempt to explain. What he proposes is a method which takes the others seriously, but which provides the reader with new tools to penetrate the Mystery Juan had met in his own life.

What he clearly offers is a new method of interpretation based upon Paul Ricoeur's philosophical hermeneutics. Carefully and convincingly, he brings the reader through the complexities of the Ricoeurian approach to a text and then presents one with the implications of this hermeneutical approach to reading Juan's incredibly passionate poem, the *Cántico espiritual*.

Not only does he give an excellent overview of the various methods employed until now, but in this very well researched study he provides both the scholars and the ordinary reader an approach which unlocks new levels of meaning found in Juan's text. I believe that Professor Perrin has superbly accomplished a task which will affirm the transformative potential found in Juan's work. As scholars study this hermeneutical method which Perrin explains and apply it to Juan's work and that of other mystical writers, I am convinced that we will find whole new vistas opening up for the scholar and the contemporary reader.

Professor Perrin has opened the door and we need but enter into the discoveries which await us.

Richard P. Hardy
Professor of Spirituality
Faculty of Theology
Saint Paul University
Ottawa, Canada

FORWARD II

The poem *Canciones entre el alma y el esposo* of Juan de la Cruz has long been an enormously rich source of Western spirituality. More than four centuries of debate and commentary have made it into a spiritual classic. Although usually named the *Cántico espiritual* or *Spiritual Canticle*, the original interpretative title of the love song(s) allows us to read the poem as a song of the soul, deeply engrossed by an Other, either within or without, who is wedded to the soul as a spouse. The anxious imagery of love and the tryst of lovers in all its sensuality and desire, graphic yet evocative, reveal the soul as a passionate search for and an abiding with a deeper Self who is more than the Self.

The interpretation of the *Cántico* has a long tradition and evinces the delicate depth of its spiritual world. To the historical-contextual, the literary-textual, the ascetico-theological, the thematic-symbolic, the philosophical, the psychological, and the phenomenological approaches with which the *Cántico* has been probed, David Perrin wishes to add the hermeneutical. From the various hermeneutical menues, he has found the textual hermeneutics of the French philosopher, Paul Ricoeur to be the most fruitful. With Ricoeur's heightened sense of the power and ontological depth of language he has sought to pry loose possible extensions of meanings of the *Cántico*, allowing the reader to see the text with new eyes. With the application of these hermeneutical resources to understand oneself through the *Cántico*, Perrin's book intends to be not so much a new examination of the content of the text as to lay the groundwork for another interpretation. Allow me to point out a few new avenues which a hermeneutical approach might open up to enrich future readings.

Perrin proposes that it is time to cease the fruitless and indecisive exercise of choosing an *editio typica* among two versions of the *Spiritual Canticle*. These versions are generally identified as *CA* and *CB*. Juan composed the original poem of 31 stanzas in 1578 while in prison and recited or sang it to the Carmelite Sisters, possibly, as Eulogio Pacho suggests, the *Descalzas* under the direction of

Teresa of Avila at Beas de Segura. This version - identified by Perrin as *CO* - is generally not considered for interpretation on its own. This is because Juan wrote a second version of the *Cántico* between 1579 and 1582, adding eight stanzas to the original *CO* (stanzas 32 - 39). The literature identifies this version as *CA*. A third edition of the *Cántico* appeared in 1584 (usually identified as *CB*). It added one stanza to the *CA* version (stanza 11) and rearranged the order of the *Cántico*, creating in effect a new song. Commentators ever since have battled over which version of the *Cántico* ought to be taken as Juan's authentic spiritual insight. But most commentators limited their choice to either the *CA* or the *CB* version. The original poem which Juan recited in prison became the Cinderella version. It received scant attention as an authentic and complete poem. Little effort has been made to explore its meaning as distinct from the later versions. In Juan de la Cruz's life the three versions were at one time each considered a complete poem. Perrin proposes to preserve this integrity of each version and challenges future interpreters to respect each version on its own. As integral poems each version has, to use Ricoeur's terminology, its own "world of the text." Perrin proposes that it might indeed be a fruitful exercise to determine how the additions and rearrangements of the text affect the meaning and change the effect of the text.

The hermeneutical approach also encourages a reinterpretation of the relationship between the song and the commentaries - even Juan's own theological, doctrinal interpretation. One might ask whether the *Cántico*'s figurative, poetic construct of reality is most adequately interpreted by the doctrinal or speculative theological genre. It is obviously - at least to Juan - one of the possible interpretations. But is it the only? It is important, according to Perrin, to recognize the ontological and epistemological difference between the literary genre of song and of theological speculative writing. Does a theological interpretation with its terms of reference clearly derived from the scholastic tradition deliver the most appropriate reading of a song? Does not the poetic genre call forth another response from a reader? Here Ricoeur's lengthy reflection in *The Rule of Metaphor* on the relation of the metaphorical to the speculative has allowed Perrin to introduce some helpful tools to shed light on genre-appropriate interpretations. Sensitivity to differences of form can then lead to a different appreciation of the traditional weight given to Juan's own theological commentary.

Finally what appears to be a most telling advance of a hermeneutical approach is its practical effect. The hermeneutics of Ricoeur is a practical hermeneutics. Its aim is to increase the practical know-how, the practical efficacy of humans in their capacity to act authentically in history. Its theory of reading and refiguration intends to activate today's reader into responding to the *Cántico*. In other words, the *Spiritual Canticle* according to a hermeneutical reading gains meaning when it comes alive for those who interact with it. The effectiveness of the *Spiritual Canticle* is felt in its ability to communicate and inform lives with its poetic vision across historical and cultural differences. Its past is not dead inasmuch as it still has the power to transmit its vitality in the present. A practical hermeneutics of a poem such as the *Spiritual Canticle* requires that the reader be able to place the song within a practical competency.

Such an interpretation of the *Spiritual Canticle* places new challenges upon contemporary interpreters. David Perrin's detailed analysis both of Ricoeur's hermeneutics and of the structure of the *Cántico* is much more persuasive than I can be in a brief forward that such a hermeneutics of a classical text is worth our effort. It can open up new ways of seeing our own reality through the delicate weave of this love song. The enduring attraction of this song in the Western spiritual tradition begs us to recreate its insight so that we too may learn to sing it.

John van den Hengel
Professor of Systematic Theology
Faculty of Theology
Saint Paul University
Ottawa, Ontario, Canada

AUTHOR'S PREFACE

This dissertation presents a hermeneutical framework within which an interpretation of Juan de la Cruz's *Cántico* may be undertaken. I call this framework a *Global Hermeneutical Method*. The phenomenological hermeneutics of Paul Ricoeur are used to construct this framework. Ricoeur's phenomenological hermeneutics of texts is based on a theory of mimesis. In following the hermeneutical arc constructed in the pre-understanding of the *Cántico* (mimesis₁), its configuration (mimesis₂), and then its reconfiguration (mimesis₃), a number of significant methodological issues for the interpretation of Juan's *Cántico* are reflected upon. These are examined to show how Juan's poem can be meaningfully interpreted for the contemporary reader, culturally and historically removed from sixteenth-century Spain.

A hermeneutical approach to the *Cántico* does not merely ask the question, "What does the text mean?" but also asks, "What does the text mean for the reader today?" With this approach there is a shift away from the predominance of the ascetical-theological approach to interpretation which has sought to objectify the meaning of the *Cántico* within the interpretation Juan gave it in his commentary, and a move towards a hermeneutical approach to interpretation that views the meaning of the *Cántico* as an event in the life of a person. Therefore, a hermeneutical interpretation of the *Cántico* explains why the *Cántico* is capable of being the place of a transformative event before the Divine, and why a multiplicity of interpretations is possible. Ricoeur's hermeneutical theory helps us understand how this is possible without losing sight of the doctrinal content of the poem.

Through the dialectic of explanation and understanding it is possible to unite within a single methodological approach the diverse ways that the *Cántico* of Juan de la Cruz has been received over the centuries. This is true even if the various approaches are at odds one with another. This is possible since interpretation is viewed not only as the objectification of information but also as a way of being-in-the-world which results from the interplay of the experience of the reader, the history of the reception of the text, and the text-world of the *Cántico*.

The methodical moment of interpretation within the dialectic of explanation and understanding asks that the reader enter into the text of the *Cántico* in a more conscious way. All the various ways of studying the *Cántico* contribute toward an explanation of the text. For example, ascetical-theological studies orient the reader within the theological content of the *Cántico* while literary-textual studies provide a description of the poetic techniques operative within the *Cántico*. Through these studies the analytical moment of interpretation constructs the objective sense of the *Cántico*. The sense of the *Cántico* orients the reader toward the ultimate reference of the text. It is this dialectic of sense and reference within the dialectic of explanation and understanding which results in the reconfiguration of a life, the ultimate project of interpretation.

In a particular way this dissertation examines the split-reference of metaphorical discourse which accounts for the legitimation of the noetic content of the *Cántico* as well as the emergence of new meaning. The dogmatic content of the *Cántico* can therefore be accounted for without excluding the possibility of new readings of the *Cántico*. Metaphor, which uses ordinary language to construct linguistic models of reality, is seen as the tool, par excellence, which produces the what-is-not-yet in the world.

In the hermeneutical approach, to put the "issue of the text" before everything, else is to stop asking the question of the inspiration of the *Cántico*, at least in the psychological sense as a "flash" of personal meaning which is projected into the text. The world-of-the-text is not revealed by the psychological intentions of the author but is mediated by the structures of the work.

A hermeneutical interpretation of Juan's *Cántico* helps us understand the originality of the text of the *Cántico*, even though, intertextually, the *Cántico* interacts with the *Song of Songs*, as well as other texts, in the production of meaning. Ricoeur's theory of sedimentation and innovation suggests that the *Cántico* is a new configuration of human action which has been born from within a particular life. We can therefore speak more of Juan's conceptual and symbolic *fields of resources* than we can speak of his *sources*.

The hermeneutical interpretation of Juan's *Cántico* suggests that neither *Cántico A* nor *Cántico B* be given priority in interpretation. Each of these two texts constructs its own meaning since the dramatic structure of each is different. The suggestion that *CA* be considered the poetic text, while *CB* be considered the theological text, becomes irrelevant in this approach. Both texts are unique poetic texts which open up unique text-worlds as is suggested by the difference in the dramatic structure of each text. There is also the possibility that the original poem, which I refer to as *Cántico O*, may also construct a different world-of-the-text than either *CA* or *CB*. Although I outline an analysis of the dramatic structure of each of these three texts, I suggest that a more thorough structural analysis needs to be done in order to surface more clearly the unique text-world which each constructs.

The hermeneutical approach to interpretation puts the enigmatic expressions of the *Cántico* to work, suggesting that temporal and poetic incongruencies in the *Cántico* are the very devices which are at work in the production of new meaning. Temporal zones of indetermination or lacunae in the text are viewed as that which plays on the reader to involve the reader in finishing the text. The text of the *Cántico*, therefore, is not viewed as a life-less object but rather as a living entity that becomes productive through the appropriation of the text.

Within the hermeneutical approach to interpretation, I also propose that the title of the *Cántico* plays a role in constructing metaphorical reference which in turn impacts the meaning of the text. This has led me to suggest that the title which appears at the top of the poem in the Sanlúcar and Jaén manuscripts: *Canciones entre el alma y el esposo* be used as the title for the poem rather than the editorial title of 1630: *Cántico espiritual entre el alma y Cristo su Esposo.* This title was later shortened to the present title *Cántico espiritual.*

The poetry-prose relationship is reassessed within the hermeneutical approach to Juan's *Cántico*. Poetic discourse (the poem) and speculative discourse (the commentary) are two radically different forms of discourse. The poem is capable of being productive of noetic content but the reader must continually return to the primordial text to "think some more." Hermeneutical interpretation of Juan's poem continually returns us to the world-of-the-text to interpret new models of being-in-the-world. New referents are opened up in the *Cántico* because of the interchange between conceptual and poetic discourse. The hermeneutical interpretation of the *Cántico* suggests a cyclical understanding of the poem which is never complete. The *Cántico* is, therefore, freed from an overdependence on the commentary which tends to interpret the poem allegorically.

The commentary, within the hermeneutical approach, is not viewed as an unpacking of the poem, a paraphrase in conceptual language of the poetic form. The commentary is not a description of the meaning of the *Cántico* itself but is a particular reception of the poem. However, it is not the only possible reception. There are other ways of receiving the poem. Both the poem and the commentary, since they are different literary forms require their own mode of reception. I suggest that an aesthetic reception of the *Cántico* is most appropriate because of its poetic form. The hermeneutical approach is seen by Ricoeur as bridging the gap between the poet and the theologian: the poetic gives rise to thought.

A hermeneutical interpretation of the *Cántico* explains how the profane or secular language of the *Cántico* can result in the conversion of the spiritual pilgrim. Ricoeur's theory of appropriation helps us understand why an aesthetic reading of the *Cántico* brings alive the transformative power of the text. The *Cántico* affects the reader through the production of mood. Mood brings the reader into contact with the deeper elements of reality. Mood characterizes reality before the object-subject split which occurs through conceptualization.

I suggest that the most significant impact of Juan's poem may be its ontological import. From Juan's poem we construct new ways of being-in-the-world. Authentic existence is displayed in the world-of-the-text of the *Cántico*. Although the reception of the *Cántico* at the level of its ontological import cannot be controlled, the various moods sketched in the *Cántico* suggest certain questions which may help us understand its ontological import. For example, I ask the question, "If appropriation of the *Cántico* is of a sexual nature, what does this say about all of our relationships, that is, with God, with our world, with others, and with ourselves?" Questions like these may open up the world-of-the-*Cántico* to new meaning.

Of singular importance, this dissertation establishes the primacy of the text of the poem for interpretation. It is the *Cántico* itself which holds hermeneutical priority. A *Global Hermeneutical Method* shifts methodological considerations from an author-centred reading of the *Cántico* to a text-centred reading. With a hermeneutical approach to the *Cántico* Juan de la Cruz's poem can be brought from the sixteenth century into the twentieth century. A hermeneutical reconfiguration of the *Cántico* would effectively guide pilgrims along their way, a work to which Juan de la Cruz dedicated his entire life.

ACKNOWLEDGMENTS

The end of a long journey such as the completion of a doctoral dissertation is an occasion for remembering and thanking those who guided the pilgrim traveler along the way. Completion of the project would have been impossible without the wisdom and insights of my director Dr. John van den Hengel, SCJ. His concern and patience kept me inspired and on track in the drafting and revision of each chapter. His thorough knowledge of Paul Ricoeur's philosophy provided for me a sure beacon of light that exposed me to the subtleties of Ricoeur's complex thought. His openness to learn about another giant thinker, John of the Cross, provided the happy mix that guided the project throughout its various stages..

A considerable debt of gratitude is due to my doctoral seminar director, Dr. Richard Hardy who first exposed me to the sixteenth-century Spanish mystic John of the Cross. Dr. Hardy carefully guided me through a systematic reading of the complete works of John of the Cross. This rich and stimulating journey gradually led me to the doctoral project set within these pages. To the jury members who read and critiqued my dissertation I owe my thanks: Dr. Sandra M. Schneiders, IHM (Graduate Theological Union in Berkeley, California), Dr. Richard Hardy, Dr. Paul Rigby, and Dr. Dale Schlitt, OMI (all at Saint Paul University, Ottawa).

To all my teachers, in and out of Saint Paul University, I owe special consideration, but especially to Dr. Michael Garanzini, SJ whose encouragement while I attended his classes at the Pontifical Gregorian University in Rome sowed the seed of future doctoral studies.

I am grateful to my religious community, the Missionary Oblates of Mary Immaculate, St. Peter's Province, Ottawa, who graciously freed me up from other ministry in order to pursue doctoral studies.

This doctoral project was made possible by three generous doctoral scholarships awarded by the Social Sciences and Humanities Research Council of Canada as well as by two doctoral scholarships provided by Saint Paul University. The publication of this book received financial support from Saint Paul University.

INTRODUCTION

1. Preamble

This is a methodological dissertation which constructs a hermeneutical framework for an interpretation of the poem commonly known as the *Cántico espiritual* of Juan de la Cruz.[1]

In constructing a hermeneutical framework for interpretation, I am suggesting not a new and original interpretation of the poem, but rather, a theoretical framework within which a hermeneutical interpretation can take place. This dissertation explores, therefore, what it means to interpret hermeneutically. A hermeneutical contextualization of the *Cántico* will also suggest why the poem is open to new and original interpretations which are consistent with Juan's own remarks concerning the interpretation of the *Cántico*.

In general a hermeneutical framework shifts methodological considerations from an author-centred reading of the *Cántico* to a text-centred reading.[2] An author-centred reading focuses on the whole world behind the *Cántico*.

---

[1] The title which appears at the top of the poem in many of the manuscripts is different (including the authoritative Sanlúcar de Barrameda and Jaén manuscripts): *Canciones entre el alma y el esposo*. Since it is the contention of this dissertation that a title of a work has bearing on its meaning, I will use *Cántico* throughout this dissertation to refer to the longer title just mentioned. Further reasons for this choice, from a hermeneutical perspective, will be discussed in Chapter Seven.

[2] The difference between an author-centred reading of a text and a text-centred reading are succinctly summarized in Walter VOGELS, *Interpreting Scripture in the Third Millennium: Author - Reader - Text*, Novalis Theological Series (Ottawa: Novalis, 1993). Although I refer to this reference in a general way to give the reader further information concerning a text-centred interpretation of a text I do not follow the method which is outlined in *Interpreting Scripture*. The reader will see that the method of text-centred interpretation which is emphasized in this dissertation is developed in such a way that neither the author, nor the reader, is ignored. All three, the author, the present reader, and the text are given a significant role to play in the hermeneutical contextualization of Juan's *Cántico* set forth in this dissertation. Although I was unable to consult the following reference the title indicates that the shift from an author-centred reading to a text-centred reading has been extensively studied in Paul Ricoeur's text theory by the author: R.E.C. JOHNSTON, *From an Author-Oriented*

2

This world includes the historical, cultural and political setting within which the text came to life, as well as the sources which may have inspired Juan, whether from his own life or from the lives of those about him. An author-centred approach, to a large degree, explores the text diachronically; it examines the various layers of the text through either source criticism or redaction criticism in the historical development of the text.[3] Priority is given to the intended meaning of the text as stated (whether implicitly or explicitly) by the author. In short, an author-centred reading focuses on the development of the text within the world of the author and how that development and that world impact the interpretation of the text. On the other hand, a text-centred reading takes into consideration that once an author has written a text, he or she, in a certain way, loses control over the text: the text takes on a certain independence from the time within which it was written, as well as from the intended meaning of the text as stated by the author. In a text-centred reading of the *Cántico* its intended meaning is subordinated to what is contained in the text itself, that is, what is actually written. We may refer to this approach as a synchronic approach to the *Cántico*, that is, an examination of the actual and present text we have before us.[4] As well, the form or genre of the text plays a significant part in the meaning of the text in a text-centred approach. This underlines the fact that Juan's *Cántico* needs to be respected as a particular form of discourse: poetry is a particular way persons choose to communicate. Poetry's capacity to communicate is different from a short story or a technical report.

We will see that the shift from an author-centred reading of the *Cántico* to a text-centred reading shifts the interpretation of the *Cántico* from an overly dogmatic interpretation that predominantly views it as an allegory describing

2

2

to a Text-Oriented Hermeneutic: Implications of Paul Ricoeur's Hermeneutical Theory for the Interpretation of the New Testament, 2 vols., Ph.D. Dissertation in Religious Studies, (Katholieke Universiteit te Leuven, Faculty of Theology, 1977).

[3] VOGELS, *Interpreting Scripture*, 78.

[4] VOGELS, *Interpreting Scripture*, 78.

the relationship between God and an individual human soul to a reading that opens up the interpretation of the *Cántico* to contemporary issues in faith life.

The dissertation also addresses a number of issues which concern an interpretation of the *Cántico*. For example, Juan wrote the originary[5] poem of thirty-one stanzas while a prisoner in Toledo in 1578. Over the next six years he added to this poem twice: the first time he brought the total number of stanzas to thirty-nine; the second time he added one more stanza, but rearranged large segments of the poem without changing anything in the stanzas themselves. The textual debate has been whether the poem of thirty-nine stanzas known as *Cántico A*, or that of forty, known as *Cántico B*, is the poem to be used for interpretive purposes. A hermeneutical approach opens up the possibility that neither *Cántico A* nor *Cántico B* should be seen as the definitive poem but that each one may have a contribution to make towards the hermeneutical understanding of Juan's *Cántico*. Furthermore, a hermeneutical approach opens up the question of the status of the originary Toledan poem, and questions the present understanding of the relationship between *Cántico A* and *Cántico B*.[6] As a corollary issue, the relationship between the poems and the commentaries Juan de la Cruz wrote on them is questioned by the hermeneutical contextualization of Juan's *Cántico* which I have set forth in this dissertation. Other issues concerning methodology and interpretation of Juan's *Cántico* are impacted by this hermeneutical framework within which the poem may

[5] "Originary" is the translation of the French *originaire*. *Originaire* is used by the French philosopher Paul Ricoeur to describe a foundational meaning-event. "Originary" is not to be found in most dictionaries. *Websters Third New International Dictionary of the English Language Unabridged*, ed. Philip Babcock Gove, (Springfield, Mass.: G. & C. Merriam Co., 1981), 1592 defines "originary" as "constituting a source."

[6] Some scholars use the same title *Cántico espiritual* to refer to the poem and the commentary either as individual works or as a combined unit. However, when using the title *Cántico* I am referring exclusively to the poem which bears the longer title *Canciones entre el alma y el esposo*. This reference to the poem is generic, that is, I am not referring to any particular version of the *Cántico*. When I am referring to a specific version of the poem, or Juan's Commentary on the poem, I will clearly state this as the case. *Cántico A* will often be referred to as simply *CA* and *Cántico B* will often be referred to as *CB*.

4

be read.[7] These are outlined below.

2. General Statement of the Problem of the Interpretation of Juan's *Cántico*

The world described in the *Cántico* of Juan de la Cruz initially appears to the reader as an obscure world. Juan de la Cruz wrote the *Cántico* in symbolic language that was charged with emotions and feelings. The poem moves freely into the past, the present, and the future, obscuring any logical progression of time as we ordinarily define it. The poem contains metaphors which arouse new and powerful images of the way two lovers are present in the world. Tradition has labelled this poem a religious poem, or, perhaps even more strongly, a "mystical" poem, describing the journey God has undertaken with the human soul. What is astonishing, however, is that not once, throughout the entire poem, does Juan de la Cruz mention God.[8] The poem itself, somehow, brings the reader into the mysterious world of the human and the divine. The power of the poem has been *felt* equally by the sixteenth-century and the twentieth-century reader, even though the cultural and historical settings of these two eras are dramatically different. The central problem

---

[7] Please note the way family names are referenced in this dissertation: Spanish family names are often a conjunction of the maternal as well as the paternal name. In order to facilitate references to these names in the BIBLIOGRAPHY at the back of the dissertation I have capitalized the full family name of all authors. For example, Baldomero Jiménez Duque is referenced as JIMÉNEZ DUQUE, Baldomero.

Some authors who have been writing over an extended number of years have either stopped using their full maternal or paternal family name, or use it in some publications but not in others. In order to facilitate reference to these authors, and to identify them as the same person, I have included the full name as it appears in at least some references. When it does not appear in full I have added the rest of the name in square brackets. For example, Federico Ruiz Salvador is sometimes published under Federico Ruiz. Some of his works can therefore be referenced under RUIZ [SALVADOR], Federico.

In one case the author has stopped using the religious name and changed back to the given family name. In order to be able to recognize this reference as one and the same person I have included the religious name with the given family name (if it was the religious name given in the publication). Eulogio de la V. Del Carmen may be referenced under PACHO. Eulogio [de la V. del Carmen].

If an author has published using only his or her religious name, this name is treated as a family name and fully capitalized. For example: GREGORIO DE JESÚS CRUCIFICADO.

[8] *Cántico A* 16 speaks of *bálsamo divino*, but this may not be a direct reference to God.

of interpretation of the *Cántico* thus does not comprise an attempt to clear away the cultural and historical debris that has accumulated over the centuries, hiding the true meaning of the text. The long-standing appeal of the *Cántico* has shown it to be meaningful to readers in a diversity of cultural and historical settings. The history of reception of the *Cántico* confirms that the poem is *meaningful*, and continues to be so for a large number of readers. Therefore, the problem is, how and why can the meaning of the *Cántico* be appropriated today, as it has been over the past four hundred years?

On the level of the text itself, the question surfaces: How does Juan access the transcendent world of the divine in such secular and, at times, erotic and passionate terms? The task is to show how the *material* and *secular* levels of the poem can possibly access the *spiritual* and the *sacred* to which the poem ultimately refers. How is the implied spiritual level of the poem supported by the familiar, cognitional structures contained within? Ostensive references to concrete objects and definite situations somehow conjure up a world of the poem that is not strictly secular in nature. But how is this done? Furthermore, has sufficient attention been paid to this "sacred world" (without referring directly to Juan's "religious" interpretation of his own poem) within the confines of the poem itself? Past readings of Juan's *Cántico* have relied heavily on Juan's own commentary to justify a "spiritual" reading of the poem. But are there other dynamics at work which open the door to the enigma of the "sacred" manifest through the "profane," in this case, through literary works?

At times the tendency has been to interpret the *Cántico* of Juan de la Cruz as if it were a theological treatise and to expect the same kinds of clarifications and logical progressions. The zeal to place Juan's *Cántico* within pre-determined theological categories has inhibited the dynamic nature of this text. As well, interpretation of the *Cántico* has fallen prey to an isolationist stance which interprets this text within the confines of Juan's own commentary on it. The reader has thus tended to isolate the *Cántico* itself from an encounter with his or her own religious experience. What role does the reader's experience bring to the task of interpreting the *Cántico*? The literature on the *Cántico* has not addressed this question, and has not suggested a theoretical framework within which we can understand the role of the reader. Juan himself was sensitive to the contribution each reader brought to his poem.

Juan de la Cruz tells us that the reader's horizon before his poem must include self-involvement at all levels. There is something operative in the life of the reader, other than just the rational intellect, which is needed to correctly understand what Juan wrote. Juan de la Cruz defined "mystical theology" not as the theological analysis of mysticism but as the experience of the mystical encounter itself.[9] He thus distinguished between scholastic theology and mystical theology, between a theology accessible only to the specialist and a theology which could be learnt through personal experience.[10] Even though Juan interpreted the *Cántico* in a particular way by writing a rather lengthy commentary on it, he explicitly tells us that the stanzas of his *Cántico* cannot be adequately interpreted rationally, not by him, nor by

---

[9] Juan makes this distinction in the Prologue of his commentary on the *Cántico* when he addresses Mother Ana de Jesús (Lobera), prioress of the discalced Carmelite nuns of St. Joseph's in Granada in 1584: "Aunque a V.R. le falte el ejercicio de teología escolástica con que se entienden las verdades divinas, no le falta el de la mística, que se sabe por amor, en que no solamente se saben, mas justamente se gustan." *CB* Prologo 3 (Rod., 573). "Rod." refers to the critical Spanish edition of Juan's collected works I will be using throughout this dissertation: *San Juan de la Cruz: Obras Completas*, ed. José Vicente Rodríguez, Introduction and doctrinal notes by Federico Ruiz Salvador, 3rd edition, (Madrid: Editorial de Espiritualidad, 1988). "Kav." refers to the English translation of *The Collected Works of St. John of the Cross*, trans. Kieran Kavanaugh and Otilio Rodriguez, Revisions and Introductions by Kieran Kavanaugh, Revised edition, (Washington: Institute of Carmelite Studies, 1991).

[10] This distinction was not new in the time of Juan. For example, Desiderius Erasmus (1469-1536) was an energetic and influential proponent of the purification of Christianity of an overly rational approach to faith life. He criticized ceremonialism and the plethora of corrupt editions of its scriptures presently in use. He exhorted Christians and the institutional church to return to the simplicity of the teachings of Christ. Colin Thompson tells us that "The introspection taught by San Juan is of a very different kind from the interior religion praised by Erasmus. But the underlying protest is perhaps the same: a protest against a religion which ties itself up in dogmatic niceties of external observances, and has nothing to offer to the deeper, inner needs of man. Mysticism, in seeking to supply those needs, is also a protest against a sterile religion." Colin THOMPSON, *The Poet and the Mystic: A Study of the Cántico Espiritual of San Juan de la Cruz*, Oxford modern languages and literature monographs (Oxford: Oxford University Press, 1977), 5.

anybody else.[11] In the end, he tells us that each person must stand before the poem of the *Cántico* her- or himself. In the Prologue to his commentary on the *Cántico* he explains that this is the case, so that each one may profit from it "according to the mode and capacity of one's own spirit. ... As a result, though we give some explanation of these stanzas, there is no reason to be bound to this explanation."[12] How, then, is the modern day reader expected to gain from a reading of the *Cántico* without being bound to Juan's own explanation?[13] What theoretical approach to the *Cántico* might help explain the diversity of readings which Juan himself is suggesting?

Scholarly studies on the *Cántico* by theologians have tended to focus on extracting and objectifying information from it which binds them to Juan's own interpretation of his poem in the commentary. This approach has not sufficiently taken into consideration the approach to the *Cántico* which Juan himself has signalled. Generally speaking there has been an exegetical approach to interpreting Juan's *Cántico*. Examples would include the classification and association of key symbols in the *Cántico*, or a distillation of central dogmatic principles of the Christian faith which Juan himself explains in his commentary. These studies are essential and have been valuable in clarifying the objective content of the *Cántico*. Juan, the "spiritual theologian," has much to offer in various areas of Christian thought. But how do these approaches to the text in fact move the reader further

---

[11] "Por haberse, pues, estas Canciones compuesto en amor de abundante inteligencia mística, no se podrán declarar al justo, ni mi intento será tal, sino sólo dar alguna luz general, pues V.R. así lo ha querido." *CB* Prologo 2, (Rod., 572). And in the paragraph before Juan says: "De donde se sigue que los santos doctores, aunque mucho dicen y más digan, nunca pueden acabar de declararlo por palabras, así como tampoco por palabras se pudo ello decir." *CB* Prologo 1, (Rod., 572).

[12] *CB* Prologue 2, (Kav., 470). "Según su modo y caudal de espíritu, que abreviarlos a un sentido a que no se acomode todo paladar. ... Y así, aunque en alguna manera se declaran, no hay para qué atarse a la declaración." *CB* Prologo 2, (Rod., 572).

[13] Juan was asked to write his own commentary on the *Cántico* by Mother Ana de Jesús (Lobera), as mentioned earlier. We also know writing commentaries on "religious" poems has a long tradition that originated with Origin and his allegorical interpretation of the biblical poem the *Song of Songs* in the third century. But can we still say more about the value of such commentaries, and in particular the commentary on the *Cántico*?

ahead in coming to understand the *Cántico* itself?

When a particular exegetical interpretation is placed on the text, is the text, in fact, opened to be appropriated? For example, in classifying and interpreting the major symbols in the *Cántico* exclusively within the perspective of the classical spiritual itinerary of purgation, illumination, and union, is there a tendency to impoverish what is to be understood in the *Cántico*? Juan himself tells us that his own explanation of the *Cántico* contains *less* than what is in the poem.[14] In this case have the symbols of the *Cántico* been reduced to an intellectual abstraction that has unwittingly impoverished them, removing them from the play of the text on the reader? The following question ultimately surfaces: Is the text of the *Cántico*, as well as the hermeneutics operative within the poem in relationship to the reader, trusted enough to allow the poem to speak to the informed reader? What is being reflected in this problematic is the shift in focus from Romantic hermeneutics to what is known today as post-Heideggerian hermeneutics.[15]

The Romanticist's perspective approaches interpretation as a search for the psychological intentions of the author which ultimately reveal the objective content of the text concealed *behind* the text. This psychological approach to interpretation is concerned with the singularity, the acumen, of the author's message. Ultimately, however, this approach focuses on the limits of understanding based on the common use and interpretation of words. A post-Heideggerian approach to

[14] "Y asi, lo que de ello se declara, ordinariamente es lo menos que contiene en si." *CB* Prologo 1, (Rod., 572).

[15] See Paul Ricoeur's analysis of this shift in hermeneutics in his article: Paul RICOEUR, "The Task of Hermeneutics," *Philosophy Today* 17 (1973), 112-128. In general, a post-Heideggerian approach to interpretation involves two fundamental shifts in the way texts are interpreted. The first is a shift from epistemology to ontology, that is, before there is any consideration of the human subject knowing, there is a more primordial level, that of Being which is to be considered: "Instead of asking 'how do we know?', the question will be 'what is the mode of being of that being who only exists through understanding?' ... What we are interpreting is the *meaning* of being." Ibid., 120-121. The second major shift is from the understanding of another person to the understanding of the world as it is brought to us through texts: "The foundations of the ontological problem are to be sought in the domain of the relation to the world and not in the domain of relation with another person. It is in relation to my situation, in the fundamental understanding of my position within being, that understanding in its principle sense is implied. ... In making understanding 'worldly', Heidegger 'depsychologizes' it." Ibid., 121-122.

hermeneutics sees interpretation as an attempt to clarify the type of being-in-the-world unfolding *in front of* the text, through a discovery of the world-of-the-text which ultimately leads toward self-understanding. Paul Ricoeur suggests that what must be interpreted in a text is a proposed world which could be inhabited and wherein one could project one's own possibilities. This is what he calls the "world-of-the-text," the world proper to this unique text. In this "new hermeneutics," to *understand* is to *understand oneself in front of the text.*

The shift from Romantic methods of interpretation to a post-Heideggerian approach signals the subordination of understanding as a "method" to understanding as a "way of being," and of relationship to being-in-the-world. It is the former which has preoccupied interpreters of the *Cántico* to date. This is to say that the general approach in interpreting the *Cántico* has been an attempt to restore the author's intention behind the text. This approach, as we will see, limits the potential of the text. For example, Romantic hermeneutics, as I have already indicated, has not sufficiently taken into consideration the religious experience which the reader brings to the reading and interpretation of the text. This is a fundamental problem often overlooked in the exegesis and interpretation of the *Cántico.* Any method used to understand religious texts needs to take into consideration the religious experience which the reader brings to a reading of the text.

Concerning the question of understanding the *Cántico* we might ask Is it the text which is ultimately to be interpreted by the reader, or is it the life of the reader which [16] gives the text the chance to actualize all the text's potentialities?[16] If emphasis is placed on the latter, what kind of hermeneutics can the reader bring to the text in order to appropriate it? Has Juan already modelled this hermeneutical approach in the relationship he sets forth between the poem of the *Cántico* and his prose commentary on it? What is suggested by these questions is that Juan is not only offering the reader objective information about his personal faith experiences,

---

[16] This question comes as a result of comments made by Jean-Paul Michaud in his written feedback after the presentation of this doctoral project at the Working Seminar, St Paul University, April 28, 1992.

or a description of the content of his belief. Interpretation of the *Cántico* cannot (at least not exclusively) be the search for facts or objective information. Interpretation of the text of the *Cántico* will involve something else. The real concern of this thesis is to set up a methodological approach to the *Cántico* to assist the reader to encounter the text as a dynamic transformative event before the Divine. To enter into this pilgrimage through the text is to "understand" the text.

An adequate approach to understanding the text of the *Cántico* includes how *it*, the *Cántico* itself, becomes operative in the life of the reader and transforms the reader's life as it did Juan's. There must be a hermeneutics operative in the text that confronts the life of the reader in order to allow this to happen. What we discover, therefore, is that the hermeneutical task is not first and foremost the work of bringing the past meaning of the text into the present, but rather, bringing the present meaning of the text into confrontation with the life of the would-be pilgrim. A hermeneutical approach to the interpretation of Juan de la Cruz's *Cántico* promises to open us up to the variety of interpretations of the *Cántico*, to which, as I have already indicated, Juan himself explicitly referred.

The problem and central question of this inquiry is thus revealed: Is a hermeneutical approach to the *Cántico* an approach that will allow us to open up the text to our present day reality and enable us to appropriate it into our life? Or to put it more succinctly: What allows us to open up the text of the *Cántico* to our own time?

3. Research Hypothesis

3.1 Statement of Hypothesis

A reading of the Cántico of Juan de la Cruz within the framework of Paul Ricoeur's hermeneutical phenomenology will shift the interpretation of the Cántico from a predominantly ascetical-theological interpretation (based on the Cántico's commentary) to an interpretation of the Cántico as the uncovering of the text-world (based on the hermeneutical priority given the poem itself) in confrontation with the life-world of the reader.

This thesis affects issues concerning methodology and interpretation of Juan's *Cántico*. Although other issues are also addressed, this thesis:

> i)   situates and unifies the role presently assigned diverse methodologies in the interpretation of the *Cántico*;
>
> ii) establishes the text of Juan's *Cántico* as a *text*, that is, accounts for the dialectic operative in the transition from the oral version of the *Cántico* to its written form and the consequences of this for interpretation;
>
> iii) accounts for the various interpretations of the *Cántico* which Juan said were possible;
>
> iv) opens up for further investigation the question of the relationship of the three versions of the *Cántico*, that is, the Toledan poem, *Cántico A* and *Cántico B*;
>
> v) situates the contribution which the reader brings to an interpretation of the *Cántico*;
>
> vi) assesses the role of the title of the poem (*Cántico espiritual*) given by the editor, although *Canciones entre el alma y el esposo* appears at the top of the poem in the majority of the manuscripts;
>
> vii) opens up for further investigation the question of the nature of the poem-commentary relationship.

3.2 Explanation of the Research Hypothesis

What I am offering is a method to help uncover what remains available to the reader today in Juan de la Cruz's *Cántico*. This implies the following questions: How can Juan de la Cruz be read today? How can the present-day reader, temporally and culturally removed from the genesis of the poem, access what is *croyable-disponible* in the *Cántico*? The problem is not just understanding Juan de la Cruz's *Cántico* in the sixteenth century; the text needs to be brought into the twentieth century. I am not, as yet, suggesting a twentieth-century interpretation of Juan's *Cántico*, but I am offering a method by which this can be achieved. In so doing, as I indicated above, I am causing certain questions to surface.

4. Methodology

My research will situate Juan de la Cruz's *Cántico* in the theory of the interpretation of texts as it is currently being pursued by Paul Ricoeur. Although I have surveyed a wide segment of Ricoeur's thought, it is his three volume work *Time and Narrative* which has provided the theoretical framework for this dissertation.[17] Ricoeur's understanding of the concept of mimesis (representation) outlined in *Time and Narrative* will be used to construct a hermeneutical approach to the *Cántico*. Why Ricoeur's theory of mimesis has been chosen to build a theoretical framework within which we can interpret the *Cántico* is explored in detail in Chapter Two. At this time I will merely make a few general comments on the value of Ricoeur's theory for my work.

Traditional conceptions of mimesis hold that all artistic and linguistic productions are diminished representations of reality. This is the view which Plato develops in his *Republic* and *Phaedrus*. According to James Dicenso, Socrates argues in the *Republic* that "the artist is at 'third remove' from reality because he imitates things, such as the products of craftsmanship, which are themselves but imitations of the forms. This tertiary status means that artistic products are very low in rank of valuation because they are far distanced from the originary sources of Being and truth."[18] However, Ricoeur's theory of mimesis stresses that art, and in particular linguistic productions, are *intensifications* of reality; they bring reality into focus in a way which it was not before.

---

[17] Paul RICOEUR, *Time and Narrative*, vol. 1, trans. Kathleen McLaughlin and David Pellauer (Chicago: University of Chicago Press, 1984); *Time and Narrative*. vol. 2, trans. Kathleen McLaughlin and David Pellauer (Chicago: University of Chicago Press, 1985); *Time and Narrative*, vol. 3, trans. Kathleen Blamey and David Pellauer (Chicago: University of Chicago Press, 1988). As indicated I have used the English translation of *Time and Narrative*, and, as well, the English translations of Ricoeur's other major works. However, Ricoeur is a French philosopher and wrote the bulk of his material in French. When deemed necessary I have consulted the French text.

[18] James J. DICENSO, *Hermeneutics and the Disclosure of Truth: A Study in the Work of Heidegger, Gadamer, and Ricoeur*, (Charlottesville: University Press of Virginia, 1990), 116-117.

A text, according to Ricoeur's concept of mimesis, contains a *surplus of meaning* beyond the intention of the author. Ricoeur's hermeneutical theory reconstructs the notion of mimesis to help us understand that even though particular historical and cultural factors gave birth to a text, its meaning is not locked within them, or limited by them.[19] What I am suggesting is that understanding the text of the *Cántico* is not dependent so much on where it came from as on where it is going, that is, on the reality that the text refers to in a current reading.

Ricoeur's theory of mimesis suggests that the text, once written, has a certain independence even from the intentionality of the author.[20] For Ricoeur, the author appears to be merely the first reader.[21] Even the author may be open to *interpreting* his or her own work as we see in the prose commentaries Juan wrote on the *Cántico*. Ricoeur's hermeneutical theory will therefore take us beyond an ideology that claims that an adequate understanding of the *Cántico* can be reached through an unravelling of the theological concepts embodied in the text. Theological analysis is necessary in Ricoeur's hermeneutical program, but it is seen only as an inadequate step toward a more sophisticated understanding of the text. In the hermeneutical theory of Ricoeur, the effect the text produces on its reader and the life-world the reader brings before the text are intrinsic components of the present or actual meaning of the text.[22] Ricoeur's interpretation theory takes into account the religious experience which the reader brings before the text. This was something of which Juan de la Cruz was also very aware. As Ricoeur tells us, "The moment of

---

[19] This problem is suggested by Paul Ricoeur in the following passage. "There is thus a problem of the interpretation of works, a problem irreducible to the step by step understanding of sentences." Paul RICOEUR, "The Hermeneutical Function of Distanciation," in *Hermeneutics and the Human Sciences*, ed., trans., and Introduction by John B. Thompson (Cambridge: Cambridge University Press, 1981), 136.

[20] RICOEUR, "Metaphor and the Central Problem of Hermeneutics," 165.

[21] RICOEUR, "What is a Text? Explanation and Understanding," in *From Text to Action: Essays in Hermeneutics II*, trans. Kathleen Blamey and John B. Thompson (Evanston: Northwestern University Press, 1991), 109.

[22] RICOEUR, *Time and Narrative*, 1:77.

14

'understanding' corresponds dialectically to being in a situation: it is the projection of our ownmost possibilities at the very heart of the situations in which we find ourselves. ... For what must be interpreted in a text is a *proposed world* which I could inhabit and wherein I could project one of my ownmost possibilities."[23] With this approach, the meaning of the *Cántico* is found in the intersection of the world of the *Cántico* with the actual and potential world of the reader.[24]

We must note, therefore, that Juan de la Cruz is not talking about the physical world as the world which is accessible to the reader through the appropriation of the *Cántico*. The problematic of interpretation enters because the world to be interpreted in the *Cántico* is a world accessed by the imagination.[25] Juan's *Cántico* is largely a fictive interplay between imaginary characters and colourful images drawn from the world of nature.

The *Cántico* of Juan de la Cruz is replete with metaphors and symbols, enigmatic expressions and poetic discourse which describe a potential world to be appropriated by the reader. Ricoeur's theory of mimesis provides the tools necessary to understand how we may appropriate a largely symbolic world such as the one contained in the *Cántico*. In short, Ricoeur's text theory of mimesis offers us an understanding of how we are to understand poetic discourse such as that of the

---

[23] RICOEUR, "The Hermeneutical Function of Distanciation," 142.

[24] The reader, therefore, receives more than mere information from a text. The reader receives a new way of being in the world through the meeting of the world-of-the-text and the world of the reader: "What a reader receives is not just the sense of the work, but, through its sense, its reference, that is, the experience it brings to language and, in the last analysis, the world and the temporality it unfolds in the face of this experience." RICOEUR, *Time and Narrative*, 1:78-79.

[25] Ricoeur distinguishes between two kinds of texts with different senses of world: the scientific text (referring to the physical world) and the poetic or literary text (referring to a potential or possible world accessed through the imagination). The former does not present a difficulty in interpretation; the latter does. It is this kind of world which Juan presents to us in the *Cántico*. As David Klemm says: "The hermeneutically unproblematic case of reference to a world by a text is that of a descriptive or scientific text. ... The hermeneutically significant sense of *world* for Ricoeur is enjoined with the interpretation of literary or poetic works, by which Ricoeur means works that refer not to the physical world but to a possible world accessible to the imagination." David E. KLEMM, *The Hermeneutical Theory of Paul Ricoeur: A Constructive Analysis*, (Toronto: Associated University Presses, 1983), 85.

Cántico of Juan de la Cruz.

5. Plan of the Dissertation

My methodological approach to the *Cántico* will be what I have chosen to call a *Global Hermeneutical Method.* I will use Paul Ricoeur's textual theory of mimesis to construct a method that examines the *Cántico* from three perspectives, or more dynamically, from the perspective of three different "mimetic moments." Ricoeur describes these three moments as that of prefiguration (pre-understanding of the text), configuration (distanciation from the text), and reconfiguration (appropriation of the text). It is this threefold mimesis which I have used to structure the dissertation, and to bring Juan de la Cruz's poem into dialogue with the text theory of Paul Ricoeur.

Chapter One: METHODOLOGICAL APPROACHES TO THE *CÁNTICO* will lay out the predominant methodological approaches to the poem currently in use. When I have shown that these approaches do make a contribution to the hermeneutical approach but do not adequately respond to questions concerning the appropriation of the *Cántico*, I will move into **Chapter Two: THE CONCEPT OF MIMESIS.** In the second chapter I will begin to develop Ricoeur's theory of mimesis which helps us respond to some of the issues concerning the appropriation of a text. This second chapter will contextualize the *Cántico* within that part of Ricoeur's theory of mimesis he calls "mimesis$_1$." We will see that what is important in this moment of my methodological construction is the pre-understanding of Juan's *Cántico* in terms of the resources Juan de la Cruz had available to him. I will refer to this as Juan's conceptual and symbolic world. I will describe this world in its cultural and historical manifestation in **Chapter Three: MIMESIS$_1$ AND JUAN'S CONCEPTUAL AND SYMBOLIC WORLD.** Since this mimesis involves Juan's life and its significant moments I will give a brief biographical outline. The literary resources Juan had available to him and the historical development of the various texts of the *Cántico* will be presented. In a particular way the western mystical tradition will be considered as one of the primary resources which helped shape Juan's *Cántico*.

I will next examine the text of the *Cántico* which Ricoeur calls its "configuration." **Chapter Four: MIMESIS$_2$ AND CONFIGURATION OF THE *CÁNTICO*** examines the text itself within the second moment of Ricoeur's theory of mimesis. Mimesis$_2$ is characterized by its function of mediation. While mimesis$_1$ considers the pre-linguistic resources available to the author, mimesis$_2$ refers to the making of a literary structure which interprets and organizes those resources into a text. Within Ricoeur's theory of mimesis the text is seen as a mimesis of human action which results in a production or form for meaningful human action beyond the text itself. At this point I will be in a position to examine the text of the *Cántico*. The following chapter, **Chapter Five: MIMESIS$_2$ AND THE TEXT OF THE *CÁNTICO*** will draw out the consequences of this mimetic moment with respect to the text of the *Cántico*. The consequences of the analysis of the dramatic structure of the *Cántico* will suggest how the Toledan poem, *Cántico A*, and *Cántico B* relate to one another in the context of Ricoeur's theory of mimesis$_2$.

After examination of the actual text of the *Cántico*, I will then explore how reading leads toward the appropriation of the text by the reader. The third moment of the hermeneutical arc, mimesis$_3$, will be explored. **Chapter Six: MIMESIS$_3$ AND APPROPRIATION OF THE *CÁNTICO*** will situate Juan's poem within text-reader theory and will suggest how one might enter into an understanding of the *Cántico* through reading the text in interaction with the reader's own horizon of experience. I will thus present a theoretical framework within which we can appreciate the diversity of readings of the text of which Juan himself spoke. This theoretical framework will also help us better understand the transformative power of reading. It is in the exploration of the dynamics of reading as an act of "play" and the production of "mood" that the transformative dynamic of the *Cántico* is confronted. These investigations will help us understand that the meaning of Juan's *Cántico* is inserted into the movements of transformation and conversion in the Christian journey.

Chapter Seven: MIMESIS₃ AND RECEPTION OF THE *CÁNTICO* will round off the dissertation with a look at three issues concerning the appropriation of the *Cántico* which are impacted by the hermeneutical contextualization of the *Cántico* I have developed throughout the dissertation. First I will examine the significance of the title which Juan gave the poem. This title is not currently used in publications of Juan's *Cántico*. The implications of this editorial choice are thus examined within the context of Ricoeur's appropriation theory. Second I will examine the issue of the relationship of the poem with the prose commentary written on it. A hermeneutical appropriation of the *Cántico* brings a unique appreciation of the relationship between these two different forms of Juan's literary output. The question of the inter-textual relationship between these diverse forms of discourse will thus be explored in view of the elements of Ricoeur's theory of mimesis and appropriation developed in the dissertation. In a third section I will raise the question of the ontological import of Juan's *Cántico*. This is to raise the question of the refiguration of existence made possible by the *Cántico*. New models of being-in-the-world are the hermeneutical interpretations of the poem which this dissertation opens up.

I will end the dissertation by reviewing the particular contribution a hermeneutical framework brings to an interpretation of Juan de la Cruz's *Cántico*. I will also summarize the various methodological issues which are opened up as a result of the hermeneutical framework I have proposed for the *Cántico*. These issues suggest the possibility of further research on the *Cántico* within this hermeneutical framework.

A single Appendix follows the body of the text. In this Appendix I have included the Spanish text of the Toledan *Cántico*, *Cántico A*, and *Cántico B*, as well as a side-by-side English translation of each stanza.

CHAPTER ONE
METHODOLOGICAL APPROACHES TO THE *CÁNTICO*

1. Introduction

In order to better understand the methodological contribution of this dissertation it would be helpful to review the main approaches which have been used to study Juan de la Cruz's work in the past. Several scholars have already classified and/or evaluated the various approaches which have been used to study Juan de la Cruz's entire corpus.[1] I will use these studies to summarize the methodological approaches to Juan's de la Cruz's corpus while citing exemplary works which characterize each methodological approach. I will refer to specific texts from these studies to help situate each method in the context of the present investigation. It is to be noted that a particular author cannot be exclusively identified with any one method in the study of Juan de la Cruz. The methods themselves overlap and are not mutually exclusive. However, most scholars fit more readily into one category than an other.

The second section of this chapter will look at methodological approaches from a different perspective. I will suggest that the movement toward the hermeneutical approach is already evident in the literature on sanjuanist studies.

---

[1] See for example: Max Huot de LONGCHAMP, *Lectures de Jean de la Croix: Essai d'Anthropologie Mystique,* ed. Charles Kannengiesser, with a Preface by Albert Deblaere, Théologie Historique 62 (Paris: Beauchesne, 1981), 391-416; Andres Rafael LUEVANO, *Endless Transforming Love: An Interpretation of the Mystical Doctrine of Saint John of the Cross According to the Soul's Affective Relation and Dynamic Structure,* Vacare Deo 9 (Rome: Institutum Carmelitanum, 1990), 13-26; Marilyn May MALLORY, *Christian Mysticism: Transcending Techniques: A Theological Reflection on the Empirical Testing of the Teaching of St. John of the Cross,* (Assen: Van Gorcum, 1977), 3-10; Federico RUIZ [SALVADOR], "Síntesis Doctrinal," in *Introducción a la lectura de San Juan de la Cruz,* ed. A. Garcia Simón (Valladolid: Junta de Castilla y León Consejería de Cultura y Turismo, 1991), 222-223. For a not too positive evaluation of de Longchamp's *Lectures* and his methodological approach see Richard P. HARDY, "Recensions - Book Reviews," *Église et Théologie* 13 (1982), 256.

This assertion will be supported by outlining the contribution Roger Duvivier has made in his use of phenomenology to study the *Cántico*. In fact, the phenomenological approach could be listed as one of the methods which has been used to study the sanjuanist corpus. However, because of the importance of Duvivier's study, and its direct link with the hermeneutical interpretation I am outlining in this dissertation, I have decided to treat it in a separate section.

In the third section of this chapter, I will begin to explore how all of the foregoing approaches to the sanjuanist corpus contribute toward the hermeneutical approach. It is the hermeneutical approach which will be expanded throughout the dissertation and used to show the methodological issues and gains that arise from this interpretation of Juan de la Cruz's *Cántico*.

2. Methodologies Used in the Study of the Corpus of Juan de la Cruz

All sanjuanist methods contribute in some way toward an understanding of Juan's *Cántico*. The plurality of methodologies which analyze the *Cántico* from various perspectives is therefore a rich resource for the hermeneutical approach developed in this dissertation. Various classifications of the approaches to Juan de la Cruz's work have been proposed. Max Huot de Longchamp divides them into two main categories: *lecture systématique* and *lecture symbolique*.[2] Federico Ruiz Salvador suggests five divisions: 1. *ascético-teológico;* 2. *metafísico-existencial;* 3. *filosófico;* 4. *teológico-existencial;* and 5. *fenomenológica.*[3] Andres Rafael Luevano also classifies them in five divisions: 1. historical; 2. thematic;

---

[2] LONGCHAMP, *Lectures de Jean de la Croix*, 391-392. In the end Longchamp rejects both these approaches (he calls them *tentations*). He suggests the *lecture systématique* and the *lecture symbolique* both misrepresent Juan. Longchamp goes on to suggest how to read Juan, but his remarks are extremely general. Ibid., 415-416. Longchamp simply indicates that he prefers a "descriptive" approach to a "speculative" approach to Juan's works. Longchamp suggests that a mystic cannot make a contribution toward systematic theology at all. Quoting A. Poulain, Longchamp says that "l'école spéculative a produit des chefs-d'oeuvre, qui probablement ne pourront pas être dépassés. On préfèrera les rééditer que de recommencer leur immense travail. En un mot, il ne semble pas que la mystique puisse faire des progrès de ce côté." A. POULAIN, *Des grâces d'oraisons,* 11th edition, (Paris: 1931), xcviii-xcic, quoted in LONGCHAMP, *Lectures de Jean de la Croix,* 415

[3] RUIZ [SALVADOR], "Síntesis Doctrinal," 222-223.

3. theological/philosophical; 4. literary/poetic; 5. psychological.[4] The classifications by Ruiz Salvador and Luevano appear to be more encompassing and, therefore, more useful than Longchamp's. However, Ruiz Salvador leaves no place for literary and textual studies, while Luevano joins together theological and philosophical studies. Literary-textual, as well as philosophical and theological studies, each have their own methodological considerations and therefore, it would appear, should have their own methodological classification. This will become clear when I examine the contribution that each of these approaches makes to the study of the sanjuanist corpus. I have therefore opted for the following divisions which allow the significant contribution of each methodological approach to be recognized: 1. historical-contextual; 2. literary-textual; 3. ascetical-theological; 4. thematic-symbolic; 5. philosophical; 6. psychological.

The purpose in presenting these methodological approaches to Juan's corpus is twofold: 1. to highlight the contribution which each one of them makes toward the study of Juan's corpus; 2. to concretize these studies using examples from their use in the study of the *Cántico*.

2.1 *Historical-contextual* Studies

Excellent biographical studies have been published on the life and times of San Juan de la Cruz.[5] Two exemplary works in this area are: José de Jesús

---

[4] LUEVANO, *Endless Transforming Love*, 13. Luevano goes on to develop a sixth methodological approach which he calls the "structural-dynamic method" of interpreting mystical texts, and in particular those of Juan de la Cruz. However, I include his own approach within a theological approach.

[5] Early biographical information on Juan de la Cruz is primarily found in the documents for his beatification. This information was recorded between 1600-30. See THOMPSON, *The Poet and the Mystic*, 21-26 for a description of this process. These so-called *dichos* come from people who knew Juan, and for this reason they are a primary source for any biographical study of Juan. Silverio de Santa Teresa has published much of this early biographical material (with the works of San Juan included): *Obras de San Juan de la Cruz*, ed. and notes Silverio de Santa Teresa, 5 vols., Biblioteca Mística Carmelitana 10-15 (Burgos, El Monte Carmelo, 1929-31). However, due to the beatification cause for which much of the information was gathered, the early biographies tend to include hagiographical material. For example, a biography by JOSÉ DE JESÚS MARIA [Quiroga], *Historia de la vida y virtudes del Venerable P. Fray Juan de la Cruz*, (Brussels: Ivan de Meerbeeck, 1628), is of this nature. The important work of BRUNO DE JÉSUS-MARIE, *Saint Jean de la Croix*, with

Maria [Quiroga], *Historia de la vida y virtudes del Vernerable P. Fray Juan de la Cruz* (1628) and Crisógono de Jesús, *Vida y obras completas de San juan de la Cruz,* (1946). However, the focus of the various biographies published over the last four hundred years has been quite disparate.[6] Early biographies, and even those written in the first part of our own century, tend to indulge in hagiography. The authors of these biographies tried to fit the life of Juan into their contemporary understanding of holiness. This biographical content often included detailed descriptions of miraculous and extraordinary events in Juan's life.[7] Conversely, the most recent biographical accounts tend to focus on Juan as he lived the common inheritance of all of humanity.[8] Of singular importance in these studies is Richard Hardy, *Search for Nothing: The Life of St. John of the Cross.*

These latter accounts reveal a more complete picture of Juan, his

a Preface by Jacques Maritain, Revised and corrected from the 1929 edition, (Paris: Plon, 1948) also contains hagiographical content, even though it is of a scholarly nature. The standard biography in Spanish by the famed CRISÓGONO DE JESÚS SACRAMENTADO, *Vida de San Juan de la Cruz,* Revised and annotated by Matía del Niño Jesús, 1st edition 1946, 11th edition, Biblioteca de Autores Cristianos 435 (Madrid: Editorial Católica, 1982) although also of a scholarly nature, it suffers from a less than critical evaluation of spectacular stories from Juan's life. For a detailed history of the reform of the Carmelite order with which Juan de la Cruz and Teresa de Avila were involved see: Allison PEERS, *Handbook to the Life and Times of St. Teresa and St. John of the Cross,* (London: Burns and Oates, 1954), 3-104. For a brief yet very helpful account of the principal personages associated with Juan and Teresa see Ibid., 107-233.

  [6] Richard Hardy has given us a good idea of the range of these various biographical accounts in Richard HARDY, *Search for Nothing: The Life of St. John of the Cross,* (New York: Crossroads Publishing Co., 1982), 147-148. I would particularly recommend this biography to the individual who would like to be in touch with Juan's personal characteristics and the events that touched him deeply in his life.

  [7] Whether these stories are true or not is not the concern of this study. However, since some stories border on the incredulous, their reliability can at least be called into question. Richard Hardy recounts of some of these extraordinary stories in "Early Biographical Documentation on Juan de la Cruz," *Science et Esprit* 30 (1978), 313-23. Hardy gives a balanced and succinct presentation of the life of Juan de la Cruz in another publication: "San Juan de la Cruz (1542-1591): A Personality Sketch," *Ephemerides Carmeliticae* 29 (1978), 507-518.

  [8] Richard Hardy's own work *Search for Nothing,* a scholarly and well researched biography written in a popularized style, is justifiably critical of the inclusion of biographical anecdotes bordering on the fantastic. Gerald BRENAN, *St. John of the Cross: His Life and Poetry,* (Cambridge: Cambridge University Press, 1973) contains a briefer biographical account but is nonetheless very informative. He also adopts a critical attitude toward the hagiographical material related in some of the principal biographical works on Juan.

human joys, as well as his struggles.[9] It is the Juan of the world common to all people who is the author of the *Cántico*. Juan was so much in touch with himself, with humanity, and creation, that he was able to create poetry that spoke to others at a very deep level of their being.

Historical-contextual studies help explain the *Cántico* because they situate Juan within the context of his family life and of personal experiences which are reflected directly or indirectly in his texts. These studies have often broadly taken the form of historical or biographical studies which include a description of the sociological, political, cultural and religious climate of Juan's time. Personal experiences, such as the nine-month internment in Toledo during which Juan wrote the first thirty-one stanzas of the *Cántico*, are used to analyse and help us understand Juan's enigmatic writings. Or, to take another example, *CB* 14 speaks of *las ínsulas extrañas*. It has been suggested that this phrase brings into the *Cántico* all the mystery and intrigue of the recent discovery of the islands of the so-called "new world" in 1492 which Juan would most certainly have heard about. Another example: although one would hardly expect to find *cuevas de leones enlazado* in the nuptial bed of *CB* 24, this expression makes sense in the context of the coat of arms of the de Yepes family to which Juan belonged.[10]

Historical-contextual studies thus aid the interpreter in situating the *Cántico* in Juan's life and help explain the presence of enigmatic phrases or expressions which may be foreign to the contemporary reader. It constructs for us a picture of Juan's life, and we can form a mental image of Juan, the man, who wrote

---

[9] Interestingly enough, current biographies still tend to fit Juan into the most recent, up-to-date, understanding of holiness (i.e. a concern for creation, focus on relationships, and a non-dualistic approach to sexuality). However, it could be argued that the contemporary appreciation of holiness is more balanced and includes a global look at the individual in the world, rather then a focus on a strictly "other-worldly" life preoccupied with the transcendent.

[10] The de Yepes coat of arms features a lion crowned with gold on an azure background. This family shield may have been seen hung over a bed of a relative when young Juan was travelling with his mother after the death of his father. See Georges TAVARD, *Poetry and Contemplation in St. John of the Cross*, (Athens: Ohio University, 1988), 44-45. For a description of the coat of arms of the Yepes family see Francisco PIFERRER, *Nobiliario de los Reinos y Señoríos de España*, vol. 3 (Madrid, 1857), 189-99, quoted in TAVARD, *Poetry and Contemplation*, 256, n. 8.

the *Cántico*. Historical studies allow us to enter into dialogue with the times in which Juan lived and thus we are assisted in contextualizing the poem in the throes of sixteenth-century Spain. Historical studies, therefore, help the reader situate the text within the climate of its production.

2.2 *Literary-textual* Studies

Literary studies recognize Juan de la Cruz as an exemplary Spanish poet and author. This method of study examines Juan's literary techniques, his style, and the possible literary sources for the *Cántico*. Textual studies ensure that the sanjuanist scholar has a reliable and accurate text with which to work, whether this be in the original Spanish or a translation. Literary and textual studies endeavour to delve into the meaning (or meanings) of individual words or phrases within the context of their historical and literary use. These studies have also provided the analytical expertise needed to determine the authenticity of both *Cántico A* and *Cántico B*.[11]

The pioneers in the area of literary studies are Jean Baruzi, *St. Jean de la Croix et le problème de l'experience mystique* (1924), Crisógono de Jesús Sacramentado, *San Juan de la Cruz, su obra científica y su obra literaria* (1929), and Damaso Alonso *La poesia de san Juan de la Cruz* (1942).[12] Their studies focus on the cultural sources which Juan wove into his poetry. For example, Alonso's contribution places Juan's corpus in the context of the popular folk songs and poetry of Juan's day, such as the work of Garcilaso. Colin Thompson offers an excellent

---

[11] A summary of the various studies which either support or deny the authenticity of *Cántico B* is presented in Chapter Five.

[12] Jean BARUZI, *Saint Jean de la Croix et le problème de l'expérience mystique*, (Paris: Librairie Félex Alcan, 1924); CRISÓGONO DE JÉSUS SACRAMENTADO, *San Juan de la Cruz, su obra científica y su obra literaria*, 2 vols., (Madrid: Editorial Mensajero de santa Teresa y de san Juan de la Cruz, 1929); Damaso ALONSO, *La poesia de san Juan de la Cruz: Desde esta ladera*, (Madrid: Consejo Superior de Investigaciones Científicas Instituto Antonio de Nebrija, 1942). These studies do not deal exclusively with the *Cántico*, but are standard in any literary study of Juan's poetry.

summary of the literary origins of the *Cántico* in *The Poet and the Mystic*.[13] One of the most extensive literary studies focused specifically on the *Cántico* is *Stylistic Relationship in the Cántico espiritual* by Rose Marie Icaza.[14] José Morales in *El Cántico espiritual de San Juan de la Cruz*, begins his own analysis of the *Cántico* with an Introduction entitled "El Problema de las «fuentes literaria» de San Juan de la Cruz."[15] His specific project is to examine the classical and popular sources of the *Cántico*. In particular his study focuses on the biblical *Song of Songs* as the primary source for Juan's own *Cántico*.[16]

There are no manuscripts of Juan's *Cántico* in his own handwriting. Publications of the *Cántico* are dependent upon the study and evaluation of the various manuscripts. A list of these manuscripts can be found in Eulogio Pacho, *Cántico espiritual: Primera redacción y texto retocado*.[17] Extensive work has been done on the determination of the critical and authoritative text of the *Cántico*, particularly by Eulogio Pacho.[18] A good introduction to the textual difficulties

---

[13] THOMPSON, *The Poet and the Mystic*, 62-80.

[14] Rose Marie ICAZA, *The Stylistic Relationship Between Poetry and Prose in the Cántico espiritual of San Juan de la Cruz*, The Catholic University of America Studies in Romance Languages and Literatures 54 (New York: AMS Press, 1969).

[15] José L. MORALES, *El Cántico espiritual de San Juan de la Cruz: su relación con el Cantar de los Cantares y otras fuentes escrituristicas y literarias*, (Madrid: Editorial de Espiritualidad, 1971), 9-22.

[16] "La mayoría de los intérpretes de San Juan de la Cruz son teólogos o escritores espirituales cuyo modo de enfocar el estudio es teológico y místico Nuestro trabajo mira en primer término a lo literario, aunque no se limita al campo lírico de San Juan de la Cruz. Hemos tomado como punto de partido las fuentes literarias, proponiéndonos demostrar la tesis de que es la Biblia, y sobre todo el libro del *Cantar de los Cantares*, la obra de mayor influencia en el *Cántico Espiritual*." MORALES, *El Cántico espiritual de San Juan de la Cruz*, 16.

[17] *Cántico espiritual: Primera redacción y testó retocado*, Introduction, editing and notes by Eulogio Pacho, Clásicos Olvidados 4 (Madrid: Fundación Universitaria Española, 1981), 5-8.

[18] A thorough analysis of the text of *Cántico A* can be found in Pacho's monumental work: PACHO, *Cántico espiritual: Primera redacción y texto retocado;* and *San Juan de la Cruz y sus escritos*, Teología y Siglo XX 10 (Madrid: Ediciones Cristiandad, 1969). A list of primary sources and an extensive bibliography concerning the textual criticism of the *Cántico* can be found in *El Cántico Espiritual: Trayectoria Historica del Texto*, Bibliotheca Carmelitica, Series II: Studia, vol. 7 (Rome: Desclée, 1967), ix-xxii.

concerning the *Cántico* can be found in his, "El «Cántico espiritual» retocado: Introducción a su problemática textual."[19] Other scholars have also done extensive work on establishing the authenticity and exactness of the sanjuanist texts. These include *Obras del místico doctor san Juan de la Cruz*[20] by Gerardo de San Juan de la Cruz and *Cántico espiritual y poesías de san Juan de la Cruz según el códice de Sanlúcar de Barrameda*[21] by Silverio de Santa Teresa.

In summary, then, the strength of the literary-textual method is that it examines the text itself as a poetic text or as a piece of literature and strives to contextualize the text within its place of production. Although it may dissect the *Cántico* in certain phases of its analysis, it tends to consider the text as a whole. The internal movements of the *Cántico* are highlighted by this approach. Therefore, literary-textual studies offer valuable insights into the technical aspects of the *Cántico*. It is easy to see that literary-textual studies show the logic of the operations that connect the text of the *Cántico* through, for example, rhyme, alliteration, or cacophony, and assure us of the integrity of the code of the text. Through them we come to appreciate the aesthetic qualities of Juan's labour.[22] Literary-textual studies assure us that we have an accurate text to interpret, and help guarantee reliable translations through the understanding of individual words and phrases in their historical contexts.

---

[19] Eulogio PACHO, "El «Cántico espiritual» retocado: Introducción a su problemática textual," *Ephemerides Carmeliticae* 27 (1976), 382-452.

[20] *Obras del místico doctor san Juan de la Cruz*, ed. Gerardo de San Juan de la Cruz, 3 vols., (Toledo: J. Peláez, 1912-1914).

[21] *Cántico espiritual y poesías de san Juan de la Cruz según el códice de Sanlúcar de Barrameda*, ed. Silverio de Santa Teresa, 2 vols., (Burgos: El Monte Carmelo, 1928).

[22] Below, in my presentation on Paul Ricoeur, we will see that the aesthetic quality so much appreciated in Juan's *Cántico* is not merely decorative but, to a large degree, provides the meaning of the text for the reader. Ricoeur states: "Contrary to the common idea that pleasure is ignorant and mute, Jauss asserts that it possesses the power to open a space of meaning in which the logic of question and answer will subsequently unfold. It gives rise to understanding--*il donne à comprendre*. Pleasure is a perceptive reception, attentive to the prescriptions of the musical score that the text is." RICOEUR, *Time and Narrative*, 3:174.

2.3 *Ascetical-theological* Studies

Ascetical-theological studies help to explain and illustrate Juan de la Cruz's doctrine in the advancement of the spiritual life. This method often uses a particular theological system to interpret Juan's writings and fosters the development of the spiritual journey in the life of the reader. Quite often scholastic theology or Thomism is used to probe Juan's thought toward this end.[23] Clarification of the spiritual journey is helpful since there are two fundamental impasses which ascetical-theological studies help us understand.[24] The first impasse is that of the self, the natural individuality of the person marked by sin. The second impasse is that of the world: full union with God is not possible in this world. The fullness of life with God comes only with physical death.

Ascetical-theological studies can thus be used to elaborate Juan de la Cruz's description of how the human person lives and grows within these two moments of impasse. The strength of this method of interpretation is therefore its pursuit of clarity concerning the traditional stages of mystical transformation of the human person. For example, these studies are used to elaborate Juan's doctrine concerning the active and passive nights of the soul. Ascetical-theological studies are also used in sanjuanist scholarship to chart the purgative, illuminative, and unitive ways to God. It is this *via mistica* which Juan uses to interpret the *Cántico*. In *St. John of the Cross: His Life and Poetry*, Gerald Brenan says of the *Cántico*: "Its general message is clear enough. ... it is an allegory representing the journey of the soul to union with the Godhead. According to it, the first twelve stanzas represent the purgative stage of the *via mistica* and express the misery and

---

[23] LUEVANO, *Endless Transforming Love*, 15.

[24] These two negations are summarized from: José Sánchez DE MURILLO, "La Estructura del pensamiento de San Juan de la Cruz: Ensayo de interpretación fenomenológica," in *Experiencia y pensamiento en San Juan de la Cruz*, ed. Federico RUIZ [SALVADOR] (Madrid: Editorial de Espiritualidad, 1990), 304.

restlessness of the soul that is filled with unsatisfied love for God."[25]

Furthermore, the ascetical-theological method strives to elucidate how traditional orthodox beliefs are reflected in the *Cántico*.[26] For example, the ascetical-theological method is capable of describing the intimate union with God possible in this life, without losing the distance which exists between creature and Creator. This is seen in Georges Morel's interpretation of stanza five of *Cántico B* in *Le Sens de l'existence selon Saint Jean de la Croix*.[27] Using this text Morel affirms the permanent distinction between God and the individual even within the "spiritual marriage."

Ruiz Salvador, using what he describes as a theological-existential[28] approach, suggests that the interpretive key to Juan's writings is the following: Christian life is a process of liberation which is realized through the obscurity of the night of the *Nada*.[29] Ruiz Salvador's approach to Juan de la Cruz suggests that to read Juan is not just to repeat what he did or to follow the same path. Rather, each person must follow their own choices, follow their own *noche*. It is not possible to merely repeat Juan's experience in the life of the contemporary reader. Juan tells us as much in the Prologue of his *Cántico* as Ruiz Salvador points out.[30] This suggests that it is not possible to construct a set process of transformation, as read into the

---

[25] BRENAN, *St. John of the Cross: His Life and Poetry*, 120-121.

[26] "Esta distancia es un abismo ontológico que no puede ser salvado ni siquiera en la visión beatífica." DE MURILLO, "Estructura del pensamiento," 305.

[27] Georges MOREL, *Le Sens de l'existence selon Saint Jean de la Croix*, Théologie 46 (Paris, 1960), 2:242-246.

[28] RUIZ SALVADOR, "Sintesis doctrinal," 223.

[29] RUIZ SALVADOR, *Introducción a San Juan de la Cruz: El escritor, los escritos, el sistema*, 49-50. "La negación es columna del sistema sanjuanista. Ocupa un lugar irreemplazable y contribuye eficazmente a la armonía del conjunto. ... La NADA de San Juan de la Cruz está bien solamente en el lugar donde él la ha colocado. La tentación de sacar de quicio este elemento del sistema se renueva constantemente." Ibid., 414.

[30] RUIZ SALVADOR, *Introducción a San Juan de la Cruz: El escritor, los escritos, el sistema*, 128.

text. Ruiz Salvador, however, falls into the temptation of constructing a sanjuanist system, and part of that system is a defined *process* of human liberation based on classical theological categories.[31]

We may also include Eulogio Pacho, the leading commentator on the *Cántico*, in our list of scholars who are proponents of the ascetical-theological method.[32] In *Vértice de la poesía y de la mística: El «Cántico espiritual» de San Juan de la Cruz*, Pacho describes exegetical principles which must be used to unearth the *Cántico*'s doctrinal content. Bord, Crisógono, Lucien-Marie, as well as other scholars, have used scholastic principles and categories from the ascetical-theological method in their investigation of the *Cántico*.[33]

In conclusion we can say that ascetical-theological studies help us to understand the progression and development of the spiritual life within the Christian tradition. They provide an opportunity for us to explore and understand theologically what is happening through God's mysterious grace present in our lives.

---

[31] This approach is evident in the subtitles which Ruiz Salvador gives his work in *Introducción a San Juan de la Cruz: El escritor, los escritos, el sistema.* For example, Section III, which consists of seven chapters, is subtitled "Il Sistema," and Section IV, with a total of eight chapters, is subtitled, "Processo Evolutivo."

[32] Among his extensive publications the following works demonstrate this approach: Eulogio PACHO, *Vértice de la poesía y de la mística: El «Cántico espiritual» de San Juan de la Cruz*, Estudios Monte Carmelo 4 (Burgos: Editorial Monte Carmelo, 1983); Ibid., *San Juan de la Cruz: Temas fundamentales*, 2 vols., (Burgos: Editorial Monte Carmelo, 1984); Ibid., "Noemática e interpretación del «Cántico espiritual»: Poesía y teologia," *Teresianum* 40 (1989), 337-362.

[33] André BORD, *Mémoire et espérance chez Jean de la Croix*, with a Preface by Henri Gouhier, Bibliothèque de Spiritualité 8 (Paris: Beauchesne, 1971). Although not dealing exclusively with the *Cántico*, *San Juan de la Cruz, su obra científica y su obra literaria* by Crisógono de Jesús is in this line. In this two-volume work by Crisógono see in particular Volume I "Principios filosóficos fundamentales en el sistema de san Juan de la Cruz," 73-103 and "Principios teológicos fundamentales en el sistema del místico Doctor," 105-123. Although the bibiography is extensive the following are also to be included among studies using the ascetical-theological approach to Juan's corpus: Réginald GARRIGOU-LAGRANGE, *Perfection chrétienne et contemplation selon saint Thomas d'Aquin et saint Jean de la Croix*, 2 vols., (Paris: Éditions de la Vie Spirituelle, 1923); LUCIEN-MARIE DE SAINT-JOSEPH, *L'expérience de Dieu: Actualité du message de saint Jean de la Croix*, (Paris: 1968); George MOREL, "Nature et transformation de la volonté selon Saint Jean de la Croix," *Vie Spirituelle*, Supplement 10 (1957), 383-398; Federico RUIZ SALVADOR "Unidad de contrastes: Hermenéutica sanjuanista," in *Experiencia y pensamiento*, ed. Federico Ruiz [Salvador], 17-52; Henri SANSON, *L'esprit humain selon saint Jean de la Croix*. Publications de la Faculté des Lettres d'Alger 22. (Paris: Presses Universitaires de France, 1953).

Within the framework of these studies, Juan's *Cántico* and its commentary are used to disclose the mystical journey with the transcendent-immanent God.

2.4 Thematic-symbolic Studies

Through intra- and inter-textual analysis, this method of study seeks to isolate key themes revealed by Juan's symbols, metaphors, expressions of thought and images. For example, José Morales isolates several key images in Juan's commentary on the *Cántico* (i.e. *el beso, las hijas de Jerusalén,* and *la bodega)* and examines these against the backdrop of one of Juan's predecessors, St. Bernard.[34] Fernande Pepin in *Noces de Feu: Le Symbolisme nuptial du "Cántico espiritual" de saint Jean de la Croix à la lumière du "Canticum Canticorum"* isolates a single symbol in the *Cántico,* that of the "spiritual marriage," and examines the meaning of it through an analysis of the *Song of Songs* and its relationship to the *Cántico.*[35] Roger Duvivier's extensive study, *Le dynamisme existentiel dans la poésie de Jean de la Croix: Lecture du «Cántico espiritual»,* is largely a symbolic analysis of Juan's *Cántico.*[36] Duvivier, through his study of Juan's symbolic expression, seeks to reveal

[34] MORALES, *El Cántico espiritual de San Juan de la Cruz,* 53-57. I would also situate within this thematic approach Federico RUIZ SALVADOR, *Introducción a San Juan de la Cruz: El escritor, los escritos, el sistema,* Biblioteca de Autores Cristianos 279 (Madrid: Editorial Católica, 1968), 295-675. Ruiz Salvador develops a series of themes drawing from Juan's entire corpus. In Chapter 8 of Ibid., 215-248 the *Cántico* is specifically dealt with. Ruiz Salvador also takes this thematic approach in his more recent work "Unidad de contrastes: Hermenéutica sanjuanista," in *Experiencia y pensamiento,* 17-52. In this article Ruiz Salvador investigates a set of ten pairs of opposites which focus on the essential unity of the sanjuanist corpus.

[35] Fernande PEPIN, *Noces de Feu: Le Symbolisme nuptial du "Cántico espiritual" de saint Jean de la Croix à la lumière du "Canticum Canticorum,"* Recherches 9 Théologie (Montréal: Bellarmin, 1972).

[36] Roger DUVIVIER, *Le dynamisme existentiel dans la poésie de Jean de la Croix: Lecture du «Cántico espiritual»,* Études de littérature étrangère et comparée (Didier: Paris, 1973), 45-46. Duvivier organises this project based on Merleau-Ponty's classic work *Phénoménologie de la perception* (Paris: Gallimard, 1945). Duvivier suggests two possible perspectives from which his phenomenological reading is analyzed. We see this in the following statement concerning Juan's poem: "L'entreprise esthétique de Jean de la Croix est soumise à deux déterminations: l'une vient du côte de l'expérience même, qui s'impose comme sujet, l'autre, l'autre tient aux matériaux littéraires disponibles et aux formes d'imagination contemporaine." Ibid., 87. Because of the phenomenological nature of this study of Juan's symbolism I will examine it again below. In another extensive work: Ibid., *La genèse du «Cantique spirituel» de Saint Jean de la Croix,* Bibliothèque de

the interior life of Juan de la Cruz. The externalization of Juan's interior life in symbols, according to Duvivier, builds a certain intersubjectivity between Juan and the reader of Juan's *Cántico*. In this way Duvivier attempts to build a formative bridge between Juan's ineffable experience of the spiritual world and the experience of the reader in the present world.[37]

Thematic-symbolic studies have often been used in conjunction with the theological-ascetical approach.[38] For example, the theme of conversion is mapped against the doctrinal progression of the *vía mística* by Federico Ruiz Salvador in *Vida teologal durante la purificación interior en los escritos de San Juan*

---

la Faculté de Philosophie et Lettres de l'Université de Liège, Fasc. 189 (Paris: Société d'Édition "Les Belles Lettres," 1971), 178-223, Duvivier outlines the development of the symbolism in the *Cántico*.

[37] Duvivier outlines his project in the following way: "Toute question de pure métaphysique mise à part, nous essayerons de rejoindre une existence réalisée dans ce monde-ci. Pour sympathiser avec la poésie du *Cántico*, nous n'avons d'autre recours que de nous interroger sur le sens existentiel des images dominantes, ce qui revient à entreprendre une sorte d'analyse phénoménologique du poème. Aucune prétention donc de toucher à l'*essence* de la vie mystique, mais tout de même un certain espoir de retrouver des directions de vie, certains intuitions de la philosophie [sic] *existentielle* de Jean de la Croix." DUVIVIER, *Dynamisme existentiel*, 45-46. In his conclusion Duvivier states: "Certes, le poète balisé du côté de ce monde, mais nous voyons bien que c'est pour mieux l'ouvrir de l'autre côté. Tel est l'intérêt de ce que nous avons appelé la géographie de l'âme, géographie dont les relevés n'atteignent que les zones limitrophes du terrestre. Sous le couvert d'un allégorisme assez simple, on y trouve tout ensemble une vision du monde sensible selon l'espace spirituel et une référence inavouée aux fondements physiques de cet espace qui, malgré tout, garde des attaches phénoménales." Ibid., 195. "En conclusion, l'imagination de Jean de la Croix passe par les archétypes, tout comme sa poésie doit se soumettre à la figuration par la nature et accueillir des formes et thèmes d'expression traditionnels: il est assez grand mystique et assez vrai poète pour user les ressources de l'inconscient à la manière dont il use de l'univers objectif ou des procédés littéraires hérités de ses prédécesseurs." Ibid., 221

[38] I would cite this as the guiding force behind the investigations in ICAZA, "Key Words and Key Symbols," in *The Stylistic Relationship in the Cántico*, 53-86. For example: "The concrete symbol of the flame may be regarded as the culminating symbol of the soul purified by love and raised to the transformation of a flame within the Fire and Light of God through love. Since the present study deals primarily with the *Cántico*, the poetic text is again the pivotal point for the discussion of the symbol of fire. In its poetic lines there are three concrete symbols of fire: a) *lumbre* (10), b) *centella* (16), c) *llama* (38). All three enclose in themselves two general connotations: fire and light. In this way, San Juan de la Cruz masterfully condenses in a simple figure *the only two ways* in which the simplified human soul can possibly be united to God, through intellect-knowledge-light and will-love-fire." Ibid., 64, (emphasis mine). Icaza refers the reader to Aquinas' *Summa* I-II, 62,3 for support of these two ways. See ICAZA, Ibid., 64, n. 20.

de la Cruz.[39] E. W. Trueman Dicken develops various themes from the writings of Juan de la Cruz in *The Crucible of Love.*[40] His study includes an examination of prayer, stages of spiritual progress, and visions, as they are reflected in Juan's corpus. In thematic-symbolic studies of the sanjuanist corpus, symbols are often looked upon as veiled manifestations of doctrinal content which reveal the classical progression of the spiritual life. Juan's literary symbols are seen as symbolic expressions of Juan's experiences.[41] The symbols are thus perceived as being representations of some other reality that pre-exists symbolic representation. It is the task of thematic-symbolic studies to unmask for the benefit of today's reader that reality or to display the dogmatic content hidden behind the symbol or image.[42]

[39] Federic RUIZ SALVADOR, *Vida teologal durante la purificación interior en los escritos de San Juan de la Cruz*, (Madrid: 1959). Ruiz Salvador's excellent study *Introducción a San Juan de la Cruz: El escritor, los escritos, el sistema* develops many themes recurrent throughout Juan's corpus. See in particular: RUIZ SALVADOR, "*«Cántico espiritual»*" in *Introducción a San Juan de la Cruz: El escritor, los escritos, el sistema*, 215-248.

[40] E.W. Trueman DICKEN, *The Crucible of Love: A Study of the Mysticism of St. Teresa of Jesus and St. John of the Cross*, (New York: Sheed and Ward, 1963).

[41] For example, the dark night, which Jean Baruzi attributes to the Toledan jail experience. Baruzi sees the symbol of the night as particularly reflective of Juan's personal experience: "Attachons-nous à ce thème de la nuit, thème qui se moule sur l'expérience au point de se confondre avec elle. Par un prodige de l'imagination mystique, la nuit est à la fois *la plus intime traduction de l'expérience et l'expérience elle-même*. Cette même nuit, que nous venons d'entrevoir comme un immense schéma symbolique, sera l'épreuve qui créera en nous un être nouveau." BARUZI, *Problème de l'expérience mystique*, 330. See Baruzi's extensive comments on Juan's symbolic representation in Ibid., 305-374. It is in this chapter entitled "L'Expression mystique et ses prolongements," where Baruzi explores the relationship between Juan's experience and his poetry. According to Baruzi the meeting point between these two resides in Juan's use of the symbol, that is, the symbol expresses Juan's experience in poetic form.

[42] We see this approach in Rosa Maria Icaza: "With the help of the prose commentary to the *Cántico espiritual* it may be concluded with certainty that in both instances the wind is the symbol of the Holy Spirit in His action of love-imparting." ICAZA, *Stylistic Relationship in the Cántico*, 70. Icaza later explains: "As it has been seen before, the wind in the later stanzas of the *Cántico espiritual* is particularly the symbol of love breathed and exchanged between the two lovers and specifically recognized as identical with its source, the Holy Spirit, Love himself and Breathing of the Father and the Son, proceeding from Both as Love Bond between Both." Ibid., 71. "If one examines the poetic symbols in the order in which they appear in the poem, and parallels them with their abstract meaning given in the prose commentary, one is able to trace again the path of the soul in her ascension to God." Ibid., 75. "In a word, the symbol has been the stepping stone to explain with simplicity one of the most profound mysteries of faith, the Triune God." Ibid., 85.

2.5 *Philosophical* Studies

Philosophical studies work to expand the meaning of Juan's writings by reflecting on them with philosophical tools that are not specifically linked to a theological system. Philosophical studies, therefore, attempt to interpret Juan's corpus from the perspective of deductive reasoning which is not overly tied to preconceived theological categories. These studies open up the possibility of allowing Juan's texts to speak in new ways. To demonstrate the contribution of the philosophical method I will cite the philosophical works of three authors: Jean Baruzi, Edith Stein, and Georges Morel.

The first major philosophical reflection on Juan's corpus was Jean Baruzi's 1924 study *Saint Jean de la Croix et le problème de l'expérience mystique.* Instead of examining Juan's corpus from a particular theological perspective Baruzi attempts to understand Juan's writings from within Juan's expression of his own personal experience. Baruzi did not situate Juan on the horizon of Juan's faith, but tried to let Juan's experience, as it is reflected in his works, speak for itself. Baruzi's approach attempted to unravel the anthropological experience of Juan expressed through Juan's symbols. It was this emphasis on exploring Juan's experience, rather than his theological doctrine, which constitutes Baruzi's methodological contribution.[43]

This approach allows an exploration of Juan's corpus which is critical in the sense that Juan's anthropological experience is seen as anterior to its expression in dogmatic or theological principles. Baruzi attempts to get at the root of Juan's metaphysical experience that supports the theological doctrine that emerges from it. Juan's experience as a human-being-in-the-world therefore comes to light in Baruzi's analysis.[44] This experience, for Baruzi, is reflected in Juan's symbolic

---

[43] DE MURILLO, "Estructura del pensamiento," 305.

[44] The success of Baruzi's project has been continually called into doubt. See, for example, the following (largely negative) evaluation of Baruzi's 1924 publication: Baldomero JIMÉNEZ DUQUE, "Una interpretación moderna de San Juan de la Cruz," *Revista Española de Teología* 4 (1944), 315-344. Jiménez Duque says of Baruzi: "La obra de M. Baruzi no ha interpretado fielmente a San Juan de la Cruz. Son dos posiciones totalmente distintas." Ibid., 338. Florencio García Muñoz has an

system. Of fundamental importance for Baruzi is Juan's symbol of *noche*.[45] Baruzi sees this nocturnal symbolism as being the dominant symbol which bridges Juan's experience and Juan's doctrinal expression. The symbol of *noche* is thus the meeting point of experience and doctrine. Baruzi therefore views the symbol of *noche* not as a "thing," but as a function.[46] For this reason Baruzi views the symbol of *noche* as the symbol which unites all of sanjuanist thought.[47]

However, Baruzi's interpretation, for all its emphasis on experience, tends to intellectualize Juan's writings.[48] Baruzi tends to secularize Juan's writings and exclude the dynamic role of grace and the presence of the Divine in his reflections.[49] He tends to reduce mystical experience to a mechanical process of self-

equally negative appreciation of Baruzi's work: "Baruzi se equivoca por completo al pensar en una Deidad vaga e impersonal en la que se pierde el alma. En San Juan de la Cruz es claro que el Dios que aparece es trinamente personal, y la permanencia en su identidad por parte del alma en ese Dios, es radical." Florencio GARCIA MUÑOZ, *Cristología de San Juan de la Cruz: Sistemática y Mística,* (Madrid: Universidad de Salamanca, Fundación Universitaria Española, 1982), 153, n. 21. Fernande Pepin says of Baruzi: "Ce gros volume offre trop de génie pour n'être pas cité. C'est le sujet d'une thèse d'une documentation extrêmement fouillée et d'un exposé qui cherche, sinon la concision du moins la précision. ... L'auteur fait de Jean de la Croix un néo-intellectualiste et ces théories ne cadrent pas avec les enseignements du Saint Docteur; dans ce déplacement des valeurs sensibles aux yeux des croyants catholiques, il n'a pu que peindre un tableau incomplet." Fernande PÉPIN, *Saint Jean de la Croix: Bibliographie et état présent des travaux,* Doctoral Dissertation presented at the University of Laval, Québec, typewritten copy, (January 1968), 580-1.

[45] BARUZI, *Problème de l'expérience mystique,* 307. See also, Ibid., 329.

[46] BARUZI, *Problème de l'expérience mystique,* 321.

[47] BARUZI, *Problème de l'expérience mystique,* 312.

[48] As I mentioned above negative critique of Baruzi's work is not lacking in the literature. The first negative critiques of Baruzi's work can be found in the *Bulletin de la Société française de Philosophie,* (Paris), (May-June 1925), quoted in DE MURILLO, "Estructura del pensamiento," 305, n. 10. For a philosophical evaluation of Baruzi's approach see: MOREL, *Le sens de l'existence,* 1:10-20.

[49] Since this extensive study was published (780 pages), it is nearly always cited in major publications on Juan. Notwithstanding the frequency with which it is cited, it is usually mentioned in a disapproving way as I have already indicated. However, the current breakdown of the predominance of the ascetical-theological approach to Juan's work may open the door for a reconsideration of Baruzi's work. This movement may be indicated in the recent first publication of Baruzi's study translated into a foreign language, in this case Spanish: *San Juan de la Cruz y el problema de la experiencia mística,* ed. José Jiménez Lozano, trans. Carlos Ortega (Valladolid, 1991).

liberation that minimized the moment of the transcendent.[50]

Edith Stein, a student of Edmund Husserl, used her philosophical background to give Juan's corpus a contemporary appeal and vocabulary in *The Science of the Cross: A Study of St. John of the Cross.*[51] To a large extent Stein uses Juan's corpus to expound on truths of the Christian faith which may not be directly reflected in Juan's corpus but flow from it.[52]

A third contribution in the philosophical arena (although it overlaps the theological) is the extensive three volume work of Georges Morel entitled: *Le sens de l'existence selon Saint Jean de la Croix* (1960-61). Morel's focus is on Juan's own experience. However, Morel, in contrast to Baruzi, included the role of faith in his study of the sanjuanist corpus.

Morel describes Juan's concept of faith as something dynamic, a faith which is in movement.[53] He suggests that it is neither faith itself nor reason (*mouvement intellectuel*)[54] which sustains this movement, but rather something which surpasses them both, that is, a fundamental attitude. This fundamental attitude

---

[50] For example, Baruzi states: "En dépit de l'apparence, Jean de la Croix traduit moins un devenir affectif qu'une recherche intellectuelle." BARUZI, *Problème de l'expérience mystique*, 277. And, "Nous pouvons être assurés que ce qui domine, chez Jean de la Croix, c'est l'activité d'analyse." Ibid., 280. See also, Ibid., 298.

[51] Edith STEIN, *The Science of the Cross: A Study of St. John of the Cross*, ed. L. Gelber and R. Leuven, trans. Hilda Graef (London: Burns & Oates, 1960).

[52] See STEIN, *The Science of the Cross*, xxi. Of the *Cántico* she says: "The Canticle introduces us to the world such as it appears to the longing soul intoxicated with love. It only goes out to seek its Beloved. It is anxious to find traces of him everywhere; everything reminds it of him and is important only insofar as it gives news of him or contains a message from him. As the hart appears for a second at the edge of the forest and vanishes as soon as it is seen by man, so did the Lord at the first meetings: he showed himself to the soul but had disappeared before it could take hold of him. The crystal fount that refreshes the wanderer is the faith: for the truth it gives is pure, not darkened by error, and from it springs the water of life that flows on to eternal life (John 4.14). Longingly the soul bends over it: may not the eyes of its Beloved shine from its clear mirror? His eyes-- this means the divine rays that have wounded, enlightened and inflamed its inmost parts. The soul always feels that these eyes see it, they are imprinted in its ground." Ibid., 187.

[53] MOREL, *Le sens de l'existence*, 2.219.

[54] MOREL, *Le sens de l'existence*, 2.221.

he describes as love, a love in which the Absolute Self-manifests.[55] Morel thus suggests that it is Love which mediates faith and reason. Faith and reason are but two moments of the transcendent dynamic of love which sustains the pilgrim on his or her path.

The self-realization of the human person is founded in the movement of Self-revelation of the Absolute through love in the world.[56] Using this basis, Morel shows the philosophical importance, as well as the contemporary importance, of sanjuanist mysticism. For example, Morel attempts to break through the ascetical-theological "stages" of Christian faith by describing the various "situations of movement" that constitute the Christian journey.[57] Morel thus describes sanjuanist mysticism as a dynamic existential movement that does not base itself exclusively on Christian tradition, but on something anterior, the Source of that tradition which is beyond all representation.[58] Morel thus divests Juan of any ideological perspective.

This is to say that Morel suggests that Juan's writings do not reflect on the *idea* of God but rather reflect Juan's *experience* of God. Morel says that Juan's focus is not "God and the human person," nor "God and God's creation," but rather "God and God's work *is* God."[59] This interpretation, suggests Morel, does not fall into contradiction with the God of Christian Revelation, but rather affirms that

---

[55] "La *Manifestation* est constitutive de l'essence divine. Être et manifester son dialectiquement identique en Dieu." MOREL, *Le sens de l'existence*, 2:222.

[56] See this entire section which treats this theme in MOREL, *Le sens de l'existence*, 2:216-228.

[57] MOREL, *Le sens de l'existence*, 2:20-21.

[58] "Saint Jean de la Croix ne s'appuie donc pas sur la tradition chrétienne comme sur quelque chose de premier: l'acte qui sous-entend le périple humain n'est pas seulement retour aux sources main retour à la Source, constante remontée à l'Origine, laquelle est au-delà de toute *représentation* même révélée. ceci sera vérifié plus tard par l'usage que le mystique fait des texte de l'Écriture, non seulement ceux de l'Ancien mais aussi ceux du Nouveau Testament." MOREL, *Le sens de l'existence*, 2:143.

[59] "Dieu et son oeuvre *sont* Dieu." MOREL, *Le sens de l'existence*, 2:148. See also Ibid., 2:156-157.

God lies beyond all representation of God.[60] Morel's reading of Juan underlined the importance of the philosophical approach and content of Juan's writings, something Baruzi was not able to convince others of during his own time.

Through these three authors, Baruzi, Stein, and Morel, we can see the richness that the philosophical approach brings to a reading of Juan's corpus. These authors read Juan without the confinement of predetermined theological categories. They have allowed Juan's writings to speak in a fresh and new way. However, the philosophical approach that allows Juan's writings to be examined from various perspectives frequently affirms the findings of an ascetical-theological reading. The philosophical approach, therefore, often deepens our appreciation of those very same findings.

2.6 *Psychological* Studies

This approach to the sanjuanist corpus is relatively new. It attempts to understand and contextualize Juan's spiritual practices and developments within the insights of modern psychology. The psychological method, therefore, attempts to develop what might be referred to as a "mystic psychology."[61] In order to explore the human workings of mysticism and its expressions, contemporary models of developmental psychology are brought into dialogue with Juan's own developmental insights.

Two exemplary works in this area both exhibit the use of Jungian psychology. The first is by James Arraj who uses Jung exclusively to guide his reflection: *Christian Mysticism in the Light of Jungian Psychology: John of the Cross and Dr. C.G. Jung.*[62] The second is by John Welch who uses insights from Jung as well as from a number of other contemporary thinkers such as Bernard

---

[60] MOREL, *Le sens de l'existence*, 2:143.

[61] LUEVANO, *Endless Transforming Love*, 17.

[62] James ARRAJ, *Christian Mysticism in the Light of Jungian Psychology: John of the Cross and Dr. C.G. Jung*, (Chiloquin, OR: Tools for Inner Growth, 1986).

Lonergan, James Fowler and Gabriel Moran: *When Gods Die: An Introduction to John of the Cross.*[63]

Although transcending the strictly psychological approach, the work of Marilyn May Mallory may be included in this section as well: *Christian Mysticism: Transcending Techniques: A Theological Reflection on the Empirical Testing of the Teaching of St. John of the Cross.*[64] Mallory weaves together the findings of psychology, various fields of theology, the social sciences, as well as the medical sciences, to empirically explore spiritual experience and to expose the reader to the practical thought of Juan de la Cruz.

Since Juan de la Cruz speaks about the fundamental spiritual journey, which is the journey of adult maturation, these studies substantially contribute toward a practical as well as a theoretical understanding of the progression and development of spiritual life within a contemporary understanding of the growth and maturation of the human psyche. For example, in his summary on the *Cántico* Welch says:

> John's process [in the *Cántico*] exemplifies Bernard Lonergan's description of the interior process of coming to consciousness and living responsibly. His psyche followed the transcendental precepts to be attentive (in prayerful listening), to be intelligent (through attempts to word his experience, first in symbolic form), to be reasonable (through discussion in his commentary), to be responsible (in urging the active nights and openness to the passive nights). This process revealed a gradual union with God in love, pointing to a final precept to be in love.[65]

Psychological studies can be very practical in nature and provide aids for persons with different personality types to mature. Maturity is seen, not as parallel to spiritual maturation, but as spiritual maturation itself. The journey

[63] John WELCH, *An Introduction to John of the Cross: When Gods Die*, (New York: Paulist Press, 1990).

[64] Marilyn May MALLORY, *Christian Mysticism: Transcending Techniques: A Theological Reflection on the Empirical Testing of the Teaching of St. John of the Cross*, (Assen: Van Gorcum, 1977).

[65] WELCH, *When Gods Die*, 177.

outlined in the *Cántico* is thus viewed as the fundamental story of humanity, a humanity transformed in its deepest desires in its movement toward God.[66]

It should now be obvious that many different methodological approaches to Juan's corpus have produced, at various levels, tremendous insight into the meaning and value of Juan's corpus. I have given examples from six different methodological approaches to Juan's corpus. Each of these approaches has its own tools and therefore exposes different areas of Juan's thought. It is the contention of this dissertation that these different methodological approaches to Juan's corpus, and, in particular, to Juan's *Cántico*, are coherently unified through a hermeneutical inquiry: hermeneutical interpretation of Juan's *Cántico* establishes a dialectic between and among the various disciplines that have been used to study the *Cántico*. The benefits from this dialectic are discussed in the last section of this chapter. For now, however, let us turn our attention to an examination of the phenomenological approach, which, as has been suggested already, is closely related to the hermeneutical approach I am investigating.

3. Toward the Hermeneutical Dialectic through Phenomenology

In addition to the preceding body of literature, I am now in a position to highlight a study which contributes in a particular way toward the hermeneutical approach I am suggesting in this dissertation: Roger Duvivier's *Le dynamisme existentiel dans la poésie de Jean de la Croix: Lecture du «Cántico espiritual»*. The unique contribution of this study lies in its use of phenomenology to analyse Juan de la Cruz's *Cántico*. The phenomenological approach is but one move away from the hermeneutical approach I am suggesting in this dissertation.

I will proceed in two steps in this section in order to link phenomenology with the hermeneutical approach. First, I will give a general definition of phenomenology and indicate why Paul Ricoeur was led from a strictly phenomenological method to include hermeneutics in his methodology. Second, I

---

[66] This is the overall approach John Welch takes in *When Gods Die*.

will summarize the particular phenomenological approach used by Duvivier and the results of his research. This will put us in a position to begin to explore more fully the particular resources which the hermeneutical approach has to offer us in order to interpret Juan de la Cruz's *Cántico*.

3.1 Phenomenology

Phenomenology "is a showing or bringing to appearance of something as it is, in its manifestness."[67] In the tradition of Husserl it constructs a method "which might lay open the processes of being in human existence in such a way that being, and not simply one's own ideology, might come into view. ... phenomenology ... [opens] up the realm of the preconceptual apprehending of phenomena."[68] "Phenomenology methodically describes objects of consciousness and correlative acts of intending."[69] The content of lived experience is, therefore, the subject matter of phenomenological inquiry.

For example, in *Fallible Man* Ricoeur uses the resources of phenomenology to investigate such phenomena as finitude, guilt, and sin.[70] Cultural experiences and cultural expressions, such as those just mentioned, are therefore viewed as disclosures of reality and investigated through phenomenology. Through our intuited consciousness and perceptions of these realities the world in which human beings live is conceptually articulated.

These phenomenological expressions of being-in-the-world are explored as laying bare reality itself. The noema of reality, that is, their specific mode of appearing, are intuited directly by the transcendental ego and described in their encounter with the human subject. In phenomenology it is not the task of the

---

[67] Richard E. PALMER, *Hermeneutics: Interpretation Theory in Schleiermacher, Dilthey, Heidegger, and Gadamer*, (Evanston: Northwestern University Press, 1969), 128.

[68] PALMER, *Hermeneutics*, 124-5.

[69] KLEMM, *The Hermeneutical Theory of Paul Ricoeur*, 47.

[70] Paul RICOEUR, *Fallible Man*, trans. Charles A. Kelby (Chicago: Henry Regnery Co., 1965).

mind to project meaning onto the phenomenon of reality; rather, "what appears is an ontological manifesting of the thing itself."[71] This approach is in contrast to dogmatism. Through dogmatism "a thing can be forced to be seen only in the desired aspect. But to let a thing appear as what it is becomes a matter of learning to allow it to do so, for it gives itself to be seen."[72] Phenomenology develops a method of inquiry which allows this to happen.[73]

Phenomenology, therefore, means a reversal of direction from that to which we are accustomed: "it is not we who point to things; rather, things show themselves to us."[74] True understanding, in the phenomenological approach, results in us being led by the "power of the thing to manifest itself."[75] We know (noesis) the phenomena of reality by the way in which the phenomena (noema) "show" themselves to us in their own way. Phenomenology is a means of being led by the phenomenon of reality through a way of access genuinely belonging *to them*.[76] The phenomenological approach is important in the theory of interpretation, since it implies that interpretation is not grounded in human categories but in the "manifestness" of whatever we encounter in reality, and, conversely, what encounters us.[77] Through phenomenology the experience of human existence is reflexively

---

[71] PALMER, *Hermeneutics*, 128.

[72] PALMER, *Hermeneutics*, 128.

[73] Husserlian phenomenology, which Ricoeur adopted, is called "phenomenological reduction." "It proceeds through these steps: (1) the *epochē*, in which one suspends belief in the existence of the object, and (2) the *eidetic* phase of reduction, which includes intuition of the essence of the phenomenon (its mode of appearing) as it is constituted by the transcendental ego. The aim of the descriptive method is to exhibit the elements and the relations between elements that make up the structure of the phenomenon as an intended object of consciousness related to an intending subject. Ricoeur's work from the beginning has taken the style of noematic analysis in Husserl's sense of phenomenological reduction, in which one reads the object, person, event, or expression for the correlate structure of consciousness." KLEMM, *The Hermeneutical Theory of Paul Ricoeur*, 47.

[74] PALMER, *Hermeneutics*, 128.

[75] PALMER, *Hermeneutics*, 128.

[76] PALMER, *Hermeneutics*, 128.

[77] PALMER, *Hermeneutics*, 128.

described. According to Heidegger, this openness to the noema of existence in themselves, opens up new possibilities of being-in-the-world.

With Heidegger, therefore, we understand that reality is dynamic and necessarily unfinished. It presents itself to us in new culturally and historically determined ways. Phenomenology is thus linked with ontology. Phenomenology, in the end, renders open "the mood and direction of human existence; it ... [renders] visible the invisible structure of being-in-the-world."[78] For Heidegger, "ontology must, as phenomenology of being, become a 'hermeneutic' of existence."[79]

Paul Ricoeur takes the phenomenological approach one step further and develops what could be called phenomenological hermeneutics. *The Symbolism of Evil* is Ricoeur's first formal hermeneutical work which benefits from this approach. From the more intuitive descriptions of the way meaning appears, Ricoeur was led to the lingual phenomena, first as symbols, then as texts.[80] For Ricoeur, reality is essentially linguistic and mediated through texts. Reality is not immediately available, that is, immediately intuited in the Husserlian phenomenological sense; rather it is subject to the process of interpretation as it is mediated through language. Meaning in human existence, not being immediately present, is mediated by the semantic disclosure of texts.

Ricoeur thus continues to use the resources of phenomenology in his investigations, but centres these investigations on the cultural deposits of the appearances of the content of lived experience *through* texts. Ricoeur thus instituted

---

[78] PALMER, *Hermeneutics*, 129.

[79] PALMER, *Hermeneutics*, 129.

[80] The development of this area of Ricoeur's thought can be found in Donald IHDE, "Toward the Philosophy of Language *Freud and Philosophy: An Essay On Interpretation*," *Hermeneutic Phenomenology: The Philosophy of Paul Ricoeur*, with a Foreward by Paul Ricoeur (Evanston: Northwestern University Press, 1971), 131-166. See also, Ibid., "Hermeneutics and the Linguistic Disciplines: New Counterfoci," 167-181; Paul CLARK, "The Hermeneutic Turn," in *Paul Ricoeur, Critics of the Twentieth Century*, London: Routledge, 1990, 90-119; and Mary GERHART, "Theory of Symbol: The Symbolic Forms of Belief," in *The Question of Belief in Literary Criticism: An Introduction to the Hermeneutical Theory of Paul Ricoeur*, (Stuttgart: Akademischer Verlag Hans-Dieter Heinz), 1979, 175-206.

a hermeneutical turn: the content of lived experience, as inscribed in texts, is opened up to *historical interpretation* of cultural traces. With this stance Ricoeur moved away from the idealist position of Husserl who believed that human existence could be intuited directly through the phenomenological method. For Ricoeur, it is language, with its polysemy of words, which reveals human being's relationship to the world in two ways: (1) the disclosure of the world, and (2) the becoming of the world. Ricoeur, through his textual hermeneutics, retained the phenomenological resources of Husserl to perceive and describe the world, as well as the ontological focus of Heidegger who holds that reality is essentially unfinished.

Ricoeur's turn to textual mediation of the phenomenon of the world claims that we cannot stand outside of time and observe reality, as the *epochē* of Husserl claims. Rather, Ricoeur holds that the noema of reality are a product of the flux of the historical situation itself. New possibilities for human being-in-the-world become possibile through reflexive hermeneutics. It is this approach to reality and its disclosure which form the critical framework for the work of this dissertation.

Ricoeur's approach is critical because it presents a reflexive hermeneutics. Ricoeur is convinced that a "relatively clear trace of human being"[81] can be discerned through texts, the medium, par excellence which dynamically discloses and shapes human existence. "Ricoeur shifts his method to the interpretation of linguistic expressions precisely in hope that he can thereby gain new and fruitful access to the meaning of human subjectivity under the conditions of existence."[82] "The guiding principle for the hermeneutical turn is that if language is the medium of experience and thought, then we can trace backward from the expression of experience and thought to the kind of self-in-a-world that '*spricht sich aus*' but is otherwise not directly accessible."[83] We must therefore get at what is expressed of being-in-the-world through the interpretation of texts rather than

---

[81] KLEMM, *The Hermeneutical Theory of Paul Ricoeur*, 45.

[82] KLEMM, *The Hermeneutical Theory of Paul Ricoeur*, 61.

[83] KLEMM, *The Hermeneutical Theory of Paul Ricoeur*, 62.

immediate and intuitive perception. The expression, through interpretation, is thereby brought to appearance. The work of this dissertation is to provide a dialectical approach to the *Cántico* to "make appear" what it expresses, that is, to interpret hermeneutically the *Cántico* of Juan de la Cruz.

As I mentioned above, one scholar, Roger Duvivier, has used a strictly phenomenological approach to investigate the *Cántico* of Juan de la Cruz. Let us briefly review his findings to reveal the richness of the phenomenological approach and continue to explore why the phenomenological approach is but one step away from the hermeneutical approach that enriches our interpretive task. We will thus be led to examine more fully Ricoeur's approach which uses the resources of phenomenology to develop the hermeneutical project.

3.2 Roger Duvivier's Phenomenological Analysis of the *Cántico*

A recent article by José Sánchez de Murillo has extended an invitation for a concerted effort to bring sanjuanist studies into the contemporary dialogue pertaining to phenomenological research.[84] In his article, de Murillo shows how the studies of Baruzi, Morel, and Ruiz Salvador, already discussed above, have contributed toward the phenomenological approach to the sanjuanist corpus.[85] There is, however, a study which uses a phenomenological method *per se* to study the *Cántico* of Juan de la Cruz. This is Roger Duvivier's *Le dynamisme existentiel dans la poésie de Jean de la Croix: Lecture du «Cántico espiritual»*.

Duvivier bases his analysis of Juan's major symbols in the *Cántico* on the existential phenomenology of Merleau-Ponty.[86] In *Le dynamisme existentiel*

---

[84] DE MURILLO, "Estructura del Pensamiento," 297-334. The anthology of scholarly articles in *Experiencia y pensamiento* is an excellent indication of the forefront of various areas of sanjuanist studies.

[85] DE MURILLO, "Estructura del pensamiento," 305-314.

[86] Maurice MERLEAU-PONTY, *Phénoménologie de la perception*, (Paris: Gallimard, 1945). Duvivier says that: "En réalité, le propos phénoménologique ne s'est pas trouvé au départ." DUVIVIER, *Dynamisme existentiel*, 47. For this reason, he says, he did not find it necessary to set out, at the beginning, the specific phenomenological principles upon which his research is based.

dans la poésie de Jean de la Croix Duvivier investigates the interior world of Juan de la Cruz as *this world appears* phenomenologically in the symbols of the *Cántico.*[87] Duvivier suggests that the *Cántico,* through its symbolic expression, allows the contemporary reader to be exposed to the interior life of Juan de la Cruz.[88] Duvivier shows how this is possible by the analysis of the existential movements of the *Cántico* as they appear in symbolic representation. Duvivier, methodically, examines the *Cántico* stanza by stanza, commenting on various expressions and phrases, symbols and images, which Juan uses to express his existential experience. Duvivier, however, does not attempt to describe a set pattern for the human journey as it may or may not be suggested by Juan. Duvivier views Juan's poetry as a source of "traces" of what Juan experienced in his mysterious journey.[89]

These "traces" point the reader toward the reality which is at the origin of the experience for Juan, that is, the Divine. The poem thus orients the reader toward the transcendent Other *in this world.*[90] Within this orientation, this journey, there is a certain liberation of the fundamental structures of life through Juan's symbolic expression of his own experience.[91] The existential dynamism of being-human within the Divine, as it is suggested by Juan's poetry, is thus recognized

Ibid., 47, n. 1. He simply refers the reader to the above text by Merleau-Ponty in a general way through a footnote.

[87] Duvivier describes his project in the following way: "Pour sympathiser avec la poésie du *Cántico,* nous n'avons d'autre recours que de nous interroger sur le sens existentiel des images dominantes, ce qui revient à entreprendre une sorte d'analyse phénoménologique du poème. Aucune prétention donc de toucher à *l'essence* de la vie mystique, mais tout de même un certain espoir de retrouver des directions de vie, certaines intuitions de la philosophie *existentielle* de Jean de la Croix." DUVIVIER, *Dynamisme existentiel,* 46.

[88] DUVIVIER, *Dynamisme existentiel,* 7-8. With Duvivier an interpretation of the *Cántico* takes as its goal the determination of Juan's interior life. It is this interiority which Duvivier suggests is mediated by the symbolic expression in the poem.

[89] DUVIVIER, *Dynamisme existentiel,* 228-9.

[90] DUVIVIER, *Dynamisme existentiel,* 45. "Cette poésie ne nous touchera qu'en semblant à tout le moins nous mener à l'Existant, ou en nous donnant un sentiment existentiel plus intense et plus général." Ibid., 228.

[91] DUVIVIER, *Dynamisme existentiel,* 228.

46

by Duvivier. Herein lies his contribution: Duvivier acknowledges as a primary source for his study of the *Cántico* the text of the poem itself. He attempts to describe the existential realities which "appear" through an examination of the symbols, images, and literary expressions of the *Cántico*.

The contribution of the phenomenological approach, as pursued by Duvivier, recognizes the existential significance of Juan's *Cántico*. Through Juan's poetry Duvivier was able to describe the movements of the Divine in the human world. The one world in which God and human beings live shows itself in a dynamic way through Juan's poetry. Duviver does not suggest that there is one system, one ideological stance from which we can view the way the Divine is present-in-the-world. The phenomenological approach thus helps liberate Juan's corpus from the excessive dogmatism within which it remained for so long.[92] This is the contribution of a phenomenological analysis of Juan de la Cruz's *Cántico*. It is also the point where we leave behind the current state of sanjuanist research on Juan de la Cruz's *Cántico*.

Duvivier's approach cannot yet be considered hermeneutical.

---

[92] De Murillo testifies to this: "La interpretación fenomenológica de la doctrina sanjuanista pretende traducir sus contenidos en categorías accesibles al lector pensante. Pero el nivel de pensamiento del místico español es tan elevado, que en el curso del trabajo la misma Fenomenología se ha sentido tocada en su esencia, obligado a purificarse, a liberarse de su dogmatismo." DE MURILLO, "Estructura del pensamiento," 297. However, I wonder if Sánchez de Murillo himself is entirely free from a dogmatic approach. In his opening remarks concerning Juan's *pensamiento fundamental* he is quite ready to sum up Juan's thought in a few sentences: "La mística sanjuanista describe la transformación del alma en el proceso de ascensión del Monte Carmelo, que simboliza el ser religiosa. Que el místico concibe el ser religiosa como una escalada--y que en este punto no quiere ser malentendido--se deduce del diseño del Monte Carmelo dibujado por él mismo. Ese dibujo le servía de esquema para exponer su doctrina." Ibid., 314. A bit later this thought is clarified even further: "El núcleo del pensamiento es: la Nada *como tal* es *al mismo tiempo* Todo." Ibid., 315. Sánchez de Murillo thus quickly formulates a central hermeneutical principle formed by the dialectic operative between the *tody y nada*. "La correlación de estos conceptos ha de ser entenada como un simultaneidad dinámica, que sostiene el proceso de transformación." Ibid., 315. And so Sánchez de Murillo arrives at the central theme of Juan's mysticism: "La unión del alma con Dios es el tema central de la doctrina sanjuanista." Ibid., 323. What we see here is that, although Sánchez de Murillo strongly recommends a phenomenological methodology in the interpretation of Juan's corpus, his philosophical method, and his terminus, are quite different from that espoused by this dissertation. My methodological approach does not start from a hermeneutical principle with which we can read Juan's *Cántico*, but rather outlines a method for reading which culminates in self-understanding in the world. This dialectic attributes a role to the text as well as the reader in the phenomenological-hermeneutical enterprise.

Duvivier uses the mediation of symbols to describe the dynamics and experience of the transcendent Other in the world but he does not yet explicitly examine the text hermeneutically: hermeneutics goes one step further and attempts to understand the movements of meaning. A hermeneutic approach asks the question of the meaning of human existence in the here and now. We can say that Duvivier is moving in the direction of hermeneutics but does not yet specifically address the questions which hermeneutics raises, that is, the questions of self-understanding in an historical world which are impacted by the text of the *Cántico*. To begin to ask questions concerning the appropriation of the self through the mediation of a text is to enter specifically into the hermeneutical task. Duvivier's approach to the *Cántico*, shaped by the existential phenomenology of Merleau-Ponty, operates on the level of perception. Ricoeur, looking for a way to have more control over meaning, focuses on reality as it shows in language. However, what shows itself linguistically calls for interpretation.

This is the hermeneutical turn which Ricoeur adopted with his hermeneutical phenomenology. With phenomenology we are able to investigate the appearing of the phenomenon of reality, but we are not yet able to ask the questions concerning their meaning and appropriation. From the way reality shows itself Ricoeur continues to ask the question of the meaning of that showing through appropriation of the human subject. Essentially the questions of hermeneutics respond to an understanding of oneself in the reality within which the self is immersed. This task is never complete. Hermeneutics presents a cyclical approach to understanding a text in the context of a life, and a life in the context of a text. Hermeneutical meaning, therefore, is both contingent and productive of the world in which one lives, acts, and has being.

From this point we can now take one step further and begin to specifically explore a hermeneutical approach to the *Cántico* which is dependent upon all that has been presented to this point. I have indicated that the approaches of the foregoing scholars are valuable in their contribution toward a deeper understanding of the enigmatic writings of Juan. Through the progressive efforts of the many scholars cited above it has been shown that the sanjuanist corpus can be profitably studied by a variety of methods. These methods have continually opened up the sanjuanist corpus. Up until the time of Baruzi the predominant interpretive approach to the sanjuanist corpus relied almost exclusively on the ascetical-theological method. Other methods, as we have seen, have developed since that time. But there is still the need and possibility of saying more. This dissertation is, in part, a response to this desire to say "more," albeit as well, still only a beginning toward a richer dialogue between our new area of investigation, that is, "hermeneutical phenomenology" and Juan's *Cántico*.

4. The Hermeneutical Concept of Interpretation

The hermeneutical interpretation being proposed for Juan de la Cruz's *Cántico* is dependent on all the previously indicated methods used to study the poem. Each of the above examined approaches to Juan's *Cántico* contributes toward the hermeneutical contextualization of the poem, but none of them terminates in the hermeneutical interpretation of the *Cántico*, a mediation of the self as a subject-in-the-world. As mentioned above, Ricoeur uses the resources of phenomenology to take this step and move the interpretive task into the realm of hermeneutics, specifically, textual hermeneutics.

In this section I want to explain two things in order to underline the importance of the hermeneutical approach to Juan's *Cántico* and show why there is a need and room for this approach in conjunction with all the other approaches. First, I will explore more extensively the hermeneutical concept of interpretation. As mentioned above, the hermeneutical approach focuses on the questions of meaning in the life of the human subject as it is mediated through texts. In a second section I will present the dialectic which Ricoeur suggests is central to textual hermeneutics: the interplay of explanation and understanding. It is this dialectic which brings into coherent play the various methodologies and findings which have been examined above.

4.1 The Focus of the Hermeneutical Approach

The hermeneutical method developed in this dissertation culminates in the interpretation of the *Cántico* understood as a deepening of *self*-understanding. From the phenomenological approach which culminates in a "showing" and "description" of the experience of being-in-the-world, we move toward a hermeneutical understanding which culminates in the appropriation of the self-in-the-world through appropriation of the meaning of the text. As David Klemm explains:

> Consciousness of the self is not a given but a task of appropriating what is lost and self-alienated in language. Reflective philosophy must reconstitute itself as hermeneutics in order to recover the meaning of the 'I' of 'I am' in its act of existing by deciphering the meaning of the self as it has become sedimented in the linguistic tradition. Hermeneutics as the outgrowth of reflective philosophy is in this sense an ethical practice to the extent that it leads from alienation to freedom and beatitude.[93]

In order to accomplish this task, Ricoeur extends the field of inquiry from "experience of appearing objects and thinking [that which phenomenology addresses *per se*] to the experience of language."[94] Ricoeur's contribution lies in the manner in which he addresses meaning in its "appearance" in texts. Through appropriation this "appearance" mediates our understanding of being-in-the-world.

Interpretation of texts, according to Ricoeur, has this dual form: (1) access to an external trace through writing (that which he calls the "world-of-the-text"), and (2) an appropriation of this world through distanciation. Because of distanciation texts are opened to be appropriated. Ricoeur's concept of distanciation is extensively developed in Chapter Four. For now we can say that distanciation allows the interpreter to bring his or her world to the text in order to interact with the world of the text. Distanciation allows "a notion of hermeneutical appropriation that is not founded upon the primacy of the subject. ... The notion of distanciation in

---

[93] KLEMM, *The Hermeneutical Theory of Paul Ricoeur*, 60-61

[94] KLEMM, *The Hermeneutical Theory of Paul Ricoeur*, 61

50

hermeneutics provides the key to maintaining the alterity of the text, stimulating the critical and reflexive transformation of subjective modes of knowing and being."[95] Following on the phenomenological and hermeneutical findings of Husserl, Gadamer, Heiddegger and others, Ricoeur makes the interaction of today's reader with a text central to interpretation and the appropriation of meaning through distanciation.[96]

It is this dynamic involvement of the reader in textual interpretation which ultimately raises the question of self-understanding in the world. This is to suggest that to understand the text of the *Cántico* is, in some respects, to deepen one's understanding of the world in which one lives and acts. This presupposes that a hermeneutical approach to Juan's *Cántico* opens the possibility of self-discovery and transformation through the text. "In hermeneutical reflection--or in reflective hermeneutics--the constitution of the *self* is contemporaneous with the constitution of *meaning*."[97] This understanding of meaning forms the basis of the hermeneutical method which is being set forth in this dissertation. In short, a hermeneutical

---

[95] DICENSO, *Hermeneutics and the Disclosure of Truth*, 138.

[96] In dialogue with Ricoeur, Richard Kearney makes this comment on the contribution hermeneutics has to make in his reflection on structural analysis: "The scientific language of structuralism, for its part, exposes the immanent arrangements of texts and textual codes, but virtually ignores the *meaning* created by these codes. A phenomenological hermeneutics, taking its inspiration from Husserl and Heidegger, addresses this central question of meaning. It acknowledges both the critical and creative functions of language by disclosing how human self-understanding occurs in and through the mediating detour of signs whereby we understand ourselves as projects of possibility. Ricoeur concludes accordingly that we need a hermeneutic approach to language, one directed neither 'toward scientific verification nor ordinary communication but toward the disclosure of possible worlds. ... The decisive feature of hermeneutics is the capacity of world-disclosure yielded by symbols and texts. Hermeneutics is not confined to the *objective* structural analysis of texts nor to the *subjective* existential analysis of the authors of texts; its primary concern is with the worlds which these authors and texts open up. It is by an understanding of the worlds, actual and possible, opened up by language that we may arrive at a better understanding of ourselves'." Richard KEARNEY, "Ideology and Religion: A Hermeneutic Conflict," in *Phenomenology of the Truth Proper to Religion,* (New York: State University of New York Press, 1990), 298, n. 22. Ricoeur says this from a slightly different perspective using Ferdinand de Saussure's terminology: "It is possible to treat the text according to the explanatory rules that linguistics successfully applies to the simple system of signs that constitute language [*langue*] as opposed to speech [*parole*]. ... Linguistics considers only systems of units devoid of proper meaning, each of which is defined only in terms of its difference from all the others." RICOEUR, "What is a Text? Explanation and Understanding," 113.

[97] RICOEUR, "What is a Text? Explanation and Understanding," 119.

understanding of Juan's *Cántico* involves a reflexive interpretation of the text which allows meaning to emerge within a life. This is, properly speaking, the hermeneutical project. To interpret the text is to appropriate the text, i.e., gain new possibilities for the self, *here and now* in a life.

Ricoeur, therefore, allows a new reading of the *Cántico* which insists that the reader today enter into the text more consciously than other interpretations do. The hermeneutical enterprise is only successful if it succeeds in opening up my self-understanding before the text. However, in doing so hermeneutics is able to incorporate the contributions of most other approaches to the text even if their results conflict with one another. It is my thesis that a hermeneutical approach to the *Cántico* is the preferred approach because it is able to incorporate more of the previous research and methodologies into its method. The hermeneutical approach uses the variety of methodological approaches to take the project of interpretation further. This unity of the methodological approaches is based on what Ricoeur calls the "dialectic of hermeneutics": there is no explanation without understanding, no understanding without explanation.[98]

4.2 The Dialectic of Explanation and Understanding

For Ricoeur, the interpretation of a text is a dialectical movement comprising the interplay between these two: explanation and understanding. This dialectic is of fundamental importance in appreciating Ricoeur's contribution to phenomenological hermeneutics. I will outline and apply this notion to a reading of Juan's *Cántico* to explain how each of the various methodological approaches to the *Cántico* cited above contribute toward a hermeneutical interpretation.

Hermeneutics, properly speaking, encompasses both the non-methodic moment of interpretation (understanding) and the methodic moment (explanation). For Ricoeur, when we first read a text we understand it at a certain level. The text cannot fail to be about something. We have already interpreted it at

---

[98] RICOEUR. "Explanation and Understanding," in *From Text to Action*, 142.

some level. Ricoeur refers to this level of understanding as "naive": we "guess" at the meaning of the text. The dialectic of explanation and understanding begins with this initial encounter and understanding of the text. However, our initial understanding of a text can be modified, authenticated, and deepened by recourse to the objective structure of the text, that is, an explanation of the text. Let us take for our example the *Cántico* of Juan de la Cruz.

Upon first reading of the *Cántico*, we encounter a story about two lovers roaming in the countryside in search of one another. They encounter various forms of nature along the way, and experience moments of trouble as well as bliss in their adventures. Eventually the poem tells us of their discovery of each other and the consummation of their love. This is, on a first reading, what we understand the *Cántico* to be about. Ricoeur suggests, however, that a first reading of a text may not reveal the full depth of its meaning. Traditional readings of the *Cántico*, the results from the various approaches above, as well as Juan's own interpretation of the *Cántico*, move far beyond the surface meaning just summarized. Ricoeur's textual hermeneutics tells us that meaning at other levels can be developed methodically through recourse to an explanation of the text. This, in turn, affects our understanding and so the cycle continues as the findings of new explanatory methods are incorported into the dialectic. Let us continue to apply this to the *Cántico*.

To explain the *Cántico* is to investigate its historical origins (historical-contextual studies), explore the sources of its metaphors and images (literary-textual studies), develop the themes which are recurrent in its verses (thematic-symbolic studies), and outline what appear to be dogmatic assertions supported by the text (ascetical-theological studies). For example, explaining the *Cántico* may involve exploring allusions to the threefold mystical way or other dogmatic categories concerning the Christian faith which surface in the text. In general, the notion of explanation involves a reading of the *Cántico* which prolongs and reinforces its explicit or implicit references. Therefore, explanation develops understanding analytically as Ricoeur tells us:

There are not two methods, the explanatory method and the

comprehensive method. Strictly speaking, explanation alone is methodical. Understanding is instead the nonmethodical moment that, in the sciences of interpretation, combines with the methodical moment of explanation. This moment precedes, accompanies, concludes, and thus *envelops* explanation. Explanation, in turn, *develops* understanding analytically.[99]

The meaning of a text is supported and developed by the explanatory investigations. Ricoeur says that "it is this second attitude [that of understanding or appropriation] that is the real aim of reading. For this attitude reveals the true nature of the suspense that intercepts the movement of the text toward meaning."[100]

Understanding a text, according to Ricoeur, results in an interpretation that culminates in the self-interpretation of the reading subject "who thenceforth understands himself better, understands himself differently, or simply begins to understand himself."[101] Explanation and understanding thus envelop one another in a singular movement of *self-appropriation*. Within this hermeneutical methodology, an interpretation of the *Cántico* moves toward the actualization of the text of the *Cántico* in the life of a person. Through interpretation, the *Cántico* is taken back up into discourse as event in the life of the reader, it becomes living speech. "Initially the text had only a sense, that is, internal relations or a structure; now it has meaning, that is, a realization in the discourse of the reading subject."[102] It is the work of the text on the reading subject and the work of the reading subject on the text through the dialectic of explanation and understanding that give ultimate meaning to the text.

Therefore, this approach to interpretation of the text of the *Cántico* works to place the reflexive subject in its meaning, that is, to orient the life of the reader toward the *Cántico*'s ultimate reference. This is quite different from an

---

[99] RICOEUR, "Explanation and Understanding," 142.

[100] RICOEUR, "What is a Text? Explanation and Understanding," 118.

[101] RICOUER, "What is a Text? Explanation and Understanding," 118.

[102] RICOEUR, "What is a Text? Explanation and Understanding," 119.

54

interpretation of the *Cántico* that terminates with an explanation of its literary structures, an outline of its theological content, or an investigation of its historical sources.[103] These various methods of approaching Juan's *Cántico* are necessary within the analytical development of understanding, but, according to Ricoeur, do not constitute the interpretation of the *Cántico*, nor do they respond to the questions of the movements of meaning in the *Cántico* itself.

Within Ricoeur's theory these theological and literary categories are necessary to convey the objective sense of the text but are, themselves, already interpretive acts which analytically develop understanding. As we will see more clearly below, it is this "sense" of the text which opens the possibility of new meaning and a new way of being-in-the-world for the reader. In short, what Ricoeur says is at stake in the understanding (interpretation) of a text is the movement toward authentic existence in the world.

The overt sense of a religious text gives way to another reference, the covert world-of-the-text, which the reader is invited to enter. This world is the world formed by the meeting of the world-of-the-reader and the world-of-the-text. In the end, what we appropriate in the *Cántico* is therefore not arbitrary, but is a recovery of what "is at work, in labor, within the text"[104] in confrontation with the life of the

---

[103] Ricoeur emphasizes the importance of historical studies: "L'herméneutique, avant d'être simplement la riposte à la distance historique, est une fonction de la continuité historique elle-même, de la mission et de la transmission qui sont à l'origine du texte. Notre postulat est celui-ci: nous appartenons à la même tradition que le texte: l'interprétation et la tradition sont l'envers et l'endroit de la même tradition. Le texte est la reprise d'une tradition et l'interprétation est la reprise du texte. Ainsi se constitue une chaîne: tradition-texte-interprétation, chaîne qu'on peut lire dans tous les sens: texte-interprétation-tradition, ou encore: interprétation-texte-tradition." Paul RICOEUR, "Esquisse de conclusion [at the Association catholique française pour l'étude de la Bible (A.C.F.E.B.) on 'Exégèse et herméneutique'], " in *Exégèse et herméneutique*, ed. Xavier Léon-Dufour, Parole de Dieu (Paris: Seuil, 1971), 291. Historical studies, Ricoeur insists, are necessary because they place the interpreter (or interpreting community) within the continuity of the tradition of the interpretation of the text: "C'est à l'intérieur de la même tradition que le texte a été écrit et qu'il est lu. L'enveloppement historique du texte et du lecteur est la condition même de l'objectivation et de la distanciation mises en oeuvre par toute méthode analytique et critique." Ibid., 292. See also: Paul RICOEUR, "Objectivity and Subjectivity in History," in *History and Truth*, trans. and Introduction by Charles A. Kelbley (Evanston: Northwestern University Press, 1965), 24.

[104] RICOEUR, "What is a Text? Explanation and Understanding," 124.

reflexive reader today. Therefore, both the life of the text and the life of the reader are involved in the hermeneutical approach to interpretation through the dialectic of explanation and understanding. The text is only understood when it is understood with respect to one's own world.[105]

Ricoeur's method of reading and understanding texts can thus be generally described in the following movements contained within the dialectic of explanation and understanding:

1. The First Non-methodical Moment: An Educated Guess: One must read the text with a certain sympathy for the text and its meaning. In this reading there exists a certain naiveté concerning the deeper meaning of the text but, nonetheless, the reading subject can make a *guess* concerning its meaning at this non-critical level. However, this *guess* is not a completely uninformed one. The text cannot fail to speak about something. This "something" is followed by the reader through a common understanding of words. The title may be an important vector orienting the reader in his or her reading.

2. The Analytical Moment: The first naive reading must be intercepted by an analysis of the text: for example, an examination of its literary structures, its symbols and metaphors. The literal meaning of the text gives way to a deeper meaning which Ricoeur refers to as the "world-of-the-text." The orientation of the reader towards the world-of-the-text is accomplished by these literary structures of the text. The *Cántico* of Juan de la Cruz is not just about a maiden in search of her lover or even the threefold *via mistica*. Literary or rhetorical studies will help inform a critical appreciation of the text in its reading at this level. Historical studies which sensitize the reader to the milieu in which it was written, or studies concerning the broader origins of certain symbols or key phrases in the *Cántico*, will all help inform the reader as to what the text says, i.e., explain the text.

3. Another Non-methodical Moment: Interpretation of the text ultimately rests in the reader's ability to appropriate the world-of-the-text opened up by the linguistic referents. The hermeneutical reading

---

[105] The accusation of too subjective an interpretation may arise in the mind of the reader of this dissertation at this point. This objection is dealt with within the hermeneutical method as it is explained in more detail further on. See Chapter Four: 3.4 "The Effect of the Distanciation of Sense and Reference."

subject is invited to appropriate this world in a step toward self-understanding of being-in-the-world. In the end, therefore, the subject matter for interpretation becomes the world-of-the-reader in confrontation with the world-of-the-text. Further explanatory work on the text within this newfound understanding may further develop one's understanding of the text.

We see, then, that the hermeneutical approach recognizes both a methodical and a non-methodical moment of interpretation that is cyclic in nature.[106]

The hermeneutical approach includes a reflexive role for the reader in the interpretive enterprise which is explained by current reading-reception theory. To interpret the *Cántico* itself is to follow the path of thought opened up by the *Cántico*, to place oneself "en route toward the *orient* of the text."[107] To interpret is not just to seek answers to questions concerning the *Cántico*, but it is also to listen, to allow the questions of *a life* to surface from within the *Cántico*. This requires a humbler stance before Juan's *Cántico*, taking as the starting point the attitude that ultimately I am not in charge even of my own reading of it. Ultimately, an interpretation of the text questions my being-in-the-world and this questioning results in an understanding that refigures my world. This openness can be described as an openness to the truth-claims of the text.

5. Conclusion

In this chapter I have presented the various approaches which have been used over the past four hundred years to contextualize and interpret the corpus of Juan de la Cruz. All these methods are seen as contributing toward an enrichment of the interpretation of Juan de la Cruz's *Cántico*. In a second step the

---

[106] "If the word *understanding* possesses such density, it is because it both denotes the nonmethodical pole, dialectically opposed to the pole of explanation in every interpretive science, *and* constitutes the index, again not methodical but genuinely truth-centered, of the ontological relation of belonging joining our being to being and to Being. This is the rich ambiguity of the word *understanding*, denoting a moment in the theory of method, what we have called the nonmethodical pole, *and* the apprehension, on a level other than scientific, of our belonging to the whole of what is." RICOEUR, "Explanation and Understanding," 143.

[107] RICOEUR, "What is a Text? Explanation and Understanding," 122.

phenomenological approach of Roger Duvivier was presented since Duvivier's phenomenological approach to the *Cántico* is but one move away from the hermeneutical approach which I am developing in this dissertation. I suggested that a further step can already be taken by using the phenomenological approach to move into the hermeneutical approach to interpret Juan de la Cruz's *Cántico*. The step from the phenomenological approach which asks the question "What aspects of reality 'appear' in the text?" to the hermeneutical approach which asks the question, "What does the text mean for the reading subject today?" is suggested by Paul Ricoeur's dialectic of explanation and understanding.

I also suggested that it is the hermeneutical approach based on Ricoeur's dialectic of explanation and understanding which is capable of bringing into a productive coherence the multitude of methodological contributions used to investigate the *Cántico* to date, even if these methods occasionally find themselves at odds with each other. The hermeneutical method also adds an integral role for the reader in the constitution of the meaning of a text. The reader's horizon of meaning impacts the actual meaning of a text in the hermeneutical approach to textual interpretation.

All of the above is by way of introduction to move us into the hermeneutical interpretation of Juan de la Cruz's *Cántico*. Having presented some of the basic ideas central to textual interpretation in Ricoeur's thought in an introductory way, as well the way in which these ideas may impact our view of the various methods in the interpretation of Juan's *Cántico*, I will now begin to set forth the hermeneutical method in much greater detail.

The possibility of the appropriation of a text based on the dialectic of explanation and understanding comes under the umbrella of a larger hermeneutical program outlined in Ricoeur's thought. This program is detailed in Ricoeur's notion of textual mimesis. The remainder of this dissertation adopts Ricoeur's notion of mimesis to explore the implications of a hermeneutical interpretation of Juan de la Cruz's *Cántico*.

CHAPTER TWO
THE CONCEPT OF MIMESIS

1. Introduction

Using the concept of mimesis Ricoeur has constructed his theory of textual hermeneutics.[1] The reason that it is a central concept in this dissertation has already been presented in the Introduction. In this chapter I will continue to examine the theoretical basis of Ricoeur's theory of mimesis. I will begin by showing how Ricoeur has adapted the concept of mimesis from its historical genesis. In a second section I will explore the implications of this theory of mimesis for the interpretation of the *Cántico*. However, many of the concepts in this presentation of Ricoeur's theory of mimesis will be revisited throughout the dissertation; each time I will go a bit further into the details of Ricoeur's interpretation theory. The theoretical tools which Ricoeur presents for his theory of interpretation are multi-faceted and at times need to be examined again from yet a different perspective in their actual application for an interpretation of the *Cántico*. This approach will gradually deepen the reader's understanding of Ricoeur's theory and its implications in the interpretation of Juan's *Cántico* as the dissertation progresses. In a third section I will present Ricoeur's concept of mimesis$_1$, the first moment of the threefold hermeneutical arc consisting

---

[1] For a presentation of the development of the notion of mimesis see: John D. BOYD, *The Function of Mimesis and its Decline*, (Cambridge: Harvard University Press, 1968). Boyd presents and evaluates the single critical notion of mimesis in the context of its tradition. The study covers the origin of the concept of mimesis in fifth-century Classical Greece with Plato and Aristotle, to what he cites as the decline of its tradition in eighteenth-century England. For a more recent study which sees the concept of mimesis very much alive in our own century see Karla L. SCHULTZ, *Mimesis on the move: Theodor W. Adorno's Concept of Imitation*, (New York: Peter Lang, 1990). On mimetic theories see Alex PREMINGER, ed., *Princeton Encyclopedia of Poetry and Poetics* (Princeton: Princeton University Press, 1974), 640-641 and Mihai SPARIOSU, *Mimesis in Contemporary Theory*, (Philadelphia and Amsterdam: John Benjamins Publishing Co., 1984). For an anthology of the expression of mimesis in western literature see Erich AUERBACH, *Mimesis: The Representation of Reality in Western Literature*, trans. W.R. Trask, (Princeton: Princeton University Press, 1953).

of mimesis$_1$, mimesis$_2$, and mimesis$_3$.

2. Mimesis in the Hermeneutics of Paul Ricoeur

As I mentioned in Chapter One, Socrates and Plato held that artistic expressions were diminished reflections of reality.[2] Socrates argues in the *Phaedrus* (274e-277e) that mimetic activity is a diminished reflection of "original" being.[3] Language, in particular, cannot provide true knowledge but can simply remind the reader of that which is known already. Language, therefore, cannot contribute "to the creative development of new knowledge and insight" nor can it be transformative.[4] Plato believed that true discourse was "written in the soul." Written texts, therefore, were viewed to be deficient with respect to the knowledge already present in the soul.

However, Ricoeur, with Derrida and Gadamer, rejects these classical formulations of mimesis. Ironically, the basis for such a rejection is found in the *Phaedrus* itself.[5] Ricoeur also rejects the purely phenomenological position which confines artistic reference "to the descriptive denomination of extra-linguistic entities that are posited 'in themselves'."[6] Instead Ricoeur holds that a text is not a diminished representation of reality, and further, it may be creative in a number of

---

[2] This brief overview of the classical understanding of mimesis and its subsequent reformulation according to the theory of Ricoeur are summarized from DICENSO, *Hermeneutics and the Disclosure of Truth*, 113-125.

[3] RICOEUR, *Time and Narrative*, 1:80.

[4] DICENSO, *Hermeneutics and the Disclosure of Truth*, 117.

[5] See DICENSO, *Hermeneutics and the Disclosure of Truth*, 119-120 for a presentation of Derrida's analysis of the *Phaedrus* which results in the deconstruction of Plato's own position. Dicenso summarizes: "Thus, even in one of the central texts that has operated historically as a source for the condemnation of mimesis, the mimetic nature of language exhibits a creative and disclosive capacity to produce new meaning and insight. Language frees itself from the mind of the author, extending beyond his or her intentions through its capacity to speak freshly to historically changing loci of appropriation." Ibid., 120.

[6] DICENSO, *Hermeneutics and the Disclosure of Truth*, 116.

ways, but only through interpretation.[7] The ultimate reference of the text is not given immediately, but must be creatively interpreted. By reference I am referring to the capacity of language to refer to an extra-linguistic reality. Language, specifically written language, is therefore held to be productive.[8] Language has the capacity to bring about a mimesis, that is, a representation of that which was not before. Ricoeur reconstructs this notion of mimesis from his reading of Aristotle's *Poetics*.[9]

Paul Ricoeur joins together the notions of muthos (plot) and mimesis (imitation) from Aristotle to begin constructing his theory concerning the imitation of human action through written discourse. Of singular importance is the fact that Ricoeur sees both these concepts as operations, not as structures. Muthos is not simply defined as the end product, a "plot" in a Greek tragedy, but rather refers to the

---

[7] Interpretation releases us from the liabilities inherent in the notion of the "hermeneutic circle," that is, we are merely in a circular relationship with Juan's *Cántico* (we interpret the text to find what we already know). Ricoeur's theory of mimesis suggests that each interpretation becomes unique within the confines of a life. Juan's symbolic pre-figuration (mimesis$_1$) is linked to the reader by the taking up of human doing (mimesis$_3$), not only human knowing. As Ricoeur explains for us: "The first mimetic relation refers, in the case of an individual, to the semantics of desire, which only includes those prenarrative features attached to the demand constitutive of human desire. The third mimetic relation is defined by the narrative identity of an individual or people, stemming from the endless rectification of a previous narrative by a subsequent one, and from the chain of refigurations that results from this. In a word, narrative identity is the poetic resolution of the hermeneutic circle." RICOEUR, *Time and Narrative,* 3:248. Ricoeur holds that the act of reading is never neutral. We are affected by what we read: "The theory of reading has warned us that the strategy of persuasion undertaken by the narrator is aimed at imposing on the reader a vision of the world that is never ethically neutral, but that rather implicitly or explicitly induces a new evaluation of the world and of the reader as well." Ibid., 3:249.

[8] Ricoeur adopts this position from Gadamer. Gadamer argues that "representation is an ontological event and belongs to the ontological level of what is represented. Through being represented it experiences, as it were, an increase in being." Hans-Georg GADAMER, *Truth and Method,* trans. Garrett Barden and John Cumming, (New York: Seabury, 1975), 228, quoted in DICENSO, *Hermeneutics and the Disclosure of Truth,* 121. "Representation is not simply 'added on' to preexistent entities determinable as such but rather divulges aspects of things heretofore obscured." Ibid., 121.

[9] Ricoeur starts his reflection with Aristotle's *Poetics* but moves beyond Aristotle in the development of the details of his theory. In volume one of *Time and Narrative* Ricoeur relates Aristotle's and Augustine's concept of time with the latter's notion of mimesis to develop his own unique threefold theory of mimesis. However, Mary Gerhart points out in her book review of *Time and Narrative* that "Neither Augustine nor Aristotle, ... attempted to tie their explanations of time (bk. 10 of the *Confessions* and the *Physics*) to their own emplotment of time in narrative (bks. 1-9 of the *Confessions* and the *Poetics*)." Mary GERHART, "Time and Narrative," *Journal of Religion* 69 (1989), 93.

dynamic organization of events into a plot, that is, emplotment.[10] Mimesis, whether one translates it by "imitation" or "representation," refers to the mimetic *activity*, "the active process of imitating or representing something."[11] This activity is what Ricoeur refers to as emplotment. Muthos and mimesis therefore come together in a production: "Imitating or representing is a mimetic activity inasmuch as it produces something, namely, the organization of events by emplotment."[12]

What is being *re*-presented through the poetic activity of muthos? Again from Aristotle, Ricoeur answers this question: mimesis is the imitation or representation of human action. "Indeed the first time that Aristotle has to give a definite correlate to what the 'imitators represent,' he defines it as the 'persons engaged in action'."[13] The two terms muthos and mimesis are thus quasi-identified: "The action is the 'construct' of that construction that the mimetic activity consists of."[14]

A consequence of the joining together of the two terms muthos and mimesis is the subordination of the characters in a plot to the primacy of the "consideration of the action itself."[15] It is this hierarchical status which "seals the equivalence between the two expressions 'representation of action' and 'organization of the events'."[16] Emplotment is an imitation of human acting, not an imitation of

---

[10] RICOEUR, *Time and Narrative*, 1:33.

[11] RICOEUR, *Time and Narrative*, 1:33. "Imitation or representation, therefore, must be understood in the dynamic sense of making a representation, of a transposition into representative works." Ibid., 1:33.

[12] RICOEUR, *Time and Narrative*, 1:34.

[13] RICOEUR, *Time and Narrative*, 1:35.

[14] RICOEUR, *Time and Narrative*, 1:35.

[15] RICOEUR, *Time and Narrative*, 1:37. Aristotle says "tragedy is not an imitation of men but of actions and of life. It is in action that happiness and unhappiness are found, and the end we aim at is a kind of activity, not a quality. ... What is more, without action there could not be a tragedy, but there could be without characterization." ARISTOTLE, *Poetics*, 50a 16-24, quoted in RICOEUR, *Time and Narrative*, 1:37.

[16] RICOEUR, *Time and Narrative*, 1:37.

human beings acting. Human action has a universal structure and, thus, the typical plot comes first; names are added later.[17] Emplotment rests first "on the connections internal to ... action and not on external accidents."[18]

In summary, the two terms muthos and mimesis are joined together in this brief formula: the imitation of action is achieved through the dynamics of emplotment.[19] The concept of mimesis as representation of human action is thus the principal idea which Ricoeur extracts from Aristotle's *Poetics*. More precisely, Ricoeur defines mimesis as "the imitating or representing of action in the medium of metrical language, hence as accompanied by rhythms (to which are added, in the case of tragedy, the prime example [for Aristotle], spectacle and melody)."[20]

Ricoeur's theory of mimesis will lead us to explore three mimetic moments of the *Cántico*. The first mimesis is the practical world of the author and the reader within which the inscription and the interpretation of the *Cántico* occurred/occurs. Ricoeur refers to this mimesis as mimesis$_1$. Mimesis$_1$ presents a generalized framework of human action which is common to the author of the *Cántico* as well as the contemporary reader. Human action has a conceptual, symbolic, and temporal framework which bridge our world to the world of Juan de la Cruz. What is at stake in hermeneutics is the intimate connection between different horizons of meaning brought together within these three fields which characterize human action universally. It is our pre-understanding of Juan's practical world which provides the trans-historical and trans-cultural bridge for our current appropriation of the poem. Our pre-understanding of Juan's world is a world of action, i.e. a practical world.

It is the general structure of human action (mimesis$_1$) which is the

---

[17] RICOEUR, *Time and Narrative*, 1:41.

[18] RICOEUR, *Time and Narrative*, 1:41.

[19] Aristotle, *Poetics*, 50a1. quoted in RICOEUR, *Time and Narrative*, 1:34.

[20] RICOEUR, *Time and Narrative*, 1:33.

same for Juan and for us. At the same time an examination of the historical details of Juan's world allows the current reader to enter into the text more consciously with respect to its literary origins and historical context. Juan de la Cruz lived in sixteenth-century Spain. This invites us to make apparent the coherence of his text with the norms of his time. I will therefore describe the historical, cultural, and spiritual world of Juan de la Cruz.

Second, there is the actual composition of the poem shaped in this conceptual framework, that is, the mimesis of the creation of the work (mimesis$_2$). This second component of mimesis calls for an examination of the text of the *Cántico* itself. But mimesis, as an activity, "does not reach its intended term through the dynamism of the poetic text alone. It also requires a spectator or reader."[21] This leads Ricoeur to a discussion of the third moment of mimesis: the appropriation of the text (mimesis$_3$). This could be described as the mimesis of the reader of the text. The literary work is again taken up into the world of human action from where it came. This third component of mimesis will lead to an exploration of how the text of the *Cántico* continues to be a meaningful text for the reader in our own time.

Following this general definition of mimesis a number of precisions concerning it must now be made. The first of these concerns the following question: Is mimesis through artistic production a weakened mirror of reality (mere imitation in the Platonic sense), or does mimetic activity represent a strengthened version of reality (in the Aristotelian sense)?

2.1 Mimesis as an Intensification of Reality

Aristotle's view of literature as mimesis surfaces the notion that the mimetic principle is operative in the poet who imitates insofar as the poet makes. The opposite is also true. "The ultimate tension in poetry, then, of subject and object is really the dynamic cooperation of the 'creative' with the 'given'."[22] Following

---

[21] RICOEUR, *Time and Narrative,* 1:46.

[22] BOYD, *The Function of Mimesis,* 305.

Kant and his concept of the "productive imagination," Ricoeur acknowledges that human beings alone can intervene in the flow and flux of reality. Human beings can find spaces in reality which can be entered in order to bring about a metamorphosis of reality through literary creations. As Ricoeur states: "If we translate mimesis by 'representation' (as do Dupont-Roc and Lallot), we must not understand by this word some redoubling of presence, as we could still do for Platonic mimesis, but rather the break that opens the space for fiction. Artisans who work with words produce not things but quasi-things; they invent the as-if. And in this sense, the Aristotelian mimesis is the emblem of the shift [*décrochage*] that, to use our vocabulary today, produces the 'literariness' of the work of literature."[23]

On the side of Aristotle, Ricoeur sees mimetic activity as a uniquely human activity that does not *re*-present reality in a weakened form, but rather, strengthens reality in its reconfiguration of human action.[24] A significant feature of mimesis, then, "is that it is directed more at the coherence of the muthos than at its particular story. Its making [faire] is immediately a universalizing 'making.' The whole problem of narrative *Verstehen* [understanding] is contained here in principle. To make a plot is already to make the intelligible spring from the accidental, the universal from the singular, the necessary or the probable from the episodic."[25] This access to the universal structure of human action through texts is a productive

---

[23] RICOEUR, *Time and Narrative*, 1:45

[24] "Platonic mimesis ... distances the work of art by twice over from the ideal model which is its ultimate basis. Aristotle's mimesis has just a single space wherein it is unfolded--human making [*faire*], the arts of composition." RICOEUR, *Time and Narrative*, 1:34. For Aristotle mimetic activity teaches us something.

[25] RICOEUR, *Time and Narrative*, 1:41. Ricoeur finds his source here in Aristotle's *Poetics:* "It is clear then from the foregoing remarks that the poet should be a maker of plots more than a maker of verse, in that he is a poet by virtue of his imitation and he imitates actions. So even if on occasion he takes real events as the subject of a poem, he is none the less a poet, since nothing prevents some of the things that have actually happened from being of the sort that might probably or possibly happen, and it is in accordance with this that he is their poet." *Poetics*, 51b27-32, quoted in RICOEUR, *Time and Narrative*, 1:42.

activity, that is, it refigures the logical structure of human acting and its meaning.[26] Through mimesis we create the possibility of focusing on patterns of human existence not before encountered.

This stance concerning the "making" of poetic texts is in direct opposition to the position most scholars hold toward Juan's *Cántico*. For example, Pacho, the leading commentator on the *Cántico*, holds that Juan's artistic intuition coincides with his mystical experience to produce poems which are *only* "pale reflections" of his "personal experience."[27] Pacho says that these "shadows" and "images" which reflect reality need to be explained in order to understand what Juan is saying. This explanation is given in the commentary which Juan himself wrote on the *Cántico*.[28] According to Pacho we have been left with a "compromised" position concerning Juan's artistic making.[29]

The exact opposite of Pacho's position is the central point in Ricoeur's analysis. Ricoeur holds that the point of entry into the possibility of the making and metamorphosis of reality is language.[30] Written language, specifically, is a fuller

---

[26] G. F. Else points out that for Aristotle the poet is "The maker of what happened! Not the maker of actuality of events but of their logical structure, of their meaning: their having happened is accidental to their being composed." G.F. ELSE, *Aristotle's Poetics: The Argument*, (Cambridge: Harvard University Press, 1957), 321, quoted in RICOEUR, *Time and Narrative*, 1:240, n. 23.

[27] Eulogio PACHO, "La estructura literaria del «Cántico espiritual»," *El Monte Carmelo* 68 (1960), 394.

[28] "Consciente de su misión de maestro espiritual, luchando contra la inefabilidad y venciendo su natural repugnancia vuelve un día sobre sus maravillosas canciones dispuesto a hacernos participantes de los recónditos *tesoros espirituales allí* [in the Cántico] *escondidos*. Nace el comentario." PACHO, "La estructura literaria del «Cántico espiritual»," 399. (emphasis mine)

[29] "El problema básico de la expresión sentido por el poeta nos coloca en situación *comprometida*, obligándonos a indagar su pensamiento a través de los «dislates» imaginativos, a no ser que, como en el *Cántico*, nos guíe él mismo, explanándonos, por «términos vulgares y usados», *el contenido doctrinal de su mensaje.*" PACHO, "La estructura literaria del «Cántico espiritual»," 394. (emphasis mine)

[30] Ricoeur relies on Husserl here as John van den Hengel explains: "In his last works Husserl provides some hints about the operation whereby language returns to the experience that lies prior to language. Husserl calls the world of experience prior to language, *Lebenswelt*. This *Lebenswelt* is a reality that is not immediately available. For him it comes into sight in the operation of language. ... Language articulates and opens up the *Lebenswelt*. The link between the reference of language to

expression of reality, not a "pale image" of reality. As Ricoeur states: "If mimetic activity 'composes' action, it is what establishes what is necessary in composing it. It does not see the universal, it makes it spring forth."[31] Written texts, therefore, probe and create a world that was not before. This is to say that texts are creative productions; they are not mere reflections of reality, but rather shape reality. The goal of mimesis is the organization of events that refigures reality in the "real domain, covered by ethics, and the imaginary one, covered by poetics."[32] Muthos thus transposes the practical world of action through literary production which is taken up again by a spectator or reader in a new way. This approach to Juan's *Cántico* opens the reader to the potential of the transformative-event that *is* the *Cántico*.

However, as van den Hengel observes, "not every language is equally capable of bringing the *Lebenswelt* [Husserl's "life-world"] to the surface. Neither scientific language nor the language of description are devoid of ontological import, but they operate on a level of knowledge which attempts to manipulate and control language."[33] In agreement with Husserl, Ricoeur sees poetic texts as being *the* medium in and through which reality is refigured and brought into focus. Poetry is not a celebration of language in itself, as many hold. Poetic language speaks of the world, but not of the world of objects.[34]

---

the extralinguistic reality is therefore not direct but indirect. ... For Ricoeur what lies prior to language is not a mute or thingified reality, ... it is not merely an *expérience vécu*, but an experience that is a dynamic act, surrounded by language." John VAN DEN HENGEL, *The Home of Meaning: The Hermeneutics of the Subject of Paul Ricoeur*, (Washington: University Press of America, 1982), 56-57.

[31] RICOEUR, *Time and Narrative*, 1:42.

[32] RICOEUR, *Time and Narrative*, 1:46.

[33] VAN DEN HENGEL, *Home of Meaning*, 57.

[34] It is to be noted here that Ricoeur adopts a very wide notion of poetry. In fact, Ricoeur speaks more of the "poetic function" or "poetic discourse." Poetic discourse (whether narrative fiction, lyricism, or the essay) "suspends a first-order referential function, whether it is a question of direct reference to familiar objects of perception or of indirect reference to physical entities." Paul RICOEUR, "Naming God," *Union Seminary Quarterly Review* 34, no.4 (1979), 218. Ricoeur holds

Mimesis is operative within a world that is both given and simultaneously created through the selective activity of the poetic artist. In the core of its meaning, mimesis does not refer to a repetitive function of doing over again, or to immediate description; but rather it is a concept integral to human life that seeks to select and name the participation of humanity in the creative dynamics of the deepest structures of human existence.[35] "Like sculpture, poetry converts language into matter, worked for its own sake. This solid object is not the representation of some thing, but an expression of [life] itself."[36]

The creative edge of this construction, the frontier through which the interface of artistic production and life is situated, is the imaginative endeavour of the poet. Through literary mimesis new imaginative possibilities for life unfold for the individual and the community in which that individual lives. The disclosure of a world through the non-ostensive references of a literary work, creates new possibilities in the life of the reader.

In a sense then, Ricoeur's valuing of the mimetic function in the tradition of Aristotle's *Poetics* can be seen as a recovery of the struggle to name the correlation that exists between texts, particularly poetic texts, and the existential realm. A second question, therefore, surfaces in Ricoeur's analysis of mimesis: how does literary production, in its mimetic activity, bring about this heightened sense of reality in the existential sphere? Ricoeur finds a response to this question in his reflection on the characteristics and function of metaphor and poetic reference.

2.2 The Tools of Mimesis: Metaphor and Poetic Reference

Dicenso states: "Ricoeur's reconstruction of the concept of mimesis

---

that poetic texts refer to the world in their own way, that is, through metaphorical reference as we will see below. "This thesis covers every nondescriptive use of language, and therefore every poetic text, whether it be lyrical or narrative." Ibid., *Time and Narrative*, 1:80.

[35] RICOEUR, *Time and Narrative*, 1:34.

[36] RICOEUR, *Rule of Metaphor*, 224.

provides the conceptual framework for understanding language as creatively disclosive of Being rather than simply as providing significations of things in the preexistent forms."[37] But how is language able to point beyond itself to disclose reality (or Being, as Dicenso states)? Ricoeur develops the thesis that the function of language is ultimately not "limited to the celebration of language for its own sake."[38] If artistic doing is a mimesis of human action, and this artistic doing is to have an impact on human existence, it must point beyond itself, that is, it must reference reality beyond itself.

The concept of reference is thus introduced into the discussion. Ricoeur addresses the problem of the relationship between language and reality by reconstructing the concept of reference. Ricoeur holds that it is especially through metaphor that reference to previously undisclosed levels of reality takes place. This valuing of the creative dimension of metaphor is important for an interpretation of Juan's poem.

Juan de la Cruz's *Cántico* is replete with metaphors to the point where one commentator, Jean Baruzi, has said that the poem is so innovative that it is closed and inaccessible to meaning.[39] However, according to Ricoeur's theory, it is this richness of metaphor in Juan's *Cántico* that provides us with an appropriate text

---

[37] DICENSO, *Hermeneutics and the Disclosure of Truth*, 125-126.

[38] RICOEUR, *Time and Narrative*, I:x. See also RICOEUR, *Rule of Metaphor*, 216-256 where Ricoeur develops a theory of text that is built on the theory of metaphor. Here Ricoeur explains that it is not only metaphors which redescribe reality but that fictional works also do so. This is done by the construction of the world-of-the-text through the interaction of the text-world and the reader. The literal meaning of the text is thus suspended in favour of its actual referent. These notions are explored in greater detail in the following chapter of this dissertation.

[39] Commenting on Juan's three major poems Jean Baruzi says: "Plus profondément, les poèmes de la «Noche» et de la «Llama», d'une part, le poème du «Cántico» d'autre part, ne nous offrent pas la même inaccessibilité. Les strophes de la «Noche» et de la «Llama» nous sont inaccessibles avant tout parce qu'elles décrivent une expérience ineffable; *mais le poème du «Cántico» nous est doublement clos*. Il se dérobe, et par l'expérience qu'il résume, et par l'état d'inspiration divine, qu'en langage à la fois déchaîné et hiératique, Jean de la Croix y voudrait perpétuer. Et certes, les poèmes de la «Noche» et de la «Llama» ne sont pas, pour Jean de la Croix, étrangers à l'état d'inspiration divine. Mais, lorsqu'il regarde son «Cántico», c'est cet état qui retient sa rêverie." BARUZI, *Problème de l'expérience mystique*, 359. (emphasis mine)

for a hermeneutical analysis. It is the use of metaphor within the *Cántico* that opens up the possibility of access to other levels of reality. Ricoeur's reformulation of mimesis brings to the surface the suspension of the direct referential claims of metaphor in order to access non-ostensive reality. How is this done?

The metaphor, in the act of language, produces "a new semantic pertinence by means of an impertinent attribution."[40] Metaphors resist the ordinary use of language and reveal resemblances where, at first, no resemblance may be perceived. Ricoeur bases this concept of metaphor on Kant's notion of the "productive imagination."[41] "The productive imagination at work in the metaphorical process is thus our competence for producing new logical species by predicative assimilation, in spite of the resistance of our current categorizations of language."[42] Metaphors, through their deconstruction of the literal sense of words, create new meaning.

Poetics texts, through the use of metaphor, speak of the world and have a particular ability to construct new meaning and lay open previously unknown aspects of reality.[43] Description of the world includes not only "descriptive reference but also nondescriptive references, those of poetic diction."[44] But in order to link the redescription of reality on the poetic level with the ontological level, Ricoeur metaphorizes the verb "to be."[45] Ricoeur suggests that "seeing-as" (accomplished by the work of metaphor) be given full ontological meaning. "Seeing-as" is thus

[40] RICOEUR, *Time and Narrative*, 1:ix.

[41] RICOEUR, *Time and Narrative*, 1:x.

[42] RICOEUR, *Time and Narrative*, 1:x.

[43] Through the use of metaphor in poetry new levels of reality surface: "Metaphorical reference, ... consists in the fact that the effacement of descriptive reference--an effacement that, as a first approximation, makes language refer to itself--is revealed to be, in a second approximation, the negative condition for freeing a more radical power of reference to those aspects of our being-in-the-world that cannot be talked about directly." RICOEUR, *Time and Narrative*, 1:80.

[44] RICOEUR, *Time and Narrative*, 1:80.

[45] RICOEUR, *Time and Narrative*, 1:80.

correlated with "being-as." This is the referential work of metaphor.

A similar kind of process occurs with narrative. "With narrative, the semantic innovation lies in the inventing of another work of synthesis--a plot. By means of the plot, goals, causes, and chance are brought together within the temporal unity of a whole and complete action. It is this synthesis of the heterogeneous that brings narrative close to metaphor."[46] New possibilities for life on the existential level are thus opened up through language. "Here a living metaphor, that is, a new pertinence in the predication, there a feigned plot, that is, a new congruence in the organization of events."[47] Narrative thus possesses a mimetic quality in the possibility of refiguring reality through the action (the play) of the plot.[48]

Both metaphor and narrative "belong to the same basic phenomenon of semantic innovation."[49] Through semantic innovation in metaphor and narrative, reality is configured. This, in turn, opens reality to refiguration in the existential sphere. Ricoeur says that the delineation between poetic composition (metaphorical utterance) and narrative (emplotment) is unstable, and Ricoeur concludes that there exists "one vast poetic sphere that includes metaphorical utterance and narrative discourse."[50] Through emplotment the writer is able to re-configure "our confused, unformed, and at the limit mute temporal experience."[51]

The abolition in poetry of the direct reference "to objects that we can manipulate allows the world of our originary rootedness to appear."[52] To emphasize the poetic form of Juan's *Cántico*, therefore, is to underline the significance of its

---

[46] RICOEUR, *Time and Narrative*, 1:ix.

[47] RICOEUR, *Time and Narrative*, 1:ix.

[48] Recall: "Plot, says Aristotle, is the mimēsis of an action." RICOEUR, *Time and Narrative*, 1:xi.

[49] RICOEUR, *Time and Narrative*, 1:ix.

[50] RICOEUR, *Time and Narrative*, 1:xi.

[51] RICOEUR, *Time and Narrative*, 1:xi.

[52] Paul RICOEUR, "Toward a Hermeneutic of the Idea of Revelation," *Harvard Theological Review* 70, no. 1-2 (January-April 1977), 26.

literary form to convey meaning in a particular way. Different literary forms have varying abilities to articulate and refigure temporal existence. What "announces itself" is, in each case, "qualified by the form of the announcement."[53] Poetry, because of its peculiar use of metaphorical reference, is the medium, par excellence which has the ability to reshape human existence. Ricoeur holds a special place for the role of "feelings" or "emotions" which surface in the reading of poetic texts.[54]

What Ricoeur calls feelings or emotions which surface in the wake of a poetic reading are "precisely modalities of our relation to the world that are not exhausted in the description of objects. Basic emotions such as fear, anger, joy, and sadness express ways of belonging to things as much as ways in which we behave in relation to them; all the more reason why feelings, temperaments, moods, and *Stimmungen*, expressed, shaped, and instructed by poetic language, should throw us into the midst of things."[55] Poetry's unique referential capacity inserts us into our originary rootedness and bring us into worlds to which, otherwise, we had no prior access. We come to belong to the world, in its deepest dimensions, through the modality of poetic discourse. Feelings, therefore, are not merely subjective. Through them we participate in the most integral aspects of human existence.

Poetic discourse, therefore, "refers to our many ways of belonging to the world before we oppose ourselves to things understood as 'objects' that stand before a 'subject'."[56] Ricoeur suggests that we have "become blind to these modalities of *rootedness* and *belonging-to* (*appartenance*) that precede the relation of a subject to objects" since we have ratified, in an uncritical way, a certain concept of truth.[57] Let us now see how Ricoeur's reformulation of mimesis benefits our

---

[53] RICOEUR, "Toward a Hermeneutic of the Idea of Revelation," 16.

[54] RICOEUR, "Naming God," 218.

[55] RICOEUR, "Naming God," 218.

[56] RICOEUR, "Naming God," 218.

[57] RICOEUR, "Naming God," 218. I present Ricoeur's reformulation of the concept of truth in Chapter Four.

interpretation of the *Cántico*.

3. Value of Ricoeur's Theory of Mimesis for Interpretation of the *Cántico*

The written text serves as the intermediary among the three operations Ricoeur names mimesis$_1$ ("reference back to the familiar pre-understanding we have of the order of action"), mimesis$_2$ ("entry in the realm of poetic composition"), and mimesis$_3$ ("a new configuration by means of this poetic refiguring of the pre-understood order of action").[58] Mimesis$_2$ serves as the pivotal point, the mediating function, between "the prefiguration of the practical field and its refiguration through the reception of the work."[59] The reader "is that operator par excellence who takes up through doing something -- the act of reading -- the unity of the traversal from mimesis$_1$ to mimesis$_3$ by way of mimesis$_2$."[60]

In due course, each of the three operations of mimesis$_1$, mimesis$_2$, and mimesis$_3$, will be described in more detail. This dissertation asserts that each of these three hermeneutical moments must be explored in pursuing an adequate interpretation of Juan's *Cántico*. As already shown in Chapter One, this trajectory affects the appreciation of other methodological approaches to the *Cántico*. However, it is hoped that the pursuit of the full hermeneutical arc described by mimesis$_1$, mimesis$_2$, and mimesis$_3$ will enrich the current understanding of Juan's *Cántico* and respond in a more helpful way to certain questions of interpretation concerning this poem. Why is this so?

Ricoeur's theory of mimesis helps us understand reality and the insertion and role of the reflexive subject in that reality. Ricoeur's theory reveals that it is through language, particularly poetic language, that the individual shapes and

[58] RICOEUR, *Time and Narrative*, 1:xi.

[59] RICOEUR, *Time and Narrative*, 1:53.

[60] RICOEUR, *Time and Narrative*, 1:53. In summary, "we are following therefore the destiny of a prefigured time that becomes a refigured time through the mediation of a configured time." Ibid., 1:54.

refigures reality. Through Ricoeur's reformulation of the concept of mimesis it can be determined that Juan de la Cruz is not merely describing an already past experience, nor a present experience, in his poem, the *Cántico*. Rather, Ricoeur's analysis of mimesis leads to the conclusion that Juan, through his poetic work, actually shapes his experience and refigures the world.

This position shifts that held by most sanjuanist scholars who describe the *Cántico* as an autobiographical account of Juan's personal ascent to God, even though this ascent is seen as paradigmatic of the human journey.[61] For example, Eulogio Pacho describes the *Cántico* in this way. He holds that even though Juan describes a universal journey, the *Cántico*, even more, describes *un sentido integramente personal.*[62]

However, in Ricoeur's hermeneutical setting, description of the experience through language *gives* the experience, an experience that wouldn't exist

[61] For example, Max Huot de Longchamp describes the challenge of the mystic in this way: "La mystique entraîne une *science*, une science d'*observation* qui se nourrit de témoignages sur *des fait*. Elle est susceptible de progrès dans la mesure où l'observation se fait plus exacte, les témoignages plus précis et plus abondants." LONGCHAMP, *Lectures de Jean de la Croix*, 416. Georges Tavard similarly sees Juan's writings as his poetic expression of sublime experience: "John of the Cross does not propose any neat theory on the degrees of spiritual life. He does not even propose a theory at all. He describes and interprets an experience." TAVARD, *Poetry and Contemplation*, 132. In as much as I can agree with Tavard that Juan is not setting out a "neat theory" of spiritual development, it is difficult to accept his position that Juan is merely describing and interpreting an experience. Something else is happening in the composition of the *Cántico*. This position will become clear in the progression of my thesis. Antonio T. DE NICOLÁS, *St. John of the Cross: Alchemist of the Soul*, with a Forward by Seyyed Hossein Nasr, (New York: Paragon House, 1989) holds a similar view to that of Tavard. After citing several verses of the *Cántico* he says: "But the mystic, San Juan de la Cruz, is not concerned with esthetics as the primary intention of his poetry. Esthetics is a happy outcome, indirectly achieved, of a larger intention, the description in poetic form of his inner experience." Ibid., 68.

[62] "Por más que la escala amorosa en su gradual elevación describa cronológicamente el desarrollo de la perfección común a todas las almas, el ejercicio del amor rimado en las sublimes estrofas de nuestra égloga divina tiene un *sentido integramente personal*; es retrato fiel del proprio fray Juan de la Cruz: historia fidedigna de sus requiebros amorosos con «el Esposo Cristo». Podemos rotular el poema con significación autobiográfica como «Canciones que tratan del ejercicio de amor entre el alma de fray Juan y el Esposo Cristo». No puede haber duda, el *Cántico* es relato vivo y personalisimo: semblanza límpida y cautivadora del arrebatado espiritu un Santo." (emphasis mine) Eulogio de la V. del Carmen [PACHO], "La Clave exegetica del 'Cántico espiritual'," *Ephemerides Carmeliticae* 9 (1958), 314.

without Juan's poetic inscription of it.[63] In short, through Ricoeur's concept of mimesis we see that Juan's poem is not the poetic description of an already known shaped into language, but is a new configuration of reality. This configuration then becomes potentially available for the reader in some other time and culture. As Ricoeur says: "Narration preserves the meaning that is behind us so that we can have meaning before us. There is always *more* order in what we narrate than in what we have actually lived; and this narrative excess (*surcroît*) of order, coherence and unity, is a prime example of the creative power of narration."[64]

The role of language is thus also shifted in a consideration of Ricoeur's theory of mimesis in the context of the interpretation of the *Cántico*. The written *Cántico* is not an impoverishment of Juan's virginal mystical experience, as if writing is a poor copy of the experience. For Ricoeur writing is "productive." Writing is seen as an enrichment of Juan's mystical experience which makes possible future meaning-events that similarly would not have been possible otherwise. The written *Cántico* is, therefore, not composed of the "inert material of language" as Pacho would have us believe.[65] Rather, the text of the *Cántico* is a dynamic text that is open to new interpretations.

Within the threefold concept of mimesis, Juan de la Cruz's commentary on his own poem becomes the first incidence of reader-text appropriation in Ricoeur's analysis. Juan's own commentary opens up some aspects

---

[63] "An end is put once and for all to the Cartesian and Fichtean--and to an extent Husserlian--ideal of the subject's transparence to itself. To understand oneself is to understand oneself as one confronts the text and to receive from it the conditions for a self other than that which first undertakes the reading. Neither of the two subjectivities, neither that of the author nor that of the reader, is thus primary in the sense of an originary presence of the self to itself." RICOEUR, "On Interpretation," in *From Text to Action*, 17.

[64] Paul RICOEUR, "The Creativity of Language," in *A Ricoeur Reader: Reflection and Imagination*, ed. Mario J. Valdés, Theory/Culture 2 (Toronto: University of Toronto Press, 1991), 468.

[65] "En ninguna de sus obras aparece con tanto relieve el dominio del pensamiento sobre la forma expresiva como en el *Cántico espiritual*. Representa dentro de su aval literario el triunfo de la idea sobre la palabra, de la forma mental sobre la materia inerte del lenguaje." PACHO, "La Clave exegética del 'Cántico espiritual'," 308.

of the poetic work, but does not, and cannot, exhaust the meaning of Juan's poem. Juan's commentary on his own poem must then be seen as one-sided and incomplete. Ricoeur's concept of mimesis leaves the poetic text capable of continuing its work of refiguring reality in new ways through being taken up again in other historical periods through the unfolding of the "world-of-the-text," Ricoeur's central concept in his hermeneutical program. Therefore, through Ricoeur's concept of mimesis, we discover that the text of the *Cántico* is "open" for readers in today's world, as it has been experienced as an "open" text for countless readers in the past four hundred years.

Ricoeur's theory of mimesis has structured this dissertation in its chapter divisions and shaped the methodology as I have already presented it. The chapter divisions within this dissertation flow from Ricoeur's threefold mimesis mentioned above. He has aptly named these three moments of mimetic activity: mimesis$_1$ (prefiguration of the text), mimesis$_2$ (configuration of the text), and mimesis$_3$ (refiguration of the text). Each of these three moments of mimesis will be explained in greater detail prior to each part of the dissertation that deals with that particular moment of mimesis and its confrontation with methodological considerations in the interpretation of Juan's *Cántico*.

4. Mimesis$_1$

Literary productions are rooted in the historical world, a particular cultural and political setting. They are born within the experience of that meaningful world of which the author is a part. However, Ricoeur suggests, "poets find not only an implicit categorization of the practical field in their cultural stock but also a first narrative organization [mise en forme]."[66] It is to this world to which mimesis$_1$ refers, that is, the world of action within which both the author and the reader live.[67] The conceptual framework for human action is what today's reader shares with Juan

---

[66] RICOEUR, *Time and Narrative*, 1:47.

[67] This presentation of mimesis$_1$ is based on RICOEUR, *Time and Narrative*, 1:54-64.

de la Cruz. Ricoeur's theory suggests that Juan's prefigurative world provided organizational principles for his poetic doing but these principles are common to the contemporary reader.

These organizational principles are themselves hermeneutical in nature.[68] This is to say that Juan's world has already been linguistically informed and hence is itself mimetic. As Ricoeur says: "The human person is part of the practical world of 'doing' before an author writes about 'doing'."[69] Therefore, the contemporary reader does not share Juan's cultural world but he or she does share Juan's world of human action.

Ricoeur refers to this moment of mimesis as "pre-understanding."[70] The features of this "pre-understanding," or what Ricoeur also refers to as "practical understanding," are described, rather than deduced.[71] Within the concept of mimesis$_1$ Ricoeur creates an inventory of the resources of human action, that is, the resources with which poetics transposes human action and suffering into a literary work (mimesis$_2$). Mimesis$_1$, therefore, refers to the conceptual and symbolic tools available to the author for the inscription of human action into a literary work. It is the conceptual and symbolic features of human action, therefore, which I want to present in the first hermeneutical moment in my interpretation of Juan's *Cántico*.

In his theory, Ricoeur sets forth three features of the pre-understanding of a text. First, if emplotment is an imitation of action, action (specifically human acting) must possess some meaningful universal structure which can be described prior to the inscription of a text. Second, if imitating is meaningful, one must be able to identify the symbolic mediations of action which convey this

---

[68] DICENSO, *Hermeneutics and the Disclosure of Truth*, 128.

[69] "To understand a story is to understand both the language of 'doing something' and the cultural tradition from which proceeds the typology of plots." RICOEUR, *Time and Narrative*, 1:57.

[70] RICOEUR, *Time and Narrative*, 1:54.

[71] RICOEUR, *Time and Narrative*, 1:54. Ricoeur goes on to say that this does not mean that the description is a closed one. Any description of some past reality, even the distant past, is not static. New insights and perspectives may reveal further accuracies in the descriptive order.

meaning. Third, these symbolic representations of action also sustain the temporal elements which allow action to be narrated. Each of these three features of mimesis$_1$, that is, the structural, the symbolic, and the temporal will now be described separately.

4.1 The Structure of Human Acting

Ricoeur suggests that human action has a universal structure which is common to all people when he distinguishes human action from mere physical movement: human action implies motivation and particular goals, it has meaning that can be conveyed.[72] We can describe human activity and contextualize it. This is to say that human action is accompanied by circumstances, effects, or consequences, by which one can explain *why* somebody did something.[73] Since something was done by someone, human action also implies actors, the *who* of *who did what*. The universal structures of human action can thus be made intelligible through response to these various queries.

Ricoeur refers to the inquiries posed by these questions of *what?*, *why?*, *who?*, *how?*, *with whom?*, or *against whom?* of any human action as the "practical understanding" of human action. The reference to any one of the parameters infers the inclusion of all the others. Although we can understand what human action is about within this practical, conceptual sphere, Ricoeur also speaks of understanding human action within the confines of "narrative understanding." Human action can be composed.

However, "narrative understanding" of human action is different; it can be linked to the practical understanding of human action through the use of two words: "It is a relation of *presupposition* and of *transformation*."[74] Literary composition of human action presupposes a familiarity with the common terms used

---

[72] RICOEUR. *Time and Narrative*, 1:55.

[73] RICOEUR. *Time and Narrative*, 1:55.

[74] RICOEUR. *Time and Narrative*, 1:55. (emphasis mine)

to describe the practical understanding of human action mentioned above. However, "narrative is not limited to making use of our familiarity with the conceptual network of action. Narrative adds discursive features to our conceptual network of action that distinguishes this network from a simple sequence of action sentences."[75] These additions do not belong to the conceptual network described in the *who?*, *why?*, *what?* and so on of practical understanding. Rather they belong to the syntactic order which engenders literary works whether they are historical or fictional. When action is composed, it is not merely in response to the questions of *Who?*, *Why*, *What?* and so on.

Although there is a need to be informed at the practical level concerning the direction and motivation of human action, there is another dynamic taking place within the articulation of human action through language. Literary "articulations of action are bearers of more precisely temporal elements, from which proceed more directly the very capacity of action to be narrated and perhaps the need to narrate it."[76] Through the telling of "doing," a text is formed from what previously were disparate parts and therefore the human experience of action takes on form through language.

Briefly then, the relationship between "narrative understanding" and "practical understanding" can be summed up as follows: "In passing from the paradigmatic order of action to the syntagmatic order of narrative, the terms of the semantics of action acquire integration and actuality. Actuality, because the terms, which had only a virtual signification in the paradigmatic order, that is, a pure capacity to be used, receive an actual [*effective*] signification thanks to the sequential interconnections the plot confers on the agents, their deeds, and their sufferings. Integration, because terms as heterogeneous as agents, motives, and circumstances are rendered compatible and work together in actual temporal wholes."[77] Language

[75] RICOEUR, *Time and Narrative*, 1:56.

[76] RICOEUR, *Time and Narrative*, 1:54.

[77] RICOEUR, *Time and Narrative*, 1:56-57.

is therefore subject to the common structures of human acting as well as the human experience of temporality in which literary production takes place.

What we become aware of here is that there is no original story. Literary creations are "a redefining of what is already defined, a reinterpretation of what is already interpreted."[78] This "makes possible a human solidarity through retrieval of a common past."[79] Through the common experience of language the human community mediates what it means to live practically in the world within a common heritage: "There is no lived reality, no human or social reality, that is not already *represented* in some sense. Therefore, the referent of narration, namely human action, is never raw or immediate reality but an action that has been symbolized and resymbolized over and over again."[80] Our human condition of being-in-the-world is expressed using the practical resources available to us in literary structures which are common to the universal experience of human acting.[81] Therefore, "practical understanding" refers to the semantics of human acting shared by all people in all times. Human action has a conceptual structure where agents and circumstances, goals and consequences, are shared in the common human condition. To live in the world is already mimetic: human doing interprets reality. As James Dicenso says, "representation per se refers to a being-in-the-world that is culturally and linguistically formed and hence is itself mimetic."[82] Juan's existential reality has already been shaped and informed by the linguistic doing of many people that have gone before him. The contributions of mimesis$_2$ and mimesis$_3$ already contribute to Juan's mimetic activity in mimesis$_1$.

---

[78] Steven H. CLARK, *Paul Ricoeur*, Critics of the Twentieth Century (London: Routledge, 1990), 154.

[79] CLARK, *Paul Ricoeur*, 154.

[80] Paul RICOEUR, *Dialogues with Contemporary Continental Thinkers*, ed. Richard Kearney, (Manchester: Manchester University Press, 1984), 23-4, quoted in CLARK, *Paul Ricoeur*, 169.

[81] RICOEUR, *Time and Narrative*, 1:52,55.

[82] DICENSO, *Hermeneutics and the Disclosure of Truth*, 122.

However, Juan's virtual experiences of being-in-the-world take on a particular shape within Juan's own poetic work, that is, they receive "actual signification" and undergo "transformation" through his poetic doing, the focus of mimesis$_2$. Juan's poetic doing is a taking up of the pre-narrative resources available to him within his own time. These are the cultural resources of his day. These resources form part of the prelinguistic structure of Juan's *Cántico*.

4.2 Symbolic Structures of Human Acting

The second feature of mimesis$_1$ abides specifically "in the symbolic resources of the practical field."[83] Every culture is drenched in its own symbolic heritage, its signs, and its rules. Human action can be symbolically communicated through the use of these cultural symbols, signs, and rules which are pervasive in every civilization.[84] When Ricoeur speaks of this symbolic communication or mediation, he is referring to cultural symbols that underlie human action and that "constitute its first signification, before autonomous symbolic wholes dependent upon speaking or writing become detached from the practical level."[85]

Here Ricoeur draws on *verstehen* sociology such as that of Clifford Geertz in *The Interpretation of Cultures*.[86] Geertz describes culture as "an historically transmitted pattern of meanings embodied in symbols, a system of inherited conceptions expressed in symbolic forms by means of which men communicate, perpetuate, and develop their knowledge about and attitudes toward life. ... sacred symbols function to synthesize a people's ethos--the tone, character, and quality of their life, its moral and aesthetic style and mood--and their world view--the picture they have of the way things in sheer actuality are, their most

---

[83] RICOEUR, *Time and Narrative*, 1:57.

[84] RICOEUR, *Time and Narrative*, 1:57.

[85] RICOEUR, *Time and Narrative*, 1:57. In this way Ricoeur distinguishes "an implicit or immanent symbolism, in opposition to an explicit or autonomous one." Ibid., 1:57.

[86] RICOEUR, *Time and Narrative*, 1:57.

comprehensive ideas of order."[87] Symbols therefore serve to articulate the experience of the human community, without which that experience would remain blind and incommunicable.[88] This symbolism, from its pre-conceptual level, is brought to the conceptual level in language.[89] Symbols lie on the frontier and mediate between the deepest structures of human reality and linguistic code.

This symbolic mediation manifests itself in the form of a structured symbolic system.[90] Individual symbols cannot be totally isolated from within the matrix of symbolic representations temporally operative in the culture. "A symbolic system thus furnishes a descriptive context for particular actions."[91] But beyond the descriptive order, symbols are also "cultural processes that articulate experience."[92] Ricoeur thus speaks of action as a sort of "quasi-text" since the symbols which are taken up in human action are already once removed from the human experience from which they rose, but they are also already interpretants of human action and

---

[87] Clifford GEERTZ, *The Interpretation of Cultures: Selected Essays*, (New York: Basic Books, 1973), 89. Ricoeur opts for the definition of symbol closest to that of E. Cassirer in his *Philosophie des formes symboliques*, (Paris: Édition de Minuit, 1972). Ricoeur summarizes Cassirer's definition in his article "Poétique et symbolique" in *Initiation à la pratique de la théologie: Tome I Introduction*, ed. Bernard Lauret and François Refoulé (Paris: Cerf, 1982), 37-61. Using Cassirer's definition Ricoeur says symbols are "des structures de l'expérience humaine dotées d'un statut *culturel* et capable de *relier (religio)* entre eux les membres de la communauté qui reconnaissent des symboles comme les *règles* de leur conduite." RICOEUR, *Initiation*, 1:38.

[88] RICOEUR, *Initiation*, 1:37.

[89] "Dès le stade oral, on peut voir le symbolisme se condenser dans des activités verbales autonomes et parfaitement identifiables. Les symboles dont nous allons maintenant parler répondent à cette double considération: d'une part, le sémitisme analogique y est clairement discernable; d'autre part, il s'incarne dans des actes de langage bien définis que l'écriture n'a pas eu de peine à fixer, même s'ils ont eu une longue existence orale avant que des *scribes* de profession les inscrivent sur un support durable et leur donnent une existence textuelle. Ce symbolisme explicite, distinct, est le symbolisme proprement dit." RICOEUR, *Initiation*, 1:44.

[90] RICOEUR, *Time and Narrative*, 1:58.

[91] RICOEUR, *Time and Narrative*, 1:58.

[92] RICOEUR, *Time and Narrative*, 1:57. Ricoeur, again, follows Cassirer in this description of symbols and symbolic systems.

behaviours.[93] Therefore, symbolism at this pre-conceptual level provides the initial availability of conferring "readability" or "meaning" on action.[94]

The symbolic dimension of life therefore represents normative dimensions of being-in-the-world.[95] To understand narrated human action, that is, to glean intelligibility from its symbols and its images, is at the same time "to light up our own situation or, if you will, to interpolate among the predicates of our situation all the significations that make a *Welt* of our *Umwelt*."[96] "While the latter represents an 'environment' in a naturalistic sense [the ostensive references of dialogue], the former gives expression to the encompassing cultural contexts that shape human existence."[97] Through this characteristic of mimesis$_1$, we value the symbolic resources (whether implicit or explicit) operative within the cultural traditions which Juan de la Cruz inherited. Juan inherited a stock of issues which were the symbols and themes of the cultural ethos predominant during his time. Cultural worlds exist before individuals and provide the context for the "referential structures through which discourse functions meaningfully."[98] Juan drew on these resources and shaped them in a unique way through his poetic making. Recognizing this will lead us to explore the symbolic climate of Juan's time in Chapter Three. In particular I will highlight certain symbols and themes of the western mystical tradition. It was within this symbolic tradition that the *Cántico* took shape.

---

[93] RICOEUR, *Time and Narrative*, 1:58.

[94] Ricoeur goes on to suggest symbols also "introduce the idea of a rule" in the sense that symbols capture and convey normative behaviours. Here Ricoeur follows Peter Winch who emphasizes this feature of symbols "by characterizing meaningful action as 'rule-governed behavior'." RICOEUR, *Time and Narrative*, 1:58. Ricoeur develops this idea in his article "The Model of the Text: Meaningful Action Considered as a Text," in RICOEUR, *From Text to Action*, 144-167.

[95] RICOEUR, "The Model of the Text: Meaningful Action Considered as a Text," 149.

[96] RICOEUR, "The Model of the Text: Meaningful Action Considered as a Text," 149.

[97] DICENSO, *Hermeneutics and the Disclosure of Truth*, 128.

[98] DICENSO, *Hermeneutics and the Disclosure of Truth*, 128.

4.3 The Temporal Elements of Human Acting

The mimesis of human action is not limited to an understanding of the conceptual framework of action or its symbolic mediations as they have just been described. A third feature is included in the pre-understanding of human action, that is, the "temporal elements onto which narrative time grafts its configurations."[99] Inasmuch as there are structures of human action that call for narration, so too are there temporal structures that require narrative embodiment.

Ricoeur does not linger on what he terms the "all too evident" correlation between a particular action and its reference to some past, present, or future experience. Rather he quickly moves on to the "exchange that real action makes appear *between* the temporal dimensions."[100] Here Ricoeur uses Augustine's concept of the threefold sense of the present.[101] "By saying that there is not a future time, a past time, and a present time, but a threefold present, a present of future things, a present of past things, and a present of present things, Augustine set us on the path of an investigation into the most primitive temporal structure of action."[102] Ricoeur thus proposes that human action has a prefigurative, temporal level which must be acknowledged before its narrative configuration. Routine daily acting "orders the present of the future, the present of the past, and the present of the present in terms of one another."[103] This becomes clear in the everyday use of language and action which reckons with the human experience of time.[104]

With Heidegger in *Being and Time*, Ricoeur sees the human relationship to time as that "within which" human action takes place. This concept

---

[99] RICOEUR, *Time and Narrative*, 1:59.

[100] RICOEUR, *Time and Narrative*, 1:60. (emphasis mine)

[101] Ricoeur develops this idea from Book 11 of Augustine's *Confessions*.

[102] RICOEUR, *Time and Narrative*, 1:60.

[103] RICOEUR, *Time and Narrative*, 1:60.

[104] RICOEUR, *Time and Narrative*, 1:62.

of within-time-ness (*Innerzeitigkeit*) Ricoeur sees as the best characterization of the temporality of human action.[105] This desubstantialization of time Ricoeur cites, with Heidegger, as the "temporal constitution of Care [*Sorge*]."[106] Human within-time-ness is described as a "basic characteristic of Care, our being thrown among things, which tends to make our description of temporality dependent on the description of the things about which we care."[107] The "now" proper to the time of Care, that is, the time of preoccupation, is significantly different from the "now" of an abstract moment.[108] Juan de la Cruz was not indifferently linked to the world about him. He was actively involved with his immediate religious community, the Carmelite order, and society at large. As we will see in his biographical sketch, he held particular responsibilities within these various spheres. The "now" proper to the time of Juan's Care is the "now" of doing shared with other human beings who similarly "do." Within-time-ness is thus irreducible to the representation of linear time, that is, a

---

[105] RICOEUR, *Time and Narrative*, 1:61.

[106] RICOEUR, *Time and Narrative*, 1:61. Heidegger's philosophical anthropology in *Being and Time* is organized around the concept of *Sorge* (Care). In *Sorge*, Heidegger, suggests *Dasein* (Human Being) discovers itself: "Because he knows that he will die, Dasein takes possession, like no other thing does, of the course of his personal destiny, even before it is in fact realized. Consequently, when Heidegger speaks of Dasein as Being-toward-death (*Sein-zum-Tode*) he signals the finite self-possession which characterizes the free being who in projecting himself unfolds the reality of his own destiny." Thomas LANGAN, *The Meaning of Heidegger: A Critical Study of an Existential Phenomenology*, (New York: Colombia University Press, 1959), 32; "The true Self, the caring Self, the Dasein who understands himself in the structural whole of his Being as temporality, realizes itself as conscience (*Gewissheit*). Conscience suggests a note of awareness, the kind of awareness that is born of a steady gaze directed at things as they are. ... Conscience understood thus fundamentally is not a voice calling from outside, but a still and resolute address of the authentic Dasein to himself. This call (*Ruf*) is the voice of care (*Sorge*)." Ibid., 35.

[107] RICOEUR, *Time and Narrative*, 1:62 Ordinary language philosophers (Austin and others) describe the content of everyday language as "those expressions that are most appropriate to what is properly human in our experience." Ibid., 1:62.

[108] RICOEUR, *Time and Narrative*, 1:63. Ricoeur emphasizes Heidegger's point that "Saying 'now' is the discursive articulation of a *making present* which temporalizes itself in a unity with a retentive awaiting." Martin HEIDEGGER, *Being and Time*, trans. John Macquarrie and Edward Robinson, (New York: Harper, 1962), 460, quoted in RICOEUR, *Time and Narrative*, 1:63. Ricoeur further quotes Heidegger on this issue: "The making-present which interprets itself--in other words, that which has been interpreted and is addressed in the 'now'--is what we call 'time'." HEIDEGGER, *Being and Time*, 460, quoted in RICOEUR, *Time and Narrative*, 1:63.

collapse of time in a linear succession of "nows."[109]

The importance of this analysis of the structure of temporality is revealed in this relationship of narrative to Heidegger's concept of within-time-ness.[110] The temporality of human action is not so much that we do things sequentially, from beginning to end: rather, what makes human action temporal is that human actions are shared in Care. In human action we are inserted within-time which results in the constitution of the self. Heidegger's concept of Care is an ontological category which refers to how the individual stands over and against the world in terms of preoccupations. When we use adverbs around time and action they are indicative that there is a linking of action to Care, i.e., human action is never neutral.[111]

All action has a temporal immersion because it is an expression of, or rooted in, Care. The poet, as well as the reader of the *Cántico*, takes up his or her doing as a function of Care, and relates to the world through the experience of within-time-ness manifest by the poetic doing. It is this experience the contemporary reader, as well as the reader of the *Cántico* down through the centuries, has in common with Juan de la Cruz. Time, in Ricoeur's analysis, does not separate us from Juan de la Cruz, but locates contemporary human experience within common preoccupations despite the temporal and cultural disparity between sixteenth-century Spain and the twentieth-century Global Village. Through Care, the human community enters into a common experience of with-in-time-ness that refigures

---

[109] "Being-'within'-time is already something other than measuring the intervals between limit-instants." RICOEUR, *Time and Narrative*, 1:62. The human capacity to put fixed periods on the experience of time reveals a dynamic relationship with the encounter of in-time-ness that called for calculations which resulted in the language of the measuring of this dynamic in the first instance. The initial measurements of the experience of time are found in the experience of the cosmic order itself: the natural rhythm of the change of day and night, the passing of seasons, the rising and setting of the sun, and so on. This primary reference to natural measures of time are essential to safeguard time from slipping into mere abstraction and lose its existential quality. See RICOEUR, *Time and Narrative*, 1:63.

[110] "Narrative configurations [of time] and the most elaborated forms of temporality corresponding to them share the same foundation of within-time-ness." RICOEUR, *Time and Narrative*, 1:64.

[111] RICOEUR, *Time and Narrative*, 1:62-63.

temporal distance. For Ricoeur, this dialectic is brought into sharp focus through the inscription of time in language.[112]

The question may now be asked: Where does an examination of the characteristics of mimesis$_1$, lead us with respect to our methodological trajectory? Since we recognize that Juan de la Cruz necessarily drew from his practical everyday living to shape the *Cántico*, we can reflect on Juan's poetic work to enter into the world of possibilities for human life shaped by that work. An examination of the historical world within which Juan wrote will allow the current reader to enter into this dynamic more consciously. This world includes his own family life, his cultural milieu, the socio-political-economic reality of sixteenth-century Spain, Juan's literary sources, as well the church to which Juan belonged. Various individuals, such as the great Teresa of Avila, shaped Juan's life profoundly. Juan, immersed in his own *Lebenswelt*, brought that experience to language in his *Cántico*. We are therefore led into the historical and cultural world of Juan.

Based on the foregoing reflection we may also ask: What is the originary preoccupation or Care of Juan's life? How does Juan de la Cruz or his *Cántico* stand within time? What characterizes him? These questions can only be responded to during the investigations pursued in the following chapter. However, we can say for now that Juan de la Cruz stands before us as, among other things, a theologian, a pastoral worker, an administrator, and a writer. In a particular way tradition has characterized Juan's preoccupation within-time-ness as "mystical."

5. Conclusion

Ricoeur's theory of mimesis has revealed its treasures in this presentation. It suggests that poetic doing imitates human action to be taken up again in some future time. Poetic mimesis is not a mere reflection of reality but is

---

[112] "As is well known, Heidegger reserves the term temporality (*Zeitlichkeit*) for the most originary form and the most authentic experience of time, that is, the dialectic of coming to be, having been, and making present. In this dialectic, time is entirely desubstantialized. The words 'future,' 'past,' and 'present' disappear, and time itself figures as the exploded unity of the three temporal extases. This dialectic is the temporal constitution of Care." RICOEUR, *Time and Narrative*, 1:61.

productive of authentic human existence. The language of the *Cántico* takes on a new role within this context. Through poetic language there is an intensification of reality which is constructed in a particular way, particularly through the use of metaphor. Therefore, Juan's *Cántico*, within Ricoeur's theory of mimesis, cannot be seen as a stumbling attempt to express Juan's personal experience. This insight frees Juan's *Cántico* to be a transformative text in the life of another human being. Juan's construction of reality becomes available *from* the text in the act of appropriation. Ricoeur's theory, therefore, includes a role for the author, the text, and the reader in the interpretation of Juan's *Cántico*. The *Cántico* cannot be interpreted as a text isolated from the experience of the reader.

Ricoeur's theory of mimesis₁ demonstrates that human action has a universal prenarrative structure which is imitated through narrative productivity.[113] Human action has been shown to have a semantic logic, is rooted in a culture's symbolic systems, and deals with the temporality of the everyday experience of life. "Upon this preunderstanding, common to both poets and their readers, emplotment is constructed, and, with it, textual and literary mimetics."[114] Configuration, or *re-presentation* of human action, can thus take place through emplotment (the making of a text): the pivotal point of analysis which joins time and narrative in Ricoeur's analysis.

In this study I am therefore examining how human action is emploted in Juan's *Cántico* only to be taken up again by the reader in a new way as he or she follows the "directedness" of the text. However, before I begin an analysis of the second moment of mimesis (that of the text), let us turn to an examination of the prefigurative world within which the *Cántico* took shape. In the following chapter, I will review the major events in Juan's life and describe the religious, political, and social climate of sixteenth-century Spain. These realities form the backdrop against

---

[113] "Literature would be incomprehensible if it did not give a configuration to what was already a figure in human action." RICOEUR, *Time and Narrative,* 1:64.

[114] RICOEUR, *Time and Narrative,* 1:64.

which he wrote the *Cántico*. All these fields of resources form the prefigurative world of Juan's *Cántico*.

CHAPTER THREE

MIMESIS₁ AND JUAN'S CONCEPTUAL AND SYMBOLIC WORLD

1. Introduction

Through sensitivity to the various elements of Juan's cultural and ecclesial heritage we are brought into the wider context of Juan's world within which the *Cántico* took shape. This description helps us become knowledgeable of Juan's historical world. There are three main areas which I will examine in order to present the conceptual and symbolic resources which were available to Juan de la Cruz in the composition of the *Cántico*. The first of these is a general introduction to the historical milieu of Juan, its political, sociological, intellectual, and religious characteristics. The second is an examination of Juan's own life and the development of the *Cántico* within that life. Here we will examine the unfolding of the various texts of the *Cántico* as well as their commentaries. The third is a presentation of the western mystical tradition from within which Juan wrote. Juan's contribution and uniqueness within that tradition will be our focal point here.

2. The Historical Milieu of Juan de la Cruz

Juan de la Cruz (1542-1591) lived during the dawn of the modern age in Europe.[1] It was a time of unparalleled importance for Spain on the world scene.[2]

---

[1] See Louis BOUYER, Dom Jean Leclercq, and Dom François Vandenbroucke, *A History of Christian Spirituality: II The Spirituality of the Middle Ages,* trans. The Benedictines of Holme Eden Abbey, Carlisle (London: Burns & Oates, 1968), 532-543 for a resume of the main political and religious currents of Juan's time. Another excellent summary with extensive bibliographical references which focuses more exclusively on the religious currents is: Melquiades ANDRÉS [MARTÍN], "Pensamiento teologico y vivencia religiosa en la reforma española (1400-1600)," in *Historia de la Iglesia en España III-2.° La Iglesia en la España de los siglos XV y XVI,* ed. Ricardo Garcia-Villoslada, Biblioteca de Autores Cristianos Serie maior 21 (Madrid: Editorial Católica, 1980), 269-361. See especially Ibid., "La espiritualidad española en los siglos XV y XVI: Movimientos y disputas," 327-361. Probably the most complete study of theological and spiritual currents during

92

The political and material prosperity of the Iberian Peninsula had been guaranteed by the marriage of Ferdinand of Aragon and Isabella of Castile in 1469 which united the whole of Spain.[3] With the discovery and conquest of the New World in 1492, new and immeasurable riches came flowing into Spain's many ports. However, many Spaniards remained untouched by this new found wealth, and dire poverty was widespread.

In response to this situation Juan worked as an orderly in the Hospital de las Bubas in Medina when he was still a young adolescent.[4] This hospital would

Juan's sixteenth-century Spain is Melquiades ANDRÉS [MARTÍN], *La teología español en el siglo XVI*, 2 vols., Biblioteca de Autores Cristianos Serie maior 13 & 14 (Madrid: Editorial Católica, 1976-77). For a presentation of the main elements from this work see his article: Ibid., "La Teología española en el siglo XVI," *Revista Española de Teología* 52 (1992), 129-153. A succinct summary of the main currents in sixteenth-century Spanish theology is given by Andrés Martín in GARCIA-VILLOSLADA, ed., *Historia de la Iglesia en España III-2.°*, 269-280. A less detailed presentation which focuses on the Carmelite movements during this time is Kieran KAVANAUGH, "Spanish Sixteenth Century: Carmel and Surrounding Movements," in *Christian Spirituality III: Post-Reformation and Modern*, ed. Louis Dupré and Don E. Saliers, World Spirituality: An Encyclopedic History of the Religious Quest 18 (New York: Crossroad, 1989), 69-92. A detailed and somewhat exhaustive study which presents a sociological, political, cultural, as well as a geographical and economical description of Juan's Spain can be found in Fernand BRAUDEL, *The Mediterranean and the World in the Age of Philip II*, 2 vols., trans. from French by Siân Reynolds (London: Collins, 1972).

[2] The prominence of the literary reputation of Spain at this time deserves special note. "Under Charles V and Philip it was the wealthiest land in Europe and was the centre of the political movements which governed the civilized world. There was everything to stimulate the development of a national literature which should guide the thoughts of mankind, even as the arms of Spain dominated both hemispheres. The ability of the race was unquestionable, the standard of culture was high, the language had been developed into a copious and flexible vehicle for the expression of thought, ... It was the golden age of Spanish literature." Henry Charles LEA, *Chapters from the Religious History of Spain Connected With the Inquisition*, reprint of 1890 edition, Research & Source Work Series 245; Selected Essay, History and Social Science 31 (New York: Burt Franklin, 1967), 140.

[3] Fernand Braudel describes this development in his very extensive work on this period in Spain. For a brief description of the accomplishments of this union and the contributions of Charles V and Philip II who followed Ferdinand in the line of the Catholic Kings of Spain see BRAUDEL, *Mediterranean and the Mediterranean World*, 2:669-681.

[4] Las Bubas, literally meaning "the tumours," was the popular name of the hospital. The official name of the hospital was Nuestra Señora de la Concepción. This job was offered to him by the administrator of the Hospital Don Alonso Alvarez de Toledo. Don Alonso Alvarez was struck by Juan's sensitivity to others and so knew he would be a good candidate for the job. However, Juan's family was also in need of financial support, and so Juan gladly accepted a position that would help all the members of his family. See HARDY, *Search for Nothing*, 13-14, passim. The impression this

have been for the very poor suffering from contagious diseases. However, this did not deter young Juan and it was a great source of personal growth for him. "Being close to the destitute taught Juan the real values of life; ... he did not see the patients as the objects of apostolic zeal. He saw them first and foremost as people."[5]

Juan would also have felt the repercussions of the expulsion from Spain of the last of the Muslims, located in the city of Granada. This event also took place in 1492 and resulted in relative peace and apparent religious unity for the first time in nearly eight hundred years.[6] This "apparent unity" came, however, at a great cost. Muslims and Jews alike were forced to renounce their religious beliefs in favour of catholicism, or face expulsion. However, despite these political tactics, the rich cultural heritage which the Jews and Muslims left behind was still very much

---

experience left on Juan is described for us by Hardy: "The physical, psychological and social suffering of the patients impressed young Juan de Yepes in the adolescent, formative years during which he lived and worked there." Ibid., 14. Juan was to intensely exercise his skills and care for the sick once again as an adult during the *catarro universal* or influenza while he lived in the south of Spain in the town of Baeza in 1580. This epidemic "killed his mother and left Teresa [of Avila] in a state of prostration from which she never fully recovered." BRENAN, *St. John of the Cross: His Life and Poetry,* 47. During this scourge Juan cared for the monks in his own charge, cooking and cleaning, changing their beds and caring for them in whatever ways he could despite his already very busy schedule as Rector of the new Carmelite College in Baeza.

[5] HARDY, *Search for Nothing,* 15.

[6] The peace and the unity was "relative" and "apparent" since the persecution wrought by the Spanish Inquisition took a heavy toll on the church as well as the state, causing destruction and division. (see page 98) Regretfully, the positive contributions of the Mohammedan culture were not always recognized by the church or state. For instance, it was the Muslims who had preserved the writings of Aristotle for the West. Aristotle had ceased to be studied in the Roman Empire since 529 when Justinian closed the schools of Athens. And thus it was the Muslims who were to be the guardians of Aristotelian philosophy for the blossoming of scolasticism after the turn of the millennium. It was the influx of Muslims to the Iberian Peninsula in 711, although threatening the very existence of Catholicism in that part of the world, which brought the superior Mohammedan culture with them. Therefore, because of the Muslims, Aristotelian philosophy had begun to flourish in twelfth-century Moslem Spain. From Spain, through translations made under the direction of the Archbishop of Toledo, this Greco-Arab philosophical and scientific culture spread through the Catholic intellectual world. During the time of Juan de la Cruz the Muslim heritage and culture was still very strong. See Philip HUGHES, *The Church in the World the Church Made: From Augustine to Aquinas,* History of the Church 2 (London: Sheed & Ward, 1961), 323-325.

in evidence during Juan's own time.[7]

The truth of the matter is that the first European Renaissance did not begin in Italy in the sixteenth century, but in the twelfth century in Spain. Within Spain the place where Juan was most prodigious in his writing was Andalusia.[8] This was the meeting place for a rich diversity of cultures and spiritualities of the East and of the Mediterranean which contributed toward a great cultural richness.[9] Superior architectural designs, aqueduct systems, medical, and astronomical advances were all firmly entrenched in Juan's Spain.

Intellectually, Spain was the bright light in European academic endeavours, founding many new universities during this time.[10] The University of

---

[7] Bruno de Jésus Marie reconstructs the predominantly Muslim setting of sixteenth-century Grenada. See BRUNO DE JÉSUS MARIE, *Saint Jean de la Croix*, 244-260. The most prominent Arabian philosopher of Musulman Spain, Averroës, was born in Cordoba in 1126 and influenced European theological schools throughout the Middle Ages and the Renaissance. He proposed that the end to mysticism was union with God by means of contemplation, a theme which can be readily discerned in Juan's own writings. See Henri POURRAT, *History of Christian Spirituality*, trans. from French by W.H. Mitchell, Jacques Attwater, and Donald Attwater of *La spiritualité chrétienne*, London: Burns, Oates & Washbourne, 1955, 3:81. Miguel Asín Palacios has studied the influences of this Muslim heritage on Juan's writings, see Miguel Asín PALACIOS, "Un précurseur hispano-musulman de saint Jean de la Croix," *Études Carmélitaines* 1 (1932), 113-167. In this article Palacios studies the doctrinal parallels concerning renouncement in the writings of Juan de la Cruz and the muslim mystique Ibn 'Abbâd de Ronda (†1394). Palacios argues that the mystics of sixteenth-century Spain were a direct result of the Islamic Mystics, the Sufis and Sadilies. This thesis was based on comparative linguistic studies to which he devoted his life. One need only tour the Jewish Quarter of Seville to get a feel for the influence of the Jewish presence in that town which persists even to today.

[8] The contrasts of the countryside in Andalusia are striking. At places there are vast planes which are nearly barren and desert like. In other places there are rolling hills and mountainous terrain. It was within the confines of this landscape that Juan wrote his *Cántico*. For an interesting reflection on how the geographical setting might affect an individual's spirituality see: Belden C. LANE, "Fierce Landscapes and the Indifference of God," *The Christian Century* 16, no. 29 (1989), 907-910.

[9] POURRAT, *Christian Spirituality*, 3:80-85.

[10] For a chronological list of the various faculties of theology which were established in over fourty cities throughout Spain from 1208-1693 see ANDRÉS [MARTÍN], "Pensamiento teologico," 270. However, Spain's central position in academic endeavours was not to retain its prominence. By the end of the seventeenth century "the nation which had seemed destined to supremacy alike in the world of letters and of arms had shrunk until in both spheres there were none so poor as to do it reverence." LEA, *Religious History of Spain*, 188. Lea attributes this decline in large part to the severe and absolute censorship exercised by the Spanish Inquisition. See Ibid., 187-211, where Lea discusses the influence of this censorship particularly on the academic life of the Spanish intellectuals.

Salamanca, at which Juan himself studied, boasted an impressive selection of scholars unrivalled by those in either France or Italy.[11] But even before his arrival at Salamanca, Juan would have been well versed in Greek, Latin and Rhetoric due to his four years of intensive study at the Jesuit college in Medina del Campo.[12] Juan was the recipient of the diversity and originality of these highly stimulating intellectual environments. Despite a renewal of Aristotelian scholasticism Juan was introduced to various schools of thought, and, even more significantly, he was exposed to the *right to*, and *value of*, original thinking.[13]

The foundation of the many colleges and universities during Juan's time provided the basis for the unification of theology and the growing influence of

---

[11] The University of Salamanca had existed since 1242 and had 8,000 students in the sixteenth century. It was divided into twenty-five colleges and fifty religious communities had students studying there. Domini de Soto (1494-1560), Francisco de Vitoria (1492 or 1493-1546) and Melchior Cano (1509-60) were among the greatest theologians of the day. See BOUYER, *A History of Christian Spirituality*, 2:533. Prominent in the Carmelite order were the theologians John Baconthorp and Michael of Bologna, see CRISÓGONO, *Vida y obras*, 75.

[12] For a brief description of life and studies at the Colegio de Medina del Campo see CRISÓGONO, *Vida y obras*, 34-48.

[13] This renewal in scholastic theology coincided with reforms launched by the Council of Trent. See Hubert JEDIN, *A History of the Council of Trent*, 2 vols., trans. from German by Don Ernest Graf (London: Thomas Nelson & Sons Ltd., 1957), 1:400. At the famed University of Salamanca Peter Lombard's *Libri sententiarum* was replaced by the *Summa theologiae* of Thomas Aquinas around 1526. See ANDRÉS [MARTÍN], "Pensamiento teologico," 275. However, scolasticism was not the only theology being used. Theology in the time of Juan was involved in a search for truth, and it was willing to use whatever methods available to attain it. Andrés Martín describes the academic approach at the University of Alcalá: "Cada profesor explicaba a su titular, sin obligación de atarse a su pensamiento. Incluso podía refutarlo. El amor a la verdad configuró de raíz a muchas personas de la generación de los descubrimientos e hizo de ellas críticos independientes. El teólogo no está obligado a seguir a ningún autor, salvo a la revelación. ... Entre 1500 y 1580, el teólogo español se distingue por su personalidad de criterio, por atender más al valor de las razones que a la persona que las dice." Ibid., 284 For a description of the method in theology employed by Melchor Cano during Juan's time at the University of Salamanca see Ibid., 284-289. This method essentially reverses the method used by Thomas Aquinas. As Cano says: "Antes de mí no se atendía todo lo debido a los argumentos de fe; los problemas teológicos se trataban casi con argumentos de razón. *Yo he cambiado el orden de Santo Tomás (Ordinem ... divi Thomae immutavi)*. En la *Suma contra los gentiles* él pone primero las razones y después los testimonios. Pero yo siempre, desde el principio, enseñé primero lo que definía la fe, y después lo que mostraba la razón. Melchor CANO, *De locis theologicis*, 1.12 c.10. quoted in Ibid., 287.

humanism in sixteenth-century Spain.[14] There was a growing awareness that theology was not just an abstract knowing of God through Revelation, but that humanity participated in the life of God personally, and the ideal of that life was union with God.[15] Creation and the human person were seen as fundamentally good, and thus Christian humanism did not focus upon the sinful nature of humanity, but rather focused upon the redemption of that humanity in the world.[16]

In their religious life the people of sixteenth-century Spain lived in various and, at times, diverse settings.[17] On the one hand there were the numerous

[14] For a description of the historical moment in which Juan lived which emphasises this humanistic influence see: Baldomero JIMÉNEZ DUQUE, *En Torno a San Juan de la Cruz*, Colleción Remanso, Section IV, 8 (Barcelona: Juan Flors, 1960), 15-31. Andrés Martín also points out the importance of the unification of theology and humanism during Juan's time. In speaking about major religious figures of the fifteenth and sixteenth centuries he says: "Ellos crearon universidades, colegios mayores y menores y les infundieron una recia base humanista, uniendo con estrechos lazos humanismo y teología. Gracias a ellos se aseguró la orientación cristiana de nuestra renacimiento y los teólogos se convirtieron en escritores correctos al menos; a veces, incluso en eximios latinistas, helenistas y hebraístas. En ellos se armoniza el conocimiento de las lenguas sagradas, la apertura y búsqueda de la verdad, la confianza en la capacidad creadora del hombre." ANDRÉS [MARTÍN], "Pensamiento teologico," 272. Further on Andrés Martín describes the limits of the influence of humanism, especially that espoused by Erasmus, on the theology and spirituality of sixteenth-century Spain. See Ibid., 350-353. See also POURRAT, *Christian Spirituality*, 3:49-62 for a description of the influence of the movement of Christian humanism during Juan's time. The important study of Marcel BATAILLON, *Erasme et l'Espagne: Recherches sur l'histoire spirituelle du XVIe siècle*, (Paris: E. Droz, 1937) demonstrates the influence of Dutch humanism in Spain during the sixteenth century. Rafael M.ª DE HORNEDO has outlined the effects of humanism in Juan's writings in his article "El Humanismo de San Juan de la Cruz," *Razón y Fe* 129 (1944), 133-150. See also Louis COGNET, "Mysticisme et Humanisme," in *Histoire de la Spiritualité Chrétienne III La Spiritualité Moderne*, (Paris: Aubier, 1966), 39-70.

[15] POURRAT, *Christian Spirituality*, 3:55-56.

[16] M. BREMOND, *Histoire littéraire du sentiment religieux en France: I L'Humanisme dévot*, (Paris: 1916), 10-12, quoted in POURRAT, *Christian Spirituality*, 3:61. Christian humanism was a widespread movement across Europe. The principal Christian humanists in the fifteenth and sixteenth centuries are: in the Rhineland, Cardinal Nicholas de Cusa; in Italy, Pico della Mirandola and Cardinal Sadolet; in England, Saint Thomas More; in France, Lefèvre of Etamples; in Germany, Erasmus of Rotterdam. Ibid., 49. Erasmus was read in Spain, for example, by Ignatius of Loyola. Ibid., 51.

[17] For an overview of the spiritual movements active in Juan's time see: ENRIQUE DEL SAGRADO CORAZON, "Espagne -- III. L'Age d'Or: Courants Spirituels et Sources," in *Dictionnaire de Spiritualité*, vol. 4², (Paris: Beauchesne: 1961), col. 1146-1159. Andrés Martín sums up the many diverse movements in spirituality: "Con el siglo XVI se afianza una nueva espiritualidad de espectro amplisimo, con lenguaje aproximativo y temas muchas veces fronterizos. De aqui dimanan tensiones, confusión e inseguridad. Ofrezco un pequeño indice de temas conflictivos: la

religious Orders, including the monasteries of the contemplatives like the Cistercians and Carthusians. There were the popular and frequent public devotions to the Blessed Virgin, and the celebrated pilgrimage to St. James of Compostela.[18] Included in late medieval devotions was the centrality of the passion of Christ and the cult of the saints. By the time of Juan de la Cruz, due to the very forward looking Alfonso X, Spain had available to it a translation of the Bible in the vernacular.[19] On the other hand there were the military Orders such as the Mercedarians and the Trinitarians whose mission it was to negotiate the ransom of prisoners with the Muslims.[20] In contrast to the brilliance of Alfonso X there was the "spectacle of the

---

llamada universal a la perfección cristiana, sacada de los conventos por nuestros místicos desde el año 1500 y abierta a todos los bautizados, sin distinción de estado y sexo; la insistencia en el puro espíritu; la crítica mordaz de las obras externas, de los ritos y de las ceremonias; el desprecio de la oración vocal y la recomendación permanente de la interioridad; la valoración de la experiencia frente a la ciencia; el amor como ley suprema cristiana, que lleva a los alumbrados a despreciar las leyes eclesiásticas y divinas y a desentenderse de las demás obras del cristiano; la estima de los místicos por la propia experiencia y la afirmación de amar más de lo que conocen. Así, el amor es un nuevo tema de fricción en el terreno de la espiritualidad, de la antropología y de la metafísica del conocimiento." ANDRÉS [MARTÍN], "Pensamiento teologico," 320.

[18] BOUYER, *A History of Christian Spirituality*, 2:533. For a summary of the main elements of late medieval devotion see Richard KIECKHEFER, "Major Currents in Late Medieval Devotion," in Jill Raitt et al., eds., *Christian Spirituality: II High Middle Ages and Reformation*, World Spirituality 17 (New York: Crossroad, 1987), 75-108. Kieckhefer notes that virtually all the manifestations of popular devotion at this time became problematic in the sixteenth century especially as they were critiqued by Luther and his followers. Caroline Walker Bynum says of the high Middle Ages: "The dominant note of piety is optimism and a sense of momentum toward a loving God. Concentration on the eucharist and on Christ's suffering in the Passion, which increases in thirteenth- and fourteenth-century devotions, is not primarily a stress on the sacrifice needed to bridge the enormous gap between us in our sin and God in his glory; it is rather an identification with the fact that Christ is what we are. Moreover, both the imaginative identification with Christ's humanity, which is so stressed by late medieval preachers and devotional writers, and the increased theological emphasis on creation and incarnation are answers to the major heresies of the twelfth to fourteenth centuries." Caroline WALKER BYNUM, *Jesus as Mother: Studies in the Spirituality of the High Middle Ages*, (Berkeley: University of California Press, 1982), 130.

[19] The Spanish translation of the Bible had been available since 1252 under his leadership. However, during Juan's time the reading of the Bible in the vernacular had been prohibited due to the edict of the Grand Inquisitor of the Spanish Inquisition Juan de Valdés in 1551. See BENEDICTINE OF STANBROOK ABBEY, *Mediæval Mystical Tradition and Saint John of the Cross*, (London: Burns & Oates, 1954), 19. For a description of the political development and prohibitions concerning the Bible see, LEA, *Religious History of Spain*, 44-56. Lea tells the story of Teresa of Avila's refusal of a novice due to the novice's desire to bring her own Bible to the convent. Ibid., 49.

[20] BOUYER, *A History of Christian Spirituality*, 2:533.

98

papacy at Avignon" and a general mediocrity of the clergy.[21]

Before and during Juan's time various Councils and individuals made many attempts at reform of the church. The Spanish Inquisition, known to be the fiercest and most severe, was established in November of 1478 during the reign of Ferdinand and Isabella. It was a permanent institution conferred with sweeping and, at times, harsh powers in everything concerning matters of the faith.[22] In reality, the severity of the Inquisition in Spain was to ensure political unity through religious conformity. Political unity was seen as threatened by the Jews, Muslims, and by the Protestant Reformation spreading across Europe.

The Inquisition also attacked the *alumbrados* who had appeared in Toledo by 1512 and had spread throughout Spain.[23] Anyone who showed signs of

[21] BOUYER, *A History of Christian Spirituality,* 2:534 An interesting description of the excesses in the sixteenth century of the clergy in Castile is given in Henry Charles LEA, *A History of the Inquisition of Spain,* 4 vols., (New York: Macmillan, 1906-1908), 1:10-11. Lea points out that efforts at church reform were somewhat ineffective and eventually it fell to Isabel and Ferdinand "to correct its more flagrant scandals." However, in reference to the church, Lea further states: "While powerless to reform itself it yet had influence enough to educate the people up to its standard of orthodoxy in the ruthless persecution of all whom it pleased to designate as enemies of Christ." Ibid., 11.

[22] See LEA, "The Influence of Censorship," in *Religious History of Spain,* 187-211. In fact, the Inquisition took its toll on all areas of life in Spain since the Church was still so closely tied to the State. Ibid., 139. Lea suggests the censorship of the Inquisition contributed toward a great decline in the Spanish culture. "The triumph of Church and State was complete over a docile people, to whom were closed the avenues of intelligence which were bringing new life and light to all other Christian nations. The deadly blight of enforced orthodox uniformity settled down upon the land and Spanish genius sought safety in slumber which lasted for two centuries." Ibid., 209. A Dominican, Thomas de Torquemada (†1498) was one of its harshest Grand Inquisitors. LEA, *A History of the Inquisition of Spain,* 534. The tribunals of the Spanish Inquisition were not officially abolished until the beginning of the nineteenth century with the Constitution of Cadiz in 1812. For an excellent overview of the founding of the Spanish Inquisition, its organization and its confrontation with the Alumbrados and Lutheranism, see José Luis GONZÁLEZ NOVALÍN, "La Inquisición Española," in *Historia de la Iglesia en Expaña III-2.° La Iglesia en la España de los siglos XV y XVI,* ed. Ricardo Garcia-Villoslada, Biblioteca de Autores Cristianos Serie maior 21 (Madrid: Editorial Católica, 1980), 107-268.

[23] Relatively little is known about this popular movement in Spain. However, like any other religious movement, it did not suddenly appear or disappear. Quite orthodox in its foundational period and most likely spirited by the *Devotio Moderna,* it later radically departed from the traditional paths of spirituality and fell into decline. See Ralph J. TAPIA, *The Alumbrados of Toledo,* (Park Falls, Wisconsin: F.A. Weber & Sons, Inc., 1974). See also POURRAT, *Christian Spirituality,* 3:108-113 for a description of the reaction of the Inquisition in confrontation with the Alumbrados. The response was often extreme. For example: "Urged on by Melchior Cano, Fernando de Valdés issued the famous Index of 1559 at Vallodolid. To the books already prohibited in 1551 was added a long list

religious fervour or departed from accepted patterns of orthodox teachings or behaviours was suspected of Illuminism and was in danger of being denounced to the Inquisition. Some of the *beatas*, with whom Juan journeyed as a spiritual director while Rector of the College in Baeza, were suspected of participation in the Alumbrado movement.[24] Those who followed the reforms initiated by Erasmus earlier in the fifteenth century were also persecuted by the Inquisition in the later part of the century.[25] The 1618 edition of the works of Juan had passages suppressed and added as a safeguard against misinterpretations or accusations of Illuminism.[26] However, despite these editorial precautions, Juan's works were still denounced before the Inquisition, although they were never placed on the Index.

Therefore, despite the theological diversity and openness being taught

of works mostly written by authors of irreproachable orthodoxy. Besides Carranza's book, it included three works by Luis of Granada, one by Francis Borgia, one by John of Avila, and the spiritual writings of Jorge de Montemayor." Ibid., 109. See also: ANDRÉS [MARTÍN], "Pensamiento teologico," 346-350; Ibid., "Alumbrados, Perfectistas y Quietistas," in *Historia de la teologia española: II Desde fines del siglo XVI hasta la actualidad,* Melquiades Andrés Martínez et al., eds., Publicaciones de la Fundación Universitaria Española Monografias 38 (Madrid: Fundación Universitaria Española, 1987), 2:271-286; V. BELTRÁN DE HEREDIA, "Los alumbrados de la diócesis de Jaén," in *Revista Española de Teologia* 9, no. 2 (1949), 161-222; 445-488; Massimo FIRPO, *Tra Alumbrados e «Spirituali»: Studi su Juan de Valdes e il Valdesianesimi nella crisi religiosa del '500 Italiano,* (Florence: Leo S. Olschki, 1990); ADOLFO DE LA MADRE DE DIOS and ROMÁN DE LA INMACULADA, "Espagne -- Déviations Spirituelles et Inquisition," in *Dictionnaire de Spiritualité,* vol. 4[2] (Paris: Beauchesne, 1961), col. 1159-1167; José Constantino NIETO, "The Alumbrados' Movement and its Significance," in *Juan de Valdes and the Origins of the Spanish and Italian Reformation,* (Genève: Droz, 1970), 56-60.

[24] The *beatas* were a group of devout laywomen who practised rigorous piety while living within the confines of their own homes. HARDY, *Search for Nothing,* 84.

[25] The Erasmists in Spain were commonly persecuted under the charge of Illuminism (condemned in 1312 at the Council of Vienne) since Erasmus held in disfavour any regard for external ceremonies. Erasmus was initially read on a popular level and, as well, had protectors in high places in the hierarchy of the Catholic Church who supported his writings. Among these were the dreaded Inquisitor General, Cardinal Alfonso Manrique, Archbishop of Seville and the Primate of Spain, Alfonso Fonseca, Archbishop of Toledo. Eventually Erasmus fell into disrepute and some of his books were put on the first Spanish Index of 1551. This Index also forbid the reading of any version of the bible in Castilian or any other language. POURRAT, *Christian Spirituality,* 3:108. By 1640 Erasmus "had come to be classed with incorrigible heretics." LEA, *Religious History of Spain,* 35-44. See also José Luis GONZÁLEZ NOVALÍN, "La Inquisición Española," 162-174 for a discussion of the confrontation of Erasmists with the Spanish Inquisition.

[26] KAVANAUGH, "Spanish Sixteenth Century: Carmel and Surrounding Movements," 90.

in the universities, ironically Juan de la Cruz lived in a time of religious intolerance in the political and ecclesial forums. After eight hundred years of Moorish occupation, the ambition of national expansion, and the lust for the wealth of the new world, religion was used to ensure political and economic success in Spain. However, Juan also lived during a time of reform and there were many great religious reformers.

The reformers existed particularly among the Orders, which genuinely sought to change the excesses of the "ecclesial state." The Franciscan, Cardinal Ximenez de Cisneros (1436-1517), confessor of Queen Isabella, Provincial of the Franciscans in Castile, and Archbishop of Toledo, launched extensive reforms of his territories.[27] The Dominicans were reformed through the work of men such as Alvaro of Cordova (1423-34). The reform of the Dominicans, at the theological level, continued into the sixteenth century as is witnessed by the prominent Dominican scholars teaching at the University of Salamanca while Juan was there. The Franciscans carried on reforms on the level of popular spirituality.[28] The Franciscan, Francisco de Osuna (c. 1492-1540), inspired Teresa of Avila in her own

---

[27] These reforms are described in NIETO, *Origins of the Spanish and Italian Reformation*, 52-56. One of Cisneros' main contributions to religious life of his day was the encouragement of translation of devotional writings from Latin into the vernacular so that the general population (largely uneducated) could have access to this literature.

[28] ANDRÉS [MARTÍN], "Pensamiento teológico," 277. Andrés Martín describes two levels of reform within this period. "La primera está caracterizada por los movimientos de las observancias. La segunda responde, desde dentro de las órdenes religiosas, a la voluntad decidida de reforma de nuestros obispos durante el concilio de Trento, del cual retornaron insatisfechos." Ibid., 278. This *segunda reforma* was characterized by the *movimiento descalzo*. Many individuals within religious Orders felt a deep need to be transformed and to return to the values of perfection, austerity, prayer, and overall humility in life. This interior disposition was exteriorly manifest by living without shoes. In books on Carmelite spirituality and history the impression is often given that the Carmelites, and specifically Teresa of Avila and Juan de la Cruz, were singular in adopting the practice of the *descalcez*. Without diminishing the importance of the Teresian Reform on both the women's and men's sides which resulted in the *descalzas* and the *descalzos*, many other religious orders at the same time had adopted this practice. Neither Teresa nor Juan were original in taking on this tradition. Andrés Martín cites Juan de Guadalupe, O.F.M. as being the precursor of this movement, along with San Pedro de Alcántara. Other orders which had adopted this practice, at least to a degree, included the Trinitarians, the Mercedarians, and the Augustinians. See Ibid., 278 and 356.

spiritual quest.[29] His positive ideas on recollection (*no pensar nada*), and movement towards simplicity (*atento a solo Dios y contento*), that focus on God alone, seem to foreshadow Juan's own famous *nada*.[30]

Equally felt during Juan's time were the reforms launched by the Benedictine abbot of Montserrat, Garcia Ximenes de Cisneros (1455-1510).[31] Cisneros is indebted to the writers of the *Devotio moderna*, such as John Mombaer and Gerard of Zutphen.[32] Cisneros' well-known and widely read anthology, *Ejercitatorio de la vida espiritual* (1500), described the three classical ways of the spiritual itinerary: the purgative, illuminative, and unitive ways to God. These are used to arrive at a fourth way, that of contemplation.[33] Cisneros' *Ejercitatorio de la vida espiritual* and Ignatius of Loyola's *Ejercicios espirituales* (1522) are prime examples of the full growth of methodical prayer in the fifteenth and sixteenth centuries. Methods of prayer, such as those of Cisneros and Ignatius of Loyola, were based on the *De triplici via* of Bonaventure which had become widespread during Juan's time.[34]

The *Devotio Moderna*, which had developed in the Low Countries in

---

[29] Osuna's famous six *Alphabets*, were read by Teresa. "The first and sixth of these treatises are devoted to the passion of Christ; the second and fifth to the ascetical life; and the third and fourth to the mystical life. It is the *Third Alphabet* that Teresa of Avila seems to have meditated upon, perhaps as early as 1537." BOUYER, *A History of Christian Spirituality*, 2:536-37. Teresa states she read Osuna's *Subida del Monte Sion* with great esteem. Ibid., 539.

[30] BOUYER, *A History Christian of Spirituality*, 2:538.

[31] Garcia Ximenes de Cisneros was related to the famous Cardinal Ximenez mentioned previously.

[32] For a general overview of the *Devotio Moderna* and further bibliographical references see Otto GRÜNDLER, "Devotio Moderna," in *Christian Spirituality*, Jill Raitt et al., eds., 2:176-193. For an examination of the writings of some of its more influential proponents such as those of the founder, Geert Grote, see *Devotio moderna: Basic Writings*, trans. and introduction John Van Engen with a Preface by Heiko A. Oberman, (New York: Paulist Press, 1988).

[33] This book was simultaneously published in Castilian and Latin in Montserrat in 1500. In fact it is hardly original in its scope but puts together writings from many universally known authors such as Bonaventure, Hugh Balma, and Gerson. BOUYER, *A History of Christian Spirituality*, 540.

[34] For the development of this systemization of the spiritual life which had its origins in the *Devotio Moderna* see POURRAT, *Christian Spirituality*, 3:1-22.

the fourteenth century, had also become the inspiration for Spanish piety during Juan's days.[35] Because of this movement the exclusivity of spirituality for only those in the convents and cloisters had been broken down and the call to holiness was extended to all Christians.[36] The development of the printing press greatly accelerated the distribution in books and manuals of this idea of the call to holiness for all people, regardless of what occupation the individual followed or to what level of society he or she belonged.

The popularity of the *Devotio Moderna* signalled a break between theology and mysticism. "Mystical experience was thought of not so much in terms of an experience of the data of Revelation in themselves, as of an experience in the framework of, and guaranteed by, these data. ... the spiritual life became a fact of experience, valid as such--no longer the experience of a fact valid in itself."[37] Paralleling the renewal in academic circles, which involved the return to the early Christian theological sources, was the loss of confidence in speculative theology at the popular level. Proponents of the *Devotio Moderna* and its subsequent movements preferred to trust in personal experience and the observance of methods in prayer which had become the practice of the commoner. Personal holiness through the development of interior prayer and recollection was seen as the basis of

---

[35] The *Devotio moderna* was a turn to the past in an effort to capture the simplicity of the message of the Gospel in its emphasis on love. However, it was distrustful of speculative mysticism and scholastic theology.

[36] Melquiades Andrés Martín sees this call to holiness of all the baptized as "la manifestación más importante" of theological reform of the day. See ANDRÉS MARTÍN, "La Teologia española en el Siglo XVI," 146.

[37] BOUYER, *A History of Christian Spirituality,* 543. The primacy of personal experience over the intellectual abstractions of scolasticism is also described for us by Melquiades Andrés Martín: "Otro tema conflictivo es el de la valoración de la experiencia, del sabor, del gusto, frente a la teologia escolástica y los profesores universitarios. Nuestros místicos recomiendan caminos o vias vividos y experimentados por ellos. Sus obras no son tratados de mística, sino experiencias puestas a la luz del día. A Dios se puede ir por camino de entendimiento o de amor. ... todos coinciden en que la mística, o ciencia de amor, está por encima de la escolástica, o ciencia del saber; que el amor penetra secretos que no alcanza el entendimiento: que ellos aman más de lo que conocen; que esto lo saben por experiencia y que no lo entenderá el que no lo pruebe." ANDRÉS [MARTÍN], "Pensamiento teologico," 334.

ecclesial reform.

However, reform of the ecclesial institution by that institution itself is most notable through the initiatives launched by the Council of Trent (1545-1563). Its main concerns focused on the healing of the confessional split in Germany (already irreversible and spreading throughout Europe), inner reform of the Church itself, and "establishment of peace so that a defense against the Ottomans could be elaborated."[38] The reforms launched by Trent were in the process of being implemented during Juan's time. These reforms included, for the first time, the establishment of formal episcopal seminaries for the training of priests. Most certainly Juan would have benefitted from this very recent development. Prior to this time it had been left to each candidate for priesthood to acquire the necessary training for ordination.[39] As Jedin has pointed out, "The new Catholic piety and mysticism, the revival of scholastic theology, the emergence of positive theology, and the art and culture of the baroque age depend upon the Council of Trent or at least are inconceivable without it. It was no mere restoration of the Middle Ages; rather it brought so many new features to the countenance of the Church that with it a new era of Church history begins."[40]

It was this revitalized church, even if still deeply troubled and divided, into which Juan was born and in which he lived. The ambitious political agenda of the Spanish monarchy further fuelled the turbulence of a church in deep division, yet the church continued to seek a new way to live the life toward which it felt called. At all levels of society and in the church there was a search for truth.[41]

---

[38] Hubert JEDIN, "Council of Trent" in *New Catholic Encyclopedia,* vol. 14, (New York: McGraw-Hill, 1967), 272.

[39] JEDIN, "Council of Trent," 275.

[40] JEDIN, "Council of Trent," 277.

[41] A great part of Spanish life at all levels was preoccupied with this search for truth. "Se busca la verdad hasta dar con ella, hasta encontrarla: se busca el Dorado, las fuentes de la juventud, el lugar del paraíso, la verdad intelectual, geográfica, humana." ANDRÉS MARTÍN, "La Teología española en el Siglo XVI," 137. Further on Andrés Martín says: "¿Y qué es la búsqueda de la verdad sino el deseo de encontrarla? Junto a los buscadores de la verdad científica, evángelica, geográfica, humana,

104

For Teresa of Avila, Juan de la Cruz's mentor, this truth took the form of humility and the transparency of oneself before the Divine. Before the truth of oneself in authentic love, one could discover *a* way to the reality of God.[42]

The spirit of *searching* and *discovery* led to a constant revision of ideas and methods which resulted in an atmosphere of tremendous creativity in Spain. However, this search for truth and progress, whether in the discovery of the "new" world through its geography and riches, or in the area of theology and spirituality in its search for the authenticity of love, was not linear and continual in an uninterrupted fashion. The search for truth goes hand in hand with periods of disorientation and crisis as if one were on a constant journey, a pilgrimage.[43] The dynamism of this age therefore served to feed Juan's deep longing for the fullness of life in which his own mysticism was centred. Perhaps the spirituality of Juan's day could thus be summed up as "incarnationalist."[44]

Humanity was created in the image and likeness of God (Genesis 1:26-30). This was a central symbol which inspired the faith life and theological systems of Juan's time.[45] In turn God had taken on this same human flesh, and God was thus formed in the image of the human. Therefore, human virtues and action

proliferan los buscadores de paraísos australes, de pasos entre mares, de quijotes de diversa índole, de emuladores de la Iglesia apostólica y de las reglas primitivas de su orden religiosa. La historia se puede concebir como deseo de entender, de poder, de poseer, de disfrutar, de descubrir, de misionar... España desde 1492 parece la gran feria del deseo en tierra, mar y casa real, en la universidad, en las órdenes religiosas, en la vida interior de muchas almas. Los hombres son sus voluntades; la voluntad, sus deseos." Ibid., 138.

[42] ANDRÉS MARTÍN, "La Teologia española en el Siglo XVI," 137.

[43] ANDRÉS MARTÍN, "La Teologia española en el Siglo XVI," 138.

[44] Andrés Martín uses the term *encarnacionista* to describe the spirituality of the Golden Age of Spain. ANDRÉS [MARTÍN], "Pensamiento teologico," 333. Caroline Walker Bynum characterizes the period immediately prior to John of the Cross in the following terms: "The affective piety of the high Middle Ages is based on an increasing sense of, first, humankind's creation 'in the image and likeness' of God and, second, the humanity of Christ as guarantee that what we are is inextricably joined with divinity. Creation and incarnation are stressed more than atonement and judgment." WALKER BYNUM, *Jesus as Mother*, 130.

[45] ANDRÉS MARTÍN, "La Teologia española en el Siglo XVI," 133 and 152.

must also be concrete, not mere intellectual abstractions or pietistic rituals of a select few. The call to holiness was seen as universal. The personal experience of all persons was valued. The responsibility of building a vibrant and relevant church was the felt responsibility of all the baptized. Within this universal call Juan grounded his own mystical writings, one of which was the *Cántico*.

3. The Life and Writings of Juan de la Cruz

For this study it is important to note that we are dealing with a man who was very much inserted in the world just described above. Juan de la Cruz involved himself intimately in other people's lives and continually gave of himself in the service of others. Juan was a contemplative, a mystic, it is true, but one who lived life fully in all its dimensions.

In order to obtain a general picture of Juan's life, the presentation below is divided into two sections. The first is "A Chronological Portrait of Juan de la Cruz." This is a general chronological description of the trajectory of Juan's life including elements from his family life, his academic background, and significant transition points. The second concerns "The Composition of the *Cántico*." Of particular interest concerning the composition of the *Cántico* is the fact that both the poem and the commentary circulated in the oral tradition before they were published.

3.1 A Chronological Portrait of Juan de la Cruz[46]

1542 Birth of Juan de Yepes y Alvarez in *Fontiveros*, the third son of Gonzalo de Yepes and Catalina Alvarez. Juan's father dies soon after his birth.

1547 Poverty forces the family to move to *Arévalo*.

1551 Again, due to dire poverty, the family moves, this time to *Medina del Campo*.

c. **1552** Juan is boarded out at an orphanage called the *Colegio de le Doctrina*.

c. **1557** He works at a hospital for the poor: *Nuestra Señora de la Concepción*.

1559-63 He attends the *Colegio de la Compañia de Jesús* where he is exposed to the humanist currents of thought of the times.

1562 Foundation by Teresa de Avila of the first reformed convent at *Avila*.

1563 Juan joins the Carmelites at *Medina* taking the name Juan de Santo Matía.

1564-68 Juan studies philosophy and theology at the University of *Salamanca*.

1567 Juan is ordained. He meets Teresa de Avila.

1568 Juan ends his studies and returns to *Medina*. He goes with Teresa in August to found the convent at *Valladolid*, and in October to *Duruelo*.

Fray Juan de Santo Matía changes his name to Fray Juan de la Cruz.

1569 Foundation of the *Pastrana* convent.

1571 Juan is appointed rector to the new Discalced college at *Alcalá de Henares*.

1572 In May he spends a few weeks at *Pastrana* to correct the excesses of the novice-master. In September he goes as confessor to the Calced convent of the Encarnación at *Avila*, where Teresa is prioress. He remains there for five and a half years.

1573 Teresa leaves *Avila*.

1576 Founding of the first Chapter of the Discalced Carmelites.

[46] The principle dates and biographical information for this presentation have been taken from the following sources: Federico RUIZ [SALVADOR], ed., *Dios habla en la noche: Vida, palabra, ambiente de San Juan de la Cruz*, (Madrid: Editorial de Espiritualidad, 1990), 376-379; BRENAN, "Principle Dates in the Life of San Juan de la Cruz," in *St. John of the Cross: His Life and Poetry*, 228-230; CRISÓGONO, *Vida y obras;* HARDY, *Search For Nothing:* DE NICOLÁS, *Alchemist.* Scholarship concerning precisions around some of the dates and events in Juan de la Cruz's life are still being pursued. An excellent article outlining some of the dates and areas now being questioned can be found in: José VICENTE RODRIGUEZ, "Lectura varia sanjuanista," *Revista de Espiritualidad* 52 (1993), 285-323. The details concerning the redactional history of the *Cántico* are taken from: Eulogio PACHO, "Primeras Ediciones del Cántico Espiritual," *Ephemerides Carmeliticae* 18 (1967), 3-48; Ibid., "Proceso Redaccional del «Cántico»," in *Vértice*, 13-40; Ibid., *Sus escritos*, 99-150 and 185-228; THOMPSON, "The Origins of the *Cántico*," in *The Poet and the Mystic*, 21-32.

Juan is present at *Almodóvar, Ciudad Real.*

1576 In January Juan is kidnapped by the Calced priors and imprisoned at *Medina,* but is released soon after.

1577 Juan is taken prisoner by the Calced at *Avila,* this time he is taken to *Toledo.* He remains there until mid-August 1578. **It is while in prison (1578) he composes the first 31 stanzas of the *Cántico* (*CA* 1-31).**

1578 In October he is named prior of the convent *El Calvario* near *Jaen.* Between 1578 and 1580 he writes the *Subida* and the *Noche Oscura.* **Either this year or the next Juan begins his written commentary on *CA* 1-31 and continues this over the next several years.**

1579 Juan goes to *Baeza* where he founds the Discalced College of Baeza and later becomes rector. **Probably sometime over the next two years *CA* 32-34 are written.** Juan journeys as a spiritual guide with many of the religious of *Baeza* as well as the townspeople, including the group of laywomen known as *beatas.* Some of the people Juan was directing would have been connected with the Alumbrado movement, putting Juan personally at risk vis-á-vis the Inquisition.

1580 Juan's mother dies in *Medina* during the Spanish epidemic known as the *catarro universal.*

1581 In March Juan attends the Chapter of the Separation at *Alcalá.* Juan becomes third definitor and prior of Los Mártires at *Granada,* while remaining for a while at *Baeza* where he is rector of the college. Juan is involved in extensive travel, visiting places such as *Baeza, Alcala de Henares, Caravaca, Beas,* and *Avila* (where he sees Teresa for the last time).

1582 A convent for nuns is founded at *Granada.* Teresa dies October 4. **Sometime during the next two years Juan writes *CA* 35-39.**

1583 At the Chapter of *Almodóvar* Juan is reelected prior of the convent of *Granada.*

1584 *Cántico* A, poem and commentary, are complete. Over the next two years the redaction of *Cántico A* into *Cántico B* takes place at Granada.

1585 Juan founds a convent for nuns at *Málaga.* In May he attends the chapter of *Lisbon.* Juan is appointed second definitor while still prior of Los Mártires. In October the chapter continues at *Pastrana.* Juan is appointed vicar-provincial of Andalucía. This gives him nearly two years of continuous travelling. Among the places he visits: *Grenada, Lisbon, Seville, Malaga, Caravaca, Baeza, Madrid, Pastrana.*

1586 Juan founds a priory at *Córdoba* in May. In August he falls seriously ill with pleurisy at *Guadalcázar.*

1587 At the chapter of *Valladolid* Juan ceases to be definitor and vicar-provincial, but he is reappointed prior of Los

108

Mártires.

1588 In June, Juan attends the first chapter-general of the reform at *Madrid.* Juan is appointed first definitor and a *consiliario* on the *consulta.* In August he becomes prior of *Segovia.* He remains at *Segovia* for nearly three years.

1591 At the chapter-general held at *Madrid* in June, Juan is deprived of all his offices and sent to *La Peñuela,* near *Baeza.* He arrives in August and soon falls seriously ill. In September Juan leaves for *Ubeda,* where he dies on December 14.

1593 Juan's body is transferred from *Ubeda* in the south, to *Segovia* in the north. In December the Congregation of the Discalced Carmelites is made a separate order by a bull of Clement VIII.

1618-19 First editions of Juan's *Obras* appear at *Alcalá* (1618) and *Barcelona* (1619), **without the *Cántico*.**

1622 First appearance of

the *Cántico* in print (Paris: René Gaultier's French translation). This edition uses the *Cántico* of thirty-nine stanzas without editing.

1627 First Spanish edition of the *Cántico* published in *Brussels.* This publication is again of the thirty-nine stanza *Cántico* only, also without editing, and contains the French translation with it. There are no other of Juan's works included.

1627 First appearance of *CB* 11 inserted in the edited primitive *Cántico* known as *Cántico A'.* This "hybrid" consisting of *CA'* and *CB 11* appeared in the Italian translation of Juan's four major works in Rome. The Madrid Spanish edition cited below used *CA'* as well.

1630 First edition of Juan's complete works published in *Madrid* in Spanish by Jerónimo de San José (Ezquerra) who gives the *Cántico* the title *Cántico espiritual entre el alma y Cristo su Esposo.* This slightly edited edition of the primitive *Cántico (CA')* includes *CB* 11. It is a

hybrid of *CA* and *CB* and becomes the new and official standard text of the *Cántico* in all translations until 1703 when it is surplanted by the text of *Cántico B.*

1675 Juan is beatified by Clement X, with the papal brief *Spiritus Domini,* Jan. 25.

1679 In *Alba de Tormes* the first church is dedicated to Juan de la Cruz.

1725 He is canonized by Benedict XIII.

1912 The first critical edition of Juan's work is published in Toledo.

1926 San Juan is declared a doctor of the universal church by Pius XI.

1991 Celebration of 400th anniversary of Juan de la Cruz's death.

1993 With a brief (*breve*) entitled *Inter praeclaros poetas* dated March 8 Pope John Paul II names Juan de la Cruz as patron of Spanish-language poets.

3.2 The Composition of the *Cántico* -- Poem and Commentary

Although the central focus of this dissertation is the actual text of the *Cántico*, its origin and redaction are also of fundamental interest to the topic of this study. The historical fact that the original poem of thirty-one stanzas written in Toledo in 1578 did not have any stanzas added to it for over a year gives it a particular hermeneutical interest. In total, *Cántico A* was written over a period of six years (1578-1584) before being redacted into *Cántico B*. This provides the initial criterion for suggesting the hermeneutical independence of *Cántico A* and *Cántico B*. Although the hermeneutical significance and analysis of these developments will be the focus of the next Chapter, the historical relatedness of these two versions of the *Cántico* will now be presented in more detail.

The development of the poems *Cántico A* and *B* is presented in a first section, while in a second section the development of the commentaries is presented. We are interested in the development of the commentaries at this point since they help anchor us in the poem itself. Recall, it is Juan's symbolic and conceptual world, in all of its facets, which provides for us the hermeneutical setting of the *Cántico*.

3.2.1 Development of the Poem

The previous section in this chapter situated the composition of the *Cántico* in the overall life of Juan de la Cruz. Further precisions now need to be made concerning the evolution of the poem of the *Cántico*. This section will summarize the main turning points in the development of the poem.[47] How this historical information provides evidence for establishing the hermeneutical independence of *Cántico A* will be dealt with in Chapter Four. What can be said for now is that this historical information points to the literary independence of each of

---

[47] The main studies used to summarize these historical developments are the following: DUVIVIER, *La genèse du «Cantique spiritual»*, 79-134 and 227-290; PACHO, *Sus escritos*, 99-139; 185-228; and 275-391; THOMPSON, *The Poet and the Mystic*, 21-59.

the texts of the *Cántico*. From the beginning, each text of the *Cántico* has been read as a dynamic text, a text which, even for the author, provided an ongoing source of self-understanding.

Although the earliest testimonies date from twenty-six years after Juan's death, the evidence is sufficiently reliable to provide certainty concerning the principal developments of the *Cántico*.[48] The first of these developments is the initial composition of the *Cántico* (what has come to be known as *CA* 1-31) during Juan's nine-month incarceration in the conventual prison in Toledo.[49] Magdalena del Espíritu Santo testifies to this in her 1630 correspondence, "Relación de la vida del S. Juan de la Cruz," sent to Jerónimo de San José, the historian of the Discalced Carmelites.[50] Juan de la Cruz was seen by her leaving the prison with a small book in which was written the *canciónes* which began with *Adónde te escondiste* and ended with *Oh ninfas de Judea*.[51] We now know these words as the opening verses of the first and last stanzas of the thirty-one stanza *Cántico*.

---

[48] THOMPSON, *The Poet and the Mystic*, 24.

[49] There is some conflicting evidence as to whether Juan actually wrote down the verses before leaving prison. For instance, Fr. Juan de Santa María, Juan's gaoler, in his own testimony does not mention giving Juan writing materials. See THOMPSON, *The Poet and the Mystic*, 27-28. However, the evidence presented by Pacho strongly supports the actual inscription of the first thirty-one verses of the *Cántico* in prison. See PACHO, *Sus escritos*, 142. See also Ibid., 112-122 and 140ff concerning the question of composition and inscription.

[50] PACHO, *Sus escritos*, 115.

[51] Madre Magdalena del Espíritu Santo relates her eye-witness account to Jerónimo de san José in 1629 of Juan leaving the Toledan prison with the original stanzas of the *Cántico* completed: "Sacó el Santo Padre, cuando salió de la cárcel, un cuaderno que estando en ella había escrito de unos romances sobre el Evangelio '*In principio erat verbum*', ... y las *canciones* o liras que dicen, *Adónde te escondiste*, hasta la que dice *Oh ninfas de Judea* ... Este cuaderno que el Santo escribió en la cárcel, le dejó en el convento de Beas, y a mí me mandaron trasladarle algunas veces." Biblioteca Nacional de Madrid, ms 12944, 132; cfr. Biblioteca Mística Carmelitana 13, 323, quoted in PACHO, *Sus escritos*, 115-116. Testimony by several others confirms this observation. As Eulogio Pacho tells us: "Los testigos que hablan de los escritos redactados en Toledo mencionan casi todos la poesía del *Cántico espiritual*, aun cuando emplean expresiones diferentes para individualizarla. ... Reuniendo las aportaciones de los numerosos testimonios históricos que aluden a las otras composiciones podemos rehacer acaso en su integridad el modesto repertorio toledano. Comprende, además del *Cántico*, el breve poema rotulado *Cantar del alma que se huelga de conocer a Dios por fe* ... y los romances sobre el *Evangelio "in principio erat verbum"* – *acerca de la Santísima Trinidad* ... y sobre el Salmo *Super flumina Babylonis.*" Ibid., 112-113. See also Ibid., 121-122.

What is remarkable is that from the confines of a dark and isolated cell, in the midst of apparently complete rejection by his community and the almost total absence of even the most basic necessities of life, Juan composed a poem speaking of freedom, beauty, blowing winds, and bright colours. Incontestable is the fact that Juan's *Cántico* cannot be divorced from his severe prison experience which was exactly the opposite of what the poem describes.[52] Somehow Juan brought together two diametrically opposed worlds into an inseparable whole. Juan's poem indicates that he was immersed in a level of reality that included the desperate experience of confinement, but, as well, the most authentic elements of human existence. However, Juan was not to remain in prison for the rest of his life: he escaped from prison after nine months. This resulted in the circulation of the works Juan had composed while in prison.

Soon after Juan's escape from prison, as the historian Jerónimo de san José confirms, Juan's writings spread rapidly in oral and written forms.[53] Juan's poems written in prison (not just the *Cántico*) had somehow captured the imagination of the men and women who came in contact with them, particularly among the *Descalzas* of Teresa of Avila.[54] They passed among the nuns orally, even from one convent to the next. It is significant that, although no commentary had yet been written on the *Cántico*, the stanzas were meaningful to those who read and heard

---

[52] Inocencio de San Andrés in his disposition of Jan. 16, 1618 states: "Su cárcel era un hueco de una pared, el cual lugar de la dicha cárcel este testigo ha visto, adonde le tuvieron apretado por espacio de nueve meses; la dicha cárcel no tenía luz ninguna, ni él la tenía, sino cuando alguna vex le daban algún candil para rezar sus Horas." Biblioteca Mística Carmelitana 14, 66, quoted in PACHO, *Sus escritos*, 103-104, n. 6. See also PACHO, *Sus escritos*, 104-106, notes 7-11 for further description of the jail and the conditions in which Juan lived while there.

[53] JERÓNIMO DE SAN JOSÉ [EZQUERRA], *Historia del venerable padre Fr. Juan de la Cruz, primer descalzo carmelita, compañero y coajutor de santa Teresa de Jesús en le fundación de la Reforma*, (Madrid: 1641), 594, quoted in PACHO, *Sus escritos*, 185.

[54] "Muy de ordinario las traian de boca en boca, hallando una celestial suavidad y eficacia en sus palabras." JERÓNIMO DE SAN JOSÉ [EZQUERRA], *Historia del venerable padre Fr. Juan de la Cruz*, 594, quoted in PACHO, *Sus escritos*, 185.

112

them, even in spite of their "incomprehensibility."[55] The diffusion and celebration of the *Cántico* continued when Juan accepted the position of spiritual director of the *Descalzas* at Beas de Segura. Eulogio Pacho even suggests that the stanzas were sung in the visiting room where Juan would have encountered the *Descalzas* for spiritual direction.[56] This suggestion, however, is not shared by all commentators. Anselmo Donazar suggests that Juan's poetry would have lost much of its effect had it been sung.[57] Whether the poetry was sung or not is uncertain, but it is known that many of the *Descalzas* at Beas memorized the stanzas and used them for their personal edification.

While living in the convent of El Calvario, John frequently visited the

---

[55] "Las aventajadas hijas de la Madre Teresa se percataron de la profundidad espiritual de aquellos versos endiosados, por más que, a pesar de sus buenos deseos, les resultaban casi ininteligibles." PACHO, *Sus escritos*, 186. "A los primeros lectores --monjas de Toledo y de Beas-- las ingrávidas estrofas les resultaban ininteligibles algo esotérico. ... Sin aclaraciones personales del autor, [es] imposible penetrar en su rico meollo espiritual." Ibid., 206.

[56] In speaking of Juan in these encounters he says: "Perduran mucho tiempo la procuerdo del traspaso espiritual, al oír las coplas cantadas en el locutorio, la intuición y el convencimiento de tratar con un alma espiritualmente extraordinaria y sublimada." PACHO, *Sus escritos*, 208. Jerónimo de San José reports the following story about Juan singing: "San Juan de la Cruz, una noche de Navidad, en Granada, arrebatado por el amor al divino Niño, se levantó impetuoso y tomando su imagen en los brazos comenzó a bailar mientras cantaba: 'Mi dulce y tierno Jesús,/ Si amores me han de matar/ Agora tienen lugar'," JERÓNIMO DE SAN JOSÉ [EZQUERRA], *Historia del venerable padre Fr. Juan*, 428, quoted in DUVIVIER, *La genèse du «Cantique spirituel»*, 119, n. 1. Francisca de la Madre de Dios reports Juan singing the *Cántico* in her Declaration: "Y que en la dicha prisión había estado como nueve meses, y que era mucho el consuelo que tenía en aquella estrecha cárcel, ... y que particularmente había comenzado a cantar aquella canción que dice: '¿Adónde te escondiste, Amado, / y me dejaste con gemido?'" Biblioteca Nacional de Madrid, ms 12738, 437-[438]; cfr. Biblioteca Mística Carmelitana 14, 173-4, quoted in DUVIVIER, *La genèse du »Cantique spirituel»*, 125, n. 1.

[57] Anselmo Donazar states that most poetry was sung in sixteenth-century Spain. In speaking of Teresa of Avila he says: "Es curioso observar que el movimiento espiritual que la Madre Teresa inaugura se mantiene con música y quien dice música dice poesía, pues en aquellos tiempos la poesía casi siempre era cantada." Anselmo DONAZAR, *Fray Juan de la Cruz: El hombre de las ínsulas extrañas*, (Burgos: Editorial Monte Carmelo, 1985), 49. However, he says Juan's poetry does not fit into this category for the following reasons: "Fray Juan de la Cruz sale de las entrañas del pueblo, cómo no; pero no va a cantar en la cuerda del pueblo. Busca la poesía cortesana, el efecto entre los cultos. Juan de la Cruz no canta; cantar salmos por los caminos (como asegura algún contemporáneo) no es cantar y, desde luego no escribe su poesía para ser cantada. ... Si tratamos de poner en música la poesía de Fray Juan de la Cruz, veremos que se pierden los efectos sibilantes y los consonánticos; el efecto tónico que le puso desaparece." Ibid., 50. Duvivier is in agreement with this position: "Non seulement saint Jean de la Croix a composé les cinq strophes par écrit, mais il ne les chante ni ne les écrit, pas plus qu'il «ne les lit ou ne les dicte», pour reprendre les termes de M. Orozco." DUVIVIER, *La genèse du «Cantique spirituel»*, 120.

nuns at Beas to preach, give spiritual direction, and hear confessions. These visits continued, albeit with less frequency as time passed, even after Juan had become rector of the college in Baeza in 1579 and prior of the convent in Granada in 1582.[58] The *Cántico* was often a subject of discussion during these visits.[59] Therefore, before the poem was completed, there evolved both an oral and written commentary on it. The nuns at Beas would question Juan on the meaning of his sublime verses and Juan would enter into dialogue with them concerning their interpretation. A similar dynamic ensued when Juan lived in Granada and visited the nuns of that town.

Starting in 1578 or 1579, Juan most likely sketched out in oral and written form commentaries on the passages. These commentaries were initiated by the questions of the nuns. The later sections of the poem (the nine stanzas added at various stages after the original thirty-one stanzas written in prison), would therefore have been written with the experience of a needed commentary in mind. According to the testimony of Francisca de la Madre de Dios, in April 1618, it was during one of the visits to the nuns of Beas, while Juan lived in Granada, that he wrote stanzas 35-39 of the *Cántico*.[60]

---

[58] See PACHO, *Sus escritos*, 192 for testimony of these many visits. See also DUVIVIER, *La genèse du «Cantique spirituel»*, 109.

[59] "A golpe de preguntas y respuestas va perfilándose poco a poco un auténtico comentario de las ya famosas liras. De hecho, en Beas nacen los primeros intentos de parafrasear doctrinalmente el poema del *Cántico*." PACHO, *Sus escritos*, 187. M. Magdalena affirms this concerning Juan's many visits to the nuns at Beas: "Las *declaraciones*, algunas las hizo en Beas, respondiendo a pregunta que las religiosas le hacian, y otras estando en Granada." Biblioteca Mística Carmelitana 10, 325, quoted in Ibid., 187.

[60] "Y asimismo, preguntándole un día a esta testigo en qué traía la oración, le dijo que en mirar la hermosura de Dios y holgarse de que la tuviese; y el Santo se alegró tanto de esto, que por algunos días decía cosas muy levantadas, que admiraban, de la hermosura de Dios; y así, llevado de este amor, hizo unas cinco canciones a este tiempo sobre esto, que comienzan: 'Gocémonos, Amado, y , Vámonos a ver en tu hermosura.'" Biblioteca Nacional de Madrid ms. 12738, 428; cfr. Biblioteca Mística Carmelitana 14, 170, quoted in DUVIVIER, *La genèse du «Cantique Spirituel»*, 105, n. 3. This testimony was repeated in a letter to the historian, Jerónimo de San José, eleven years later in November of 1629. This datation of the addition of *CA* 35-9 is thus generally accepted over the contradictory witness of Magdalena del Espíritu Santo (Biblioteca Mística Carmelitana 10, 325) who testifies to the existence of these verses during Juan's time at Baeza, that is, sometime between 1579 and 1582. See DUVIVIER, *La genèse du «Cantique Spirituel»*, 105-112 for a discussion on this matter.

114

This places the composition of *CA* 35-9 between 1582 (when Juan left Baeza for Granada) and 1584, when they appear in the definitive manuscript of *Cántico A* of Sanlúcar de Barrameda.[61] In contrast to the solitude and quiet of the Toledan cell where *CA* 1-31 took shape, it was during a period of numerous apostolic commitments that Juan wrote these later five stanzas. When Juan was prior of the convent at Granada the demands on his time would have been great. As well, he had many other commitments: Juan was spiritual director to the nuns in Beas de Segura and the local convent; he was involved in formation in his own community; he held offices of government in the Carmelite community which required him to travel extensively; and he was even involved in various building projects for the convent at Granada.[62]

Whether Juan was in isolation or in the midst of many people, in deprivation or in times of relative plenty, he continued his work on the *Cántico*. Thirty-six stanzas (*CA* 1-31 & *CA* 35-39) were written in two periods at least four years apart and in very different settings. The first period of composition took place in the confines of prison, the second amidst the stark beauty of the countryside of Andalusia. However, there still remain four stanzas (*CA* 32-4, and *CB* 11) which have not been accounted for.[63]

There is some disagreement as to when *CA* 32-4 was added to the original thirty-one stanzas. While the historical information surrounding the composition of *CA* 35-9 is well documented, the determination of when *CA* 32-4 was

---

[61] THOMPSON, *The Poet and the Mystic*, 29.

[62] Federico Ruiz Salvador relates this intense period of activity of Juan's life: "En Granada asistimos a la mayor explosión de vitalidad concentrada en la existencia de Juan de la Cruz. Venimos observando un *crescendo* continuo de madurez en diferentes planos: vocación personal, tareas de formación, responsabilidades de gobierno, creación literaria, viajes... sus cuarenta años de existencia intensa y variada alcanzan su culminación desbordante en estos seis años del período granadino (1582-1586). ... Fray Juan está a punto de cumplir los 40 años. En lo mejor de su edad, se siente pletórico, decidido, dispuesto a todo: contemplación, gobierno, dirección, negocios, soledad, construcción, fraternidad, viajes interminables ... Y en medio de esta baraúnda, la creación de una obra mística y literaria de la máxima calidad." RUIZ [SALVADOR], ed., *Dios habla en la noche*, 221-222.

[63] Pacho presents various pieces of evidence that would also place the composition of these verses during Juan's stay in Granada. See PACHO, *Sus escritos*, 128-33.

added to the *Cántico* is almost a matter of speculation due to a lack of information.[64] Duvivier suggests that this unit formed part of the addition of *CA* 35-9 and therefore *CA* 32-9 is a complete unit.[65] Pacho proposes *CA* 32-4 was written independently, and at an earlier date, than that of *CA* 35-9.[66] In the end, given the lack of manuscript evidence, Thompson suggests it is impossible to know anything for certain about the composition and insertion of *CA* 32-4 into the primitive *Cántico*. Thompson suggests what can be said is that *CA* 32-4 must have been written after the original *CA* 1-31 had begun to be disseminated and before *CA* 35-39 were added.[67] When a copy of all the stanzas in existence was made the two units were most likely added together.[68]

[64] In contrast to the anecdotes that give some evidence (even though conflicting) as to when *CA* 35-9 may have been written, no testimony surfaces giving witness to the composition of *CA* 32-34. See DUVIVIER, *La genèse du «Cantique spirituel»*, 110.

[65] "L'acquis le plus sûr et le plus important de la moisson du P. Eulogio me paraît être la concordance substantielle de l'ensemble des faits réunis avec la teneur des trois strophes en cause. Et pour moi, j'élargirais volontiers cette constation à la totalité des huit dernières strophes du *Cantique*, trente-deuxième à trente-neuvième." DUVIVIER, *La genèse du «Cantique spirituel»*, 112-113. Duvivier then summarizes: "Nous pouvons considérer que le «groupe des trois» et le «groupe des cinq», probablement quelque peu distants sur le plan chronologique, ont une certaine parenté." Ibid., 115.

[66] "Aunque no podamos precisar ni la fecha exacta ni el lugar, en fuerza de los documentos aducidos, debemos admitir que el poema inicial de Toledo fue ampliado por el Santo en dos ocasiones con sendos grupos estróficos. ¿Cuál de ellos es el primero? ... Desprovistos de segura información documental podemos considerar acorde con su génesis histórica el orden temático de las canciones desde el momento en que el *Cántico* se presenta como obra conclusa en 1584. En un momento dado, sin que sepamos ni el cuándo ni el porqué, san Juan de la Cruz acopla los dos grupos estróficos a las estancias compuestas en la cárcel y forma un todo poético de admirable armonía y de perfecta unidad literaria." PACHO, *Sus escritos*, 204. For the textual and historical reasoning behind this conclusion ses Ibid., 188-198.

[67] "There is no manuscript evidence for a thirty-four-stanza *Cántico* except BNM MS 868, which gives *CA* 33, 32, and 34 as a sonnet of rather unusual form in a corrupt text. So this interim stage between thirty-one and thirty-nine stanzas is not well enough attested except to be noted with interest. At some point probably in 1582-3 *CA* 35-9 were added to a poem which San Juan had already expanded to include *CA* 32-4. But when the time came to make a fair copy of this longer poem and the prose commentaries which now accompanied it, the eight additional stanzas seem to have been included together." THOMPSON, *The Poet and the Mystic*, 30.

[68] No copies of the *Cántico* in the handwriting of Juan de la Cruz are in known existence. However, the Sanlúcar manuscript, bearing the date 1584, must represent *Cántico A* soon after the final eight verses were added. Its prime position among the six manuscripts of *Cántico A* is not disputed. It contains corrections and additions believed to be in the handwriting of Juan de la Cruz.

116

The unit of *CA* 32-34 was thus written in an environment similar to that of *CA* 35-39, most likely while Juan was living in the convent of Los Martires in Granada. Whatever the exact sequence of composition, what is certain is the fact that the composition of the *Cántico* was dynamic and not static. This is affirmed by the re-arrangement of the completed *CA* and the further addition of one more stanza to *CB*, that of *CB* 11.

Cántico B 11 did not appear in print until the Italian edition of 1627 in Rome. The next appearance was shortly after, in Madrid, in the Spanish edition of 1630. However, its existence is attested to in the oral tradition as far back as 1614 by Francisca de Jesús, a Discalced nun from Medina, who knew the stanza by heart along with other sections of Juan's poetry.[69] The *Cántico*, both *A* and *B*, was therefore known for over thirty-five years largely through the oral tradition, but also through the handwritten manuscripts that had been duplicated and passed around before its official publication.

As is noted above in "A Chronological Portrait of Juan," the first complete published Spanish edition of Juan's literary output appeared in 1630 in Madrid. With this publication, the editor, Jerónimo de San José (Ezquerra), gave the

---

For a discussion on this manuscript see Eulogio PACHO, "Un Manuscrito Famoso del 'Cántico Espiritual' -- Las notas del códice de Sanlúcar de Barrameda y su valor crítico," *El Monte Carmelo* 62 (1954), 155-203. Silverio de Sta. Teresa edited and published in 1928 a *fototipográfica* (photocopy) edition of the Sanlúcar manuscript with notes in: *Cántico Espiritual y poesias de San Juan de la Cruz según el códice de Sanlúcar de Barrameda*.

[69] In the beatification process of 1614 Francisca de Jesús' testimony is recorded concerning the writings of Juan de la Cruz: "Esta testigo ha tenido y tiene gran consuelo cuando oye algunas cosas de los escritos del dicho venerable Padre que le causan grandísima ternura y gozo en su alma; en especial cuando se le ofrece a la memoria y refiere algo de las *Canciones* que compuso del trato del almo con Dios, como de esta que se sigue que compuso entre las demás el dicho venerable Padre, que esta testigo de memoria y es en esta manera ... lo cual hace gran efecto en esta testigo que la hace derramar lágrimas de devoción aunque indigna y pecadora." Vatican MS 2838 (S25),f. 29, quoted in PACHO, *Sus escritos*, 336-337. The declaration says Francisca de Jesús recitó by heart *CA* 8 (¿Mas cómo perseveras, ...) and *CB* 11 (Descubre tu presencia, ...). See also PACHO, "Primeras ediciones del Cántico Espiritual," 3-48.

Cántico (CA´) the title: *Cántico espiritual entre el alma y Cristo su Esposo.*[70] The title was soon shortened to *Cántico espiritual* in subsequent publications. This is the common title used today to refer to Juan's poem. As we will see below it is important to note that Juan's own title on the Sanlúcar de Barrameda manuscript is different: *Canciones entre el alma y el esposo.*[71]

3.2.2 Development of the Commentary

The first indications that a commentary was developing on the stanzas of the poem come from the witness of M. Magdalena del Espíritu cited above.[72] Pacho suggests that even during the sessions at the convent in Beas, the nuns may have taken notes which were possibly used later by Juan for his own written commentary.[73] The nuns at Beas saw something extraordinary in the stanzas of the *Cántico* and so they requested Juan to explain them. Thus the first steps were taken toward a complete commentary on the entire poem.

It is generally accepted that Juan did not write the stanzas with a commentary in mind.[74] However, the nuns sensed something alive and dynamic

---

[70] For a brief discussion on the history of the title given by the historian Jerónimo de San José see the edition of Juan's *Cántico* edited by Eulogio Pacho: *Cántico espiritual: Primera redaccion y texto retocado*, 12, n. 2. See also Ibid., 193-267 for more complete details concerning the titles of the various earliest editions of the *Cántico*. See also DUVIVIER, *La genèse du «Cantique spirituel»*, xxxiii and MORALES, *El Cántico espiritual de San Juan de la Cruz*, 63-64. *Canciones entre el alma y el esposo* is the title which appears at the top of the Sanlúcar de Barrameda manuscript. The Sanlúcar manuscript has corrections to the text in the hand of Juan de la Cruz himself. It is therefore held to be the most authoritative manuscript of *CA*.

[71] PACHO, ed., *Cántico espiritual: Primera redaccion y texto retocado*, 583.

[72] See footnote number 59. See also Roger Duvivier's detailed presentation of the historical emergence of the commentaries: DUVIVIER, "Premières traces historiques," in *La genèse du «Cantique Spirituel»*, 227-238.

[73] "No aventurariamos mucho suponiendo que algunos de los comentarios pasaron de la simple respuesta oral al papel, sea redactados por el mismo Santo, sea transcritos de oído por las monjas. La interpretación más obvia del testimonio referido así lo insinúa." PACHO, *Sus escritos*, 187.

[74] Eulogio Pacho says this clearly: "Se torna inadmisible suponer que la disposición de las estrofas se basa en un esquema doctrinal riguroso establecido a priori." PACHO, *Sus escritos*, 205. Donazar suggests that the beginning of the written commentaries was the "fall" of the poem. In commenting on the influence popular folk songs may have had on Juan and the nuns who heard his poetry he says:

within Juan's *Cántico*, and they wanted to hear more. Over a period of time Juan became involved in a dialogue with the nuns concerning various stanzas and sections of the poem. At times the nuns requested explanations of the stanzas from Juan, but also Juan, in turn, asked the nuns to explain the stanzas.[75] The nuns took notes on what they wanted to retain for themselves. These notes, in the context of the dialogue between Juan and the nuns, were the beginnings of the first commentary in its written form.[76] Over the years, starting in 1578, Juan himself wrote on the stanzas and used the written commentary to instruct and guide various groups, including the *Descalzos*.[77] The commentary is therefore a result of Juan's contact with many Carmelite communities, those in Toledo, Beas, El Calvario, Baeza, and Granada. Eventually, at the request of one of the nuns at Beas, Madre Ana de Jesús, Juan put together the complete written commentary.[78] At this time, in 1584, the poem of

---

"Tengamos por cierto que el santo las buscaba donde precisamente estaban: en el aire, en los Cancioneros. ¡Admirable intuición de las monjas! Ellas vieron la profunda intención de las canciones, pues en sus manos estuvieron antes de caer desangradas (esa es la palabra) en los comentarios." DONAZAR, *Fray Juan*, 60. This point will be dealt with below in the discussion on the relationship between the poem and the commentary.

[75] Here is an excerpt from a letter of Francisca de la Madre de Dios, which spoke of this dynamic even during recreation periods with the nuns: "Para afervorar y enseñar el verdadero espíritu y ejercicio de virtudes, hacía algunas preguntas a las religiosas, y sobre las respuestas trataba de suerte que se aprovechaba bien el tiempo y quedaban enseñadas." Biblioteca Mística Carmelitana 10, 326, quoted in PACHO, *Sus escritos*, 209.

[76] Eulogio Pacho refers to this process as a kind of "socratic dialogue." See PACHO, "El Prologo y la hermenéutica del 'Cántico espiritual'," 26.

[77] "En Granada siguen las mismas relaciones entre padre e hijas espirituales. Es simple prolongación del contacto establecido en la villa de Beas." PACHO, *Sus escritos*, 224. See also Ibid., 211. Pacho outlines the various groups of verses which may have had commentaries written on them prior to the redaction of 1584 in Ibid., 211-218. However, it is very difficult to ascertain with certainty what exactly was in written form prior to 1584. Pacho concludes: "A la fin de cuentas, hemos de reconocer que no disponemos de suficiente documentación para precisar las estrofas glosadas por separado, antes de que el Santo determinase ordenarlas en un todo orgánico." Ibid., 218.

[78] Such was their friendship that Juan writes this acknowledgement into the *Prologo* of the commentary, which in fact, is the only title Juan himself gave to the commentary: "Declaración de las canciones, que tratan de el ejercicio de amor entre el alma y el esposo cristo; en la cual se tocan y declaran algunos puntos y efectos de oración, a petición de la Madre Ana de Jesús, priora de las descalzas en San José de Granada. Año de 1584 años." Prologo *CA* (Rod., 861.) This "title" follows with the authentic signature of Fray Juan de la Cruz.

thirty-nine stanzas was joined together with its completed commentary into an organic whole.

It is significant that the development of the commentary on *CA* followed the same process as the poem: its elaboration came slowly over a period of time and in various steps. The first commentary was the animated dialogue Juan had with various individuals and groups. Brief written commentaries on particular sections followed the oral discussions. At one point however, the pieces were put together, and written down as a whole, despite Juan's uncertainty about such a venture.

In the *Prologo* of the commentary Juan de la Cruz alludes to this resistance to write down the meaning of the sublime stanzas.[79] Since these stanzas "were composed in a love flowing from abundant mystical understanding," he suggests that each individual "may derive profit from them according to the mode and capacity of one's own spirit."[80] Notwithstanding Juan's hesitation, the first commentary began to circulate in handwritten copies in a manner Juan had not anticipated.[81] On some of these copies appeared corrections and annotations until Juan eventually decided to make an entirely new redaction. Juan reordered the stanzas of *Cántico A* and enlarged the original commentary on it. Sometime between 1585-86, while Juan lived in Granada, these changes resulted in what has come to be known as *Cántico B*.

There are three principal differences between *Cántico A* and *Cántico B*.[82] The first notable change is the addition of stanza 11 in *Cántico B* with its

---

[79] "Estas *Canciones* compuesto en amor de abundante inteligencia mística, no se podrán declarar al justo ni mi intento será tal, sino sólo dar alguna luz en general ... porque los dichos de amor es mejor dejarlos en su anchura, para que cada uno de ellos se aproveche según su modo y caudal de espíritu, que abreviarlos a un sentido a que no se acomode todo paladar." *CA* Prologo 2, (Rod.,862).

[80] *CB* Prologue 2, (Kav., 470).

[81] PACHO, *Sus escritos*, 227.

[82] These are given in: PACHO, *Sus escritos*, 280. During the seventeenth century neither of these texts were those used by the general population. In circulation at the time was a text which has come to be known as *CA'*. This text contains minor revisions of the original *CA* finalized in 1584. The

corresponding commentary. This pushes back the subsequent numbering of the stanzas and corresponding commentaries by one count. The second major change is the reordering of the stanzas and their commentaries from 14/15 onward. The order of the stanzas in *CA* and *CB* are identical from stanza 1 through 13. The third notable change is the addition in the commentary of *Cántico B* of some lengthier paragraphs that have no corresponding paragraphs in the commentary on *Cántico A*. As well, the commentary of *Cántico B* has been extensively reworked. In both redactions the text of the poem is almost identical, with some minor revisions, except

primary difference between *CA* and *CA'* is that *CA'* stops giving the Latin texts of scripture in *CA* 13, line 4 whereas in *CA* of the Sanlúcar manuscript (the most authentic manuscript of *Cántico A*), these are given throughout. As noted in the chronological presentation on page 107 *CA'* was used for the Italian and Spanish editions with the further addition of verse 11 taken from *CB*. This later redaction was an editorial insertion whereas the minor revisions are known to be the work of Juan de la Cruz. However, they are not significant enough to be considered a new redaction of the work as is *CB*. Thirteen manuscripts of this revised text (*CA'*) are known today, while only six manuscripts of the primitive CA are known. *CA'* with CB 11 began to circulate with official sanction given by the Carmelite order with the Spanish publication of 1630 and retained its preeminence until 1703 when it was supplanted by P. Andrés de Jesús María's edition of *CB* based on the Jaén manuscript. For a detailed account of the reasons behind the publications of the various editions and the rather tardy publication of the first Spanish official edition of the *Cántico* only in 1630 (the 1618-19 Spanish edition **excluded** the *Cántico*, while the French and Italian editions appeared in 1622 and 1627 respectively), see Eulogio PACHO, "Primeras Ediciones del Cántico Espiritual," in *Ephemerides Carmeliticae* 18 (1967), 3-48. See also DUVIVIER, *La genèse du «Cantique Spirituel»*, 239-290. Duvivier, for the most part, cites Pacho on this matter but adds some interesting details including those from Jean Krynen's publication of 1948: Jean KRYNEN, *Le Cantique spirituel de saint Jean de la Croix commenté et refondu au XVIIe siècle: Un regard sur l'histoire de l'exégèse du cantique de Jaén*, (Salamanca, Universidad de Salamanca, 1948). Duviver suggests, however, that the conspiracy not to publish Juan's works actually started while Juan was still living and did not begin with the various administrative roles of Alonso de Jesús María who evidently was against the publications. See DUVIVIER, *La genèse du «Cantique Spirituel»*, 246-7.

Since 1912 the only two recognized texts are those of *CA* and *CB*, although the authenticity of *CB* was first seriously challenged by Dom Chevallier in his article of 1922: Phillipe CHEVALLIER, "Le 'Cantique spirituel' de saint Jean de la Croix a-t-il été interpolé?" *Bulletin Hispanique* 24 (1922), 307-342. He restates this position in Phillipe CHEVALLIER, *Le "Cantique spirituel" de saint Jean de la Croix*, (Bruges, Belgium: Desclée de Brouwer & Cie, 1930), LXXXV-XCIV. However, in the light of modern textual criticism *CA'* is not sufficiently different to be considered a new redaction and CB is considered to be genuinely the work of Juan de la Cruz. Dom Chevallier also later changed his position in his works posterior to 1938. These changes are related in PACHO, *Sus escritos*, 285 and 288. A detailed history of the development of the text of the *Cántico* is presented in: PACHO, Eulogio, *El Cántico espiritual: Trayectoria histórica del texto*, Bibliotheca Carmelitica. Series II: Studia, vol. 7, Rome: Desclée, 1967. Pacho presents a summary of this position in: PACHO, *Sus escritos*, 283 ff. See also Eulogio Pacho's bibliographical summary: Eulogio PACHO, "La cuestión crítica del 'Cántico espiritual': Nota bibliográfica," *El Monte Carmelo* 65 (1957), 309-323.

for the mentioned addition of stanza 11 and the reordering of the stanzas. The result has been that the commentary on *CB* incorporates a lot of new material, making the commentary on *CA* only about three-quarters the length of that of *CB*.[83]

4. Juan de la Cruz and the Western Mystical Tradition

As has been previously noted, Juan de la Cruz came on the scene during a time characterized by change and renewal in the church as well as in society in general. Politics and religion were inseparable during Juan's time. Exploration and discovery at the political level, as well as reform and reorganization at the ecclesial level, were the norms of the day. Yet Juan's literary output did not find its inspiration solely in the historical moment of his own life, nor in his own personal experience. Juan's writings form part of a larger picture, that of the western mystical tradition.

The task at hand, then, is twofold: the first, to note that Juan necessarily was inserted into the plethora of resources that were common to the development of the western mystical tradition;[84] and the second, to suggest how Juan contributed to this already well-developed tradition and how he further helped shape it. Three questions will guide the inquiry into both how Juan is inserted into a well established mystical tradition and how he contributed to that tradition in a unique and original way: 1. What were Juan's "resources"?; 2. How did he use them?; 3.

---

[83] THOMPSON, *The Poet and the Mystic,* 34. Thompson presents in summary form the main arguments outlining the authenticity of *Cántico B* in Ibid., 33-59.

[84] See especially the foundational work of Cuthbert BUTLER, *Western Mysticism,* (New York: E.P. Dutton, 1924). Butler gives a summary of the characteristics of the western mystical tradition as he reads them in Augustine, Gregory and Bernard: Ibid., 179-192. See also Thomas KATSAROS and Nathaniel Kaplan, *The Western Mystical Tradition: An Intellectual History of Western Civilization,* 2 vols., (New Haven: College & University Press, 1969). Volume I of this latter work presents the historical development of the Western mystical tradition from its early Greek beginnings to the Renaissance. Although Juan de la Cruz is not mentioned, it sets the historical context within which his own mysticism developed. Also of interest concerning the foundations of the western mystical tradition within which Juan lived is: Andrew LOUTH, "Patristic Mysticism and St. John of the Cross," in *The Origins of the Christian Mystical Tradition: From Plato to Denys,* (Oxford: Clarendon Press, 1981), 179-190.

What is Juan's original contribution to the western mystical tradition?

The purpose in exploring the first two of these questions is not to produce an exhaustive study. Ample information is already available on Juan's possible literary influences and sources.[85] Rather, the intention is to note that although Juan has made a significant and original contribution to the western mystical tradition (as well as to other mystical traditions),[86] he nonetheless forms part of a greater symbolic reality which shaped that which he lived and wrote. Further to this we can begin to describe Juan's particular contribution to the western mystical tradition.

4.1 Juan's Literary Resources and their Use

Juan inherited the wealth of the classical texts of the Patristic writers, the Scholastics, the mystics who preceded him, as well as other literary resources.[87]

---

[85] For a presentation of possible sources and literary influences on the *Cántico* (poem and commentary) see especially: Dámaso ALONSO, "Raiz biblica. El 'Cantar de los Cantares'," in *La poesía de San Juan de la Cruz*, 149-161 (Alonso also investigates in detail other literary sources in Juan); Helmut A. HATZFELD, "Sobre la Prosa Sanjuanista en el 'Cántico Espiritual'," in *Estudios literarios sobre mística española*, 3rd edition, Biblioteca Románica Hispánica II, Estudios y ensayos 16 (Madrid: Gredos, 1976), 306-317 (Other chapters dealing with various symbolic and literary sources in Juan's writings are also of great value in Hatzfeld's work); R.A. HERRERA, *Saint John of the Cross: Introductory Studies* (Madrid: Editorial de Espiritualidad, 1968), 29-39 (Herrera presents a detailed discussion regarding the influences of Aquinas on Juan de la Cruz); and MORALES, *El "Cantico espiritual" de san Juan de la Cruz*. Two foundational works which treat the question of sources in Juan's writings overall are: BARUZI, *Problème de l'expérience mystique*, and CRISÓGONO DE JESÚS SACRAMENTADO, *Obra científica*. For more extensive bibliographical references on the question of sources and influences in Juan's work see: DUVIVIER, *La genèse du «Cantique spirituel»*, 513-517 and Eulogio PACHO, *Iniciación a S. Juan de la Cruz*, Colección Karmel 11 (Burgos: Editorial Monte Carmelo, 1982), 282-286.

[86] See Swami ABHAYANANDA, *History of Mysticism: The Unchanging Testament*, (Fallsburg, New York: Atma Books, 1987), 335-355, for some suggestions as to how Juan reflects elements present in the mystical tradition of various other religions.

[87] Antonio T. de Nicolás suggests Juan's creations were autonomous with respect to any exterior influence. This extreme position must be rejected. He states: "San Juan de la Cruz composed his poetry out of the development of a faculty unknown to them: he used pure imaginings, so that by creating images out of nothing, rather than borrowing them from anything existing around him, a new world of sensation, feeling, memory, and will was created and it is this which is responsible for the power of his poetry." DE NICOLÁS, *Alchemist*, 6. However, de Nicolás appears to modify this position in his suggestion that Juan borrowed "a number of symbols of Sufi origin." Ibid., xi. He further modifies this position in his discussion on the texts Juan uses from both the old and the new

Of prime importance is the frequent use of scripture, *the* text upon which Christian orthodoxy and Juan's own mystical experience is based.[88] However, in the case of the *Cántico* of Juan de la Cruz, the most important single source is a particular scriptural text which inspires its foundational symbolism, the biblical *Song of Songs*.[89]

Juan was not the first to be inspired by this text, nor was he the last.[90]

testament. Ibid., 22-23.

[88] For the role scripture plays in Juan's writings see: Barnabas AHERN, "The Use of Scripture in the Spiritual Theology of St. John of the Cross," *Catholic Biblical Quarterly* 14 (1952), 6-17; Francisco de BRÄNDLE, *Biblia en San Juan de la Cruz*, Logos 39 (Madrid: Editorial de Espiritualidad, 1990); Stanislaus FUMET, "Saint Jean de la Croix et la Bible," in *Saint Jean de la Croix: Docteur de l'Eglise,* (Lyon: 1942), 24-26; Felix GARCIA, "San Juan de la Cruz y la Biblia," *Revista de Espiritualidad* 1 (July-December 1942), 372-388; Jean VILNET, *Bible et mystique chez Saint Jean de la Croix,* (Desclée de Brouwer, 1949), especially 34-61.

[89] Fernande Pepin dedicates an entire work to the relationship of the *Song* to the *Cántico*. See PEPIN, *Noces de Feu.* Pepin includes an extensive bibliography: Ibid., xxi - xliii. These references deal with the various developments of the *Song of Songs* as well as the *Cántico* of San Juan de la Cruz. In Part I, Chapter I, Pepin follows the development of the nuptial symbol from its Jewish roots as it is reflected in the Old Testament, to how it is used by certain New Testament writers. She then outlines its development in Origin, Gregory of Nyssa, and Bernard of Clairvaux. Bernard of Clairvaux (1090-1153) wrote eighty-six sermons on the *Song of Songs* yet his commentary on it was still incomplete. The eighty-six sermons composed over a period of eighteen years only covered to the beginning of the third chapter. See Jean LECLERCQ, *The Love of Learning and the Desire for God: A Study of Monastic Culture,* trans. Catharine Misrahi, 2nd edition, (New York, Fordham University Press, 1974), 107. For a translation of Bernard's sermons see BERNARD OF CLAIRVAUX, *On the Song of Songs,* trans. K. Walsh, (Shannon: I.U.P., 1971). José Morales has also dedicated an entire volume to the link between the *Cántico* and the *Song.* See MORALES, *El Cántico espiritual de San Juan de la Cruz.* Morales summarizes the relationship between these two in the following way: "No obstante, lo que hemos comprobado es que, a pesar de esta dependencia, la labor original de San Juan de la Cruz está en la elaboración de los temas bíblicos hasta hacer que el *Cántico* sea una entera recreación poética." Ibid., 249. However, the original contribution of Juan's poem may be more than a simple "elaboration of biblical themes" as Morales seems to suggest. The relationship of the *Song* and the *Cántico* will be briefly examined from a hermeneutical perspective below in Chapter Four.

[90] Concerning the history of the imagery of the "spiritual marriage" Butler says: "The idea that Jesus Christ or the Divine Word is the Bridegroom, and the devout soul the Bride of the Canticle goes back to Origen, and became acclimatized in the West by the translations of his Commentary on the Canticle made by Jerome and Rufinus. It is found not infrequently in Augustine, and at least once in Gregory; but the idea is not emphasized or elaborated, as by Bernard. That consecrated virgins are the `spouses of Christ` is a very early Christian conception, found, equivalently, in Cyprian (*Ep.* 4). Though a natural step, it is a step forward in allegory to look on the union of the soul with God in contemplation as a spiritual marriage, ... The first, ... to give utterance to the realities of mystical experience in terms of sublimated human love was the austerely intellectual Plotinus ... . Mystical writers in the West from the time of St. Bernard onwards use the imagery of the `spiritual marriage` freely, and as a matter of course. I do not know that it was so definitely used by any writer before

124

The *Song of Songs*, with its rich and highly affective nuptial symbolism, has its own particular place in the development of the western mystical tradition,[91] as well as in the tradition of the Carmelite order.[92] Jean Leclercq says that the *Song of Songs* "was the book which was most read, and most frequently commented in the medieval cloister."[93]

Leclercq points out that the commentaries on the *Song of Songs* were written in a variety of ways. The Scholastic writers tended to allegorize the Bride

him. It is found, however, and in an accentuated form in his young contemporary, Richard of St Victor (died c. 1173), *de quatuor Gradibus violentae Caritatis* (Migne, Patr. Lat. cxcvi). It passed into the common stock of mystical writers in later times, notably B. John Ruysbroeck, St John of the Cross, St Teresa." BUTLER, *Western Mysticism*, 161. For a brief yet excellent history of the mystical interpretation of the *Song of Songs* see: William Ralph INGE, *Christian Mysticism*, 5th edition, The Bampton Lectures 1989 (London: Methuen & Co., 1921), Appendix D. See also the foundational work of Evelyn UNDERHILL, *Mysticism*, 1st edition 1911, (New York: E.P. Dutton, 1961), 162 ff., and 509 ff..

[91] See PEPIN, *Noces de Feu*, as well as P. PARENTE, "The Canticle of Canticles in Mystical Theology," *Catholic Biblical Quarterly* 6 (1944), 142-158. For more recent information on how this text has been used throughout the Christian tradition see: Roland E. MURPHY, *The Song of Songs: A Commentary on the Book of Canticles or the Song of Songs*, ed. S. Dean McBride, Hermeneia Commentary Series, (Minneapolis: Fortress Press, 1990) and Max ENGAMMARE, *Le Cantique des cantiques à la Renaissance: étude et bibliographie*, (Genève: Droz, 1993). Both these latter references contain extensive up to date bibliographical materials.

[92] See D. ROMANUS RIOS, "The Canticle of Canticles Among the Early Discalced Carmelites," *Ephemerides Carmeliticae* 2 (1948), 305-313. For a brief but excellent overview of Carmelite history and spirituality see Keith J. EGAN, "The Spirituality of the Carmelites," in *Christian Spirituality*, ed. Jill Raitt et al., 2:50-62. To put Juan's literary output into some perspective concerning the Carmelite mystical tradition Egan says: "The contemplative orientation of Carmelite spirituality during the Middle Ages did not have, however, the strong mystical elements that would be so pervasive in the writings of Teresa of Jesus and John of the Cross. Interest in the specifically mystical was only occasional during this era." Ibid., 53; "The literary activity of the Carmelites did not get underway in earnest until the second quarter of the fourteenth century." Ibid., 58. For a more extensive study see: Joachim SMET, *The Carmelites: A History of the Brothers of Our Lady of Mount Carmel*, 3 vols., (Darien, IL: Carmelite Spiritual Centre, 1975, 1976, 1982). Of particular interest in Smet's study is Volume II which covers the history of the Carmelite order in the post-tridentine period 1550-1600. For an interesting study which actively combines the historical developments of the *Order of Our Lady of Mount Carmel* with popular Carmelite spirituality see Titus BRANDSMA, *Carmelite Mysticism: Historical Sketches*, (Chicago: Carmelite Press, 1936). Crisógono de Jesús Sacramentado traces the development of Carmelite mysticism from its origins into modern times in CRISÓGONO DE JESÚS SACRAMENTADO, *L'Ecole Mystique Carmélitaine*, trans. D. Vallois-del Real from the Spanish *La escuela mística carmelitana*, (Madrid: Editorial Mensajero: 1930), (Paris: Emmanuel Vitte, 1934).

[93] LECLERCQ, *The Love of Learning*, 106.

with the collectivity of the Church, emphasizing the revelation of divine truth and the presence of God in the world through the Incarnation.[94] This style of commentary furnished clear and concise doctrine addressed to the intelligence.[95] "On the other hand, the monastic commentary's object is rather God's relations with each soul, Christ's presence in it, the spiritual union realized through charity. ... Monastic commentary is addressed to the whole being; its aim is to touch the heart rather than to instruct the mind."[96]

Juan's text of the *Cántico* is more consistent with this monastic approach to the biblical text of the *Song of Songs*.[97] Generally speaking, scriptural exegesis occurred in the following manner: "First came literal or historical exegesis, then the moral sense, the allegorical and finally the analogical or mystical."[98] However, not all texts needed to be examined at each of these levels of exegesis, since sometimes one or more levels may not apply to a particular text. This left Juan free to use the scriptural texts as he saw fit. Based on his own experience within the tradition Juan brought to life scriptural texts in a new way. In conclusion, we can say that the use of the *Song of Songs*, by Juan and by others, "must be understood in the

[94] LECLERCQ, *The Love of Learning*, 107.

[95] LECLERCQ, *The Love of Learning*, 107.

[96] LECLERCQ, *The Love of Learning*, 107. Leclercq asks the question: "What is the significance of the interest that the medieval monks took in the Canticle of Canticles?" To his own question he replies: "The Canticle is the poem of the pursuit which is the basis for the whole program of monastic life: *quarere Deum*, a pursuit which will reach its end only in eternity but which already obtains fulfillment here in an obscure possession; and the latter increases desire which is the form love takes here below. The Canticle is the dialogue between the bridegroom and the bride who are seeking each other, calling to each other, growing nearer to each other and who find they are separated just when they believe they are finally about to be united. ... The Canticle of Canticles is a contemplative text: *theoricus sermo*, as St. Bernard would say. It is not pastoral in nature; it does not teach morality, prescribe good works to perform or precepts to observe; nor even purvey exhortations to wisdom. But with its ardent language and its dialogue of praise, it was more attuned than any other book in Sacred Scripture to loving, disinterested contemplation." Ibid., 108.

[97] See AHERN, "The Use of Scripture in the Spiritual Theology of St. John of the Cross," 6-17; Robert M. GRANT, *The Bible in the Church*, 4th edition (c1948), (N.Y., Macmillan, 1960); and Gillian Rosemary EVANS, *The Language and Logic of the Bible*, (Cambridge: Cambridge University Press, 1984).

[98] THOMPSON, *The Poet and the Mystic*, 15.

light of some fifteen hundred years of Jewish and Christian exegetical practice. ...
From the Song came many of the images used by the mystical tradition to describe
the spiritual life: bride and bridegroom, lover and beloved, betrothal and marriage,
wound, spark, wine, and so on; and from it too comes that mixing of love sacred and
profane so characteristic of the language of mysticism."[99]

The question of what non-scriptural literary resources inspired Juan
cannot be answered as easily, or with the kind of precision that may be preferred.
This is primarily due to the fact that Juan de la Cruz rarely mentions by name any
authors he cites.[100] Juan had formally studied the Patristic and Scholastic writings,
the medieval mystics, and scripture during his time at Salamanca. After that time his
personal study and liturgical practice would have enriched those earlier
beginnings.[101] During that time and subsequently, Juan memorized numerous
fragments of various writings and worked them into his texts making them his own.
A richness of citations, similes, metaphors, images, and exhortations was readily
available to Juan, as was frequently the case for learned theologians of his day. As
one anonymous writer tells us, Juan is "at once original and traditional, and certain
figures of speech and expressions had long become the common property of all
spiritual theologians. We find the same language century after century; all the later

---

[99] THOMPSON, *The Poet and the Mystic*, 16.

[100] In responding to the question of why Juan rarely cites his sources, or in only a general way,
Max Milner says: "La critique des sources ne nous permet pas encore de répondre. Et d'ailleurs ce
n'est pas cela qui nous importe. Quelles que soient les occasions de cette évasion, saint Jean de la
Croix échappe aux fatalités de son milieu et de son époque, il refuse la facilité; il retrouve dans une
synthèse plus vaste que celles de ses compatriotes des êtres qui ont pensé et prié à des siècles de
distance et dans des milieux complètement différents du sien." Max MILNER, *Poésie et vie mystique
chez Saint Jean de la Croix*, with a Preface by Jean Baruzi, La Vigne du Carmel, (Paris: Seuil, 1951),
59.

[101] Recall Juan had ended his formal studies in 1568. He begins to write only about ten years later.
During this time he would have benefitted greatly from further personal study as well as scriptural and
other readings required by the Carmelite way of life. On this question see especially Joachim SMET,
"The Spiritual and Intellectual Life of the Order," in *The Carmelites*, 2:229-254 and SIMEON DE LA
SAGRADA FAMILIA, "Fuentes doctrinales y literarias de San Juan de la Cruz," *El Monte Carmelo*
69 (1961), 104.

writers draw upon the earlier authorities."[102] Juan's purpose was practical in nature, rather than academic, and he saw no reason for giving his readers references for what he wrote.[103]

Differing from his contemporaries in Spain and elsewhere in Europe, Juan does not cite series of quotations, except in the case of Scripture.[104] Without feeling a need to reference the non-scriptural texts which he used, Juan simply wove sources together with his intuitive and creative mind making them into an original synthesis.[105] However, even given this difficulty in precisely situating Juan within the literary tradition, several key studies have located some of those authors whom Juan would most certainly have read and whose ideas, images, and symbols he would have incorporated into his own writings.[106] One of the most eminent experts on Juan de la Cruz, E. Allison Peers, summarizes the matter in this way:

> Though the precise extent of his debt to this Salamancan training in philosophy has not yet been definitely assessed, the fact of its influence is evident to every reader. It gives massiveness, harmony and unity to both the ascetic and the mystical works of St. John of the Cross--that is to say, to all his scientific writing. Deeply, however,

---

[102] BENEDICTINE OF STANBROOK ABBEY, *Mediæval mystical tradition and Saint John of the Cross,* 23.

[103] The reason why Juan de la Cruz did not fully cite his sources can also be attributed to, at least in part, the audience for whom he was writing. On the question "For whom did Juan de la Cruz write?" see: Edgar Allison PEERS, *St. John of the Cross and Other Lectures and Addresses,* (London: Faber and Faber, 1946), 43-50. Concerning Juan's intended audience Peers asserts: "Primarily, he is, without the slightest doubt, addressing a small group of Carmelites." Ibid., 43.

[104] BENEDICTINE OF STANBROOK ABBEY, *Mediæval mystical tradition and Saint John of the Cross,* 23.

[105] E. Allison Peers describes this dynamic in the following way: "We have not read St. John of the Cross for long before we find ourselves in the full current of mystical tradition. It is not by means of more or less literal quotations that the Saint produces this impression; he has studied his precursors so thoroughly that he absorbs the substance of their doctrine and incorporates it so intimately in his own that it becomes flesh of his flesh." E. Allison PEERS, *The Complete Works of Saint John of the Cross, Doctor of the Church,* trans. and ed. E. Allison Peers from the critical edition of Silverio de Santa Teresa, 3 volumes in one, 1st edition 1935, (Wheathampstead, Eng.: Anthony Clarke, 1974), xxxiii.

[106] Along with those references given in footnote number 85 see in particular: SIMEON DE LA SAGRADA FAMILIA, "Fuentes doctrinales y literarias de San Juan de la Cruz," 103-9.

as St. John of the Cross drew from the Schoolmen, he was also profoundly indebted to many other writers. He was distinctly eclectic in his reading and quotes freely (though less than some of his Spanish contemporaries) from the Fathers and from the medieval mystics, especially from St. Thomas, St. Bonaventure, Hugh of St. Victor and the pseudo-Areopagite. All that he quotes, however, he makes his own, with the result that his chapters are never a mass of citations loosely strung together, as are those of many other Spanish mystics of his time.[107]

Peers' list is not exhaustive, but it is representative of what were most likely Juan's non-scriptural resources.[108] For example, Crisógono de Jesús also argues that the German mystical school of the fourteenth century would have had a

---

[107] PEERS, *The Complete Works of Saint John of the Cross,* xxvii-xxviii. Peers gives his own assessment of probable non-scriptural sources of Juan de la Cruz: "The Saint's chief non-scriptural sources seem to be St. Thomas, St. Augustine, and St. Gregory. Apart probably from the pseudo-Dionysius, I believe that there is no proof of his having used any other writers, and such external evidence as exists supports internal evidence here." PEERS, *St. John of the Cross and Other Lectures and Addresses,* 40-41. Jordan Aumann gives a slightly different list of those authors whom John would have read, but nonetheless both collaborate in their assessment that even though Juan drew greatly from his predecessors he did not merely copy them: "Having studied at Salamanca, St. John of the Cross was trained in Thomistic theology, but he also read the works of pseudo-Dionysius and St. Gregory the Great. However, the author that most influenced St. John seems to have been Tauler, although it is quite certain that he was familiar with the works of St. Bernard, Ruysbroeck, Cassian, the Victorines, Osuna, and, of course, St. Teresa of Avila. Nevertheless, John of the Cross was not a slavish imitator of others; his works have a distinctive character all their own." Jordan AUMANN, *Christian Spirituality in the Catholic Tradition,* (San Francisco: Ignatius Press, 1985), 195-196. Aumann takes this information from CRISÓSOGONO, *Obra científica,* 1:51. For the same idea expressed by another Sanjuanist scholar who has extensively studied Juan's poetry and prose see ICAZA, *The Stylistic Relationship in the Cántico,* 53. A well known sanjuanist scholar who holds that the "worldly" influences on Juan's poetry are exaggerated is José L. Morales. Commenting on the study by ALONSO, *La poesia de san Juan de la Cruz,* Morales says (in agreement with Lucinio del SS. Sacramento): "Nosotros compartimos de todo corazón la opinión del escritor carmelita y añadiremos por nuestra parte que el haber querido Dámaso Alonso estudiar a San Juan de la Cruz «desde esta ladera» era ya, en sí, plantear el problema de su estudio sobre una base equivocada. Porque hay que advertir que San Juan de la Cruz no tiene laderas, puesto que los místicos no tienen dimensiones horizontales, sino verticales. Hay que estudiarlos desde donde se sitúan: desde la altura." MORALES, *El Cántico espiritual de san Juan de la Cruz,* 17.

[108] A more recent article which synthesizes Juan's literary sources and influences from a number of perspectives is: Cristóbal CUEVAS, "Estudio literario," in *Introducción a la lectura de San Juan de la Cruz,* ed. A. García Simón, (Valladolid, Junta de Castilla y León Consejería de Cultura y Turismo, 1991), 125-201. See especially Ibid., 127-148 which summarize Juan's work as a writer and presents how his intellectual formation contributed toward his literary work.

strong influence on Juan.[109] E. A. Peers strongly disagrees with this position.[110]

Beyond the use of scripture and various theological texts from the Patristic writers, there are two other sources which most certainly would have influenced Juan although frequently they are not included in the list of Juan's main literary resources. Perhaps this is so since their influence would have been more indirect. These are, the *Rule of the Order of Our Lady of Mount Carmel* approved by Innocent IV in 1247,[111] and *De institutione primorum monachorum* (1379 - 1391).[112] The *Rule* would have regulated Juan's general style of life: personal prayers, liturgical customs, use of material goods, and so on. Of singular importance, however, was the modification of the *Rule* in 1281 that had approved both the contemplative life and the involvement in pastoral ministry for the

---

[109] CRISÓGONO, *Obra cientifica*, 40-45, quoted in PEERS, *St. John of the Cross and Other Lectures and Addresses*, 40. For a detailed study affirming the influence of the German mystical school on Juan's writings see: Jean ORCIBAL, *Saint Jean de la Croix et les mystiques rhéno-flamands*, Présence du Carmel 6 (Bruges: Desclée de Brouwer, 1966).

[110] PEERS, *St. John of the Cross and Other Lectures and Addresses*, 40.

[111] This first *Rule*, granted under the approval of Albert, Patriarch of Jerusalem, was a revision of the original, *Vitae Formulam* of 1206-1214, which had guided the fledgling Carmelite eremitical community. Because of the involvement of Albert, it was frequently known as the *Rule of Saint Albert*. The *Rule* was adapted to suit a more mendicant lifestyle in 1247 under the approval of Innocent IV. Although it remained essentially the same, further mitigation of the *Rule* was approved by Eugene IV in 1432 in response to the requests of the Carmelites themselves. Keith J. EGAN, "The Spirituality of the Carmelites," in *Christian Spirituality: II High Middle Ages and Reformation*, ed. Jill Raitt et al., World Spirituality 17 (New York: Crossroad, 1987), 51-54. In part it was in response to the already twice mitigated *Rule* of 1432 which Teresa of Avila had launched her own reform and had enlisted the services of Juan de la Cruz to aid her. Unaware of the already mitigated rule of 1247, Teresa believed her reform was a return to the *regla primitiva* of the earliest Carmelite foundations. For a description of some of the details of the *Vitae Formulam* and the *Rule of Saint Albert* see Domenico LOMBARDO, "Gli stratti del testo e loro significato," in *La Regola del Carmelo oggi*, ed. Bruno Secondin (Rome: Edizioni Institutum Carmelitanum, 1983), 151-156. The Latin text of the *Rule* approved by Innocent IV in 1247 by the Bull *Quae honorem Conditoris* is available in Ibid., 11-25 with its Italian translation. It is also available in its latin form in Bruno SECONDIN, ed., *La Regola del Carmelo: per una nuova interpretazione*, Quaderni di "Presenza del Carmelo" 5 (Rome: Edizioni Institutum Carmelitanum, 1982), 46-67, also with the Italian translation.

[112] EGAN, "The Spirituality of the Carmelites," 254. An English translation of *De institutione primorum monachorum* is *Book of the Institution of the First Monks*, trans. B. Edwards (Boars Hill: Oxford, 1969).

Carmelite community.[113] This change in the *Rule* would have removed potential barriers to the Carmelite mendicant style of life which would later allow Juan invaluable freedom of contact with the world outside the monastery walls.[114] This also opened the way in the fourteenth century for the Carmelites to launch a plan of studies for their members.[115] This contact further immersed Juan into the life of his contemporaries as well as the socio-political climate of his day. It cannot be said that Juan lived his life, not even the major part of it, closed off from the society in which he lived. Juan was rooted in the historical climate of his day on both sides of the monastic cloister. The *De institutione* may have played an equally important role in Juan's life, even if in an indirect way as is the case with the *Rule*.

Otger Steggink has called the *De institutione primorum monachorum* the "chief book of spiritual reading in the Carmelite order" up until the seventeenth century.[116] Keith Egan claims that it was this book, holding within it the memory of

---

[113] Cristóbol CUEVAS GARCÍA, "San Juan de la Cruz y la transgresión de la norma expresiva," in *Actas del Congreso Internacional Sanjuanista*, Prepared by: Centro Internacional Teresiano-Sanjuanist de Avila (Valladolid: Junta de Castilla y León, Consejería de Cultura y Turismo, 1993), 1:58. Up until this time there had been difficulty in accepting pastoral involvement outside the community by those who favoured a strictly contemplative lifestyle.

[114] Given the mobility of Juan, and his involvement in various apostolates, I wonder if the observation of Colin P. Thompson is accurate. Concerning the "secular" influences, literary and otherwise, on Juan's life during his time at the Jesuit college as a layman he says: "These formative years must have left their mark on Juan, and they represent the *only period of his life when he was open to various secular influences.* From the time he left Medina for Salamanca, already a Carmelite novice, his life was one of self-discipline and renunciation, and one must suppose that his exposure to secular literature would have been minimal." (emphasis mine) THOMPSON, *The Poet and the Mystic,* 3. For an excellent summary of Juan's travels in the "secular" world see especially, RUIZ [SALVADOR], ed., *Dios habla en la noche.* Chapters 9 and 10 summarize the voyages Juan made in the later part of his life. In total it is estimated Juan travelled 25,000 kms., much of this on foot. Ibid., 254.

[115] CUEVAS GARCÍA, "San Juan de la Cruz y la transgresión de la norma expresiva," 58.

[116] See Otger STEGGINK, *La reforma del Carmelo español: La visita canónica del general Rubeo y su encuentro con Santa Teresa (1566-1567),* (Rome: Institutum Carmelitanum, 1965), 357 quoted in EGAN, "The Spirituality of the Carmelites," in *Christian Spirituality,* ed. Jill Raitt et al., 2:54. Egan goes on to say: "Modern Carmelites have neglected this text, which is the first part of a four-part work from the late fourteenth century and which was almost certainly composed by Philip Ribot, Catalonian Carmelite provincial. Ribot passed off his work as a collection of earlier writings that he merely edited. The purported author of the *Institution* is John XLIV, supposedly patriarch of Jerusalem, who allegedly wrote this text in Greek in 412. The *Institution* tells of the founding of the

the eremitical solitude of the first Carmelites located near the medieval port of Haifa at the wadi 'Ain es-Siāh,[117] that "laid the groundwork for the sixteenth-century mysticism of Teresa and John." It was this book which intimated the identity of a subsequent Carmelite mystical tradition, which, up to the time of John of the Cross and Teresa of Avila, had been developed minimally.[118] The *De institutione* portrays Carmelite spirituality

> as a withdrawal from the usual preoccupations of life and an entering into solitude, as a purification of the heart and finally as the reception of the gift of union with God in love. The culmination of Carmelite life is experiential union with God, according to the *Institution*. This Carmelite journey one lives in the prophetic spirit of Elijah. These themes of the *Institution* are both a manifestation of a spiritual doctrine about the personal experience of God held up as an ideal for medieval Carmelites and are a prelude to post-Reformation mystical doctrine of both the Teresian reform and the Touraine Reform, which so creatively built on the spiritual doctrine of the *Institution*.[119]

Further on Egan says:

> There was ever present in Carmelite life an inspiration for an intense life of solitude and prayer. Somewhere below the surface of Carmelite consciousness, there was always half-forgotten and half-remembered the heritage of the simple lay penitents who had sought solitude on Mount Carmel. This elusive memory, nonetheless, gave rise during the Middle Ages to various albeit inconclusive, reforms. Eventually this remembering of the spirit of the original Carmelites

Carmelite order by the prophet Elijah and of a fanciful history of the order in the pre- and early Christian era." Ibid., 2:54.

[117] EGAN, "The Spirituality of the Carmelites," 51. For a very detailed and quite fascinating history of the eremitical foundations of the original lay penitents at wadi 'Ain es-Siāh see Elias FRIEDMAN, *The Latin Hermits of Mount Carmel: A Study in Carmelite Origins*, Institutum Historicum Teresianum, Studia I (Rome: Teresianum, 1979).

[118] "The contemplative orientation of Carmelite spirituality during the Middle Ages did not have, however, the strong mystical elements that would be so pervasive in the writings of Teresa of Jesus and John of the Cross. Interest in the specifically mystical was only occasional during this era." EGAN, "The Spirituality of the Carmelites," 53.

[119] EGAN, "The Spirituality of the Carmelites," 56.

inspired the magnificent Teresian reform.[120]

To determine whether in fact this "remembering" of the primitive Carmelite spirit as it was reflected in the De institutione was one of the major influences on Juan's mysticism, as is suggested by Egan, is not the purpose of this inquiry. Again, the purpose here is not to establish a definitive list of sources and inspirations for Juan's Cántico, but rather it is to put the reader in touch with the elements of the symbolic and conceptual world of Juan de la Cruz as it would have been reflected in the tradition that opened up his personal mystical experience. Juan is indebted to the "accumulated tradition" rather than to specific sources or authors per se. As Colin Thompson tells us: "It is the developing tradition, rather than individual authors which needs to be appreciated."[121] And so a brief look at some of the main themes of medieval mysticism would readily situate the reflection within elements of Juan's symbolic and conceptual inheritance of the western mystical tradition. This is the fifth area which I present in order to obtain a sense of Juan's symbolic and conceptual environment.

Some of the main themes in late medieval mysticism of the western tradition which are reflected in Juan's work are the following:[122]

1. The division of the spiritual life into **three ways**: purgation (for beginners), illumination (for proficients), and union (for perfects), presented by Juan in his opening argumento in the commentary on the Cántico. This division is already a very ancient one present in Origen and Dionysius.

2. The **seven degrees of love** which Juan interprets from CB 26. This imagery was used by Augustine, Bernard and the Victorines. "To these he adds his own analysis through the dark nights, active and passive, of sense and spirit, original, though with many

---

[120] EGAN, "The Spirituality of the Carmelites," 59.

[121] THOMPSON, The Poet and the Mystic, 9.

[122] The following summary is, in large part, taken from THOMPSON, The Poet and the Mystic, 1-20.

traditional elements."[123]

3. The distinction between **contemplation and action**. Origen, Augustine, Gregory, and Bernard allegorized many scripture stories using this division. Osuna and Laredo use it as well in their treatises.

4. The **renunciation of self and every created thing for God**. Thompson notes that this theme has its roots in pre-Christian antiquity and it occurs in other faiths. "Bonaventure links this with the Dionysian paradox: 'Forgetting all created things and liberated from them thou shalt rise above thyself and beyond all creation to find thyself within the shaft of light that flashes out from the divine, mysterious darkness'."[124] Chapter Five of the *Institution* is reminiscent here. The monk is urged to "flee from familiarity with crowds" and "mourn in solitude for your own sins and the sins of others."[125]

5. The experience of **union with God** at the end of the mystical journey. "Clement of Alexandria (2nd century) and Origen (3rd century) are both early witnesses to the Christian tradition, with roots in Greek philosophy but under the discipline of Christian revelation. Origen was the first writer to interpret the union symbolized in the *Song of Songs* between Bride and Bridegroom as between the Word of God (the Logos) and the individual soul--an interpretation which was to become immensely influential."[126] Bernard of Clairveaux adopted this interpretation in his sermons on the *Song*, which Juan in turn adopted.

6. The **created order is disproportionate with God**. Aquinas held this position as well. "But he [Juan] is more thoroughgoing than Aquinas and insists that even the partial knowledge of things immaterial gained through contemplation of the creation must be negated in the dark nights."[127] "Yet it is surely important to recognize the philosophical and theological debt of San Juan to Thomist

---

[123] THOMPSON, *The Poet and the Mystic,* 10.

[124] THOMPSON, *The Poet and the Mystic,* 10.

[125] *Book of the Institution of the First Monks,* Chapter 5, quoted in THOMPSON, *The Poet and the Mystic,* 11.

[126] THOMPSON, *The Poet and the Mystic,* 12.

[127] THOMPSON, *The Poet and the Mystic,* 14.

thinkers, for it dictated the way in which he set about analysing the experiences referred to in his prose commentaries and related him firmly to the intellectual outlook of Spanish Catholicism in the second half of the sixteenth century."[128]

7. The use of **metaphors and images**. A few examples will serve as an indication of what Juan had available to him: Juan's favourite image "is that of the sun shining through glass either revealing the specks of dust which cannot otherwise be seen, or as a demonstration of the same light that is in the sun streaming from it in rays without diminishing it. The analogy of the river flowing into the sea is not confined to Christian writers, and the bird pining for her mate, and the nightingale, have centuries of use behind them. The analogy of fire burning and consuming the wood appears to come from Hugh of St. Victor, though San Juan may have found it elsewhere, and a very beautiful example of it occurs in Luis de León. Paradox and antithesis also played an important part in the language of mysticism, full of notions of light and darkness, living and dying, pain that is pleasure, suffering that is joy."[129]

These few examples do not exhaust the rich symbolic heritage Juan received. Neither have they been a thorough indication of which authors may or may not have primarily influenced Juan. For our purposes it is significant to know that Juan was writing within a rich cultural and religious symbolism. These are the resources which Juan takes up into his own writings.

I have briefly described these resources. They include: 1. scriptural sources, especially the *Song of Songs*; 2. Patristic sources; 3. the *Rule;* 4. the *De institutione;* 5. mystical themes and symbols prevalent during Juan's day. Notably absent from this list is the resource Juan would have had in the popular folk-literature, songs, and poetry in common circulation at the time. Since this resource greatly impacts the determination of the *Cántico*'s literary genre, a determination which belongs to the second hermeneutical moment, mimesis$_2$, it is included in that discussion in Chapter Five.

---

[128] THOMPSON, *The Poet and the Mystic*, 15.

[129] THOMPSON, *The Poet and the Mystic*, 19-20.

Using a reflection of Colin Thompson I can, for now, summarize Juan's involvement with the symbolic systems of his day as follows:

San Juan has drawn on a vein of inherited wisdom running rich and deep for some fifteen hundred years. New authorities were constantly being added to the old ones, so that new insights and ideas came to replenish the tradition. Where we might see different schools of theology or mystical teaching, and note many changes and developments, San Juan and his contemporaries saw one body of authoritative literature guarding the truth from contamination. Individual authors were important as contributing members of this distinguished tradition. The broad outlines of the mystical journey had been drawn, and many details were already in place. This had given rise to a recognizable form of literature, using the kind of techniques we have looked at. These are all present in San Juan, not because he created a new kind of literature, but because he worked within a defined tradition. To them he added what he himself had acquired from his Jesuit education and his training at Salamanca, notably scholastic theology, a grounding in rhetoric, and a profound love of the Bible. His last and most intimate source was his own extraordinary mystical experience. What he could never have known was that with the blending of all these ingredients he too in time would become one of the greatest of all the authorities for those who followed his footsteps in the soul's ascent to God.[130]

Clearly, then, Juan wrote within a well established tradition. But he did not simply repeat, or merely organize this tradition in an original way. He had his own specific and original contribution to make to it.[131]

4.2 Juan's Contribution to the Western Mystical Tradition

In the previous section it was emphasized that Juan composed within a dynamic and well founded symbolic system which I have referred to as the western mystical tradition. However, Juan also helped fashion that tradition in a new way. Rather than fall into oblivion, his writings went on to inspire and be celebrated by

[130] THOMPSON, *The Poet and the Mystic*, 20.

[131] THOMPSON, *The Poet and the Mystic*, 11.

many people.[132] What was Juan's specific contribution to the western mystical tradition? The suggestions here concerning Juan's contribution are from the doctrinal perspective.[133] Further contributions to that tradition will be uncovered in the analysis below where I will discuss the appropriation and reception of the *Cántico*.

The presentation here will unfold in two sections. The first section deals with Juan's synthesis of themes, language, and method in his spiritual writings. The second section briefly describes the uniqueness of Juan's own contribution at the doctrinal level, that is, the doctrine of the passive and active nights of the senses and spirit which emerged from the synthesis of the three areas. The dialectic of the active and passive nights are Juan's most striking contribution to the western mystical tradition.

However, a text such as Juan's *Cántico* transcends its own era and remains meaningful for successive generations because the text has a capacity to create a world which it projects "in front of itself." This is the possible world which Ricoeur calls "the world in front of the text,"[134] as opposed to the world out of which the text came. This releases the time-boundedness of the text and allows it not merely to be informative, but transformative.

4.2.1 Juan's Synthesis

In the beginning of the sixteenth century, as already stated, there was an incredible upheaval and general reexamination of religious practices and

---

[132] For example the celebrated Sainte Thérèse de L'Enfant-Jésus and Charles de Foucauld were inspired by Juan de la Cruz. See: Charles A. BERNARD, "L'influence de saint Jean de la Croix sur Sainte Thérèse de l'Enfant-Jésus," *Revue d'Ascétique et de Mystique* 32 (1956), 69-80; Pierre BLANCHARD, "Sainte Thérèse de l'Enfant-Jésus fille de saint Jean de la Croix," *L'Année Theologique* 8 (1947), 425-438; Ibid, "Le Père de Foucauld, fils de saint Jean de la Croix," *Carmel* 1 (1959), 15-26; GREGORIO DE JESÚS CRUCIFICADO, "Las noches sanjuanistas vividas por santa Teresa del Niño Jesús," *Ephemerides Carmeliticae* 11 (1960), 352-382.

[133] The innovations Juan brought to the western mystical tradition, ideally, belong to mimesis$_2$. However, there is an initial discussion of these in this chapter since I am emphasizing that Juan wrote within a well established tradition. The fact that Juan received and lived within a particular tradition is the main point here.

[134] RICOEUR, *Hermenuetics and the Human Sciences*, 140-142.

structures at all levels. Renewal and reform were the dominant calls of the day in the church as well as in society at large. Hubert Jedin points out that with the Council of Trent a "new era of church history begins."[135] Concerning Juan de la Cruz, Hilda Graef states: "With St. John of the Cross we have reached the heights of Western mystical theology; to approach the seventeenth century will mean a descent from the rarefied air surrounding the heights of Mount Carmel to the lesser peaks of the mystical landscape."[136] Thus, within this environment of flux, change, and renewal, there is a culminating point within the western mystical tradition which is centred around Juan de la Cruz.

Several other authors describe Juan's mysticism and his contribution in this way: Colin Thompson in his insightful and concise study of Juan's place in the western mystical tradition says: "San Juan's indebtedness to the theological and mystical literature and tradition of the West must be considered; and he will then appear not as an isolated phenomenon but as a culminating point in an ancient and influential tradition which has left its mark on the literature of the Golden Age."[137] An anonymous writer describes the culminating point of Juan's writings in a slightly different way: "What he did do was to clear away the long, often contradictory digressions and repetitions of the mediaevalists, separate the essential from the non-essential, and in short do for mystical theology much of what St. Thomas Aquinas did for the subject in general."[138] E. Allison Peers emphasizes the same point: "Everything in his [Juan's] writings is fully matured: he has no *juvenilia*. The

[135] JEDIN, "Council of Trent," 277.

[136] Hilda Charlotte GRAEF, *The Story of Mysticism*, (Garden City, New York: Doubleday, 1965), 248. Graef continues: "Though the seventeenth century still produced some attractive mystics and a certain amount of mystical theology, it, and even more the eighteenth century of rationalism and 'enlightenment,' was a period of decline. The originality and mystical drive of a Catherine of Siena or Teresa of Avila as well as the theological and psychological penetration of a St. John of the Cross were no longer present in their successors." Ibid., 249.

[137] THOMPSON, *The Poet and the Mystic*, 2.

[138] BENEDICTINE OF STANBROOK ABBEY, *Mediæval Mystical Tradition and Saint John of the Cross*, 24.

mediaeval mystics whom he uses are too often vague and undisciplined; they need someone to select from them and unify them, to give them clarity and order, so that their treatment of mystical theology may have the solidity and substance of scholastic theology. To have done this is one of the achievements of St. John of the Cross."[139] Elsewhere Peers emphasizes Juan's unique contribution: "So far as my own reading goes, in fact, St. John of the Cross, considered as a mystic, has only two rivals in the whole history of Christian literature. One of these is St. Augustine. ... The other is the fourteenth-century Fleming Blessed John Ruysbroeck."[140]

Melquiades Andrés Martín suggests that Juan's unique contribution to the western mystical tradition lies in his clarification of new concepts, style of language, and methodology in the changing spiritual tradition.[141] Juan's mysticism is seen as bringing together the new and, at times, divergent movements reflected in these three areas of the tradition. Each of these areas will now be briefly presented separately.

4.2.2 New Themes in Spirituality

Many of the new themes that were surfacing in religious practice during Juan's time have already been mentioned. In large part these are related to the popularity of the *Devotio Moderna* and the rise in methodical prayer during the sixteenth century. A brief summary of these would include the following:[142] the universal call to perfection; a valuation of the interior spiritual life and a disvaluation of exterior works; integration of the entire person into mystical life; a valuation of one's personal existence and one's own conscience; a valuation of personal liberty;

---

[139] PEERS, *The Complete Works of Saint John of the Cross*, xxxiii.

[140] Allison E. PEERS, *Spirit of Flame: A Study of St. John of the Cross*, (London: Student Christian Movement Press, 1944), 95.

[141] Melquiades ANDRÉS MARTÍN, "Teresa y Juan de la Cruz: Contribución al proceso de clarificación en la mística española," *Revista de Espiritualidad* 36 (1977), 481.

[142] This summary is taken from ANDRÉS MARTÍN, "Teresa y Juan de la Cruz: Proceso de clarifación en la mística," 481.

mediation of humanity and divinity in the person of Christ; harmony of the active and contemplative lives; and the acceptance that knowledge can be attained through love.

Juan integrated these current themes into his own synthesis.[143] As Juan wove the symbolic and conceptual heritage of a diversity of writers into his own original work, so did he weave these themes together in a unique way. Juan de la Cruz and Teresa of Avila both worked within the tradition, and at the same time broke away from it. They transformed and reordered much of the spiritual terrain of their day in their spiritual writings and practices.[144]

4.2.3 New Style of Language

Within the western mystical tradition, mystics tended not to use predominantly conceptual or scientific language to express their experience. Instead they freely used symbolic language replete with metaphors, comparisons, and similes. However, with the rise of the *alumbrados* and Protestantism there was a need to more concretely systematize and clarify the language of mystical expression and popular piety.[145] With the Spanish Inquisition in full force, the threat of having

---

[143] For example, Cuthbert Butler, in his classic text, *Western Mysticism,* comments on Juan's unique appreciation of the active and contemplative ways to God as Juan introduces them from the Eastern mystical tradition into the Western: "[Juan] strikes another note, out of harmony with the trend of the Western tradition, but akin to that of Cassian and the East. ... There is no need to pursue the subject through later writers: what has been adduced suffices to delineate the great Western tradition on the contemplative life and the necessary admixture with it of the active life. In modern times this life has come to be called the 'mixed life,' and the ideal expressed by St. John of the Cross, the old Oriental conception, has tended to come into general acceptance as the ideal of the contemplative life." BUTLER, *Western Mysticism,* 275-276.

[144] "Ambos han sido declarados doctores de la Iglesia y todavía son clásicos en las tareas del espíritu. Ambos se formaron en la mística del recogimiento, ambos partieron de ella, buscaron nuevas fórmulas, rompieron a veces con las precedentes, las ordenaron y transformaron." ANDRÉS MARTÍN, "Teresa y Juan de la Cruz: Proceso de clarifación en la mística," 482.

[145] "Existe ... un claro proceso de clarificación en símbolos, imágenes, temas, lenguaje, que en muchos casos se convierte en proceso de esencialización. ... Lenguaje e ideas antropológicas, metafísicas y a veces teológicas, constituyen campos de rozamiento entre escolásticos y místicos. ... El problema de la clarificación de ideas y lenguaje se convirtió en céntrico a mitad del siglo XVI en relación con la herejía protestante, como se deduce del proceso de Carranza, del libro sobre la oración de Juan de la Cruz (1555), de la censura de biblias, del índice de libros prohibidos de 1559."

one's books put on the Index --or worse-- the threat of personal condemnation and severe discipline, was very real. Authors needed to be clear and careful in their writing since at times there was little difference between the practices of popular piety of Juan's day, and the doctrines being espoused by the rejected Alumbrado movement and Protestantism. Juan de la Cruz had to tip-toe his way between the pitfalls of these two camps.[146]

Paradoxically, Juan's mysticism emerged from within the spiritual tradition of *recogimiento* which had much in common with the *alumbrados:* the respect of quiet and tranquillity and the focus on a methodical and interior life of prayer. However, the tradition of *recogimiento* and the *alumbrados* differed in some important aspects. For example, the *alumbrados* despised participation in a church community and external works. Instead, they gave great importance to the extreme details of prayer. It was the severity of the practices of the *alumbrados* which often resulted in Quietism and led to their condemnation.

Juan de la Cruz recognized the importance of both an active and contemplative life within the *recogido* tradition. This is witnessed to in his commentary on *CB* 29.[147] Without the acknowledgement of Juan's debt to the

---

ANDRÉS MARTÍN, "Teresa y Juan de la Cruz: Proceso de clarifación en la mística," 482. Andrés Martín further suggests that it is in large part due to Teresa of Avila and Juan de la Cruz that this clarification process took place. In his description of sixteenth-century theological thought he says: "A lo largo del siglo XVI es claramente perceptible un proceso de clarificación en los conceptos y en el lenguaje místico, que alcanza cimas espectaculares en las obras de Santa Teresa y de San Juan de la Cruz. Las *Moradas*, la *Subida del monte Carmelo*, y el *Cántico* son modelo de claridad, ideológica y formal, y distinción de los grados de oración, en la purificación activa y pasiva de los sentidos y potencias ... . Con su experiencia mística y su ciencia teológica, San Juan de la Cruz respondió prácticamente, con su vida y obras escritas, a la teoría de Cano, Cuevas, Fernando de Valdés y cuantos oponían escolástica y mística como insociables." ANDRÉS [MARTIN], "Pensamiento teologico," 321-322.

[146] "Los dos genios más grandes en el campo de clarificación de las ideas y lenguaje místico son Santa Teresa, especialmente en lo referente a los grados de oración, y San Juan de la Cruz en lo tocante a la sistematización del progreso en la purificación y de la vida divina en el alma." ANDRÉS MARTIN, "Teresa y Juan de la Cruz: Proceso de clarificación en la mística," 482.

[147] For an excellent history and a description of the differences between *recogidos* and *alumbrados* see: ANDRÉS [MARTIN], *La teología española en el siglo XVI*, 2:198-259.

tradition of *recogimiento,* it is difficult to situate Juan within his own time.[148] It was upon this tradition that Juan's mysticism was based. This tradition emphasized personal, affective, and methodical prayer through the practice of love which led to union with the Divine in this world. It emphasized the inseparability and importance of the entire person: the bodily senses and the faculties, together with the soul. It also acknowledged the need to know oneself as part of one's journey to God. The *alumbrados* had been condemned due to their extreme pursuit of these goals through Quietism. Quietism often separated the faithful from any active participation in ecclesial life.[149]

However, despite Juan's radical appreciation of the contemplative life, he never had any of his books placed on the *Index* of the Inquisition. Juan stayed within the orthodoxy of the tradition of *recogimiento.* Juan's ability to clarify and his ability to emphasize the best of the tradition while shaping it through language in a unique yet orthodox way is evident here.

4.2.4 New Method in Description of the Mystical Journey

Juan was able to use his understanding of the spiritual journey as presented through the structures of scholasticism. However, he used and adapted these structures to write his poetry. His other resources included scripture, tradition,

---

[148] "La vía del recogimiento produjo los primeros grandes místicos de nuestra edad de oro, influyó en San Juan de Avila, Santa Teresa y San Juan de la Cruz y pervivió llena de vitalidad hasta fines del siglo XVII. Sin conocerla debidamente es imposible la inteligencia de la espiritualidad española de la edad de oro. Ella constituye la mística española primaria y fundamental." ANDRÉS [MARTÍN], *La teología española en el siglo XVI,* 2:198.

[149] The possibility that Juan's doctrine of "acquired contemplation" is Quietist in nature is discussed in ROMÁN DE LA INMACULADA, "¿Es quietista la contemplación enseñada por san Juan de la Cruz?," *Revista de Espiritualidad* 8, no. 30-31 (1949), 127-155. Contrary to two authors which he cites (Juan de la Anunciación and Gabriel de San José who identify "acquired contemplation" with "quietism" in Juan's corpus) Inmaculada concludes: "San Juan de la Cruz, restaurador insigne de la contemplación adquirida, afirmativa y negativa, no tiene ningún parentesco con el quietismo. Más aún, su doctrina pugna con la quietista, porque lleva caracteres irreductibles, que nunca permitirán fusionarlos." Ibid., 155.

and his personal experience.[150] Therefore, Juan brought theory and practice together into a single synthesis. Of particular interest here is his conception of the passive and active nights of the senses and the spirit. His conception of the passive and active nights safeguards the gratuitousness of God's grace in our lives, but also leaves an active role for the individual to play in the spiritual journey. This approach has often been viewed as Juan's most significant contribution to the western mystical tradition.

4.2.5 Juan's Unique Doctrinal Contribution

Juan's synthesis of concepts, language, and method coalesce in his crowning achievement within the western mystical tradition.[151] That is, Juan's unique contribution to the western mystical tradition at the doctrinal level was his ability to clearly present the *natural* movement of the union of the human person with God in his presentation of the dialectic of the active and passive nights of the senses and the spirit.[152] With this synthesis he retained the theological and doctrinal

---

[150] "San Juan de la Cruz puso luz en temas complicados con lenguaje nuevo, aunando el método de intuición experiencial del místico con el riguroso análisis conceptual del universitario." ANDRÉS [MARTÍN], "Pensamiento teologico," 358; "El santo Doctor sistematizó una doctrina y una experiencia, armonizó en ellas la tradición y el sentido de progreso, respondió desde las entrañas de la teología universitaria a los que disociaban escolástica y mística y, por miedo a posibles desviaciones, aconsejaban sistemáticamente caminos llanos, comunes y carreteros." Ibid., 359.

[151] A study which is beyond the focus of this dissertation, but nonetheless related, would be to examine how Juan's synthesis was (or was not) successful in bringing back together the approach to the spiritual life which "may be characterized as one of separation and division" from the twelfth century onwards. See Philip SHELDRAKE, *Spirituality and History: Questions of Interpretation and Method*, (New York: Crossroad, 1992), 40-44 for a discussion of the various splits in spirituality which resulted from the rise of scolasticism. The three major divisions which he cites are the following: "There was, first of all, a division of spirituality from theology, of affectivity from knowledge. Secondly, there was a gradual limitation of interest to interiority or subjective spiritual experience. In other words, spirituality became separated from social praxis and ethics. And finally, ... there was a separation of spirituality from liturgy, the personal from the communal, expressed most graphically by a new attention to the structures of personal prayer and meditation." Ibid., 44.

[152] In discussing the progression of the purification of the soul Andrés Martin says: "Se trata de una dialéctica en dos tiempos: vacio y lleno, renuncia de sí y posesión de Dios, tiempo y contratiempo. Pero en ellas se afirma con fuerza incoercible *la potencialidad de la naturaleza humana*, del hombre concreto en su espiritu de empresa y de lucha." ANDRÉS MARTÍN, "Teresa y Juan de la Cruz: Proceso de clarificación en la mistica," 490. (emphasis mine) For an article focusing on the description of Juan's doctrine of "acquired contemplation" (operative within the active night of the

richness of his scholastic training and the contribution of his own personal experience.[153] Juan's synthesis thus achieved theological precision without the errors of Quietism or the *alumbrados,* or without abandoning the uniqueness of his own personal journey or the uniqueness of the journey of others. In Juan's dialectic, involving the passive and active nights of the senses and spirit, he joined together human experience and the experience of the Divine, while safeguarding the transcendence and the immanence of God.[154] Melquiades Andrés Martín suggests nobody during Juan's time, or since, has surpassed Juan's synthesis in this regard.[155]

senses and spirit) see ADOLFO DE LA MADRE DE DIOS, "Estado y acto de contemplación la contemplación adquirida, según San Juan de la Cruz," *Revista de Espiritualidad* 8, no. 30-31 (1949), 96-126. An article which affirms the "naturalness" of mystical life and which refers frequently to Juan de la Cruz to affirm this position is: CLAUDIO DE JESÚS CRUCIFICADO, "Aclarando posiciones acerca del 'concepto de mística sobrenatural': La naturaleza de la vida mística," *Revista Española de Teología* 9 (1949), 105-122. The opposite position is given in: Antonio ROYO MARÍN, "El concepto de mística sobrenatural," *Revista Española de Teología* 8 (1948), 59-79.

[153] Baldomero Jiménez Duque affirms this strongly: "Porque en San Juan de la Cruz confluyen las antiguas corrientes espirituales de una manera ecléctica, original y única. Por una parte los elementos son tradicionales, viejos como el mundo y como el cristianismo. ... por otra parte San Juan de la Cruz ha sabido hacer un preparado suyísimo; aquello es de la mano propia de San Juan de la Cruz: Hay un sabor personal que, agradable, trasciende. Hay una impresión de madurez, de cosa lograda, casi definitiva. Pero, todo ello está asegurando que el fondo es el fondo clásico, tradicional, cristiano, un esquema preconcebido, trabajado después con agilidad y con soltura de forma y de expresión. Viejo y nuevo." Baldomero JIMÉNEZ DUQUE, "La perfección cristiana y San Juan de la Cruz," *Revista Española de Teología* 9, no. 2 (1949), 442.

[154] The literature on this subject is extensive. Following are a few references which deal with the theological and ascetical description of the progression of union with God as Juan reflects it in his dialectic of the passive and active nights of the senses and spirit: Bede FROST, Saint *Saint John of the Cross 1542-1591: An Introduction to his Philosophy, Theology and Spirituality,* (London: Hodder & Stoughton, 1937); JÉROME DE LA MÈRE DE DIEU, *La Doctrine du Carmel d'après Saint Jean de la Croix,* 2 vols., (Vienne: Carmel de Vienne, 1959-1961); RUIZ SALVADOR, *Introducción a San Juan de la Cruz: El escritor, los escritos, el sistema;* EULOGIO DE SAN JUAN DE LA CRUZ, *La transformación total del alma en Dios según San Juan de la Cruz,* Extract from doctoral dissertation presented in the Faculty of Theology at the Pontifical University of Salamanca, Madrid: Editorial de Espiritualidad, 1963; A more contemporary and psychological reading of these movements can be found in: WELCH, *When Gods Die,* 70-168.

[155] ANDRÉS MARTÍN, "Teresa y Juan de la Cruz: Proceso de clarificación en la mística," 489. "El santo sistematizó una doctrina, armonizó en ella el sentido de progreso y respondió desde lo más profundo de la teología escolástica a todos aquellos partidarios de Melchor Cano, Domingo Cuevas y Fernanado de Valdés que oponían escolástica y mística como insociables." Ibid., 489. Juan, "Con su esfuerzo, con su experiencia y con la gracia de efabilidad recibida de Dios, ha construido una exigente mística, encuadrada en una exigente escolástica. Así respondió al reto antimístico de Cano y de otros profesores de la Universidad de Salamanca. Luis de León, Antolínez y otros siguieron

According to Andrés Martín the most original part of the dialectic of the active and passive nights of the senses and spirit is the following: the human person is not only purified of one's faults but the very roots of those faults are purified.[156] This takes place during the passive nights of the senses and spirit. The human person is "transformed" into Divine life resulting in the passive contemplation described in the commentary on the *Cántico*.[157] Andrés Martín cites this schema as the most complete synthesis of the western mystical tradition in its description of the soul's transformation and union with God, a tradition, as we saw above, which has been part of the Christian and pre-Christian literature for millennia.

camino diferente." Ibid., 491. Herein lies the paradox: Juan did not set out to accomplish this singular feat in the development of western mysticism. Juan had a far simpler project in mind. As discussed previously, Juan's writings were geared in large part toward the uneducated nuns at Beas. Juan was not writing theory or setting out doctrine as a scholastic writer might, but rather his effort was to bring to those whom he guided a practical experience and discovery of God within their world and to help them discover themselves within God's world. In Juan's dialectic the two worlds are in fact one.

[156] "Es la segunda parte de la obra maestra de San Juan de la Cruz, llamada tradicionalmente *Noche oscura*, que es lo más original de su mística. En ella el alma no es purificada de sus faltas, sino de las raíces de las mismas, que han resistido el esfuerzo personal y la gracia ordinaria. Es la purificación pasiva de los sentidos y potencias o del espíritu." ANDRÉS MARTÍN, "Teresa y Juan de la Cruz: Proceso de clarificación en la mística," (1977), 490. Claudio de Jesús Crucificado says: "San Juan de la Cruz en mistica fué original con un grado que probablemente hasta ahora no ha sido superado ni siguiera igualado." CLAUDIO DE JESÚS CRUCIFICADO, "Originalidad de la doctrina mística de San Juan de la Cruz," *El Monte Carmelo* 39 (1935), 354-355. A succinct summary of Juan's other main doctrinal contributions and clarifications gathered from his various writings can be found in RUIZ [SALVADOR], ed., *Dios habla en la noche*, XI. As a preliminary list Ruiz Salvador presents these under the following eight categories: 1. The revealed and hidden God; 2. Jesus, the Word made human; 3. The human person in transformation; 4. Faith, light in the night; 5. Communion of Love; 6. Prayer and Contemplation; 7. Beauty; 8. Word and silence.

[157] Andrés Martín describes this "new state" as the *introduction* of divine life in the soul: "La contemplación pasiva es la plenitud del acto de fe, cima de la desnudez y de la introducción de la vida divina en el alma." ANDRÉS MARTÍN, "Teresa y Juan de la Cruz: Proceso de clarificación en la mística," 490. The simplest schema of Juan's mystical progression, according to this doctrinal model, can therefore be summarized in the following way: 1. Active purification of the senses and spirit. (the "work" of the individual); 2. This leads to active contemplation; 3. Passive purification of the senses and spirit (the "work" of God); 4. This leads to passive contemplation. "Pues bien, este esquema de lógica mística: purificación activa de los sentidos y potencias --> contemplación activa; purificación pasiva de los sentido y potencias --> contemplación pasiva o infusa constituye en sí mismo la cima más alta de la tematización de la mística; la clarificación más maravillosa de los procesos de purificación del alma y de su transformación en Dios." Ibid., 490-491.

5. Conclusion

With the perusal of the first moment of Ricoeur's hermeneutical trajectory, I have described the resources Juan had available to him in order to write the *Cántico*. I have done this at two levels. In Chapter Two I described the pre-narrative resources which Ricoeur defines as mimesis₁. Within the concept of mimesis₁ Ricoeur lists the resources of human action with which authors transpose being-in-the-world into texts. Both Juan and the current reader of the *Cántico* share resources at this level. In the present chapter I have described Juan's unique cultural and symbolic heritage. Awareness of these resources allow the contemporary reader to enter more consicously into Juan's text. These resources include the historical milieu of Juan, its political, sociological, intellectual and religious characteristics. They also include Juan's own life experience, his involvement in a diversity of ministries, and his personal commitment to the Carmelite way of life. Overall, Juan was inserted into the western mystical tradition, a tradition which he drew from, but also shaped in a unique way. Within this tradition he had a plethora of literary resources available to him, both scriptural and non-scriptural.

His particular contribution to the mystical tradition in the west is his description of the purification of the human soul through the active and passive nights of the senses and spirit. Juan's original contribution at this dogmatic level was publicly recognized when he was declared a Doctor of the universal church by Pius XI in 1926.[158]

However, Juan's doctrinal contribution to the western mystical tradition has resulted in his work being interpreted from a largely ascetical-theological approach as was shown in Chapter One. This approach, used by the majority of sanjuanist scholars, has tended to highlight a linear progression of the spiritual journey as they read it in the commentary on Juan's *Cántico*. This linear

---

[158] Pope Pius XI made this proclamation in his apostolic letter *Die vicesima septima* of August 26, 1926 (*A.S.S.*, vol. SVIII, 380); cfr. De GUIBERT: *Documenta ecclesiastica christianae perfectionis studium spectantia*, (Rome: 1931), quoted in Baldomero JIMÉNEZ DUQUE, "Problemas místicos en torno a la figura de san Juan de la Cruz," *Revista Española de Teología* 1 (1941), 963.

approach (usually characterized by the threefold way of purgation, illumination, and union) does not sufficiently take into consideration the uniqueness of the experience of the individual, nor does it take into consideration the role of the experience of the reader in the interpretive enterprise. The ascetical-theological approach has focused on doctrine which is distilled from Juan's *Cántico*, rather than the free movement of God's grace in the life of the person. Furthermore, the ascetical-theological approach implicitly distances God from humanity: the focus of interpretation tends to be on absolute (dogmatic) truth rather than the present truth of God alive in the life of the individual and the community. These consequences are inconsistent with Juan's own approach and method which, instead, foster a profound intimacy between the human and the divine. Without negating Juan's theological clarifications at the doctrinal level of the western mystical tradition, I would like to suggest another way of talking about Juan's contribution to this tradition, a way that is more consistent with Juan's personal approach and method.

In short, I would like to suggest that Juan's contribution to the western mystical tradition is not exclusively the formation of doctrine that balances in harmony the subjective and objective movements of the passive and active nights of the soul for which Juan is so famous. Juan's primary language was not doctrinal -- it was poetic. Its genre alone indicates that Juan had another interest at heart. Juan's contribution also consists in the bringing of "a world" to the western mystical tradition through poetic discourse. This "world" is a way of being-in-the-world which could not exist otherwise; a configuration of authentic human existence which transcends the immanence and transcendence of God reflected in the active and passive nights. Juan has achieved the projection of this "world" through the mimetic activity of his poetry. I have already suggested how the creation and possibility of this world is described through Ricoeur's concept of mimesis.

The inscription of this text is the second of the three hermeneutical moments being developed within the hermeneutical setting I am constructing for the *Cántico*. It is in the configuration of Juan's *Cántico* that we encounter a text which is more than a product of its own historical rootedness, or its doctrinal precisions.

CHAPTER FOUR
MIMESIS$_2$ AND CONFIGURATION OF THE *CÁNTICO*

1. Introduction

I will now present the second moment of mimesis as it is envisioned by Paul Ricoeur: mimesis$_2$, otherwise known as configuration or emplotment of a text. Mimesis$_2$ is the mediatory step which takes the reader from mimesis$_1$ (prefiguration of the action), to mimesis$_3$ (appropriation of the action) via the text itself. When the *Cántico* was written down it passed from its prefigured state to its configured state. It is the dynamics involved when a text is written which Ricoeur refers to as mimesis$_2$. These dynamics affect the way the *Cántico* is interpreted. Ricoeur's theory of mimesis continues to assist us to get at the meaning of the text of the *Cántico* which comes to us in its written form.

The presentation of mimesis$_2$ will take place in two sections. The first will deal directly with the mediatory function of mimesis$_2$ and the tools available to achieve this goal. I will thus examine the main characteristics of mimesis$_2$. Of singular importance is the dialectic of "sedimentation and innovation" which is operative in the configuration of a text. The relationship of Juan's *Cántico* to the scriptural *Song of Songs* will be explored as an example of this dialectic. A second section will introduce Ricoeur's theory of text. In this second section I will reflect on the characteristics of texts and the effect that the writing of discourse has on the communicative function. Essentially, I will respond to the following two questions: "What does writing do?" and "What makes a written text different from oral discourse?" The results of this investigation will be applied to methodological issues which need to be considered when interpreting the *Cántico*. This application will provide insights into the referential shifts which need to be considered when using

148

a hermeneutical approach to interpretation. In my conclusion of this chapter I will suggest that writing allows meaning (understanding) to manifest itself through explanatory analysis. The distinction between explanation and understanding suggests that there is a special role for exegesis and structural analysis in the interpretation process but these do not, in themselves, bring the reader to an "understanding" of the text. It is the dialectic of explanation and understanding, already introduced in Chapter One, which makes productive the various methodological approaches in the study and interpretation of the *Cántico*.

2. The Mediatory Function of Mimesis₂

Of utmost importance is Ricoeur's insistence on the mediatory value of a text. Written texts, the product of mimesis₂, mediate the operation that joins mimesis₁ to mimesis₃.[1] Mimesis₂, in its mediating function, refers to the configuration of human action in poetic composition.[2] In our case we are considering the text of Juan de la Cruz's *Cántico*. As already shown, preunderstanding (mimesis₁) refers to the first side of the composed text which seriously considers the resources available to Juan for the inscription of his text. From these resources the act of composing the *Cántico* makes "appear" Juan's unique meaning-event. The noema of reality are configured and "show" through inscription. Reality is configured through the composition of the *Cántico* such that Juan's experience is objectified and made available for others. Through the mediation of the text, aspects of reality, hitherto unknown, become available.[3] Mimesis₂ thus refers to the making of a literary structure which interprets and organizes the field of human action, opening up new possibilities for human action and knowledge through

---

[1] RICOEUR, *Time and Narrative*, 1:65.

[2] "This passage from the paradigmatic to the syntagmatic constitutes the transition from mimesis₁ to mimesis₂. It is the work of the configuring activity." RICOEUR, *Time and Narrative*, 1:66.

[3] As we will see below, the first "reader" to benefit by the production of the text may be the author herself/himself.

interpretation.[4]   Mimesis$_2$ is therefore characterized by this mediating function which makes available, in an objectifiable form, Juan's unique experience of being-in-the-world.[5]

Specifically, then, what is mediated by the act of composition? Briefly stated, mimesis$_2$ mediates between the "opaque depths of living, acting, and suffering" of an author and the receiving of the text by the reader.[6] Mimesis$_2$ refers to the act of emploting human action into a written text. By the production of a text, an author emplots the experience of being-in-the-world in a dynamic representational form. This form is then available for analysis in various ways which, in the end, are productive of new meaning.

The author's composition of human action constructs a text that is a mimesis of a unique interpretation of being-in-the-world. This, in turn, creates a form for an original meaning-event in the life of another person. If the act of composition is author oriented, the product is reader oriented.

Juan, therefore, in constructing the *Cántico*, configured a certain life-experience into a text. However, the *Cántico* is not just the expression of his own experience; it is more. Juan's *Cántico* mediates his *lebenswelt*, his experience of being-in-the-world which opens up the experience for others. Ricoeur's theory distinguishes between the act of composition and the product which is the configuration of being-in-the-world. The inscription of the *Cántico* is that intermediary step that provides the reader with an open door into an authentic human

---

[4] Care must be taken not to put a too restrictive sense on the word "knowledge" in this context. Knowledge in this context is meant to refer to the whole range of human knowing and experience that includes sensitivity to the rational as well as to the intuitive, to the affective as well as the cognitive.

[5] RICOEUR, *Time and Narrative*, 1:53. In short, what Paul Ricoeur is referring to in mimesis$_2$ "is the concrete process by which the textual configuration mediates between the prefiguration of the practical field [mimesis$_1$] and its refiguration through the reception of the work [mimesis$_3$]." Ibid., 1:53.

[6] RICOEUR, *Time and Narrative*, 1:53. This expression of Ricoeur's emerges from his study of Freud's concept of the unconscious. See Paul RICOEUR, *Freud and Philosophy: An Essay on Interpretation*, trans. Denis Savage (New Haven: Yale University Press, 1970), especially Chapter 3: "Instinct and Idea in the 'Papers on Metapsychology'," 115-151.

experience of being-in-the-world modelled in the *Cántico*.[7] The production of this "form for human action beyond the text" depends on the literariness of the text. The written text itself is required to appropriate Juan's meaning-event in the realm of human action today.

What I want to underline here is the importance of the text of Juan's poem. It is the text itself of the poem which is at work in mediating the production of future meaning-events in the reactualization of the text through reading. But if it is the text itself which mediates Juan's unique experience of being-in-the-world, the structure of the text itself should provide important indications as to the meaning of this experience. In mimesis$_2$ the interest is not so much in the alleged creation process of the text of Juan's *Cántico* as the techniques by means of which a work is made communicable.[8] Part of that communicability is the originality of the specific literary techniques employed by Juan to construct the *Cántico*. The work is also made communicable through its rootedness in what is already familiar, that is, in the existant tradition. However, what is already familiar is made, by mimesis$_2$, "unfamilar" in order to set the text to work in the mediation of new meaning events for other people. It is this dialectic which calls forth the interpretive task. Ricoeur thus describes a relationship between tradition and innovations within that tradition which are set to work in a text to produce new meaning.

2.1 The Dynamic Characteristics of Mimesis$_2$:

Schematization, Traditionality, and Innovation

Mimesis$_2$ semantically mediates the depths of human acting, thereby providing an open door for an original meaning-event for the reader. We saw in the overall introduction on mimesis in Chapter Two that emplotment is not a mere

---

[7] Recall that emplotment can be described as an act of judgement which intervenes in the flow and flux of reality in order to bring about an intensification and a metamorphosis of it.

[8] RICOEUR, "Between the Text and Its Readers," 391. Ricoeur goes on to say: "These techniques can be discerned in the work itself. The result is that the only type of author whose authority is in question here is not the real author, the object of biography, but the implied author." Ibid., 391.

mirroring of the original meaning-event of the author, but rather it is a production of an original meaning-event as well as a metamorphosis of it mediated through the text. The originality of future meaning-events is thus based on the uniqueness of the text which mediates these possible future meaning-events. No literary structure is absolutely identical to any other. Therefore, each act of emplotment is founded on the interplay of known literary technique and creative innovation.

Throughout history, various literary genres have proven to be adequate frameworks within which an author has emplotted the reality of being-in-the-world. Love ballads were popular with the troubadours in medieval times, while the epic drama was used by Homer in antiquity. The literary genre is therefore a significant key to the meaning of the text and must be identified in any adequate interpretation. The genre clues the reader as to what a text might mean. For example, a poem is read differently than a scientific report. However, an author is also free to innovate within the genre.[9]

Each author has a different style which gives a text a unique configuration even though the genre of the text may be quite common in the literary tradition. It is here, in the style of an author, that the originality of any one text shines forth.[10] Within the genre tradition, an author innovates and creates a slightly different schema of the meaning-event through his or her individual style. The unique style of an author may provide important clues to the uniqueness of the meaning-event which is inscribed in the text. Therefore, it is important to get at the objectivity of the *Cántico*, that is, to do an adequate exegesis that takes into

---

[9] "Innovation remains the opposite pole of tradition. There is always room for innovation to the extent that whatever is produced in composing the poem is, ultimately, always a singular work, this particular work. The rules that together form a kind of grammar direct the composition of new works--new before becoming typical. Every work is an original production, a new being within the realm of discourse." RICOEUR, "Life: A Story in Search of a Narrator," 430.

[10] "By producing discourse as such and such a work taking up such and such a genre, the composition codes assign to works of discourse that unique configuration we call style. This shaping of the work concurs with the phenomenon of writing in externalizing and objectifying the text into what one literary critic has called a 'verbal icon'." RICOEUR, "Toward a Hermeneutic of the idea of Revelation," 23.

consideration its structure, the images it uses, and other various literary techniques of the author which constitute a unique writing style. All these provide the "landscape" for the potential meaning-event in the life of the reader. Ricoeur describes the play between the tradition and the literary work in the following way:

> Emplotment [composition] ... engenders a mixed intelligibility between what has been called the point, theme, or thought of a story, and the intuitive presentation of circumstances, characters, episodes, and changes of fortune that make up the denouement. ... This schematism, in turn, is constituted within a history that has all the characteristics of a tradition. Let us understand by this term not the inert transmission of some already dead deposit of material but the living transmission of an innovation always capable of being reactivated by a return to the most creative moments of poetic activity.[11]

Schematization thus refers to the capacity to use the paradigms inherent within a particular tradition to fashion a new linguistic work. Traditionality refers to the ability to be able to recognize the work as belonging to a particular tradition while contributing to it and shaping it in an original way through an author's particular style. Juan used the resources available to him within the western mystical tradition but he did not merely copy them. Of particular note within this tradition is the longstanding interest in the *Song of Songs*, a fundamental symbolic field which Juan draws from for his own *Cántico*.[12]

In the context of Ricoeur's interpretation theory, Juan's *Cántico* is not a mere retelling of that story from scripture or from within its various configurations present within the tradition. Juan did not transmit "some already dead deposit of material" but, through poetic activity, reactivated the most critical and creative paradigms of the tradition while shaping them in a new way for that very tradition. Ricoeur cites this reflective capacity as the central dialectic operative in

---

[11] RICOEUR, *Time and Narrative*, 1:68.

[12] Colin Thompson gives an excellent summary of the connections between the *Song of Songs* and the *Cántico* in THOMPSON, *The Poet and the Mystic*, 60-80. Even though he cites the *Song* as a major influence on Juan's own poem, he still holds the distinct originality of Juan's work.

building up a literary tradition. He describes this as an "interplay of innovation and sedimentation":

> In fact, a tradition is constituted by the interplay of innovation and sedimentation. To sedimentation must be referred the paradigms that constitute the typology of emplotment. These paradigms have issued from a sedimented history whose genesis has been covered over. The sedimentation is produced on multiple levels, and this requires of us a broad discernment in our use of the term paradigmatic.[13]

> These paradigms, themselves issuing from a previous innovation, furnish the rules for subsequent experimentations within the narrative field. These rules change under the pressure of new inventions, but they change slowly and even resist change, in virtue of the very process of sedimentation. As for the other pole of tradition, innovation, its status is correlative to that of sedimentation. There is always a place for innovation inasmuch as what is produced, in the *poiēsis* of the poem, is always, in the last analysis, a singular work, this work.[14]

The paradigms which Juan inherited, whether they were linguistic, conceptual, symbolic, or otherwise, can be considered the "grammar" of what constituted a new and original work, even though his *Cántico* rests within a well established and long-standing tradition.[15] Although Juan's *Cántico* bears great resemblance to the *Song of Songs*, a "previous innovation" which has furnished (in part at least) "the rules for a subsequent experimentation," we can affirm that Juan's *Cántico* is an original work that has been produced within the tension of the two poles of sedimentation (those paradigms belonging to the tradition) and innovation (a new configuration of those paradigms born in its semantic content). Ricoeur affirms this dialectic in the following statement: "The labor of imagination is not

---

[13] RICOEUR, *Time and Narrative*, 1:68.

[14] RICOEUR, *Time and Narrative*, 1:69.

[15] "This is why the paradigms only constitute the grammar that governs the composition of new works--new before becoming typical. In the same way as the grammar of a language governs the production of well-formed sentences, whose number and content are unforeseeable, a work of art--a poem, play, novel--is an original production, a new existence in the linguistic [*langagier*] kingdom." RICOEUR, *Time and Narrative*, 1:69.

born from nothing. It is bound in one way or another to the tradition's paradigms. But the range of solutions is vast. It is deployed between the two poles of servile application and calculated deviation, passing through every degree of 'rule-governed deformation'."[16] I will use several examples to demonstrate the innovations which Juan brought in configuring the *Cántico* with respect to the *Song*.

The overall structure of the *Cántico* and the *Song* are very similiar.[17] Both are a colloquy between *esposa* and *esposo* with a chorus of creatures which occasionally interject comments or are asked questions. The parts spoken by each of the two main characters in the *Cántico* and the *Song* vary in length and are not always addressed to one another. The *Song* and the *Cántico* both abruptly change tense and context frequently. "Above all, both move around a focal point--the union of the lovers--rather than in linear progression from their meeting to the consummation of their love."[18] On the literary level the two texts share a common vocabulary: they both use abundant images from nature and the animal-world. However, Juan uses complete liberty in fashioning his own poem which shares so much with the *Song*. The following are examples which demonstrate the innovations Juan undertook in the *Cántico* with respect to the *Song*:

> In CA 18 the Bride reports in the third person and a past tense what Song 7:12 and 8:2 refer to the future and in direct speech: 'ibi dabo tibi ubera mea' and 'ibi me docebis' become 'allí me dio su pecho' and 'allí me enseñó', as the soul looks back to her betrothal. The image of Song 1:5 is altered in CA 19 from the Bride no longer tending her vineyard to the neglect of her sheep. Although the pastoral is strongly characteristic of the Bible (Psalm 23; John 10:1-16), there is no need to dwell on its significance in sixteenth-century

[16] RICOEUR, *Time and Narrative*, 1:69. Elsewhere Ricoeur describes this in a similar way: "The emplotment process oscillates between servile conformity with respect to the narrative tradition and rebellion with respect to any paradigm received from that tradition." Ibid., 208.

[17] This summary of the similiarities and differences between the *Cántico* and the *Song* is taken from THOMPSON, *The Poet and the Mystic*, 60-68. Thompson gives an excellent side by side comparison of passages which are similiar in the two texts: Ibid., 62-63 as well as a side by side expose of words used in common: Ibid. 64-65.

[18] THOMPSON, *The Poet and the Mystic*, 61.

literature. And although there are viticultural references elsewhere in the *Cántico* (CA 16,25), here, for some reason best known to himself, San Juan has chosen to alter the imagery. Further examples are not hard to find. The Bridegroom's words in Song 4:9 are given to the Bride in CA 21-2. In Song 4:16, both north and south winds are summoned; CA 25 calls on the 'cierzo muerto' ... to cease and the south wind only to blow--more understandable perhaps in Spain than in Palestine. ... In other places, his freedom in altering has a more directly poetic function: changes in vocabulary, omissions and amplifications, to aid scansion and rhyme.[19]

From the above examples the *Cántico*'s rootedness in the *Song* is clear. However, these examples show that Juan took significant liberties with the scriptural text in writing his own poem. Nonetheless, Juan's recourse to various resources, for example the *Song* or other texts, is assessed differently by various scholars examining his work. This is evidenced by the recent comments by Antonio T. de Nicolás who says, "San Juan de la Cruz composed his poetry out of ... pure imaginings, so that by creating images out of nothing, rather than borrowing them from anything existing around him, a new world of sensation, feeling, memory, and will was created and it is this which is responsible for the power of his poetry."[20] A little further on he underlines this point even more: "It might help to bear in mind ... that the project embarked upon by San Juan de la Cruz was to remove from his body any taste for the sensation coming to him from the outside--to be *sensitized exclusively from the inside out*. His poetry and prose are the narrative of this journey."[21] De Nicolás recognizes the newness of Juan's contribution but does not appear to give due merit to the resources which Juan had available to him for its composition. That Juan composed his poetry out of "pure imaginings" or "out of nothing" is questionable.

Pikaza describes the *Cántico* as a mere redaction of the *Song of Songs*

---

[19] THOMPSON, *The Poet and the Mystic*, 67-68. Thompson continues to give more details concerning Juan's innovative use of the *Song*. Ibid., 68ff.

[20] DE NICOLÁS, *Alchemist*, 6.

[21] DE NICOLÁS, *Alchemist*, 7. (emphasis mine)

and in fact says it contains nothing new.[22] Crisógono's perspective is also similar.

He suggests that many verses of Juan's *Cántico* are nothing more than beautiful translations of those from the *Song*, and therefore he does not undertake any detailed discussion of the *Cántico-Song* relationship.[23] Damaso Alonso also does not pay as much attention to the *Cántico*'s link to the *Song* as one might expect.[24] Instead Alonso focuses on the *Cántico*'s origins in secular literary sources. José Morales undertook a more thorough examination of the *Cántico-Song* relationship. Morales describes the relationship of the *Song* to the *Cántico* as one of "direct and close influence" whereby many of the themes of the *Song* are "recreated" in the *Cántico*.[25] These are "recreated" in such a way that they are used by Juan to reflect the three stages of the different mystical states, that is, the purgative, illuminative, and unitive states.[26] Pacho sees the *Song* as providing Juan de la Cruz with a "medium of expression" for his personal "interior life" since the *Song* was written by another who

---

[22] "Podemos decir, en un cierto sentido, que el Cántico empezó siendo una traducción del *Cant* que SJCruz fue haciendo vida y recreando en su propia entraña de poeta. No quiso crear algo distinto; no intentó encontrar motivos nuevos. Revivió desde su memoria selectiva, sin libros de consulta, los aspectos más salientes del *Cant* de la Escritura, expresando su camino de hombre perseguido en las palabras de un *Cántico* de amor." Xabier PIKAZA "Introducción al Cántico Espiritual: Anotaciones filosófico-teológicas," *Cuadernos Salmantinos de Filosofía* 18 (1991), 210. Strangely enough Pikaza cites Colin P. Thompson as a source for this affirmation, Ibid., n. 29, 210. However, although Thompson very much affirms the rootedness of Juan's *Cántico* in the *Song*, his perspective concerning the *Cántico - Song* relationship is quite different than the one suggested by Pikaza.

[23] "Muchas estrofas del *Cántico espiritual* no son más que bellísima traducción de versillos del epitalamio ... por eso, no hay poesía que tanto se parezca a la hebrea como la de San Juan." CRISÓGONO DE JESÚS SACRAMENTADO, *Obra científica*, 2:31, quoted in THOMPSON, *The Poet and the Mystic*, 61.

[24] ALONSO, *La poesia de San Juan de la Cruz*, 149-161.

[25] "Resumiendo el punto central de este estudio podemos ver que San Juan de la Cruz ha recreado genialmente muchos temas del *Cantar de los Cantares*. La estructura, el contexto y otras circunstancias en ambos poemas, prueban la directa y próxima influencia del *Cantar* bíblico." MORALES, *El Cántico espiritual de San Juan de la Cruz*, 251.

[26] "San Juan de la Cruz, que se inspira frecuentemente en el *Cantar* bíblico, trata de acomodarlo en sus partes a los tres diferentes estados místicos. Ya vimos como toma las imágenes del matrimonio espiritual para el desposorio y aun para el enamoramiento, y viceversa. Es decir, el Santo usa de los *Cantares* como de los *Salmos* o de los *Profetas* o del *Nuevo Testamento*, tomando sus sentencias como de cualquier libro sagrado, y porque vienen bien a la letra con su pensamiento." MORALES, *El Cántico espiritual de San Juan de la Cruz*, 249.

had an experience similar to Juan's own.[27] However, in the end, Pacho suggests that during Juan's *supremo trance de creación poética,* he had nothing before him but his personal mystical inspiration and vague literary memories.[28]

Taking a different approach, Ferdinande Pepin spiritualizes the profane love of the *Song* through Juan's adaptation of it in the *Cántico.* She suggests that if the biblical poem remains the love poem modelling all human love, Juan de la Cruz takes this nuptial symbolism to describe a transcendent love which comes *d'en-haut.*[29] She thus describes the *Cántico* as an "echo" of the biblical *Song.*[30]

However, regarding the relationship between the *Cántico* and the *Song,* Ricoeur's theory more readily aligns with Colin P. Thompson's comments: "Sometimes, he [Juan] takes a phrase and does little more than translate it or arrange it so that it will scan or rhyme. ... But more often, San Juan allows himself complete

---

[27] "El *Cantar de los Cantares* y la Biblia en general es fuente poética para el Santo en cuanto le sirve de medio de expresión de su vivencia interior, en cuanto soporte de otra experiencia enteramente similar a la suya. El maravilloso mundo de absorta belleza descrito en el *Cántico espiritual* no es un simple trenzado de bellas imágenes pedidas de prestado a las fuentes poética de la secular tración [sic] literaria. Según decíamos arriba, en el supremo trance de creación poética, el místico San Juan de la Cruz no tiene delante modelo alguno, sufre la carga de la inspiración y con ella se infiltran desvaídas reminiscencias, aletargados recuerdos de la formación literaria. En fin de cuentas, no hay más que esto: «Su pensamiento poético trabaja creando y sueña recreando»." Eulogio PACHO, "El 'Prologo' y la hermenéutica del 'Cántico espiritual', *El Monte Carmelo* 66 (1958), 85-86.

[28] PACHO, "El 'Prologo' y la hermenéutica del 'Cántico espiritual'," 86.

[29] "Si le poème biblique demeure le poème d'amour sur lequel se modèleront toutes les amours humaines, il garde cette résonance spirituelle où le nouvel homme biblique, Jean de la Croix, trouve le pur itinéraire d'Élie. Sous les termes amoureux du symbolisme nuptial, le poète carmélitain authentifie ce qu'il éprouve et interprète le poème biblique à la lumière de sa lumière intérieure: l'expérience de Dieu qu'il fait en son âme. La signification nouvelle du symbolisme conjugal qui se lit au «Cántico espiritual» continue la signification traditionnelle, mais reprise et polarisée dans un sens transcendant par l'amour qui vient d'en-haut." PEPIN, *Noces de Feu,* 406. Pepin describes Juan's use of the symbolism from the *Song* as a "transposition" and a "recreation:" "Nous avons conclu de la plus grande facilité de Jean de la Croix à transposer et recréer le symbolisme nuptial du «Canticum Canticorum» dans ce domaine à la fois esthétique et mystique du «Cántico espiritual»." Ibid., 409. Further she adds: "Sensibilisé à tous les éléments terrestres et divins, Jean de la Croix absorbe la mystique essence du «Canticum Canticorum»; il insère, dans le poème qui de toute nécessité lui est inspiré, de nouvelles harmoniques au-delà même de l'ancienne mélodie biblique. C'est ce que nous avons voulu lire au long du «Cántico espiritual»." Ibid., 411. Because of this *profondeur mystique* Pepin concludes that the *Cántico* has a *valeur supérieure* over that of the *Song.* Ibid., 415.

[30] PEPIN, *Noces de Feu,* 412.

liberty. Not only does he integrate material from the *Song* with passages from secular traditions, he also makes considerable alterations to the Latin texts themselves, changing speaker, context, tense and meaning at will."[31] Thompson's comment describes the dynamics which were at work in the production of the *Cántico* based on tradition and linguistic elements from that tradition.

Ricoeur's hermeneutical framework, therefore, gives us a way to understand how the *Cántico* is new even though it is heavily anchored in a previous literary tradition. Juan's *Cántico* is not a mere copy of the *Song* (de Nicolás, Pikaza, and Crisógono), nor is it a re-creation for doctrinal purposes (Morales), nor a mirroring of his own interior experience (Pacho). Neither is the *Cántico* a mere transformation of the *Song* (Pepin).

Through innovation of the tradition (the dialectic of sedimentation and innovation) Juan's *Cántico* can be described as a new and original work. As we saw in Ricoeur's reformulation of the concept of mimesis, literary texts, particularly poetic texts, access levels of reality which, hitherto, were unknown. This is the configuring work which suggests that the *Cántico* configures a different text-world than the *Song* as well as reflects more than Juan's personal experience. Texts are productions, that is, they are productive of reality. As an innovative text the *Cántico* is a *representative activity*. This creativity of the *Cántico* will be more extensively examined when I explore the consequences of "The Act of Writing" below. At this point I will briefly summarize where we have arrived in describing the mediatory function of mimesis$_2$ with respect to Juan's *Cántico*.

In this chapter I am developing the various characteristics of mimesis$_2$ which will help us understand the textuality of Juan's *Cántico* and its mediating function of a new meaning-event through the neology of the text and its anchorage in the conceptual and symbolic fields of mimesis$_1$. The main characteristic of mimesis$_2$ is the production of a text capable of mediating future meaning-events. Of particular significance in the mediation of meaning through the text will be the

---

[31] THOMPSON, *The Poet and the Mystic*, 67.

indications of creative innovation within Juan's literary tradition. As one example we have examined its relationship to the *Song of Songs*. However, Juan's *Cántico* is an original work. Through innovation Juan used the sedimented paradigms of his day and configured a new text. This is where we have come thus far.

Now that we have situated the *Cántico* generally into that level of interpretation which Ricoeur refers to as mimesis$_2$, we must return to an even more basic question: What specifically does writing do? Or, to ask the same question in a different way: what are the repercussions of configuring a text such as the *Cántico*? A response to this question will deepen our appreciation of the textuality of Juan's *Cántico* and begin to expose us to the importance of the poetic form which Juan used to configure his life-world. I will then be in a position to move into section two where I will explore the expansion of meaning of the configuring event through Ricoeur's fourfold distanciation which takes place when orality is inscribed.

2.2 The Consequences of the Act of Emplotment[32]

What does the production of a text do? This is to ask: what are the repercussions of configuring a text? Juan's emplotment produced a specific schema which drew upon the resources available within his literary tradition. Yet he manipulated these resources to configure a unique meaning-event in the structure of the *Cántico*. Ricoeur outlines three major consequences of this process of composing:[33] 1. Individual action sequences are brought together to complete a text which configures a beginning, a middle, and an end; 2. Disparate elements are configured to belong to, and build, the cohesiveness of this text; 3. The experience and aporia of temporality are reckoned with through writing. Each of these will now be briefly described with a comment concerning the overall text of Juan's *Cántico*.

First, the operation of emplotment is a "mediation between the

---

[32] For an overall introduction and reference to the content of this section see RICOEUR, "What is a Text?: Explanation and Understanding," 105-124; Ibid., *Interpretation Theory: Discourse and the Surplus of Meaning*, (Fort Worth: Texas Christian Press), 1974, 19-22.

[33] RICOEUR, *Time and Narrative*, 1:65-68.

individual events or incidents and a story taken as a whole."[34] Singular events are transformed into a meaningful whole through the dynamic of emplotment. Each event gets its definition and meaning from its contribution towards the composition taken as a whole. "In short, emplotment is the operation that draws a configuration out of a simple succession."[35] The various metaphors, symbols, and other literary devices all play a role interacting with each other as a *single* network to mediate a new meaning event in the life of the reader.

This function of emplotment allows us to affirm the singularity and cohesiveness of the entire poem of the *Cántico*. No individual action sequence or event within the text of the *Cántico* can be viewed as *the* event. *The* event of the poem is the entire creative production opened up by the poem.[36] It is the complete semantic content of the text, the interaction of the various characters, their activities, and the individual sub-plots, which make up the configuring dynamic. Any singular exegetical study, such as a thematic or a symbolic study, would be seen only as a needed step in a more complete hermeneutical interpretation of the *Cántico*.

Second, "emplotment brings together factors as heterogeneous as agents, goals, means, interactions, circumstances, [and] unexpected results."[37] Even apparent contradictions and reversals in the *Cántico* belong to the configuration of Juan's meaning-event. What seems not to belong together in the text is brought into a unified whole through emplotment.[38] Ricoeur describes this characteristic of

---

[34] RICOEUR, *Time and Narrative*, 1:65.

[35] RICOEUR, *Time and Narrative*, 1:65.

[36] This production is the world of *as if* inscribed in the work. Ricoeur describes it as the world-of-the-text which we will be examining in the next section. It creates the literary nature of the text. "Artisans who work with words produce not things but quasi-things; they invent the as-if. And in this sense, the Aristotelian mimesis is the emblem of the shift [*décrochage*] that, to use our vocabulary today, produces the 'literariness' of the work of literature." RICOEUR, *Time and Narrative*, 1:45.

[37] RICOEUR, *Time and Narrative*, 1:65.

[38] Ricoeur extends this analysis of literature to his concept of history: "If we define what counts as a plot broadly enough, even quantitative history reenters its orbit. There is a plot whenever history brings together a set of goals, material causes, and chance. A plot is 'a very human and very

emplotment as "concordant discordance."[39] Everything belongs to the plot; there is nothing in the text which is extraneous to it.

This second consequence of emplotment will be especially significant in our consideration of the text of *Cántico A* where there are apparent reversals and contradictions which led Juan de la Cruz to redact the *Cántico* into what has come to be known as *Cántico B*.[40] By the third stanza, Juan himself discovered that it was simply not possible to doctrinally outline the progression of the spiritual life following the text of *Cántico A*.[41] However, a hermeneutical framework suggests a different appreciation of the incongruencies of *Cántico A*. Ricoeur's hermeneutical approach to a text suggests that, ultimately, Juan's poem may not be strictly doctrinal in nature. Ricoeur's theory of mimesis holds that aporia present in a text

---

unscientific mixture of material causes, ends, and chance events.' Chronological order is not essential to it. In my opinion, this definition is completely compatible with the notion of the synthesis of the heterogeneous." RICOEUR, *Time and Narrative*, 1:170. Here Ricoeur is appealing to Paul Veyne to support his perspective: Paul VEYNE, *Comment on écrit l'histoire*, (Paris: Seuil, 1971), 46. Ricoeur thus affirms the continuity between the concept of "story" and that of "history." Ricoeur comments on this coherence with respect to the epistemological break usually cited between story ("fiction") and history ("fact"): "If this narrative continuity between story and history was little noticed in the past, it was because the problems posed by the epistemological break between fiction and history, or between myth and history, turned attention to the question of evidence, at the expense of the *more fundamental question* of what accounts for the interest of a work of history. It is this interest that assures the continuity between history based on historiography and ordinary narration." RICOEUR, *Time and Narrative*, 1:151. (emphasis mine)

[39] This concept is developed in RICOEUR, *Time and Narrative*, 1:42-45. Ricoeur states: "Discordant concordance is intended still more directly by the analysis of surprise. Aristotle characterizes it by an extraordinary expression in anacoluthic form, which is lost in the English translation: 'when they come unexpectedly and yet occur in a causal sequence in which one thing leads to another [para tēn doxan di'allēla]' ([*Poetics*] 52a4). The 'marvelous' things (*to thaumaston*) (ibid.)--the height of the discordant--are those strokes of chance that seem to arrive by design." Ibid., 1:43.

[40] Eulogio PACHO describes the temporal and logical disorder of *Cántico A* in this way: "Hay rodeos, sinuosidades, vueltas y revueltas, que entorpecen la marcha regular del orden cronológico." PACHO, "La Clave exegetica del 'Cántico espiritual'," 329.

[41] Eulogio Pacho describes this discovery of Juan: "Pensando, sin duda, al redactor el prólogo que el orden de la poesía refleja con suficiente rigor el progreso espiritual en alas del amor, el comentarista [Juan] no encuentra de momento dificultad en combinar ambos elementos. Por eso no alude a ellos explícitamente, convencido de que el ritmo poético, cual tenue hilo que engarza unas con otras las estrofas, sirve también para ordenar en sistemática unidad su respectiva declaración doctrinal. La ilusión se descubre muy pronto." PACHO, "La Clave exegetica del 'Cántico espiritual'," 329.

are part of the metaphorical reference of the text. These incongruencies are thus put to work to mediate to the reading subject meaning that is not strictly doctrinal in nature. The *Cántico* makes use of metaphorical reference to speak of other levels of reality, not only the doctrinal.

The incongruencies of *Cántico A*, in this perspective, are not seen as roadblocks to understanding what the *Cántico* is about, but rather are the very vehicle which the text uses to mediate meaning. This approach to the *Cántico* assists in opening up access to new meaning within the *Cántico*. Poetic texts, through metaphorical reference, do not merely convey information but bring into focus through interpretation new possibilities of being-in-the-world.

The issue of the relationship of *Cántico A* to *Cántico B* is also opened up in this approach to the aporia of *Cántico A*. Within a hermeneutical framework *Cántico A* cannot be assumed to be a "less perfect" form of the *Cántico* that eventually found its completion in *Cántico B*. The significance and role of both the *Cánticos* must thus be questioned within a hermeneutical approach to the text. This will be part of the work of Chapter Five, where we will examine in more detail both of these texts.

Third, emplotment reorients the human experience of temporality through the interweaving of the cosmological (Aristotelian) and the phenomenological (Augustinian) experience of time.[42] Aristotle measured time in a linear way through the natural rythmes of the cosmos, for example, the setting and rising of the sun. Aristotle thus clearly distinguished between a past, present, and future. Augustine dealt with time in a pyschological way, collapsing Aristotle's threefold temporal divisions into "a present of future things, a present of past things, and a present of present things."[43] "The aporetics of the Augustinian and Aristotelian conceptions lies in the fact that the one cannot show how cosmic time is derivable from psychological time and the other cannot show how psychological

---

[42] RICOEUR, *Time and Narrative*, 1:7-16; 1:66-68.

[43] RICOEUR, *Time and Narrative*, 1:60.

time is derived from the cosmological. From the Augustinian 'present' we cannot get an Aristotelian 'instant,' nor conversely."[44] However, poetic composition is particularly efficacious in dealing with the aporia arising from these two approaches to time. Configuration, the work of mimesis$_2$, manages the dialectic operative between these two poles.[45] Although there is no common ground between the cosmological and phenomenological explanations of time, "there is a poetic mediation between the two."[46] The aporia of time are thus brought to productivity and used to create meaning through poetic discourse.

Jorge Guillén observes that the overall temporal reference of the *Cántico* is toward a "very real present": "The things that happen, throughout the *Canticle* are set before us in a very real present. This is not a past already concluded that the poet reconstructs. Nothing in the poem is alien to the burning actuality which here and now--within the compass of the poem--sets forth its present acts of love."[47] How is this "very real present" constructed in the *Cántico*? The *Cántico* constructs this temporal whole by weaving together various tenses that jump back and forth throughout the poem. The past is not followed by the present, nor is the future preceded by the present.

---

[44] Robert P. SCHARLEMANN, "The Textuality of Texts," in *Meanings in Texts and Actions: Questioning Paul Ricoeur*, ed. David E. Klemm and Willam Schweiker, Studies in Religion and Culture (Charlottesville and London: University Press of Virginia: 1993), 16. The difference between Augustine's and Aristotle's notion of time is developed by Ricoeur in "The Dispute Between Augustine and Aristotle," in *Time and Narrative*, 3:12-22.

[45] Recall, Aristotle did not consider this temporal characteristic of emplotment in his *Poetics* but dealt with it separately in his *Physics*. Similarly, Augustine did not tie his explanation of time in the *Confessions*, bk. 11, to his discussion on narrative, in bks. 1-9 of the *Confessions*. Ricoeur's project is to bring time and narrative together into a single theory that explains the production of new meaning effected through the threefold movement of mimesis. The question which Ricoeur is struggling with here in the refiguration of time is the following: "In what way is the ordinary experience of time, borne by daily acting and suffering, refashioned by its passage through the grid of narrative?" Ricoeur, *A Ricoeur Reader*, 338. See as well: RICOEUR, *Time and Narrative*, 3:241-249 which summarizes Ricoeur's struggle with the phenomenological aporia of time and how emplotment deals with these.

[46] SCHARLEMANN, "The Textuality of Texts," 17.

[47] GUILLÉN, *Language and Poetry*, 87.

For example, the temporal sequence from stanza 35 through stanza 37 shows no logical progression.[48] The bride in stanza 35 uses the present subjunctive in the first person plural (*gocémonos, Amado, y vámonos*). She uses the future in stanza 36 (*nos iremos / entraremos / gustaremos*), while in stanza 37 the bride uses conditionals with an imperfect and a preterite (*mostrarías / pretendía / darías / diste*). The whole poem is constructed in this way: changes of speaker, tense, and location are associated, at times, with torrents of unrelated images and illogical progressions from one scene to the next. Colin Thompson describes the results of Juan's composition in the following manner:

> In parts it is almost impressionistic in feel; in other parts, it seems to be using a sixteenth-century equivalent of modern cinematographic technique: flashbacks introduced without warning, events implied rather than stated, characters introduced in passing, focused upon briefly, then discarded. No sequence of events can be followed except through small groups of stanzas, because the thematic progress of the poem is constantly being interrupted by glances into the future or past, and by fragments of conversations and comments.[49]

The *Cántico* combines in alterable proportions both of the temporal dimensions described above to achieve a temporal unity that holds the poem together. The first temporal dimension is chronological (the episodic dimension characterized by the linear passing of time) the other is not (the phenomenological dimension characterized by the temporal unity of the poem considered as a whole).[50] The episodic dimension of a text characterizes the text since it is made up of various events or episodes which can be followed, more or less, by the reader. However, note that the episodes involving the bride and the bridegroom, although presented in some sequential fashion, do not express a linear progression of the movements within the poem. We will see this in more detail in the various reversals and abrupt shifts in the *Cántico*, particularly *Cántico A*, which are examined in Chapter Five.

---

[48] THOMPSON, *The Poet and the Mystic*, 86.

[49] THOMPSON, *The Poet and the Mystic*, 86.

[50] Ricoeur describes these in RICOEUR, *Time and Narrative*, 1:66.

However, the text is presented in such a way that it can be followed "proper to the configurational act."[51]

The second temporal dimension of the text, the phenomenological dimension, transforms the assorted events into a unified temporal whole.[52] The entire temporal configuration of the text is capable of being present (ontologically) in the life of the current reader. In this context, time is no longer perceived as flowing from the past toward the future, but rather its threefold dimension is reoriented.[53] The linearity of historical time is refigured by this poetic temporality in the way we are present to the entire text at the behest of the text. It is such a stance before time that is demanded by Juan's *Cántico* because of the undulating and cyclic nature of time sequences presented in the poem. Historical time stands refigured, or reoriented through phenomenological time. The present and eternity are thus brought into tension through the poetic act. Particularly in *Cántico A*

> there is no ordered progression in time, place, or argument, except the very basic one that at the beginning the Bride is searching for her beloved and at the end she is united with him. The over-all impression is one of a large number of beautiful fragments pieced together but never fitting properly. In this the *Cántico* faithfully reflects it [sic] model [the *Song of Songs*], but manages to be more complex and elusive in a much shorter span.[54]

Since we stand in time moving towards death, in confrontation with eternity, the poet's task is to mediate between these two poles. It is the text which

---

[51] RICOEUR, *Time and Narrative*, 1:66. More will be said about this in the presentation of reader-reception theory in Chapter Six.

[52] "By mediating between the two poles of event and story, emplotment brings to the paradox a solution that is the poetic act itself. This act ... extracts a figure from a succession, reveals itself to the listener or the reader in the story's capacity to be followed." RICOEUR, *Time and Narrative*, 1:66. Ricoeur notes, therefore, "that it is in the act of *retelling* rather than in that of telling" that the structural function of the "thought" or "point" can be discerned. Ibid., 1:67. (emphasis mine)

[53] "As soon as a story is well known ... to follow the story is not so much to enclose its surprises or discoveries within our recognition of the meaning attached to the story, as to apprehend the episodes which are themselves well known as leading to this end. A new quality of time emerges from this understanding." RICOEUR, *Time and Narrative*, 1:67.

[54] THOMPSON, *The Poet and the Mystic*, 87.

confronts the aporetic elements of phenomenological time in confrontation with the smooth linearity of cosmological time. Poetic activity alone can respond, not theoretically, but poetically, to the insoluble enigmas of time.[55] It is this "reckoning with time" which also forms part of the meaning mediated by Juan's poetic doing in the *Cántico*.

In writing the *Cántico*, Juan could have given us a pure narrative form, but he did not. Narrative temporality intersects more readily with historical temporality. Poetic temporality shifts temporality making the three extensions of time (past, present, and future) very *strong* in the present.

This effect of poetic configuration, as suggested by Ricoeur, reinforces my thesis that the referential dimension of Juan's *Cántico* is not exclusively doctrinal in character, but rather includes something else.[56] If Juan's *Cántico* projects a world before the text that deals with time, the "temporal space" opened up by the text and habitable by the human person is an integral part of the text's meaning. To restrict Juan's *Cántico* to its doctrinal referents, would, again, impoverish its richness.

2.3 Summary

So far in this chapter I have examined two points: the mediatory function of mimesis$_2$ and the effects of the act of emplotment. We have seen that mimesis$_2$ shapes, expresses, and mediates authentic human existence through the

---

[55] "A constant thesis of this book will be that speculation on time is an inconclusive rumination to which narrative activity alone can respond. Not that this activity solves the aporias through substitution. If it does resolve them, it is in a poetical and not a theoretical sense of the words. Emplotment, ... replies to the speculative aporia with a poetic making of something capable, certainly, of clarifying the aporia ... but not of resolving it theoretically." RICOEUR, *Time and Narrative*, 1:6.

[56] The temporal configuration of Juan's *Cántico* within the context of Ricoeur's discussion on the Aristotilian and Augustinian approaches to time deserve more attention. The above presentation brings to the fore the question of the productive capacity of the refiguration of time with respect to the poem's meaning. The refiguration of time within the poem forms part of the ultimate reference of the poem.

medium of a text. This text affects discourse[57] in three ways: first, through emplotment each individual event is seen as contributing toward the entire production of the text; second, apparent contradictions and unexpected results are also seen as an integral part of the production of the text and not aberrations; and third, mimesis₂ alters the various dimensions of temporality. These characteristics of mimesis₂ offer several key affirmations concerning the hermeneutical setting of Juan's *Cántico* which can briefly be summarized at this point:

> 1. It is the literariness of the *Cántico* itself which mediates to the reader Juan's unique experience of being-in-the-world. The *text* of the *Cántico* is an original meaning-event which configures the depths of this human acting and suffering.
>
> 2. If composing a text is a *production*, Juan's *Cántico* is not a finished product. It is a construction of being-in-the-world, a mimesis, which is a vibrant reality. Therefore, the meaning of Juan's *Cántico* cannot be so clearly established that the text is dead. The text is *not complete* and bears an openness to completion through appropriation in changing historical and cultural moments.
>
> 3. The entire content and all the movements within the poem are a necessary part of the disclosure of Juan's unique experience of being-in-the-world. No particular event can be excluded, even if it appears to suggest a contradiction or insert a "break" into the flow of the poem. The configuring mediation is a product of the *entire poem*. This conclusion will have repercussions for the way we later assess Juan's redaction of *Cántico A* into *Cántico B*.
>
> 4. Juan's *Cántico*, as suggested by Ricoeur's mimetic theory, configures time in a unique way. It is this configuration of time which helps reassess the current preoccupation with the poem's doctrinal referents. Meaning in Juan's *Cántico* is also integrally involved with temporal space, a constitutive part of the *Cántico's* meaning, which Juan's poem opens up.

In general, therefore, the act of writing the *Cántico* has stabilized as

---

[57] Recall, discourse, according to Heidegger, is the way human beings articulate significantly the intelligibility of being-in-the-world. Discourse could therefore refer to a number of mediums whereby human beings express this reality of *Dasein*. For Ricoeur, however, the privileged medium for the appearance of *Dasein* is language, specifically poetic language shaped in a text.

well as configured the meaning-event of Juan's being-in-the-world. The text can now potentially enter the lives of whoever can read. Writing, therefore, opens up the life-experience of the author in a new way and makes the author's unique meaning-event accessible to others. But once the text is written the author loses control over its meaning. The author, literally, is distanced from the text when it passes into the hands of others.

Ricoeur refers to the distance the author takes with respect to the written text, as well as to the originary meaning-event of discourse, as "distanciation." Distanciation through writing both fixes the meaning of a text anchored in the resources of mimesis$_1$, and at the same time allows it to be open to expanded meaning in the life of the reader. This dialectic of distanciation and expanded meaning is what I will now begin to explore. What I want to examine here is a verification of the possibility of expanded meaning within the text of the *Cántico* *mediated through its textuality.* The same possibility of meaning is not available strictly through oral discourse, nor through narrative composition. Let us now see how and why this is true.

3. The Act of Writing: The Significance for Interpretation of Distanciation through Writing

Several key concepts must be examined to present this section of Ricoeur's theory that explains how writing and the absence of the author through the presence of the text actually enriches the interpretive task. Ricoeur describes a fourfold removal from the original setting of production and reception of a text which results in an enrichment of the original event of discourse. The enrichment of discourse through writing is first of all based on the dialectic of the separation of the event of speaking from its meaning.[58] This is the primary distanciation of which Ricoeur speaks.

---

[58] For a general overview of this notion see RICOEUR, "The Hermeneutical Function of Distanciation," 131-144.

This dialectic affirms that meaning is virtual when structured in a text, and through the text there exists the potentiality of this meaning to become event in the life of another person. Based on this dialectic, a further threefold distanciation occurs when oral discourse becomes inscribed. This distanciation alienates the text from the author, from the original audience, and from the original life-situation from which the text arose.[59]

Set in this interpretive context the inscription of Juan's *Cántico* enriches the originary meaning-event. It also frees the poem to speak in new ways to other audiences within different historical and cultural settings. This latter point implies that Juan's *Cántico* can have an unlimited number of valid interpretations. We will see then, that Juan's *Cántico* does not merely describe the classical spiritual itinerary of the *via mistica* but can be open to other interpretive possibilities.

3.1 The Effect of the Distanciation of Meaning From the Event

What happens when oral discourse becomes written discourse? What happens to its meaning? It has already been shown that the *Cántico* existed in an oral form prior to its inscription by Juan de la Cruz. Recall that Juan committed the first thirty-one stanzas of the poem to memory while in the prison at Toledo even though he most likely wrote down these stanzas before his escape. Following this, while living in El Calvario, Juan frequently visited the nuns at Beas, many of whom had also memorized Juan's sublime poetry. Juan first gave his poem to the nuns in its oral form and through this event of discourse the nuns found the poem to be meaningful. Dialogue with the nuns allowed an exchange which would have facilitated clarification concerning the meaning of the stanzas. But oral discourse eventually terminated, and Juan's *Cántico* was committed to a written form. It is this

---

[59] See especially RICOEUR, "Speaking and Writing," in *Interpretation Theory*, 25-44. I am indebted to Sandra Schneiders for her presentation of Ricoeur's notion of distanciation in Sandra SCHNEIDERS, *The Revelatory Text: Interpreting the New Testament as Sacred Scripture*, (San Francisco: Harper, 1991), 142-144.

written discourse, among other things, which Ricoeur refers to as a text.[60]

This written form of discourse has provided audiences entry into Juan's unique meaning-event over the past four hundred years. Contemporary audiences are not in a position to dialogue with Juan, nor with the nuns, but the inscription of Juan's *Cántico* makes possible the continuation of the originary meaning-event. What I want to investigate here is what happened when the oral form of Juan's *Cántico* was written down, as well as what continues to happen with the poem due to its inscription. This is important since this written form is the only available form of the poem we have.

Hermeneutic interpretation really begins and becomes possible only when dialogue ends, that is, when there is a certain distance from the discourse event.[61] This distance becomes possible through writing. "What happens in writing is the *full manifestation* of something that is in a virtual state, something nascent and inchoate, in living speech, namely, the detachment of meaning from the event."[62] Often it is assumed that the inability to dialogue with the author of a text about its meaning is a disadvantage. This stance, from the perspective of Ricoeur's interpretation theory, is a naive one. It wrongly assumes that written discourse is simply a substitution for oral discourse. Furthermore, it does not consider any of the other dynamics operative when oral discourse assumes a written form.[63]

Ricoeur emphasises that discourse is "not merely preserved from destruction by being fixed in writing, but that it is deeply affected in its

---

[60] See RICOEUR, "What is a Text?: Explanation and Understanding," 105-124; Ibid., *Interpretation Theory*, 19-22; Ibid., *Rule of Metaphor*, 219. Briefly stated, a "text" for Ricoeur is any object that can be subjected to hermeneutical inquiry, "even human existence." VAN DEN HENGEL, *Home of Meaning*, 111. Therefore, a "text," in the thought of Ricoeur, refers to a much broader reality than merely written texts.

[61] "Hermeneutics begins where dialogue ends." RICOEUR, *Interpretation Theory*, 32. What we clearly see here is that, for Ricoeur, hermeneutics is a *textual* hermeneutics.

[62] RICOEUR, *Interpretation Theory*, 25. (emphasis mine)

[63] For a more detailed description of what happens when speaking becomes writing, see RICOEUR, *Interpretation Theory*, 25-44 and more briefly Ibid., "The Hermeneutical Function of Distanciation," 139-140.

communicative function."[64] The text, in its written form, serves as an enrichment of discourse and not an impoverishment. This is to say that writing is not *only* "a question of a change of medium, where the human voice, face, and gesture are replaced by material marks other than the speaker's own body."[65] Emplotment fixes through semantic autonomy the *fullness* of the meaning of discourse, which, previously, only existed in a virtual state. Something new happened in the fixing of Juan's *Cántico* in writing; it is not merely oral discourse *re*-presented through the written form. Rather, the written *Cántico accentuates* the original meaning-event.

I have already said that this first moment of Ricoeur's fourfold distanciation is referred to as the separation of meaning from the event of discourse.[66] As is often experienced, the event of speaking and hearing gives voice to something meaningful to the interlocutors. But, the question must be asked, what is left *after* speaking and hearing? What happens when discourse terminates and silence perdures? When the event of speaking terminates *meaning remains* in the lives of those who were involved in the oral discourse. According to Ricoeur, if, after speaking, it is meaning which remains in the lives of the interlocutors, the meaning of discourse can also be fixed through writing and takes on permanence.[67] Through writing the meaning of discourse takes on a certain materiality that can be recalled later.[68] Thus, language, and specifically written language, provides the framework

---

[64] RICOEUR, *Interpretation Theory*, 28.

[65] RICOEUR, *Interpretation Theory*, 28. Ricoeur states elsewhere: "In my view, the text is much more than a particular case of intersubjective communication: it is the paradigm of distanciation in communication. As such, it displays a fundamental characteristic of the very historicity of human experience, namely, that it is communication in and through distance." Ibid., "The Hermeneutical Function of Distanciation," 131.

[66] Meaning, according to Ricoeur, is an *event*, it is something that happens through discourse, *the* event of language. See RICOEUR, *Interpretation Theory*, 8-12.

[67] "It is because discourse only exists in a temporal and present instance of discourse that it may flee as speech or be fixed as writing." RICOEUR, *Interpretation Theory*, 26.

[68] "Only discourse is to be fixed, because discourse as event disappears." RICOEUR, *Interpretation Theory*, 27. See further Ibid., 26-29.

from within which the *event of meaning* can potentially be made accessible to another person. Ricoeur explains, using the language theory of J.L. Austin and John Searle:

> What in effect does writing fix? Not the event of speaking, but the 'said' of speaking, where we understand by the 'said' of speaking that intentional exteriorization constitutive of the aim of discourse thanks to which the *sagen*, the saying, wants to become *Aus-sage*, the enunciation, the enunciated. In short, what we write, what we inscribe, is the noema of the speaking. It is the meaning of the speech event, not the event as event.[69]

What is being emphasized here is that language has a "force." Ordinary Language Philosophy suggests that "acts of discourse do things with words;" language is performative.[70] Ricoeur picks up on the traits of language suggested by Ordinary Language Philosophy in order to explain why this is the case.

> The act of speaking, according to these authors [Austin and Searle], is constituted by a hierarchy of subordinate acts distributed on three levels: (1) the level of the locutionary or propositional act, the act of *saying*; (2) the level of the illocutionary act or force, that which we do *in* saying; and (3) the level of the perlocutionary act, that which we do *by* saying.[71]

Ricoeur agrees with Austin and Searle that all three of these characteristics of language are taken up in written discourse:

> The locutionary act exteriorizes itself in the sentence. The sentence can in effect be identified and reidentified as being the same sentence. ... But the illocutionary act can also be exteriorized through grammatical paradigms (indicative, imperative, and subjunctive modes, and other procedures expressive of the illocutionary force) which permit its identification and reidentification. ... Without a doubt we must concede that the

---

[69] RICOEUR, "The Model of the Text: Meaningful Action Considered as a Text," 146.

[70] VAN DEN HENGEL, *Home of Meaning*, 31. That language is performative was first suggested by J.L. Austin. See J.L. AUSTIN, *How to Do Things with Words? (Oxford Conferences)*, (Oxford: The Clarendon Press, 1962), quoted in Ibid., 31, n. 11.

[71] RICOEUR, "The Model of the Text: Meaningful Action Considered as a Text," 146-7.

perlocutionary act is the least inscribable aspect of discourse and that by preference it characterizes spoken language. But the perlocutionary act is precisely what is the least discourse in discourse. It is the discourse as stimulus. It acts not by my interlocutor's recognition of my intention, but sort of energetically, by direct influence upon the emotions and the affective dispositions. Thus the propositional act, the illocutionary force, and the perlocutionary action are susceptible, in a decreasing order, to the intentional exteriorization that makes the inscription in writing possible.[72]

To summarize, when the sound fades something objective is left. Through emplotment the meaning of an event, or events, is captured, albeit in some ideal form, so that later it can be reactualized by another person through the act of reading.[73] Language, and its expression through texts, thus allows the human person to break through his or her own solitude and enter into the experience of another human being in a new way.[74] It is, at least in part, this dynamic which explains why the *Cántico* is found to be meaningful for readers today.

3.2 The Effect of the Distanciation of the Text From its Author

The second distanciation occurs in the detachment of the text from its author. In oral discourse, the speaker can be questioned if a participant fails to understand what is said, as we saw with Juan and the nuns at Beas. The author is in a position to correct misinterpretation and regulate the meaning of what is said. However, with written discourse this regulation is lost, "the author's intention and the meaning of the text cease to coincide. This dissociation of the verbal meaning of the

---

[72] RICOEUR, "The Model of the Text: Meaningful Action Considered as a Text," 147.

[73] Ricoeur states it this way: "Only the message gives actuality to language, and discourse grounds the very existence of language since only the discrete and each time unique acts of discourse actualize the code." RICOEUR, *Interpretation Theory*, 9.

[74] "Language is itself the process by which private experience is made public. Language is the exteriorization thanks to which an impression is transcended and becomes an ex-pression, or, in other words, the transformation of the psychic into the noetic ... There the solitude of life is for a moment, anyway, illuminated by the common light of discourse." RICOEUR, *Interpretation Theory*, 19.

text and the mental intention of the author gives to the concept of inscription its decisive significance, beyond the mere fixation of previous oral discourse."[75] Inscription assures the semantic autonomy of the text, thus separating the mental intention of the author from the actual meaning of the text. As Ricoeur states, "The text's career escapes the finite horizon lived by its author. What the text means now matters more than what the author meant when he wrote it."[76]

The result of this second distanciation is that the text now begins to live a life of its own, beyond the intention of the author. The author is no longer in full control of the meaning of the text. Its meaning is now extended to the full range of possibilities opened by the structure of emplotment and the polysemy of words. Therefore, any interpretation of Juan's *Cántico* which limits its meaning to the intention of its author, limits the fullness of its actual meaning. Interpretation of meaning absolutely restricted to authorial intentionality is not desirable and impoverishes access to the meaning of texts. The limitation of interpretation based on the intention of the author is a predominant characteristic of the Romanticist's approach to interpretation. This has resulted in the almost exclusive prominence given to the ascetical-theological interpretation of the *Cántico*. In Chapter One we have already seen how this approach is limited in opening up Juan's *Cántico* for the contemporary reader. However, there are other limiting characteristics to the interpretive methods which have resulted from the Romanticist's approach.

The Romanticist's approach to the poem moves within the concept of understanding based on the meeting of two minds, that of Juan de la Cruz, and that of the reader, which ultimately come to share a common perspective informed by the poem. This approach is founded on the belief that the psychological intentions of the author concealed *behind* the text are available to some degree and provide the necessary interpretive principle for an understanding of the text. This interpretive principle is usually seen as primarily available through the conceptualization of the

[75] RICOEUR, *Interpretation Theory*, 29.

[76] RICOEUR, *Interpretation Theory*, 30.

Cántico in the commentary on it.

Eulogio Pacho is a primary proponent of the intentionalist approach to the *Cántico*. Pacho says that the "primordial intention" of Juan de la Cruz is to *teach* the spiritual itinerary that results in the union of the human with the divine.[77] The primacy and importance of this intentionality, as it is expressed in the commentary, is the key to an understanding of the *Cántico*.[78] In other words, if the reader has no direct point of access to the doctrinal content of the *Cántico* through the commentary, Pacho seems to be suggesting that no understanding of the poem can take place. The commentary, Pacho says, presents us with a more "natural" way of understanding.[79] Pacho suggests that there is a richness of expression in poetry, but a poverty of understanding, because the doctrinal content is not accessible through the poetic medium. Conceptual expression of the poetic experience through the commentary is the pathway to "natural" understanding. This conceptual approach to the *Cántico* is concerned with the singularity, the acumen, of the author's

---

[77] "Sin refugiarse en sutilezas peligrosas pueden asentarse algunas conclusiones seguras. La intención primordial de fray Juan persigue la enseñanza del itinerario espiritual que culmina en la unión divina. A ese «intento» subordina y ordena todo lo demás." Eulogio PACHO, "Lenguaje y Mensaje," in *Experiencia y Pensamiento en San Juan de la Cruz*, ed. Federico Ruiz Salvador (Madrid: Editorial de Espiritualidad, 1990), 62. Elsewhere in this same article Pacho writes: "[Es] fáciles de espigar, se deduce que fray Juan no persigue en su prosa el arte por el arte. Su finalidad no es estilística ni literaria, sino espiritual. ... Busca la elegancia y la pulcritud sin sacrificar por ello la eficacia pedagógica, que es norte y guía supremo de sa pluma." Ibid., 64. See also Ibid., 55, 58, 59, 61, and 63 where this same basic idea is presented.

[78] "Desde esta ladera humana penetramos mejor el discurso razonador, el minucioso análisis del comentarista, que los sublimes dislates del poeta. Nos acercamos mas a la sabrosa inteligencia interior a través de largos y complicados razonamientos que por medio de las intuiciones plásticas profundas del poeta." PACHO, *Vértice*, 125.

[79] "Aparte los mil pormenores carentes de consistencia mental en el momento de la creación poética, y que luego se van acumulando a lo largo del comentario, son estas disquisiciones doctrinales las que alargan el contenido doctrinal de la paráfrasis respecto al poema y *le hacen mas asequible a nuestro modo natural de comprender*." PACHO, *Vértice*, 120. (emphasis mine) This is true for Pacho at the level of "understanding." However, Pacho does affirm that at the level of expression poetic-symbolic language is the *most conatural* way for the human person to bring experience to **expression**. "Si se tiene en cuenta la condición inefable de lo místico no resulta extraño que un artista como Juan de la Cruz se refugie en la poesía al momento de traducir su emoción y su sentimiento; lo que él llama «noticia amorosa». Lo figurativo y simbólico es lo más connatural a la experiencia profunda, lo mismo que para la capacidad creadora del poeta." PACHO, "Lenguaje y Mensaje," 71. See also PACHO, *Vértice*, 68.

message as it is clarified in Juan's commentary. Conceivably, within this approach, the meaning of the *Cántico* would eventually be exhausted.

However, the availability of historical intentionality of an author must at least be called into question. Also, this approach does not take into consideration the unique referential capacity of poetic discourse. Nor does this approach take into consideration the expansion of meaning which occurs when oral discourse is committed to a written form. This dynamic results in the fourfold distanciation we are now exploring which profoundly affects the interpretation of the *Cántico*. Furthermore, an exclusive intentionalist approach does not give sufficient consideration (if any) to reception or reading theory which affects the meaning of a text. I will take up this dynamic in Chapter Six. Ultimately, therefore, the intentionalist approach to textual interpretation focuses on the *limits* of understanding, born from the common interpretation of words, rather than recognizing that the *Cántico* has been meaningful to many generations since its origin due to other dynamics at work within the text itself.[80]

Given the distanciation which takes place through the inscription of a text, not to mention a further distanciation which takes place if an author interprets her or his own work as did Juan de la Cruz, authorial intention cannot be used to divine the absolute meaning of the text. Interpretation, at least in an exclusive way, cannot be the search for indubitable information pursued by the light of the intention of the author. As Ricoeur says: "Thanks to writing, the 'world' of the *text* may [even] explode the world of the *author*."[81]

For example, to return to the *Song of Songs*, scholars hold little doubt that the *Song of Songs* was not written as a religious text.[82] Yet this text was

---

[80] See RICOEUR, *Interpretation Theory*, 46 ff. Here Ricoeur presents his theory of metaphor which negatively critiques this positivist tradition.

[81] RICOEUR, "The Hermeneutical Function of Distanciation," 139.

[82] Roland E. Murphy outlines the history of this book of the Old Testament in Roland E. MURPHY, "The Song of Songs: Critical Biblical Scholarship Vis-à-vis Exegetical Traditions," in *Understanding the Word: Essays in Honor of Bernhard W. Anderson*, ed. James T. Butler, Edgar W.

accepted as a profoundly religious text not only by the Jewish people but subsequently by Christians as well. The *Song of Songs* displays a surplus of meaning that goes beyond authorial intentionality and continues to inspire countless people today. The *Song* is no longer available through the author. In its being set free from the author, the text achieves an objectivity which allows it to enter into different contexts. The possibility of this "surplus of meaning," to use Ricoeur's term, becomes especially obvious when we consider the nature and characteristics of language. Several characteristics of language are relevant to our inquiry to make this point clear.[83]

First, what is said in language, including written discourse, stands always against the backdrop of the vast unsaid to which it is related.[84] The absolute expression of something through language is simply not possible. Language is always charged with a *range of meaning* located beyond its own sense which becomes explicit only in different circumstances, thereby evoking the depth of meaning contained within. Second, language is integrally symbolic. Language, as "the body of thought and feeling," accesses and symbolically displays those realms of reality which are otherwise not perceivable. "But because language is symbolic, it simultaneously reveals and conceals that which it renders present."[85] This characteristic of language discloses that language is ambiguous and opens up the possibility of misinterpretation, thus surfacing the hermeneutical task which is opposed to an absolute interpretation of a text. Third, and finally, we see that

Conrad, and Ben C. Ollenberger, *Journal for the Study of the Old Testament*, Supplement Series 37 (Sheffield: JSOT, 1985), 63-69.

[83] The following is a summary from SCHNEIDERS, *The Revelatory Text*, 138-140. To a large extent Schneiders summarizes these characteristics of language from Hans-Georg GADAMER, *Truth and Method*, trans. J. Weinsheimer and D. Marshall, 2nd edition (New York: Crossroad, 1989).

[84] SCHNEIDERS, *The Revelatory Text*, 138.

[85] SCHNEIDERS, *The Revelatory Text*, 139.

178

language, even ordinary everyday language,[86] is essentially metaphoric.[87] Whereas

symbolism is tied to a multiplicity of forms (for example, dreams, cosmic entities,

and archetypal images), metaphor is inserted into the flow of the semantic

possibilities of symbolism.[88] Symbolism, therefore, is a broadly encompassing

reality that uses language as *one* of its various embodiments. Metaphors, as

linguistic referents, point toward a primordial level, the as yet unappropriated world

of symbolism.[89] In short, as we will soon see in greater detail, the metaphoric

character of language changes the ordinary use of words and identifies potentially

new meaning through the redescription of reality.[90] "In metaphor the mind 'feels'

toward meaning with a reach that exceeds the grasp of pure rationality."[91]

These three basic characteristics of language reveal the fallacy of the

---

[86] It is significant that Ricoeur also affirms the basic continuity of everyday language and metaphoric language. This is in opposition to Wittgenstein who argues that various language games are all radically distinct and autonomous. Even Heidegger parallels this position of Wittgenstein with his dichotomy between nonobjectifying and objectifying discourse. In more popular terms this distinction has often been seen as "reasons of the heart" versus "reasons of the head." This brief comment on the connection between metaphor and everyday language is summarized from Frank Burch BROWN, "Transfiguration: Poetic Metaphor and Theological Reflection," *The Journal of Religion* 62, no. 1 (January 1982), 44. Brown states: "Metaphor, even in its most poetic forms, typically exhibits both continuity and discontinuity with ordinary language and thought. Its world of meaning is world in dialogue, being neither 'wholly other' nor wholly familiar. Metaphor thereby constitutes a linguistic transfiguration the meaning of which both draws on, and contributes to, language and thought as a whole." Ibid., 44.

[87] This question is dealt with in RICOEUR, "Metaphor and the Central Problem of Hermeneutics," 165-181, as well as in RICOEUR, *Interpretation Theory*, 45-69.

[88] "The symbol, in effect, only gives rise to thought if it first gives rise to speech. Metaphor is the appropriate reagent to bring to light this aspect of symbols that has an affinity for language." RICOEUR, *Interpretation Theory*, 55. For a more detailed discussion of the distinction between symbols and metaphors see RICOEUR, *Interpretation Theory*, 45-69, especially 53-59.

[89] "Metaphor occurs in the already purified universe of the *logos*, while the symbol hesitates on the dividing line between *bios* and *logos*. It testifies to the primordial rootedness of Discourse in Life. It is born where force and form coincide." RICOEUR, *Interpretation Theory*, 59.

[90] "This redescription is guided by the interplay between differences and resemblances that gives rise to the tension at the level of the utterance. It is precisely from this tensive apprehension that a new vision of reality springs forth, which ordinary vision resists because it is attached to the ordinary use of words. The eclipse of the objective, manipulable world thus makes way for the revelation of a new dimension of reality and truth." RICOEUR, *Interpretation Theory*, 68.

[91] SCHNEIDERS, *The Revelatory Text*, 139.

positivistic tendency to affirm that texts have a univocal meaning that is identified with the intention of the author. But the question may be asked: with so much more being brought to the text, and expected of it, what happens to the intentions of the author who *meant* the text to *mean* a particular thing, or, even after the text was written, as is the case with Juan de la Cruz, explained the text and *ascribed a particular meaning* to it?

The approach to interpretation, which Ricoeur properly calls hermeneutics, sees interpretation as an attempt to clarify the type of being-in-the-world which unfolds *in front of* the text through a discovery of the world-of-the-text[92] interacting with the world-of-the-reader. In this approach, the author's presence is not totally excluded from the text. The author has left indications *in* the text through written language, that is, its textuality. Therefore, interpretation of the text is not located *behind* the text, but rather *within* and *in front of* the text itself.[93] When additional information concerning the text is available, in this case Juan's own commentary on the *Cántico*, it must be considered in view of what is in the primordial text, that is, the poem. Juan is "present" in the text, not through a psychic presence behind the text, but rather is present through the structure and style of the text, that is, through the schematization of the text.

However, the semantic autonomy of the text and polysemy of words provides the basis for a surplus of meaning which opens up the possibility and

---

[92] The "world-of-the-text" is an expression which Ricoeur uses and will require further explanation. It is introduced here, however, since it is the world-of-the-text which is substituted for authorial intentionality as the main issue confronting the interpretive task: "It is the final consequence of a critique of Romanticist hermeneutics, at the end of which the concept of the world of the text has taken the place of the authors's intention." RICOEUR, "Toward a Hermeneutic of the Idea of Revelation," 30.

[93] "The nature of reference in the context of literary works has an important consequence for the concept of interpretation. It implies that the meaning of a text lies not behind the text but in front of it. The meaning is not something hidden but something disclosed. What gives rise to understanding is that which points towards a possible world, by means of the non-ostensive references of the text. Texts speak of possible worlds and of possible ways of orientating oneself in these worlds. In this way, disclosure plays the equivalent role for written texts as ostensive reference plays in spoken language. Interpretation thus becomes the apprehension of the proposed worlds which are opened up by the non-ostensive references of the text." RICOEUR, "Metaphor and the Central Problem of Hermeneutics," 177.

richness of a *range* of legitimate interpretations of a text.[94] It is this characteristic of the *Cántico* which has kept the text alive and relevant in various moments of history and diverse cultural settings. Given the semantic autonomy of a text, the question may be asked whether there can be any "objectivity" in the interpretation of Juan's *Cántico*? What, therefore, governs the adequacy of a particular interpretation? Furthermore, against what "norm" are differing interpretations of Juan's *Cántico* to be judged?

Given the variety of interpretations made possible through the semantic autonomy of the text from its author, legitimate interpretations are still not limitless. According to Ricoeur the meaning of a text is a function of the dialectic between sense and reference. It can be affirmed that the text itself regulates these interpretations and provides a common orientation available to all interpreters of the *Cántico*.[95] Put another way, there is access to an "objective" interpretation of Juan's *Cántico* which resides in the semantic structure of the text itself operative within the dialectic of sense and reference.

3.3 The Effect of the Distanciation of the Text From its Original Audience

The third distanciation due to the inscription of a text is the distance the text assumes with respect to its original audience. The hearer becomes the reader and hence allows for a temporal distanciation. Time now separates the text from those who originally received it. Therefore, the written *Cántico* now "free-floats" through history. It has been definitively removed from sixteenth-century Spain and now lives in different cultural and historical settings which are nearly oblivious to the originary meaning-event. However, Juan's *Cántico* continues to be meaningful as a product of the enriching dynamic of the separation of the text from the original audience. The new hearers of the text will hear new things.

However, Juan did write using the symbols, images, and language

---

[94] RICOEUR, *Interpretation Theory*, 57.

[95] The dialectic of sense and reference is presented in detail below.

current in his day. He was sensitive to what would be meaningful language for his audience. As we have already seen, he especially used the popular imagery and symbols contained within the *Song of Songs* to write his own *Cántico*. However, once the *Cántico* was written, it was detached from its original audience, and, in a certain way, from the *Song of Songs*, as well as from the other sources which we have discussed. It thus became a new and original literary work available to anyone who can read. Through writing, Juan's *Cántico* was alienated from its original centre of production to become available, at least potentially, to a universal audience.

Although the first audience would have had a particular appreciation of the religious imagery used by Juan for them, subsequent audiences are able to open up the text, through interpretation, in a new way. Because of the new experiences of the new audience, later readings of the text may be even richer in meaning than earlier readings because of the surplus of meaning available in the text. The original audience understood the *Cántico* subject to the perspective they brought to the text within their own cultural-historical moment. In this case the full hermeneutical dialectic of distanciation may not allow the expansion of meaning available to later audiences when the speaker-author is not present. This is not to say that the author is necessarily a roadblock to interpretation and understanding of the text. Rather, the text is enriched by the additional experience brought to the text by a new audience.[96] This is in contrast to the restricted meaning available to the original audience which may have been in contact with Juan, the speaker-author, who may have explained the text on site.

Ricoeur describes this shift in the following way:

> Whereas spoken discourse is addressed to someone who is determined in advance by the dialogical situation--it is addressed to you, the second person--a written text is addressed to an unknown reader and potentially to whoever knows how to read. This universalization of the audience is one of the more striking effects of

---

[96] This further emphasizes that transcription of dialogue is not a mere *re*-presentation of the what was said in written form. As we see here the communicative function is radically altered when it assumes a written form. For example, the aporia in the text are put to work to construct new meaning in a different setting.

writing and may be expressed in terms of a paradox. Because discourse is now linked to a material support, it becomes more spiritual in the sense that it is liberated from the narrowness of the face-to-face situation.[97]

Once written, the *Cántico* escaped the confines of the nuns at Beas and *created for itself* a new public. As Ricoeur says: "A work also creates its public. ... it enlarges the circle of communication and properly *initiates new modes of communication.* To that extent, the recognition of the work by the audience created by the work is an unpredictable event."[98] We have already seen how this is true for Juan's *Cántico*. During his lifetime Juan's audience was limited to those with whom he had contact in relatively few places, for example, El Calvario, Baeza, and Granada. His writings were used to further the pastoral care of those in his charge. However, even during Juan's own lifetime his audience began to grow due to handwritten copies of Juan's poems which were distributed by those inspired by the text. It was the text of the *Cántico* itself which procured for Juan a place in the western mystical tradition and the hearts of generations. It was not Juan himself, nor his immediate and personal relationship with his audience (however personable he may or may not have been), which formed Juan's place in the western mystical tradition. The paradox of the written *Cántico* lies in its universality due to inscription, yet this universality has no real meaning if it does not realize contingency in some way in the lives of the readers.[99]

Ricoeur describes this dynamic as follows: "On the one hand, it is the semantic autonomy of the text which opens up the range of potential readers and, so

---

[97] RICOEUR, *Interpretation Theory*, 31.

[98] RICOEUR, *Interpretation Theory*, 31. (emphasis mine)

[99] Ricoeur ties this emergence of meaning to the play of metaphor in texts: "So even if metaphorical meaning is something more and other than the actualization of one of the possible meanings of a polysemic word (and all of the words in natural languages are polysemic), nevertheless this metaphorical use must be solely contextual, that is, a meaning which emerges as the unique and fleeting result of a certain contextual action." RICOEUR, "Metaphor and the Central Problem of Hermeneutics," 169.

to speak, creates the audience of the text. On the other hand, it is the response of the audience which makes the text important and therefore significant."[100] It was Juan's audience-response which led to the eventual publication of Juan's *Cántico* on a larger scale more than thirty years after his death. Due to the new experiences brought to the text by the changing audience in different historical and cultural settings, new meaning which Juan himself could not possibly have imagined may be ascribed to the text of the *Cántico*. The distanciation from the original audience due to writing, therefore, effects an enrichment of Juan's *Cántico* and further underlines the impoverishment of any interpretation of the text that would limit the meaning of the text within the context of authorial intentionality.

3.4 The Effect of Distanciation Upon Sense and Reference

In a fourth way there is a change when oral discourse is fixed through writing. In oral discourse the speaker can directly point to what is being talked about or discussed. In oral discourse both the speaker and the hearer have

> the possibility of showing the thing referred to as a member of the situation common to both [of them] ... This situation surrounds the dialogue, and its landmarks can all be shown by a gesture ... Or it can be designated in an ostensive manner by the discourse itself through the oblique reference of those indicators which include the demonstratives, the adverbs of time and place, and the tenses of the verbs. Finally they can be described in such a definite way that one, and only one, thing may be identified within the common framework of reference.[101]

However, because of the effect of the inscription of oral discourse, there is an absence of ostensive pointers which were available in oral discourse.[102] "It is this

---

[100] RICOEUR, *Interpretation Theory*, 31.

[101] RICOEUR, *Interpretation Theory*, 34.

[102] "In the same manner that the text frees its meaning from the tutelage of the mental intention, it frees its reference from the limits of situational reference." RICOEUR, *Interpretation Theory*, 36.

grounding of reference in the dialogical situation that is shattered by writing."[103]

Ricoeur rhetorically asks and responds: "Does this mean that this eclipse of reference, in either the ostensive or descriptive sense, amounts to a sheer abolition of all reference? No. My contention is that discourse cannot fail to be about something."[104] When Ricoeur says that every text refers to something, he is saying that every text potentially has the ability to make truth claims about reality. It is the text itself which must take over the signs and signals of oral discourse to refer to this "something."

Ricoeur shows that this objective side of interpreting a text may be taken in two different ways. "We may mean the 'what' of discourse or the 'about what' of discourse. The 'what' of discourse is its 'sense,' and the 'about what' is its 'reference'."[105] In other words, the "sense" of a sentence, or a larger lexical unit, is determined by virtue of what the unit actually says. Sense, therefore is immanent to the text, and "objective in the sense of the ideal."[106] Reference, on the other hand, is what the text is about. However, this ultimate reference of the text is dependent on the sense of the text and is constructed by it.

Objectivity with respect to any interpretation of Juan's *Cántico* is thus safeguarded through the backdrop of the immanent sense of the text. The sense of the *Cántico is* accessible through the poem itself. The ideal meaning is what is preserved in the act of emplotment and, therefore, provides the basis for the objectivity and normative interpretation of the text. Ideal meaning inscribed through the structure of Juan's *Cántico* provides the basis for the interaction between the

---

[103] RICOEUR, *Interpretation Theory*, 35.

[104] RICOEUR, *Interpretation Theory*, 36.

[105] RICOEUR, *Interpretation Theory*, 19. For a discussion of this same point which also includes the function of metaphor in the dynamic see, RICOEUR, "Metaphor and the Central Problem of Hermeneutics," 167. The distinction between "sense" and "reference" Ricoeur has adapted from the mathematician Gottlob Frege in his famous article "Ueber Sinn und Bedeutung." which was translated into English as "On Sense and Reference."

[106] RICOEUR, *Interpretation Theory*, 20.

content of the text and any interpretation of its ultimate reference ascribed to it.[107] Therefore, we see the necessity of an adequate exegesis of the text in order to unearth the "ideal structure" of the sense. Exegesis of the text sets up this dialectic between sense and reference.

It is not the sense of a text which can make truth claims vis-à-vis reality. Rather, it is the text's ultimate reference which can say something about the world which can be verified. For example, the sentence, "Birds do not fly." makes sense, that is, the sentence is grammatically correct, but on the basis of its *ultimate reference*, its claim to reflect some aspect of the real world, this statement is false. What then, is the text ultimately about? Language has this peculiar capacity to refer to something else other than what is immanent, or ostensively referred to, in the text.

It is this ultimate "something else" *in front of* the text which Ricoeur refers to as the world-of-the-text. However, this "something else" can only be referenced by what is written, i.e. by what is said in the text. "The world of the text designates the reference of the work of discourse, not what is said, but about what it is said. Hence the issue of the text is the object of hermeneutics. And the issue of the text is the world the text unfolds before itself."[108] The world-of-the-text is therefore that world to which the ultimate reference of the text points or configures, composes or produces. Ricoeur explains this further: "By this I mean that what is finally to be understood in a text is not the author or his presumed intention, nor is it the immanent structure or structures of the text, but rather the sort of world intended beyond the text as its reference. In this regard, the alternative 'either the intention or the structure' is vain. For the reference of the text is what I call the issue of the text or the world of the text."[109] That is to say that the semantic content of the text (its sense) projects beyond itself some authentic structure of human existence.

---

[107] RICOEUR, *Interpretation Theory*, 20.

[108] RICOEUR, "Toward a Hermeneutic of the Idea of Revelation," 23.

[109] RICOEUR, "Toward a Hermeneutic of the Idea of Revelation," 23.

186

This is the ultimate reference of the text.[110]

Sense is thus "spiritualized" to construct this world-of-the-text. Reference, therefore, "expresses the movement in which language transcends itself. In other words, the sense correlates the identification function and the predicative function within the sentence, and the reference relates language to the world. It is another name for discourse's claim to be true."[111] The ultimate role of language is, therefore, its capacity to unearth a new human condition of being-in-the-world through the construction of the world-of-the-text.

The possible world which the *Cántico* constructs is based on Juan's poem about two lovers and their relationship. Juan used certain symbols, metaphors, and linguistic devices to construct the world in which the lovers live. This is the sense of the text. Many helpful exegetical studies have already been done on the *Cántico* to reveal this level of the text. A significant number of these references have been cited in the literature survey of Chapter One.

Particularly efficacious in the construction of the world-of-the-text is the unique accomplishment of the poetic function of discourse and its use of metaphorical reference.[112] How does poetic discourse use metaphorical reference?

---

[110] See a very concise and clear account of Ricoeur's central hermeneutical category "the world-of-the-text" in RICOEUR, "The Hermeneutical Function of Distanciation," 140-142.

[111] RICOEUR, *Interpretation Theory*, 20.

[112] Ricoeur speaks of the "poetic function" of discourse as opposed to a "poetic genre" or a "mode of poetic discourse." See RICOEUR, "Toward a Hermeneutic of the Idea of Revelation," 23 ff. Ricoeur's major work on the role of metaphor is Paul RICOEUR, *The Rule of Metaphor: Multidisciplinary Studies of the Creation of Meaning in Language*, trans. Robert Czerny with Cathleen McLaughlin and John Costello, Toronto: University of Toronto Press, 1977. In *Rule of Metaphor* Ricoeur demonstrates that fundamentally there is a *linguistic* imagination which generates and regenerates meaning through the activity of metaphoricity: language undergoes creative transformations to create new meaning in life. (The original title, *La Métaphore vive*, is far more suggestive of this direction of Ricoeur's thought than its English translation.) For our purposes see in particular Study 7 in Ibid., "Metaphor and Reference," 216-256. Ricoeur states: "It may be, indeed, that the metaphorical statement is precisely the one that points out most clearly this relationship between suspended reference and displayed reference. Just as the metaphorical statement captures its sense as metaphorical midst the ruins of the literal sense, it also achieves its reference upon the ruins of what might be called (in symmetrical fashion) its literal reference. If it is true that literal sense and metaphorical sense are distinguished and articulated within an interpretation, so too it is within an interpretation that a second-level reference, which is properly the metaphorical

"As a first approximation, we may say that the poetic function points to the obliterating of the ordinary referential function, at least if we identify it with the capacity to describe familiar objects of perception or the objects which science alone determines by means of its standards of measurement. Poetic discourse suspends this descriptive function. It does not directly augment our knowledge of objects."[113] The poetic function of language obliterates primary reference to liberate access to "a more primitive, more originary function, which may be called a second order reference."[114] Ricoeur believes that poetic language, and poetic language alone, is capable of restoring the human subject to a participation in that profound level of reality which "precedes our capacity to oppose ourselves to things taken as objects opposed to a subject. Hence the function of poetic discourse is to bring about this emergence of a depth-structure of belonging-to amid the ruins of descriptive discourse."[115]

> The power of the text to open a dimension of reality implies in principle a recourse against any given reality and thereby the possibility of a critique of the real. It is in poetic discourse that this subversive power is most alive. The strategy of this discourse involves holding two moments in equilibrium: suspending the reference of ordinary language and releasing a second order reference, which is another name for what we have designated ... as the world opened up by the work. In the case of poetry, fiction is the

reference, is set free by means of the suspension of the first-level reference." Ibid., 221. See also Ibid., *Interpretation Theory*, 45-69.

[113] RICOEUR, "Toward a Hermeneutic of the Idea of Revelation," 23.

[114] RICOEUR, "Toward a Hermeneutic of the Idea of Revelation," 24.

[115] RICOEUR, "Toward a Hermeneutic of the Idea of Revelation," 24. As Ricoeur says elsewhere: "Poetic language also speaks of reality, but it does so at another level than does scientific language. It does not show us a world already there, as does descriptive or didactic language. In effect, ... the ordinary reference of language is abolished by the natural strategy of poetic discourse. But in the very measure that this first-order reference is abolished, another power of speaking the world is liberated, although at another level of reality. This level is that which Husserlian phenomenology has designated as the *Lebenswelt* and which Heidegger has called "being-in-the-world." It is an eclipsing of the objective manipulable world, an illumining of the life-world, of non-manipulable world, which seems to me to be the fundamental ontological import of poetic language. ... It is the heuristic fiction which bears the function of discovery in poetic language." Paul RICOEUR, "Biblical Hermeneutics," in *Semeia: Experimental Journal for Biblical Criticism*, 4 (1975), 87.

path of redescription; or to speak as Aristotle does in the *Poetics*, the creation of a *mythos*, of a "fable," is the path of mimēsis, of creative imitation.[116]

The poetic function has this power since it suspends ostensive reference to reach into this primordial ground of human existence and reality.

At this level "the poetic function incarnates a concept of truth that escapes the definition by adequation as well as the criteria of falsification and verification. Here truth no longer means verification, but manifestation, i.e. letting what shows itself be."[117] What "shows" is what Ricoeur has referred to above as the world-of-the-text.[118] Through the poetic function of discourse what shows itself is a proposed world mediated by the world-of-the-text, a world which an individual may inhabit and wherein one can project one's own possibilities.[119] This is the connection between the world-of-the-text and the real world: through the world-of-the-text a *possible* world is manifest which can in fact be lived in by the reader.[120] Informative, descriptive, and didactic discourse is suspended by poetic discourse to allow "the world of our originary rootedness to appear."[121] Through the poetic disclosure of everyday existence wrought by Juan's *Cántico*, the power of the opaque depths of ordinary human acting reveal the fundamental aspects of reality.

---

[116] Paul RICOEUR, "Hermeneutics and the Critique of Ideology," in *The Hermeneutic Tradition: From Ast to Ricoeur*, ed. Gayle L. Ormiston and Alan D. Schrift, (Albany: State University of New York Press, 1990), 326.

[117] RICOEUR, "Toward a Hermeneutic of the Idea of Revelation," 25.

[118] Each literary genre has a different way of "showing" the world.

[119] RICOEUR, "Toward a Hermeneutic of the Idea of Revelation," 25.

[120] "May we also not say, ... that the poetic world is just as hypothetical a space as is the mathematical order in relation to any given world? The poet, in short, operates through language in a hypothetical realm. In an extreme form we might even say that the poetic project is one of destroying the world as we ordinarily take it for granted." RICOEUR, *Interpretation Theory*, 61.

[121] RICOEUR, "Toward a Hermeneutic of the Idea of Revelation," 26.

The root of this linguistic disclosure of being[122] is especially made possible through the destruction of ostensive references by metaphorical reference as we already saw in Chapter Two. Through the metaphoric process, the literal meaning of the text is opened to a deeper meaning.[123] The semantic innovation construed by the split-reference of metaphor moves the reader from the level of the literal to that of the figurative, from the level of *is* to the level of *is like*.[124] Ricoeur correlates *seeing-as* through the metaphor with *being-as* in reality.[125]

Ricoeur constructs this evaluation of metaphorical discourse based on his theory that reality is essentially linguistical. Through language we participate in Being, and Being is focused in language. Through metaphorical language models of reality are constructed that cause Being to spring forth, that is, be-present in the here and now. Consequently, metaphors are not mere decorations in a poetic text, but are the central vehicle by which the meaning of concrete human experiences, and

---

[122] Double meaning, the condition of the metaphoric process, is the "means of detecting a condition of being." See, RICOEUR, "The Problem of Double Meaning as Hermeneutic Problem and as Semantic Problem," in *The Conflict of Interpretations: Essays in Hermeneutics*, ed. Don Ihde, trans. Willis Domingo et al. (Evanston: Northwestern University Press), 1974, 66-67.

[123] For Ricoeur metaphoric language is closely tied to his theory of symbols. "Metaphor is just the linguistic procedure--that bizarre form of predication--within which the symbolic power is deposited. The symbols remains a two-dimensional phenomenon to the extent that the semantic face refers back to the non-semantic one. The symbol is bound in a way that the metaphor is not. Symbols have roots. Symbols plunge us into the shadowy experience of power. Metaphors are just the linguistic surface of symbols, and they owe their power to relate the semantic surface to the presemantic surface in the depths of human experience to the two-dimensional structure of the symbol." RICOEUR, *Interpretation Theory*, 69.

[124] RICOEUR, *Interpretation Theory*, 68. The strength in Ricoeur's position on this point does not end with "mere" poetic description which flounders for words to describe a particular experience. Rather, Ricoeur's theory of metaphor consists in the very metamorphosis of reality through the construction of the text. The articulation of a "metaphorical reference on the metaphorical sense cannot be clothed with a full ontological meaning unless we go so far as to metaphorize the verb 'to be' itself and recognize in 'being-as' the correlate of 'seeing-as,' in which is summed up the work of metaphor." RICOEUR, *Time and Narrative*, 1:80.

[125] "Poetic language does not say literally what things are, but what they are like. It is in this oblique fashion that it says what they are." RICOEUR, "Biblical Hermeneutics," 88.

the metamorphosis of that experience are augmented, retained, and revealed.[126] The tension created at the literal level by metaphoric innovation moves the reader to the non-signified level of meaning of the text where the text projects images of possible new modes of being-in-the-world.[127] Therefore, metaphor, in the peculiarity of its reference and the impossibility of its literal interpretation, redescribes reality[128] and opens for the reader a new way of perceiving reality and of being-in-the-world.[129] Poetic texts are the arena, par excellence, for this type of discourse.

Since the *Cántico* is a poem replete with metaphors and symbols, its reference is also metaphorical. The primacy of this type of reference within poetic discourse calls into question the primacy of the doctrinal reference which has traditionally been given Juan's *Cántico*. The *Cántico*, as a poem, has a specific kind of reference which is *different* from the commentary on it.[130] It is not conceptual knowledge which is the primary reference of poetic discourse, but, rather, the construction of a possibility of being-in-the-world suggested by the text and effected

[126] "The poem is bound by what it creates, if the suspension of ordinary discourse and its didactic intention assumes an urgent character for the poet, this is just because the reduction of the referential values of ordinary discourse is the negative condition that allows new configurations expressing the meaning of reality to be brought to language. Through those new configurations new ways of being in the world, of living there, and of projecting our innermost possibilities onto it are also brought to language. ... What binds poetic discourse, then, is the need to bring to language modes of being that ordinary vision obscures or even represses. And in this sense, no one is more free than the poet. We might even say that the poet's speech is freed from the ordinary vision of the world only because he makes himself free for the new being which he has to bring to language." RICOEUR, *Interpretation Theory*, 60.

[127] RICOEUR, *Interpretation Theory*, 55.

[128] "The entire strategy of poetic discourse plays on this point: it seeks the abolition of the reference by means of self-destruction of the meaning of metaphorical statements, the self-destruction being made manifest by an impossible literal interpretation." RICOUER, *Rule of Metaphor*, 230.

[129] RICOEUR, *Rule of Metaphor*, 230.

[130] The poetry-prose relationship will be investigated in detail as the subject of the last chapter of this dissertation (Chapter Seven). The discontinuity of narrative reference with respect to poetic reference will be the main criterion used to affirm the diversity of interpretations possible for Juan's *Cántico* within a hermeneutical framework.

through "mood."[131]

Metaphor creates an indirect reference described as a particular mood, affect, or feeling. Ricoeur describes this reference as a "'state of soul' ... a way of finding or sensing oneself in the midst of reality."[132] The indirect reference of mood provides access to a level of reality other than the conceptual.[133] Mood is virtual in the text, a part of the sense of the text. However, this mood becomes actual in the work of reading and is productive in the reader's own life.[134] Interpretation, in this context, results in the possibility of a new vision of reality which is itself this affective level of which I am speaking.[135] This is to refute the error of logical positivism which holds that emotion has only an inside and not an outside.[136]

---

[131] "The conjunction of *muthos* and *mimêsis* is the work of all poetry. Let us recall Northrop Frye's linking of the poetic and the hypothetical. Now what is this 'hypothetical'? According to his perspective, poetic language, with its 'internal' and not 'outward' turn, constructs a mood, which has no existence outside the poem itself: this is what receives form from the poem as an arrangement of signs. ... The feeling articulated by the poem is no less heuristic than the tragic tale. The 'internal' movement of the poem, therefore, could not be opposed purely and simply to 'outward' movement. What it signifies is only the disconnection of customary reference, the elevation of feeling to the hypthetical [sic], and the creation of an affective fiction. The paradox of the poetic can be summed up entirely in this, that the elevation of feeling to fiction is the condition of its mimetic use. Only a feeling transformed into myth can open and discover the world." RICOEUR, *Rule of Metaphor*, 245.

[132] RICOEUR, *Rule of Metaphor*, 229.

[133] "If this heuristic function of mood is so difficult to recognize, it is doubtless because 'representation' has become the sole route to knowledge and the model of every relationship between subject and object. Yet feeling has an ontological status different from relationship at a distance; it makes for participation in things." RICOEUR, *Rule of Metaphor*, 245-6.

[134] "It would seem that the enigma of metaphorical discourse is that it 'invents' in both senses of the word: what it creates, it discovers; and what it finds, it invents. What must be understood, therefore, is the interconnection of three themes. In the metaphorical discourse of poetry referential power is linked to the eclipse of ordinary reference; the creation of heuristic fiction is the road to redescription; and reality brought to language unites manifestation and creation." RICOEUR, *Rule of Metaphor*, 239.

[135] "The suspension of reference in the sense defined by the norms of descriptive discourse is the negative condition of the appearance of a more fundamental mode of reference whose explication is the task of interpretation." RICOEUR, *Rule of Metaphor*, 229.

[136] "This is why the opposition between exterior and interior ceases to be valid here. Not being internal, feeling in like measure is not subjective. Metaphorical reference links rather ... 'poetic schemata of inner life' and 'the objectivity of poetic textures.' ... It is enough to say for now that the poetic verb metaphorically 'schematizes' feeling or emotions only in depicting 'textures of the world,'

192

Ricoeur, following Mikel Dufrenne, says that "To feel is to experience a feeling as a property of the object, not as a state of my being."[137] Feelings are not merely subjective, they are also a way of knowing reality. Ricoeur, therefore, equates "feeling" with an experience of learning.[138] Through the dynamic of poetic images and symbols, through the interplay of a *network of metaphors* which suspend the world of ostensive references, a new "state of soul" is possible through a hermeneutical reading of Juan's *Cántico*.[139]

What Ricoeur is referring to here is the concept of "metaphorical truth."[140] This truth can be described in the following way: "Poetic feeling itself ... develops an experience of reality in which invention and discovery cease being opposed and where creation and revelation coincide."[141] This is the power of the metaphor, but in order to exercise this power it must sacrifice its claim for truth value normally understood within the positivist tradition.[142] Without sensitivity to this

'non-human physiognomies,' which become actual portraits of our inner life,' which would be equivalent to those 'moods' that, for Northrop Frye, substitute for every referent." RICOEUR, *Rule of Metaphor*, 246.

[137] Mikel DUFRENNE, *The Phenomenology of Aesthetic Experience*, trans. from French by E.S. Carey et al., (Evanston, Ill.: Northwestern University Press, 1973), 442, quoted in RICOEUR, *Rule of Metaphor*, 227.

[138] "Learning, concluding, recognizing the form--here we have the skeleton of meaning for the pleasure found in imitation or representation." RICOEUR, *Time and Narrative*, 1:40.

[139] Colin Thompson describes the overall "mood" developed in the *Cántico* as mysterious: "A mood of mystery pervades the *Cántico*, and while there is a richness of language in many stanzas, there is also a stammering, uncertain language, imprecise, indistinct, which is deliberatley employed to help in creating this mood." THOMPSON, *The Poet and the Mystic*, 91.

[140] RICOEUR, *Rule of Metaphor*, 254-6.

[141] RICOEUR, *Rule of Metaphor*, 246.

[142] Paul RICOEUR, "Philosophy and Religious Language," *Journal of Religion* 54 (1974), 71-72. Elsewhere Ricoeur says: "The question is precisely whether poetic language does not break through to a pre-scientific, ante-predicative level, where the very notions of fact, object, reality, and truth, as deliminated by epistemology, are *called into question* by this very means of the vacillation of literal reference." Ibid., *Rule of Metaphor*, 254. See also Ibid., "Philosophical Hermeneutics and Biblical Hermeneutics," in *From Text to Action*, 89-101; Ibid., "Toward a Hermeneutic of the Idea of Revelation," 1-37. Ricoeur asks: "Do we actually know what 'reality,' 'world,' and 'truth' signify?" Ibid., *Rule of Metaphor*, 221.

dynamic, certain consequences result in the way the *Cántico* is interpreted. For example, Eulogio Pacho takes Juan de la Cruz's statement concerning the content of the *Cántico* literally: the *Cántico* deals "with the exchange of love between the soul and Christ, its Bridegroom."[143] The soul-Bridegroom relationship is metaphorical and thus we are dealing here with metaphorical, not ostensive reference. Neither the soul, Christ, or Bridegroom (in this context) can be referred to in a real way, that is, as real persons. But Pacho says that without this literal affirmation the *Cántico* is pure "rhetoric." This in turn leads him to affirm that the *Cántico*'s main "message" concerns the soul's journey to union with God via the way of purgation, illumination and union.[144]

However, according to Ricoeur, the truth of metaphorical statements is that which is enlivened in the life of the reader, rather than that subject to the scientific criterion of verification.[145] Reality is drawn out of hiddeness through metaphorical discourse which is revealed in metaphorical truth-being-present through mood in the life of a human being. This poetic approach opens the *Cántico* because metaphorical reference at work within the text makes its meaning unstable. This dialectic, in turn, is productive of meaning in the life of the reader since new possibilities for the text are opened up in changing interpretive contexts. To interpret the *Cántico* too quickly within known theological categories closes the text, as we just saw with Pacho, and does not allow its metaphorical reference to effect *new* meaning.

---

[143] "Empeñando su palabra, el místico poeta asegura que el lector está ante unas «canciones espirituales entre el alma--de fray Juan--y el esposo Cristo». Sacadas de ese reino del espíritu no tienen sentido, son pura retórica." Eulogio PACHO, "Cántico espiritual," in *Introducción a la lectura de San Juan de la Cruz*, ed. A. Garcia Simón, Valladolid: Junta de Castilla y León Consejería de Cultura y Turismo, 1991, 469.

[144] "Como en otros escritos, intenta encajarla en los clásicos estados o vías de principiantes, aprovechados y perfectos: vía purificativa, iluminativa y unitiva." PACHO, "Cántico espiritual," 479. Further on he says: "El *Cántico* desarrolla todo el proceso de la vida espiritual como crecimiento ininterrumpido en el amor divino. En torno a ese eje gira todo lo demás: un programa completo de vida cristiana en la totalidad de su recorrido." Ibid., 481.

[145] "The central argument is that, with respect to the revelation of reality, metaphor is to poetic language what the model is to scientific language." RICOEUR, *Rule of Metaphor*, 240.

Ricoeur's textual hermeneutics is thus clearly a hermeneutics not of epistemological verifications but rather of praxis which challenge the ordinarily understood truth value of poetic discourse. Each mode of discourse must be seen as having its own particular claim to truth value. It is this principle which I will develop further in Chapter Seven to suggest the radical discontinuity between Juan's poem, the *Cántico*, and his subsequent commentary on it. We can thus appreciate Juan's poem for its poetic form of discourse and the possibility of a plurality of interpretations (or in the context of the previous discussion, a *plurality of showings*) through contemporary readings.

Juan's *Cántico*, happily freed from ostensive references because of its poetic function and the use of metaphoric reference, is open to the possibility of "speaking" to new and different historical and cultural situations through the reference of the text itself.[146] As Ricoeur relates, the poetic form breaks away from its originary setting to become alive in other settings:

> An essential characteristic of a literary work, and of a work of art in general, is that it transcends its own psycho-sociological conditions of production and thereby opens itself to an unlimited series of readings, themselves situated in different socio-cultural conditions. In short, the text must be able, from the sociological as well as the psychological point of view, to "decontextualize" itself in such a way that it can be "recontextualised" in a new situation -- as accomplished, precisely, by the act of reading.[147]

Juan's *Cántico* can therefore be read meaningfully (interpreted) in the twentieth century as it was in the sixteenth because of the text's innovative metaphorical references.

The dialectic of sense and reference, therefore, has provided us with three significant characteristics of written texts which are important for the

---

[146] "The literary work through the structure proper to it displays a world only under the condition that the reference of descriptive discourse is suspended. Or to put it another way, discourse in the literary work sets out its denotation as a second-level denotation, by means of the suspension of the first-level denotation of discourse." RICOEUR, *Rule of Metaphor*, 221.

[147] RICOEUR, "The Hermeneutical Function of Distanciation," 139.

hermeneutical interpretation of Juan de la Cruz's *Cántico*. First, this dialectic affirms a pole of objectivity which safeguards limits within which the *Cántico* may be interpreted. This pole is grounded in the immanent sense of the text captured in its linguistic structure.

Second, we have seen that Ricoeur's use of the dialectic of sense and reference also undermines the primacy of authorial intentionality which we have already examined through the distanciation of the author from the text. The notion of an absolute text which can be finally and completely "understood" is also destroyed by this dialectic. The true meaning of a text cannot be equated with what the author intended to say, nor can a text be completely objectified. With the world-of-the-text meeting the horizon of the world-of-the-reader, new and varied meanings may be ascribed to the text as the audience, historical and cultural setting, or appreciation of the content of particular words, changes. This quality allows us to understand why Juan's *Cántico* has remained relevant and meaningful for countless numbers of people throughout history, and in different cultural and linguistic settings.

The third, and very significant affirmation resulting from the dialectic of sense and reference, is the emergence of the world-of-the-text which unfolds *in front of* the text as a result of the split-reference of metaphorical discourse in the poem. The category of the world-of-the-text affirms that written discourse is extra-linguistic, that is, it ultimately refers beyond itself to reality through the linguistic construction of mood. The following question thus surfaces: What might be the "reference" of the *Cántico* constructed by its "sense"? Is the reference constructed by the sense of Juan's *Cántico* only "doctrinal reference"? Based on Ricoeur's appreciation of the split-reference of metaphorical discourse, I am led to affirm that Juan's *Cántico* can both speak to doctrinal considerations and speak to other truth claims in the construction of the world-of-the-text. The notion of the split-reference of metaphor will be explored further in Chapter Seven when I examine more specifically the relationship between the poem and the commentary from the perspective of Ricoeur's hermeneutical phenomenology. For now I can say that the language of "spiritual marriage," as used by Juan in his *Cántico* and elsewhere in the western mystical tradition, is not ostensive reference, that is, it is not descriptive language. Rather it is metaphorical reference which posits a way of being-in-the-world. The question of the *Cántico*'s form surfaces once again in this context.

The mistaken assumption is that the form of discourse has little to do with "what the text is about." Literary form is often neutralized or not included in the interpretive task in a simple yet naive attempt to extract the theological content of discourse from the examination of isolated words or fragments of discourse. We have seen how this is often true of the ascetical-theological method of interpreting the *Cántico* examined in Chapter One. However, Ricoeur asserts that what announces itself in discourse is qualified by the *form* of the announcement.[148] We saw from the above discussion on the poetic function of discourse that poetry is unique in its capacity to obliterate the world of ostensive reference in order to open up the more opaque depths of reality. We can readily affirm that the *Cántico* is a poetic text, but we are led to do further exegetical work in order to more specifically describe the genre of the *Cántico*, which may further orient us to its ultimate reference. This work will be part of our investigations in the next chapter.

3.5 Summary

We have seen that the full meaning of discourse becomes possible only when it is ultimately committed to a written form. In Romantic hermeneutics the emphasis was placed on the ability to get behind the mind of the author and render his or her thought meaningfully present in the present. However, this prospect is no longer possible once we embrace the consequences of the communicative dynamic which is radically changed through writing. Distanciation and objectification by structure provide new access to a world of meaning not attainable through an exclusive dependence on the intention of the author. Instead, ultimate reality is what is referenced through the poetic function. The sense of the

---

[148] RICOEUR, "Toward a Hermeneutic of the Idea of Revelation," 16. (emphasis mine)

text, safeguarded through its structure, limits the valid interpretations. Yet these interpretations in themselves are countless since, ultimately, meaning is an event in the life of the reader.

The mediatory function of mimesis$_2$ has been emphasized in the above presentation. The act of emplotment mediates between the existential meaning-event of discourse within time and its future appropriation by the reading subject. Emplotment virtually "fixes" discourse, preserving its meaning while the event of speaking falls into silence. What is preserved in mimesis$_2$ through the text is not the event of speaking but rather the "said" of speaking, its meaning.[149] It has been important to demonstrate the textuality of Juan's *Cántico* because it reveals how this meaning can be preserved and communicated over the temporal and cultural distance which separates the contemporary reader from Juan's sixteenth-century Spain. The textuality of a text shows that language can still be meaningful long after the original meaning-event, even though interpretation is required.

We saw, then, how writing separates meaning from the event of discourse. The preservation of the meaning of the event of discourse in the text also effects a distanciation which eludes the author's intention, and similarly, Juan's *Cántico* escapes both its original audience and its originary context. The *Cántico* thus becomes autonomous with respect to the intention of its author, its original audience, and the historical period in which it was written. Furthermore, rather than being an impoverishment of the text, distanciation was seen as an enrichment, since it makes the text virtually universally available. Juan's *Cántico* is now available to anybody that can read. The question surfaced whether the reference of the *Cántico* is doctrinal or something else. This is to ask the question: What is the *Cántico* about? It was concluded that the *Cántico* eludes the world of ostensive reference

---

[149] "What in effect does writing fix? Not the event of speaking, but the 'said' of speaking, where we understand by the 'said' of speaking that intentional exteriorization constitutive of the aim of discourse thanks to which the *sagen*, the saying, wants to become *Aus-sage*, the enunciation, the enunciated. In short, what we write, what we inscribe, is the noema of the speaking. It is the meaning of the speech event, not the event as event." RICOEUR, "The Model of the Text: Meaningful Action Considered as a Text," 146.

because it is immersed in a network of metaphorical reference which constructs potential new ways of being-in-the-world through the world-of-the-text. To interpret the *Cántico* as being exclusively a linear description of the classical spiritual itinerary resulting in the "spiritual marriage" has therefore been called into question.

However, there is a place in Ricoeur's interpretive theory where the descriptive or exegetical work on a text plays a role in constructing the world-of-the-text. This process surfaces the dialectic of *explanation* and *understanding*. Explanation describes the exegetical work characteristic of mimesis$_2$ whereas understanding concerns the dynamics involved when the reader appropriates the text in his or her life.

4. Conclusion

The autonomy of the text discussed previously gives rise to two possible poles in one's approach to the *Cántico*. "We can, as readers, remain in the suspense of the text, treating it as a worldless and authorless object; in this case, we explain the text in terms of its internal relations, its structures. On the other hand, we can lift the suspense and fulfill the text in speech, restoring it to living communication; in this case, we interpret the text."[150] The first type of approach to the text Ricoeur refers to as the "explanation" of the text; the second is what happens when the text is truly "understood." It is within this dialectic of explanation and understanding that the hermeneutical framework for Juan's *Cántico* is being built: there is no understanding without explanation and no explanation without understanding.

As we already know, an initial reading of Juan's *Cántico* could reveal the text's "interception of all the relations to a world that can be pointed out and to subjectivities that can converse."[151] This reading would explain the various inter-relations within the text as well as its inter-textuality, the flow and development of

---

[150] RICOEUR, "What is a Text? Explanation and Understanding," 113.

[151] RICOEUR, "What is a Text? Explanation and Understanding," 113.

its story, and its literary uniqueness. Explanation tends to sort out the "facts" of the text. Within this explanatory approach the reader is confined within the "place of the text."[152] "On the basis of this choice, the text has no outside but only an inside; it has no transcendent aim, unlike speech that is addressed to someone about something."[153] Ricoeur affirms that this structural approach to the text is legitimate and constitutes the primary mode of investigation of linguistic inquiry.[154] "Thus arises the possibility of an explanatory attitude in regard to the text."[155] This explanatory mode gives rise to the determination of the genre of the text, its specific stylistic features whereby we can identify the individuality of an author, as well as the author's innovative production. We have already seen the importance of these investigations in the discussion on "Schematization, Traditionality, and Innovation" earlier in this chapter.

The explanation of Juan's *Cántico* would provide the panorama of the work, the movements of the text which inform the reader of the "logic of action" that "together constitute the structural continuity" of the poem.[156] Explanation includes the constitution of an integral and critical text, the determination of the meaning of individual words, and an appreciation of the historical times in which Juan lived. At this level of reading we can say that we have explained Juan's *Cántico* but that we have not yet interpreted it. We have already encountered this distinction in Chapter One concerning various methodological approaches to the *Cántico* which analyze the text at this level. These methods constitute the analytical moment of interpretation in Ricoeur's theory, that is, the objectification of the text. But, it must be stressed,

---

[152] RICOEUR, "What is a Text? Explanation and Understanding," 113.

[153] RICOEUR, "What is a Text? Explanation and Understanding," 113.

[154] In affirming this "explanatory" approach to the text Ricoeur benefits from Saussure's distinction between the system of signs that constitute language (*langue*) as opposed to living speech (*parole*). RICOEUR, "The Hermeneutical Function of Distanciation,"133.

[155] RICOEUR, "What is a Text? Explanation and Understanding," 113.

[156] RICOEUR, "What is a Text? Explanation and Understanding," 116.

explanation is already a product of our understanding of the text. We read a text with a certain "horizon of meaning" before us which already affects how we explain it. This, in turn, affects how we understand it.

The aim of understanding a text is to "lift the suspense [of the text] and fulfill the text in present speech. The text calls to be read. It is this second attitude that is the *real* aim of reading."[157] This approach to the text brings meaning back into the realm of living experience.[158] "If reading is possible, it is indeed because the text is not closed in on itself but opens out onto other things. To read is, on any hypothesis, to conjoin a new discourse to the discourse of the text. This conjunction of discourses reveals, in the very constitution of the text, an original capacity for renewal that is its open character. Interpretation is the concrete outcome of conjunction and renewal."[159]

Understanding the *Cántico* therefore culminates in the appropriation of the text, that is, self-interpretation of the reading subject who "thenceforth understands himself better, understands himself differently, or simply begins to understand himself."[160] This second mode of reading identifies understanding of the *Cántico* with some degree of self-understanding. "In short, in hermeneutical reflection--or in reflective hermeneutics--the constitution of the *self* is contemporaneous with the constitution of *meaning*."[161] Understanding a text is therefore not an end in itself. A text "mediates the relation to himself of a subject who, in the short circuit of immediate reflection, does not find the meaning of his

---

[157] RICOEUR, "What is a Text? Explanation and Understanding," 118. (emphasis mine)

[158] "Thus, in living speech, the *ideal* sense of what is said turns toward the *real* reference, toward that 'about which' we speak. At the limit, this real reference tends to merge with an ostensive designation where speech rejoins the gesture of pointing. Sense fades into reference and the latter into the act of showing." RICOEUR, "What is a Text? Explanation and Understanding," 108.

[159] RICOEUR, "What is a Text? Explanation and Understanding," 118.

[160] RICOUER, "What is a Text? Explanation and Understanding," 118.

[161] RICOEUR, "What is a Text? Explanation and Understanding," 119.

own life."[162]   To understand a text is to allow the text to mediate personal meaning in life. Through the act of reading meaning is therefore joined back together with the event of discourse.

Mediating the dialectic between explaining the text and understanding the text is the significant role of exegesis. It is the exegesis of the text which assists the reader in the dialectic of explanation and understanding. Understanding a text is therefore not mere reproduction of the text in the life of the reader, but is an original meaning-event in the life of the reader informed by a methodical analysis of the text.

I have already demonstrated how a text initially has only a "sense" constructed through the literariness of the work, that is, "the immanent pattern of discourse."[163]   To explain the text is to unveil the surface semantics of the text. This is what is done through exegesis. The text itself uses particular literary techniques to place the reader along the path of its meaning, that is, within the world of its depth semantics which Ricoeur calls the world-of-the-text.[164]   Recall that it is the "sense" of a text which constructs the world-of-the-text through the act of reading. Understanding of a text is thus mediated by explanation and explanation is mediated by understanding.[165]

Ricoeur assigns a particular role to the explanatory analysis of a text

---

[162]   RICOUER, "What is a Text? Explanation and Understanding," 119.

[163]   RICOEUR, "Metaphor and the Central Problem of Hermeneutics," 171.

[164]   RICOEUR, "What is a Text? Explanation and Understanding," 121.

[165]   Ricoeur parallels this structural analysis of a text in the process of interpretation with the analysis of metaphors which are subjected to a similar dialectic. "In both cases, the construction rests upon 'clues' contained in the text itself. A clue serves as a guide for a specific construction, in that it contains at once a permission and a prohibition; it excludes unsuitable constructions and allows those which give more meaning to the same words. Second, in both cases, one construction can be said to be more probably than another, but not more truthful. The more probably is that which, on the one hand, takes account of the greatest number of facts furnished by the text, including its potential connotations, and on the other hand, offers a qualitatively better convergence between the features which it takes into account." RICOEUR, "Metaphor and the Central Problem of Hermeneutics," 175-176

which has come to be known as structural analysis.[166] Through an analysis of the structures in the text, that is, the interplay of characters, transitions in the text, and so on, structural analysis submits the reader to what is actually in the text; it supports the entry into the objective content of the text. Semiotic structures, therefore, displace the primacy of the intention of the author of the text, as well as refutes the accusation of a subjective reading. However, beyond the depth analysis of the text developed by the structuralist method, Ricoeur is aware that the question of the appropriation (understanding) of the text remains.

> If ... we regard structural analysis as a stage--and a necessary one-- between a naive and a critical interpretation, between a surface and a depth interpretation, then it seems possible to situate explanation and interpretation along a unique *hermeneutical arc* and to integrate the opposed attitudes of explanation and understanding within an overall conception of reading as the recovery of meaning.[167]

> The reader is thus invited to follow the path of thought opened up by

---

[166] "It must be stressed that the function of structural analysis is not to provide an objective knowledge of the text through application of a scientific methodology, but to disclose a diachronic kernel by means of achronic structures." CLARK, *Paul Ricoeur*, 97. Structural analysis, therefore, exposes the boundary situations of human existence which are operative within the text. RICOEUR, *Interpretation Theory*, 87.

[167] RICOEUR, "What is a Text? Explanation and Understanding," 121. Once again Ricoeur underlines here the fallacy of the primacy given to authorial intentionality in the interpretation of a text: "Now what we have just said about the depth semantics unveiled by the structural analysis of the text invites us to say that the intended meaning of the text is not essentially the presumed intention of the author, the lived experience of the writer, but rather what the text means for whoever complies with its injunction." Ibid., 121. An excellent summary of the historical development of structural analysis and its contribution toward the hermeneutical approach is given in RICOEUR, "Biblical Hermeneutics," (see especially pages 29-73). Concerning the limits of interpretation imposed on the text by structural analysis Ricoeur says: "The least thing to be said is that, after structuralism, it is no longer possible to connect a structural analysis either with an *historical* approach like Jeremias' one (even one rebaptized *historico-literary* as with Via), or with an *existential* approach, even under the complex headline of 'literary-existential analysis.' What collapses is precisely the *link* between historical and literary analysis and the *link* between literary and existential approaches." Ibid., 64. "Structuralism, to my mind, is a dead end the very moment when it treats any 'message' as the mere 'quotation' of its underlying 'code.' This claim alone makes structural method structuralist prejudice. Structuralism as ideology started with the reversal in the relation between code and message which makes the code essential and the message unessential. And it is because this step is taken that the text is killed as message *and* that no existential interpretation seems appropriate for a message which has been reduced to a pure epiphenomenon of the 'codes.' Only the way back from code to message may both do justice to the message as such *and* pave the way to the move from structure to process." Ibid., 65.

the semantics of the text, to "place oneself en route toward the *orient* of the text" supported by structural analysis.[168] This approach emphasizes that interpretat.on is not a subjective process of interpretation as an act *on* the text by the reader, but rather it is an objective process of interpretation that underlines the act *of* the text on the reader.[169] "What is interesting here is that interpretation, before being the act of the exegete, is the act of the text."[170] To interpret is to place oneself "in the meaning indicated by the relation of interpretation that the text itself supports."[171] But this meaning, this world-of-the-text, is not constructed by the text in isolation from the reader. The world-of-the-reader is also brought into confrontation with the text. Therefore, to understand the *Cántico* is not merely to reproduce its conceptual contents unearthed through exegesis, but to follow these toward their ultimate reference. We will set ourselves further along on that course with respect to Juan's *Cántico* in the following chapter when we actually examine the text of the *Cántico*.

In summary, then, mimesis$_2$ has brought us into confrontation with what it means to have available to us the text of Juan's *Cántico* and how its literariness affects the mediation of meaning. Although Juan's *Cántico* is a work resembling in many ways the biblical *Song of Songs*, I have suggested that it is an original work born from the interplay of tradition and innovation, as Ricoeur understands these terms; Juan's *Cántico* is not a reproduction nor a mirroring of the *Song*. The literariness of the text of Juan's *Cántico* has also called into question the

---

[168] RICOEUR, "What is a Text? Explanation and Understanding," 122. Elsewhere Ricoeur emphasis this dialectic between explanation and understanding: "Strictly speaking, explanation alone is methodical. Understanding is instead the nonmethodical moment that, in the sciences of interpretation, combines with the methodical moment of explanation. This moment precedes, accompanies, concludes, and thus *envelops* explanation. Explanation, in turn, *develops understanding analytically*." RICOEUR, "Explanation and Understanding," 142.

[169] RICOEUR, "What is a Text? Explanation and Understanding," 122.

[170] RICOEUR, "What is a Text? Explanation and Understanding," 122. "Hence interpretation is, ... the work of the *vox significativa per se ipsam aliquid significans, sive complexa, sive incomplexa.* Thus it is the noun, the verb, discourse in general, that interpret in the very process of signifying." Ibid., 122.

[171] RICOEUR, "What is a Text? Explanation and Understanding," 122.

relationship of *Cántico A* to *Cántico B*. Are the incongruencies of *Cántico A* really a roadblock to meaning that necessitated the redaction of *Cántico B*, or is there another way that the relationship between these two *Cánticos* can be understood? Although this question deserves further examination, to this point I have suggested that the aporia of *Cántico A* are precisely those literary elements which Ricoeur suggests are set to work by emplotment to convey meaning. *Cántico A*, as it stood, was found very meaningful by the nuns at Beas. Any attempt to neutralize these textual aporia through dogmatic conceptualization is a hindrance to understanding the text, even if this is done by the author.

Through Ricoeur's fourfold distanciation we have seen that the *Cántico* ultimately refers to its own "world," that is, the world-of-the-text, not the world of the author, nor the historical world within which the text arose. It is this world projected by Juan's *Cántico* which is to be existentially understood as a possible world in which the reader may live and project his or her own possibilities for living. The timeless world-of-the-text posits a potential mode of existing *within* time. It refigures reality positing a new way for the reading subject to complete the hermeneutical circle by joining together meaning and event through discourse. This is what is to be interpreted in Juan's *Cántico*: the world-of-the-text and its meaning as brought back into the realm of human action in a *new* existential situation. The exclusively doctrinal reference of the *Cántico* is thus brought into question.

To raise the question of the referential capacity of the *Cántico* intimates that its meaning and reference are not conveyed in the same way as in spoken discourse. In conversation, inflection of the voice and gestures produce meaning. Speech also makes use of ostensive reference through predication. Since posture, intonation, direct reference and so on, are not available in written discourse, there must be other ways to convey meaning which are present in the text in order to produce the world-of-the-text. Metaphorical reference in poetic discourse was seen as especially efficacious toward this end. Metaphorical reference obliterates the ordinary referential function of predication to reveal a secondary order of reference which configures the world-of-the-text. Therefore, a text cannot be understood simply by analysing it in terms of its constitutive elements. For example, Juan's *Cántico* cannot be reduced to a series of symbols which, by analogy, seem to outline the progression of the threefold classical spiritual journey of purgation, illumination, and union.

However, this is not to say that the linguistic elements and the various movements within Juan's *Cántico* are not significant in its interpretation. The possibility of following the story and the highly symbolic language of the *Cántico* are the conditions which open up the way for understanding the text. The genre of the *Cántico* must also be seen as an element which aids in understanding it, as well as being a linguistic classification. Furthermore, style bears the author's unique presence in the text, and the examination of the use of various linguistic tools in the text is an important part of the analysis of the text. The aporia present in the text are seen as especially efficacious in the mediation of meaning.

Interpretation of Juan's *Cántico* must take all these literary factors into consideration. This is to say that the door of entry to understanding Juan's *Cántico* includes explanation of these structural elements. But we also know that explanation is prompted and affected by an initial understanding of the text. It is this dialectic of explanation and understanding that makes productive the methodological approaches to Juan's *Cántico* which were outlined in Chapter One. Understanding of a text can be developed analytically. These various approaches all make significant contributions to the meaning of the text within the dialectic of explanation and understanding. A hermeneutical understanding of Juan's *Cántico* is achieved when the text is brought back into discourse, that is, into the living reality of a human life. The exegetical moment provides only part of the dynamic operative in understanding the *Cántico*. However, exegesis is necessary, and it is to a preliminary and general exegesis of the *Cántico* we now turn to help open up more questions when Juan's *Cántico* is placed within a hermeneutical framework.

CHAPTER FIVE

MIMESIS₂ AND THE TEXT OF THE *CÁNTICO*

1. Introduction

The previous chapter emphasized that the literary analysis of a poetic text is, in large part, a key to understanding the text. This is true since it is the sense of the text, available through various literary analyses of the text, which mediates meaning. I suggested in an introductory way that the literary genre, also part of the sense of a text, is an important indication of its meaning. Genre forges meaning into a literary form and hence insists that a specific meaning is linked to a specific form. Genre is the specific configuration of sense which opens up a specific type of reference. It is in the context of genre that sense is produced. Therefore, different text genres significantly impact the construction of the world-of-the-text. My focus in this chapter will be a more detailed examination of the literary genre of the *Cántico* as well as the impact of the structure of the *Cántico* on its meaning. An examination of the genre of the *Cántico* will stress the primacy of the poem itself in a hermeneutical interpretation. An examination of the structure of the *Cántico* will show that each of the *Cánticos* is, to a certain extent, a unique work. Each *Cántico* contributes toward the mediation of meaning in a different way.

A complete structural analysis of the *Cántico* is beyond the scope of this dissertation.[1] In order to situate the *Cántico* within a hermeneutical framework, an analysis of structure will be confined to one aspect only, that is, the dramatic structure of the *Cántico*. If metaphorical redescription is crucial to the projection of

---

[1] The basis and orientation of such an analysis could be found in one of Ricoeur's foundational discussions on genre and structure in RICOEUR, "Biblical Hermeneutics," 29-148. See especially the section on "Narrative Form," Ibid., 37-73. For a more extensive discussion on the *stage* which structuralism plays in Ricoeur's theory of interpretation see RICOEUR, "The Model of the Text: Meaningful Action Considered as a Text," 164-167.

the world-of-the-text and is contingent on dramatic structure, then a change in dramatic structure will support the thesis that each *Cántico* projects a different world-of-the-text. If the dramatic structure of each of the *Cánticos* is different, the need for a more complete structural analysis in a hermeneutical interpretation will be indicated. Such an analysis would be helpful if an actual interpretation of the *Cántico* were undertaken.

2. The Literary Genre of the *Cántico*

The role of literary genre in interpretation is not held to be important by all sanjuanist scholars. Some scholars see it as important, but do not give it a significant role in the interpretation of the poem. I will, therefore, review various positions concerning literary genre in sanjuanist scholarship, and describe its importance from a hermeneutical perspective before describing the genre of the *Cántico*.

The indication that literary form is merely incidental and does not directly impact the meaning of Juan's work is held by one of the preminent sanjuanist scholars, E. Allison Peers. Reflecting on the qualities of Juan's literary work he says:

> His style reflects his thought, but it reflects the style of no school and of no other writer whatsoever. This is natural enough, for thought and feeling were always uppermost in the Saint; style and language take a place entirely subordinate to them. Never did he sacrifice any idea to artistic combinations of words; never blur over any delicate shade of thought to enhance some rhythmic cadence of musical prose. Literary form (to use a figure which he himself might have coined) is only present at all in his works in the sense in which the industrious and deferential servant is present in the ducal apartment, for the purpose of rendering faithful service to his lord and master. This subordination of style to content in the Saint's work is one of its most eminent qualities. He is a great writer, but not a great stylist. The strength and robustness of his intellect everywhere predominate.[2]

---

[2] PEERS, *The Complete Works of St. John of the Cross*, xxxv. The suggestion that Juan's work does not reflect the style of any school or thought whatsover must also be called into question. My presentation on Juan's rootedness in the literary resources available in his day as well as the western mystical tradition show that this is not true. See Chapter Three. This question is also dealt with in the analysis of the literary genre of the *Cántico* below.

In this statement of Peers we see that the role of literary form, or to use our term, genre, is given a very secondary role in the configuration of Juan's poetry. The "artistic combination of words," shaped by literary genre and structure, does not appear to be recognized by Peers as the very vehicle by which meaning is mediated.

Eulogio Pacho, though stressing the importance of genre[3], appears to give, at best, an ambiguous evaluation of its place in the mediation of meaning and its role in interpretation.[4] For example, the dialogical form of the *Cántico* is not given any importance in Pacho's interpretation. Although this form is unique among Juan's three major poems, for Pacho it does not merit any particular attention, nor does it pose any problems of any significance.[5] He says that this form of the *Cántico* is *solamente externa cobertura* (only external covering).[6] In the end, according to Pacho, to interpret the *Cántico* is to understand the "authentic declaration" on it. The

---

[3] "Teniendo presente el indiscuso principio exegético de que el sentido y la verdadera doctrina se determinan según el género literario y la intención del escritor, se comprende la necesidad de fijar la peculiaridad expresiva de cada obra. ... La clasificación literaria no es más que un primer paso para adentrarse en la exégesis de los textos." Eulogio PACHO, "La estructura literaria del «Cántico espiritual»," *El Monte Carmelo* 68 (1960), 388.

[4] Even though, in the end, Pacho's position remains ambiguous, at times he comes close to affirming the role of literary genre in its capacity to mediate meaning. "La interpretación genuina, profunda, total, de una obra es algo así como su recreación, o reproducción por el lector. Tanto más exacta será, cuanto mayor sea la compenetración entre autor e intérprete." PACHO, "La estructura literaria del «Cántico espiritual»," 385. However, in this reference he adopts somewhat the Romanticist perspective that the text is the vehicle of communication between the author and the reader. As we will see in the other references cited, Pacho does not affirm the value of the poetic form of the *Cántico* in itself.

[5] "Con frecuencia desaparece el escritor tras los personajes que exponen sus afectos propios en forma de conversación, en apartes y monólogos en que el alma (del Santo) descubre sus íntimos sentimientos. Pero el diálogo como tal, y precisamente por ser una categoría estilística mixta, participa de muchas formas e invade todos los géneros literarios. En orden a la exégesis del *Cántico* no merece atención particular ni ofrece dificultades importantes." PACHO, *Vértice*, 109. However, Pacho appears to contradict this position a little bit earlier when he says: "En el *Cántico* —el que nos interesa por ahora directamente— advertimos inmediatamente notas específicas que determinan su fisonomía peculiar: es una composición mucho más extensa que todas las demás; ofrece la particularidad de la forma dialogada." Ibid., 90.

[6] Pacho thus states that the form or dynamic of the poem which results in its literary genre and structure has little to do with the meaning of the *Cántico*: "Quiere decir que la forma literaria es solamente externa cobertura. Los profanos amores de la égloga y del idilio se tornan amores divinos." PACHO, *Vértice*, 91.

"authentic declaration" refers to Juan's commentary on the *Cántico*.[7] Pacho says that when we speak of literary genre with respect to the *Cántico*, our main point of reference is the commentary, not the poem. Pacho's very helpful work on the genre of the poem, as we will see below, is limited to the "classification approach" to genre. As a result, Pacho does not link genre with a particular function in the production of new meaning.[8]

Cristóbol Cuevas, another leading literary commentator on Juan de la Cruz, has a similarly ambiguous attitude toward the literary genre of Juan's *Cántico*. He, likewise, affirms the importance of literary genre.[9] However, he sees the commentary and the poem together as constituting a singular literary genre which he describes as a "hybrid."[10] The poem, he says, is the "emotional moment" while

---

[7] "Interpretar el *Cántico espiritual* significa, en última instancia, entender esa «declaración auténtica» hecha por el Santo para uso de las almas. La determinación del género literario en función de exégesis se refiere principalmente al comentario, o al comentario y poesía en cuanto designan un todo complejo, tal como entendemos la obra al llamarla sin determinaciones ulteriores «Cántico espiritual». ... No pretende admirar con creaciones artísticas, sino enseñar el camino del espíritu a las almas necesitadas de luz y guía. Fin y elementos literarios están subordinados en el *Cántico* a la intención didáctica del maestro que suplanta al poeta." PACHO, *Vértice*, 107.

[8] However, this is not entirely true, since Pacho does come very close to affirming this more dynamic role for literary genre. Again, Pacho's ambiguous stance surfaces here: "Respecto al autor, o artista, el género literario existe y pervive como una institución, o como una estructura preexistente, que se le presenta como posibilidad, si no ve obligado a seguirla, o está en grado de crear una nueva. Para el lector, género literario significa un punto de referencia ideal en que puede establecer contacto con el autor." PACHO, "La estructura literaria del «Cántico espiritual»," 389. In the end, however, he continues to see it as a classification that establishes contact with the author, not the textual production of new meaning.

[9] "No podremos pues, entender con precisión la obra literaria de nuestro escritor sin averiguar el género que eligió para ella, y lo que de él pensaba obtener con vistas a sus propósitos comunicativos." Cristóbol CUEVAS, "Estudio literario," in *Introducción a la lectura de San Juan de la Cruz*, ed. A. García Simón, 148.

[10] Cuevas underlines the importance of literary genre and its importance in sanjuanist research. However, in the end he appears to dismiss the importance of genre in the production of meaning when he says: "Un género literario no es sino un sistema de signos capaz de transmitir mensajes complejos." CUEVAS, "Estudio literario," 148. This evaluation seems to be reinforced since from here he goes on to combine the poem and the commentary into a single literary "hybrid": "La obra sanjuanista se configura en su totalidad como una canción en la que los materiales lingüístico-literarios se usan en tanto que signos eficaces de un mensaje ideológico que, surgido de experiencias emocionales, pretende arrebatar también a los lectores. ... San Juan de la Cruz, con su formación humanística, sabe que el vehículo adecuado para «racionalizar lo cordial» es la prosa, mientras el verso hace perdurable la vivencia intuitiva. De ahí que, por la dinámica misma de los hechos, se vea

the commentary is the "conceptual moment." The poem and the commentary thus form a single system of thought which is a *"continuum de intuiciones emocionadas."* Cuevas does not go any further than this to describe the genre of the *Cántico* (the poem-commentary) as a *"gloxa-tratado."*[11] Even though he emphasizes the importance of literary genre I would question his sensitivity to the unique role the genre of the poem plays in the mediation of meaning and his appreciation of the unique genre of the commentary. Genre appears to be at the service of relating complex messages. This approach on the part of Cuevas causes him later to describe *Cántico A* simply as "mystical emotion" and *Cántico B* as the basis for Juan's mature "doctrinal explanation."[12] The genre question therefore also impacts and probes both our understanding of the relationship between *Cántico A* and *Cántico B* and our appreciation of the function of the *Cántico* as a production of meaning within the confines of its own linguistic form.

Since Ricoeur's theoretical framework emphasizes the importance of genre in a hermeneutical reading of a text and since there is a diversity of evaluations of genre by different sanjuanist scholars, my purpose here is to establish the role of genre as an important and significant part of a hermeneutical interpretation of Juan's

abocado a un género literario mixto: la «glosa» doctrinal contaminada con las características del «tratado». Y así, olvidando la pureza de los géneros tradicionales, no sólo resucita una de las formas didácticas más cultivadas en la Edad Media, sino que, en actitud prebarroca, combina dos formas expresivas opuestas para deducir un sistema de pensamiento a partir de un *continuum* de intuiciones emocionadas. ... Dentro de esta estructura *híbrida*, el verso representa el momento emotivo, configurándose como intuición mística existencial, casi siempre en clave simbólica." Ibid., 150-151. (emphasis mine)

[11] CUEVAS, "Estudio literario," 164.

[12] "No todos sus poemas tenían para él [Juan] la misma capacidad de signo. La prueba la tenemos en la reelaboración a que sometió el primitivo *Cántico espiritual* para hacerlo vehículo apto de exposición doctrinal y parenética. Nos parece que este hecho ha de ser considerado como un síntoma decisivo de la convicción sanjuanista de que una cosa es el verso lírico de simple emoción mística [*CA*] --apto par el desahogo personal o la comunicación de apasionadas vivencias--y otra [*CB*] el poema que ha de servir de base a une explicación doctrinal." CUEVAS, "Estudio Literario," 154. (emphasis mine) Elsewhere Cuevas thus describes *Cántico B* as the "definitive" poem, since it represents the maturity of his thought: "De esa manera, y con las alteraciones estructurales de todos conocidas, el poema definitivo de cuarenta estrofas [*CB*] queda terminado al cabo de nada menos que ocho años de reflexiva maduración." Cristóbol CUEVAS, "La poesía de san Juan de la Cruz," in *Introducción a la lectura de San Juan de la Cruz*, ed. A. García Simón, 288.

Cántico.

Why is sensitivity to the genre question of the poem, as a poem, so important in hermeneutics? It is important since a hermeneutical reading of Juan's *Cántico* sees genre research as an attempt not only to "look back" and classify the text, but also to recognize genre as a form for the production of meaning which, by its very nature, "looks to the future." How one approaches genre, whether as a classification tool or as a form for the production of meaning, will thus determine the importance genre plays in the mediation of meaning. For example, is genre merely a function of the author's style, content of the work, its structure, metre, or the various themes within?[13] Wellek and Warren suggest that every culture has its own preferred genres and approach to genre, whatever established definition of genre one is working out of.[14] Aristotle, on the other hand, limits the number of genres to three: tragedy, comedy and epic. Northrop Frye, in his *Anatomy of Criticism*, suggests that it is because a specific genre is recognized by the reader that readers know how to

---

[13] An historical sketch of the theory of literary genres is presented in Delfín LEOCADIO GARASA, *Los Géneros literarios*, 2nd edition, (Buenos Aires: Editorial Columbia, 1971). Garasa outlines the complexity of the problem of literary genre and surveys various perspectives in the development of the theory and classification of texts with respect to literary genre. He makes the point that the specific criteria used for classification of genres in a particular context must be clear. He concludes: "Lo que importa, en última instancia, es saber en qué sentido se utiliza en cada caso: si nos referimos a convenciones o categorías, caracterizadas por rasgos generales que permiten agrupar las obras literarias con diversos criterios ... o si nos referimos a formas de contornos más circunscritos, que se imponen a la materia configurándola o modelándola según pautas más o menos precisas." Ibid., 29-30. Adrian Marino also reflects the complexity of the problem in his article "A Definition of Literary Genres." Marino concludes: "The major, essential genre of the creative self is therefore by definition the *poly-genre*. This conclusion rejects the whole traditional theory of literary genres. Nevertheless, in its internal or historical development the unity and the categorial solidarity of literature does not exclude moments of instability and unbalance, expressed by strong accents in one field or another. The conclusion is that literary genres have only a transient, fragmentary, and hierarchical existence." Adrian MARINO, "A Definition of Literary Genres," in *Theories of Literary Genre*, ed. Joseph P. Strelka (University Park: Pennsylvania State University Press, 1978), 49. In the context of Ricoeur's theory one might take exception to a comment made by Johannes A. Huisman: "As for the lack of interest shown by recent scholarship, we must note that neither the method of history of ideas nor that of hermeneutic interpretation has much need for genre theory." Johannes A. HUISMAN, "Generative Classification in Medieval Literature," in *Theories of Literary Genre*, ed. Joseph P. Strelka, 124.

[14] René WELLEK and Austin Warren, *Theory of Interpretation*, 3rd edition, (San Diego: Harcourt, Brace, Jovanich, 1977), 225. See the entire chapter entitled, "Literary Genres," 226-237. See Ibid., 231 concerning what criteria might be used to judge genre.

read them in a particular way. In *Anatomy of Criticism* Frye examines several specific literary genres which can be recognized by the reader.[15] Whatever the approach to the number of possible genres, a hermeneutic approach focuses on the second approach I have cited above, that is, genre as a means by which meaning is shaped into a literary form and which works toward establishing communication between the reader and the text. It is this approach to genre which is important for a hermeneutical interpretation of Juan's *Cántico*.

Ricoeur summarizes for us several reasons why the determination of the genre of a work is important as a form for the production of meaning in the dialectic of communication between the text and the reader.

> Literary genres fulfill several functions as concerns communication: first, they provide a common ground of understanding and of interpretation, thanks to the contrast between the traditional character of the "genre" and the novelty of the message. Second, they preserve the message from distortion, thanks to the autonomy of the form as regards speaker and hearer. ... Third, the "form" secures the survival of the meaning after the disappearance of its *Sitz im Leben* and in a way that starts the process of "decontextualization" which opens the message to fresh reinterpretation according to the contexts of discourse and of life. In this sense the "form" not only establishes communication, thanks to its *common* character, but it preserves the message from distortion thanks to the *circumspection* which it imposes upon the work of art, and it *opens* it to the history of its interpretation.[16]

Genre is, therefore, not only a means of classification of the *Cántico*, but it is also a determination of the nature of the *Cántico*'s capacity for the production of new meaning.[17] Determination of the genre of the *Cántico* is important

---

[15] Northrop FRYE, "Rhetorical Criticism: Theory of Genres," in *Anatomy of Criticism: Four Essays*, (Princeton: Princeton University Press, 1971), 243-337.

[16] RICOEUR, "Biblical Hermeneutics," 71.

[17] "In the same way as the function of grammar is to preserve the grammaticality of discourse and on that basis to insure the communication by guiding the semantic interpretation of the message, so is it the function of literary genres to provide rules for encoding and decoding a message produced as a poem, a narrative, or an essay." RICOEUR, "Biblical Hermeneutics," 69-70.

because what is written is qualified and mediated by the specific mode of discourse operative in a text. This is to say, "the medium is the message." What a poem can "do" is determined by its form. Genre structures the *Cántico* and directs it toward a particular reference. Genres are thus "conventional patterns of formulation" which are distinguished according to their function in the process of communication.[18]

However, "genres in the strict sense are never capable of being identically realized. They are capable of merely showing certain common characteristics as they are realized, which are connected with the exemplarity of their communicative function."[19] Therefore, text genres never appear in a pure form. Let us recall at this point the dialectic of sedimentation and innovation which was discussed in the last chapter. According to Ricoeur genre plays a role between sedimentation and innovation. The sedimented genre undergoes innovation in the configuring process which brings a uniqueness to both form and content. Juan exhibits a particular *style* within the genre medium which is personal to the *Cántico*.[20] It is the style of the *Cántico* which individuates the text, putting an original stamp on it.[21] But this originality is never completely dissociated from the conditioned norms of the genre form. Therefore, the circumstances of distanciation on the part of the reader of the *Cántico* are, to some extent, "compensated for by text

---

[18] Werner G. JEANROND, *Text and Interpretation as Categories of Theological Thinking*, (New York: Crossroad, 1988), 97.

[19] JEANROND, *Text*, 98. Jeanrond goes on to give a simple yet clear example which demonstrates his point: "For example, 'a newspaper-advertisement-spot' can be identified as text genre to the extent that slogans can be continually published in newspapers which have in common the communicative function 'to persuade the reader to buy a product'." Ibid., 98.

[20] Damaso Alonso witnesses to the originality of Juan's work in his extensive work on the style and artistic merit of Juan's poetry: "San juan de la Cruz no vacila, pues, en usar alguna vez los artificios estilísticos que le ofrecía la tradición literaria. Pero en él no resultan nunca fórmulas exteriores, fríamente sobrepuestas, sino que le sirven de atinados, intuitivos refuerzos de la expresión afectiva o del desarrollo conceptual." ALONSO, *La Poesia de san Juan de la Cruz*, 171. For a more extensive description of Juan's literary style and techniques see Ibid., 165-194.

[21] "Estilo es todo lo que individualiza a un ente literario: a una obra, a un escritor, a una época, a una literatura. El estilo es el único objeto de la critica literaria." ALONSO, *La Poesia de san Juan de la Cruz*, 167.

genres. For these offer the reader a semantic framework ... grounded in conventions and thus predictable. This framework consists in the exemplification of the major communicative function of a text (for example, political information, act of prayer, love song)."[22] Genre thus awakens and prompts certain expectations from the text on the part of the reader of the *Cántico* which are productive of meaning.

These expectations may be multiple according to the hierarchy of functions served by the text. "Such functions are: informative, meditative, aesthetic, documentary, confessional, entertaining, didactic, etc. ... In the case of literary text genres the aesthetic function stands in the foreground and locates the other text functions relative to the central one."[23] Since, in Ricoeur's text theory, all texts interpret and mediate reality, we need to direct our attention to the specific function of Juan's *Cántico* through our reflection on genre.[24]

---

[22] JEANROND, *Text*, 98. Jeanrond goes on to signal the importance of even the title of a text which may provide important clues concerning the function and genre of the text. Ibid., 98. We are thus alerted to the importance of the *title* of a work and its contribution toward its overall understanding. Since the title of the *Cántico*, for the most part, has not been a part of the presentation of the published poem since 1630 I will address this question below in Chapter Seven.

[23] JEANROND, *Text*, 100.

[24] As we have already seen the concept of literary genre is not always easy to define and is approached in different ways. Eric Donald Hirsch makes this point. He states: "Literary critics when discussing genre have tended to fall into two camps, which for simplicity can be called the Aristotelean and the Crocean. Aristoteleans have held that genres are limited in number (whether by convention or the nature of things or a combination of both). Croceans have held that genres are fictitious entities that arbitrarily break up the infinite continuum of expressions, each expression being potentially sui generis." Eric Donald HIRSCH, *The Aims of Interpretation*, (Chicago: University of Chicago Press, 1976), 67-68. This situation is also reflected in the comments of René Wellek and Austin Warren: "That genres are distinct--and also should be kept distinct--is a general article of Neo-Classical faith. But if we look to Neo-Classical criticism for definition of genre or method of distinguishing of genre from genre, we find little consistency or even awareness of the need for a rationale." WELLEK, *Theory of Interpretation*, 219. Later on they are a little more emphatic in what they mean by genre: "Theory of genres is a principle of order: it classifies literature and literary history not by time or place (period or national language) but by specifically literary types of organization or structure." Ibid., 226. However, Ricoeur critiques Wellek's and Warren's "classification approach" to literary genre in the following way: "Rene Welleck and Austin Warren have great difficulty in finding the proper place for the notion of literary genre in their theoretical framework (which follows more or less Ingarden's theory of the literary work). The difficulty stems from an improper concept of what a literary genre is. It is not a class in a taxinomy, it is not a means of classification, but a means of production." RICOEUR, "Biblical Hermeneutics," 69.

In summary, then, Ricoeur tells us that the construction of the meaning of the text is assisted by this delineation of genre.[25] The naming of genre is a part of the dialectic of explanation and understanding which aids toward construing the meaning of the text as a whole.[26] Our interest in genre is therefore based on the following affirmation: genre points the reader in a particular direction concerning the meaning of a text and is itself a judgement about its meaning.

Having reviewed the contribution genre makes toward meaning, let us now locate the genre of the *Cántico* within the classical genres in use during Juan's time. What we are concerned with here is locating the genre of the *Cántico* within the genre categories established by text genre theory. Research from two key sanjuanist scholars will help us in this regard.

To explore the literary genre of the *Cántico* I will summarize the findings of Eulogio Pacho, the contemporary leading expert on the text of Juan's *Cántico*.[27] I will also refer to an earlier work by Damaso Alonso. Alonso's *Poesía de San Juan de la Cruz* (1942) is still one of the most extensive analyses of the literary origins of Juan's poetry. In their presentations of the literary genre of the *Cántico* both of these scholars refer to its structure and type. Structure in this case refers to the metric pattern and type refers to the classification of the poem within the

---

[25] "As an individual it can only be reached by a process of narrowing the scope of generic concepts concerning the literary genre, the class of text to which this text belongs, the structures of different kinds that intersect in this text. The localization and the individualization of this unique text is still a guess." RICOEUR. "The Model of the Text: Meaningful Action Considered as a Text," 158.

[26] "The reconstruction of the text as a whole necessarily has a circular character, in the sense that the presupposition of a certain kind of whole is implied in the recognition of the parts. And reciprocally, it is in construing the details that we construe the whole." RICOEUR, *Interpretation Theory*, 158. It is here that Ricoeur makes another point which I have discussed, that is, because of this construction of the text at the level of explanation, no part of the text can be seen to be more important than another part. Ricoeur says: "There is no necessity and no evidence concerning what is important and what is unimportant, what is essential and what is unessential." Ibid., 158.

[27] PACHO, *Vértice*, 88-97. Although Pacho discusses literary genre and style at length in the forementioned reference, in a later publication he makes the following statement concerning the inability to pinpoint the literary genre of Juan's work: "Su talante y su talento logran adaptaciones singularisimas en busqueda de formas expresivas eficaces. De ahí que los géneros sanjuanistas resulten extraños, excepcionales, hibridos y casi inclasificables." PACHO, "Lenguaje y mensaje," 55.

popular categories of literature in Juan's day. I will use both these criteria to classify the genre of the *Cántico*.

According to Pacho, Juan's poetry can be divided into three central categories of literature: 1. *canciónes* (*estancias, liras,* or *líricos)*; 2. *coplas;* and 3. *romances.* The *Cántico* belongs to the first group, that is, *canciónes.*[28] In Juan's day *cancióne* referred to a broad spectrum of poetic writings, almost like the way we refer to a "poem" today.[29] Within this broad categorization the *Cántico* is described as a hendecasyllabic lira poem.[30] This form of verse had been newly introduced into Spain during Juan's time and made popular by the famous "secular" poet Garcilaso de la Vega. Garcilaso was born in Toledo; however, due to political banishment, he spent some time in Naples where he encountered various Italian and Latin poets. Jones explains how the name "lira" is associated with Garcilaso: "Some time during

---

[28] PACHO, *Vértice,* 89.

[29] "«Canción» no indica un tipo único de poesía, cortado según el limitado patrón propuesto hoy en nuestras modernas preceptivas a esa forma específica de poesía lírica. San Juan de la Cruz usa la palabra en el sentido que se dio a la *canzone* italiana implantada en España por la corriente petrarquista." PACHO, *Vértice,* 89.

[30] Damaso Alonso discusses whether Juan de la Cruz encountered this form of poetry through Fray Luis while at the University of Salamanca since traditional castilian poetry was written in octosyllabic metre. Whether Juan de la Cruz read Garcilaso directly or encountered the style through Fray Luis or through Córdoba's book (cited in footnote number 36) is open for discussion. See ALONSO, *La Poesía de san Juan de la Cruz,* 29-46. For example, Alonso suggests as one possibility the following sequence: "La lira, estrofa pagana de Garcilaso, se espiritualiza en fray Luis, se diviniza en San Juan de la Cruz." Ibid., 31. Latter he concludes more definitively: "Hay en la obra del Santo elementos que vienen directamente, unos, de Garcilaso; otros de Sebastián de Córdoba; otros, en fin, que proceden probablemente sólo de este último ... San Juan de la Cruz leyó a Garcilaso; leyó también su refundición por Córdoba." Ibid., 93. Allison Peers seems to leave the question open: "That St. John of the Cross, consciously or unconsciously, echoes Boscán, Garcilaso and Sebastián de Córdoba I am convinced: the parallels alleged, though no one of them is individually conclusive, are in the sum total far too numerous to be disregarded. But the reminiscences might quite well be the result of impressions formed by reading these authors in boyhood ... . To believe, with Baruzi, that the Saint 'made a technical study of Garcilaso' would surely be highly untrue to his character." PEERS, *St. John of the Cross and other Lectures and Addresses,* 37. Perhaps Juan did not read Garcilaso directly, however, since there was opposition to this new form of verse introduced by Garcilaso, we can at least conclude that Juan made a very conscious decision to adopt the *lyra.* Jones records for us this opposition to the form which Juan used for the *Cántico:* "However, though the new Italianate style gained ground very rapidly, it was not accepted immediately by all. Many remained attached to the older Castilian metres and the styles associated with them, either for nationalistic reasons or because they genuinely regretted the loss of the peculiar poetic experience which the older poetry offered." JONES. *The Golden Age,* 47.

218

his Neapolitan period Garcilaso composed his *Cánción* V, 'Oda a la flor de Gnido', a plea on behalf of his friend Mario Galeota addressed to Doña Violante Sanseverino. ... Apart from its instrinsic poetic merits it has a further historical importance in that it introduced into Spanish the stanza-form in which Luis de León and St John of the Cross were to write some of their best poetry, and gave the stanza a name, *lira*, taken from the last word of the ode's first line: 'Se de mi baja lira'."[31] The lira was also adopted by another renowned poet Fray Luis de León. Tavard summarizes the structure of the hendecasyllabic lira form and comments on the effect of this arrangement:

> Adoption of the stanza called a *lira*, presumably inspired by the fifth canto, Flor de Gnido, of Garcilaso, ascribed strict formal boundaries within which the author had to function. The stanzas in question have five verses and two rhymes: the first one connects the first verse and the third; the second one is common to the remaining three verses. Thus the entire poem follows a double rhythm, related on the one hand to syllabic length -- *a b a a b* -- on the other to rhyme -- *a b a b b*.[32]

> The periodic recurrence of the syllabic rhythm within that of the rhymes conveys to the whole poem the appearance of light dancing. Far from being an orgiastic dance modeled on the bacchanals of Dionysian mysticism, this dance is strictly controlled. Enthusiasm is held in check by the evanescence of the rhymes. These are chiefly feminine, ending in a vowel: they open the soul at the sound of its words, yet with a certain monotony, since the Spanish language, which has few words ending in *u*, forces the poet constantly to fall back on the three basic vowels, *a, e, o*. As to the masculine rhymes, closed on a consonant, they end with *s* (mostly plural nouns, with some verbs in the second person singular), interspersed with a few *n*'s (verbs in the third person plural). In this way the simplicity of rhymes puts the brakes on the rich flow of words, as the double rhythm of the verses introduces a dancing motion into the music of

---

[31] Royston O. JONES, *The Golden Age: Prose and Poetry II The Sixteenth and Seventeenth Centuries,* A Literary History of Spain (London: E. Benn, 1971), 46. For a more extensive history of the origins of the lira see Damaso ALONSO, "Sobre los orígenes de la lira," in *Poesia Española: Ensayo de metodos y limites estilisticos,* 2nd edition, Biblioteca Romanica Hispanica II. Estudios y Ensayos (Madrid: Editorial Gredos, 1952), 611-618.

[32] TAVARD, *Poetry and Contemplation,* 41.

the discourse.[33]

The *Cántico* is also described as an *égloga* (eclogue), that is, a poetic pastoral dialogue in the same style as that of Garcilaso.[34] Thus, the literary genre of the *Cántico* is described by Pacho as a pastoral love poem *a lo divino*, that is, a human love poem which is slightly modified by a subsequent writer to reflect the love relationship between God and humanity. The term "pastoral" refers to the bucolic setting of the poem, that is, the rustic world of nature, shepherds, rivers, countryside, and so on. In the case of the *Cántico* the "profane" dialogue of the Lover and the Beloved is taken to be an analogy of the "divine" dialogue between the human soul and God.[35] This practice of taking the images of profane literature and transforming them *a lo divino* was a common one during Juan's time.[36] Jones

---

[33] TAVARD, *Poetry and Contemplation*, 41-42.

[34] "El *Cántico* es un requiebro amoroso, una versión a lo divino de los amoers pastoriles morosamente descritos en las mejores églogas o idilios de la edad dorada de nuestras letras." PACHO, *Vértice*, 90. On this point see also ALONSO, *La Poesía de san Juan de la Cruz*, 63. Jorge Guillén, in his chapter devoted essentially to Juan de la Cruz refers to the *Cántico* in this way, calling it as well a "Canticle-eclogue." A little later he refers to it as an "epithalamium." Jorge GUILLÉN, "The Ineffable Language of Mysticism: San Juan de la Cruz," in *Language and Poetry: Some Poets of Spain*, (Cambridge, Mass., Harvard University Press, 1961), 84, 88. See also Marcial JOSE BAYO, "Aspecto lírico de San Juan de la Cruz," *Revista de Espiritualidad* 1 (1941-42), 300-308, especially pages 301-302 concerning the possible influence of Garcilaso on Juan de la Cruz.

[35] Jerónimo de San José describes it thus: "El asunto es (como queda dicho) un íntimo coloquio del alma con Dios, donde se representan las correspondencias amorosas entre ambos." JERÓNIMO DE SAN JOSÉ [EZQUERRA], *Historia del venerable padre Fr. Juan de la Cruz*, 276, quoted in PACHO, *Vértice*, 91.

[36] For support attesting to the influence of this practice on Juan's *Cántico* see: Pacho, *Vértice*, 90. Carlos Dominguez wrote a doctoral dissertation on the sixteenth century practice of *contrafactum* in relationship to Juan's use of *poemas a lo divino*: Carlos DOMINGUEZ, *Contrafactum as Allegory: The Religious Recasting in Sixteenth Century Italy and Spain, From Girolamo Malpiero to San Juan de la Cruz*, Ph.D. Thesis, Stanford University, 1983. Dominguez describes the use and purpose of *contrafactum* in relationship to the *a lo divino* practice in this way: "The reductive tendency of the *contrafactum* mostly operates at the referential level, forcing the ambiguous and suggestive secular referent to be brought down to a graspable reality. As a result the contrafactors turn polysemic texts into monosemic entities. It is their means of extracting the 'germane sense' from secular lyric poems-- purging, says Malipiero, 'da ogni veleno antico i leggiardi sonetti del Thosco poeta.' It is their way of hindering language from signifying more than the Establishment permits. Because of their polemic configuration, these recastings behave like 'pentimenti,' allowing the original poem to come to the surface in the purged text. San Juan's *poemas a lo divino*, on the other hand, resemble a palimpsest, successfully effacing the original--at least to the extent that a poetic sign can efface its own diachrony. Having his gaze fixed upon the Other-world, he perceives secularity as a void--an ever-empty

describes the growth of this movement during Juan's lifetime:

The Counter-Reformation accentuated a phenomenon which before the end of the fifteenth century had little importance in Spain (though much in certain other countries): religious parody, or the rewriting of profane literature in religious terms. ... The practice grew in the sixteenth century, reaching its climax in the later years of the century and the beginning of the next. The movement petered out towards 1625. In that time countless poems were recast, or *contrahechos a lo divino*, as the phrase went. *Contrafacta* were made of all kinds of poetry; though *villancicos*, *romances*, and other traditional forms predominated since these were sung and music played a crucial part in the movement. Almost all *contrafacta*, indeed, were composed to be sung to popular tunes.[37]

receptacle that lives in hope of what is to come, making the friction between the two realms irrelevant." Ibid., 3. See also ALONSO, *La Poesía de san Juan de la Cruz*, 47 ff on the practice of *a lo divino*, and Ibid., 115-116. Alonso cites as an example Sebastián de Córdoba's 1575 "religious" publication of the work of two "secular" poets: Boscán y Garcilaso. Ibid., 47. Jorgé Guillén, however, stresses the purely human reference of Juan's three major poems: *Noche oscura*, *Llama de amor viva*, and *Cántico espiritual*: "We know that San Juan de la Cruz conceived these poems in accordance with a Biblical tradition (the supreme eclogue of the *Song of Songs*) and the Graeco-Latin-Italian tradition flowering in the eclogues of Garcilaso de la Vega, who was the point of departure for all Spanish poetry of the sixteenth century. These various reminiscences having been fused in San Juan's 'integrating lyricism,' we find here three magnificent expressions of human love, love in absence and in presence, in anxiety and in fulfillment. The poems, when they are read as poems--and that is what they are--signify nothing but love, the intoxication of love, and their terms of reference are invariably human. No other 'poetic' horizon is perceptible." GUILLÉN, *Language and Poetry*, 89.

[37] JONES, *The Golden Age*, 87. See also, B.W. WARDROPPER, *Historia de la poesia lírica a lo divino en la Cristiandad occidental*, (Madrid: 1958), quoted in Ibid., 89. However, Anselmo Donazar is of the opinion that this transformation of poems *a lo divino* had little to do with Juan's poetry: "Según lo que vengo diciendo, la poesía del Santo ... nada tiene que ver con lo que, en la historia de la literatura, se llaman las 'versiones a lo divino'. Al fijarse en la raíz sacramental del amor, el poeta místico ha quitado al género el aire de las velas. La obra clásica de W. Wardropper 'Historia de la poesia lírica a lo divino en la Cristiandad occidental' no sirve aquí de poco, pues el autor no considera la raíz mistérica de los poemas de San Juan de la Cruz." DONAZAR, *Fray Juan*, 179. Donazar softens this position somewhat on the following page explaining what he means by mysticism. See Ibid., 180-181. However, his conclusion in this chapter titled "El Cántico espiritual y las versiones a lo divino," (pp. 165-186) leaves little doubt that he does not make a direct connection between Juan's poetry and the *a lo divino* movement of Juan's day: "Fray Juan entiende y atiende a esas criaturas que cantan como gorriones; pero sus versos van por otro camino. El no es dueño de su inspiración." Ibid., 186. The evidence cited by other sanjuanist scholars supports the influence of the *a lo divino* movement on Juan's poetry. See my footnote number 36 in this chapter for literature to support this point. That Juan would have written outside the influence of this extremely popular as well as courtly practice is unlikely.

Alonso situates the *Cántico* within popular *cancioneros cortesanos*.[38]

These were collections of popular poems and love ballads from the countryside of Castilla.[39] We thus discover that Juan adopted forms for his poetic expression that would have been well known during his day.[40] The *Cántico* reflects a style of Italian verse made popular at that time in Spain by such famous poets as Fray Luis de León, Garcilaso de la Vega, and Sebastián de Córdoba.[41] From this we know that Juan was

[38] "Hemos visto cómo una parte de la poesía de San Juan de la Cruz --la caracterizada por el uso de temas iniciales desarrollados en estrofas y parcialmente repetidos al fin de cada estrofa como estribillo-- está profundamente enraizada en la vieja tradición de Castilla, ya directamente sobre la base popular, sobre la de los cancioneros cortesanos. ... Después del análisis que hemos hecho, comprendemos que, si la anécdota es cierta, todo lo más que la cancioncilla pudo hacer, sería reavivar en la imaginación del cautivo una palabra de la poesía tradicional y rústica, poesía en la que, como hemos visto, estaba profundamente empapado. Así es como no explicamos que la palabra *carillo*, procedente de la pastoral rústica --repetida una y otra vez en las canciones populares --esté ahí, en los versos endecasílabos, chocando entre las dulzuras de égloga garcilasesca y los hieratismos provinientes del *Cantar de los Cantares*, que forman el ambiente externo y el fondo temático del *Cántico espiritual*, compuesto, precisamente, en parte, durante la prisión toledana." ALONSO, *La Poesía de san Juan de la Cruz*, 135-36.

[39] "El alma castellana y tradicional del poeta de Hontiveros [sic] rezuma también en expresión y se condensa en ambiente, hasta en un poema culto como el *Cántico espiritual*, donde la huella bíblica y el rastro garcilasesco son innegables y evidentes. San Juan de la Cruz, que en sus poesías de tema inicial y estribillo, muestra su enraizamiento en la tradición popular castellana, nos deja ver también cómo hasta su misma poesía en endecasílabos le llegan emanaciones, temas, vocabulario de ese mismo campo popular, cómo a veces en él la tradición literaria culta y la popular del siglo XVI se entermezclan y quizá mutuamente se reinfluyen, cómo, en fin, una oscura fuerza selectiva pone antes al alcance de la imaginación del poeta los elementos populares y aun vivos de su Castilla creadora." ALONSO, *La Poesía de san Juan de la Cruz*, 143. Allison Peers supports this position in PEERS, *Spirit of Flame*, 105-106.

[40] Juan's poetry: "Pertenecen al tipo de romance aconsonantado, sumamente monótono, usado desde el siglo XV; y prolongan giros y expresiones de los viejos y de los juglarescos." ALONSO, *La Poesía de san Juan de la Cruz*, 105. This opinion seems to be in contradiction to that of Pacho who gives Juan's work a certain independence from the literary forms of his day despite the above stated indications. He states: "Nadie como él ha sabido presentar las realidades espirituales conabsoluta independencia de formas literarias, prescindiendo de los clásicos cánones de exposición." PACHO, *Vértice*, 127. Anselmo Donazar remarks more in the line of Alonso: "San Juan de la Cruz como poeta místico es un fenómeno de confluencia venturosa. ... Supuesto que en este hombre actúa una densificación típica del proceso idealizador del amor." DONAZAR, *Fray Juan*, 168.

[41] Allison Peers generally supports the research of Alonso and praises his work *La Poesía de san Juan de la Cruz*. At the same time Peers cautions that the influence Alonso attributes to Luis de León, Garcilaso de la Vega, and Sebastián de Córdoba on Juan de la Cruz may be excessive. PEERS, *St. John of the Cross and Other Lectures and Addresses*, 51. However, even if Alonso sees Juan as having been influenced by Garcilaso, he also readily admits that there is a great difference between the two: "Mas el lenguaje no es sino (con la terminologia de Saussure) un sistema de signos expresivos. La alteración de cualquier orden de estos signos trae como consecuencia la profunda

thoroughly steeped in his own popular, as well as intellectual, tradition.[42] Both are reflected in the literary genre of the *Cántico*.[43] Therefore, the literary genre of the *Cántico* of Juan de la Cruz can be described as pastoral hendecasyllabic love poetry. This genre classification combines both the literary components of genre categorization as well as a hint of its productive capacity. I will now briefly examine the productive capacity of this form of text by linking the genre of Juan's *Cántico* with that of the *Song of Songs*.

If the structure of the *Cántico* is closely linked with the *Song*, as I have indicated in Chapter Four, might the genre of the *Cántico* also be linked with the *Song* in a similiar way? If the *Cántico* and *Song* share a similiar genre, then we could expect that the genre of the *Song* would also be a clue to the productive capacity of the *Cántico*.

In Chapter Three I indicated that the *Song* was a main symbolic field of reference for the *Cántico*. In Chapter Four I showed how the *Cántico* was an innovation of the sedimented paradigms of the *Song* that resulted in an original work.

modificación de todos los valores del sistema. Si llamamos habla poética *A* a la de Garcilaso, y *B* a la de San Juan de la Cruz, el paso del sistema *A* al *B* está definido por una total subversión del orden de los signos adjetivos: por la enorme disminución de esta serie de valores, por la casi desaparición del adjetivo analítico, por la intensa revalorización de los signos adjetivales que sobreviven, y la consiguiente revitalización con valor poético activo de su fuerza semántica, por sus movimientos ondulares de enrarecimiento o agrupación." ALONSO, *La Poesia de san Juan de la Cruz*, 193.

[42] The study by Allison Peers expresses this well in his general comments on Juan's poetry: "Our great cause for satisfaction must be that he caught the poetical language of Spain, as it were, at a moment when with richness of conception and a capacity for imaginative and emotional flight--even for sustained flight--it combined simplicity, dignity and restraint. And those characteristics of his age are synthesized and carried to a most intense degree in his own poetry. He was, I believe, a supremely skilful artist endowed in the highest measure with natural ability. It is by no mere chance that those epithets of his--notably in the 'Spiritual Canticle'--are so perfect in themselves and yield so much to the imagination. Either his stanzas were kneaded, pulled to pieces and refashioned again and again in the cell of his mind-- ... or he was possessed of the most marvellously intuitive poetic faculty imaginable and developed what the Catalan Maragall was later to call the art of the 'living word' (*paraula viva*) to an extent heretofore unknown. To me the former hypothesis seems by far the more credible and fully borne out by such admittedly slender external evidence as we have." PEERS, *Spirit of Flame*, 105.

[43] ALONSO, *La Poesia de san Juan de la Cruz*, 145.

But the two texts are both described as "canticles."[44]   In the context of a hermeneutical interpretation of the *Cántico* I might ask the following questions: What do canticles do? Or, to ask the question in another way, what aspects of reality do canticles uniquely generate and how do they do it? A complete response to these questions are beyond the scope of this dissertation. My purpose is simply to indicate that the *Cántico* and the *Song* are also linked at the level of genre as a form for the production of meaning. Exploration of how they are linked may provide some indications of the kind of productivity we may expect of Juan's *Cántico*.

The *Song of Songs* is often described as Hebrew love poetry,[45] even though its oriental origins are well documented.[46] Since the end of the nineteenth century it has been recognized as a collection of popular wedding or love poems that were sung and have subsequently been joined together into a single text.[47] For example, some segments of the *Song* are known as *wasfs*. *Wasfs* are expressions of mutual love, often in the form of a sung dialogue, that describe "through a series of images the parts of the male and female body."[48] *Wasfs* were still sung in Palestine

---

[44]   The primary meaning of canticle is "little song" and secondarily it refers to a "song, poem, hymn." *Webster's Third New International Dictionary of the English Language Unabridged*, ed. Philip Babcock Gove et al., (Springfield, Mass.: G. & C. Merriam Company, 1981), 329.

[45]   E. Ann MATTER, *The Voice of My Beloved: The Song of Songs in Western Medieval Christianity*, (Philadelphia: University of Pennsylvania Press, 1990), 10.

[46]   Dalmazio COLOMBO, "Alle origini del Cantico," in *Cantico dei Cantici*, (Brescia: Editrice Queriniana, 1985), 23-37.

[47]   A. ROBERT, "Le genre littéraire du Cantique des Cantiques," *Revue Biblique*, 52 (1943-44), 192.

[48]   Marcia FALK, "The *Wasf*," in *The Song of Songs*, ed. with an introduction by Harold Bloom (New York: Chelsea House Publishers, 1988), 67. *Wasf* is an Arabic word which means "description." "Not only is the form of the wasf fairly rigid and its subject matter determined at the outset, its treatment of the subject also follows a pattern: each part of the physique is described by means of specific, often unlikely images drawn from the realms of nature and artifice. While the imagery in the wasf is usually visual, it sometimes appeals to other senses, as in the tactile 'breasts like fawns' or the olfactory and tastelike associations of 'lips like lilies.'" Ibid., 68. The possibility that Juan's *Cántico* contains some form of these *wasfs* is a study yet to be undertaken.

as recently as our own century.[49]

Roland Murphy describes the basic characteristics and purpose of the various love songs (or poems) which make up the *Song*:

> The technique of the author is to present various scenes or episodes in the intimate life of his characters. ... the Canticle [*Song*] is more an expression of mood than a carefully constructed theme. There is really no climax in the poem and none was needed. The marrige relationship itself was the climax; the author intended only to give it expression. There is no plot, no conflict, but a series of scenes on an imaginative plane. There is no question, therefore, of the development in the mutual love of the man and the woman. ... The pair are as much in love at the beginning as at the end. ... The sentiments [of love] uttered there are a general philosophy of love and come quite naturally within the scope of the poem.[50]

In its religious reception by the Jews the *Song* speaks of the new Israel and Yahweh in terms of human marriage.[51] For Christians the religious reception of the *Song* revolved around the union of the Incarnate Word with the Church or the individual soul.[52] The human experience of love, reflected in the *Song*, is therefore shown to be a model or paradigm of how God is present in the human community. In its religious reception this would appear to describe what canticles "do." They provoke, bring alive, and celebrate the dynamic relationship of God within the believing community through the creation of affect or mood.

At this point let us go back to the definition of literary genre with which we started our discussion on the naming of the literary genre of the *Cántico*. I stated that interest in the determination of genre is not merely to classify the *Cántico* as we look back, but it is also the determination of the medium which is productive of a particular kind of meaning. It is this approach to genre as a means

---

[49] H. STEPHAN, "Modern Palestinian Parallels to the Song of Songs," *The Journal of the Palestine Oriental Society*, 2 (1922), 199-278, quoted in Roland E. MURPHY, "The Structure of the Canticle of Canticles," *Catholic Biblical Quarterly*, 16 (1954), 383.

[50] MURPHY, "The Structure of the Canticle of Canticles," 383.

[51] ROBERT, "Le genre littéraire du Cantique des Cantiques," 196.

[52] ROBERT, "Le genre littéraire du Cantique des Cantiques," 196.

of production (rather than classification) which has caused us to question the limiting approach some sanjuanist scholars hold toward genre and its role in the production of meaning. Sensitivity to genre affects our interpretation of Juan's *Cántico*.

The *Cántico* was written in the form of a pastoral love poem *a lo divino*. This form of literature was popular in its reception, yet technical in its composition. It used the common language of the time, its symbols and imagery, to speak of the religious experience of the community. There is reason to believe that these poems were often sung, as were the *wasfs* of the *Song*. Accompanied by music, poems *a lo divino* "embodied more," thus making their insertion into the life of the faithful vibrant and colourful. Alonso associates the *Cántico* with popular love songs known as *cancioneros cortesanos*. Juan was surrounded by various forms of expression, both religious and secular in nature that shaped his world and, similarly, come to shape ours through the *Cántico*. The two canticles, the *Cántico* and the *Song*, are productive of mood which draws the reader into the text-world. How and why mood is a way of knowing and is productive of meaning was discussed in Chapter Four where I considered the productive capacity of "mood" and "feelings." I will return to the productive capacity of mood in Chapter Seven where I discuss in more detail the unique referential capacity of the *Cántico* in relationship to the commentary. However, there is already an important consequence which comes from this appreciation of the genre of Juan's *Cántico* as a pastoral hendecasyllabic love poem, a canticle, which operates at the level of mood.

This approach to genre releases us from limiting the meaning of the *Cántico* to a description of the threefold classical spiritual itinerary outlined in the *Cántico*'s commentary. The referential capacity of the genre of the *Cántico*, therefore, does not appear to be strictly doctrinal in nature, but also includes the production of mood. Sensitivity to this referential capacity of the *Cántico* opens up the poem to other meanings according to what canticles such as Juan's *Cántico* "do." Let us now examine more closely the configuration of Juan's "pastoral hendecasyllabic love poem" to orient ourselves toward these possible "doings."

226

3. The Configuration of the *Cántico*

A number of studies have been done on the structural and literary composition of Juan's *Cántico*. Among the more significant literary studies are those of Damaso Alonso, Roger Duvivier, Rose Marie Icaza, and Eulogio Pacho.[53] Since I determined in the last chapter that literary analysis is but a step toward a more complete understanding of the *Cántico*, our task here is to show how structure *does* affect the meaning of the *Cántico*, but without doing a complete structural analysis. Therefore, I have chosen a more recent author, George Tavard, who has benefited from the work of these earlier scholars and has gone on to make his own contribution concerning the relationship of structure and meaning in the study of the *Cántico*. The other aforementioned scholars will be used to complement Tavard's position.

It is Tavard who has most explicitly demonstrated the contribution of the structure of the *Cántico* towards its meaning.[54] This has moved him in the

---

[53] A list of contributions in this area would include the above-stated authors as well as the others listed here. Many of these have already been cited frequently throughout this dissertation: ALONSO, *La Poesia de san Juan de la Cruz;* Anselmo Donazar has a brief, yet inciteful chapter on literary devices in "Perfección formal y valores literarios del Cántico," in *Fray Juan,* 77-83; DUVIVER, *Dynamisme existentiel;* ICAZA, *Stylistic Relationship in the Cántico;* MORALES, *El "Cántico espiritual" de San Juan de la Cruz;* PACHO, "La Estructura literaria del «Cántico espiritual»,"; PACHO ed., *Cántico espiritual: Primera redacción y testo retocado;* PEPIN, *Noces de Feu;* RUIZ SALVADOR, "El Cántico espiritual" in *Introducción a San Juan de la Cruz: El escritor, los escritos, el sistema,* 215-248.

[54] See especially Chapters 3, 7, and 12 in TAVARD, *Poetry and Contemplation,* 37-51; 117-136; 217-228. Although a significant number of authors have offered elements of a structural analysis, no scholar has taken the *Cántico as a whole* and done an indepth structural analysis on the entire text of the poem *in itself* using the theory of the structuralist school of thought as pioneered by Greimas, Lévi-Strauss, Propp, and others. See for example two well known works that set out the basis for the French-language structuralist school of thought: Algirdas Julien GREIMAS, *Sémantique structural: Recherche de méthode,* (Paris: Larousse, 1966) and Claude LÉVI-STRAUSS, *Anthropologie structurale,* (Paris: Plon, 1958). Roger Duvivier has pursued a general study of the structure and meaning of *C4* in conjunction with the commentary in DUVIVIER, *Dynamisme existentiel.* Eulogio Pacho published an article in 1960: PACHO, "La estructura literaria del «Cántico espiritual»," However, the focus of this article concerns more literary genre, the poetry-prose relationship, and the relationship between the *Cántico* and Juan's other major works. Pacho describes the purpose of this article in the following words: "Tal es el propósito del presente artículo: precisar las formas expresivas en que San Juan de la Cruz nos transmite su doctrina espiritual." PACHO, "La estructura literaria del «Cántico espiritual»," 384. Pacho did little work on the structure of the poem, *per se,* and its contribution to the meaning of the *Cántico.* Literary analysis in the literature tends more toward an examination of major symbols and themes that contribute toward an understanding of the *Cántico,* or studies have focused on biblical, popular and classical sources. Although these studies are

direction of the hermeneutical approach to Juan's *Cántico*, although he does not explicitly include many elements from the hermeneutical method that I am suggesting.[55] However, before I begin the investigation of the structure and meaning of the *Cántico*, which *Cántico* will be the focus of the study?

Thus far I have been able to avoid the problem of choice posed by the various forms of the *Cántico* of Juan de la Cruz. Although I presented a brief historical review of the context of the emergence of the various forms of the *Cántico* in Chapter Two, I have not yet needed to choose among these various forms for my methodological analysis. According to the traditional way of approaching the *Cántico*, I would now be at the point where I would be forced to make the choice between what has come to be known as *Cántico A* and *Cántico B*.[56]

Recall that the original *Cántico* of thirty-one stanzas was written while Juan was in prison in Toledo during the first half of 1578. Sometime between 1579 and 1584, in two stages, Juan added eight more verses to the *Cántico*. This poem of thirty-nine stanzas became known as *Cántico A*. Subsequently, between 1584 and 1586, *Cántico A* had one more verse added to it and was further re-

---

invaluable, they are still only a step in completing a thorough *structural analysis* of the *Cántico*. There is still much more work to be done in this area. For Ricoeur, recuperation of meaning is contingent on the deep structure of the text as it is revealed using the methods of structural analysis in the structuralist school of thought.

[55] For example, Tavard readily admits the diversity of interpretations which are possible for Juan's *Cántico*. He mentions "sense" and "semiotic levels," although he does not use these words with a hermeneutical connotation. He therefore implies the possibility of interpretions which are free from the author's intention. In commenting on the *Cántico* he says: "From the standpoint of pure poetry, there is of course no valid objection against the idea that a text may potentially apply to other situations and contexts than those of its original composition, that it must be read, in diverse context, at different semiotic levels, and that it has, consequently, several senses." TAVARD, *Poetry and Contemplation*, 226-227. On the "non-hermeneutical" side Tavard does not include text or reading theory in his analysis. The role of the reading subject in interpretation is therefore eclipsed from the "several senses" of the text to which Tavard refers.

[56] Fairly complete bibliographical information concerning which of these two forms of the *Cántico* constitutes *the Cántico* can be found in: PACHO, "La cuestión crítica del 'Cántico Espiritual': Nota bibliográfica," 309-23. Pacho gives a concise literary and historical commentary in support of the authenticity and primacy of *CB* in PACHO, "El «Cántico Espiritual» retocado," 382-452. However, in this thesis I will suggest that neither *CA* or *CB* can be considered *the Cántico* of Juan de la Cruz. Both are free of each other in certain ways and each are productive of meaning.

arranged into what has become known as *Cántico B*. Those scholars who affirm the authenticity of both *CA* and *CB* generally cite *CB* as *the Cántico* for any course of investigation on the *Cántico*.[57] Few today would deny the authenticity of both accepted versions of the *Cántico*.[58] However, several scholars either have not accepted the authenticity of *CB*, or at least have called it into question, and therefore use *CA* for their inquiries.[59] Or some scholars use *CA* because of its poetic or

[57] The preeminent scholar which upholds the authenticity of both *CA* and *CB* is Eulogio Pacho. See PACHO, *Sus escritos*, 325-392. Colin P. Thompson also supports the authenticity of *CB*. See Thompson's concise and excellent review of the literature concerning the pros and cons of the authenticity of *CB* in THOMPSON, "The Questions of *Cántico* B," in *The Poet and the Mystic*, 33-59. In reference to the additions of *CB* he concludes: "Thus the evidence these additions provide is, in my view, decisive in demonstrating that CB is the work of San Juan and, together with the failure of its opponents to construct a coherent, consistent, and methodical case against it, sufficient to scotch the idea that anyone other than San Juan was responsible for the second redaction of the *Cántico*." Ibid., 54.

[58] The most recent critical Spanish edition of Juan's collected works (the 1988 edition which I am using for this dissertation) includes both *CA* and *CB* as authentic works of the saint: *San Juan de la Cruz: Obras Completas*, ed. José Vicente Rodríguez.

[59] Dom Chevallier opened the debate in this century questioning the authenticity of *CB* in his controversial article of 1922: CHEVALLIER, "Le 'Cantique spirituel' de saint Jean de la Croix a-t-il été interpolé?," 307-342. Jean Baruzi went on to categorically reject the authenticity of *CB*: BARUZI, *Problème de l'expérience mystique*, 16-35. Baruzi summarizes his position as follows: "Les arguments d'ordre historique, d'ordre esthétique et d'ordre philosophico-théologique nous conduisent à la même conclusion. Seule la prudence nous peut interdire une affirmation sans nuances. Mais nous ne pouvons guère hésiter qu'entre deux solutions: ou bien Jean de la Croix, brisé par les persécutions, affaibli en son audace, a lui-même substitué un texte appauvri à son oeuvre véritable ou bien--ce que toutes les données historiques et critiques nous engagent à admettre--la deuxième rédaction du «Cantique spirituel» est un ouvrage apocryphe." Ibid., 34-35. Accepting the critique of Baruzi, Damaso Alonso also rejects *CB* on the grounds that the rearrangement of *CA* into *CB* with the addition of verse 11 is aesthetically a disaster: "La segunda ordenación del poema, comparada con la primera desde el punto de vista estético, me parece una verdadera catástrofe." ALONSO, *La Poesía de San Juan de la Cruz*, 289, n. 20. Without seriously questioning the relationship between *CA* and *CB* Fernande PEPIN also uses *CA* because of its aesthetic appeal, suggesting, without further discussion, that it is closer to the "author-poet." She says: "Pour ce qui est du «Cántico espiritual», nous avons suivi le texte de la première rédaction, du manuscrit de Sanlúcar, qui nous a paru plus artistique et donc plus près de l'auteur-poète." PEPIN, *Noces de Feu*, ix. Such a methodological assumption, although it does not reject outright *CB*, can at least be called into question. Is the writer of *CB* not also an "author-poet?" Among others who reject the authenticity of *CB* are: LONGCHAMP, *Lectures de Jean de la Croix*. A summary of his position is given in Ibid., 417-420; KRYNEN, *Le Cantique spirituel commenté et refondu*. Krynen attributes the second *Cántico* to a Carmelite priest-theologian who lived in the early part of the 17th century, Thomas de Jésus (Ibid., 229), although this has not been a very well accepted hypothesis; Rose Marie Icaza, does not outright reject *CB*, but uses *CA* because of the work of Dom Chevallier. Icaza also gives an excellent short commentary on the bibliography available concerning this debate in ICAZA, *Stylistic*

historical primacy before the redactions of *CB*.

As I have already mentioned, nearly all scholars make a choice for either *Cántico A* (based on the manuscript of Sanlúcar de Barrameda) or *Cántico B*, the "revised" *Cántico* (based on the manuscript at the *Carmelitas Descalzas* in Jaén). Yet, when interpreting the *Cántico* of Juan de la Cruz, one may question whether it is *methodologically correct* to simply choose between *Cántico A* and *Cántico B*, disregarding one or the other completely? Further to this point, might there be an authentic "third" *Cántico*, complete in itself, which is the first *Cántico* Juan de la Cruz wrote in the prison at Toledo? In short, is there only one *Cántico* which merits the attention of the sanjuanist scholar, or are there in fact three inter-dependent *Cánticos*, each having its own contribution to make toward the overall sanjuanist opus?

I stated earlier that Juan de la Cruz most likely left prison with the thirty-one stanza *Cántico*. Whether it was actually written in some form is not absolutely certain, but the fact of the completion of this initial composition in at least its oral form (which I will refer to as *Cántico O* = *CO* = *Cántico original*), is undisputed. What reasons could we cite to suggest that this original poem of thirty-one stanzas is not a complete poem in itself? Juan would have had sufficient time to complete the poem while in his Toledan cell. Given the fact that this originary composition existed independently of any additions for perhaps up to three years, why would we want to assume that this composition was not a completed poem when Juan escaped from prison? However, virtually all sanjuanist scholars have assumed that the primitive poem was not a complete poem. The first complete poem is assumed to have come with its written form and with the addition of eight more stanzas known today as *Cántico A*. As already mentioned, Juan redacted *CA* into *CB*

Relationship in the Cántico, 2-4; Roger Duvivier, even with his rejection of *CB* curiously includes the famous verse 11 of *CB* in his analysis of *CA*: "La strophe «*Descubre tu presencia*» sera admise, non sans réserves, au sein du plan A." DUVIVIER, *Dynamisme existentiel*, 44; José Morales also uses *CA* citing for his reason: "Nuestra preferencia por el manuscrito de Sanlúcar está basada en el hecho histórico de que, de todas las copias que han llegado hasta nosotros, la más preciada e interesante es el códice que está en posesión de la monjas Carmelitas Descalzas de Sanlúcar de Barrameda." MORALES, *El Cántico espiritual de San Juan de la Cruz*, 21.

230

with revisions and the addition of one more stanza. To ask the question again, might all three of these texts (*CO*, *CA* and *CB*) be considered to have a unique role to play in the mediation of meaning?

As far as I know, only one scholar, George Tavard, has suggested that there are three *Cánticos*, the first being the poem of thirty-one stanzas, with which Juan left prison.[60] Tavard cites the temporal distance among the three poems (the Toledan poem, *CA*, and *CB*) as being one of the main reasons to support the independence of each literary creation.[61] A second reason which Tavard gives in support of the literal independence of the primitive *Cántico* of thirty-one stanzas is based on the quality of the ending which Juan gave the Toledan poem: "stanza 31 provides a perfect ending to what John had composed in Toledo. The *Canticle* must have been in the same shape as the other poems written during captivity: they were finished works."[62] Besides the arguments of temporal distance and the integrity of the ending which support the independence and completeness of *CO*, can further support be added if we consider the poem in light of Ricoeur's theory of mimesis and metaphorical reference which has already been examined in Chapter Four? Recall that metaphoricity of a poem is not operative only within the interplay of words in a phrase or a particular expression, but it is operative at the level of the entire text.[63] It is the metaphorical reference of each text which constructs the singularity and uniqueness of the world-of-the-text. But Ricoeur says that the metaphoricity of a

---

[60] TAVARD, *Poetry and Contemplation*, 37-38.

[61] Since the commentary on *CA* was a project initiated much later by Madre Ana de Jesús at Beas, the Toledan poem, as a complete poem may be read and interpreted without being strictly tied to a subsequent commentary. This approach liberates the primitive *Cántico* from Juan's own analysis and commentary, something which cannot be said of the two subsequent "versions."

[62] TAVARD, *Poetry and Contemplation*, 38.

[63] "The bearers of the metaphor are not the individual sentences of the narratives, but the whole structure, the narrative as a whole, what Aristotle had called the *mythos* in the poem." RICOEUR, "Biblical Hermeneutics," 94.

text is in turn supported by the dramatic structure of the text.[64]

It is the clues given by the *plot*, "in the challenge which this plot displays for the main characters, and in the answer of these characters to the *crisis* situation" which provide the basis for the metaphorical referent of the text.[65] The dramatic structure thus forms the dynamism of a text and is integral to its meaning. What *happens* in a text is homogeneous to this meaning.[66] "In other words, it is the 'plot' as such which is the bearer of the metaphoric process."[67] "Any existential transparities which can be advocated later have to be rooted in the dramatic structure itself. It is this dramatic structure which *means* that the existence may be 'lost' or 'gained.' Existence, as it were, has to be redescribed according to the basic plot movements."[68]

Since metaphorical redescription determines the world-of-the-text, and metaphorical redescription is contingent on dramatic structure, then a difference in dramatic structure supports the possibility that a different world-of-the-text is configured by each of the *Cánticos*. This would lend support to the hermeneutic autonomy, as well as the inter-dependence, of each of the three texts which have come down to us. A hermeneutic interpretation of Juan's *Cántico* would then consider all three of the texts and the contribution each has to make toward new meaning.

---

[64] RICOEUR, "Biblical Hermeneutics," 97. Ricoeur is developing his argument here concerning the metaphorical reference of parabolic discourse in scripture. However, the process of poetic redescription which he finds operative in the parables may be applied to the poetic redescription operative in poetry as well, i.e. Juan's *Cántico*. Let us recall at this point the salient characteristic of what we have already referred to as "metaphorical reference" in Chapter Four. Metaphorical reference divests discourse of its ordinary descriptive function in order to serve its heuristic function of re-description. It is precisely this characteristic of poetic discourse which poetry and parables share in common. See "The Metaphorical Process," in Ibid., 75-106.

[65] RICOEUR, "Biblical Hermeneutics," 97.

[66] "The surface-structure of the 'plot' is not an epiphenomenon, but the message itself." RICOEUR, "Biblical Hermeneutics," 71.

[67] RICOEUR, "Biblical Hermeneutics," 98.

[68] RICOEUR, "Biblical Hermeneutics," 98.

232

In summary, therefore, a dramatic analysis may suggest a different referential capacity for each of the *Cánticos*, may point to their inter-dependence or complementarity, and may lead us to exclude the possibility of choosing one text of the *Cántico* over and against the other(s) in a complete hermeneutical reading of Juan's *Cántico*. Let us now turn to the project of an examination of the dramatic structures of *CO*, *CA*, and *CB*.[69]

3.1 Dramatic Structure of *CO*

As already mentioned above Juan did not write a commentary on *CO*; his first commentary was begun on *CA* only a few years after the poem was completed. This opens up the possibility of reading *CO* as a poem without the influence of a commentary. The commentary simply did not exist at the time of the completion of *CO*. This fact, however, does not exclude the use of inter-textual criticism or the relatedness of *CO* to the texts of *CA* and *CB*.

In light of the fundamental theme of *CO*, that of the relationship between the Bride and Bridegroom, *CO* can be divided into the following sections to highlight its dramatic structure:[70]

I. *CO* Dramatic Structure: The Bride-Bridegroom Relationship[71]

Search by the *Bride* for the Bridegroom in creatures   st. 1-4
    Response of the *Creatures*   st. 5

---

[69] Note that henceforth I shall use the following abbreviation to refer to Juan's originary poem: *CO* = the thirty-one stanzas of the *Cántico original* written while in prison in Toledo in 1578. I will continue to use the traditional abbreviations for the two accepted versions of the poem: *CA* = the thirty-nine stanzas of the *Cántico* most likely completed in either Baeza or Granada sometime between 1579 and 1581; *CB* = the fourty stanzas of the *Cántico* which emerged in Granada sometime between 1584 and 1586. Use of "*Cántico*" will continue to refer to all three poems in a generic fashion.

[70] Although I have modified some of the language used and expounded on many of the main ideas, the following analysis is based, in large part, on TAVARD, *Prayer and Contemplation*, 39-51.

[71] Again, I have clarified somewhat the language which Tavard uses to express the bride-bridegroom relationship. The italics indicate who the protagonist is in that section of the poem.

Desire expressed by the *Bride* for the presence
of the Bridegroom himself (rather than via the
mediation of creatures)   st. 6-12
    Response of the *Bridegroom*   st. 12

Song of the *Bride* -- encounter of the Bride and Bridegroom
    The Bridegroom is found by the Bride through the encounter
        with Creatures   st. 13-16
    The Bridegroom is found in himself   st. 17-26

    Narration by *Creatures*   st. 27

    Response by the *Bridegroom*   st. 28-30

Conclusion by the *Bride*   st. 31

Although the sections differ significantly in length, they are united thematically through the dynamics expressed by the singular movement of desire-search-encounter which is repeated throughout the poem. The following structure thus surfaces when we consider this fundamental movement of the poem:

II. *CO* Structure According to the Movement of Desire-Search-Encounter

Search (I)   st. 1-4
    Preliminary answer (1)   st. 5

Search-desire (II)   st. 6-11
    First full answer (2)   st. 12

Encounter (I), responding to search (I)   st. 13-16

Encounter (II), responding to search-desire (II)   st. 17-27
    Second full answer (3)   st. 28-30

Conclusion   st. 31

Regarding the overall dramatic structure of *CO*, several observations

234

can be made with respect to the significant role that nature plays.[72] Following this one element in several key places in *CO* will allow us to affirm the completeness of the poem and will give us a sense of its overall meaning.

Very early in *CO*, we see the importance nature plays in the journey of these two lovers. It is the response of nature (the creatures in stanza 5), which invites the Bride to go further in her search:[73]

Pouring out a thousand graces,	Mil gracias derramando
he passed these groves in haste;	pasó por estos sotos con presura
and having looked at them,	e yéndolos mirando
with his image alone,	con sola su figura
clothed them in beauty	vestidos los dejó

The Bride is lured on by natural beauty which reflects the love which she seeks. The expression of her desire for the Bridegroom in stanzas 6-11 is likewise followed by the appearance of nature in the crystalline fountain which, again, appears to spur on her hope. As the Bride says:[74]

O spring like crystal!	¡Oh cristalina fuente:
If only, on your silvered-over faces,	se en esos tus semblantes plateados
you would suddenly form	formases de repente
the eyes I have desired,	los ojos deseados
which I bear sketched deep within my heart.	que tengo en mis entrañas dibujados!

---

[72] The dramatic analysis presented here does not take into consideration the complexity and detail of the poem. However, it satisfies our purpose in that it situates the need for a more detailed *structural analysis* within the hermeneutical approach to Juan's *Cántico*. Further work is yet to be done on the structural analysis of *CO as a complete text in itself*. The same is true of *CA* and *CB*. Because of the poem's narrative movement a semiotic approach to the text might provide some valuable insights into the text. Walter Vogels gives a general, and very practical, introduction to this method of analyzing a text. See Walter VOGELS, *Reading and Preaching the Bible: A New Semiotic Approach*, Background Books 4, (Wilmington, DE: Michael Glazier, Inc., 1986). See especially Chapter Two, Ibid., 30-75 where Vogels presents the basic movements of a narrative text. These are: **Beginning State** (negative state usually characterized by some lack) -> **Transformation** (manipulation, competence, performance, sanction) -> **End-state** (positive state where the lack has disappeared). Given the dynamics operative within the "story" of the *Cántico*, this approach could provide valuable information in the context of a hermeneutical reading.

[73] *CO* 5

[74] *CO* 11

Her hope lies in the capacity for these waters to be transformed into a truer reflection of the love which she seeks. But even now there is deep within her heart the kind of presence which she seeks in the *cristalina fuente*. This presence is already "sketched," yet the fullness of the image is yet to come. And then, as if her request is immediately fulfilled, causing her to move into ecstasy, she begs the Bridegroom to withdraw "the eyes" she has desired:[75]

Withdraw them, Beloved,	¡Apártalos, Amado,
I am taking flight!	que voy de vuelo!

Beyond the mere "sketching" which lies in the depths of the Bride's heart, the experience of encounter proves to be too much for her at this point. Nature, even in all of its "earthliness," is not so "natural," and so she sings its glorious praise as the Beloved which she seeks. The contradistinction of the "natural" and the "divine" seems to become meaningless in this context. We thus come to the eruption of adjectives in the *Cántico*, which, to this point, were practically absent:[76]

My Beloved, the mountains,	Mi Amado las montañas
and lonely wooded valleys,	los valles solitarios nemorosos
strange islands,	las ínsulas extrañas
and resounding rivers,	los ríos sonorosos
the whistling of love-stirring breezes,	el silbo de los aires amorosos.

---

[75] *CO* 12

[76] *CO* 13-15. This peculiar absence of adjectives (virtually none are present in the first ten stanzas of the *Cántico*) has not gone unnoticed by sanjuanist scholars. Damaso Alonso summarizes the effect of this: "Las consecuencias inmediatas de la escasez en el empleo del adjetivo por San Juan de la Cruz, se comprenden en seguida: se aumenta la velocidad, la cohesión y la concentración de todo el período poético; resulta resaltada la función del nombre. Resaltada en dos sentidos: porque los sustantivos se adensan, se suceden con una mayor rapidez, y, aun más importante, porque el nombre aislado, desnudo, tiene que multiplicar sus valencias afectivas, recargándose al mismo tiempo de su original fuerza intuitiva, que en la poesía del Renacimiento había cómodamente abandonado a la función adjetival." ALONSO, *La Poesía de san Juan de la Cruz*, 187-88. Alonso goes on to describe this "salvific" use of the adjective in the context of Renaissance poetry where the adjective was "monótonamente usado:" "Y es que el adjetivo, monótonamente usado por la poesía renacentista, se redime así, se salva otra vez. Tras del ardor requemado de las primeras estrofas, ¡cómo volvemos a gustar el efecto mágico del adjetivo, que prolonga y enriquece la dulce estela del nombre!." Ibid., 190.

the tranquil night	la noche sosegada
at the time of the rising dawn,	en par de los levantes de la aurora
silent music,	la música callada
sounding solitude	la soledad sonora
the supper that refreshes, and deepens love.	la cena que recrea y enamora.

	Nuestro lecho florido
Our bed is in flower,	de cuevas de leones enlazado
bound round with linking dens of lions,	en púrpura tendido
hung with purple,	de paz edificado
built up in peace,	de mil escudos de oro coronado.
and crowned with a thousand shields of gold.	

The Beloved is no longer just the "wounded stag ... in sight on the hill,"[77] but now *is* the mountains, the lonely wooded valleys, the strange islands, resounding rivers and so on.[78] This determination has clarified the content of "I-don't-know-what" of stanza 7:

All who are free	Y todos cuantos vagan
tell me a thousand graceful things of you;	de ti me van mil gracias refiriendo
all wound me more and leave me dying	y todos más me llagan
of, ah, I-don't-know-what behind their stammering	y déjame muriendo
	un so sé qué quedan balbuciendo.

Previously "creatures" were experienced as a "stammering" reflection of the Beloved. However, by stanza 17 a transformation has taken place in the perception of the Bride. Creatures are now seen as participating in an intimate way in the life of the Beloved. Tavard picks up on this metamorphosis in the context of what happens next:

> Then, through an unexpected reversal, in stanza 18 the bridegroom gives his breast to the bride. How bold the poet for whom all is pure! He stammers; he vainly attempts to express directly the "sweet and living knowledge." And the bride responds through her unreserved

---

[77] "El ciervo vulnerado por el otero asoma," *CO* 12

[78] TAVARD, *Poetry and Contemplation*, 47.

self-gift. Stanza 19 echoes back the theme of love. Once more the bride turns to the creatures. For she realizes that she cannot always remain in the inner wine cellar. When she leaves it she will seem to be lost, yet in reality she will have been found (st. 20). With the bridegroom she will take the creatures and make a garland with them, which she will tie together with one of her hairs (st. 21).[79]

This arrangement of beauty captivates the Bridegroom (st. 22), and then in another astonishing reversal, it is the eye of the Bride that wounds the Beloved Bridegroom:

You considered	En solo aquel cabello
that one hair fluttering at my neck;	que en mi cuello volar consideraste
you gazed at it upon my neck	mirástele en mi cuello
and it captivated you;	y en él preso quedaste
and one of my eyes wounded you.	y en uno de mis ojos te llagaste.

Both have now been wounded by the love of the other, but the Bride readily admits that she is capable of such a love only because of the love which the Bridegroom first bestowed upon her:

When you looked at me	Cuando tú me mirabas
your eyes imprinted your grace in me;	tu gracia en mí tus ojos imprimían;
for this you loved me ardently;	por eso me adamabas
and thus my eyes deserved	y en eso merecían
to adore what they beheld in you.	los míos adorar lo que en ti vían.

The Bride and Bridegroom then recline in an intimate embrace (st. 27), not in the wine cellar, but in the "sweet garden" of the Bride's desire.[80]

---

[79] TAVARD, *Poetry and Contemplation,* 48. Helmut Hatzfeld also notes that this is a reversal of the drama in the *Song of Songs*: "Diferente del *Canticum* (7, 10-13) donde es la Esposa la que ofrece sus pechos al Esposo, mientras que, en el *Cántico* es el Esposo el que da sus pechos a la Esposa, un *tour de force*, justificado por Isaías (60, 12): 'A los pechos de Dios seréis llevados'." HATZFELD, "Sobre la Prosa Sanjuanista en el 'Cántico Espiritual'," 316.

[80] *CO* 27, 1 and 2. As Tavard has pointed out in TAVARD, *Poetry and Contemplation,* 256, n. 28, it is interesting to note in the commentary on *CA* that Juan de la Cruz locates the following narration of stanza 27 in the discourse of the Bridegroom:

The bride has entered	Entrado se ha la esposa
the sweet garden of her desire,	en el ameno huerto deseado
and she rests in delight,	y a su sabor reposa
laying her neck	el cuello reclinado

In stanza 28, with an allusion to the story of the Fall in Genesis 3, the Bridegroom speaks of the "restoration of his Bride" beneath the apple tree. It was here where the Bride's mother had once been "corrupted." This union of love between the Bride and Bridegroom thus brings harmony to an order which had previously been perverted. The Bridegroom then returns his attention to nature and calls to creatures in a succession of nouns that is accompanied by not a single verb and only by three adjectives (st. 29). In the following stanzas the Bridegroom instructs these creatures not to disrupt the Bride as they previously had done in stanza 6. Therefore the Bride may "sleep in deeper peace" (st. 30).

The examination of the last verse of *CO*, stanza 31, is important since I am suggesting that the original *Cántico* of thirty-one stanzas is a complete text.[81] Stanza 31 appears to be the *last* stanza of *CO* because of the role it plays in the overall structure of *CO*. Let us now take a closer look at this stanza and its link to the overall structure and meaning of the poem.

It is evident that stanza 31 alludes to the *Song of Songs*, 8:4. *CO* 31 is a loose paraphrase of the discourse of the Bridegroom in the *Song*. The passage from the *Song of Songs* reads:[82]

I charge you,
daughters of Jerusalem,
not to stir my love, nor rouse it,
until it please to awake.

on the gentle arms of her Beloved.   sobre los dulces brazos del Amado.

Commenting on this verse in *CA*, Juan de la Cruz begins: "In this stanza, where the Bridegroom speaks." However, this does not make sense in the flow of the poem, nor with the reference to both the Bride and the Bridegroom by the inferred narrator. We see in this instance that the meaning of the poem contradicts the author's commentary. Here we have a case where the text must stand by itself in opposition to what even the author says about it. It is the narrator, presumably the chorus of creatures whose discourse has been woven throughout the drama, who speaks stanza 27. The Bridegroom's discourse only begins in stanza 28.

[81] The analysis of this verse is taken from TAVARD, *Poetry and Contemplation*, 49-51.

[82] Taken from *The Jerusalem Bible*, Standard Edition, (London: Dartman, Longman & Todd, 1966), 1002. "The 'nymphs of Judea' of John of the Cross are easily recognizable as the 'daughters of Jerusalem' of the Bible." TAVARD, *Poetry and Contemplation*, 49.

Stanza 31 of *CO* reads:[83]

You nymphs of Judea, while among flowers and roses the amber spreads its perfume, stay away, there on the outskirts: do not so much as seek to touch our thresholds.	¡Oh ninfas de Judea! en tanto que en las flores y rosales el ámbar perfumea, morá en los arrabales y no queráis tocar nuestros umbrales.

What becomes immediately apparent is the reversal that has taken place between the *Song of Songs* and *CO* 31. In the biblical passage it is the Bridegroom who speaks; however, in Juan's poem it is the Bride. In stanza 30 of *CO* the Bridegroom has ordered the creatures not to disturb the Bride since she is deep in sleep! The Bride responds in the following stanza which is *CO* 31. But how can the Bride speak if she is sleeping? The Bride must therefore be dreaming.[84] To speak, as the Bride does here while sleeping, is to be in a state of dreaming. This is why the "daughters of Jerusalem" have become the "nymphs of Judea": this signals the emergence of another level of reality in which the Bride now participates. Nymphs are imaginary, semi-divine mythological maidens who animate and inhabit seas, rivers, hills, fountains, woods, and trees. These creatures that signal the dream-like state are silenced since the Bridegroom is now communicating with the Bride at another level of her being. It is not the iconic quality of nature or creatures that will speak to the Bride of her Beloved, but now it will be the silent whispers from the Bridegroom himself which come in the stillness of her deep sleep, that is, the depths of her person. The Bridegroom's word does not disturb the slumber of the Bride since the Bridegroom speaks in silence at this level. Here the Bride experiences the apophatic way, that of negative knowledge, of knowing her Beloved. Within the

---

[83] Kavanaugh and Rodriquez translate "ninfas" from the Spanish into "girls" in their *Collected Works* (Kav., 474). However, I have used the English word "nymphs" as does the Spanish. This change in translation is important since it is the role played by this mythological semi-divine maiden which brings *CO* to its conclusion as we will see in the following analysis. Although "girls" is an acceptable translation of "ninfas" into English, it destroys the function stanza 31 holds as the "completing" stanza of *CO*.

[84] TAVARD, *Poetry and Contemplation*, 49.

bosom of her Beloved, where all is silenced, the only *reality* the Bride experiences is the Bridegroom himself.

In this way stanza 31 brings *CO* to a logical conclusion. The Bride is close to the fullness of the mystery of the love of her Beloved. In the depths of her being she drinks sweetly from his word and experiences the intensity of his being. The poem is complete in the tranquillity of this setting. I will now make a number of observations concerning the overall structure of *CO*.

The structure of *CO* is characterized by recapitulations, transformations, and reversals. Images and symbols of nature are revisited throughout the poem, but each time in new and varied forms which reveal a different depth of the relationship which is growing between the lovers. The use of the nature images is not mere poetic decoration, but, rather, it constructs a movement within the poem which is cyclic and reciprocal, as opposed to a strictly linear movement. The Bride and Bridegroom do not terminate individual states of relationship, passing from one "level" to another, but rather move more deeply within those which exist already. Nor is the movement of the relationship one-sided; there is a certain mutuality that develops between the giving and accepting of love both on the part of the Bride and of the Bridegroom. Again, it is the use of the nature images that carries these dynamics for the reader. In summary, examples which we have already seen will suffice to show these points.

The "eyes" of the Bridegroom in the fountain (st. 11) which caused the Bride to "take flight" appear again in the "eyes" of the Bride which, this time, *wound the Bridegroom* (st. 22). The Bride and the Bridegroom are capable of wounding each other with their intense love for each other. The stag that appeared on the hill (st. 12) is told sometime later not to appear (st. 25). The overwhelming presence of nature, indicated in the plethora of adjectives in stanzas 13-15, is lessened in the admonition of stanza 30. "Nature" thus takes on a different role in the Bride-Bridegroom relationship as the relationship deepens in itself.[85] And lastly, a striking example of reversal which confirms the completeness of *CO* is the dream-speech of the Bride (st. 31). The dream-speech of CO 31 tells us of the harmony of the Bride's present state. The iconoclasm of nature is now complete. It is only in silence that the Beloved can speak and impart the intensity of the love which the Bride so desired and in which she now rests. The state of the Bride in stanza 1 characterized by anxiety and searching has been transformed into one of serenity and calm in stanza 31. The Bride now rests in a state of hope. Her dreamed-of future, however, is not yet fully realized in her present reality.

3.2 Dramatic Structure of *CA*

The second *Cántico*, referred to as *CA*, had eight stanzas added to the originary *Cántico*, *CO*. These are the stanzas Juan added in two successive steps after his escape from the prison in Toledo.[86] We already know the fundamental story of *CA* which contains thirty-nine stanzas. The poem is about a woman in search of her Beloved. Her journey in this pursuit takes her to woods and thickets, to hills and valleys. What I would like to show is that the addition of these eight stanzas has changed the world of the poem: it has not merely extended and completed the journey which *CO* began. Again, I will show this by a dramatic analysis of the poem.

We know *CO* was composed while Juan was in the confines of the Toledo prison. Let us review the conditions under which *CA* would have taken shape. The addition of the eight new stanzas was effected amidst a great amount of bustling activity in Juan's life. During this time, that is sometime between 1582 and 1584, Juan laboured to meet the demands of his pastoral and administrative work in

---

[85] It could be said that "nature" simply mediates in a different way, it has become more transparent to the divine nature which called it forth. However, we have seen in stanza 17 "nature" intimately participates in the life of the Beloved.

[86] See my presentation of the history of these additions in Chapter Three: 3.2 The Composition of the *Cántico* -- Poem and Commentary.

the countryside of Andalucía. The Teresian Reform was well underway. However, Juan's great mentor and foundress of the Reform, Teresa of Avila, died in October of 1582. Juan had seen her for the last time in 1581. Therefore, this period was a time of intense change and transition for Juan. His journey had taken him from the despair of prison to the beauty of the countryside of Andalucía, and then to the grief of personal loss. A new text was forming in this context for which Juan chose to use *CO* as the basis. The new text comprised all of *CO* plus eight new stanzas added at the end.

Tavard describes the first stanzas of this addition, that is, stanzas 32-34:

> Stanzas 32-34 exhibit characteristics of a purposeful adjunction. This is clear from the first verses. After the dream of stanza 31, where, in the guise of nymphs, the soul evoked the daughters of Judea, asking them not to wake her up by making noise in the garden for she was asleep in her Beloved's arms, the soul now turns to her Beloved. Her first words, "Hide yourself," reverse the perspective of the first stanza of the poem: "Where are you hiding ... ?" In other words we are at a new departure; we begin a new reading.[87]

At the beginning, the Bride thought it was the hiding place which separated her from her lover, yet now, in stanza 32, it is precisely the hiding place which becomes the place of intimate encounter.[88] Now awakened from her dream-speech in the midst of reality, the Bride knows she can be united with her Bridegroom only in the most secret of places. Indeed, the Bride has awakened to a new level of being in the world and within her own self. The pattern of recapitulations surfaces again here. Juan uses images in *CA* 32, already familiar in *CO*, to signal the new level of being where the lovers now reside:[89]

---

[87] TAVARD, *Poetry and Contemplation*, 120.

[88] Again, this analysis is based on Tavard's presentation in TAVARD, *Poetry and Contemplation*, 117-136.

[89] *CA* 32. Kavanaugh and Rodriguez translate *carillo* here as "my love" in their *Collected Works* (Kav., 474). However, given the sequence of diminuitives that follow in response in stanza 33, and the fact that *carillo* itself is the diminutive in Spanish, a more acceptable translation, it seems to me,

Hide yourself, dearest one;	Escóndete, Carillo,
Turn with your face to the mountains,	y mira con tu haz a las montañas
and do not speak;	y no quieras decillo,
but look at those companions	mas mira las compañas
going with her through strange islands.	de la que va por ínsulas extrañas.

The "mountains" of stanza 32 remind us of the "mountains" of stanza 3 where the Bride went in search of her Beloved. But this time she exhorts her Beloved not to speak. This call to silence is reminiscent of the creatures of stanza 6 who also did not speak. While the creatures of stanza 6 were incapable of speaking of the secret place of encounter, the Beloved is quite capable of speaking of it but is urged not to. This time the Bride uses silence to protect that which she has discovered. The Bride invites her lover to "look at those companions," recalling the nature-companions of stanza 4. Under the gaze of the Beloved, creatures have taken on a new role: they are now companions along the journey who go with the Bride to "strange islands." We have already seen these "islands" in stanza 13, where the Bride found her Beloved amidst "mountains, and lonely wooded valleys, strange islands and resounding rivers."[90]

The Bridegroom goes on to affirm this new situation. Calling the Bride "dove," as he did in stanza 12, he says in stanza 33:

The small white dove	La blanca palomica
has returned to the ark with an olive branch;	al arca con el ramo se ha tornado
and now the turtledove	y ya la tortolica
has found its longed-for mate by the green river banks.	al socio deseado
	en las riberas verdes ha hallado.

However, whereas in stanza 12 the noun *paloma* is used, stanza 33 uses the more endearing diminutive *palomica*, (small white dove) and *tortolica*, (turtledove). The use of these endearing terms respond to the Bride's diminutive *carillo* (dearest one)

would be "dear" or "dearest one." Therefore, I have used "dearest one" in the translation in my own text.

[90] CA 13

in stanza 32.

These added stanzas lead the reader to encounter the intensified relationship of the Bride and Bridegroom. The "sounding solitude" of the "tranquil night" and of the "silent music" of the Bride alone in stanza 14 becomes the shared solitude of the lovers in stanza 34:

She lived in solitude,	En soledad vivía
and now in solitude has built her next;	y en soledad ha puesto ya su nido
and in solitude he guides her,	y en soledad la guía
he alone, who also bears	a solas su querido
in solitude the wound of love.	también en soledad de amor herido.

The Beloved himself has been wounded by love; in stanza 12 he was described as a "wounded stag" high on the hill, but the Beloved now resides within the nest of the Bride. A reversal of roles between the Bride and Bridegroom has taken place: he goes forth to search for her as her companion in the mountains, on the hill, in the purity of waters, and in the thicket. This is accentuated in stanza 35:

Let us rejoice, Beloved,	Gocémonos, Amado,
and let us go forth to behold ourselves	y vámanos a ver
in your beauty,	en tu hermosura
to the mountain and to the hill,	al monte o al collado
to where the pure water flows,	do mana el agua pura;
and further, deep into the thicket.	entremos más adentro en la espesura,

This journey of the Bride and Bridegroom recalls images already familiar to the reader. The "high caverns in the rock" (st. 36) remind us of the "dens of lions" (st. 15) and the "cellar" of stanza 17. It was here, in this "cellar," that the Bridegroom gave his love his Beloved breast. However, in stanza 37, he gives her "life:"

There you will show me	Allí me mostrarías
what my soul has been seeking,	aquello que mi alma pretendía
and then you will give me,	y luego me darías
you, my life, will give me there	allí tú, ¡vida mía!
what you gave me on that other day:	aquello que me diste el otro día:

The Beloved now give more than his breast, he gives life itself, that which he already gave "on that other day,"

Noted here, in these most intimate terms exhibiting the love between the Bride and Bridegroom, are many "indeterminate expressions." For example, demonstrative pronouns are left undetermined by not linking them to specific nouns: in stanza 37 there are the phrases *aquello que me alma pretendía* ("what my soul has been seeking") and *aquello que me diste el otro día* ("what you gave me on that other day"). What is shown and given in stanza 37 is not described other than "what was given" and "life." Stanzas 36 and 37 use the indeterminate expression of time *y luego* ("and then"). Space is also relativized and has become indeterminate. This is seen in stanzas 36 and 37 with the use of *allí* ("there").[91] In the entire poem it is not indicated who these lovers are, or where they live. They are not named, they could be anybody. Other vague expressions throughout *Cántico A* include: stanza 2 *aquel que yo más quiero* ("him I love most"); stanza 7 *un no sé qué* ("I-don't-know-what"); stanza 17 *ya cosa no sabía* ("I no longer knew anything")" and stanza 18 *allí me enseño ciencia muy sabrosa* ("there he taught me a sweet and living knowledge").

Damaso Alonso suggests that these generalities are due to the incapacity of Juan to be more precise, that is, his mystical experience is essentially indescribable and therefore Juan cannot give all the details.[92] However, within Ricoeur's theory of text, it is precisely these indeterminate expressions which

---

[91] The English term "there" does not seem to have the same indeterminate sense as the Spanish "allí." The significance of the term "alli" in Juan's *Cántico* has, to a large extent, gone unnoticed by sanjuanist scholars. An exception would be THOMPSON, *The Poet and the Mystic,* 88. Thompson notes the repitition of "alli" in *CA* 18, 28, 36, and 37. Speaking of the many places for which "alli" is used he says: "Each place must have a more than a literal meaning; you don't get betrothed in a wine-cellar and under an appletree, nor is a dark cave a good place for showing anyone anything. For this reason, and through its insistent repetition, 'allí' acquires a power of its own, a combination of all these places and more, as the locus of some extraordinary event which must continually be approached in different ways because it is so momentous." Ibid., 88.

[92] In his study of Juan's style of writing Alonso notes certain characteristics, one of which are these vague indications of time and place: "Aqui notaría primero el contraste que ofrecen los lugares de gran vaguedad conceptual, plasmados a veces en fórmulas del lenguaje corriente, y aquellos otros en que un sutil concepto se expresa con alambicada y a la par matemática precisión. Abunden lo bastante para que no se escapen ni al lector más ligero los ejemplos de la primera clase. Son expresiones, vagas, indeterminadas, borrosas: 'aquello que mi alma pretendía', 'aquello que me diste el otro día,' 'un no sé qué que quedan balbuciendo', ... *Todas ellas fórmulas expresivas de la imposibilidad de expresión de lo inefable.*" ALONSO, *La Poesia de san Juan de la Cruz,* 175. (emphasis mine)

mediate meaning in the act of reading. It is up to the reader to "fill in" the lack of information around time, space, and nouns. Thus the time of the poem becomes the time of the reader;[93] the space of encounter, the space of the reader; and that which is received is that which is given to the reader. In this structure we have an excellent example of what will be discussed in more detail in Chapter Six on the "Interpretive Dynamics Operative Between the Text and Its Reader" and "Reading as the Production of Play." For now we can say that the text and its structure are open and available for the reader to interpret in a variety of ways.

It is also to be noted that stanzas 35-37 are written projecting the dynamic of the poem into the future: *gocémonos* ("let us rejoice") and *vámonos* ("let us go forth") (st. 35); *y luego a las subidas* ("and then we will go on") and *y allí nos entraremos* ("there we shall enter") (st. 36); *allí me mostrarías* ("there you will show me"); *y luego me darías* ("and then you will give me") (st. 37). The use of the future tense accentuates further the indeterminate nature of this part of the poem. The future tense expresses the longed-for fullness of what the Bride has already come to know. The Bride invites the Bridegroom to the completeness of what the "soul has been seeking" (st. 37). The Bride thus expresses a certain hopefulness in what she has not yet fully lived. The Bride and the Bridegroom can go still "further, deep into the thicket" (st. 36).

What has been give is stated in stanza 38:

the breathing of the air,	el aspirar de el aire
the song of the sweet nightingale,	el canto de la dulce filomena
the grove and its living beauty	el soto y su donaire
in the serene night,	en la noche serena
with a flame that is consuming and painless.	con llama que consume y do da pena.

This listing calls to mind the sudden arrival of the Beloved equated with nature in stanzas 13-15: "My Beloved, the mountains, and lonely wooded

---

[93] Jorge Guillén observes: "The things that happen, throughout the *Canticle* and the *Flame*, are set before us in a very real present. This is not a past already concluded that the poet reconstructs. Nothing in the poems is alien to the burning actuality which here and now--within the compass of the poem--sets forth its present acts of love." GUILLÉN, *Language and Poetry*, 87.

valleys, strange islands and resounding rivers" and so on. Once again, nature, signalling the here and now, reflects the intensity of the relationship shared between the Bride and the Bridegroom. The Bride and the Bridegroom have finally arrived at the possibility of giving one another the completeness of each other's life. In the dream-speech of stanza 31, the Bride thought she had passed the threshold into the reality of this fullness. It was this experience which terminated *CO*. The intensity of the Bride-Bridegroom relationship no longer exists as if in a dream, but instead is a *lived reality*. It is this experience which brings to an end *CA* with stanza 39:

No one looked at her,	Que nadie lo miraba;
nor did Aminadab appear;	Aminadab tampoco parecía
the siege was still;	y el cerco sosegaba
and the cavalry,	y la caballería
at the sight of the waters, descended.	a vista de las aguas descendía.

In the absence of anybody who could possibly see, away from all evil, symbolized in Aminadab, absolute goodness prevailed. The cavalry, normally a noisy, ferocious, and fast moving group, becomes the image of silence, passivity, and stillness before the descent into the waters. All that was in turbulence is now quieted, submerged in the waters of life.

We see then that Juan has constructed a different dramatic structure with the addition of the eight new stanzas. The poem is different since a different situation or relationship between the Bride and Bridegroom is constructed with *CA*. The dramatic structure of *CA*, like *CO,* can be described by paying attention to the desire-search-encounter movement in the poem, as well as to the identification of the speaker and responder.

Topical and Dramatic Structure of *CA*
According to the Movement of Desire-Search-Encounter[94]

Search (I) -- *Bride*		st. 1-4
Preliminary answer (1)	-- *Creatures*	st. 5

[94] Again, this structure is based on Tavard's analysis in TAVARD, *Poetry and Contemplation,* 128-129. I have combined Tavard's topical and dramatic structure into the one presentation shown here.

248

Notice here that there is a dialogical situation shared among three parties: the Bride, the Bridegroom and nature or creatures. Each actant[96] speaks in a particular way. The Bride speaks mainly in the future, orienting the movement of the poem to the eventual consummation of union with her Beloved. The poem ends with this future still open ended, even though there is a certain realization of the union which the Bride desires with her Beloved. The Bridegroom speaks

---

[95] It might seem logical that these stanzas, *CA* 33 and *CA* 34, are spoken by someone other then the Bridegroom (or the Bride) since the Bride and Bridegroom are referred to in the third person. However, it is commonly accepted that these stanzas are a summary of the situation made by the Bridegroom. This is due to the fact that Juan de la Cruz would have written, if not completed, a major portion of the commentary of *CA* when these stanzas were written. They were written, therefore, having in mind that a commentary would eventually be written on them as well. Therefore, it is accepted that Juan's own designation of these stanzas to the Bridegroom in the commentary of *CA* is accurate. Furthermore, this designation complements the flow of the poem in its overall structure as I have outlined it above.

[96] I have borrowed the term "actant" from the vocabulary used in the semiotic study of texts. It refers to that entity which directs "the subject operator to act." This can happen under many different forms: "invitation, temptation, command, provocation, seduction, and the like. But whatever form it takes, the manipulation is always at the cognitive level and is, more precisely, a persuasive operation. The manipulation consists in influencing the subject-operator to get interested in the object to assure that he is going to act." VOGELS, *Reading and Preaching the Bible*, 50.

predominantly in the past, summarizing what has taken place and at times connecting it to some distant past (st. 28). Creatures or nature also summarize on two different occasions what has taken place (st. 5 and 27). It is also to be noticed that creatures are now in a more intimate relationship with the Bride than before. Each time they speak it is in response to her longings. The response of creatures in the Bride's life gives her hope to further her quest.

We see, then, that Juan de la Cruz did not merely add eight new stanzas to *CO* as a sort of supplement to create *CA*. He constructed a different text with his new poem, even though both poems obviously share much in common. This poem has an original configuration because of the eight final stanzas which *CO* does not have. What new configuration is this? Let us go back and examine again the ending of *CO* to respond to this question.

It was pointed out that *CO* terminated with the hope-filled dream-speech of the Bride. This ending signalled a longed-for union with the Beloved that was realized in some fashion, but, as in a dream, was not fully inserted into the lived experience of the Bride. The awakening of the Bride in *CA* grounds the drama of her quest further in reality. The Bridegroom confirms this in the third encounter of stanzas 33 and 34. The Bride has been touched by a beauty which is ecstatic and realizes her own beauty at the same time as being a reflection of the beauty of the Bridegroom (st. 35). Yet, and now awake, she exhorts the Bridegroom to go even further with her into the thicket. There is more yet to come, a fullness of their love which was not indicated in the ending of *CO*. Even though there has been a consummation of the love of the Bride for her Beloved, the deepest place of this encounter is projected into the future (st. 37). However, this time the quest is pursued in some type of mutual relationship which the two lovers share with one another.

This is a very different text-world than that constructed by *CO*. First, the ending of *CO* leaves nature at a distance isolating the Bride from those companions who accompanied her on the quest. Secondly, it assumes that the Bride and Bridegroom have arrived at the fullness of their relationship. This latter stance implies the lack of openness to future possibilities and encounters.

The ending of *CA* is quite different. First, as opposed to *CO* it invites the nature-companions along in the continuation of the journey. Second, it projects the couple into an unknown, yet dynamic, future. Yet, is this ending not similiar to the beginning of the poem? Had not the Bride had some sort of encounter with her lover that left her wounded and moaning (st. 1)? Does she not journey with these nature-companions along the way, seeking from them counsel and hope, in attempting to find that love which had already been given her? And, once she finds him the second time, does she not set out again with her lover and those nature-companions that first accompanied her? The story moves forward but, in many ways, remains the same. The Bride has arrived at the unknown place she seeks, but then, in the end, sets off for another unknown place (the indeterminate *allí* of stanzas 36 and 37) with the lover she has known all along.

What we are left with is a sense that the end is what is happening at every moment. In a certain sense, history has been abolished in *CA* through its circular movement causing the poem to end at a point which has been visited before (at least once). *CA* has moved us toward an expected future already realized in the present and in the past.

Thus, Juan has found out about our world in flux and emplotted a way for us to be in this world. There has been an ordering, an emplotment, which brought about a certain concordance from the dissonance of human experience within time. However, this concordance is not so smooth that the aporias of reality are levelled beyond the need for interpretation. Thus, the "sense" of the text points the reader to another "reference" which ultimately becomes operative in the life of the reader. Whereas *CO* is characterized by hope, *CA* is characterized by a realized betrothal and marriage in the lived reality of the lovers. And, as is known, the series is not yet finished. Juan went on to write a third *Cántico* to which we now turn our attention.

3.3 Dramatic Structure of *CB*

I have already presented the controversy regarding the authorship of

CB. Internal and external evidence confirms that Juan de la Cruz is indeed the author of *CB*.[97] Sometime between 1584 and 1586 Juan added another stanza to *CA* (st. 11), and he rearranged the order of the other stanzas to form *CB*. This new poem and its commentary were concluded within just two years of the completion of *CA* and its commentary. What is to be made of this radical reorganization and addition to *CA* to create the text of *CB*? I want to show here, as with the passage from *CO* to *CA*, that a different dramatic structure of the text would lend support to the textual originality of *CB* and therefore a different text-world.

Topical and Dramatic Structure of *CB*
According to the Movement of Desire-Search-Encounter[98]

Search-desire (I) -- *Bride*	st. 1-4
Preliminary Answer -- *Creatures*	st. 5
Search-desire (II) -- *Bride*	st. 6-12
Full Answer -- *Bridegroom*	st. 13
Encounter (I) in creatures, responding to search (I)	st. 14-19
-- *Bride*	
Appeal to creatures -- *Bridegroom*	st. 20-21
Narration -- *Creatures*	st. 22
Remembrance -- *Bridegroom*	st. 23
Encounter (II) in the Bridegroom, responding	
to search-desire (II) -- *Bride*	st. 24-33
Responding to search-desire (II) -- *Bridegroom*	st. 34-35
Desire expressed for the eternal encounter -- *Bride*	st. 36-39
Final Rest -- *Creatures*	st. 40

---

[97] See Thompson's excellent summary of this evidence in THOMPSON, *The Poet and the Mystic*, 33-59.

[98] TAVARD, *Poetry and Contemplation*, 220-221.

252

The modifications Juan made which resulted in *CB* are not haphazard. Juan de la Cruz carefully configured a new text with a number of key changes. To highlight these changes, Tavard has divided *CA* and *CB* into units. Each unit contains from one to three stanzas and each unit has been assigned a capital letter to designate it.[99] These units are then grouped into four blocks. The differences between *CA* and *CB* can therefore be easily followed when we view these divisions schematically:

	CA		*CB*
Block I	A (st. 1-2)	**Block I**	A (identical)
(not moved,	B (st. 3-4)		B (identical)
changes in	C (st. 5)		C (identical)
numbering	D (st. 6-7)		D (identical)
start with	E (st. 8-9)		E (identical)
addition of	F (st. 10-11)		F (st. 10-12 = 10-11 of *CA*; new 11)
st. 11)	G (st. 12)		G (st. 13 = st. 12 of *CA*)
	H (st. 13-14)		H (st. 14-15 = st. 13-14 of *CA*)
Block II	I (st. 15-16)	**Block III**	N (st. 16-17 = 25-26 of *CA*)
(moved,	J (st. 17-18)		Q (st. 18-19 = 31-32 of *CA*)
order not	K (st. 19-20)		P (st. 21-21 = 29-30 of *CA*)
changed)	L (st. 21-22)		O (st. 22-23 = 27-28 of *CA*)
	M (st. 23-24)		
Block III	N (st. 25-26)	**Block II**	I (st. 24-25 = 15-16 of *CA*)
(moved,	O (st. 27-28)		J (st. 26-27 = 17-18 of *CA*)
inverted	P (st. 29-30)		K (st. 28-29 = 19-20 of *CA*)
from O on)	Q (st. 31-32)		L (st. 30-31 = 21-22 of *CA*)
			M (st. 32-33 = 23-24 of *CA*)
Block IV	R (st. 33-34)	**Block IV**	R (st. 34-35 = st. 33-34 of *CA*)
(not moved,	S (st. 35-36)		S (st. 36-37 = st. 35-36 of *CA*)
order not	T (st. 37-38)		T (st. 38-39 = st. 37-38 of *CA*)
changed)	U (st. 39)		U (st. 40 = st. 39 of *CA*)

Block I and Block IV were neither rearranged nor relocated in the

[99] TAVARD, *Poetry and Contemplation*, 222.

new text, except that Block I had a new stanza (st. 11), added to it. This addition resulted in the numbering difference noted in *CB*. Block II was moved toward the end and Block III moved closer to the beginning of the poem. A number of observations can now be made concerning this new structure.

Block II is still in the central part of the poem but instead of being a reflection of the initial movements of the poem, it now serves as an introduction to the finale of the poem. "From witnesses to the past he [Juan] has made them heralds of the future."[100] Furthermore, Block II was displaced without any modification of its internal structure, whereas Block III was rearranged considerably. The verbs used in the displaced Block II remain, for the most part, in the past, although stanza 25 is in the present tense and stanza 30 is in the future tense.[101] Stanzas 29 and 33 contain a mixture of tenses. Tavard notes that although the stanzas are displaced without changing the tenses for the most part, this is not problematic: "As the future is naturally rooted in the past, the latter may be perceived as an anticipation of the former. Moreover, these stanzas are now set in a new context, defined by what comes before, and on which they depend."[102]

Block III, as was mentioned, was moved closer to the beginning of the poem with considerable modifications of its internal structure. These changes can be viewed easily in the above schema. The sequence of O-P-Q in Block III (*CA*) is completely reversed in *CB* to become Q-P-O. Unit N remains in its initial place in Block III. Tavard notes:

> Here again the change has taken the shape of a reversal of direction. Just as block II (units I-M), once transposed to a subsequent locus, is reoriented in a teleological sense, so block III (units N-Q), being displaced toward the beginning to occupy the place left vacant by the removal of block II, is nonetheless interiorly reversed.[103]

[100] TAVARD, *Poetry and Contemplation*, 221.

[101] TAVARD, *Poetry and Contemplation*, 221.

[102] TAVARD, *Poetry and Contemplation*, 222.

[103] TAVARD, *Poetry and Contemplation*, 222.

These changes dramatically point the movement of the poem toward the future.[104]

Stanza 11, the only addition to *CA* in the making of *CB*, marks this movement in a striking way:

Reveal your presence,	¡Descubre tu presencia,
and may the vision of your beauty be	y máteme tu vista y hermosura;
my death;	mira que la dolencia
for the sickness of love	de amor, que no se cura
is not cured except by your very presence and image.	sino con la presencia y la figura!

Stanza 11 expresses that the desire of the Bride can be completely fulfilled only through death. This death is accompanied by the beauty of the presence and image of the Beloved. No longer are we involved in a poem that tactfully tells the story of the search of two lovers in the fields, valleys, and hills of the countryside. The backdrop for the encounter suddenly becomes death itself and the satisfaction of the Bride's desire in that death. But with this stanza the poem is oriented toward "what may be foreseen, this side of dying by love, of what will happen beyond."[105] The Bridegroom responds with an expression of a similiar desire (st. 13). However, whereas in *CA* we encountered a long monologue of the Bride (st. 13-26) we now have a "reciprocal chanting" of the Bride and the Bridegroom (st. 14-21). The Bride begins by celebrating the identification of her Beloved with nature. The Bride continues evoking various images from nature until we encounter the "nymphs of Judea." This time the Bride is wide awake. Are these nymphs now the "companions" referred to in stanza 19 who accompany the Bride on her journey?

Whoever they are,[106] the Bridegroom responds to the Bride's

---

[104] Tavard interprets this new orientation of the poem to reflect the end-point experiences of Juan's own life: "Altogether, the remaking of the poem has thus taken place under the sign of the poet's tension toward the future, which, at this moment of John of the Cross's [sic] life and experience, could scarcely be less than the eschatological future." TAVARD, *Poetry and Contemplation*, 223. Tavard cites the eschatological orientation of the *Living Flame of Love* as that which "must have brought about the new teleology of the third *Canticle*." Ibid., 223. The poem of the *Living Flame* was written sometime between 1582-84, just before the time Juan redacted *CA* into *CB* (1584-86).

[105] TAVARD, *Poetry and Contemplation*, 226.

[106] Again, I see this as another "zone of indetermination" discussed earlier.

companions, who, at this point, have "become all the scenic manifestations of created nature."[107] He tells them to be quiet in silence. The Bridegroom's response in these two stanzas of 20 and 21 echo the Bride's discourse of stanzas 14 and 15.[108] Both erupt with a plethora of nouns taken from nature, followed by images of peacefilled tranquillity evoked through music. Against the backdrop of the fullness of love after death introduced with stanza 11, Juan presents us with the immanence of that love in the here and now. Therefore, it is stanza 11 which has given *CB* its entirely new flavour and has structured a new text. With the introduction of stanza 11 a new text-world was created which necessitated the reordering of other sections of the poem. The being-in-the-world proposed by *CB* is different from the proposed being-in-the-world of *CA*. Juan has carefully constructed this reference through various linguistic tools. Tavard gives us an indication of the devices Juan has used to construct this text-world:

> [Stanza 11] ... opened on a delicate call to the Beloved to "unveil his presence." It continued with lines in which initial M sounds (in Spanish of course: *y mateme* [sic] ..., *mira que* ..., *de amor que* ...) led to a redundance of guttural sounds (*que ... que ... con* ...), which fit well in the sequence of *que* that marks the betrothed's whole discourse in stanzas 6 to 13. Taking account of such words as *quien* [sic], *quiero, aqueste*, the guttural sound recurs five times in stanza 6, three times in stanza 7--with its famous line, "*un no sé qué que quedan balbuciendo*"--three times in 8, four times in 9, twice in 10. It occurs twice inside stanza 11, once being grammatically redundant, though one could disagree on which one. The breathing of the request seems to halt, to stutter, after syllables articulated on M and on R sounds (mira que .../ amor que ...). Awe brings about hesitancy before the desired presence; yet such hesitancy can only feed the desire and its prayer. Only the "presence" and the "image" can bring to fruition the bride's stammering. The solitary *que* featured at the last line of stanza 12 precisely acts as a hyphen between the desire and its fulfilment, the outline of which is already being drawn in the soul:

[107] TAVARD, *Poetry and Contemplation*, 225.

[108] TAVARD, *Poetry and Contemplation*, 225.

> The desired eyes
> Whose sketch I bear in my inside!
> *(Que tengo en mis entrañas dibujados!)*[109]

The new text, *CB*, shows signs of poetic tools at the service of the new text-world. Did Juan de la Cruz sacrifice poetry for doctrine, as we have been led to believe by Pacho, in the passage from *CA* to *CB*?[110] It does not appear that this is the case. Neither is the new text of *CB* a "poetic disaster" as Alonso has suggested.[111] Rather, *CB* is a highly crafted entity which creates a new text-world through linguistic technique, as has been demonstrated above. It is a *different* text-world from *CO* or *CA*.

Let us then summarize our findings by suggesting what each of the text-worlds might look like because of the different dramatic structures of each of *CO*, *CA*, and *CB*. If *CO* is characterized by hope, and *CA* by the nuptial union in the present life, then we can say *CB* once again returns to the theme of hope. But this time the theme of hope occurs in a new way. Stanza 11 has shifted the locus of this hope. The realization of the object of the hope of *CB* is not perceived in its fullness in the present reality. *CB* points the lovers toward an eschatological hope that it seems only death can satisfy.

4. Conclusion

I have examined two things in this chapter. First, I examined the literary genre of the *Cántico*. What is important to retain from this discussion on

---

[109] TAVARD, *Poetry and Contemplation*, 227

[110] PACHO, *Sus escritos*, 379-80.

[111] I have cited a text earlier (footnote 59) concerning this matter. However, Damaso Alonso returns to this depreciation of *CB* in several places. For example, elsewhere he says of the poem: "Notemos --no recuerdo haber leído esta observación-- que en la redacción primera, que es la que seguimos, todo el estado de desposorios es un prolongado canto de la Esposa, lleno de juegos, de gozos y de graciosos remilgos. El estado de unión perfecta --en cambio-- es un cántico alterno de ambos amantes. Esta traza clara y significativa (que no creo deje de tener profundo sentido místico) *está malamente destruida en la segunda redacción*." ALONSO, *La poesía de San Juan de la Cruz*, 210. (emphasis mine) Alonso says the same thing about the commentary in Ibid., 219.

genre is that genre is not only a means of classification as we look back to the structure of a literary work, but it is also a means of production for future meaning-events in the life of the reader. Interpretation of the *Cántico* needs to take this into consideration. Genre provides the common ground of understanding and interpretation of the *Cántico* and preserves the content of the text from distortion. The form of the *Cántico* preserves meaning in a particular way after the disappearance of the meaning-event. What a text can "do" is indicated by its genre.

The *Cántico* was determined to be a pastoral hendecasyllabic love poem, a canticle. Canticles are highly productive of mood, of feelings. Feelings are not merely subjective but also operate at a cognitive level. Feelings shape our world and inform us of its deeper dimensions. It will be this productive capacity of the *Cántico* which I will use further in Chapter Six and Chapter Seven when I examine the appropriation and the reception of the text. The approach to genre which I have outlined in this chapter liberates us from confining the meaning of the *Cántico* to a description of the threefold classical spiritual itinerary.

Second, Ricoeur's literary hermeneutics has led us into the investigation of the dramatic structure of *CO*, *CA*, and *CB*. Within Ricoeur's theory of mimesis, a difference in dramatic structure (muthos) would reorient metaphorical redescription which constructs the world-of-the-text. Since we have been led to a different dramatic structure through our analysis, the unique contribution to meaning by each text seems to be supported. Besides affirming the contribution each poem may make, the difference in dramatic structure of each poem raises certain questions which concern the use of *CA* and *CB* in scholarly research.

The individual nature of *CB* with respect to *CA* from a textual perspective has been supported by the difference of the dramatic structure. This opens up the question of the nature of the two poems, the relationship between *CA* and *CB*, and their respective contributions towards the mediation of meaning in the world. We know that Juan de la Cruz redacted *CA* into *CB* in order to organize the poem into a doctrinal systematization of the development of the classical spiritual itinerary which corresponded more closely to the "real" world.[112] But does that mean that the value of *CA* is reduced and is simply seen as a beautiful piece of poetry which does not correspond to the "real" world at all?[113] Given the various text-

---

[112] Pacho explains this in the following way: "Intentó, ante todo y sobre todo, *una organización sistemática del progreso espiritual* a despecho del encanto literario del poema. De ello no hay duda. Tampoco la hay de que para lograr su intento siguió las insinuaciones del CA, volviendo explícito y manifiesto el esquema latente, alterado por 'súbitas regresiones'. Consumado el trastrueque imprescindible, las fisuras entre las piezas dislocadas, desde el punto de vista estructural o redaccional, eran inevitables. Está claro, el CB no hace otra cosa que poner orden doctrinal en el desorden del CA. ... San Juan de la Cruz, en ocasión solemne, sin preocuparse por el encanto de su creación poética, trastrueca las canciones ordenándolas según el esquema doctrinal que ha madurado en su mente mientras redacta el primer comentario y que perfecciona a lo largo de su carrera de maestro espiritual. El trazado del CA está motivado por el ritmo poético de la creación lírica; la ordenación de CB es fruto de la sistematización doctrinal ... . Incluso para quienes rechazan la intervención sanjuanista no existe otra razón suprema que explique la existencia del CB si no es la estructuración más sistemática la canciones espirituales." (emphasis mine) PACHO, *Sus escritos*, 379-80. This reasoning for the redaction of *CA* into *CB* is the common view held by sanjuanist scholars. See, for example, Thompson who says much the same thing: "This more systematic delineation of the stages in the spiritual life is the clue behind the reorganization of the stanzas. As the soul progresses San Juan's clear teaching is that disturbances and demonic interferences recede. But the order of stanzas in CA makes this difficult to maintain, because the 'raposas' of CA 25 and the 'ninfas de Judea' of CA 31 represent just such troubles. This creates a tension between the CA poem and the commentary it has generated. CA 25 offers on the one hand 'turbaciones', on the other, 'suave deleite'. CA 31 urges the nymphs to grant the soul a peace she is long since supposed to have gained. Here the tension is explicit, and San Juan feels obliged to explain why the nymphs are distracting the soul which has already entered the 'ameno huerto desseado'." THOMPSON, *The Poet and the Mystic*, 57. Thompson concludes a little later: "The best guide to San Juan as a poet is CA, because it reflects more nearly the original impulse to sing the divine love. But to appreciate his thought, there is every justification for turning to CB, because there is his *final word* on the *Cántico*, the word of a poet who is also a theologian." Ibid., 59. (emphasis mine) Fernande Pepin reflects a similar attitude stating that later redactions of Juan's *Cántico* were "corrections:" "Si Jean de la Croix ne demeura pas satisfait une fois pour toutes de son oeuvre accomplie, la revisant, la corrigeant, l'amplifiant et la refondant dans une second rédaction, c'est que la généralisation du poème révélait un tracé plus logique et rectiligne, ainsi qu'un ajustement des strophes dû à une plus vaste réflexion scientifico-didactique." PEPIN, *Noces de Feu*, 322.

[113] Pacho suggests, in line with Juan de la Cruz's own struggle to align the poetic sequence of *CA* with the unfolding of "mystical love:" "Todo radica en ese hecho indubable: la trama poética del primer *Cántico* no se corresponde exactamente con el proceso real del amor místico. Manteniendo su orden estrófico, el comentarista tiene que desentrañar en cada estrofa y lugar lo que alli se canta, se lo impone el método adoptado; no le queda otro remedio que denunciar las incongruencias y alteraciones, tratando de situar cada cosa en su sitio sin alterar el orden de los versos. El resultado no puede ser más amplio aunque interferido con el poético. Para descubrir el proyecto definitivo de fray Juan hay que recurrir a la declaración. Si se quiere identificar en la propuesta madurada con los años, debe asumirse el CB." Eulogio PACHO, "Cántico espiritual," in *Introducción a la lectura de San Juan de la Cruz*, ed. A. Garcia Simón, 471. Pacho, however, also attests to Juan's struggle in making even *Cántico B* "fit" the threefold way: "El *Cántico* y la *Llama* semejan un impetuoso torrente de ideas sin conexión [sic], ni armónica estructura doctrinal. Conviene no exagerar esta visión que se funda más en apariencias externas que en el estudio metódico de la contextura literaria y, que, en

worlds which have surfaced from our dramatic analysis, are we to limit Juan's *proyecto definitivo* with *CB*? At this point let us recall that it was the texts of *CO* and *CA* (before there was even a commentary on *CA*), that caught the imagination and wonder of the nuns at Beas. Even though they may not have been able to completely "explain" the poems, as neither could Juan, they found great meaning in them. If *CA* lacks precision in systematizing the progression of the purgative, illuminative, and unitive states associated with the classical spiritual itinerary, does it have another contribution to make? And, because of *CB*'s doctrinal alignment, does that mean that it is not a poetic creation, as Pacho suggests?[114] Poetic beauty was sacrificed for doctrinal precision, according to Pacho.[115] Given all these questions arising from a hermeneutical approach to Juan's *Cántico* the relationship of *CA* with *CB* needs to be investigated further to explore the contribution both poems may make with respect to the mediation of meaning.[116] We have already seen that *CA* and *CB* are still being used for scholarly research on the *Cántico* depending

buena parte, no responde a las explícitas afirmaciones del mismo Santo." PACHO, "La Estructura literaria del «Cántico Espiritual»," 402. Later on he emphasis this point even further: "La lucha entre el esquema teórico y el ritmo impuesto por las estrofas es tan manifiesta, que se trasparenta [sic] a cada paso, sobre todo en la *Noche* y en el *Cántico.*" Ibid., 405.

[114] "La ordenación nueva de las 40 canciones *no es creación poética*, es obra del maestro espiritual que intenta presentar un esquema fiel del crecimiento del amor divino. Las disonancias entre marcha poética y programa real del comentarista desaparecen, por lo menos en los puntos más conflictivos. Por algo el poema del CB responde a un orden más lógico. Ha perdido la frescura de la espontaneidad y de la inmediatez a la experiencia mística, pero se ha estructurado con mayor reflexión y dominio del argumento." PACHO, "Cántico espiritual," 471. (emphasis mine)

[115] Furthermore, Pacho suggests that Juan's real contribution was at the doctrinal level reflected in his didactic commentary, rather than in his artistic genius which is captured in the poem: "No pretende admirar con creaciones artísticas, sino enseñar con sólida doctrina el camino del espíritu a las almas necesitadas de luz y guia. Fin y elementos literarios están subordinados en el *Cántico* a la intención didáctica del maestro que suplanta al poeta." PACHO, "La Estructura literaria del «Cántico espiritual»," 400. We also see here the lack of importance Pacho places on literary structure and its contribution toward meaning.

[116] See the comments on such a project suggested in footnote number 72, page 233.

on the approach of the researcher.[117]

For example, an ascetical-theological approach to the text, characterized by Pacho, has affirmed the singularity of the reference of all three texts, that is, Juan was trying to get across the same "message" in each of the three *Cánticos*. Pacho suggests that among the primitive Toledan "nucleus," the text of *CA*, and that of *CB*, there is no referential difference which points to the individual contribution each text might be able to make.[118] From Pacho's perspective, each text was an attempt of Juan de la Cruz to improve the clarity of his doctrinal program. Since *CB* is more closely aligned with the doctrinal progression of the spiritual life, the ascetical-theological approach would use *CB* for its research. Another approach, the literary approach, seems to favour the text of *CA* for its artistic merit. Pepin, Icaza, and Morales all have recently used *CA* for their studies.[119] Thus, methodologically, within the ascetical-theological approach, as well as the literary approach, there has been the practice of choosing one text.

A hermeneutical approach to the *Cántico* seems to challenge the exclusive use of one text of the *Cántico*. The hermeneutical approach suggests that

---

[117] Some scholars choose to work with *CA* since they doubt the authenticity of *CB*. However, since the authenticity of *CB* is no longer disputed, some scholars still choose *CA* because of its poetic dynamism. See footnotes 57 and 59, page 228, for these positions. Since we have seen that each text surfaces a different dramatic structure, a hermeneutic approach to the *Cántico* does not force this kind of decision on the researcher. Each text can be invited into the dialogue from its various perspectives to contribute toward a hermeneutical understanding of Juan's *Cántico*.

[118] "Entre el núcleo poético de Toledo y las agregaciones posteriores no existe diferencia alguna en lo que a la estructura de composición se refiere. La armoniosa unidad del conjunto mantiene el origen incontaminado de poesía pura, al margen de imposiciones doctrinarias." PACHO, "Cántico espiritual," 451.

[119] Morales testifies to this choice available to researchers. He says in his introduction: "Los que prefieren el manuscrito de Sanlúcar [*CA*] mantienen que en él se encuentra la espontánea creación y, por lo tanto, parece éste el orden de las estrofas más cercano a las fuentes de su inspiración. Los que prefieren el manuscrito de Jaén [*CB*] dicen que en este códice la creación poética está hecha a través del esfuerzo y de elaborado y concienzuda elaboración." MORALES, *El Cántico espiritual de San Juan de la Cruz*, 21. However, he himself goes on to say that he uses *CA* due to historical reasons. Ibid., 21. Ferdinande Pepin uses *CA* because of its artistic completeness, PEPIN, *Noces de Feu*, ix. Icaza uses *CA* as well, citing it as "the most reliable." ICAZA, *Stylistic Relationship*, 5.

each text may have a contribution to make in our understanding of the *Cántico*.[120] The differences in dramatic structure which we have described in the three texts would suggest a unique contribution towards a mediated meaning of each of the *three Cánticos*. In order to support this position further, let us now come back to the question: What is a text?

What is important to stress here is that we have considered *CO*, *CA* and *CB*, as *texts* in the context of Ricoeur's analysis of a text.[121] It would be useful at this point to review Ricoeur's main characteristics of a text. These can be applied to the three poems to support my thesis that all three *Cánticos* have a contribution to make to a hermeneutical reading of the *Cántico*.

We can recall some of the main characteristics of a written text from the earlier presentation.[122] These are: 1. meaning is separated from the event of discourse and is fixed through writing, 2. the text is freed from the mental intention of the author, 3. the written text has a universal range with respect to whom it may address, and 4. texts display nonostensive references. Going back to the first characteristic, let us recall what is fixed by written discourse: it is the objective meaning in discourse which is fixed by writing. If the writing changes, then the objective meaning likewise changes. Rearrangement (as in *CA* to *CB*), or addition to a text (as in the eight stanzas added to the Toledan poem), changes the text

---

[120] What might be questioned, therefore, is the absence of *Cántico A* in the recent critical edition in 1991 of Juan de la Cruz's collected works translated into English by Kavanaugh and Rodriguez: *Collected Works*, trans. Kieran Kavanaugh and Otilio Rodriguez. This is all the more surprising, since the authors state in their Foreword that they have "made continual use of two particularly valuable Spanish editions of the works of St. John of the Cross," Ibid., 8. One of the Spanish editions used is the recent 1988 critical edition: *San Juan de la Cruz: Obras Completas*, ed. José Vicente Rodriguez. This work includes both *CA* and *CB*. There was obviously a clear choice made not to include *CA* in the "collected works" edited by Kavanaugh and Rodriguez.

[121] As Tavard also notes, there are obvious relationships between these three poems, "but *no identity*." TAVARD, *Poetry and Contemplation*, 38. (emphasis mine)

[122] See especially my Chapter Four: 3. "The Act of Writing: The Significance for Interpretation of Distanciation through Writing."

profoundly as we have seen.[123]

The second characteristic likewise frees us from assuming that the redaction of *CA* into *CB* was only an attempt by Juan de la Cruz to clarify the religious concepts contained in the poem. As an example we could cite the often used reason for the redaction of *CA* into *CB*: the clarification of the steps associated with the classical spiritual journey (the purgative, illuminative, and unitive ways). However, the original author does not have full possession of his or her own intentionality. There are conscious dimensions, but also unconscious dimensions of intentionality that need to be considered in composing a text. Subsequent interpretations of a text cannot always be attempts to get back at the intention of the author, even if the author has indicated what he or she had in mind in the composition of the text. The intentionality of the author of a text is also a question of interpretation on the part of the current reader. Therefore, if the text is freed from the mental intention of the author, then interpretation of the text allows new readings that may be life-giving beyond the expectation of the author and even the current interpretor.

The third characteristic suggests that a written text is available to whoever can read. The text can therefore be available to produce meaning in a vast number of contexts simply because it is written. The fourth characteristic of a text suggests that a text is more than a linear succession of sentences objectifying what the author intended to say. This approach opens up the potential universality of the text based on its non-ostensive references. Recall: "The depth semantics of the text is not what the author intended to say, but what the text is about, that is, the

---

[123] Anselmo Donazar is overly nonchalant when it comes to determining the number of verses in the *Cántico* as if it really didn't matter. He states: "El Cántico es abierto. Como tiene 40 canciones, podia tener 50 ó 60 ó podria tener 20 ó 25. La última canción del poema aparece como un broche por separado. . . Así como el autor añadió más tarde una canción, pudo haber añadido otras, pues en el poema hay espacios abiertos. Si no intervino más veces para completarse o continuarse, sería porque no encontró el aire o la inspiración o porque le parecieron bastantes 39 canciones para cerrar con la 40." DONAZAR, *Fray Juan*, 61 Such a position does not give sufficient importance to the fact that each of the three *Cánticos are complete texts*, each has a certain completeness. Juan could have added other verses to the *Cántico*, but the fact is, he didn't; we have the texts as they exist today.

nonostensive reference of the text. And the nonostensive reference of the text is the kind of world opened up by the depth semantics of the text."[124] Therefore, a written text "is a cumulative, holistic process."[125] Understanding a text is not an end in itself. Understanding a text passes through the investigation of the "cultural signs in which the self documents and forms itself;"[126] however, hermeneutical understanding culminates in the retrieval of the meaning of one's own life.[127] This meaning of the reader's life is oriented through the reference supplied by the semantics of the text.

Thus Juan de la Cruz does not merely say "more" in his addition of eight verses to the primitive poem in the construction of *CA*. Nor is he saying "more," or saying it "better," or even "more completely," in his rearrangement of *CA* to form *CB* with the addition of stanza 11. With each of the three poems Juan de la Cruz is presenting something *different*. We have seen Juan constructed a different dramatic structure each time.[128] Each poem (text) proposes a new way of looking at things, that is, "an injunction to think in a certain manner."[129]

Placing Juan's *Cántico* within the context of Ricoeur's hermeneutical theory, therefore, significantly shifts the objective of both "the written" and "the read" text of Juan's *Cántico*. The purpose of interpreting Juan's *Cántico* from a hermeneutical perspective is not to allegorize the "secular" images of the poem to arrive at traditionally religious or ethical themes which are already known. It is

---

[124] RICOEUR, "The Model of the Text: Meaningful Action Considered as a Text," 165.

[125] RICOEUR, "The Model of the Text: Meaningful Action Considered as a Text," 159.

[126] RICOEUR, "What is a Text? Explanation and Understanding," 119.

[127] "In short, in hermeneutical reflection--or in reflective hermeneutics--the constitution of the *self* is contemporaneous with the constitution of *meaning*." RICOEUR, "What is a Text? Explanation and Understanding," 119.

[128] As mentioned above, even Juan's own commentaries on *CA* and *CB* emphasize only one side of the *Cántico*. See RICOEUR, "The Model of the Text: Meaningful Action Considered as a Text," 158. The question of the multiplicity of interpretations of the *Cántico* is examined further in Chapter Seven where I discuss the impact of the hermeneutical approach on the poetry-prose relationship.

[129] RICOEUR, "The Model of the Text: Meaningful Action Considered as a Text," 165.

Ricoeur's concept of mimesis which allows us to affirm that Juan's *Cántico* is not the poetic description of an "already known" brought to language, but is a refiguration of a particular aspect of reality which becomes available to the reader. Everyday reality is transformed with the help of the metamorphoses of that reality effected through literature. Logos is transformative.

An analysis of the dramatic structure of the texts of the *Cántico* suggests that the three poems cannot be viewed as the linear description, development, or progression of Juan's personal journey.[130] According to Ricoeur's theory of mimesis, poetic discourse is not the revealed landscape of the author's inner journey. We are not dealing here with either the external signs of Juan's inner mental life or exclusively the lived experience of the author.

If a text is only the expression of personal experience, a reaching for words to communicate the ineffable during a systematic analysis, then interpretation consists of bridging the gap between the mind of the reader and the experience of the author. If a text is primarily the expression of personal experience, or the attempt to find a common horizon for the meeting of two minds (that of the author and that of the reader), then all distanciation from a text is alienating. This, as we have seen in Chapter Four, is not the case. Distanciation is a resource for access to meaning in a text as I have defined it according to Ricoeur's hermeneutical method. A text, as already explained, "fixes" discourse, preserving its meaning when the event of speaking passes away. A text therefore expresses, preserves, and conveys meaning over temporal and cultural distance. A text refers to its own "world," "where this world is to be understood in an existential sense as a possible world for self-understanding and a potential mode of existing. It is, in a word, a new way of

---

[130] Fernande Pepin is an author who holds this position. It is clearly stated in reference to *Cántico A*. Referring to the *Cántico* she says: "Le poème sanjuaniste suit une marche linéaire, lente et sévère tout au cours des trente-neuf strophes que se déroulent sous nos yeux; Jean de la Croix, suivant une théorie qui lui est propre, bâtit son poème comme, dans un travail ordonné et pierre sur pierre, on élève un édifice, sans laisser aucun interstice, suivant les plans de l'architecte qui rêve d'un monument à demeurer." PEPIN. *Voces de feu*, 381.

understanding reality."[131]

The difference in the dramatic structure of *CO*, *CA*, and *CB* seems to indicate the difference which lies in the text-worlds of the three *Cánticos*. The judgement whether these text-worlds are radically different or not must wait for a more complete structural analysis of all three texts. Structural analysis would reveal the deep-structures (the "codes" of the *Cántico*) that are bearers of meaning.[132] This analytical moment depsychologizes the interpretation of the *Cántico* since these structures are unearthed from within the text itself. It is the "codes" within the text which result in the production of discourse once the reader returns to the surface-structures of the "plot" (muthos). This means that in order to interpret the *Cántico* the following question must eventually be asked: What does the *Cántico* say about our fundamental existence?[133] Therefore, a totally subjective reading of the *Cántico* is avoided when the results of structural analysis are included as part of the hermeneutical interpretation of Juan's poem.

---

[131] David PELLAUER, "The Significance of the Text in Paul Ricoeur's Hermeneutical Theory," in *Studies in the Philosophy of Paul Ricoeur,* ed. E. Reagan, (Athens: Ohio University Press, 1979), 104.

[132] Ricoeur acknowledges the invaluable contribution of structuralism: "The invaluable contribution made by structuralism was to offer an exact scientific description of the codes and paradigms of language. But I do not believe that this excludes the creative expression of consciousness. The creation of meaning in language comes from the specifically *human* production of new ways of expressing the objective paradigms and codes made available by language." RICOEUR, "The Creativity of Language," 465.

[133] I have paraphrased this question from VAN DEN HENGEL, *Home of Meaning,* 136. Van den Hengel asks: "What does the story say about our fundamental existence?" Ibid., 136. Concerning story and meaning Ricoeur says: "A text has an entirely different significance from that which a structural analysis, deriving from linguistics, accords to it; it is a mediation between man and the world, between man and man, between man and himself. Mediation between man and the world is called *reference*; mediation between man and man is *communication*; mediation between man and himself is *self-understanding*. A literary work brings together these three dimensions of reference, communication, and self-understanding. Thus, the work of hermeneutics begins where linguistics stops. Hermeneutics would uncover new traits of non-descriptive reference, of non-utilitarian communication, of non-narcissistic reflexivity--traits engendered by the literary work. In a word, hermeneutics takes hold of the hinge between the (internal) configuration of a work and the (external) refiguration of a life. As I see it, everything said ... concerning the dynamics of composition proper to a literary creation is nothing but a lengthy preparation to understanding the real problem, i.e. that of the dynamics of transfiguration proper to the work. In this regard plotting is the work of the text and the reader jointly." RICOEUR, "Life: A Story in Search of a Narrator," 431-432.

The work of structural analysis on the *Cántico* is yet to be done. For now, however, in the context of the dramatic analysis based on Ricoeur's hermeneutical theory, it can be suggested that the rearrangement of Juan's *Cántico A* into *Cántico B* may not merely have resulted in a clearer text or a more accurate way to express what *Cántico A* failed to adequately communicate. Ricoeur's theory of mimesis cautions us that we should not amalgamate too quickly *CO*, *CA* and *CB*. This is to say that it is not enough to give only one reading to the *Cántico*. *CO*, *CA*, and *CB*, need to be brought into dialogue with one another to plumb the depths of the texts. Each text may have a particular vision of spiritual life to offer. As David Pellauer summarizes:

> Ricoeur maintains that a text cannot be simply analysed into its elements. It is more than a mere collection of sentences as can be demonstrated if we recall that the *sequence of a text cannot be altered without affecting its meaning*, nor may a poem be reduced to a series of propositions that "say the same thing."[134]

A hermeneutical approach to Juan's *Cántico* suggests that its meaning may not be exclusively the outlining of the doctrine of *CB*. Rather, Ricoeur tells us that understanding Juan's *Cántico* will be a project of self-understanding in one's present existential reality which is constructed by the text. All three *Cánticos*, interacting with each other, may have something to contribute toward this project.

It has already been said that a text decontextualizes the original meaning-event of discourse and makes possible the consequent recontextualization of its meaning through the redescription and metamorphosis of reality. Reality itself is as yet unfinished. A text *gives* reality in its process of becoming. Therefore, a text is an expression of "being." It is not a mere passing on of information, although this can be part of the function of a text. As Ricoeur says: "Language in the making celebrates reality in the making."[135] Temporality is a structure of existence that is

---

[134] PELLAUER, "The Significance of the Text," in *Studies in the Philosophy of Paul Ricoeur*, ed. E. Reagan, 105. (emphasis mine)

[135] Paul RICOEUR, "Poetry and Possibility," in *A Ricoeur Reader*, 462.

bound to language, especially in the poetic form of language.

Ricoeur also leads us to question whether each of the three texts of the *Cántico* succeeds the other in some progressive, developmental fashion. It would be difficult to judge one text as better than the other, one more complete, more detailed or unique.[136] This language may be inappropriate to discuss what is occurring in the configuration of the three texts. Rather the preceding analysis suggests that all three texts stand together, yet each one is unique with a unique contribution to make.

In summary, the text of Juan's *Cántico* cannot remain as a lifeless entity against the backdrop of the paper upon which it is written. The interaction of the text with the life of the reading subject completes the hermeneutical framework which I am developing. It is the incorporation of the life-world of the reader with the text-world which completes the hermeneutical arc. This step comprises the third moment of mimesis in Ricoeur's hermeneutical methodology. It is to this third mimesis, called mimesis$_3$, that we now turn.

---

[136] The correspondence between the two systems: betrothal and marriage, and the three ways of the classical spiritual journey, are not so neat and tidy in *CB* as some suggest. This becomes evident in reading the commentary on *CB* which reveals Juan's own struggle to match them. Referring to the commentary on *CB* Tavard remarks: "To tell the truth, the plan is not so clear as the author suggests. The notes or annotations that are characteristic of version (B) show the text swinging back and forth between the sequence of three ways and some experiences or graces that may be anterior or posterior to the state of the soul that is being considered. One gets the impression that the narrative comes back several times to already bygone moments of the spiritual journey, or at times jumps ahead toward states that are yet to come for the soul." TAVARD, *Poetry and Contemplation*, 235. See this reference for some examples concerning Juan's struggle in this regard.

CHAPTER SIX
MIMESIS₃ AND APPROPRIATION OF THE *CÁNTICO*

1. Introduction

The third hermeneutical moment concerns the appropriation of textual meaning which Ricoeur refers to as mimesis$_3$. With this moment I come to the goal of the hermeneutical contextualization of Juan's *Cántico* which I have been investigating. Appropriation completes the hermeneutical process because at this point the meaning of the text is removed from estrangement to be brought into the realm of understanding.

The understanding process is launched with a methodical laying out of the sense of the text. This dynamic, as was shown in Chapter Four through Ricoeur's dialectic of sense and reference, is necessary in order to determine the ideal meaning of a text, but interpretation cannot be limited to this. Ideal meaning (sense) must be engaged as real meaning (reference) grounded in the life of the reader. The methodical moment (explanation) orients the reader of the text to personalize its meaning but does not yet result in the appropriation (understanding) of the text.

Appropriation of a text, in Ricoeur's theory, could be described as the non-methodical moment of interpretation. Understanding a text is not an explanation of its literary elements, a history of its genesis, or an intuitive grasping of textual meaning, that is, a meeting of the mind of the reader with the mind of the author.[1]

---

[1] Eulogio Pacho sees just such a "meeting of minds" as the goal of the interpretation of the *Cántico*. In commenting on the interpretation of Juan de la Cruz's *Cántico*, Pacho states: "La interpretación genuina, profunda, total, de una obra es algo así como su recreación, o reproducción por el lector. Tanto más exacta será cuanto mayor sea la compenetración entre el autor e intérprete. La postura del exégeta ante un escrito doctrinal no puede ser idéntica a la del espectador, o admirador, de una pieza artística. Requiere y exige mayor movimiento personal de acercamiento. Tiende y establece una comunicación directa entre ambos: autor e intérprete." PACHO, "La Estructura literaria del «Cántico Espiritual»," 385. Further on he says that the goal of interpretation is to recreate the

Such a Romantic understanding of "understanding" is eliminated by the work of literary and structural analysis as was suggested in the last chapter. The tools of historical analysis, textual criticism, literary criticism, structural analysis, and so on, give the interpreter the competence to enter into the text, but the understanding of the text or its appropriation does not end with them.

Ricoeur's theory of interpretation takes us beyond the linguistic or theological analysis of a text. With the methodical (or analytical) moment, Ricoeur includes another dynamic. For Ricoeur, understanding or appropriation is the dialectic operative when an imagined possible world shaped by the text is made actual through reading. This is to say that appropriation of the world-of-the-text results in the metamorphosis of the reading subject.[2] In the process of reading the narcissistic self is challenged to let go of the central place it guards for itself as a being-in-the-world.[3] A new dimension of life is exposed for the reading subject according to the prescription of the text. Exploration of Ricoeur's theory of reading will expose this relationship which the reader shares with the *Cántico* of Juan de la Cruz so that this human transformation is possible.[4]

In this chapter I will follow a definite procedure. First, I will give a general introduction to the concept of mimesis₃. Ricoeur suggests that understanding a text, in this case Juan's *Cántico*, means restoring the poem to the time of action and suffering whence it came, *according to the act of the text itself.* Second, I will examine several components of Ricoeur's theory of reading which is

situation of the author in the life of the interpreter: "Se intenta sorprender directamente la actitud, la postura del autor desde dentro y en el momento de crear su imagen, su alegoría, su símbolo. Para abarcar todo el significado de la imagen es necesaria una especie de reincidencia en la situación en que aquélla se fragua. Hay que asistir a su forja en la mente del escritor; así será fácil y segura la caracterización de su tropología." Ibid., 389.

[2] RICOEUR, "Appropriation," in *Hermeneutics and the Human Sciences*, 187.

[3] RICOEUR, "Appropriation," 191.

[4] Clarity about the relationship the reader shares with a poetic text will also set the stage for the analytic in the next chapter which will allow an examination of three corollary issues concerning the interpretation, appropriation, and reception of Juan's *Cántico*. These are: 1. the role of the title of Juan's poem; 2. the poetry-commentary relationship; and 3. the ontological import of the *Cántico*.

the basis for the passage from mimesis$_2$ to mimesis$_3$. It is this movement, under the guise of "play," which opens the reader to the appropriation of texts and thus the conversion of human subjectivity. Third, because Juan's *Cántico* is lyrical, I will suggest how we may appropriate the *Cántico*. Lyric poetry has a unique ability to refigure human subjectivity through mood. I have already presented this concept in several places. I will develop it further here to suggest what might be an appropriate reception of Juan's *Cántico* for our time.

2. Mimesis$_3$: The Meaning of Understanding

Mimesis$_3$ brings us to the end point of the trajectory which we began with mimesis$_1$. We arrive at mimesis$_3$ having already explored the pre-understanding of human action in mimesis$_1$ and, subsequently, the emplotment of human action in mimesis$_2$. Through the reading of the text, mimesis$_2$ passes over into mimesis$_3$ and we encounter the return to time of the metamorphosis of reality configured by the text. Ricoeur clearly states this thesis in the following quote: "The process of composition, of configuration, does not realize itself in the text but in the reader, and under this condition configuration makes possible reconfiguration of a life."[5] Once the discourse of existence is fixed in a text, the text becomes the point of access to that discourse in another life in the present. The poetic act is therefore only completed in the life of the reader.[6] Mimesis$_3$, in this context, can be described as "the intersection of the world unfolded by fiction and the world wherein actual action unfolds."[7]

---

[5] RICOEUR, "Life: A Story in Search of a Narrator," 430.

[6] The possible critique that Ricoeur's interpretation theory simply leads to a vicious circle, i.e. that the end point of mimesis$_3$ is already anticipated where we began in mimesis , is responded to in RICOEUR, *Time and Narrative*, 1:71-76. Ricoeur sums up his position with the following statement: "The manifest circularity of every analysis of narrative, an analysis that does not stop interpreting in terms of each other the temporal form inherent in experience and the narrative structure, is not a lifeless tautology. We should see in it instead a 'healthy circle' in which the arguments advanced about each side of the problem aid one another." Ibid., 1:76.

[7] RICOEUR, "Mimesis and Representation," in *A Ricoeur Reader*, 148.

Just as the function of mediation is the predominant characteristic of mimesis$_2$, the refiguration of a life, that is, the presentation of new existential possibilities, is the hallmark of mimesis$_3$. The poetic text has its full meaning only "when it is restored to the time of action and of suffering."[8] Mimesis$_3$ thus marks the "intersection of the world of the text and the world of the hearer or reader, the intersection, therefore, of the world configured by the poem and the world wherein real action occurs and unfolds its specific temporality."[9] Especially through poetic making, the world is transformed "to the extent that recounting or narrating remakes action following the poem's invitation."[10] In this way Ricoeur's interpretive theory overcomes the limitations of a theory of interpretation that would divide the text into an "inside" and an "outside."[11]

Ricoeur says that "we must stop seeing the text as its own interior and life as exterior to it. Instead we must accompany that structuring operation that begins in life, is invested in the text, then returns to life."[12] The invitation for the text to "return to life" comes from the act of the text on the reader, not the act of the reader on the text.[13] This is true even though, in the final analysis, it is the reader

---

[8] RICOEUR, *Time and Narrative*, 1:70.

[9] RICOEUR, *Time and Narrative*, 1:71.

[10] RICOEUR, "Mimesis and Representation," 151.

[11] "For hermeneutics, ... seeks to reconstruct the whole arc of operations by which practical experience is turned into works, authors, and readers, there is neither an inside nor an outside to the work--the distinction of inside and outside being a methodological artefact--instead, there is a concrete process in which the textual configuration conjoins the practical prefiguration and the practical transfiguration." RICOEUR, "Mimesis and Representation," 140. Ricoeur places this movement in contrast with semioticians, such as those who follow Greimas' narrative semiotics, who have "given up the representative illusion by having constituted the text as an inside without an outside, or rather as an inside whose outside (be it author, audience, or socio-cultural circumstances) has become irrelevant. The referent of the text has become a function of the text. Within the narrative field, it is the narrated story as narrated and nothing more." Ibid., 144.

[12] RICOEUR, "Mimesis and Representation," 151.

[13] "The text, as writing, *awaits and calls* for a reading. If reading is possible, it is indeed because the text is not closed in on itself but opens out onto other things. To read is ... to conjoin a new discourse to the discourse of the text. This conjunction of discourses reveals, in the very constitution of the text, an original capacity for renewal that is its open character. Interpretation is the concrete

who is the operator of the "unceasing passage from mimesis$_1$ to mimesis$_3$ through mimesis$_2$."[14] In the context of Ricoeur's theory of mimesis it is the reader who *completes* the work of Juan's *Cántico* through appropriation of the world-of-the-text, but it is the work of the text before it is the work of the reader.[15]

To appropriate the world-of-the-text is to bring the discourse of the text back into an event of discourse in a life. It is the effects of reading, and the dynamics behind textual appropriation which primarily effect the reconfiguration so characteristic of mimesis$_3$. Ricoeur's theory of reading will now be examined in order to determine how the act of reading Juan's *Cántico* forms the basis for the transformation of the individual through the appropriation of the poem. One must remember that mimesis, in its singular threefold movement, "is an action about action. What it prefigures in the first stage and configures in the second, it transfigures in the third."[16]

3. The Act of Reading: The Significance of Reading in Interpretation

Several components of Ricoeur's theory of reading are significant for the hermeneutical interpretation of Juan's *Cántico*. First, I will investigate the relationship between the reader and the author through the reader's act of reading. Ricoeur suggests that the task before the reader is not to enter into the psychological space of the author, but rather to appropriate the world-of-the-text which is projected before the text *through* the act of reading. Second, I will investigate the relationship between the *Cántico* itself and the reader. Clarification of these issues will reveal that it is only through the reading and the appropriation of Juan's poem that the

---

outcome of conjunction and renewal." RICOEUR, "What is a Text? Explanation and Understanding," 118.

[14] RICOEUR, "Mimesis and Representation," 151.

[15] Ironically, this work of the text, actualized by the text, results in the completion of the text by the reader. As Ricoeur says: "Ultimately it is true that the reader composes the text." RICOEUR, "The Creativity of Language," 468.

[16] RICOEUR, "Mimesis and Representation," 150.

destiny of Juan's *Cántico* is fulfilled.[17]   Third, I will explore the dynamics of the transformative process which occurs in reading through the model of "play." The model of reading as "play" helps us to understand the invitation towards self-relinquishment that occurs through reading. Through reading, the primacy of the *cogito* (the conscious, self-constituting self) is subordinated to the possibility of transformation of all levels of the *self.*

Ricoeur's hermeneutical program abandons the primacy of the *cogito* and holds that "all reflection is mediated, there is no immediate self-consciousness."[18]   "Reflection is never first, never constituting--it arrives unexpectedly like a 'crisis' within an experience that bears us, and it constitutes us as the subject of the experience."[19] "Where consciousness posits itself as the origin of meaning, hermeneutics brings about the abandonment of this pretension."[20]   The dynamic of transformation and conversion effected by reading suggested by Ricoeur is astonishingly similar to the project that Juan cites for the individual in the world before God.[21]

3.1 The Focus of the Reader-Author Relationship

Ricoeur's reader-author relationship is a direct result of the decisive shift which he signals in interpretation theory and the impact that this shift has on his understanding of the hermeneutical circle.   In the tradition of Romantic hermeneutics, as we have already seen, the task of the reader was to place himself or herself into the spiritual life of the writer. The task at hand was to delve into the

---

[17] RICOEUR, "What is a Text? Explanation and Understanding," 124.

[18] Paul RICOEUR, "Toward a Hermeneutic of the Idea of Revelation," *Harvard Theological Review* 79, no. 1-2, (January-April 1977), 28.

[19] RICOEUR, "Toward a Hermeneutic of the Idea of Revelation," 29.

[20] RICOEUR, "Toward a Hermeneutic of the Idea of Revelation," 30.

[21] This dynamic is investigated in Juan's commentaries on two other poems: *The Ascent to Mount Carmel* and the *Dark Night.*

psychological space of the author, that is, to understand what the *author* intended to say. The text in this instance was a mere bridge to the perceived goal, that is, to understand the *author*. However, the emphasis in post-Heideggerian hermeneutics "is less on the other [the real author] as a spiritual entity than on the world which the work [of the text] unfolds."[22]

This world has already been presented as the world-of-the-text. "Beyond the situation of the author," the reader comes before the text to offer himself or herself "to the possible mode of being-in-the-world which the text opens up."[23] With this approach, the understanding of a text cannot be an objective procedure which unearths the mind of the author, but must include "the way in which the reader *already* understands himself and his work. Hence a sort of circularity is produced between understanding the text and self-understanding."[24]

With this statement we encounter Ricoeur's understanding of the hermeneutical circle which further emphasizes the kind of relationship the author and reader share. As just mentioned, understanding the author is not the goal of reading, but instead reading leads to an increase in *self*-understanding. It is true that, for Ricoeur, as in Romantic hermeneutics, the interpretation of a text is not authentic unless "it culminates in some form of appropriation (*Aneignung*)."[25] But what is appropriated is not the foreign experience of an *other*.[26] What the reader appropriates is not the "alien experience" of the author, but "the horizon of a world

---

[22] RICOEUR, "Metaphor and the Central Problem of Hermeneutics," 177.

[23] RICOEUR, "Metaphor and the Central Problem of Hermeneutics," 177.

[24] RICOEUR, "Metaphor and the Central Problem of Hermeneutics," 178. (emphasis mine)

[25] RICOEUR, "Metaphor and the Central Problem of Hermeneutics," 178.

[26] Ricoeur does not believe that the hermeneutical circle is correctly understood "when it is presented, first as a circle between two subjectivities, that of the reader and that of the author; and second, as the projection of the subjectivity of the reader into the reading itself." RICOEUR, "Metaphor and the Central Problem of Hermeneutics," 178. Ricoeur thus wishes to adjust a significant feature of the hermeneutical circle through what he believes is the nature of the author-reader relationship and the object of appropriation of the reading subject.

towards which a work directs itself."[27] Furthermore, the appropriation of the reference of the text is not even an empathy or a sympathy which the reading subject feels with the author of the text. As Ricoeur says: "the reference of a text in language is the coming to language of a world and not the recognition of another person."[28] This world is the inexhaustible world-of-the-text and not that of the author. It is the objectification of meaning through the reference of the text which mediates the interaction between the writer and the reader.[29]

3.2 The Interpretive Dynamics Operative Between the Text and its Reader

I have already said that it is reading which concretizes the transition between mimesis$_2$ and mimesis$_3$.[30] In Ricoeur's theory the reception of the work through reading is an integral part of the constitution of its meaning.[31] The world-of-the-text is only produced through the act of reading by *someone*.[32] The encounter of the world-of-the-text with the world of the reader through reading actualizes the reference of the sense of the text. The reading of Juan's *Cántico*, in the context of Ricoeur's theory, is therefore the connection to the poem's capacity to refigure

---

[27] RICOEUR, "Metaphor and the Central Problem of Hermeneutics," 178.

[28] RICOEUR, "Metaphor and the Central Problem of Hermeneutics," 178. Elsewhere Ricoeur says: "Nothing has more harmed the theory of understanding than the identification, central in Dilthey, between understanding and understanding *others,* as though it were always first a matter of apprehending a foreign psychological life behind a text. What is to be understood in a narrative is not first of all the one who is speaking behind the text, but what is being talked about, the *thing of the text,* namely, the kind of world the work unfolds, as it were, before the text." RICOEUR, "Explanation and Understanding," 131.

[29] RICOEUR, "Appropriation," 185.

[30] See RICOEUR, "Between the Text and Its Readers," 390-424.

[31] RICOEUR, "Mimesis and Representation," 150.

[32] "After all, libraries are full of unread books, whose configuration is, none the less, well laid out, and yet they refigure nothing at all. ... Without the reader who accompanies it, there is no configurating act at work in the text; and without a reader to appropriate it, there is no world unfolded before the text. Yet the illusion is endlessly reborn that the text is a structure in itself and for itself, and that reading happens to the text as some extrinsic and contingent event." RICOEUR, "Between the Text and Its Readers," 395.

experience in the life of the reader.[33] The potential for new existential possibilities by the appropriation of the poem is ultimately the hermeneutical interpretation of Juan's *Cántico*. The impact of the text on the individual reader or the reading community, and their impact on the text, are significant.

In this section, therefore, I will therefore affirm two things: 1. That the actual meaning of Juan's *Cántico* is influenced by the present reality of the reader, his or her experiences, expectations, hopes, and so on. This is often referred to as the "horizon of the reader." The actual meaning of the *Cántico* is also impacted by the previous history of its reception by the reading public. 2. That there is a potential effect of the *Cántico* on the reader which moves the reader to assume a new way of being-in-the-world according to the prescription of the *Cántico*. In reading there is an aesthetic experience of the text that gives rise to a catharsis of the reader which in turn opens the door to this pre-figured way-of-being of the text.

First, then, I will discuss the impact of prior readings of the *Cántico* on the present meaning of the text. Ricoeur suggests that through reading, written discourse is taken up again and allowed to fulfil the configurational act through human action.[34] This is done by the reader following the directedness of the text.[35] In Chapter Four and Chapter Five I have already explored how the structure of the text produces the reference of the text and "directs" the reader through its sense.[36] The received paradigms of the text structure the reader's expectations concerning the text, but the act of reading actualizes the capacity of the text to be meaningful in new

---

[33] RICOEUR, *Time and Narrative*, 1:76.

[34] Ricoeur says that the very structure of a text is but "an effect of reading," that is, the "reading to come is the unknown that the writing puts into perspective." Therefore, reading is not that which the text prescribes, "it is that which brings the structure of the text to light through interpretation." RICOEUR, "Between the Text and Its Readers," 397.

[35] RICOEUR, *Time and Narrative*, 1:76.

[36] RICOEUR, *Time and Narrative*, 1:76.

278

ways.[37]   However, the reader does not read the text from within a vacuum.   The reader of Juan's *Cántico* participates "in the sedimented expectations of the general reading public" who have read the text previously.[38]   This position contrasts with that of Federico Ruiz Salvador. Ruiz Salvador says that "the reading of a great mystic like Saint John of the Cross is of a strictly individual character, a dialogue between the author and the reader."[39]   However, Ricoeur holds that a text is read within a *tradition* of readings which impacts the actual reading.[40]   A strictly private reading of the *Cántico* is not possible in a hermeneutical interpretation. The history of the reception of the work is "at work" in the actual meaning of the text.[41]   And so are the personal expectations which the actual reader brings before the text, which, in part, have been shaped by this "sedimented history."[42]

---

[37]   RICOEUR, *Time and Narrative*, 1:76. Elsewhere Ricoeur says: "To follow a story is to reactualize the act of configuration which gave form to it. Furthermore, it is the act of the reader who accompanies the play between innovation and sedimentation. ... It is the act of reading which completes the work, which transforms it into a reading *guide* with its zones of indetermination, its latent richness of interpretation, its ability to be reinterpreted in novel ways within historical context that are always new." RICOEUR, "Life: A Story in Search of a Narrator," 432.

[38]   RICOEUR, "Between the Text and Its Readers," 399.

[39]   "La lectura de un gran místico como San Juan de la Cruz es de carácter estrictamente individual, diálogo entre el autor y el lector." RUIZ SALVADOR, "Introducción," 127. (translation mine) Further comment could be made on this position held by Ruiz Salvador. For example, how is it possible to have a dialogical situation when the author of a text is deceased? As we have already seen in Chapter Four, it is distanciation from the text through the absence of the author which makes the text more productive of meaning.

[40]   Recall this point which was made earlier in Chapter Three: "To say that the narrative schema has a history of its own, and that this history possesses all the characteristics of a tradition, is not at all to defend tradition understood as an inert transmission of dead sediment. On the contrary, it is to point to tradition, as a living passing-on of innovation which can always be re-activated by a return to the most creative moments of the poetic composition." RICOEUR, "Life: A Story in Search of a Narrator," 429.

[41]   RICOEUR, "Between the Text and Its Readers," 399.

[42]   "We must say that the reception of the work and the welcome given what Gadamer likes to call the 'issue' of the text are extracted from the sheer subjectivity of the act of reading only on the condition of being inscribed within a chain of readings, which gives a historical dimension to this reception and to this welcome. The act of reading is thereby included within a reading community, which, under certain favourable conditions, develops the sort of normativity and canonical status that we acknowledge in great works, those that never cease decontextualizing and recontextualizing themselves in the most diverse cultural circumstances." RICOEUR, "Between the Text and Its

Ricoeur again moves away from a psychological understanding of interpretation that subjectifies the meaning of the text. Instead he embraces a theory of interpretation that is connected with the process at work in the production of the text itself. This production takes place through various readings which have produced a history of the reception of the text. "The entire theory of hermeneutics consists in mediating this interpretation-appropriation by the series of interpretations that belong to the work of the text upon itself. Appropriation loses its arbitrariness insofar as it is the recovery of that which is at work, in labor, within the text. What the interpreter says is a resaying that reactivates what is said by the text."[43]

Down through the past four centuries Juan's *Cántico* has enjoyed a large audience within the western mystical culture. Today it continues to be the most widely read of Juan's works.[44] At different times particular academic disciplines, such as those of philosophy, theology, and literary studies have focused upon specific aspects of the *Cántico*.[45] From the various points of interest demonstrated in these academic disciplines we can see that the *Cántico* has had its own history of reception.[46] In the context of Ricoeur's hermeneutical theory we can appreciate why

---

Readers," 413.

[43] RICOEUR, "What is a Text? Explanation and Understanding," 124.

[44] PACHO, "Cántico espiritual," 491.

[45] Examples of all of these can be easily gleaned from the review of the literature in Chapter One.

[46] A more detailed study of the history of reception of Juan's *Cántico*, especially at the popular level, is yet to be done. However, we know of the diversity of the reception of Juan's opus as a whole. An interesting article reflecting on the influence of Juan's writings in various aspects of North American life dating back to the 1800's, including Juan's influence on the famous poet T.S. Eliot, is Steven PAYNE, "The Influence of John of the Cross in the United States: A Preliminary Study," in *Carmelite Studies IV: John of the Cross*, ed. Steven Payne (Washington: I.C.S. Publications, 1992), 167-195. An example of the shift taking place in the reception of Juan's work today is found in an article by Gerald May. May includes writings by Juan de la Cruz in his research on addictions counselling: Gerald MAY, "Lightness of Soul: From Addiction Toward Love in John of the Cross," *Spiritual Life* 37, (Fall 1991), 139-147. A couple of quotes from May's article serve to show how the reception of Juan's work has become significant in the field of psychology: "Western psychological science did not even entertain the idea of the unconscious until Freud introduced it in the early 20th century. Yet centuries earlier John, ... and other contemplatives were describing in fierce detail the inner life of the soul that goes on beneath our surface awareness. They seemed to know all about what Freud would eventually call defense mechanisms--the tricks our minds play on us--and the subtle ways

Juan's *Cántico* is open to speak to people from these different perspectives in different cultures and time periods. Juan's writings have been read and appropriated in various ways and continue to be read (received) today in new and original ways. Because of this timelessness of the *Cántico*, its interpretation calls for the hermeneutical approach. The richness of the text requires a variety of receptions. The ongoing interpretation of the *Cántico* cannot be reduced to a single reading, or to a deciphering of the message of the text in the form of theological concepts.

Psychologists, addiction therapists, or feminist theologians[47] are just as apt to turn to the *Cántico* for new insights into their being-in-the-world, as is the traditional spiritual theologian. Juan's *Cántico* is continually being given a new voice at the behest of the text itself because of the different circumstances and contexts in which it is being read. Ricoeur describes this quality of a text as its "surplus of meaning." This is the "unwritten" part of the text.[48] Juan's *Cántico*

---

selfishness can masquerade as spirituality." Ibid.,140; "What John describes as attachment is precisely what modern psychology calls conditioning and addiction. ... In addressing addictions, psychology advocates the substitution of 'better,' more efficient conditioning. John goes much deeper than this. He sees the *objects* of our attachment as good in themselves. But no *attachment*, ... no matter how noble or efficient, can really be seen as good. ... The radical point of John's psychology *for our time* is his conviction that human beings are capable of growth beyond addiction, toward absolute freedom for love. " Ibid., 142. On addictions and Juan de la Cruz see also, Marie Theresa COOMBS and Francis Kelly Nemeck, *O Blessed Night: Recovering From Addiction, Codependency and Attachment Based on the Insights of St. John of the Cross and Pierre Teilhard de Chardin*, (New York: Alba House, 1991). On the use of Juan's writings from the viewpoint of a feminist theologian see, Constance FITZGERALD, "A Discipleship of Equals: Voices from the Tradition--Teresa of Avila and John of the Cross," in *A Discipleship of Equals: Towards a Christian Feminist Spirituality*, ed. Francis A. Eigo (Villanova, PA: Villanova University Press, 1988), 63-97. On Juan de la Cruz and Liberation Theology see: Richard HARDY, "Liberation Theology and Saint John of the Cross: A Meeting," *Église et Théologie* 20 (1989), 259-282. From the perspective of an ethical reflection see, David SANDERLINE, "Charity According to St. John of the Cross: A Disinterested Love for Interesting Special Relationships, Including Marriage," *The Journal of Religious Ethics* 21, no. 1 (Spring 1993), 87-115. An article which connects Juan de la Cruz and Paul Ricoeur from the philosophical, as well as the theological, perspective is: Pierre MASSET, "Que suis-je? Qui suis-je? Que sommes-nous? De Ricoeur à St. Jean de la Croix," *Filosofia Oggi* 57, no. 1 (January-March 1992), 31-46.

[47] The term "theologian" is becoming very current in feminist studies. It refers to the use of mythologies which have feminine deities. These mythologies are used to construct anti-patriarchal religious systems.

[48] RICOEUR, "Between the Text and Its Reader," 401.

demonstrates a surplus of meaning because it is possible to read it in ways hardly dreamed of during the time of its composition.

Therefore, it is the *Cántico* itself, its history of reception, and the personal horizon of the reader, which furnish the guidelines for the encounter between the *Cántico* and the reader. This dynamic dispels the accusation of absolute subjectivity in the hermeneutical interpretation of Juan's *Cántico*. It is to be noted, however, that even though I have affirmed the importance of the history of reception of Juan's *Cántico* which affects and effects its actual meaning, the future interpretation of the *Cántico* is not limited to past or even current interpretations. The text is open for the future production of new meaning-events which in turn are shaped by its actual meaning.

Second, in what way does the text affect the reading subject? Ricoeur says: "Through fiction and poetry, new possibilities of being-in-the-world are opened up within everyday reality. Fiction and poetry intend being, not under the modality of being-given, but under the modality of power-to-be. Everyday reality is thereby metamorphised by what could be called the imaginative variations which literature carries out on the real."[49] The hermeneutical interpretation is that interpretation which affects *existentially* the life of the reader because of its ability to *engage* the life of the individual. Transformation, self-understanding, and new ways of being-in-the-world, are made possible through the appropriation of Juan's *Cántico*. Through reading, the text is freed to become grounded within the actual circumstances of the reality of the reading subject.

Through reading, the subject stands before the work of the text with his or her own capacity for receptivity of the imaginative variations of being-in-the-world which are presented by the text. Therefore, it is not the work of the reading subject to limit the text by projecting her or his own limitations onto the text. Through the analysis of the text explored in mimesis$_2$ the reader has already passed

---

[49] RICOEUR, "The Hermeneutical Function of Distanciation," 142. Recall the discussion on metaphorical reference and poetry. Poetic language, according to Ricoeur, is *par excellence* that which effects what Aristotle called the *mimesis* of reality.

beyond a naïve reading of the text. Rather, that which has *not* been disclosed becomes the work of the text in the life of the reader.[50] Or what has been lost in experience is "salvaged" in the reception of the text, that is, sedimented in the text as a "deposit of traces" of what is.[51] This reception is possible proportionate to the self-*availability* that the reading subject brings before the text . As Ricoeur says:

> If appropriation is the counterpart of disclosure, then the role of subjectivity must not be described in terms of projection. I should prefer to say that the reader understands himself in front of the text, in front of the world of the work. To understand oneself in front of a text is quite the contrary of projecting oneself and one's own beliefs and prejudices; it is to let the work and its world enlarge the horizon of the understanding which I have of myself. ... Thus the hermeneutical circle is not repudiated but displaced from a subjectivistic level to an ontological plane. The circle is between my mode of being--beyond the knowledge which I may have of it--and the mode opened up and disclosed by the text as the world of the work.[52]

Given this approach to the question of the relationship between the text and the reader, the question of denying the subjective dimension of reading and understanding Juan's *Cántico* disappears. This dimension forms the very heart of understanding Juan's *Cántico*, but it must be understood within Ricoeur's theory of author-subject and subject-text relationship. The task of understanding is to bring back to action the reference of the work of the poem, not to reconstruct the psychological experience of the author. The reader, however, is not to simply project his or her own subjectivity onto the text. Understanding only occurs when *someone*

---

[50] Due to the surplus of meaning in the text, that is, there is always *more* in the text then what the author actually lived. The reader is the one who, in the end, *composes* the text. On this point, see RICOEUR, "The Creativity of Language," 468-469. Ricoeur also uses this point to emphasize the task of hermeneutics: "The task of hermeneutics is to charter the unexplored resources of the to-be-said on the basis of the already said." Ibid., 471.

[51] "To rework language is to rediscover what we are. What is lost in experience is often salvaged in language sedimented as a deposit of traces, as a thesaurus. ... To rediscover meaning we must return to the multilayered sedimentations of language, to the complex plurality of its instances, which can preserve what is said from the destruction of oblivion." RICOEUR, "The Creativity of Language," 474.

[52] RICOEUR, "Metaphor and the Central Problem of Hermeneutics," 178.

appropriates the meaning for himself or herself in real life *according to the directions of the text*. Appropriation occurs when someone's world is enlarged, when one's self-understanding is moved beyond the actual limitations of the ego-subject. This enlargement of one's world is the purpose of writing and reading. Ricoeur, citing Jauss, asserts that a significant part of the increase in self-understanding is due to the effect of the "pleasure of the text" and the subsequent catharsis of the reading subject.[53]

"Contrary to the common idea that pleasure is ignorant and mute, ... it possesses the power to open a space of meaning."[54] Ricoeur says that pleasure is a "perceptive reception" which gives rise to understanding. In a way similar to the pleasing attentiveness one gives when listening to a musical score which effects a certain self-relinquishment, the pleasure of reading releases one from everyday perception and opens up new ways of being-in-the-world according to the "instructions" of the text.[55] "The text asks its readers, first of all, to entrust themselves to this perceptive understanding, to the suggestions of meaning that a second reading will thematize, suggestions of meaning that will provide a horizon for this reading."[56]

From the first reading of Juan's *Cántico*, that is, the aesthetic reading "just for pleasure," comes a certain pre-understanding of the text. In a first reading

---

[53] See RICOEUR, "Between the Text and Its Readers," 408-410. Ricoeur comments: "If the specific nature of literary understanding in terms of enjoyment has been neglected, this is due to the curious convergence between the interdiction uttered by structural poetics, forbidding us to step outside the text or to move beyond the reading instructions it contains, and the disfavour cast on enjoyment by Adorno's negative aesthetic, which sees in it merely a 'bourgeois' compensation for the asceticism of labour." Ibid., 408.

[54] RICOEUR, "Between the Text and Its Readers," 408.

[55] "If fiction is a fundamental dimension of the reference of the text, it is no less a fundamental dimension of the subjectivity of the reader. As reader, I find myself only by losing myself. Reading introduces me into the imaginative variations of the *ego*. The metamorphosis of the world in play is also the playful metamorphosis of the *ego*." RICOEUR, "The Hermeneutical Function of Distanciation," 144.

[56] RICOEUR, "Between the Text and Its Readers," 408.

the reader has an idea what the text is about and who the main characters are. However, this naive reading, as we have already seen, is displaced and intercepted by the work of *explanation*. The original "guess" is displaced by critical readings which may validate or adjust the initial "guess."[57] For example, historical studies will clarify the meanings of particular words within the context of Juan's sixteenth-century Spain. Literary studies will highlight the literary techniques used to construct the *Cántico* and lay bare the subtleties of the text. Through investigation of the dramatic structure of the *Cántico*, I have revealed the possibility that there is a deeper meaning to the text which needs to be uncovered through structural analysis. A more complete structural analysis of the *Cántico* would reveal the deep-structures of the text that are the "paradigmatic codes of language" which convey meaning. Genre orients the reader toward the kind of meaning available in that particular form.

All this work on the text of the poem, within the dialectic of explanation and understanding, involves the act of reading which *orients the reader* toward its potential meaning. Subsequent readings, again at the level of the aesthetic surface-structures, move the reader further toward an *understanding* of the text. Through the various readings, the reader follows the movement of the text from its sense to its reference, from what the text says to what it talks about.[58] This

---

[57] Ricoeur says that we need an art of "divination" because of the metaphorical nature of language and the polysemy of words. "A text has to be construed because it is not a mere sequence of sentences, all on an equal footing and separately understandable. A text is a whole, a totality. The relation between whole and parts--as in a work of art or in an animal--requires a specific kind of 'judgment' for which Kant gave the theory in the third *Critique*. Correctly, the whole appears as a hierarchy of topics, or primary and subordinate topics. The reconstruction of the text as a whole necessarily has a circular character, in the sense that the presupposition of a certain kind of whole is implied in the recognition of the parts. And reciprocally, it is in construing the details that we construe the whole. There is no necessity and evidence concerning what is important and what is unimportant, what is essential and what is unessential. The judgment of importance is a guess." RICOEUR, "The Model of the Text: Meaningful Action Considered as a Text," 158. The kind of validation of the "guess" is based more on a logic of qualitative probability than a logic of verification. See Ibid., 159.

[58] RICOEUR, "The Model of the Text: Meaningful Action Considered as a Text," 165. This mediation is orchestrated by the text itself in conjunction with the horizon of the reader. This prevents the reader from "identifying understanding with some kind of intuitive grasping of the intention underlying the text. What we have said about the depth semantics that structural analysis yields

movement from sense to reference is the activation of the invitation of the text for the subject to think in a certain manner. Ricoeur describes the injunction of the text to think in a certain manner as a catharsis of the reading subject that frees the reader to be present in the world in a new way: "*Aisthēsis* frees the reader from everyday concerns; catharsis sets the reader free for new evaluations of reality that will take shape in rereading."[59]

Catharsis, therefore, designates the effect of the work of the text: "new evaluations, hitherto unheard-of norms, are proposed by the work, confronting or shaking current customs."[60] Through catharsis of previously held values or norms, the work "teaches."[61] This effect of reading is achieved by the beauty of the work, a characteristic readily recognized in even a superficial reading of Juan's *Cántico*. Ricoeur notes an even more subtle effect which results from catharsis. "Thanks to the clarification it brings about, catharsis sets in motion a process of transposition, one that is not only affective but cognitive as well, something like allégorèse."[62] This allegorization is the translation of the meaning of the text into the field of human action. Or, in the words of Ricoeur, to allegorize the text is "to translate the meaning of a text in its first context into another context, which amounts to saying: to give it a new signification which goes beyond the horizon of meaning delimited by the intentionality of the text in its original context."[63]

---

invites us rather to think of the sense of the text as an injunction starting from the text as a new way of looking at things, as an injunction to think in a certain manner." Ibid., 165.

[59] RICOEUR, "Between the Text and Its Readers," 410.

[60] RICOEUR, "Between the Text and Its Readers," 410.

[61] RICOEUR, "Between the Text and Its Readers," 410. Ricoeur goes on to say: "What we find here is not simply a notation from Aristotle but a major feature of Kantian aesthetics--the contention that the universal nature of the beautiful consists in nothing else than in its *a priori* communicability. Catharsis thus constitutes a distinct moment from *aisthēsis*, conceived of as pure receptivity; namely, the moment of communicability of perceptive understanding." Ibid., 410.

[62] RICOEUR, "Between the Text and Its Readers," 410.

[63] RICOEUR, "Between the Text and Its Readers," 411.

Interpretation is not a subjective appropriation whereby the reading subject possesses the "key" to the text. If there is a key, it is the semantic content of the text.[64] The *Cántico itself*, in interaction with the world of the reader, opens up possible paths to transformation in real action by the reader.[65] The aesthetic-catharsis dynamic places the *Cántico* and the reader in a "synergetic relation."[66] *Mediating* between the *Cántico* and the reader is the mimesis of action of the world-of-the-text which expands the horizon of the reader and makes *new* meaningful action possible for the reading subject. Ricoeur describes this dialectic as a shift from the individual *merely* living in the *world existing around the human subject* (*Umwelt*) to the creation of a meaningful and *personal world* (*Welt*) strengthened with the mimesis of the text:

> The concept of horizon and world does not just concern descriptive references but also nondescriptive references, those of poetic diction. ... The world is the whole set of references opened up by every sort of descriptive or poetic text I have read, interpreted and loved. To understand these texts is to interpolate among the predicates of our situation all those meanings that, from a simple environment (*Umwelt*), make a world (*Welt*). Indeed, we owe a large part of the enlarging of our horizons of existence to poetic works. Far from producing only weakened images of reality--shadows, as in the Platonic treatment of the *eikōn* in painting or writing (*Phaedrus* 274e-77e)--literary works depict reality by *augmenting* it with meanings that themselves depend upon the virtues of abbreviation, saturation,

---

[64] Recall that the meaning of a text is stabilized in its semantic content such that it can be identified and reidentified over again: "It is necessary to understand by the meaning of the speech act, or by the noema of the saying, not only the sentence, in the narrow sense of the propositional act, but also the illocutionary force and even the perlocutionary action in the measure that these three aspects of the speech act are codified, gathered into paradigms, and where, consequently, they can be identified and reidentified as having the same meaning. Therefore I am here giving the word *meaning* a very large acceptation that covers all the aspects and levels of the intentional exteriorization that makes the inscription of discourse possible." RICOEUR, "The Model of the Text: Meaningful Action Considered as a Text," 147.

[65] "The reader belongs to both the experiential horizon of the work imaginatively, and the horizon of his action concretely. The awaited horizon and the horizon meet and fuse without ceasing. In this sense Gadamer speaks of the 'fusions of horizons' (*Horizontverschmelzung*) essential to the act of understanding a text." RICOEUR, "Life: A Story in Search of a Narrator," 431.

[66] RICOEUR, "Between the Text and Its Readers," 412.

and culmination, so strikingly illustrated by emplotment.[67]

To the extent that readers subordinate their expectations to those developed by the text, they themselves become unreal to a degree comparable to the unreality of the fictive world towards which they emigrate. Reading then becomes a place, itself unreal, where reflection takes a pause. On the other hand, inasmuch as readers incorporate--little matter whether consciously or unconsciously--into their vision of the world the lessons of their readings, in order to increase the prior readability of this vision, then reading is for them something other than a place where they come to rest; it is a medium they cross through.[68]

Therefore, Ricoeur's theory of reading makes the confrontation between the world-of-the-*Cántico* and world of the reader "at once a stasis and an impetus," that is, an alteration between moments of stepping back from the text and other moments of moving with it.[69] Ideally, reading involves a synergetic play between the world-of-the-text and the world of the reader. The transformative power of the text lies in its ability to prefigure an experience yet to come in the life of the reader.[70] Hence the paradox surfaces; the reader becomes unreal with the unreal of the text and subsequently enters more profoundly into the authentic depths of human reality.

We have been following the movement of the production of Juan's *Cántico* from its first roots in the pre-understanding of human action through to its consequent emplotment and subsequent reading. In the general introduction to mimesis in Chapter One, I stressed that Juan's participation in the *lebenswelt*, that which gives rise to the world-of-the-*Cántico*, is itself a metamorphosis of reality. In

---

[67] RICOEUR, *Time and Narrative*, 1:80. Ricoeur supports this position by reference to François Dagognet's work *Ecriture et Iconographie* which contests Plato's argument that writing and *eikōns* are weakened representations of reality. Instead, Dagognet characterizes the productions of writers and artists as "iconic augmentations" which reconstruct reality through artistic work.

[68] RICOEUR, "Between the Text and Its Readers," 414.

[69] RICOEUR, "Between the Text and Its Readers," 414.

[70] RICOEUR, "Between the Text and Its Readers," 405.

Chapter Four, I emphasized the fact that the interpretation of that experience through the inscription of a poetic text is also a production, that is, an objectification of Juan's participation in Being. Therefore, the metamorphosis of the reading subject results from the metamorphosis of reality which takes place through emplotment.[71] The text mediates subsequent discourse-events through the configurational act and the succeeding reading of the text by others. I have said that the reading subject appropriates this metamorphosis of reality configured by the *Cántico* through the effects of *aisthēsis* and *catharsis*. But, more precisely, how does Ricoeur suggest that this occurs with respect to the reading subject? What kind of interaction between the text of Juan's *Cántico* and the reader *effects* the metamorphosis of the individual which we have just explored?

It is the concepts of "play" and "mood" which are at the heart of Ricoeur's understanding as to how reading impacts and refigures the life of the reading-acting subject.[72] Ricoeur, following Gadamer, suggests that reading is transformative as play is transformative. It is an exploration of the dynamic of play which I now turn to deepen the understanding of Ricoeur's theory of reading and the appropriation of Juan de la Cruz's *Cántico*.

3.3 Reading as Playful Production

The protagonist at work in reading is usually described as the reader. Frequently the text is only seen as a life-less objectifiable entity subjected to the exploitation of the reading subject. However, this approach leaves little room for the possibility of transformation of human lives which we know has occurred since the production and reading of texts. "The accomplishment of reading is its power to transform the otherness of the text into an event of discourse for me. The event of discourse of the reader is a new event; that is, not a repetition of the original event,

---

[71] RICOEUR, "Appropriation," 186.

[72] Ricoeur uses Hans-Georg Gadamer's concept of "play" in *Truth and Method*. See for example: GADAMER, "The Ontology of the Work of Art and its Hermeneutic Significance: Play as the Clue to Ontological Explanation," in *Truth and Method*, 101-134.

but a creation produced at the behest of the text."[73] It is the concept of "play" in Ricoeur's interpretation theory which makes the reader an active and willing partner in the dynamics of reading and the refiguration of a life according to the *Cántico's* prescription.

Ricoeur describes play in the following way: "Play is not determined by the consciousness which plays; play has its own way of being. Play is an experience which transforms those who participate in it. It seems that the subject of aesthetic experience is not the player himself, but rather what 'takes place' in play."[74] We see then that the human subject can play, but can also be "played upon."[75] Through play, the playing subject is removed from his or her immediate conscious self to be engaged in play by the "game." "Play shatters the seriousness of a utilitarian preoccupation where the self-presence of the subject is too secure. In play, subjectivity forgets itself; in seriousness, subjectivity is regained."[76] The activity of being-played can even take place with an unknown partner, such as the risk of playing against "all the odds!" In our case the engaging *other* is Juan's *Cántico*.

If I apply this brief analysis of play to reading, we see that the *Cántico* and the reader are both "living" entities which interact through the act of reading. Juan's *Cántico*, in Ricoeur's theory of text and reading, can therefore be described as a "form of life." Reading produces a distanciation of the reading subject from his or her own self allowing a playful entry into the life of the *Cántico*.

It is this distanciation which Ricoeur suggests is the precondition for self-understanding. This distanciation also provides the mutual meeting space for

---

[73] VAN DEN HENGEL, *Home of Meaning*, 201.

[74] RICOEUR, "Appropriation," 186.

[75] "On the one hand, the presentation of a world in a poem is a heuristic fiction and in this sense 'playful'; but on the other hand, all play reveals something true, precisely because it is play. To play, says Gadamer, is to play at something. In entering a game we hand ourselves over, we abandon ourselves to the space of meaning which holds sway over the reader." RICOEUR, "Appropriation," 187.

[76] RICOEUR, "Appropriation," 186.

the world-of-the-text and the human subject which creates the possibility for transformation in the realm of action.[77] What we come to see, then, is that self-understanding is not immediate. Self-understanding is mediated by the text interacting with the reading subject. Self-distanciation through reading provides the possibility of self-transformation. It is this latter point which I would like to explore further in our model of reading Juan's *Cántico* looked upon as "play."

The shattering of illusions in life is made possible through reading. New possibilities of the real are proposed in the mode of play.[78] The playfulness of reading can shatter illusions because in reading we set free our imaginations and temporarily live in an imaginary world. We live in an "as if" mode which breaks down our defences and makes our imagination dwell in possible new ways of being-in-the-world. However, in the act of reading, the reader must play within the constraints of the text as the reader enjoys "the pleasure of the text."[79] In this way it is the reader who completes the work of the text "inasmuch as ... the written work is a *sketch* for reading."[80] The written work "consists of holes, lacunae, zones of indetermination, which ... challenge the reader's capacity to configure what the author seems to take malign delight in defiguring. ... It is the reader, almost abandoned by the work, who carries the burden of emplotment."[81] I examined some of these lacunae in Juan's *Cántico* in the study of its configuration in Chapter Five.

---

[77] RICOEUR, "The Hermeneutical Function of Distanciation," 142-144.

[78] RICOEUR, "Appropriation," 186. "A balance is sought between the signals provided by the text and the synthetic activity of reading. This balance is the unstable effect of the dynamism by which ... the configuration of the text in terms of structure becomes equal to the reader's refiguration in terms of experience. This vital experience, in turn, is a genuine dialectic by virtue of the negativity it implies: depragmatization and defamiliarization, inversion of the given in image-building consciousness, illusion-breaking." RICOEUR, "Between the Text and Its Readers," 402-403. Also, "Play is formidable precisely because it is loose in the world, planting its mediations everywhere, shattering the illusion of the immediacy of the real." Ibid., 470.

[79] RICOEUR, *Time and Narrative*, 1:77.

[80] RICOEUR, *Time and Narrative*, 1:77. (emphasis mine)

[81] RICOEUR, *Time and Narrative*, 1:77.

Ricoeur sees these "zones of indetermination" as instigators of the work of interpretation for the reader. Incongruencies in the text are not necessarily inhibitors to understanding but, in Ricoeur's model, may be productive of meaning since they participate in the construction of the metaphorical reference of the text. This concept of reading allows the text to be appreciated as a set of instructions that the reader executes in a creative way in the mode of play.[82]

In this way, the reader receives the work according to his or her own receptive capacity.[83] The reader "plays" the text as best he or she can. This stance of Ricoeur is similar to that held by Juan de la Cruz in the guidelines that he suggests for the reading and interpretation of his *Cántico*. Juan states: "It is better to explain the utterances of love in their broadest sense so that each one may derive profit from them according to the mode and capacity of one's own spirit, rather than narrow them down to the meaning unadaptable to every palate."[84]

The play which is enacted in reading and whereby the reading subject loses immediate subjectivity effects a metamorphosis whereby "everyday reality is abolished and yet everyone becomes himself."[85] The subject's true being is thus realized through the playful act of reading:

[82] RICOEUR, *Time and Narrative*, 1:77. Ricoeur follows the theory of Ingarden. A text is *necessarily* incomplete first, because "it offers different 'schematic views' that readers are asked to 'concretize.' They strive to picture the characters and the events reported in the text. It is in relation to this image-building concretization that the work presents lacunae, 'places of indeterminacy.' However well-articulated the 'schematic views' proposed for our execution may be, the text resembles a musical score lending itself to different realizations. A text is incomplete, second, in the sense that the world it proposes is defined as the intentional correlate of a sequence of sentences (*intentionale Satzkorrelate*), which remains to be made into a whole for such a world to be intended. Turning to advantage the Husserlian theory of time and applying it to the sequential chain of sentences in the text, Ingarden shows how each sentence points beyond itself, indicates something to be done, opens up a perspective." RICOEUR, "Between the Text and Its Readers," 399-400.

[83] "The listeners or readers receive it, [the text] according to their own receptive capacity, which itself is defined by a situation that is both limited and open to the world's horizon." RICOEUR, *Time and Narrative*, 1:77.

[84] *CB* Prologue 2 "Y esto tengo por mejor, porque los dichos de amor es mejor declararlos en su anchura, para que cada uno de ellos se aproveche según su modo y caudal de espíritu, que abreviarlos a un sentido a que no se acomode todo paladar." *CB* Prologo 2

[85] RICOEUR, "Appropriation," 187.

> The player is metamorphosed 'in the true'; in playful representation, 'what is emerges'; but 'what is' is no longer what we call everyday reality; or rather, reality truly becomes reality, that is, something which comprises a future horizon of undecided possibilities, something to fear or to hope for, something unsettled. Art only abolishes non-metamorphosed reality. Whence the true *mimesis*: a metamorphosis according to truth.[86]

The essential true being thus emerges through poetic composition and the subsequent act of reading. Through reading Juan's *Cántico*, the subject is invited to undergo an "imaginative variation of his *ego*. ... The reader is this imaginary 'me', created by the poem and participating in the poetic universe."[87] This universe is the world-of-the-*Cántico* to be appropriated by the reading subject. The actualized *Cántico* thus resumes the referential movement of the world-of-the-text as constructed by its semantic "rules." As Ricoeur says: "Reading is like the execution of a musical score; it marks the realization, the enactment, of the semantic possibilities of the text."[88] But, as we have just seen, not only does the reader *produce* the production of the text, but the text also plays or *produces* the reading subject. "For the work itself has constructed the reader in his role."[89] To enter into a work of art such as Juan's *Cántico* is to divest oneself of the former "I" in order "to receive, as in play, the self conferred by the work."[90]

This concept of appropriation, as presented by Ricoeur, once again emphasizes certain fallacies of the Romanticist's approach to interpretation and understanding of a text. We can review several of these quickly here. First, appropriation is not the recovery of the genius of the author, whether it be through

---

[86] RICOEUR, "Appropriation," 187.

[87] RICOEUR, "Appropriation," 189.

[88] RICOEUR, "What is a Text? Explanation and Understanding," 119. Ricoeur goes on to say that this feature "is the most important because it is the condition ... of overcoming cultural distance and of fusing textual interpretation with self-interpretation." Ibid., 119.

[89] RICOEUR, "Appropriation," 189.

[90] RICOEUR, "Appropriation," 190.

a recovery of the message of the text or an analysis of its depth structures. Second, appropriation is not the discernment of the true intention of the author. We have already seen how written discourse escapes the narrow boundaries of authorial intentionality. Third, appropriation is not a discovery of the original audience of the text whereby one attempts to identify oneself with that first original group. Let us now return to the line of thought presented above: the production of the reading subject through the act of reading.

In the process of reading there is the potential for the appropriation of a text as well as the fundamental relinquishment of the self.[91] This is the twofold movement which is the paradoxical result of reading. Hermeneutics is thus securely linked with fundamental ontology. In the end, appropriation of the *Cántico*

> is the process by which the revelation of new modes of being--or, if you prefer Wittgenstein to Heidegger, new 'forms of life'--*gives* the subject new capacities for knowing himself. If the reference of a text is the projection of a world, then it is not in the first instance the reader who projects himself. The reader is rather broadened in his capacity to project himself by receiving a new mode of being from the text itself.[92]

Therefore, within the context of Ricoeur's theory of mimesis, the only interpretations which satisfy the admonition of Juan's *Cántico* are those interpretations which follow

> the 'arrow' of meaning [of the text] and endeavors to 'think in accordance with' it, engenders a new *self*-understanding. By the expression '*self*-understanding', I should like to contrast the *self* which emerges from the understanding of the text to the *ego* which claims to precede this understanding. It is the text, with its universal power of unveiling, which gives a *self* to the *ego*.[93]

Understanding the meaning of Juan's *Cántico* is thus irreversibly

---

[91] David Klemm gives a succinct description of this movement: "The self finds itself and gains its true destiny only in the willingness to withdraw itself from the position of constituting consciousness in order to allow the text-tradition to confer that consciousness in belongingness to and dependence on that tradition." KLEMM, *The Hermeneutical Theory of Paul Ricoeur*, 156-157.

[92] RICOEUR, "Appropriation," 192.

[93] RICOEUR, "Appropriation," 193.

linked with self-understanding and the revelatory power of the text. Juan's *Cántico* is a manifestation, an epiphany, of a particular way of being-in-the-world which the text invites the reader to appropriate. Appropriation of this world is, in the end, what it means to interpret Juan's *Cántico*.[94] This bringing back to the event of discourse the meaning of the text will be unique in the lived experience of each individual. This approach to interpretation suggests that interpretation does not result in the certainty of absolute knowledge. Therefore, "between absolute knowledge and hermeneutics, it is necessary to choose."[95]

4. Appropriation of the *Cántico* Through its Unique Productive Capacity

We have seen through the preceding presentation that reading is the act by which mimesis$_2$ passes to mimesis$_3$. The text is not meaningful unless it is read. Through the dynamics of play the text interacts with the reading subject orienting the reader toward the ultimate reference of the text. But we have already seen in Chapter Four that lyric poetry has a unique referential capacity to construct "mood." Feelings constructed by the poetic text are, to a large extent, what the text is about. We will continue to explore the truth of this thesis in this section. Ultimately we must question the unique referential capacity of Juan's *Cántico*.

The question, therefore, to be responded to in this section is the following: based on the *Cántico*'s particular literary form, its genre, and Ricoeur's reading/reception theory which we just examined, how might Juan's *Cántico* be appropriated for our own time? I have already stressed in several places (Chapter Two, Chapter Four, and Chapter Five) the importance of the form of the text in the construction of meaning. In each instance what is to be appropriated from a literary work is qualified by the form or genre of the work. The genre of a work determines what a work can "do." Genre suggests the kind of appropriation which may be

---

[94] "Above all, the subordination of the theme of appropriation to that of manifestation turns more towards a hermeneutics of the *I am* than a hermeneutics of the *I think*." RICOEUR, "Appropriation," 193.

[95] RICOEUR, "Appropriation," 193.

suitable to that particular work.

In Chapter Four, I described the genre of the *Cántico* as a pastoral hendecasyllablic love poem. I also linked the genre of the *Cántico* with the genre of the *Song of Songs*, describing both of them as canticles. I asked the question: What do canticles do? Canticles have the capacity to create mood, to evoke feelings. If this is what canticles do, then their reception must be such that this productive capacity of the text is allowed to shine forth. The question, therefore, is what kind of reception through reading is appropriate for this form of literature which is highly metaphorical?

Metaphorical truth recognizes that language can divest itself of direct description in order to discover levels of reality that are not accessible through ostensive reference. Language, therefore, has the potential to schematize feelings which link us to the world. Feelings are a way of knowing the world which precede the subject/object dichotomy characteristic of scientific knowing. In as much as feelings or mood insert us into levels of reality not before known, feelings are productive; they discover and create reality. To interpret a text in this context, is to understand this new vision of reality schematized by the text.

We have therefore returned to the questions of genre, the function of metaphorical reference, and the role of mood, in order to lead us toward the kind of reception appropriate for Juan's *Cántico*. How are we to appropriate the *Cántico* for today? In Chapter One we reviewed many ways the *Cántico* has been received and appropriated. These various ways of approaching the *Cántico* are all different receptions of the text which resulted in a particular appropriation. But if the *Cántico*'s genre is directed toward the production of mood, as love poems or canticles are, then it appears that there are other possible receptions and appropriations which may not yet have been explored, or at least formally recognized in the appropriation of Juan's *Cántico*.

I would now like to examine further the significance of the *Cántico*'s production of mood in order to explore how the *Cántico* may be appropriated. I have already examined this question in a preliminary way in Chapter Four where I connected feeling with an experience of learning. I stressed there that to feel is to experience a feeling as a property of the felt object. Feelings are not merely subjective. Since metaphorical reference directs us toward non-ostensive reality, feelings connect us with the deeper dimensions of existence. Appropriation of the *Cántico* through feeling or mood can be described as an aesthetic reception of the *Cántico*. I will now return to the question of the relationship of feeling and knowing in order to strees the importance of an aesthetic appropriation of Juan's *Cántico*.[96]

Ricoeur says that feeling and knowing "explain each other."[97] Feelings connect me to the world and insert me into reality. We are attached to the realities being presented through affective levels of our being. I therefore come to know reality in a new way. Feeling and knowing have a shared genesis whereby one promotes the other. We are affected by what we know; we also know through our affections. Knowing something engenders various levels of feeling about that which we know. We feel qualities *on* things, *on* persons, *on* the world.[98] What we know, therefore, is not before us without some level of feeling about that which we know. On the other hand, feeling directs the intention of our knowing. Feeling, in its intentionality, leads us to know more. Feeling is an awareness of "something"--the lovable, the hateful.[99] Feelings are organized around what we know of something, and what we feel of this something directs our knowing of it. We are thus led to a paradox: intention and affection are held together within the same experience.

But whereas knowing holds the something known at a distance,

---

[96] In order to further explore the relationship of feelings and knowing, I will use a chapter of Paul RICOEUR, *Fallible Man*, trans. Charles A. Kelby, (Chicago: Henry Regnery Co., 1965), 122-202. It is here that Ricoeur most clearly develops his understanding that feeling, through mood, develops our belonging to the world objectified as an intention toward the world.

[97] RICOEUR, *Fallible Man*, 126.

[98] This is a paraphrase of an expression Ricoeur uses to describe the shared intentionality of feelings and knowledge: "But it is a very strange intentionality which on the one hand designates qualities felt *on* things, *on* persons, *on* the world and on the other hand manifests and reveals the way in which the self is inwardly affected." RICOEUR, *Fallible Man*, 127.

[99] RICOEUR, *Fallible Man*, 127.

perpetuating the subject and object dichotomy, feeling is understood, "by contrast, as the manifestation of a relation to the world which constantly restores our complicity with it, our inherence and belonging in it, something more profound than all polarity and duality."[100] "By means of feelings, objects touch me."[101] This kind of relation to the world, effected through feeling, "is irreducible to any *objectival* polarity and can only be achieved indirectly."[102] "Feeling is the privileged mode through which this pre- and hyper-objective relation is revealed."[103] Feelings express my belonging to the world objectified as an intention toward the world and an affection of the self.[104] "This paradox, however, is only the sign pointing toward the mystery of feeling, namely, the undivided connection of my existence with beings and being through desire and love."[105]

If we say feelings are merely "subjective," we miss the intentional dimension of feelings; feelings *aim* at something, are focused *on* something. Ricoeur brings this insight to bear on the significant relationship of feelings and knowledge:

> If feeling manifests what life aims at, if it reveals the orientation of tendencies which direct our lives toward the world, feeling must *add* a new dimension to the merely transcendental understanding of human reality. Furthermore, if feeling manifests its meaning only by contrast with the work of objectification proper to knowing, if its

---

[100] RICOEUR, *Fallible Man*, 129.

[101] RICOEUR, *Fallible Man*, 135.

[102] RICOEUR, *Fallible Man*, 129.

[103] RICOEUR, *Fallible Man*, 129. Ricoeur explains that scholastic theology was sensitive to this dynamic: "The scholastics had an excellent word to express this mutual coaptation of man to goods which suit him and to bads which do not suit him. They spoke of a bond of connaturality between my being and other beings. This bond of connaturality is silently effected in our tendential life; we feel it in a conscious and sensory way in all our affections, but we do not understand it in reflection except by contrast with the movement of objectification proper to knowing. Consequently feeling can be defined only by this very contrast between the movement by means of which we 'detach' over and against us and 'objectify' things and beings, and the movement of which we somehow 'appropriate' and interiorize them." Ibid., 133-4.

[104] RICOEUR, *Fallible Man*, 134.

[105] RICOEUR, *Fallible Man*, 134.

general function is to interiorize the reality that we objectify over against us, then the advent of feeling is necessarily contemporary with that of knowledge.[106]

Feelings are therefore revelatory about that which we feel. But Ricoeur says we must say more about this revelatory capacity of feelings if we are not to fall back into mere formalism which would "allow the essence of the revelation of feeling to escape."[107] For Ricoeur, based on Kant, it is a question of recognizing that we are already *inserted* in that reality which we feel and *in* which we may continue our existence. "Feeling is wholly itself only through that consciousness of being already in ..., through that primordial *inesse*. Feeling is more than the identity of existence and reason in the person; it is the very belonging of existence to the being whose thinking is reason."[108]

Whatever exists, feeling confirms that we are part of it: "it is not the Entirely-Other but the medium or primordial space in which we continue to exist. This fundamental feeling, this Eros through which we are in being, is particularized in a diversity of feelings of belonging which are, as it were, the schematization of it. These feelings, called 'spiritual,' are no longer adaptable to any finite satisfaction; they make up the pole of infinitude of our whole affective life."[109]

Ricoeur refers to the above schematization as "ontological feeling,"[110] feeling that shapes our world and anticipates that which is to come. However, not all feeling takes on ontological import. Feelings are capable of being felt without effecting any ontological change. As Ricoeur states:

> All feelings are capable of acquiring form or of returning to a formless state; this is a consequence of the intentional structure of feeling in general: in turn, it takes on form in accordance with the

---

[106] RICOEUR, *Fallible Man*, 137.

[107] RICOEUR, *Fallible Man*, 155.

[108] RICOEUR, *Fallible Man*, 156.

[109] RICOEUR, *Fallible Man*, 156.

[110] RICOEUR, *Fallible Man*, 157.

objects of knowledge to which it fastens its felt epithets, or returns to the formless in accordance with the law of interiorization, of introception, the plunging back into the ground of life from which intentional acts emerge.[111]

It is the particularization of feeling in mood which mediates between the ontological level of feeling and intellectual knowing. Feeling, potentially, serves to instruct us about that which we feel and through various moods to shape our world. They, therefore, open up new possibilities for existence, for knowing reality in a new way. Moods create new possibilities for being-in-the-world which did not exist before. The ontological manifests itself through mood.

The particularization of "ontological feeling" is named joy, delight, serenity, exultation, and so on. Moods such as these are often elicited by a reading of Juan's *Cántico*. These particularizations of feeling are what Ricoeur says characterize our openness to being, that is, our feelings are open to acquiring form in their particularization. Mood holds a special place in bringing together two sets of poles: the coincidence of the transcendent with intellectual determinations, and the interiority of the human person with existential movement.[112]

Feeling (as particularized in mood), therefore, mediates between living and thinking, between bios and logos.[113] It is in this intermediate region that the *self* is constituted. Through feelings, my world is enlarged and I come to know myself as different from natural beings and other selves.[114] Feelings betray my adherence to and my inherence in aspects of the world that I no longer set over against myself as objects.[115] New existential possibilities therefore become possible because I am bound to that which my feelings feel. As mentioned, this mode of

---

[111] RICOEUR, *Fallible Man*, 160.

[112] RICOEUR, *Fallible Man*, 160.

[113] RICOEUR, *Fallible Man*, 163.

[114] RICOEUR, *Fallible Man*, 163.

[115] RICOEUR, *Fallible Man*, 171.

300

being has the potential to take on ontological import in my life. In conclusion
Ricoeur states:

> The universal function of feeling is to bind together. It connects what
> knowledge divides; it binds me to things, to beings, to being.
> Whereas the whole movement of objectification tends to set a world
> over against me, feeling unites the intentionality, which throws me
> out of myself, to the affection through which I feel myself existing.[116]

If feeling, or mood, is so essential a part of existential movement and
self-understanding, then Juan's *Cántico* which is productive of mood, needs to be
received in such a way that this production is not only possible, but enhanced. This
becomes especially significant since the reception of Juan's *Cántico* has largely been
religious in nature. If the *Cántico*'s referential capacity through mood is uniquely
directed toward the reality of the Divine present in our world, and if it is mood which
unites us with that reality, then mood becomes the operator, par excellence, to plunge
us into the productive depths of Juan's poem. Although the doctrinal elements of the
poem are important, they are not productive of life and existence in the same way as
mood.

I therefore am now in a position to respond to the question concerning
the appropriation of Juan's *Cántico*. Given the significance of mood and its
productive capacity, how might Juan's *Cántico* be appropriated? How might we
receive Juan's *Cántico* such that its productive capacity is set free?

It was suggested by some commentators that Juan's *Cántico* may have
been sung during Juan's own time. As I pointed out in Chapter Three the literature
on this question is not decisive one way or another, even though there is one eye
witness account of Juan singing his own *Cántico*.[117] However, the research on the
genre question in Chapter Five lends support to the possibility that Juan's *Cántico*
may have been sung, or is at least based on literary forms that were sung (i.e., recall

---

[116] RICOEUR, *Fallible Man*, 200.

[117] As I noted in Chapter Three Francisco de la Madre de Dios reported Juan singing the *Cántico* in her Declaration during the gathering of information for Juan's canonization.

the *a lo divino* movement). The fact that Juan's *Cántico* is referred to as a *canción* by Eulogio Pacho, and is situated within popular *cancioneros cortesanos* by Damaso Alonso, supports the possibility that Juan's *Cántico* was indeed sung during Juan's own day. Poetic discourse, coupled with music, has a unique capacity to evoke mood, to surface feeling, to get us in touch with the affective level of our being. Is it, therefore, an aesthetic reception of Juan's *Cántico* through music and song which would set free its ultimate referential capacity? If reading Juan's poem orients us toward the metaphorical reference of the poem, might singing open up the poem even more, allowing the singer/listener to exploit its rhythmic patterns, its poetic movements, its particular literary devices? Through music the poem would be allowed to "embody more."

This aesthetic reception of Juan's *Cántico* takes seriously that it is a canticle, possibly even a song in its earliest reception. Various musical settings would obviously interpret the *Cántico* differently, each one making unique use of the *Cántico*'s metaphorical referential capacity. I am aware that some of the *Cántico* has recently been set to music and song. The *Grupo Polifonico San Juan de la Cruz* set *CA* 1, 6, and 19 to music and song for the fourth centenary of the anniversary of Juan de la Cruz's death.[118] The song is titled "Canción 15." Other stanzas of the *Cántico* are included within other songs on the same cassette.

In order to take advantage of the metaphorical reference of the *Cántico* it is also possible to receive the poem through recitation. Such was the situation with the nuns at Beas and Granada. Juan shared his poem with those nuns, they memorized it, and used it for their personal edification and reflection. Juan's poem, it seems, is opened to its full referential capacity, when the poem itself is the central focus of our attention. Such is the conclusion which comes from Ricoeur's

---

[118] *Grupo Polifonico San Juan de la Cruz*, (Montilla [Córdoba], Spain: Sonsisur, 1991), CO 1412, sound cassette. Why "Canción 15" is the title of the song is not obvious. Stanza 15 from either *CO*, *CA* or *CB* is included in the setting. Other musicians have recently set other pieces of Juan's poetry to music: Paul GURR, *Paul Gurr Sings Vol. 2: Still Waters: Poetry of the John of the Cross*, trans. of poems Marjorie Flower (Richmond Vic, Australia, 1992), sound cassette; Loreena McKENNITT, "The Dark Night of the Soul," on *The Mask and Mirror*, (Scarborough: Warner Music Canada, 1994), 99 52964, sound cassette.

reading-reception theory which suggests that we enter into the depths of the text through its metaphorical reference. The primary access to the world of Juan's *Cántico* is not through the commentary which Juan wrote, but is through the poem itself. It appears that an aesthetic reading, whether, sung or memorized, is the reception of the poem which would free up its referential capacity to "do" what the poem is capable of doing.

5. Conclusion

What becomes apparent in Ricoeur's theory of textual interpretation is that the "meaningful patterns that a depth interpretation wants to grasp cannot be understood without a kind of personal commitment similar to that of the reader who grasps the depth semantics of the text and makes it his or her 'own'."[119] Understanding Juan's *Cántico* has little to do with an *immediate* grasping of Juan's psychic life or with an *emotional* identification with his mental intention.[120] "Understanding is entirely *mediated* by the whole of explanatory procedures that precede it and accompany it. The counterpart of this personal appropriation is not something that can be *felt* in sympathy with the author of the text; it is the dynamic meaning released by the explanation which we identified earlier with the reference of the text, that is, its power of disclosing a world."[121] This world-of-the-*Cántico* is ultimately what is to be appropriated through reading.

Ricoeur's theory of reading and appropriation accounts for the dynamic reception of Juan's *Cántico* over the past four hundred years by a very diverse public. Juan's *Cántico* has had a large "following" through a variety of receptions. These receptions have been in a plethora of cultural and historical settings. This testifies to the readers' ability to enter into the surplus of meaning contained in the text. Ricoeur's concept of appropriation, as developed in his theory

[119] RICOEUR. "The Model of the Text: Meaningful Action Considered as a Text," 167.

[120] RICOEUR. "The Model of the Text: Meaningful Action Considered as a Text," 167.

[121] RICOEUR. "The Model of the Text: Meaningful Action Considered as a Text," 167.

of reading, also accounts for the *present* character of interpretation and for the continued reception of Juan's *Cántico* by a wide spectrum of people. Reading actualizes the possibilities of the *Cántico for today*, thus overcoming cultural and historical distance, two main roadblocks often cited in the interpretation of Juan's *Cántico*. In Ricoeur's theory it is because of historical and cultural distance that the referential power of the *Cántico* is resumed through appropriation and once again becomes living speech (discourse) in today's world.

Ricoeur's theory of reading and reception, particularly his emphasis on the configurational capacity of mood, accounts also for the self-involvement in the interpretation of the *Cántico* which Juan de la Cruz signalled in his commentary. Juan was sensitive to the "mystical understanding" which gave birth to the *Cántico* as well as to the "mystical understanding" which each person brings to its reading. Therefore, in his commentary on the *Cántico*, Juan did not pretend to define once and for all the meaning of the poem, rather he knew that meaning would vary according to the disposition of the individual. Juan says in the Prologue of his commentary on the *Cántico*:

> I do not plan to expound these stanzas in all the breadth and fullness that the fruitful spirit of love conveys to them. It would be foolish to think that expressions of love arising from mystical understanding, like these stanzas, are fully explainable. ... Who can describe in writing the understanding he [referring to the "Spirit of the Lord"] gives to loving souls in whom he dwells? ... Certainly, no one can! Not even they who receive these communications. As a result these persons let something of their experience overflow in figures, comparisons and similitudes, and from the abundance of their spirit pour out secrets and mysteries rather than rational explanations. ... The saintly doctors [referring to scholastic theologians], no matter how much they have said or will say, can never furnish an exhaustive explanation of these figures and comparisons, since the abundant meanings of the Holy Spirit cannot be caught in words. Thus the explanation of these expressions usually contains less than what they embody in themselves.
>
> Since these stanzas [referring to the *Cántico*], then, were composed in a love flowing from abundant mystical understanding, I cannot explain them adequately, nor is it my intention to do so. I only wish

304

to shed some general light on them. ... I believe such an explanation
will be more suitable. It is better to explain the utterances of love in
their broadest sense so that each *one may derive profit from them
according to the mode and capacity of one's own spirit,* rather than
narrow them down to a meaning unadaptable to every palate. As a
result, though we give some explanation of these stanzas, there is *no
reason to be bound to this explanation.* For mystical wisdom, which
comes through love and is the subject of these stanzas, *need not be
understood distinctly in order to cause love* and affection in the soul,
for it is given according to the mode of faith through which we love
God *without understanding him.*[122]

In Juan's own approach to interpretation of the *Cántico* there is an
indication of a hermeneutical approach to the *Cántico.* If we consider the dialectic
of explanation and understanding in Ricoeur's theory of mimesis, Juan's own
commentary on the poem can be included as a particular reception and appropriation
of the poem. Juan's commentary is *an* interpretation but in itself does not constitute
the fullness of meaning contained in the *Cántico.* Juan himself suggests that
understanding the stanzas of his *Cántico* results only from the interaction of the
poem and reader, since each person "may derive profit from them according to the
mode and capacity of one's own spirit." Juan appeared to be sensitive to the
hermeneutical dialectic of interpretation when he suggests that his commentary on
the *Cántico* contains "less than what they [the stanzas of the *Cántico*] embody in

---

[122] Prologue *CB* 1,2 (emphasis mine) "No pienso yo ahora declarar toda la anchura y copia que
el espíritu fecundo del amor en ellas lleva; antes sería ignorancia pensar que los dichos de amor en
inteligencia mística, cuales son los de las presentes *Canciones* con alguna manera de palabras se
puedan bien explicar; ... Porque ¿quién podrá escribir lo que a las almas amorosas, donde él mora,
hace entender? ... Cierto, nadie lo puede; cierto, ni ellas mismas, por quien pasa, lo pueden. Porque
ésta es la causa por que con figuras, comparaciones, y semejanzas, antes rebosan algo de lo que
sienten y de la abundancia del espíritu vierten secretos y misterios, que con razones lo declaran. ... De
donde se sigue que los santos doctores, aunque mucho dicen y más digan, nunca pueden acabar de
declararlo por palabras, así como tampoco por palabras se pudo ello decir. Y así, lo que de ello se
declara, ordinariamente es lo menos que contiene en sí.
    Por haberse, pues, estas *Canciones* compuesto en amor de abundante inteligencia
mística, no se podrán declarar al justo, ni mi intento será tal, sino sólo dar alguna luz general. ... Y
esto tengo por mejor, porque los dichos de amor es mejor declararlos en su anchura, para que cada uno
de ellos se aproveche según su modo y caudal de espíritu, que abreviarlos a un sentido a que no se
acomode todo paladar. Y así, aunque en alguna manera se declaran, no hay para qué atarse a la
declaración; porque la sabiduría mística, la cual es por amor, de que las presentes *Canciones* tratan,
no ha menester distintamente entenderse para hacer efecto de amor y afición en el alma, porque es a
modo de la fe, en la cual amamos a Dios sin entenderle." Prologo *CB* 1,2

themselves." To use Ricoeur's term, there is a "surplus of meaning" in the *Cántico*
which is accounted for by his theory of mimesis and his reading/reception theory.
The *Cántico* only becomes meaning-*ful* when its meaning is appropriated in a human
life. In a particular way we saw that mood, as constructed through metaphorical
reference, brings the *Cántico* to bear on the life of the receiver of the poem.

Therefore, appropriation involves a reader who places himself or
herself within the world-of-the-*Cántico* and understands its mysteries in the context
of authentic human life, rather than "rational explanations," as Juan himself
appreciated. The reader who understands the *Cántico* will understand better his or
her place in-the-world before the mysteries of that world. The mimesis of the text
thus takes place in the context of a life. The story of the bride and bridegroom is
what the *Cántico* relates.

> Beyond this, the reader finds something non-sensical at the literal
> level that overturns the primacy of literal meaning even while it
> points to a second, metaphorical meaning that appears 'on' or
> 'through' the literal meaning. This new sense and referent is first
> understood apart from its appropriation by a reader. But when the
> reader actualizes the 'semantic virtualities' in the meaning by
> identifying with the signified mode of being so that the reader
> encounters a figure who represents 'I' as I ... [*could be*], then we
> reach the stage of appropriation. Where the reader can see himself
> reflected in the text so that he can say 'I understand my own
> authentic being through this text-world,' the text-world is
> appropriated.[123]

Authentic appropriation of the *Cántico* therefore culminates in self-
understanding but this is not knowledge that is objectifiable in a strictly scientific
way. This self-understanding exteriorizes itself in personal commitment to the
project of the text-world in conjunction with the present text-situation of our lives.
It is this fusion which gives rise to what I have already referred to as the world-of-
the-text. A new life-project, or at least a reoriented one, is embarked upon when
textual understanding in the form of the world-of-the-text occurs. Christian theology

---

[123] KLEMM, *The Hermeneutical Theory of Paul Ricoeur*, 148.

calls this dynamic conversion: the turning of the egocentric self towards another Centre, another way of being-in-the-world not dictated by the *cogito*. Conversion "dislocates our project of making a whole of our lives"[124] and makes possible a "life-lived for others."[125] A new way of being-in-the-world which questions the status quo ultimately surfaces with authentic understanding of a text. This new way of being-in-the-world is not conceptually described, nor "mapped" out by the text, but rather it is made available to the imagination in such a way that the ordinary way-of-being is disrupted to make way for a more authentic grounding in existence.[126]

The understanding of the text therefore *shows itself* in the life of the individual. Ricoeur refers to this dialectic as "testimony."[127] Through testimony the individual's life takes up the discourse of the text in exterior action which shows the individual's interior convictions. In religious discourse, testimony ultimately reveals the immanence of the transcendent Other. This revelation is bound to the divestment the individual makes with respect to his or her personal destiny in accordance with

---

[124] RICOEUR, "Biblical Hermeneutics," 125.

[125] RICOEUR, "Biblical Hermeneutics," 126.

[126] RICOEUR, "Biblical Hermeneutics," 125.

[127] According to Ricoeur the issue of testimony is both a philosophical issue as well as a religious one: "The term testimony should be applied to words, works, actions, and to lives which attest to an intention, an inspiration, an idea at the heart of experience and history which nonetheless transcend experience and history. The philosophical problem of testimony is the problem of the testimony of the absolute or, better, of absolute testimony of the absolute." Paul RICOEUR, "The Hermeneutics of Testimony," *Anglican Theological Review* 51, no. 4 (October 1979), 436; "The religious meaning of testimony arises ... [in] an absolutely new dimension that we are not able to deploy starting with the profane use of the word. But--and this counterpart is not less important ... the profane sense is not simply abolished but in a certain fashion conserved and even exalted." Ibid., 444. Ricoeur uses a text from Second Isaiah (43:8-13; 44:6-8) to explore this new dimension of testimony within the religious sphere. Four points are noted: 1. a "witness is not just anyone who comes forward and gives testimony, but the one who is sent in order to testify;" 2. the witness does not "testify about isolated and contingent fact but about the radical, global meaning of human experience;" 3. "the testimony is oriented toward proclamation, divulging, propagation" for all peoples; 4. "this profession implies a total engagement not only of words but of acts and, in the extreme, in the sacrifice of a life." Ibid., 445.

the generosity of a God who appears through contingency.[128]   "Testimony, each time singular, confers the sanction of reality on ideas, ideals, and modes of being."[129] Ultimately, in the extreme, testimony may involve the sacrifice of a life. It is this act which Ricoeur refers to as the absolute testimony of the Absolute.[130] This ultimate divestment disposes reflection to receive the meaning of events which would attest that the encounter with evil (the "unjustifiable") is overcome in the here and now.[131]

Ricoeur's theory of mimesis, therefore, accounts for the "materiality" as well as the "spiritualization" of the *Cántico*: through the use of "secular" and "profane" imagery, Juan conjures up a "spiritual" world, that is, a world which submerges the reader in the most authentic structures of human reality and turns the subject toward the *limits* of authentic forms of human life in the present.[132] Ultimately, Ricoeur paradoxically points out, the living of authentic human life may result in the loss, or radical transformation of one's life modelled on the testimony

---

[128] "It is by this 'divestment' that reflection is brought to the encounter with contingent signs that the absolute, in its generosity, allows to appear of itself." RICOEUR, "The Hermeneutics of Testimony," 436.

[129] RICOEUR, "The Hermeneutics of Testimony," 438. "What we can recognize in testimony--not in the sense of the story of a witness who tells what he has seen but of a work that attests--is that it is the expression of the freedom that we desire to be. I recognize as existing what is only an idea for me. What I recognize outside myself is, in its effectiveness, the movement of liberation that I posit only as an ideal." RICOEUR, "The Hermeneutics of Testimony," 460.

[130] RICOEUR, "The Hermeneutics of Testimony," 436.

[131] RICOEUR, "The Hermeneutics of Testimony," 437. This ultimate divestment "waits for words and especially actions which would be absolute actions in the sense that the root of the unjustifiable will be more manifestly and visibly uprooted." Ibid., 437.

[132] "The *eruption of the unheard of* in our discourse and *in* our experience constitutes precisely one dimension *of* our discourse and of our experience. To speak of a limit-experience is to speak of our experience. This expression in no way says that there is nothing in our common human experience and in our common language which corresponds to speech about the extreme. If this were not so, the claim of the Scriptures that Christian self-understanding in fact is the understanding of authentic human existence would fail entirely. It is precisely as extreme that religious language is appropriated. And it is this appropriateness of limit-expressions to limit-experiences which is signified by our affirmation that religious language, like all poetic language, in the strongest sense of the words, redescribes human experience." RICOEUR, "Biblical Hermeneutics," 127. A little further Ricoeur states: "The [ordinary] human condition as such includes experiences which baffle discourse and praxis." Ibid., 128.

of Jesus Christ.[133] "We also understand that testimony, at the human level, is dual: it is internal testimony, the seal of conviction, but it is also the testimony of works; that is, it is modeled on the passion of Christ, the testimony of suffering."[134]

The use of theological categories may aid the reader in his or her sensitivity to these realities surfaced by a text, but theological categories do not constitute the revelatory power of the texts. The revelatory power of the *Cántico*, within Ricoeur's theory of mimesis, lies within the power of the text to refigure a life by "indirectly informing" the subject of the limits of *reality itself*. We have already seen how this indirect informing takes place in the text through metaphorical discourse which redescribes reality in the mode of "as if." The specific redescription of reality in the mode of "as-if" by Juan's *Cántico* will be examined in the last section of Chapter Seven. Metaphorical discourse creates "models" of what the deepest structures of reality "are like" but does not disclose what they "are."

The inability to conceptually know the depths of the divine reality present within the world, yet the ability to live meaningfully within this not-knowing, has been referred to as the "apophatic way of knowing" or *theologia negativa* in the Christian tradition. Juan de la Cruz has been traditionally labelled as an "apophatic mystic." Although it has usually been his poem entitled *Noche oscura* which has given him this reputation, the *Cántico* can also be appreciated within the same apophatic tradition when it is approached from within the context of Ricoeur's theory of mimesis and his theory of reading/reception. Not-knowing in the mode of "as-if" opens up the space for divine self-manifestation, a mimesis of the divine in the world characterized by the dialectic of testimony. "For the apprehension of the divine, the divestment (dépouillement) essential for mystical experience and the link of the

---

[133] "The 'confessional' kernel of testimony is certainly the center around which the rest gravitates. The confession that Jesus is the Christ constitutes testimony par excellence. Here again the witness is sent, and his testimony does not belong to him." RICOEUR, "The Hermeneutics of Testimony," 447.

[134] RICOEUR, "The Hermeneutics of Testimony," 452.

divine to a historic manifestation are mutually complementary."[135]

The refigured subject, therefore, may not "know conceptually" but nonetheless finds himself or herself committed to the meaningful project founded by the text. Christian theology has described this phenomenon as "faith." For his part Ricoeur states that "faith never appears as an immediate experience, but always as mediated by a certain language which articulates it. ... I should link the concept of faith to that of *self-understanding* in the face of the text. Faith is the attitude of one who accepts being interpreted at the same time that he interprets the world of the text."[136] Faith is to be lived by being-in-the-world within the unknown horizons which the text opens up. Juan's *Cántico*, in this context, could therefore be described as "subversive." This is true since religious discourse involves the imaginative refiguration of discourse in all categories: speculative, practical, ethical, and political.[137] Refiguration of a life-world, at all levels, is what takes place in Ricoeur's theory of appropriation, or mimesis$_3$.

Based on the role Ricoeur assigns to metaphorical reference, genre and mood, I have suggested that an aesthetic reception of Juan's text might be the way of appropriating the *Cántico* which best suits its unique literary form. New and varied interpretations would become possible through setting the poem to music, exploiting its unique rythmic movements. Minimally, it needs to be recognized that

---

[135] Jean NABERT, *Le desir de Dieu*, (Paris: Aubier, 1966), 265, quoted in RICOEUR, "The Hermeneutics of Testimony," 457.

[136] RICOEUR, "Philosophy and Religious Language," 84. Ricoeur goes on to say: "In this sense, faith is the limit of all hermeneutics and the nonhermeneutical origin of all interpretation. The ceaseless movement of interpretation begins and ends in the risk of a response which is neither engendered nor exhausted by commentary. It is in taking account of this prelinguistic or hyperlinguistic characteristic that faith could be called 'ultimate concern,' which speaks of the laying hold of the necessary and unique thing from whose basis I orient myself in all my choices. It has also been called a 'feeling of absolute dependence' to underscore the fact that it responds to an initiative which always precedes me. Or it could be called 'unconditional trust' to say that it is inseparable from a movement of hope which makes its way in spite of the contradictions of experience and which turns reasons for despair into reasons for hope according to the paradoxical laws of a logic of superabundance. In all these traits the thematic of faith escapes from hermeneutics and testifies to the fact that the latter is neither the first nor the last word." Ibid., 84.

[137] RICOEUR, "Biblical Hermeneutics," 126.

it is the text itself which is to be given primacy for the interpretive project. The referential capacity of mood, as sketched by the text through reading, is only set-free through the text itself.

New existential possibilities are presented through the world-of-the-text as constructed through mood in the mode of "as-if." The question of the *Cántico*'s particular ontological significance will be examined in Chapter Seven. The question to be addressed there is : What is the significance of existence, seen as being understood as a dialogue between lovers? Through the mystery of human love, as lived and expressed through the interaction of the poem's two main characters, Juan's *Cántico* is revelatory of the Divine. This revelation is a unique mimesis of the *Cántico*, a return of the text to discourse, since the text has found its reconfiguration in a life.

CHAPTER SEVEN

MIMESIS₃ AND RECEPTION OF THE *CÁNTICO*

1. Introduction

In the conclusion of the last chapter I suggested that Juan conjures up a *religious* world by turning the reader toward what we might call the *limits* of the authentic structures of human life. Through metaphor and image we "think" beyond the conceptual limits of human existence. In poetic form the *Cántico* tells of two lovers and their search for each other, a search which models a way of being-in-the-world which is beyond human knowing.[1] The extra-linguistic "appearance" of human reality through the refiguration of the poem is effected by metaphorical reference.[2] Ultimately, however, reconfiguration of the ultimate reference of the

---

[1] Ricoeur, agreeing with Crossan, says that we are sensitized to the extra-linguistic, through metaphorical reference, because of the "normalcy" of the story. RICOEUR, "Biblical Hermeneutics," 98. But, "if this normalcy was not symbolic, ... the telling of the story would be pointless. As we assume that it is not pointless--perhaps because we listen to the warning: 'let those who have ears hear'!--we look for an interpretation which makes sense." Ibid., 98. Not yet satisfied Ricoeur asks again: "But, once more, how do we know that someone is speaking ironically if he gives us no further clues of his double-talking?" Ibid., 98. His hypothesis, complementing the previous one, is stated equally as simply with reference to the metaphoricity of parables (which is the context within which he is developing his discussion on metaphorical reference): "The trait which invites us to *transgress* the narrative structures is the same as that which *specifies* the parable as a 'religious' kind of 'poetic' discourse. This trait is, to my mind, the element of extravagance which makes the 'oddness' of the narrative, by mixing the 'extraordinary' with the 'ordinary.'" Ibid., 99. Ricoeur continues: "Could we not say that this dimension of extravagance delivers the *openness* of the metaphorical process from the *closure* of the narrative form?" Ibid., 99.

[2] For Ricoeur it is not so much the metaphorical or poetic function that constitutes *religious language* per se "but a certain intensification of the metaphorical function." RICOEUR, "Biblical Hermeneutics," 108. It is not my intention here to present in depth Ricoeur's criterion for what constitutes a "religious text." Such an analysis would remove us from the main purpose of this chapter, that is, to suggest the importance of the title of Juan's *Cántico* and to assess the role of the commentary in a hermeneutical reading of the same. That the *Cántico is* such a text is affirmed in the context of this dissertation by two main criteria: the intensity of the text or its "extravagence" to use Ricoeur's term, and its history of reception. An introduction to the criteria which Ricoeur outlines to identify specifically "religious texts" may be found in RICOEUR, "Philosophy and Religious

312

Cántico "shows" in the life of another human being, a dialectic which Ricoeur refers to as "testimony."

In this chapter I am interested in reflecting on three specific issues which involve, or are a result of, the reception and appropriation of the *Cántico*. These three issues orient the reader in the reception of the text and therefore affect the metaphorical reference of the text and the text's ontological import according to Ricoeur's reader-reception theory which I explored in the last chapter. The three issues to be investigated in this chapter are: 1. the hermeneutical role of the title of the *Cántico*; 2. the poetry-prose relationship and the role of the commentary in the reception of the *Cántico*; 3. the ontological import of the *Cántico*. The first is intra-textual, the second is inter-textual, while the third issue relates to the existential significance of Juan's poetic act.

As we already know, it is metaphorical reference in conjunction with the reading subject which constructs the world-of-the-text. The title of the *Cántico* is being investigated in this context since it has been virtually ignored by sanjuanist scholars as an integral component of the text which contributes toward the meaning of the *Cántico*, and, in Ricoeur's theory, the world-of-the-text. Therefore, I will suggest that the title of the *Cántico* needs to be appreciated for its role in the dialectic of sense and reference which constructs the world-of-the-text. The commentary needs to be contextualized within a hermeneutical approach to the *Cántico* since it may impede the hermeneutical interpretation if it is read as *the* paradigm for the *Cántico's* interpretation. Within a hermeneutical perspective, the commentary is described as a particular reception of the *Cántico*, but is not considered to be the only possible one. Examination of the ontological import of the *Cántico* will lead us to ask the question of the way of being-in-the-world which is modelled by Juan's *Cántico*.

Language," 71-85. Ibid., "Philosophical Hermeneutics and Biblical Hermeneutics," 89-101; Ibid., "Biblical Hermeneutics," especially "The Specificity of Religious Language," 107-145. David Klemm treats this question in KLEMM, *Hermeneutical Theory of Paul Ricoeur*, 109-139 as well as VAN DEN HENGEL, *Home of Meaning*, 220-246.

2. The Importance of the Title of the *Cántico*

Little attention has been paid to the role of the title in the interpretation of Juan's *Cántico*.[3] Aside from the historical notes referred to in Chapter Three which discuss the various titles given the *Cántico* in different editions of the work, the title of the *Cántico* has not been considered as a significant part of the text of the poem. Discussion concerning the title's contribution toward meaning is virtually absent from the literature. This point is of interest since the present title used for the poem, *Cántico espiritual*, is not the title which Juan gave it.

Juan de la Cruz gave his poem the title: *Canciones entre el alma y el esposo*.[4] Given the dialectic of "sense" and "reference" which is central in Ricoeur's interpretive theory, might not the title be seen as playing a significant role in the constitution of the "sense" of the *Cántico*? If this is true, then a reassessment of the use of the title Juan gave his work seems to be in order.

It is the title, from the beginning of reading, which orients the *muthos* toward something extraordinary within the confines of a love story which has been told countless times down through the ages. From the beginning, the title begins to form the mindset of the reader, orienting the reader toward the nature of the muthos. With Juan's title, "Songs Between the Soul and the Spouse," from the beginning, the reader is alerted to the two main protagonists in the story (the "soul" and the

---

[3] The importance of the title of a work is signalled by Werner Jeanrond. "We find in the headings and title of the text, indications or even precise explanations of the theme [of the text]." JEANROND, *Text*, 87. "The major function of a text can be announced through different strategies: --by the heading (title); --by the manner of presentation; --by being embedded in a larger context of action." Ibid., 98.

[4] Kieran Kavanaugh and Otilio Rodriguez translate this title as "Stanzas between the Soul and the Bridegroom," (Kav., 471.) However, the more literal translation by E. Allison Peers is preferable: "Songs Between The Soul and the Spouse." PEERS, *The Complete Works of Saint John of the Cross*, 2:25. The use of the word "songs" is closer to the Spanish meaning of "canciones," which, as I explained in Chapter Three is more in tune with two of the primary sources for the *Cántico*: the *Song of Songs* and popular folk songs of Juan's day (*cancioneros*). To use the word "bridegroom" already in the title is to interpret the text of the *Cántico* in a direction which may alter its metaphorical reference. "Esposo" means "husband" or "spouse" indicating that a union has *already taken place*! This is an interesting detail considering that the classical interpretation of the poem has the "spiritual marriage" only taking place toward the end of the poem.

"spouse") as well as the dynamic nature of their relationship: "song." The title also provides a clue for the reader to the genre of the *Cántico*. Again, the above title suggests that the *Cántico* is a canticle.

The use of the terms "songs," the "soul," and the "spouse" all construe metaphorical reference which orients the mindset of the reader toward the real meaning of the poem. The "soul" and the "spouse" are never named as persons, they could be anybody, and, as well, the two never "sing" to each other during the entire poem. The use of the predicates "songs," "soul," and "spouse," therefore, constitute metaphorical reference, not literal or ostensive reference. We have already seen how the "ruin" of primary literal reference is achieved by metaphor in order to construct a second-order reference, that of the world-of-the-text. The title *Canciones entre el alma y el esposo* begins to bring into focus this second-order reference, and therefore orients the entire discourse which is to follow.[5] It does this in a way which *Cántico espiritual* does not do.

In Chapter Three I mentioned that it was Jerónimo de San José (Ezquerra) who gave Juan's poem the title, *Cántico espiritual entre el alma y Cristo su Esposo*, in the first Spanish publication of Juan's complete works in 1630. Subsequent publications shortened this title to what we know it as today, simply, *Cántico espiritual*. This is the title most often used when the poem is published with or without the commentary. Given the importance that a hermeneutical interpretation places on the "sense" of the poem as it is constructed by the title of a work, it may be appropriate to consider the title as it appears in the critical edition of the Sanlúcar manuscript which is dated 1584 and personally signed by Juan de la Cruz, as *the* title of Juan's poem. The title *Canciones entre el alma y el esposo* is an essential part of the text since it plays an irreplacable role in constructing the poem's

---

[5] Critical editions of both Spanish and English publications of the *Cántico* usually precede the stanzas by Juan's own title, yet still refer to the poem as *Cántico espiritual* in any other context. Both critical editions which I have used throughout this dissertation, that of Kavanaugh and Rodriguez in English, as well as that of Rodriguez in Spanish, use Juan's own title for the poem itself within the context of the poem-commentary complex. The suggestion around use of the the title *Canciones entre el alma y el Esposo* is made especially with respect to the publication of the poem outside the context of the poem-commentary complex.

ultimate "reference" in orienting the reader toward *what the text is about*. The use of *Cántico espiritual* could be restricted to refer only to the poetry-commentary complex.

However, given the question of which title to use in the naming of Juan's poem, there is one commentator who would prefer not to allow the title of the *Cántico* to play *any* role in its interpretation. Let us briefly examine the comments Jorge Guillén makes on the titles of Juan de la Cruz's poetry. Guillén's perspective will be used to emphasize the importance of the title in the hermeneutical interpretation of Juan's poem.

Jorge Guillén's appreciation of the role which the title plays in the interpretation of the *Cántico* appears to be lacking. Guillén would like to read and interpret Juan's poetry from a "purely literary perspective," that is, without the bias of the commentaries or any other supplementary information such as the historical circumstances within which the poetry was written. Guillén goes as far as placing the title of the *Cántico* in the category of "supplementary information."[6] Cutting the text in this fashion is not appropriate within a hermeneutical setting, as we have seen, since we lose an important piece of the "sense" of the text. The *Cántico*, in its capacity as a canticle and as a *text*, creates meaning of a particular kind. The current meaning of the *Cántico* is linked to its history of reception, and, therefore, to read it without sensitivity to the work of the text throughout the ages is to remove the text from its productive capacity.

Again, I cite Jorge Guillén who opposes this position as he consistently follows the "profane" stance. Of Juan's *Cántico* he says:

> The symbolic import of these verses is clear. It is entirely within the order of the profane, for this poetry does not offer any other. The reader, alone with the poem, cannot pass beyond to the order of the

---

[6] Referring to Juan's three major poems Guillén says: "In order to feel and understand these texts purely as poems, we must approach them directly, not as if they were anonymous, but still disregarding for the moment the supplementary information available about them." GUILLÉN, *Language and Poetry*, 80. Concerning the titles which he would also like to insert into this category of "supplementary information" he says: "In our reading of the three poems, let us pay no attention as yet to the titles, which incline us toward the author's interpretation." Ibid., 81.

divine. It is not here, in such symbols as these, that the allegory is to be found which the author, and only the author, can indicate, for it exists only in his private mind, and not objectively in the text.[7]

We have already seen in Chapter Four that it is precisely in the inscription of discourse that meaning separates itself from the event of discourse to be objectively available in the text. This was Ricoeur's first moment of distanciation which I examined. The text of the *Cántico*, within Ricoeur's hermeneutical theory, is not a roadblock to understanding but, rather, it is an enhancement. Meaning, previously only existing in a virtual state, can be fixed through the semantic autonomy of the text, and can be recalled later. This shapes the stance we bring before Juan's *Cántico*. Guillén's stance before Juan's *Cántico* impoverishes the productive capacity.

Suggesting that the title of Juan's *Cántico* is a necessary and significant part of the text helps recover the reference of the text which is construed by the entire and complete text through metaphorical reference. As well, the text needs to be read within its history of reception. The *Cántico*'s history of reception is an integral part of the current meaning of the poem.

3. The Poetry-Prose Relationship of Juan's *Cántico*

Unlike the title of Juan's *Cántico*, the relationship between the poem and the commentary has been given considerable attention in the literature.[8] To a great degree the discussion has focused on the doctrinal meaning of the poem as it

---

[7] GUILLÉN, *Language and Poetry*, 108-109. On the following page, where Guillén further presents some of the symbols from the *Cántico* and the interpretation Juan gives them in his commentary, he says: "Only the author can present these elucidations. From the poetic phrasing it is impossible to infer the allegory, for it is not located within, like the marrow of its bones, but is mounted on air." Ibid., 110.

[8] See for example ICAZA, *The Stylistic Relationship in the Cántico*; PACHO, *Vértice*, 41-126; RUIZ SALVADOR, *Introducción a San Juan de la Cruz: El escritor, los escritos, el sistema*, 99-128; THOMPSON, "The Poem and the Commentaries," in *The Poet and the Mystic*, 118-145; Elizabeth WILHELMSEN, "Beauty and Truth, or the Poetry and the Prose," in *Cognition and Communication in John of the Cross*, European University Studies, series 23 Theology, vol. 246. (Europäische Hochschulschriften. Reihe xxiii. Theologie: Band 246), (Frankfurt a.M/New York P. Lang, 1985), 121-143.

has been clarified by Juan himself in the commentary. The commentary is seen as a transposition or a paraphrasing of the symbolic images found in the poem which makes the "message" of the poem more accessible to the reader. In order to suggest how this appreciation of the poetry-prose relationship is better understood by using a hermeneutical approach, I will examine the poetry-prose relationship of the *Cántico* in three steps.

First, I will present the findings of Eulogio Pacho, the leading sanjuanist scholar on the *Cántico*, who represents the most common perspectives concerning the poetry-prose relationship and who has given this topic the most attention.[9] Pacho characterizes the poem as Juan's artistic outburst in the form of symbols and images. These images and symbols are explained in the commentary and thus their noetic content becomes accessible to the reader through the commentary Juan himself wrote on the *Cántico*. Therefore, Pacho describes the commentary, in large part, as an *extension* or unpacking of the poem through its conceptualization of the symbols Juan uses in the poem. Pacho explores an analogical relationship between the poem and the commentary.

In a second step I will present Ricoeur's theory of the basic *discontinuity* of poetic discourse (the poem) and conceptual discourse (the commentary). Study Eight in *The Rule of Metaphor* constitutes Ricoeur's central study on this issue and therefore will be the principle source for what follows.[10]

In a third step I will bring the theory of Ricoeur into dialogue with the position of Eulogio Pacho as presented in the first step. Based on Ricoeur's theory, I will suggest: 1. that there is a radical discontinuity between Juan's poem and his

---

[9] Occasionally I will cite from other authors. These citations will lend support to my introductory remarks concerning the predominant approach to the poetry-prose relationship in the *Cántico* which is exemplified by Pacho.

[10] RICOEUR, *Rule of Metaphor*, 257-313. I have used the following references to help guide my reading of Study 8: CLARK, *Paul Ricoeur*, 137-151; Leonard LAWLOR, "Intersection: A Reading of Ricoeur's 'Eighth Study" in *The Rule of Metaphor*" in *Imagination and Chance: The Difference Between the Thought of Ricoeur and Derrida*, (New York: State University of New York Press, 1992), 29-50; Loretta DORNISCH, *Faith and Philosophy in the Writings of Paul Ricoeur*, Problems in Contemporary Philosophy 29 (Lewiston, New York: Edwin Mellen Press, 1990), 311-314.

318

own commentary on it; 2. that Juan be considered the "first reader" who appropriates his own poem; and 3. that the commentary continually sends us back to the poem to "think some more." These three findings suggest the possibility that the poem is open to new interpretations which do not take as their starting point the doctrinal agenda of the commentary which is often viewed as *the* interpretation of the *Cántico* of Juan de la Cruz.

3.1 The Poetry-Prose Relationship in the *Cántico*: Eulogio Pacho

3.1.1 Introduction

Eulogio Pacho attests that the *Cántico* is the most harmonious, representative, complete and attractive work of Juan de la Cruz.[11] Over the past forty years he has written extensively on the *Cántico* and today is considered one of the leading scholars in this area of sanjuanist research.[12] Pacho has published on various issues which impact the interpretation of the *Cántico*. As well, his textual and literary studies have contributed enormously toward current scholarly work on the *Cántico*. Many of Pacho's publications on the *Cántico* have already been cited throughout this dissertation.

However, at this time I will present a more systematic approach to his thinking on the interpretation of the *Cántico* using as the focal point the poetry-prose relationship. Pacho's appreciation of the poetry-prose relationship cannot be isolated from his overall interpretive approach to the *Cántico*. I will, therefore, explore a number of issues impacting the interpretation of the *Cántico* from Pacho's perspective. These, in turn, will help clarify the poetry-prose relationship as he sees

---

[11] "Parece ser que en esa obra se ve la propuesta más armónica, representativa, completa y atrayente del autor." PACHO, "Noemática e interpretación," 337. In a much earlier writing Pacho comments on the literary value of the *Cántico*: "En ninguna de sus obras aparece con tanto relieve el dominio del pensamiento sobre la forma expresiva como en el *Cántico espiritual*. Representa dentro de su aval literario el triunfo de la idea sobre la palabra, de la forma mental sobre la materia inerte del lenguaje." PACHO, "La Clave exegética del 'Cántico espiritual'," 308.

[12] Pacho wrote his doctoral dissertation on *Cántico A*: Eulogio PACHO, "*El primer Cántico espiritual" de san Juan de la Cruz: Introducción crítica y síntesis doctrinal*, Doctoral Dissertation, Rome: Facultad Teológica del Colegio Internacional, o.c.d., 1957-1958.

it. The following areas of Pacho's thought concerning the *Cántico* will thus be explored: 1. Pacho's *clave exegética*: the *doble visión* of Juan de la Cruz; 2. Corollary exegetical premises; 3. Conclusion: The poetry-prose relationship.

3.1.2 Pacho's *clave exegética*: The *doble visión* of Juan de la Cruz

Pacho's first publications on the exegesis of the *Cántico* appeared in 1958.[13] In one of the 1958 articles, entitled "La Clave exegetica del «Cántico espiritual»" Pacho presents a central exegetical principle which has since remained the foundation for all of his exegetical work on the *Cántico*: the *doble visión* (twofold vision) of Juan de la Cruz. Briefly stated, the *doble visión* of Juan de la Cruz refers to "Juan the poet" versus "Juan the theologian." The *doble visión* approach focuses on coming to a description of how the *Cántico* and its commentary (whether we are discussing *Cántico A* or *B*) describe the stages of the spiritual journey as it is reflected in the purgative, illuminative, and unitive ways. This exegetical key falls within the category of the ascetical-theological approach to interpreting Juan's writings.

Pacho terms his *clave exegetica* (exegetical key) the *doble visión del «ejercicio de amor»* (double vision of the excercise of love) of the *Cántico*.[14] This key, used to interpret the *Cántico*, is based on the following principle: there are two visions of the spiritual journey, the first vision (that of the poet) appears externally in the poem as well as in the commentary made directly from the poem; the second vision (that of the spiritual theologian) develops independently from the poem, but follows the basic content and ordering of the verses of the poem. The first conception is that which predominantly appears externally in *Cántico A*, the second dominates that of *Cántico B*.

What Pacho suggests, then, is that beneath the irregular and

---

[13] The two articles Eulogio Pacho published concerning exegesis of the *Cántico* in 1958 are: "El Prólogo y la hermenéutica del *Cántico espiritual*," and "La Clave exegética del 'Cántico espiritual'."

[14] PACHO, "La Clave exegetica del 'Cántico espiritual'," 309.

undulating course of *Cántico A*, lies another pathway which is more direct and decisive, but *oculto* (hidden). The first pathway, or *visión*, as Pacho refers to it, reflects the initial artistic creative moment of the poet; the second comes from the discerned reflexive process of the theologian in the commentary. It is this fusion of experience and theoretical science which defines the peculiar doctrinal structure of the *Cántico* for Pacho.[15] From time to time these two pathways cross or run parallel, but then separate once again. According to Pacho an understanding of this dynamic is foundational in order to interpret the *Cántico* of Juan de la Cruz.

At the core of this idea is the metamorphosis of the poem that took place in its transposition into commentary. The spiritual theologian, author of the commentary, penetrated the depths of the almost impalpable intuition of the poet, author of the poem.[16] I will now summarize the issues related to this *doble visión* which will, in turn, surface corollary exegetical principles which I will outline in the next section. Two citations, one from the 1958 publication "La Clave exegetica del 'Cántico espiritual'," and one from a more recent publication in 1983, *Vértice de la poesía y de la mística: El 'Cántico Espiritual' de San Juan de la Cruz*, summarize the main elements in this *doble visión* of Juan de la Cruz.[17]

From Pacho's 1958 publication "La Clave exegetica del 'Cántico

---

[15] "Fusión de la noticia experimental con la ciencia teorizante define la peculiar estructuración doctrinal del *Cántico*." PACHO, "La Clave exegetica del 'Cántico espiritual'," 317.

[16] Pacho describes this movement in a few words: "Se ha realizado una especie de metamorfosis en que la concepción del maestro de teologia espiritual se ha sobrepuesto a la casi impalpable intuición del poeta. ... lo consideramos de capital importancia para todo exégesis racional de obra. En realidad es la llave mágica para penetrar seguros en el santuario del *Cántico espiritual*." PACHO, "La Clave exegetica del 'Cántico espiritual'," 310-311.

[17] Two of Pacho's foundational articles on the interpretation of the *Cántico*, both of which were published in 1958 later surfaced (with minor revisions) in Pacho's 1983 publication *Vertice de la poesia y de la mistica: El 'Cántico Espiritual' de San Juan de la Cruz*. Pacho's, "El «prologo» y la hermeneutica del «cántico espiritual»" was divided into two sections to became Chapter I and Chapter II in *Vertice*: pages 1-33 became Chapter I "Proceso redaccional del 'Cántico'" in *Vertice*, while pages 33-108 became "El 'Prologo' y la hermeneutica del 'Cántico espiritual'," in *Vertice*. Chapter III in *Vertice* ("Claves interpretativas") is essentially a reprint of the other 1958 publication: PACHO, "La Clave exegetica del 'Cántico espiritual'."

espiritual'" the following points are summarized:[18]

 i. SPONTANEITY OF *CÁNTICO A* -- The doctrinal commentary of *Cántico A* closely follows the doctrinal order spontaneously established in the poem.

 ii. INCONGRUENCE OF EXPERIENCE AND THEORY -- This spontaneous order of *Cántico A* does not respond to the theoretical perspective established by scholastic theology as the normal and ordinary path to spiritual perfection.[19]

 iii. "CORRECTION" OF INITIAL IMPULSE -- Due to the incongruence of experience and theory, Juan develops a separate spiritual itinerary based on scholastic principles which Pacho says is

---

[18] "El *Cántico espiritual*, en cuanto comentario o glosa de las canciones, en su *primer redacción* sigue la ordenación doctrinal libremente establecida en la poesía; tal ordenación, aunque pautada por una genérica concepción del camino espiritual, no responde exactamente en sus detalles al trazado que San Juan de la Cruz establece, desde el punto de vista teórica, como normal y ordinario para las almas que caminan a la perfección bajo el signo del amor. De ello se da cuenta el mismo Santo, y por eso, sin destruir la senda vitalmente marcada por el ritmo poético, traza soterrañamente otra más recta y más conforme con la realidad, según sus conocimientos y su experiencia. Obligado a seguir el orden de los versos, no puede hacer patente este segundo trazado más que en contadas ocasiones, sirviéndose de digresiones o aclaraciones incidentales.

No se trata de dos caminos divergentes, sino de dos trazados diversos del mismo itinerario que corren paralelos, aunque en muchos lugares se separan para volver a encontrarse más tarde. Mientras el primero es tortuoso, zigzagueante; el segundo, aunque oculto, es directo y rectilíneo. El primero domina la estructura del *primer Cántico*, el segundo motiva y dirige la composición de su *nueva redacción*.

Sin este presupuesto juzgamos comprometida radicalmente cualquier interpretación doctrinal de la obra. No existe otra base segura para explicar satisfactoriamente las irregularidades que sorprendemos a cada paso en el *primer Cántico*: esas aparentes contradicciones que dificultan su comprensión global." PACHO, "La Clave exegetica del 'Cántico espiritual'," 311.

[19] Pacho views the itinerary of the poem as giving a panoramic view of the Christian journey to perfection, but it does not give the detail that the commentary gives. Lacking in the poem are allusions to specific stages of progression in the journey and temporal orientations. Pacho seems to be suggesting that the general trajectory described in the poem is other then that of "real" life. The poem "Describe la práctica del 'ejercicio de amor' en visión panorámica casi sin perspectivas temporales. No hay que buscar el orden progresivo en la graduatoria del amor estrofa por estrofa, verso por verso. Se da sólo entre varios grupos estróficos o entre zonas sobrepuestas que, delimitando momentos y situaciones clave, recortan la graduada ascensión espiritual escala arriba del amor.

Cuando leemos en la glosa que el camino trazado en el poema responde al que ordinariamente siguen las almas para llegar a la perfección del amor, comprendemos que san Juan de la Cruz no alude a esa vaga y genérica trayectoria espiritual, vista sin relieves definidos ni perfiles temporales por el poeta en el momento de alumbrar las canciones; se refiere al itinerario metódico que, basándose en las estrofas, ha establecido el comentarista." PACHO, *Vértice*, 132.

more in conformity with Juan's "reality" and "experience."[20]

iv. TWO SEPARATE TRAJECTORIES -- one indirect (but manifest), the other direct (but hidden). These two trajectories form but one spiritual itinerary.

v. TWO COMPOSING PRINCIPLES -- *Cántico A* is dominated by poetic spontaneity; *Cántico B* is ordered by the classical spiritual itinerary.

vi. NO OTHER EXEGETICAL PRINCIPLE -- only the above *doble visión* is adequate to explain the irregularities of *Cántico A*, as well as its relationship to *Cántico B*.

In 1983 Pacho slightly reworked the 1958 article and added several other points. In addition to points i. - vi. the following elements surface from the 1983 description of the *doble visión*:[21]

vii. THE IDEA IS SUPERIOR TO THE WORD -- Pacho celebrates the mind able to master the expression of concepts through the passive medium of language.

---

[20] Pacho suggests it would be irreverent to suggest Juan had to correct himself, even though the redactional problem is obvious: "¿Qué explicación dar a tamaña urdimbre redaccional? El problema es de grandes proporciones, porque los señalados son sólo algunos de los muchos casos que podríamos elencar. Todo la trama del *primer Cántico* está involucrada en este desconcertante procedimiento redaccional. ¿Se contradice, se corrige el Santo? Sólo pensar que la obra cumbre del Doctor Místico es un zurcido de mal avenidos pensamientos en continuada oposición, parece, mas que atrevido, irreverente." PACHO, "La Clave exegetica del 'Cántico espiritual'," 326.

[21] "En ninguna de sus obras aparece con tanto relieve el dominio del pensamiento sobre la forma expresiva como en el *Cántico espiritual*. Representa dentro de su aval literario el triunfo de la idea sobre la palabra, de la forma mental sobre la materia inerte del lenguaje.

Por este motivo es también la obra doctrinalmente más imprecisa, de contornos más difusos; la que menos se amolda a nuestros hábitos mentales de ordenación lógica, la más reacia a la síntesis. Nada de extraño que su interpretación doctrinal haya seguido con frecuencia derroteros extraviados. El hecho tiene su explicación. No se han sentado convenientemente las bases científicas de su exégesis. La clave interpretativa del *Cántico espiritual* se basa en este principio: en la composición de la obra hay dos visiones del camino espiritual: la que aparece externamente es la del poema y su comentario directo; la segunda es la del tratadista metódico que elabora su concepción independiente del poema, pero sujetándose voluntariamente en la disposición material al orden estrófico, hasta que decide redactar de nuevo el escrito ordenando de otra forma las estrofas. La primera concepción es la que aparece externamente en el *Cántico A*, la segunda la del *Cántico B*." PACHO, *Vértice*, 127-128. The ideas in this quotation, beginning with "Por este motivo ...." are also essentially repeated in a later (1989) publication PACHO, "Noematica e interpretación." 342.

viii. COMPLEXITY OF THE *CÁNTICO* -- doctrinally it is Juan's most imprecise due to the effort it took to conform the irregularities of the poem to the scholastic doctrinal system.

ix. NEED FOR JUAN TO INTERPRET -- the complexities of Juan's work necessitated explanation. To date no adequate scientific base has been developed to explain Juan's own method of interpretation in his passage from the poem to the commentary.[22]

x. REORDERING OF THE INITIAL POEM -- due to the inability of Juan to adequately conform *Cántico A* to the classical spiritual itineray, *Cántico B* is written as a reordering of *CA* plus one more stanza (st. 11) to bring it into conformity with the threefold itinerary of the *purgative, illuminitive* and *unitive* way to God.[23]

These ten elements are revelatory of other exegetical principles which Pacho sees as necessary to explain the incongruencies and irregularities of the *Cántico* as well as the poem-poetry relationship within the *doble visión* of Juan. The corollary exegetical principles are essentially principles of composition and of redaction, precepts which help explain the dynamics behind Juan's presentation of his own work.[24] I will now present these exegetical principles, four in total, one at a time.

---

[22] The work of this dissertation could be considered as a contribtion toward an "adequate scientific base" to explain Juan's own method of interpretation in his passage from the poem to the commentary.

[23] Despite the continual changes which Juan made to his work Pacho seems to suffer from the Romanticist's bias that Juan knew all along exactly what he was doing and where he was going with his literary creations: "Tenemos noticias seguras para comprobar que en la lenta elaboración no se da progreso más que en el género literario y en las formas redaccionales; el pensamiento no sufre alteración alguna; tan seguro y definitivo aparece desde un principio. De la *Subida* a la *Llama*, pasando por el *Cántico espiritual* en su doble redacción corre la misma concepción de la vida espiritual; subsiste idéntico sistema doctrinal. " PACHO, "La Clave exegetica del 'Cántico espiritual'," 308.

[24] Pacho develops his own list of corollary exegetical principles. These include: i. the relationship of mysticism to poetry; ii. the relationship of poetry to theology; iii. the incomprehensibility and ineffability of mystical experience; and iv. an indication of how the classical spiritual itinerary is linearly reflected in the *Cántico*. These are presented in, among others: PACHO, "Claves interpretativas" in *Vértice*, 127-191. See also: PACHO, "Noematica e interpretación" and PACHO, *Iniciación*, 24-33. My presentation here focuses on the principles behind his central *clave exegetica*, that is, Pacho's *doble visión*. My presentation is not an attempt to summarize all the *claves interpretativas* as Pacho has presented them in the above listed references.

324

3.1.3 Corollary Exegetical Premises

As can be deduced from Pacho's *clave exegetica*, the ten points stated above surface principally from the following relationships: (i) the connection *Cántico A* and *B* have with their respective commentaries, and (ii) the correlation which *Cántico A* and *B* have with each other. A third factor of utmost importance for Pacho in interpretation of the *Cántico* comes from the ineffability and non-communicability of mystical experience.[25] These three elements provide the organizing structure for the reflection which is developed below concerning corollary exegetical premises related to Pacho's *doble visión* of Juan de la Cruz.

3.1.3.1 Juan the Poet and Juan the Theologian

As can be seen from the presentation above, Pacho repeatedly casts two basic roles for Juan, Juan the poet and Juan the theologian. Awareness of the point at which Juan is operating in either mode Pacho sees as an important exegetical principle. The functions of the poet and the theologian are complementary but he suggests there exists an inherent tension which definitively separates the two. For example, in commenting on the apparent disruption in moving from stanzas *CA* 29 and *CA* 30 in the harmony of the spiritual marriage just spoken of in stanzas *CA* 27 and *CA* 28, Pacho suggests it is the poet who has introduced the incongruence and not the theologian.[26] Again, he sees this dynamic strongly expressed in the

---

[25] "Entre los puntos clave considerados como presupuestos necesarios de su exégesis, el de la inefabilidad es el que mayor desarrollo y amplitud adquiere en el prólogo." PACHO, *Vértice*, 68.

[26] Pacho is very explicit about this point: "Es la visión del poeta la que crea esa ambientación de temores y suspicacias, que, se doctrinalmente resulta inexacta, artísticamente considerada aporta sensaciones muy bellas." PACHO, *Vértice*, 169. "Es evidente que el poeta no se ha preocupado por el esquema que ahora le atribuye el comentarista. Ha visto el progreso «en el ejercicio de amor» sin precisa perspectiva cronológica, en mirada panorámica, en clara anamórfosis. Lo que canta en cada estrofa no puede adaptarse al punto clave de la ordenación teórica ni sujetarse a un esquema reiurosos del camino espiritual." Ibid., 138. See also PACHO, "La Clave exegetica del 'Cántico espiritual'," 318-319 for a discussion of this issue. Another example of this incongruence is noted in the interruption of the unified and quiet state of the soul previously described in *Cántico A* 18,5 and 19,4 by the anxiety of the soul expressed in *Cántico A* 31,1. In the previous stanzas the soul was already "«tan entera y unida» en Dios, que no hay obra ni actividad de las potencias que la llegue a turbar; ni siquiera tiene 'primeros movimientos' de la parte inferior contra la superior." PACHO, "La Clave exegetica del 'Cántico espiritual'," 319-320.

progression from *CA* 25 to *CA* 26. In the passage from *CA* 25 to *CA* 26 Pacho says that these stanzas describe diverse stages of the spiritual life without sensitivity to their real connection to linear time.[27] I have already referred to these poetic points of transition in Chapters Five and Six as "zones of indetermination" which the text works on the reader in the production of meaning. Pacho views them as points of tension, or impediments to an understanding of the poem, which Juan the theologian needs to reconcile in the commentary. We therefore see the opposition between the poet and the theologian which Pacho accentuates.

What then is to be interpreted from the poem? In the context of the above statement we once again see Pacho's focus on the doctrinal content of the poem as it is presented in the commentary. A correct reading of the *Cántico* would reveal doctrinally correct information. Inconsistencies with this pre-determined doctrinal system are dismissed as being artistic expressions of the poet and must be adjusted by the theologian who wrote the commentary.

This *doble visión* of poet versus theologian is fundamental in Pacho's interpretation of the *Cántico* and the relationship of the poem to the commentary. Pacho appears to present Juan's primary role as that of teacher, *maestro*, in opposition to a secondary role, that of *artista*.[28] Pacho goes as far as suggesting that Juan gave more value to the doctrine reflected in the commentary than he did to the

---

[27] "La progresión o, se se prefiere, la demarcación cronológica de la vida espiritual dentro de este ciclo poético es manifiesta. También es claro que no corre paralela a la secuencia estrófica. Se describen diversos estadios de la vida espiritual sin atender a su verdadero y real enlace temporal. Se interfieren de tal manera en la visión poética que, ni aun con la explicación del comentaristas, resulta fácil su identificación.

...

En la ordenación teorética de la obra se ha de distinguir con cuidado lo que pertenece a la visión poética, con sus requisitos artísticos, y lo que hace referencia a la sistematización doctrinal intentada en la glosa posterior." PACHO, *Vértice*, 168.

[28] "El comentario hecho para nosotros no lleva intención literaria sino doctrinal. La actitud del autor es la del maestro que enseña, no la del artista que crea, o, si se prefiere, al artista que crea sucede el maestro que adoctrina. ... El Cántico, obra sustancialmente didáctica, cae en los dominios del arte en cuanto realiza su fin pragmático en formas de exquisita belleza." PACHO, *Vértice*, 108.

artistic quality of the stanzas.[29] Juan the artist, in opposition to Juan the theologian, is given second place with respect to the reader's ability to appropriate the *Cántico*. The vision of the poet is beautiful, but lacks precision and is therefore inadequate.[30]

3.1.3.2 Similarity of Experience Necessary for Understanding

As already mentioned, Pacho recognizes that at one level the commentary is a regression of the *abundante inteligencia mística* sung in the poem, but at another level the commentary signifies an enrichment of the doctrinal content concentrated in the poem. Even though the poetry is more intense and "contains more," it is inaccessible to the non-mystic.[31] Pacho says the poem does not communicate as much to us as the commentary even though it contains more. It is a question of accessibility governed by two classes of readers, those who have had experiences similiar to Juan's and those who have not.[32] For those who have had

---

[29] "San Juan de la Cruz concede más valor a la doctrina de la paráfrasis que al mérito artistico de sus versos. Sacrifia voluntariamente su poesía en aras de un caritativo magisterio espiritual." PACHO, *Vértice*, 108.

[30] "Naturalmente, la magnífica visión anamórfica del poeta no encaja con precisión en la concepción del teólogo escondido tras el comentarista. ... Magnifica la visión del poeta, pero no satisface al meticuloso maestro de espiritualidad oculto bajo los repliegues y sinuosidades de la paráfrasis." PACHO, "La Clave exegetica del 'Cántico espiritual'," 323.

[31] "El lirismo cuanto más intenso, menos comunicativo." PACHO, *Vértice*, 124.

[32] "Se basa en la distinción de dos clases de receptores: quienes han tenido experiencias similares y quienes carecen de ellas. Para los primeros el comentario o explicación doctrinal es casi ocioso. Les basta ponerse en sintonía con el portador de la experiencia para captar la autenticidad y densidad de su mensaje. Para ellos es mucho más sugestivo y apropiado el lenguaje figurativo, la comunicación simbólica (supuesta la comprensión lingüística) que la terminologia doctrinal. Esta achica y reduce la realidad al marco angosto de lo denotativo. La expresión figurada la mantiene en la virtualidad y vitalidad de lo connotativo.

En contrapartida, para quienes carecen de experiencia mística, la riqueza opulenta de lo simbólico puede quedarse en «dislates»; no pasar de sugerencia y atisbo. Les dice mucho más la explicación razonada y la terminología «vulgar y usada», es decir, técnica y corriente." PACHO, "Noemática e interpretación," 353. Juan de la Cruz himself seems to hold this as being true. See Ibid., 353. This position is also held by Elizabeth Wilhelmsen: "Among the almost infinite possibilities [in response to Juan's writings], there is only one sharp dividing line to be recognized, and that is between non-mystic and mystic readers. Among the former, the understanding yielded by such readings always pertains to that we have called the noetic *via affirmationis*. The resulting cognition will always be in terms of creatures, and is applicable to God or the mystical communion with Him only by analogy.

similiar mystical experiences to Juan's, the commentary on the *Cántico* is pointless; it is sufficient to read the figurative and symbolic language of the poetry. Those who have not had a similiar kind of experience need the commentary to understand the poem.[33]

Pacho believes that to truly understand the poem, to have access to the "more," one would need to have an experience similiar to that of Juan. Access to the "abundant mystical understanding" is best obtained through rational analysis for non-mystics. This seems to be the case for the bulk of humanity.[34] The vast majority of humanity are outsiders that look in upon an experience of God (contained in the poem) which is not available to us, even through the artistic mediation of the poem. According to Pacho, the experience is most available to us through an analysis of the commentary.

I have already stated how Pacho gives priority to the commentary because of its doctrinal content. We once again see why this is so. Access to the doctrinal content leads to an understanding of the poem and is simultaneously the door of entry to the mystical journey as Juan lived it. The only other way to understand the poem is to have an experience similiar to Juan's. Pacho himself sees little, if anything, which can be understood from the poem directly unless one has had a mystical experience similiar to Juan's. In this latter case the poem simply stirs up what is already "known."

The non-mystic's potentiality for any higher mode of knowing has not yet been actualized. For the mystic, on the other hand, the reading or hearing of texts dealing with a preeminent communion with and experience of God can evoke and reactualize those very same experiences." WILHELMSEN, *Cognition and Communication*, 122-3.

[33] "Quien no haya «gustado el adobado vino de los viejos amadores», como el Santo, es inútil que intente vivir desde dentro la experiencia mística vertida en la poesía lírica del *Cántico*." PACHO, *Vértice*, 124.

[34] "Miramos, pues, la vital experiencia desde fuera, llegamos a ella por proceso estrictamente racional." PACHO, *Vértice*, 124.

3.1.3.3 Literary Genre of the Poem and Commentary

In Chapter Five I examined the literary genre of the *Cántico* in order to emphasize the significance that the form of the *Cántico* plays in the mediation of the meaning. At that time I briefly included Eulogio Pacho's findings on the question of the literary genre of the poem and its implications for mediation of meaning. How Pacho views literary genre is also significant for his understanding of the poetry-prose relationship. I will therefore quickly review his position here on literary genre including, this time, further details on his appreciation of the literary genre of the poem and the commentary.

Early in his discussion on the literary genre of the *Cántico*, Pacho states what it means to ultimately interpret the *Cántico* of Juan de la Cruz: "To interpret the *Cántico espiritual* means, in the end, to understand the «authentic declaration» [the commentary] done by the Saint for the use of souls."[35] Since interpretation of the *Cántico* is ultimately an understanding of the commentary, Pacho goes on to say that the determination of the literary genre of the *Cántico* refers principally to the commentary, or to the poem and the commentary when it is designated as a single work.[36] For Pacho, then, the commentary occupies centre-stage with respect to the question of the genre of the *Cántico* and is also given exegetical priority.

However, even given this focus on the commentary, Pacho treats separately the literary genre of the poem and the commentary. As I said previously in Chapter Five, Pacho seems to suggest that the literary genre is not an essential part of a study on the *Cántico* since genre research contributes little toward our doctrinal

---

[35] "Interpretar el *Cántico espiritual* significa, *en última instancia*, entender esa «declaración auténtica» hecha por el Santo para uso de las almas." PACHO, *Vértice*, 107. (emphasis and translation mine)

[36] PACHO, *Vértice*, 107.

understanding.[37] This appreciation of genre helps, once again, clarify Pacho's position concerning the poetry-prose relationship and the role of each in understanding the *Cántico* of Juan de la Cruz. I will now briefly examine the genre of the poem and the commentary, each in turn, from Pacho's perspective.

a) The literary genre of the poem.

As I specified in Chapter Five, Pacho describes the poem as an "égloga," a style of poem common in sixteenth-century Spain which contained some pastoral dialogue.[38] But Pacho seems to indicate later that this form is a mere covering for what is truly important, implying that the determination of the literary genre of the poem is not so essential. The message is not conveyed within the literary form itself, but only somehow incidentally mediated through it.[39]

Pacho thus seems to suggest that one form or another for the poem, one literary genre or another, would have made little difference with respect to the creative productivity taking place in Juan de la Cruz's poem. Pacho's focus is on noetic content, not the poetic content or the specific form of the *Cántico*. Of primary

---

[37] Pacho's apparent lack of concern with literary genre is not due to his lack of discussion of it in his work. Some of his publications deal specifically with the literary genre of Juan as we have already seen in Chapter Five. However, the point I made there is that one is left with the impression that Pacho believes that the literary genre does not contribute specifically towards the central purpose of Juan de la Cruz: his doctrinal program. An exception in this attitude of Pacho's may be found in the recent article "Lenguaje y Mensaje." However, the same overriding sentiment is still present as will be shown in the following discussion. For example Pacho suggests the literary genre was practically imposed, thus not giving it the value which a hermeneutical approach to literary genre would give: "Entre las abundantes posibilidades ofrecidas a fray Juan para comunicar su mensaje, la elección del género literario se ha visto prácticamente impuesta en las llamada obras mayores. Sólo en los escritos breves en prosa ha decidido con entera libertad o autonomia. ... Juan de la Cruz se ha puesto a escribir a ruegos de personas interesada en conocer lo que se encerraba en sus herméticas poesías." PACHO, "Lenguaje y mensaje," 73.

[38] "El *Cántico* es un requiebro amoroso, una versión a lo divino de los amoers pastoriles morosamente descritos en las mejores églogas o idilios de la edad dorada de nuestras letras." PACHO, *Vértice*, 90.

[39] "Quiere decir qua la forma literaria es solamente externa cobertura. Los profanos amores de la égloga y del idilio se tornan amores divinos." PACHO, *Vértice*, 91. "No debemos olvidar jamás que la unidad temática y la estructura literaria del poema están supeditadas a la situación o actitud creadora del poeta." Ibid., 92.

importance is the existence of the *Cántico*, whatever form it may have taken. Pacho does not seem to be genuinely concerned with the details of the literary genre of the poem even though he does consider this in his own work. Pacho's tendency is to see the form of art, literary art in this case, as not being essential in an interpretation of the *Cántico*. Pacho suggests that more than one interpreter has exaggerated the artistic form of the poem and, in so doing, has compromised its doctrinal value.[40] The poem is described as a "purely artistic creation" implying that it stands outside the real business of the *Cántico*, that is, the business of the doctrine which is contained in the commentary.[41]

b) The literary genre of the commentary.

Pacho's determination of the literary genre of the commentary seems to produce two different ways of describing it, depending on which criterion one uses to determine the literary genre. In terms of literary form Pacho describes the commentary in a general way as *religioso-místico*.[42] With respect to the purpose of the commentary, Pacho describes it as *sustancialmente didáctico*. These two ways of treating the literary genre of the commentary are dealt with together in his work.[43]

---

[40] "Más de un intérprete ha desorbitado su fisonomía artística —amén de comprometer su valoración doctrinal— por olviar sistemáticamente el incontaminado nacimiento del *Cántico* como pura reación artística." PACHO, *Vértice*, 129. In Ibid., 129 n. 2 Pacho cites some sanjuanist scholars who have exaggerated the artistic merit of the *Cántico*. For example he cites Dom Chevalier and Henri Sanson in this category.

[41] I suggest this is true even though Pacho himself says elsewhere: "El símbolo y la alegorización en la poesía sanjuanista no son invenciones retóricas o simples recursos artisticos; son medios comunicativos directos e inmediatos de la experiencia indecible, aunque escogidos de intento." PACHO, *Iniciación*, 25. The emphasis keeps coming back to the real importance of the doctrine contained in the commentary.

[42] PACHO, *Vértice*, 108.

[43] "San Juan de la Cruz reduce sus escritos a dos métodos de exposición o dos géneros literarios: *el tratado* y la declaración o *comentario*." PACHO, *Vértice*, 109. The *tratado* is a commentary "libre de las trabas impuestas por los versos," while the *comentario* serves to "dar alguna luz en general" to the stanzas of the poem. *CB* Prologo 2, (Rod., 572). The method of the *tratado* leaves Juan free to include comments on many themes not directly associated with the poem (such as those on prayer or spiritual direction), while the *commentario* keeps Juan closer to the presentation of the actual stanzas.

Pacho tells us that within the commentary we encounter *formas complejas o mixtas*.[44] These complex or mixed forms are the objective-descriptive form and the subjective-expository form.[45] However, within these two categories the determination of the literary genre of the commentary is described with primary reference to the first, that is, the *objectivo-descriptiva* elements of the spiritual life, and only secondarily with respect to the *subjectivo-expositiva* elements which are more autobiographical.[46]

Because the prose commentary presents the abstract analysis of the poem in combination with the personal experience of its author, Pacho suggests that the commentary does not respond to a single category of classification, but overall the genre of the commentary can be described as "didactic."[47]

In the final analysis, therefore, Pacho describes the literary genre of the *Cántico* as a *declaración* or *commentario* since the intention of the author is to teach about the spiritual life.[48] Pacho states that Juan's intention is to give useful

---

[44] PACHO, *Vértice*, 108. In describing Juan's work Pacho says: "Su talante y su talento logran adaptaciones singularísimas en búsqueda de formas expresivas eficaces. De ahí que los géneros sanjuanistas resulten extraños, excepcionales, híbridos y casi inclasificables." PACHO, "Lenguaje y mensaje," 55. Pacho's emphasis on the uniqueness of Juan's literary style seems a little exaggerated.

[45] "Se entrecruzan en él [the commentary], con alterno predominio, la forma objetiva y la subjetiva, o, si se prefiere la moderna terminología, la categoría estética objetivo-descriptiva y subjectivo-expositiva." PACHO, *Vértice*, 108.

[46] "Prevalece en general la forma expositiva, pero no en su pura dimensión objetiva, porque corren parejos el análisis abstracto del tema y la narración de la personal experiencia del autor. La exposición doctrinal se contrapuntea constantemente con la vida concreta del Santo, con su modo personal de ver y sentir la doctrina que está desentrañando." PACHO, *Vértice*, 108-109.

[47] "Se entrecruzan y combinan en él diversas formas literarias menores con mayor o menor predominio entre sí, pero siempre dentro del género didáctico." PACHO, *Vértice*, 107. "El intento del Santo es claro: dar una breve explicación en forma de comentario o declaración de las canciones anteriormente compuestas. Establece primero en el *Cántico* un módulo literario que mantiene luego en los escritos posteriores. ... Todo ellos los presenta al lector como paráfrasis, comentarios o declaraciones de sus versos, cuajados de doctrina espiritual." Ibid., 111.

[48] PACHO, *Vértice*, 109. Alejo Venegas describes what a "declaración" meant in the literary terms of sixteenth century Spain: "Declaración es una desenvoltura de la cosa encogida; quiero decir, que así como la cosa envuelta no se conoce hasta que se descoge, así el libro por claro que sea se dice que está encogido." quoted in Ibid., 125 n. 87.

information through the commentary for the spiritual development of the reader.[49] We thus conclude, according to Pacho, that the literary form of the commentary is *religiosa-místico* and *sustancialmente didáctico*.[50] When Pacho attributes to Juan the central role of *maestro* in the form of this *declaración* he says that the intention of Juan is clear, art and literary technique are subordinated to his didactic purposes.[51]

Pacho thus seems to infer that Juan does not teach through art: the role of poet needs to be replaced by that of theologian for didactic purposes. We once again see Pacho's focus on the extraction of the doctrinal principles which describe the spiritual journey in the commentary rather than the artistic content in the poem.

3.1.3.4 Priority Given to the Author's Intention

For Pacho the poetry-prose relationship, as signalled by Juan himself, is absolutely essential in any interpretation of the *Cántico*.[52] Central to all of Pacho's *claves interpretativas* is his understanding of Juan de la Cruz's intentionality: "The

[49] "No se trata de comentario literario, sino doctrinal-espiritual. Sería un contrasentido escribirlo sin la persuasión de que consigue comunicar realidades y conocimientos de utilidad para los demás." PACHO, "Noemática e interpretación," 354.

[50] "Estamos, pues, ante un género literario peculiar bien definido; género que se prolonga sin interrupción por toda la obra. Tiene sus afinidades con el de la *Noche* y la *Llama*, pero no puede confundirse con el de esos escritos. En la suma sanjuanista el *comentario* es propio y privativo del *Cántico espiritual*, o, usando su misma terminología, la 'declaración' escueta. Podemos considerarlo *comentario literal* en cuanto explica todos los versos del poema y se ciñe siempre a la interpretación directa de los vocablos, aun en los casos en que más se extiende en la justificación teológica. ... La aplicación doctrinal se basa casi siempre en la declaración semántica de las palabras empleadas en la poesía, cosa que no sucede en la misma medida ni en la *Noche* ni en la *Llama*." PACHO, *Vértice*, 114.

[51] "El commentario hecho para nosotros no lleva intención literaria sino doctrinal. La actitud del autor es la del maestro que enseña, no la del artista que crea, o, si se prefiere, al artista que crea sucede el maestro que adoctrina. ... El *Cántico*, obra sustancialmente didáctico, cae en los dominios del arte en cuanto realiza su fin pragmático en formas de exquisita belleza." PACHO, *Vértice*, 108. "La intención del autor es clara. No pretende admirar con creaciones artísticas, sino enseñar el camino del espíritu a las almas necesitades de luz y guía. Fin y elementos literarios están subordinados en el *Cántico* a la intención didáctica del maestro que suplanta al poeta." Ibid., 107.

[52] "Quiere decirse que la comprensión literaria y poética de los versos no puede prescindir absolutamente de la conexiones señalades por el autor entre poem y comentario." PACHO, "Noemática e interpretación," 338.

primary intention of brother Juan is to endeavor to teach the spiritual itinerary that culminates in union with the Divine. To this intention everything else is subordinated and ordered."[53]

A knowledge of this pedagogical intention of the author is essential to the interpretation of the *Cántico*, according to Pacho. The pedagogical intention of Juan determines how the poetry-prose relationship can be described. However, I have already examined in Chapter Six Juan's approach to his own commentary.[54]

Several elements are worth noting again in Juan's description of the commentary:

i. Juan himself admits he cannot explain the verses of the poem adequately in the commentary.

ii. Juan indicates that he will "shed some general light on them," which seems to be a better approach.

iii. This approach is seen as better, since, each person may benefit from them according to the mode and capacity of one's own spirit.

iv. Not to follow this general approach, Juan says, would narrow the stanzas down to a meaning unadaptable to the variety of persons that would read them.

v. Therefore, Juan does not bind us to the "explanation" he gives. Mystical wisdom, he says, need not be understood distinctly and clearly.

vi. Mystical wisdom is a way of loving God without necessarily understanding God.

Within Juan's description of his own commentary, Pacho has tended

---

[53] "La intención primordial de fray Juan persigue la enseñanza del itinerario espiritual que culmina en la union divina. A ese «intento» subordina y ordena todo lo demás." PACHO, "Lenguaje y mensaje," 62. (translation mine) Pacho writes a little later that it is "fáciles de espigar, se deduce que fray Juan no persigue en su prosa el arte por el arte. Su finalidad no es estilística ni literaria, sino espiritual. ... Busca la elegancia y la pulcritud sin sacrificar por ello la eficacia pedagógica, que es norte y guia supremo de sa pluma." Ibid., 64. See also Ibid., 55, 58, 59, 61, and 63 where this same basic idea is underlined.

[54] See the Conclusion of Chapter Six.

334

to focus on the pedagogical interest of Juan. Pacho's focus is on the message Juan intended to bring to the reader, that is, the "explanation" of the stanzas.[55] In second place is the linguistic and artistic accomplishment of Juan. In no place does Pacho mention the ontological import of the poem. Pacho thus separates the "message" (in the commentary) from the linguistic and artistic "doings" (of the poem).[56]

The commentary is intended to bring a message, to transmit and communicate, to educate.[57] The poem is seen to operate on the creative plane, where no pedagogical dynamic takes place, that is, there is no "message" to be interpreted at this level. Pacho describes the poem as *el signo artístico*, and *not* as a *medio o instrumento pedagógico*. For Pacho this distinction of the status of the poem in relationship to the commentary is foundational for his exegesis.[58]

What is interesting to recall, however, is that the sequence of the stanzas of both *CA* and *CB* presented difficulties to Juan when he went to outline the

---

[55] Pacho does relativize this focus on the pedagogical intentionality of Juan: "Situar adecuadamente propósitos y actitudes obliga a reconocer la primacía de lo magisterial o pedagógico; pero sólo la primacía, no la exclusividad." PACHO, "Lenguaje y mensaje," 62.

[56] "La finalidad-motivación pedagógica de la prosa (incluidos los escritos breves) es manifiesta. No serían necesarias las declaraciones prologales para descubrirlo. Si acaso, para identificar el ámbito y el campo de actuación.

Esto quiere decir que, en los escritos en prosa, los signos expresivos son ante todo medios e instrumentos del mensaje. Sólo en segundo plano tienen función de signos lingüísticos y artísticos. Se han seleccionada en virtud de su eficacia comunicativa y educativa. En esos escritos el esfuerzo es más de transmisión y comunicación que de creatividad.

Muy diferente es el caso de las poesías. En ellas lo prioritario es la creación. Lo fundamental y esencial es el signo artístico, no el medio o instrumento pedagógico. ... El mensaje es casi elusivo, no lleva referencias extrañas del autor, por lo menos en la mayoría de la poesías. A diferencia de la prosa, no reclama destinatarios concretos. En este sentido, la poesía es virgen, libre y exenta, según suele decirse para excluir la ausencia de intencionalidad pedagógica." PACHO, "Lenguaje y mensaje," 58-59.

[57] Pacho does recognize the breadth and possibility with which Juan indicates his poems may be interpreted, that is "según su modo y caudal de espíritu." This is indicated in his discussion on this question in PACHO, "Noemática e interpretación," 344. However, even given this evidence Pacho's major focus is still on Juan's "explanation" as being *the* explanation for the poem.

[58] "La historia nos documenta con plena garantia que la última razón de la obra es la de instruir espiritualmente a las almas confiadas a la dirección de fray Juan de la Cruz." PACHO, *Vértice,* 107.

classical spiritual itinerary.[59] Thus, even given Juan's own intentionality, the question whether he in fact did what he intended to do is open for assessment. Pacho himself tells us of Juan's struggle in intending to do what he had originally wanted.[60] In Chapter Four I examined the freedom of a text from the intentionality of the author. Pacho's priority of intentionality with respect to the interpretation of Juan de la Cruz can be called into question in this context. Ironically, Pacho centres his exegetical principles on Juan's intentionality and simultaneously on the failure of that intentionality. This issue is particularly significant for the commentary on *Cántico A*.

Cántico B came into being because of the struggle ("failure") Juan faced in making a commentary on *Cántico A*. *Cántico A* would not fit into the classical spiritual itinerary. The fact that Juan de la Cruz did redact *Cántico A* into *Cántico B*, gives some strength to the pedagogical priority of *Cántico B*. The structure of *Cántico B* accommodated the transitions associated with the traditional classical itinerary which are reflected by Juan in his commentary. However, at the same time, the need to redact *Cántico A* to fit that itinerary suggests something else was going on in *Cántico A*. What is this "something?" The findings of Chapter Five

---

[59] "En la zona más profunda de su espíritu se enciende la lucha entre la expresión despersonalizada del tratado sistemático y la elevación de la propia experiencia a categoría de doctrina, universalmente valedera, mediante el comentario verso a verso de las principales poesías. En la solución concreta influyen tan poderosamente las preferencias del Santo como las imposiciones externas del ambiente." PACHO, *Vértice*, 112. Elsewhere Pacho says: "Cuando avanzan en la declaración y se da cuenta de que a pesar del relativo orden cronológico-doctrinal que llevan los versos no concuerdan plenamente con el plan teórico que él tiene concebido de la vida espiritual trata de armonizar ambos esquemas, pero sin subyugar el primero al segundo, de forma que altere el ordenamiento del poema y la fisonomía del comentario." Ibid., 114.

[60] "Sirviéndose de sus conocimientos adquiridos, como de espejo retrovisor, el Santo Doctor comprueba las desviaciones, las vueltas y revueltas del trazado poético y se pone a la brega de corregirlo sin cambiar el orden estrófico, sin deformarlo materialmente. Al término de la jornada *se da cuenta de que su intento ha resultado en part fallido*. Se decide entonces por el único procedimiento válido a su propósito: cambiar la disposición de la estrofas dándolas otra ordenación y disponiéndolas según el esquema parte fraguado mentalmente por el teólogo. Entonces sí que se puede decir que el poema describe con fidelidad la senda de la perfección siguiendo las etapas establecidas por los maestros de teología espiritual; pero cuando se adopta esta solución nace el *Cántico B*, es decir, la segunda redacción de la obra." PACHO, "La Clave exegética del 'Cántico espiritual'," 326. (emphasis mine)

point to a different world-of-the-text in both *CA* and *CB*. Juan's own struggle in writing a commentary, especially on *CA*, may also point to the difference in the metaphorical reference which these two *Cánticos* construct. Again, a structural analysis, yet to be done, would help clarify these questions. That could be the work of another study on Juan's *Cántico*. For now, let us summarize the relationship of the poem and the commentary as envisioned by Eulogio Pacho and outlined in the above discussions.

3.1.4 Conclusion: The Poetry-Prose Relationship

3.1.4.1 Essential *Unity* of the Poem and the Commentary

Pacho's exegetical approach to any study of the *Cántico* lies in an appreciation of the integral relationship between the poem and the commentary on the poem. Commenting on the different exegetical approaches to the *Cántico*, he says that the point of convergence of all of them is the radical connection between the poem and the commentary.[61]

Essentially, Pacho views the poem and the commentary as an inseparable unit. He does admit, however, that the possibility exists of studying the poem and its commentary independently when one is examining *Cántico A*. From an artistic and literal perspective the relative autonomy of *Cántico A* with respect to its commentary is acknowledged, because of the problems Juan experienced in fitting *Cántico A* into the threefold spiritual way.[62] The interpretive unity of *Cántico B* with its commentary is safeguarded.[63] In both cases Pacho suggests that the commentaries

---

[61] "Punto de convergencia desde los diferentes enfoques es el de la conexión radical entre poema y comentario en prosa." PACHO, "Noemática y interpretación," 337.

[62] In a later work Pacho appears to nuance this stance. In discussing the intentionality of the author he says: "Los poemas son perfectamente autónomos, con o sin comentarios explicativos." PACHO, "Lenguaje y mensaje," 59. In this context he does not differentiate between the poem of *Cántico A* or *B*. However, given his doctrinal interest in the reordering of *Cántico A* into *Cántico B*, Pacho's emphasis on the artistic autonomy of *Cántico A* just does not seem to hold for *Cántico B*.

[63] "La relativa autonomía del poema ha de referirse en exclusiva a su primera redacción, a la composición genuina o auténtica (la de 39 estrofas), no a la segunda (la de 40 estrofas)." PACHO, "Lenguaje y mensaje," 59.

do not stand in any way on their own. Since they both originate from their poems, their absolute dependence on their respective poems is clearly indicated.[64]

The reason for the different relationship between *Cántico A* and its commentary and *Cántico B* and its commentary comes from Pacho's appreciation of the relative doctrinal value of each of the two poems. *Cántico A* is a result of the original poetic outburst of Juan, according to Pacho. It reflects spontaneously his lived experience as expressed through art. *Cántico B*, born from the restructuration of *Cántico A* as well as the addition of stanza 11, became a poem designed to reflect the doctrinal progression of the spiritual journey based on the threefold classical division of the purgative, illuminative and unitive ways to God.[65]

Despite this redaction, as has already been stated in Pacho's *clave exegetica*, Pacho affirms that the two works do not deal with two divergent journeys but rather speak of two parallel itineraries which eventually arrive at the same spot.[66] However, the journey to "the spot" differs in each case. The medieval spiritual progression of the purgative, illuminative, and unitive ways (*Cántico B*) Pacho describes as *direct* and *in a straight line*, while the trajectory of the poem of *Cántico*

---

[64] "Los escritos en prosa (fuera de los breves) carecen de personalidad al margen de la poesía. Subsisten gracias a ella. ... La vinculación de la prosa a la poesía atañe por igual al lenguaje y al mensaje." PACHO, "Lenguaje y mensaje, 59. And elsewhere Pacho says: "Es legítimo, sin duda, el estudio analítico de cada una de las partes y de cada uno de los elementos. La síntesis comprensiva no puede prescindir de ninguno de ellos." PACHO, "Noemática y interpretación," 337.

[65] "Como es sabido, la tradición espiritual, fundada en textos patrísticos, particularmente en el Pseudo-Dionisio Areopagita, distingue tres estadios en la vía espiritual: principiantes, proficientes o aprovechados y perfectos. A partir de la Edad Media prevalece la terminología correlativa de las llamadas vía purgativa, iluminativa y unitiva, aclimatadas y divulgadas por la famosa *Theologia mystica* (hacia el año 1250), atribuida modernamente a Hugo de Balma." PACHO, *Vértice*, 147 n. 7. Pacho says Juan fits his writings into this classical spiritual itinerary. Ibid., 176. Pacho shows how we would have to reorder the stanzas of *Cántico A* in order to give a true doctrinal schema which reflects the classical threefold way. Ibid., 183.

[66] PACHO, *Vértice*, 129. As previously mentioned (refer to page 321) this idea is also expressed word for word in his 1958 article: PACHO, "La Clave Exegetica del 'Cántico espiritual'," 311. Pacho continues saying that this understanding of the *Cántico* is the only sure base to explain the irregularities which surface in the first *Cántico*. "Sin este presupuesto juzgamos comprometida radicalmente cualquier interpretación doctrinal de la obra. No existe otra base segura para explicar satisfactoriamente las irregularidades que sorprendemos a cada paso en el *primer Cántico*: esas aparentes contradicciones que dificultan su comprensión global." Ibid., 311.

338

A is *tortuous* and *zigzags*.

The relationship of *Cántico A* and its commentary could thus be described as "poetic-doctrinal," while *Cántico B* and its commentary would reflect a "doctrinal-doctrinal" relationship. Pacho describes the shift from a predominantly artistic arrangement of *Cántico A*, to a more doctrinal one in *Cántico B*, as a legitimate sacrifice of art for science, and criticizes those authors who would diminish the overall value of *Cántico B* due to its restructuration based on the doctrinal itinerary.[67]

Pacho supports his negative criticism of those scholars who would give priority to *Cántico A*, since *Cántico B* is the fullest expression of where things were moving in *Cántico A*, that is, an accurate description of the itinerary of the spiritual life. Therefore *Cántico B* brings Juan's overall project to its ultimate completion. He thus infers that the real agenda all along was a doctrinal description of progression in the spiritual life, and this is more easily outlined from the commentary based on *Cántico B*.

Pacho thus establishes the doctrinal content, or as he refers to it, the "scientific" explanation of the *Cántico*, as occupying exegetical priority, and in so doing establishes the preeminence of *Cántico B* for the study of the *Cántico* of Juan de la Cruz. Criteria for understanding the *Cántico* are thus focused on criteria which establish clarity for the possibility of objective discourse concerning the doctrinal elements of the *Cántico*. The essential link of the poem to its commentary, whether it be *CA* or *CB*, is thus the mutual reflection of their doctrinal content. *Cántico A* is given poetic primacy, while *Cántico B* is given preeminence in the doctrinal sphere.

---

[67] "Es incomprensible esa mania de eminentes críticos que siguen contra la segunda redacción del *Cántico* por su inferioridad literaria. La postura del Santo al redactor por segunda vez la obra, es la misma que sorprendemos al extender el primer comentario; es la actitud del que sacrifica el arte por la ciencia, solo que en el segundo *Cántico* lleva los cosas hasta sus ultimas consecuencias." PACHO, *Vértice*, 108.

3.1.4.2 Essential *Disunity* of the Poem and the Commentary

In Pacho's thought the various oral and literary forms which Juan used to write about his experience of being-in-the-world are seen as increasingly distancing the reader from Juan's mystical experience. Pacho seems to posit an experience that is "pure," i.e., with no admixture of language. The language then, is a lessening, a loss of the original "pure" experience. However, in Ricoeur's theory of mimesis, as we have examined in Chapter Two, it is language that *gives* the experience. Poetic discourse, in the sense of *poiēsis*, both discovers and creates new experiences, experiences of "new things."

Pacho suggests the opposite. He indicates that the poetry in itself is a degradation of Juan's mystical experience.[68] The commentary is seen as a further step away from the primordial mystical moment.[69] The progression of events which lead to the poem and the commentary could therefore be described as follows: Juan is first living a sustained and intense relationship with God;[70] then comes an expression of this enduring experience through the poem (art); this is followed by the commentary on the poem (essentially doctrine). Pacho sees each subsequent expression of Juan's mystical experience as less than the previous expression.

---

[68] "La poesía es en sí misma una degradación respecto al fenómeno místico; el comentario implica a su vez otra degradación de lo poético, resultando así el postrer grado de regresión o separación del «amoroso lance»." PACHO, *Vértice*, 123. This comment seems to be in tension with what he says elsewhere: "Cuando se decide a explicar su experiencia inicial y poetizada pone a servicio de la comunicación--por tanto, del comentario--la riqueza acumulada posteriormente por vía de mística y de ciencia. El resultado final acumula, por convergencia, ciencia y experiencia. Ofrece una condensación, sin duda, superior a la referencia inicial del poema." PACHO, "Noemática e interpretación," 361.

[69] "Intenta en ellos [the commentaries] una síntesis lógica, conforme a la concepción teórica que tiene mentalmente estructurada, y que es, en parte, independiente de la experiencia mística cantada en los poemas." PACHO, *Vértice*, 111.

[70] Pacho describes the unfolding of Juan's experience in these terms: "La manifestación, siempre precaria y limitada, tiende a realizarse de manera impulsiva y en forma reflexiva. La primera adopta de inmediata el ropaje simbólico o figuratico: la segunda, el descriptivo o explicativo. La primera es, ante todo, comunicación en clave vital; la segunda, comunicación en clave conceptual o doctrinal. La primera se vuelve poesía; la segunda, teología. En el caso del *Cántico*, la primera se corresponde con el poema; la segunda, con el comentario en prosa." PACHO, "Noemática e interpretación," 342. Pacho says the above are unequivocal affirmations drawn from the *Prologo* 1-3 of the *Cántico*.

However, as we arrive at the commentary our access to Juan's experience is greater due to the increased conceptualization of that experience.[71] There is an increase in understanding with the commentary, since, as Pacho says, the figurative and symbolic world of Juan is nearly impossible to penetrate.[72]

Ironically, with respect to the mystical experience, even though this literary movement betrays a *degradación*, Pacho suggests that we, as readers, have greater access to an understanding of the mystical experience through the actual *regressión* of the various interpretive and literary moments. The possibility of understanding the *Cántico* increases from the reader's perspective due to the increased conceptualization of the experience which comes with the commentary.[73]

[71] This may be true with the possibility of conceptualizing and objectifying the experience, but is it true with respect to "understanding" (in Ricoeur's sense) one's own initial mystical or religious experience? Perhaps further expressions of experience, even though poorer conceptually, may bring a fuller "understanding" of the experience, that is, move the individual closer to "self-understanding."

[72] "Pese a la inmediatez, frescura y plasticidad de la manifestación figurativo-simbólica, su mensaje resulta o puede resultar difuso, impreciso y hasta incomprensible. Corre el peligro de quedarse en pura exteriorización sin recepción ni percepción alguna. La enorme virtualidad de su capacidad de connotación puede inducir, en sentido contrario, a diluir y difuminar tanto su contenido que acoga hasta sentidos contradictorios." PACHO, "Noemática e interpretación," 343. "La verificación natural de que sólo a través de conceptos precisos y concretos es posible la comprensión y la enunciadión de la realidad explíca que el místico sienta también impulso a manifestar su experiencia a través de categorías mentales y enunciados conceptuales. Es el paso de la connotación figurada a la expresión denotativa. Tiene conciencia de un achicamiento de su experiencia, pero a la vez persuasión de una clarificación de cara a los demás. Pasa de poesía a la teología, de la mística poetizada a la mística teologizada." Ibid., 344.

[73] "Si para el propio autor la poesía supera con creces al comentario, para nosotros el poema, sin la declaración, apenas significa nada desde el punto de vista doctrinal." PACHO, *Vértice*, 120. A similar position is expressed by Elizabeth Wilhelmsen: "The deepest limitation of the poetry is that it is such a remote and improper incarnation of the reality represented. It could not be otherwise, given that it depends upon imagery and the material phantasms, whereas the reality symbolized is wholly spiritual. If the function of the poetry is to reproduce the experience in the reader, which it can only do in a distant and remote way, that of the prose is to disclose some of the intelligibility of said mystical encounter. The prose sacrifices the positive qualities of the poetry for the sake of yielding an intellectual grasp of the symbolized reality: of what it is and how it can be; of how it is to be sought; of how it is rational and in harmony with reality as we know it. The prose allows us to understand the mystical act itself, although in an abstract, partial and limited manner, whereas the far more concrete experience which the poetry engenders is only a remote echo of that mystical act. At the necessary price of losing the sense of concretion, proximity and sensible beauty, the prose gains in that other beauty which is the splendor and radiance of truth." WILHELMSEN, *Cognition and Communication*, 142. For Wilhelmsen Juan's poetry appears to have been relegated to the *mere* expression of "beauty," while the prose commentary contains "truth."

What becomes increasingly available to the reader through the *degradaciónes*, therefore, is the doctrinal content of the mystical experience.[74] The above statement again emphasizes Pacho's focus on the doctrinal content of the *Cántico* as the main focus of "understanding" the *Cántico*. This is true whether we are discussing *Cántico A* or *Cántico B* and their respective commentaries.

The meaning of the *Cántico* is available through understanding its doctrinal content as reflected in the commentary. Since, for Pacho, we have no doctrinal understanding of the poem without the commentary, we have no point of access to understand the poem more immediately. In other words, if the reader has no point of access to the doctrinal content, Pacho seems to be suggesting that there is no understanding of the poem that takes place. Pacho gives primacy to the originial experience, but this experience is best understood in the doctrine. For him the doctrine is the best articulation of the experience.

Pacho is therefore suggesting that there is a basic disunity that exists between the poem and its commentary. This disunity focuses on the task of locating what is to be understood. For Pacho, what is to be understood is the doctrine. The commentary thus provides the reader with all that can be understood in the *Cántico*. Our inability to understand the poem is rectified only through the doctrinal commentary.[75] The disunity of the poem and the commentary is also suggested by the way Pacho perceives the concept of understanding.

The commentary, he says, presents the individual with a more

---

[74] But the questions then surface: Is this *all* that is to be understood from the *Cántico*? Or is it even the central "message" of the *Cántico*?

[75] "La doctrina del *Cántico* no es otra que la resellada en los versos, perio tal como la desentraña la paráfrasis en prosa." PACHO, *Vértice*, 132. Note that Pacho does suggest that the doctrine is somehow present in the poem although he also curiously says that *Cántico A* was *not* composed with the doctrinal commentary in mind. See PACHO, "La Clave exegetica del `Cántico espiritual`," 327; Ibid., "Lenguaje y mensaje," 69 n. 23; and Ibid., *Vértice*, 97-107; 128-132. Despite this affirmation Pacho indicates the radical and primary access to the meaning of the *Cántico* is through its commentary.

342

"natural" way of understanding.[76] To "know" what the *Cántico* means is to be able to rationally objectify the doctrinal content of the poem as it is expressed through the commentary on it.[77] Again this is true whether we are talking about *Cántico A* or *Cántico B*. Pacho suggests that from this side of human experience we penetrate rational discourse better than we penetrate poetic discourse.[78]

Poetic understanding is given second place to the ability to objectify and make explicit in conceptual language the content of the *Cántico*.[79] Explication of concepts provides us with the meaning of the *Cántico*. The real treasure is the

[76] "Aparte los mil pormenores carentes de consistencia mental en el momento de la creación poética, y que luego se van acumulando a lo largo del comentario, son estas disquisiciones doctrinales las que alargan el contenido doctrinal de la paráfrasis respecto al poema y *le hacen mas asequible a nuestro modo natural de comprender.*" PACHO, *Vértice*, 120. (emphasis mine) This is true for Pacho at the level of "understanding." However, Pacho does affirm that at the level of expression poetic-symbolic language is the *most connatural* way for the human person to bring experience to **expression**. "Si se tiene en cuenta la condición inefable de lo místico no resulta extraño que un artista como Juan de la Cruz se refugie en la poesía al momento de traducir su emoción y su sentimiento; lo que él llama 'noticia amorosa'. Lo figurativo y simbólico es lo más connatural a la experiencia profunda, lo mismo que para la capacidad creadora del poeta." PACHO, "Lenguaje y mensaje," 71. Pacho seems to suggest there is a richness of expression, but a poverty of understanding, because the doctrinal content is not accessible through the poetic medium. Conceptual expression of the poetic experience is the pathway to "natural" understanding. See also PACHO, *Vértice*, 68 which affirms this idea.

[77] "La idea central del pensamiento sanjuanista gira en torno a los «hábitos de ciencia», es decir, a la capacidad radical y los conocimientos adquiridos con el estudio, la reflexión, el progresivo enriquecimiento. De todo eso no hay evaporación ni disminución con el advenimiento de la experiencia mística, incluso la más elevada." PACHO, "Noemática e interpretación," 359. "La intención pedagógica y la atadura material a los versos han producido cierto alegorismo e incontables «acomodaciones» espirituales. Frente a ese dato marginal y secundario se ofrece la interpretación auténtica, la comunicación válida y la enunciación teológica de la experiencia mística." Ibid., 362.

[78] "Desde esta ladera humana penetramos mejor el discurso razonador, el minucioso análisis del comentarista, que los sublimes dislates del poeta. Nos acercamos mas a la sabrosa inteligencia interior a través de largos y complicados razonamientos que por medio de las intuiciones plásticas profundas del poeta." PACHO, *Vértice*, 125.

[79] This statement seems to be in opposition to what he says later concerning the ability to understand the poem if one has had mystical experiences similiar to that of the author of the *Cántico*. In this case, "intuition," I assume, would play a major role in understanding. See PACHO, *Vértice*, 124.

doctrinal content in the commentary as it describes the spiritual pilgrimage.[80] The two basic elements of the *tesoro doctrinal* which Pacho sees as central in an interpretation of any section of the commentary are the description of which state the soul is in at any particular moment and the doctrine which can be formulated from this state.[81]

In conclusion, then, Pacho suggests that the poem contains many *intuiciones plásticas profundas* (profound expressive intuitions) which are not accessible to the reader. What is accessible, *a través de largos y complicados razonamientos* (through lengthy and complicated rationalizations), is the doctrinal content of the *Cántico* as expressed in the commentary.[82] What we are led to believe, therefore, is that there exists a disunity of the poem and commentary due to two central factors: i) the content of what is to be understood, and ii) the capability of the human person to understand this content. This disunity seems to surface from Pacho's assignment to Juan de la Cruz of two central roles, that of poet and that of theologian.

According to Pacho, therefore, the poem is in relationship to the commentary as the basic symbolic art form whose noetic content is conceptualized in the commentary. The noetic content of the commentary, in turn, helps the reader enter into the symbolic meaning of the poem, through the concepts explicated in the commentary. This interplay between the poem and the commentary is basically supported by Ricoeur. However, for Pacho, the commentary appears to be a "remedy" for the enigmas of the poem. The understanding of Juan's *Cántico* takes

---

[80] "Efectivamente, por mas que los comentarios en prosa produzcan, al contacto con la poesía, una vaga sensación de enfriamiento, es innegable que sin ellos se nos esfuma el tesoro doctrinal." PACHO, *Vértice*, 125.

[81] "Una cosa es el estado del alma, descrito en cada canción, y orta, muy distinta, el contendido doctrinal de su declaración respectiva. Son postulados básicos para la interpretación de la obra." PACHO, *Vértice*, 116.

[82] Elisabeth Wilhelmsen appears to support a similiar perspective when she says: "The numerous enigmatic paradoxes which appear in the Sanjuanist lyrics are resolved in the prose into propositions devoid of contradictory elements." WILHELMSEN, *Cognition and Communication*, 138.

place through a synergetic play between the two literay forms, but for Pacho the meaning of the *Cántico* is limited to an understanding of the progression of the classical spiritual itinerary: the purgative, illuminitive, and unitive ways to God as it is clarified in the commentary. The *Cántico* is reproduced, albeit in different language, through the conceptualization of the commentary.

Conceivably, due to the upward movement that constitutes the formation of the concept, and the wearing down of the metaphor through substitution, the commentary replaces the poem as the primary point of reference in understanding the *Cántico*. It is this latter position which is challenged by Ricoeur's theory of the radical discontinuity of discourse to which we now turn.

3.2 Poetic and Speculative Discourse: Paul Ricoeur

What I want to investigate here is Ricoeur's thinking about the relationship between poetic discourse and speculative discourse. An investigation of the relationship between these two types of discourse will cast light on the relationship of Juan's poem (poetic discourse) to the commentary (speculative discourse) as well as the implications of that relationship in a hermeneutical interpretation of the *Cántico*.

Briefly stated, Ricoeur develops the position that conceptual thought does not reproduce the semantic functioning of poetic discourse, that is, poetic discourse and speculative discourse are two radically different forms of discourse.[83] Only by safeguarding this principle, Ricoeur acknowledges, do we make metaphoricity possible. Speculative discourse is based within a single referential field, that is, it draws from the conceptual field of discourse. Metaphorical discourse, on the other hand, works in two distinct referential fields simultaneously, within the conceptual field (a known field of reference), as well as within the field

---

[83] At the beginning of this study Ricoeur states: "Taking the notion of discursiveness as such as our theme, I should like to plead for a relative pluralism of forms and levels of discourse. Without going as far as the notion, suggested by Wittgenstein, of a radical heterogeneity of language games ... it is important to recognize in principle the *discontinuity* that assures the autonomy of speculative discourse." RICOEUR, *Rule of Metaphor*, 257-8.

of non-ostensive reference (the field which opens up new meaning). However, it is to be noted that this radical difference between poetic and speculative discourse does not, as we will see, exclude the "interanimation between modes of discourse" required for interpretation.[84] Let us now pursue further details of Ricoeur's thesis concerning the discontinuity of poetic and speculative discourse.

Ricoeur begins his study by examining three *counter-examples* which, potentially, could be used to refute his own thesis. The formidable opposition to his thesis which each of these *counter-examples* presents and the detailed anlaysis he uses to refute them, bring home the fact that Ricoeur's own position is not as obvious as it may initially look. It is not my intention to follow the labyrinth which Ricoeur constructs in his analysis of each of these *counter-examples*. I will present only, and very briefly, each of these three *counter-examples* to put us in a position to appreciate the gains from Ricoeur's analysis which are summarized at the end. I will then be in a position to bring these gains into dialogue with Pacho's position which I summarized above.

Ricoeur first goes to Aristotle's *Categories* and *Metaphysics* (books Γ, E, Z, and Λ) which explore the points of greatest divergence and greatest convergence between philosophy (speculative discourse) and poetry.[85] Aristotle discovered a bridge between these two in the concept of *ousia*, "being which is shared somehow by all that exists."[86] Aristotle then applies this concept to discourse: we can talk about things that we do know, and by extension attribute this knowledge to things which we do not know.[87] Ricoeur then reviews the conclusion at which Aristotle eventually arrives: "being is said in several ways." Aristotle thus testifies that there is an ordered diversity of the categories of being. This leads Aristotle to

---

[84] RICOEUR, *Rule of Metaphor*, 258.

[85] RICOEUR, *Rule of Metaphor*, 260.

[86] DORNISCH, *Faith and Philosophy*, 311.

[87] DORNISCH, *Faith and Philosophy*, 311.

formulate the doctrine of the "analogical unity of the multiple meanings of being."[88] However, does this discovery imply the generic unity of being and thus the "simple dispersion of its meanings"?[89] In other words, does Aristotle's thesis put in peril Ricoeur's theory?

After a detailed analysis of the potential threat posed by Aristotle's findings concerning analogy and the multiple ways of the saying of being, Ricoeur concludes that poetic and speculative discourse are not merged by Aristotle's notion of analogical attribution. Aristotle, even in his own project, had failed since his theories of ontology were inadequate and therefore could not support his conclusions.[90] Aristotle attempted to find a unity of the various ways of saying being which were beyond the metaphorical, that is, to establish a properly philosophical discourse over and against the mythical discourse of Greek civilization. Ricoeur suggests that Aristotle did not succeed in excluding the metaphorical because the doctrine of analogy at which Aristotle had arrived could not exclude it.

In typically Ricoeurian style, Ricoeur ultimately used Aristotle's threatening conclusion of the analogical unity of the multiple meanings of being, even though flawed, to reinforce his own thesis: "the plurivocity that is ... brought to philosophical [speculative] discourse is of a different order than the multiplicity of meaning produced by metaphorical [poetic] utterance."[91] Aristotle's own doctrine provided for Ricoeur "the occasion for showing that there is no direct passage from the semantic functioning of metaphorical expression to the transcendental doctrine of analogy. On the contrary, the latter furnishes a particularly striking example of the autonomy of philosophical discourse."[92]

---

[88] RICOEUR, *Rule of Metaphor*, 258.

[89] RICOEUR, *Rule of Metaphor*, 273.

[90] RICOEUR, *Rule of Metaphor*, 272.

[91] RICOEUR, *Rule of Metaphor*, 260.

[92] RICOEUR, *Rule of Metaphor*, 258.

In a second *counter-example* Ricoeur reviews the Thomist doctrine of *analogia entis* (the analogy of being born from Aristotle's position stated above). Ricoeur wonders whether his own thesis concerning the radical separateness of the modes of discourse can stand up against the composite of ontology and theology ("onto-theology")?

The express purpose of onto-theology "is to establish theological discourse at the level of science and thereby to free it completely from the poetical forms of religious discourse, even at the price of severing the science of God from biblical hermeneutics."[93] This project concerns the "possibility of speaking rationally of the creative God of the Judeo-Christian tradition."[94] An attempt to speak rationally of the Judeo-Christian God leads to two radical positions concerning discourse. On one hand, if discourse is essentially held to be of a singular nature then "to impute a discourse common to God and to his creatures would be to destroy divine transcendence."[95] On the other hand, "assuming total incommunicability of meanings from one level [of discourse] to the other would condemn one to utter agnosticism."[96] The concept of "analogous attribution" was thus born as a third and median way between these two extreme and unacceptable positions.[97] However, "many critiques culminating in the physics following from Galileo and the postulates formulated by Hume made it clear that Aquinas's concept of analogy and consequent participation would no longer hold."[98] After this investigation Ricoeur once again affirms the radical divide that separates poetic and speculative discourse "at the very

---

[93] RICOEUR, *Rule of Metaphor*, 273.

[94] RICOEUR, *Rule of Metaphor*, 273.

[95] RICOEUR, *Rule of Metaphor*, 273.

[96] RICOEUR, *Rule of Metaphor*, 273.

[97] "The doctrine of the analogy of being was born of [the] ... desire to encompass in a single doctrine the horizontal relation of the categories of substance and the vertical relation of created things to the Creator." RICOEUR, *Rule of Metaphor*, 273.

[98] DORNISCH, *Faith and Philosophy*, 312.

point of their greatest proximity."[99]

In a third step Ricoeur examines "an entirely different sort of implication" which surfaces between speculative discourse and poetic discourse when they are confronted at "the level of their hidden presuppositions rather than at the level of their stated intentions."[100] The two previous *counter-examples* "involved only the semantic intentions of each type of discourse that are capable of being taken up in reflection."[101] This third *counter-example* explores the possibility that poetic and speculative discourse are joined together at the level of metaphysics. Ricoeur finds the potential source of this affirmation in Heidegger's statement: "The metaphorical exists only within the metaphysical."[102] Ricoeur goes on to explain the challenge to his own position that this statement may suggest:[103] 1. The ontology implicit in the entire rhetorical tradition is that of western metaphysics of the Platonic type: reality as we know it is a transfer of the fullness of *true reality* located elsewhere; 2. Metaphor means a transfer from the proper sense to the figurative sense; 3. Both of the above-stated transfers assume a simple transfer of equivalence between the visible and the invisible.

What is essentially at stake in affirming these corollary assertions "is the claim of reflective philosophy to retain its traditional prerogative as governing metadiscourse."[104] Ricoeur examines each of the three assertions stated above by

---

[99] RICOEUR, *Rule of Metaphor*, 280.

[100] RICOEUR, *Rule of Metaphor*, 280.

[101] RICOEUR, *Rule of Metaphor*, 280.

[102] Martin HEIDEGGER, *Der Satz vom Grund*, (Pfullingen: Neske, 1957), 89, quoted in RICOEUR, *Rule of Metaphor*, 280.

[103] "This saying suggests that the trans-gression of meta-phor and that of meta-physics are but one and the same transfer. Several things are implied here: first, that the ontology implicit in the entire rhetorical tradition is that of Western 'metaphysics' of the Platonic or neo-Platonic type, where the soul is transported from the visible world to the invisible world; second, that meta-phorical means transfer from the proper sense to the figurative sense; finally, that both transfers constitute one and the same *Über-tragung*." RICOEUR, *Rule of Metaphor*, 280.

[104] CLARK, *Paul Ricoeur*, 137.

making use of references to metaphor in Heidegger's work which are different from the concept of metaphor which Heidegger himself rejects. In the end Ricoeur concludes that "the supposed collusion between the metaphorical pair of the proper and figurative and the metaphysical pair of the visible and invisible" is not necessary and unfounded even in Heidegger's own work.[105] This collusion of the "proper and figurative" and the "visible and invisible" is a common idea which Heidegger shares with Derrida.

Ricoeur, therefore, next examines Jacques Derrida's position in *White Mythology*, a position that claims there is a wearing away of metaphor which eventually leads toward absolute knowledge or idealization. With this position, poetic and speculative discourse are once again fused. However, Ricoeur argues in great detail that even "dead metaphors," those metaphors stripped of their creative potential through the apparent entropy of language achieved in the "'elevation' of the concept," can be revivified by means of a new act of discourse.[106] In the end Ricoeur holds that philosophy must "recognize its own secondariness and refuse to succumb to the tempation of 'binding metaphorical and speculative discourse'."[107] The role of philosophical discourse is to set itself up "as the vigilant watchman, overseeing the ordered extensions of meaning; against this background, the unfettered extensions of meaning in poetic discourse spring free."[108] Once again, therefore, Ricoeur affirms the distinctness of speculative and poetic discourse.

By an examination of these three *counter-examples* Ricoeur places his thesis concerning the radical separateness of poetic and speculative discourse on solid ground. However, distinctness does not imply the inability for these two modes of discourse to be related in some way, or at some level. To show how the two

---

[105] RICOEUR, *Rule of Metaphor*, 294.

[106] RICOEUR, *Rule of Metaphor*, 259.

[107] CLARK, *Paul Ricoeur*, 137.

[108] RICOEUR, *Rule of Metaphor*, 261.

modes of discourse are related is Ricoeur's next task of Study Eight in *Rule of Metaphor*. In this section he wishes to show that speculative discourse has a condition of *possibility* based on poetic discourse.[109] However, speculative discourse does not, of necessity, spring forth from poetic discourse. It is this *epoché* which makes poetic discourse possible.

Speculative discourse is generated on its own terms from within the resources of the concept of which the mind is capable on its own. Speculative discourse has its own base referents which, Ricoeur says, "belong to the mind itself." Metaphorical discourse, however, may also give rise to the conceptual order.[110]

It is metaphorical reference which forms the bridge between these two forms of discourse. Ricoeur suggests that it is the construction of the "similar" in metaphor which gives rise to the "same" in the concept, despite a clash of differences.[111] Conversely, as the "same" is articulated in some fashion through the concept, new possibilities surface for invention of the world of "as if" discovered in the metaphor. The figurative in the form of the metaphor gives rise to the speculative in the form of the concept. "To the imaginative power of thought-full poetry, the poet replies with the speculative power of poeticizing thought."[112]

It is this creation of metaphorical reference which girds the primacy of the poetic text in interpretation. The primacy of the poetic text is established

---

[109] "Speculative discourse has its condition of *possibility* in the semantic dynamism of metaphorical utterance, and that, on the other hand, speculative discourse has its *necessity* in itself, in putting the resources of conceptual articulation to work. These are resources that doubtless belong to the mind itself, that are the mind itself reflecting upon itself. In other words, the speculative fulfils the semantic exigencies put to it by the metaphorical only when it establishes a break marking the irreducible difference between the two modes of discourse." RICOEUR, *Rule of Metaphor*, 296.

[110] "Far from the concept's being reduced to an abbreviation, by reason of some principle of thrift and economy, some play of substitution, it is the concept that makes this play of re-presentation possible." RICOEUR, *Rule of Metaphor*, 301.

[111] "To see the similar, in Aristotle's words, is to apprehend the 'same' within and in spite of 'difference'." RICOEUR, *Rule of Metaphor*, 296. "If the *imagination* is the kingdom of 'the similar,' the *intellectio* is that of the 'the same.' In the horizon opened up by the speculative, 'same' grounds 'similar' and not the inverse." Ibid., 301.

[112] RICOEUR, *Rule of Metaphor*, 310.

because in the *possible* movement from metaphor to concept a limit that is unsurpassable is reached in the concept. Metaphor, on the other hand, constantly urges us on to "think again." Hermeneutics constantly brings us back to the world-of-the-text to interpret its proposals for new modes of being-in-the-world. New projects for existence are available through interpretation of poetic texts. Speculative discourse, within the confines of the concepts, also has the potential to expand the meaning of poetic discourse. "The dynamism of meaning is shown to be a dual and intersecting dynamism where any progress towards concepts has as its counterpart a more extensive exploration of the referential field."[113] Recall that in the dialectic of explanation and understanding meaning can be developed analytically.

New referents are constantly opened up in metaphorical discourse by this interchange between speculative and metaphorical discourse. This is true even though speculative discourse frees "itself from the play of double meaning" characteristic of the poetic order.[114] The semantic tensions inherent in the metaphorical order cannot be reduced to absolute knowledge nor do they allude to some "primordial meaning" as neo-Platonic thought might assume.[115] However, the concept has its role to play in expanding meaning at the level of the metaphorical.

"Thus the referential field can extend beyond the things we are able to show, and even beyond visible, perceptible things."[116] New aspects of reality are therefore shaped and given through language when conceptual exploration is used to delve further into the metaphorical. As Ricoeur says: "On the one hand, as

---

[113] RICOEUR, *Rule of Metaphor*, 297.

[114] RICOEUR, *Rule of Metaphor*, 302.

[115] "My inclination is to see the universe of discourse as a universe kept in motion by an interplay of attractions and repulsions that ceaselessly promote the interaction and intersection of domains whose organizing nuclei are off-centred in relation to one another; and still this interplay never comes to rest in an absolute knowledge that would subsume the tensions." RICOEUR, *Rule of Metaphor*, 302. Ricoeur's investigations have led him to believe that "this language ploy involves no mystique of 'primordial meaning.' A buried sense becomes a new meaning in the present instance of discourse. This is all the more true when speculative thought adopts the new meaning in order to blaze a path to the 'thing' itself." Ibid., 311.

[116] RICOEUR, *Rule of Metaphor*, 298.

regards its sense, the metaphorical utterance reproduces the form of a movement in a portion of the trajectory of meaning that goes beyond the familiar referential field where the meaning is already constituted. On the other hand, it brings an unknown referential field towards language, and within the ambit of this field the semantic aim functions and unfolds."[117] Poetic discourse posits being in the realm of the "similar," while speculative discourse thinks of it as being in the realm of the "same."

New possibilities of meaning in the poetic text are therefore made actual by meanings that have already been established in the speculative order. To state it once again, the history of reception of a work is a significant component of its actual and present meaning: "This semantic dynamism, proper to ordinary language, gives a 'historicity' to the power of signifying."[118] What is "known" is used to plunge the depths of that which is "not known." This dialectic is based on the instability of meaning. Speculative discourse is, therefore, not in a linear relationship to poetic discourse. Gains in meaning (understanding) in the metaphorical field may not "pay back" with an equivalent gain in the conceptual field. Gain in meaning, Ricoeur says, is not necessesarily "a *conceptual* gain."[119] Rather, the indications of speculative discourse are at the service of new meaning that is potentially inexhaustible in the present metaphorical potential of the text. As Ricoeur says: "It is always in a particular utterance ... that the sedimented history of assembled meanings can be recovered in a new semantic aim. Placed in the perspective of its use, meaning appears less like a determined content, to take or to leave, than ... like an inductive principle capable of guiding semantic innovation."[120]

Gain in new meaning is therefore inseparable from the tension of the

---

[117] RICOEUR, *Rule of Metaphor*, 299. Later Ricoeur uses a phrase from Heidegger to describe this situation: "The 'flowers' of our words -- *Worte, wie Blumen* - utter existence in its blossoming forth." Ibid., 309

[118] RICOEUR, *Rule of Metaphor*, 298.

[119] RICOEUR, *Rule of Metaphor*, 296.

[120] RICOEUR, *Rule of Metaphor*, 298.

schema of the text that mediates the meaning in the life of the reader.[121] Meaning is ultimately bound to the poetic text itself, although it invites a conceptualization that is, to some degree at least, coherent. As we have already examined in Chapter Four, ultimately meaning is "in search of itself in the twofold direction of sense and reference."[122] Interpretation cannot "help but be a work of elucidation, ... and consequently a struggle for univocity."[123] "Every interpretation aims at relocating the semantic outline sketched by metaphorical utterance inside an available horizon of understanding that can be mastered conceptually."[124] Ricoeur thus arrives at a paradox which affirms at one level the importance of the rational content of interpretation, but, at the same time affirms that rationalization *may* destroy the primacy of metaphorical reference.[125] But we already know this is not the terminal point in Ricoeur's understanding of interpretation. Understanding for Ricoeur does not rest within the noetic content of the text.

Metaphoricity functions in two referential fields at the same time, that of the known or speculated to be known (noetic content) and that of the other field "for which we consequently are unable to make identifying descriptions by means of appropriate predicates."[126] Ricoeur thus refers to the "split reference" of

---

[121] "This is another way of saying that the gain in meaning is not carried to the concept, to the extent that it remains caught in the conflict of 'same' and 'different,' although it constitutes the rough outline and the demand for an instruction through the concept." RICOEUR, *Rule of Metaphor*, 297.

[122] RICOEUR, *Rule of Metaphor*, 299.

[123] RICOEUR, *Rule of Metaphor*, 302.

[124] RICOEUR, *Rule of Metaphor*, 302-3.

[125] "Whereas the metaphorical utterance leaves the second sense in suspension, while its reference continues to have no direct presentation, interpretation is necessarily a rationalization that at its limit eliminates the experience that comes to language through the metaphorical process. Doubtless it is only in reductive interpretation that rationalization culminates in clearing away the symbolic base." RICOEUR, *Rule of Metaphor*, 302.

[126] RICOEUR, *Rule of Metaphor*, 299.

poetic discourse which becomes apparent in interpretation.[127] "On one side, interpretation seeks the clarity of the concept; on the other, it hopes to preserve the dynamism of meaning that the concept holds and pins down."[128] The dynamic category which has been used throughout this dissertation to describe the intersection of these two referential fields is discourse at the level of the world-of-the-text. The world-of-the-text, referenced by metaphorical discourse, is serviced by the tools of language.[129]

The prejudice that scientific discourse alone discovers and describes reality is therefore challenged.[130] This challenge was already implicit in Chapter Four and Chapter Six where I discussed the dynamics of reading and the heuristic function of "mood." In the present context, Ricoeur again reaffirms his belief that "feeling is not less ontological than representation."[131] The opposition, often assumed, between descriptive discourse focused on the "outside" of a text and poetic discourse focused on the "inside" of a text (feelings), is also challenged.[132]

We have, therefore, come back full circle to where we started from at the beginning of this dissertation. I began this dissertation by suggesting Ricoeur's notion of mimesis had implications for the methodological issues associated with the interpretation of Juan's *Cántico*. In Ricoeur's understanding of the relationship

---

[127] RICOEUR, *Rule of Metaphor*, 305. "Split reference ... signifies that the tension characterizing metaphorical utterance is carried ultimately by the copula *is*. Being-as means being *and* not being. Such-and-such was and was not the case." RICOEUR, *Rule of Metaphor*, 306. I referred to this quality in the last chapter as capable of describing the apophatic nature of poetic discourse.

[128] RICOEUR, *Rule of Metaphor*, 303.

[129] RICOEUR, *Rule of Metaphor*, 304.

[130] RICOEUR, *Rule of Metaphor*, 305.

[131] "Poetical textures, ... are no less heuristic than fictions in narrative form; feeling is no less ontological than representation." RICOEUR, *Rule of Metaphor*, 305.

[132] "Must we not forgo the opposition between a discourse turned towards the 'outside,' which would be precisely descriptive discourse, and a discourse turned towards the 'inside,' which would portray only a mood and raise it to the hypothetical level? Is it not the very distinction between 'outside' and 'inside' that is shaken along with that between representation and feeling?" RICOEUR, *Rule of Metaphor*, 306.

between poetic and speculative discourse we have discovered a central methodological issue in the interpretation of the *Cántico*, that is, the reception of Juan's own commentary in the reception of the poem. Within Ricoeur's analysis the commentary cannot be considered as the exclusive point of reference for a hermeneutical interpretation of the *Cántico*. Through his understanding of the dialectic operative between speculative and poetic discourse, Ricoeur has restored to poetic discourse its "twofold task of both discovery and creation."[133] This position dismantles the reign of speculative discourse in interpretation. This is not, as we have already seen in the careful work that needs to be done on the level of "explanation," a plea for the irrational.[134] Rather it affirms the creative power of the poetic text in itself, while maintaining the valuable contribution which speculative discourse offers the creative process. Both the poet and the philosopher discover and create; each have their own and unique linguistic tools.

It now remains for me to show what has been gained by the affirmation that poetic and speculative discourse operate on separate planes and the way in which their relationship affects a hermeneutical understanding of the relationship between Juan's *Cántico* and his commentary. It is to this task I will now turn by bringing Ricoeur's understanding of the relationship of poetic and speculative discourse into dialogue with Eulogio Pacho's understanding of the poetry-prose relationship in the *Cántico*.

3.3 A Reflection on Pacho's Position From Ricoeur's Perspective

Pacho's key exegetical principle which accounts for the poetry-prose relationship is something which he describes as Juan's *doble visión*. This *doble visión* puts at odds Juan the poet and Juan the theologian: the poet describes an irregular and undulating course toward the "spiritual marriage," while the theologian describes a direct and sequential course known as the classical spiritual itinerary.

---

[133] RICOEUR, *Rule of Metaphor*, 306.

[134] RICOEUR, *Rule of Metaphor*, 306.

The poem is therefore metamorphosized or simply transposed by the theologian into the commentary.[135] However, at stake here is whether a metaphor can ever be translated. Pacho's *doble visión* appears to support the eventual translation of metaphor into concept.

Pacho's assessment of the poetry-prose relationship accounts for the noetic content of the *Cántico* and Juan's significant contribution to Western dogmatic theology which we reviewed in Chapter Three. For Pacho, the reader has access through the commentary to the concepts that are latent in the poem. Pacho therefore relies on a substitution theory, based on allegory, which "fuses" the poetic and theological into a singular vision in the commentary.[136] Conceivably, and with enough work, the *Cántico* would be transposable from the poetic level to the predicative level. In other words, Pacho's understanding of the poetry-prose relationship, even within the dialectic of the poetry-prose interplay, ultimately leads to conceptual categories and the possibility of exhaustive paraphrase. Pacho is therefore able to account for the noetic content of the poem to a certain degree but further exploration of the metaphorical referents does not appear to be possible. New

---

[135] "Es imperioso mantener firme y presente el proceso evolutivo de creación y comunicación; primero es la experiencia mística, a la vez teofánica y apofática; viene luego la manifestación en clave, que es la poesía; se le añade posteriormente una traducción y una explicación, que es el comentario. De ese modo el mensaje inicial --de sentido indefinido y universal, como creación-- se convierte en mensaje concreto, orientado en dirección determinada." PACHO, "Lenguaje y Mensaje," 77. Thompson holds a similar view. Of the poetry-prose relationship in the *Cántico* he says: "The *Cántico* wavers between poetic commentary and spiritual treatise because it is much longer than the other poems and because its imagery is so much more varied. The prose commentaries have to create order out of a lyrical outburst. Images, metaphors, and symbols have to be cashed. The instinct of the poet has to yield to the studied refelction [sic] of the theologian." THOMPSON, *The Poet and the Mystic*, 59.

[136] According to Juan de la Cruz's stated intention in the Prologue of the *Cántico* Pacho fuses together the poetic and theological content of Juan's literary output: "En la *introducción o* «*declaración*» *sumaria* que precede a la paráfrasis de los versos sueltos de cada estrofa, y en esas divisiones o esquemas del número anterior, es donde trata de intento de fusionar ambas concepciones: la anamórfica y panorámica del poeta y la diferencial y detallista del teólogo. Es aquí sobre todo donde se pretende hacer ver cómo las estrofas se suceden en riguroso orden, marcando el progreso de la perfección según los peldaños de la escala mística diseñada por los tratadistas de la vida espiritual. Lo que *aquí*, lo que en cada estrofa «canta el poeta» o «cuenta el alma», encuadra perfectamente en la graduatoria del «ejercicio del amor entre el alma y el Esposo Cristo»." PACHO, "La Clave exegetica del `Cántico espiritual`," 335.

meaning is eclipsed by his understanding of the poetry-prose relationship.

Pacho's understanding of the poetry-prose relationship, therefore, subtly distances the reader from the poetic text. By putting the poem at the service of the commentary and not the commentary at the service of the poem, the metaphorical play of the poetic text on the reader is impeded.[137] The noema of the text, the "thing" itself, as Ricoeur loves to say, becomes inaccessible to the reader.

Pacho's theory of the poetry-prose relationship, therefore, appears to have several disadvantages: 1. His approach restricts the split-reference constructed through the dialectic of sense and reference operative in metaphorical discourse; 2. It does not account for the potential contribution each of the *Cánticos* may make toward the mediation of self-understanding (being-in-the-world); 3. It does not account for *new* meaning, that is, the enigma of the transformative event of the *Cántico* in the life of the reader who may or may not be a mystic. How might we, therefore, account for the contribution the commentary makes towards understanding the *Cántico* (à la Ricoeur) without hampering the ultimate reference of the *Cántico* which is constructed not in its reference to the commentary but in the poem's ultimate metaphorical reference, the world-of-the-text?

We already know this ultimate reference is constructed in conjunction with the reading subject who stands before the *Cántico* as one who ultimately brings the poem back into discourse and thus understands himself or herself better as a being-in-the-world. Discourse, in Ricoeur's theory, ultimately refers to the world, not to conceptual systems. However, we know from the above presentation that hermeneutical interpretation functions precisely at the place of intersection of poetic and speculative discourse.

It is because of this understanding of interpretation that Ricoeur would suggest a different relationship between the poem (poetic or metaphorical

---

[137] Elizabeth Wilhelmsen makes an interesting comment concerning the particular contribution of Juan's poems and their commentaries. Concerning the play of either the poetic text or the commentary on the reader she says: "Within the writings of San Juan de la Cruz no absolute differentiation should be made between the poetry and the prose regarding either style or effect upon the reader." WILHELMSEN, *Cognition and Communication*, 123.

discourse) and the commentary (speculative discourse). Within Ricoeur's theory, the poem, ultimately, does not have as its primary reference the conceptualization of the poem which is undertaken by Juan in the commentary. As well, the poem-prose relationship does not reflect a mutual dialectic which deepens the understanding of the commentary and the poem in a strictly reciprocal fashion. Rather, the commentary provides *a* conceptualization of the poem, but ultimately the poem points *elsewhere* to the world which is lived in by beings-in-the-world. The commentary conceptualizes that which has been "discovered" and "created" through the metaphoricity of the poem, but returns the reader to "think again" *within the context of the poem.*

The commentary's challenge is to continually assist in the discovery of this "more" by exploring the referential fields of metaphorical discourse in the current act of discourse. The commentary, therefore, is a speculative or theological appropriation of the poem which, in turn, helps form the referential structure of the poem. Appropriation of the poem at the level of the world-of-the-text is the poetic or aesthetic appropriation of the *Cántico* which is based on the poem's metaphorical reference. This approach to the poetry-prose relationship values the poetic as well as the speculative appropriations of the *Cántico*. As well, it liberates the referential capacity of the poem to account for the mediation of *new* meaning integral to the nature of poetic discourse.

In the poetry-prose relationship, as defined by Pacho, we arrive at the end of discourse, with the attempt to define "sameness" within the poem and the commentary. Pacho's stance subtly assumes that the poem is ultimately translatable: figurative meaning is substituted for conceptual meaning. Pacho, ultimately, is therefore working within a closed system (that of the visible and invisible), whereby the poem and the commentary mutually enlighten each other, but allow no other interpretations.

Semantic innovation, as I developed it within Ricoeur's thought in Chapter Four, is not possible within Pacho's poetry-prose dialectic. No new information about reality is discovered, nor is it deemed possible. Pacho's theory leads the reader along the lines of the increased conceptualization of the poem. This noetic content, however, does not account for the emergent meaning which can only occur in the present through the noema of the poem.

The poetry-prose relationship, as defined by Ricoeur's theory, also describes the mutual relationship between the poem and commentary but adds a vector pointing the poem toward the world-of-the-text which is constructed in conjunction with the reader. Because of the split-reference of metaphorical discourse there is a rift between the "similiar" (based on metaphor) and the "same" (based on the concept) which allows the reader to play a role in the emergence of the meaning of the *Cántico*. The reader is continually sent back to the poem for more thought. This "more" is not a mere unpacking of what is already in the poem, but, because of the referential capacity of the metaphor, the poem continues its poeticizing work, its work of discovery and creation. Sedimented predicates are used by the metaphor to keep the creative act alive. The "similar/same" rift, therefore, allows for other interpretive elements to enter into the poetry-prose dialectic which opens up the meaning of the *Cántico* for the "mystic" as well as the "non-mystic."

The distinction between the "mystic" and the "non-mystic" fades and loses its significance in the context of Ricoeur's interpretation theory. Each reader brings a unique experience of being-in-the-world before Juan's *Cántico*. Each reader comes with his or her own horizon of meaning within the contextualization of the current sociological, political, cultural, and religious milieu. We have already seen how all these contribute toward the emergence of metaphorical truth in a poetic text, mystic or not. Within Ricoeur's theory, the commentary is selected as *one* of the semantic fields that orients meaning for each reader, but the commentary does not eliminate the truth which is virtually present in the poem. The poem is therefore freed from an overdependence on the commentary which tends toward interpreting the poem as an allegory describing the threefold classical spiritual itinerary. Even though Juan interprets the poem within the confines of the purgative, illuminative, and unitive ways (although he says himself it is only one possibility for interpretation) we already know of the freedom of the poetic text from the intentionality of the author.

In Ricoeur's theory, the poem is therefore left open to explore the full range of its semantic possibilities, even given Juan's own interpretation or reception. Juan is the first reader of his own *Cántico* which brings into play the dialectic operative between poetic and speculative discourse which we have been examining. Metaphor, which mediates between these two forms of discourse, does not close the poem in upon itself, but rather opens it up to new and varied meanings and continually gives rise to new thought.

Ricoeur's theory of the relationship between poetic and speculative discourse acknowledges that the *Cántico* gives rise to the noetic content of Juan's commentary, but Ricoeur's theory keeps the poem open to other previously unknown fields of meaning. Poems have their own type of reference, that is, indirect reference. Indirect reference in poetry reverts back upon the reader and touches upon our affective attachment to the world. Hermeneutical interpretation functions on the edge which exists between the clarifications of the speculative field (the noetic content of the commentary) and the deconstruction/construction of the metaphorical field (the symbolic world of the poem) in relationship with the world. Interpretation can never be displaced from this productive place of tension, which, in the end, creates the world-of-the-text. Only here do the various fields or horizons of meaning intersect and allow new meaning to emerge from the interplay of sense and reference, explanation and understanding. The enigma of why Juan's *Cántico* continues to be read across cultural, historical, as well as religious traditions, is therefore accounted for by Ricoeur's theory of the basic discontinuity of poetic (metaphorical) and conceptual (speculative) discourse.

It would be helpful at this point to recall from Chapter Three that the threefold classical itinerary did not originate with Juan de la Cruz. This paradigmatic description of growth and progression in the spiritual life had been used long before Juan wrote the *Cántico*. However, metaphors and metaphorical systems, such as that found in Juan's *Cántico*, make and remake the world. According to Ricoeur's dialectic of sedimentation and innovation, metaphors virtually posit a new way of existence. Juan's innovations were not a redescription of already known concepts in the categories of classical spirituality.

Juan's innovations from the sedimented past brought to life a new way of visioning and being alive in the world. From Juan's poem we come in touch with a certain way of seeing and acting in the world. To describe this new way of being-in-the-world suggested by Juan's *Cántico* is to describe the ontological import of Juan's *Cántico*. Ricoeur says that hermeneutics has done its job only when it "has opened the eyes and ears, i.e., when it has displayed before our imagination the figures of our authentic existence."[138] Ricoeur's theory of the poetry-prose relationship allows this dialectic of sedimentation and innovation to continue even in the present. This is the ontological import of the *Cántico* I will now explore.

4. The Ontological Import of the *Cántico*

The metaphorical redescription of existence by the *Cántico* has ontological bearing. Juan's creation of a resemblance of human existence to a song of dialogue between lovers says something about the ontological status of existence and reality. What is the significance of existence seen as *being as a dialogue between lovers*? To ask this question is to pass from the *sense* to the *reference* of the discourse of the *Cántico*. The *world-of-the-text* or, in our case, the *world-of-the-Cántico* has ontological significance: that may be its most significant aspect. With this approach to the *Cántico* we move beyond the simple transposition of the *Cántico* from poem to commentary by the way of analogy. Paul Ricoeur states:

> Through fiction and through poetry new possible modes of being-in-the-world are opened up in the midst of reality. Fiction and poetry intend being not as given being but as potentiality of being. Consequently everyday reality undergoes a metamorphosis, thanks to what could be called the 'imaginative variations' which literature displays. Metaphorical language is the kind of discourse which is most able to generate these imaginative variations and thus to redescribe reality according to the new mode created by the poet.

---

[138] RICOEUR, "Biblical Hermeneutics," 144.

Metaphorical -- and, more generally -- poetic -- language aims at a *mimesis* of reality. However this language 'imitates' reality only because it recreates reality by means of a *mythos*, a 'plot,' a 'fable,' which touches upon the very essence of things.[139]

Metaphorical redescription sustains new referential fields that are lost if the text is restricted to its analogical interpretation. We have already seen how metaphorical redescription, in the mode of "as if," posits new possibilities for being-in-the-world.[140] A new way of seeing the world emerges through metaphorical redescription. However, Ricoeur holds that to metaphorize well, is at the same time, to posit the proximity between the things themselves.[141] Through metaphorical redescription in the mode of "as if," a world is discovered and created. The appropriation of the ontological significance of the *Cántico*, therefore, moves us beyond analogy and calls us toward a different kind of reception of Juan's text.

Ricoeur says that "under the name of mood, an extra-linguistic factor is introduced, which is the index of a manner of being."[142] Because of the *Cántico's* construction of mood, we are capable of discovering new ways of being-in-the-world. As well, through mood we remake and discover new things about the world: "in aesthetic experience the *emotions function cognitively*."[143] Lyric muthos is joined by a lyric mimesis in the sense that the mood created in metaphorical redescription of the world is a model for "seeing as" and "feeling as."[144]

What can we say about the mood of the *Cántico* which allows us to

---

[139] Paul RICOEUR, "Philosophical Hermeneutics and Theological Hermeneutics," *Studies in Religion* 5 (1975), 26.

[140] Recall: "It would seem that the enigma of metaphorical discourse is that it 'invents' in both senses of the word: what it creates, it discovers; and what it finds, it invents." RICOEUR, *Rule of Metaphor*, 239.

[141] RICOEUR, *Rule of Metaphor*, 230.

[142] RICOEUR, *Rule of Metaphor*, 229.

[143] Nelson GOODMAN, *Languages of Art: An Approach to a Theory of Symbols*, (Indianapolis: Bobbs-Merrill, 1968), 248, quoted in RICOEUR, *Rule of Metaphor*, 231.

[144] RICOEUR, *Rule of Metaphor*, 245.

"see" and "remake" the world in a new way? Ricoeur asks: "is it not the function of poetry to establish another world -- another world that corresponds to other possibilities of existence, to possibilities that would be most deeply our own?"[145] The author of the *Cántico* cannot control the level of appropriation of each reader. However, we can describe in some fashion the world-of-the-*Cántico* toward which the text is directed through a description of its mood. Mood, or "state of soul" as Ricoeur says, is a way of finding or sensing oneself in the midst of reality.[146] How do I find myself among things *in* the *Cántico* through mood?

In Chapter Five I pointed out that the particular rhythmic pattern which Juan used in the *Cántico*, that of the hendecasyllablic lira, gives the whole poem the appearance of "light dancing." Tavard notes that the double rhythm of the lira "introduces a dancing motion into the music of the discourse."[147] All this "dancing" takes place in the context of the highly affective and erotic exchange of the two principal protagonists of the *Cántico*. The movement of the poem, in the form of dancing and light music, takes the reader along a varied pathway of moods. Although we have already followed the dramatic unfolding of each of the three *Cánticos* in Chapter Five, let us now briefly recapitulate the pathway of the principal moods of one of the *Cánticos* as an example in our present context. This will help describe the mood of the existential backdrop before which the Divine-human drama takes place according to the *Cántico* of Juan de la Cruz. Since *CO* has received the least amount of attention in the literature, I will use *CO* for my example in order to indicate the variety of moods sketched in the *Cántico*.

Stanza 1 of *CO* is marked by torment and anguish. The Bride is searching for her Beloved. She already is very much in love with the one whom she seeks. After expressing her pain and distress, due to the absence of her lover (st. 2), the Bride is filled with desire and hope (st. 3). With determination, she sets off into

---

[145] RICOEUR, *Rule of Metaphor*, 229.

[146] RICOEUR, *Rule of Metaphor*, 229.

[147] TAVARD, *Poetry and Contemplation*, 42.

the world without fear, to search for her love. In a moment of reprieve the Bride discusses the situation with those she meets along the way. They assure her that her world is clothed in her Beloved. Not sure of this herself, she is suddenly thrust back again into a distressing search (st. 6-8) that leaves her feeling that she is dying. Her desire is focused on her Lover, not the things he has left behind, and so her misery is great. But has she discounted too soon the genuine presence of her Lover in the world about her, in those things he has touched and "left behind"?

We are then told, again, of the deep love shared between the two main characters of the *Cántico* (st. 8-9). The Bride once more expresses her longing (st. 10) and she comes close to recognizing her Beloved in the world of nature which surrounds her (st. 11). As this insight forms in her mind, she is moved to ecstasy, but her euphoria proves overwhelming and she retreats. The calming presence of the Lover suddenly comes upon her from nowhere (st. 12). Was he there all along, but she could not see him?

Stanza 13 ushers in a new depth of feeling. The Bride now recognizes her Lover in the world about her (st. 13-15). As this realization takes hold, there is a mood of serenity, calm, and quiet. These silent moods deepen love and refresh the Bride. She is happy (st. 15-23) and the setting is tranquil. However, in stanza 24 there are hints of trouble which become explicit in stanza 26. There are still problems to deal with. Consternation is expressed by the Bride before she settles down in peaceful repose (st. 27). But again, there is the expression of fear over the possibility of an intrusion in the relationship between the Bride and Bridegroom (st. 29). The source of these problems is admonished so that peace may prevail (st. 30). Restful repose again comes with the distancing of all that would interfere with the love of the two (st. 31). However, vigilance is still necessary. While the Bride and Bridegroom rest in solitude, there is an anxious chord which is struck by the near presence of that which caused apprehension earlier. The poem ends with this admixture of tension and peace.

What are we touching through these moods of the poem? What picture of our world in relationship with the Divine does this sketch give us? How does this tableau shape the way we experience God alive-in-the-world? Does the *Cántico* give us a world, based on the appropriation of scripture, on Juan's experience, and on the tradition of the community, which invites a vital and new way of being-in-the-world? If appropriation of the *Cántico* is of a sexual nature, what does this say about all of our relationships, that is, with God, with our world, with others, with ourselves? These are some questions on which we can reflect and which may open up the world-of-the-*Cántico* to new meaning.

If this world is valued by the Christian community, and, according to the reception which Juan's *Cántico* has received through the years, it is highly valued, might it be time to explore the world-of-the-*Cántico* more integrally through an aesthetic reception of the text rather than a strictly doctrinal one?

A hermeneutical appropriation of the *Cántico* opens up my self-understanding in the world. An aesthetic reception of the text through mood creates this possibility. Through metaphorical redescription which constructs mood, Juan has liberated us from the limitations of descriptive reference and opened up access to reality in the mode of fiction and feeling.[148] Perhaps it is time to allow Juan's *Cántico* to speak to us about reality in new and varied ways in order to allow the productive capacity of Juan's text to shape and reshape our lives.

5. Conclusion

In this Chapter I have examined three separate issues which affect the reception of Juan's *Cántico*. All three of these issues come under the umbrella of mimesis$_3$ in Ricoeur's threefold concept of mimesis. These three issues are: 1. the role of the title of the *Cántico*; 2. the poetry-commentary relationship; 3. the ontological import of the *Cántico*.

The first issue was the role of the title in the context of a hermeneutical interpretation. Within Ricoeur's theory of metaphorical reference, the

---

[148] This is a partial paraphrase of "The creation of a concrete object -- the poem itself -- cuts language off from the didactic function of the sign, but at the same time opens up access to reality in the mode of fiction and feeling." RICOEUR, *Rule of Metaphor*, 229.

title becomes an important player within the dialectic of sense and reference. The title orients the reader in his or her approach to the text and forms part of the metaphorical tension inherent in the text which is productive of meaning. I suggested, therefore, that the title which appears at the top of the Sanlúcar and Jaén manuscripts: *Canciones entre el alma y el esposo*, be considered an integral part of the text and be used to title the poem itself, even when it is not accompanied by the commentary. The title *Cántico espiritual* could be used to refer only to the poetry-prose complex.

The second issue concerned the poetry-prose relationship. Eulogio Pacho's theory concerning the poetry-prose relationship was first reviewed. Although Pacho suggests a dynamic relationship between Juan's poem and the commentary, ultimately Pacho's approach leads to a linear substitution theory: the commentary is a paraphrase or an unpacking of the symbols and images in the poem. No new meaning can be accounted for in the way Pacho describes the poetry-prose relationship. Pacho leads the reader to believe that there is *a* meaning in the symbols of the poem and that this meaning is exposed in the conceptualization of the commentary and not in the referential capacity of the text of the *Cántico* itself. However, the commentary is less helpful if one is already a mystic or has had a similar experience to that of Juan de la Cruz. Meaning in the poem is therefore relegated to that which is already known by the mystic, or yet to be discovered in the commentary by the non-mystic. For Pacho the poem's metaphorical and symbolic language generates the noetic content of the commentary which is what can be ultimately "known" by all, but only through the concept. The commentary is the "natural" way for most people to enter into the mysterious ineffability of the poem.

However, Ricoeur's theory of mimesis opens up the availability of the meaning-event virtually present in the poem to all readers. The commentary is given a role in appropriating this meaning-event, but it is not given exclusive priority. The commentary is only one resource which the reader brings to his or her reading of the *Cántico*. The commentary, exemplified as speculative discourse and characterized by the concept, sends the reader back to the poem to "think some more." The poem is *the place* where the mediation of meaning takes place within the split-reference of metaphorical discourse. The split-reference of metaphor allows for the conceptualization of discourse, but its other semantic vector finds its home ultimately in the world constructed by the interaction of the reading subject with the poetic text. The world-of-the-text, resting on the in-between place of the metaphorical and the speculative, becomes the place of hermeneutical interpretation for the poetry-prose complex. Interpretation, as Ricoeur says, is a composite discourse, and as such one cannot help but feel the tension produced by metaphorical and speculative fields of reference.

The third issue which I have surfaced is the ontological import of the *Cántico*. My purpose here was to suggest some questions which come from the realization that mood constructs the primary referential field of lyrical poetry such as Juan's *Cántico*. In the mode of "as-if" of mood we appropriate the world-of-the-*Cántico*, that is, new existential possibilities for being-alive-in-the-world. The question which we are left with from this section concerns the significance of existence seen as a dialogue between lovers. The deeper structures of existence resemble in some way the intimate relationship of two people passionately in love. It is this ontological aspect of the *Cántico* which deserves further reflection. I have merely raised the question in the context of a hermeneutical interpretation of the *Cántico* of Juan de la Cruz.

CONCLUSION

This dissertation has constructed a hermeneutical framework within which an interpretation of Juan de la Cruz's *Cántico* may be undertaken. The phenomenological hermeneutics of Paul Ricoeur have been used to construct this framework. Ricoeur's phenomenological hermeneutics of texts is based on a theory of mimesis. It is Ricoeur's mimetic theory which has been used to construct the threefold framework within which interpretation of the *Cántico* can take place. In following the hermeneutical arc constructed in the pre-understanding of the *Cántico* (mimesis$_1$), its configuration (mimesis$_2$), and then its reconfiguration (mimesis$_3$), a number of significant methodological issues for the interpretation of Juan's *Cántico* were reflected upon. These have been examined to show how Juan's poem can be meaningfully interpreted for the contemporary reader, culturally and historically removed from sixteenth-century Spain.

Ricoeur's hermeneutical approach has allowed an appropriation of the *Cántico* for the reading subject today. We have seen that a hermeneutical approach to the *Cántico* does not merely ask the question, "What does the text mean?" but also asks, "What does the text mean for the reader today?" With this approach there is a shift away from the predominance of the ascetical-theological approach to interpretation which has sought to objectify the meaning of the *Cántico* within the interpretation Juan gave it in his commentary, to a hermeneutical approach to interpretation that views the meaning of the *Cántico* as an event in the life of a person. Therefore, the hermeneutical interpretation of the *Cántico* explains why the *Cántico* is capable of being the place of a transformative event before the Divine, and why a multiplicity of interpretations is possible. This is something Juan de la Cruz was sensitive to when he suggested in his Prologue to the commentary on the

Cántico that each person will benefit from the poem according to his or her own capacity. Ricoeur's hermeneutical theory has helped us understand how this is possible without losing sight of the doctrinal content of the poem.

Through the dialectic of explanation and understanding it is possible to unite within a single methodological approach the diverse ways that the *Cántico* of Juan de la Cruz has been received over the centuries. This is true even if the various approaches may be at odds with one another, or may produce conflicting results. This is possible since interpretation is viewed not only as the objectification of information but also as a way of being-in-the-world which results from the interplay of the experience of the reader, the history of the reception of the text, and the text-world of the *Cántico*. The dynamic interplay of the experience which the reader brings to the text and the text itself forms the world-of-the-text. Interpretation of the *Cántico* has therefore been viewed as the interplay of the discourse of the *Cántico* with that of the reader and the reception of the text over the centuries. This dynamic results in the reconfiguration of discourse in a life. A hermeneutical approach to the *Cántico* thus provides a role in interpretation for the experience which the reader brings before the text and the experience which is produced from within the text. Ricoeur's theory recognizes that interpretation of the *Cántico* does not take place outside the concrete circumstances of a life, nor outside the history of the reception of the *Cántico*, nor outside of the confines of the text itself.

The methodical moment of interpretation within the dialectic of explanation and understanding asks that the reader enter into the text of the *Cántico* in a more conscious way. All the various ways of studying the *Cántico* contribute toward an explanation of the text. For example, I have said that ascetical-theological studies orient the reader within the theological content of the *Cántico* while literary-textual studies provide a description of the poetic techniques operative within the *Cántico*. Through these studies the analytical moment of interpretation constructs the objective sense of the *Cántico*. The sense of the *Cántico* orients the reader toward the ultimate reference of the text. It is this dialectic of sense and reference within the dialectic of explanation and understanding which results in reconfiguration of a life, the ultimate project of interpretation.

In a particular way I have examined the split-reference of metaphorical discourse which accounts for the legitimation of the noetic content of the *Cántico* as well as the emergence of new meaning. The dogmatic content of the *Cántico* can therefore be accounted for without excluding the possibility of new readings of the *Cántico*. Metaphor, which uses ordinary language to construct linguistic models of reality, was seen as the tool, par excellence, which produces the what-is-not-yet in the world. The noema or thing-of-the-text is made present through metaphorical reference and therefore the thing-of-the-text cannot be eclipsed by dogmatic formulations.

In the hermeneutical approach to put the "issue of the text" before everything else is to stop asking the question of the inspiration of the *Cántico*, at least in the psychological sense, as a "flash" of personal meaning which is projected into the text. The world-of-the-text is not revealed by the psychological intentions of the author but is mediated by the structures of the work.

A hermeneutical interpretation of Juan's *Cántico* has helped us understand the originality of the text of the *Cántico*, even though, intertextually, the *Cántico* interacts with the *Song of Songs*, as well as other texts, in the production of meaning. Ricoeur's theory of sedimentation and innovation suggests that the *Cántico* is a new configuration of human action which has been born from within a particular life, a particular *lebenswelt*. We can therefore speak more of Juan's conceptual and symbolic *fields of resources* than we can speak of his *sources*. The use of the word "sources" suggests a more static approach to Juan's poetic resources which, in the end, does not account for the surplus of meaning which Juan's *Cántico* has enjoyed in Christian as well as non-Christian traditions.

The hermeneutical interpretation of Juan's *Cántico* suggests that neither *Cántico A* nor *Cántico B* be given priority in interpretation. Each of these two texts construct their own meaning since the dramatic structure of each is different. The suggestion that *CA* be considered the poetic text, while *CB* be considered the theological text, becomes irrelevant in this approach. Both texts are unique poetic texts which open up unique text-worlds as was suggested by the difference in the dramatic structure of each text. There also arose the possibility that the original poem, which I have referred to as *Cántico O*, may also construct a different world-of-the-text than either *CA* or *CB*. Although I outlined an analysis of the dramatic structure of each of these three texts, I suggested that a more thorough structural analysis needs to be done in order to surface more clearly the unique text-world which each constructs. A structural analysis might also reveal the possibility that the three *Cánticos* are ultimately in metaphorical tension with each other and it is the three texts, together, which construct a singular and unique text-world.

The hermeneutical approach to interpretation has put the enigmatic expressions of the *Cántico* to work, suggesting that temporal and poetic incongruencies in the *Cántico* are the very devices which are at work in the production of new meaning. Temporal zones of indetermination or lacunae in the text are viewed as that which plays on the reader to involve the reader in finishing the text. The text of the *Cántico* was therefore not viewed as a life-less objectifiable object but rather as a living entity that becomes productive through the appropriation of the text. The enigmatic expressions and movements in the *Cántico* do not need to be explained away, but rather appreciated for the unpredictable role they play in the production of new meaning and the transformation of the reading subject.

Within the hermeneutical approach to interpretation, I have also proposed that the title of the *Cántico* plays a role in constructing metaphorical reference which in turn impacts the meaning of the text. This has led me to suggest that the title which appears at the top of the poem in the Sanlúcar and Jaén manuscripts: *Canciones entre el alma y el esposo* be used as the title for the poem rather than the editorial title of 1630: *Cántico espiritual entre el alma y Cristo su Esposo*. This title was later shortened to the present title *Cántico espiritual*.

The poetry-prose relationship has also been reassessed within the hermeneutical approach to Juan's *Cántico*. Poetic discourse (the poem) and speculative discourse (the commentary) are two radically different forms of discourse. The commentary draws from a single referential field, that is, it draws from the conceptual field of discourse. However, poetic or metaphorical discourse works within two semantic fields simultaneously: within the conceptual as well as the poetic. Metaphorical reference forms the bridge between Juan's poem and his commentary. The poem is capable of being productive of noetic content but the reader must continually return back to the primordial text to "think some more." Hermeneutical interpretation of Juan's poem continually returns us to the world-of-the-text to interpret new models of being-in-the-world. New referents are opened up in the *Cántico* because of the interchange between conceptual and poetic discourse. The hermeneutical interpretation of the *Cántico* suggests a cyclical understanding of the poem which is never complete. The *Cántico* is, therefore, freed from an overdependence on the commentary which tends to interpret the poem allegorically.

The commentary, within the hermeneutical approach, is not viewed as an unpacking of the poem, a paraphrase in conceptual language of the poetic form. The commentary is not a description of the meaning of the *Cántico* itself but is a particular reception of the poem. However, it is not the only possible reception. There are other ways of receiving the poem. The *Cántico*, therefore, is opened up to new meaning because of the primacy given to the poem. The commentary may be viewed as a secondary form of discourse which helps us understand the poem but does not eclipse the poem's metaphorical referential function. Both the poem and the commentary, since they are different literary forms, require their own mode of reception. I have suggested that an aesthetic reception of the *Cántico* is most appropriate because of its poetic form and all that implies.

Within a hermeneutical setting Juan the poet and Juan the theologian can abide comfortably with one another without incongruence or opposition. The hermeneutical approach is seen by Ricoeur as bridging the gap between the poet and the theologian: the poetic gives rise to thought. Within a hermeneutical setting these two functions, the poetic and the speculative, have been assigned complementary roles. The poet who invents a particular model of reality also discovers that which can be known about that reality. This dynamic turns the reflexive subject back to explore further within the poetic or metaphorical sphere.

A hermeneutical interpretation of the *Cántico* explained how the profane or secular language of the *Cántico* can result in the conversion of the spiritual pilgrim. Ricoeur's theory of appropriation has helped us understand why an aesthetic reading of the *Cántico* brings alive the transformative power of the text. The *Cántico* affects the reader through the production of mood. Mood brings the reader into contact with the deeper elements of reality. Mood characterizes reality before the object-subject split which occurs through conceptualization.

I have suggested that the most significant impact of Juan's poem may be its ontological import. From Juan's poem we construct new ways of being-in-the-world. Authentic existence is displayed in the world-of-the-text of the *Cántico*. What is the meaning of existence portrayed as a loving dialogue between two lovers? Although the reception of the *Cántico* at the level of its ontological import cannot be controlled, the various moods sketched in the *Cántico* suggest certain questions which may help us understand its ontological import. For example, I asked the question, "If appropriation of the *Cántico* is of a sexual nature, what does this say about all of our relationships, that is, with God, with our world, with others, and with ourselves?" Questions like these may open up the world-of-the-*Cántico* to new meaning.

The hermeneutical approach also suggests further areas for exploration. Some of these I have touched on during the course of the dissertation but they could be further investigated from a hermeneutical perspective. Areas for further study from within the hermeneutical framework I have constructed in this dissertation might include: exploration of the relationship of Juan's *Cántico* to the *Song of Songs*, using the concept of innovation and sedimentation; a study on the zones of indetermination and lacunae in the text of the *Cántico* which mediate meaning; a study of the temporal movements within the three *Cánticos* and the metaphorical tension they produce; further exploration of the genre of the *Cántico* as a form of production (rather than a classification) particularly with respect to its relationship to medieval love poetry and wasfs; and a thorough structural analysis of all three *Cánticos*.

Of singular importance this dissertation has established the primacy of the text of the poem for interpretation. It is the *Cántico* itself which holds hermeneutical priority. A *Global Hermeneutical Method* shifts methodological considerations from an author-centred reading of the *Cántico* to a text-centred reading. With a hermeneutical approach Juan de la Cruz's *Canciones entre el alma y el esposo* can be brought from the sixteenth century into the twentieth century in order to continue their dynamic transformative potential.

APPENDIX

CANCIONES ENTRE EL ALMA Y EL ESPOSO

by

Juan de la Cruz

The Spanish text is the critical edition of José Vicente RODRÍGUEZ, *San Juan de la Cruz: Obras Completas,* 3rd edition.

The English text is the critical translation of Kieran KAVANAUGH, and Otilio Rodriguez, *The Collected Works of St. John of the Cross,* rev. edition.

In presenting *CO, CA,* and *CB* in English I have used as a sole source the translation cited above even though it does not present *CO* or *CA* as separate texts. Using the redactional changes which I outlined in Chapter Five I worked backwards from *CB* to reconstruct *CA* and subsequently *CO.* Since the Spanish edition gives both *CA* and *CB* I used the first 31 stanzas of *CA* to construct the Spanish text of *CO.*

Three translation changes have been made in *CO* with the corresponding changes in both *CA* and *CB*:

1. Kavanaugh and Rodriquez translate *ninfas* into "girls" in their *Collected Works* (Kav., 474). However, I have used the English word "nymphs" as does the Spanish. This change in translation is important since it is the role played by this mythological semi-divine maiden which brings *CO* to its conclusion as was shown in the analysis of Chapter Five. Although "girls" is an acceptable translation of *ninfas* into English, it destroys the function stanza 31 holds as the "completing" stanza of *CO;*

2. Kavanaugh and Rodriguez translate *carillo* in *CO* 32 as "my love" in their *Collected Works* (Kav., 474). However, given the sequence of diminuitives

378

that follow in response in stanza 33, and the fact that *carillo* itself is the diminutive in Spanish, a more acceptable translation, it seems to me, would be "dear" or "dearest one." Therefore, I have used "dearest one" in the translation in my own text.

3. Kavanaugh and Rodriguez translate *canciones* (which is used in the title above the poem in the Sanlúcar de Barrameda and Jaén manuscripts) as "stanzas." I have translated *canciones* into "songs" as does Allison E. Peers in his *The Complete Works of Saint John of the Cross, Doctor of the Church.*

CÁNTICO O

CANCIONES ENTRE EL ALMA Y EL ESPOSO	SONGS BETWEEN THE SOUL AND THE BRIDEGROOM
ESPOSA	BRIDE

1. ¿ Adónde te escondiste,
Amado, y me dejaste con gemido?
Como el ciervo huiste,
habiéndome herido,
salí tras ti clamando, y eras ido.

2. Pastores los que fuerdes
allá por las majadas al otero,
si por ventura vierdes
Aquel que yo más quiero,
decilde que adolezco, peno y muero.

3. Buscando mis amores
iré por esos montes y riberas,
ni cogeré las flores
ni temeré las fieras
y pasaré los fuertes y fronteras.

4. ¡ Oh bosques y espesuras
plantadas por la mano del Amado!
¡Oh prado de verduras
de flores esmaltado!
¡Decid se por vosotros ha pasado!

1. Where have you hidden,
Beloved, and left me moaning?
You fled like the stag
after wounding me;
I went out calling you, but you were gone.

2. Shepherds, you who go
up through the sheepfolds to the hill,
if by chance you see
him I love most,
tell him I am sick, I suffer, and I die.

3. Seeking my Love
I will head for the mountains and for watersides,
I will not gather flowers,
nor fear wild beasts;
I will go beyond strong men and frontiers.

4. O woods and thickets,
planted by the hand of my Beloved!
O green meadow,
coated, bright, with flowers,
tell me, has he passed by you?

5. Mil gracias derramando
pasó por estos sotos con presura
y yéndolos mirando
con sola su figura
vestidos los dejó de hermosura.

6. ¡ Ay, quién podrá sanarme?
¡ Acaba de entregarte ya de vero;
no quieras enviarme
de hoy más ya mensajero
que no saben decirme lo que quiero!

7. Y todo cuantos vagan
de ti me van mil gracias refiriendo
y todo más me llagan
y déjame muriendo
un   no   sé   qué   que   quedan
balbuciendo.

8. Mas ¿cómo perseveras,
¡oh vid!, no viviendo donde vives
y haciendo porque mueras
las flechas que recibes
de lo que del Amado en ti concibes?

9. ¿Por qué, pues has llagado
aqueste corazón, no le sanaste?
Y pues me le has robado,
¿por qué así le dejaste,
y no tomas el robo que robaste?

10. ¡Apaga mis enojos,
pues   que   ninguno   basta   a
deshacellos,
y véante mis ojos,
pues eres lumbre dellos
y sólo para ti quiero tenellos!

11. ¡Oh cristalina fuente,
si en esos tus semblantes plateados
formases de repente
los ojos deseados
que tengo en mis entrañas dibujados!

5. Pouring out a thousand graces,
he passed these groves in haste;
and having looked at them,
with his image alone,
clothed them in beauty.

6. Ah, who has the power to heal me?
now wholly surrender yourself!
Do not send me
any more messengers,
they cannot tell me what I must hear.

7. All who are free
tell me a thousand graceful things of you;
all wound me more
and leave me dying
of, ah, I-don't-know-what   behind   their
stammering.

8. How do you endure
O life, not living where you live,
and being brought near death
by the arrows you receive
from that which you conceive of your
Beloved?

9. Why, since you wounded
this heart, don't you heal it?
And why, since you stole it from me,
do you leave it so,
and fail to carry off what you have stolen?

10. Extinguish these miseries,
since no one else can stamp them out;
and may my eyes behold you,
because you are their light,
and I would open them to you alone.

11. O spring like crystal!
If only, on your silvered-over faces,
you would suddenly form
the eyes I have desired,
which I bear sketched deep within my heart.

12. ¡Apártalos, Amado, que voy de vuelo!	12. Withdraw them, Beloved, I am taking flight!

ESPOSO

BRIDEGROOM

¡Vuélvete, paloma, que el ciervo vulnerado por el otero asoma al aire de tu vuelo, y fresco toma!	Return, dove, the wounded stag is in sight on the hill, cooled by the breeze of your flight.

ESPOSA

BRIDE

13. Mi Amado las montañas los valles solitarios nemorosos las ínsulas extrañas los ríos sonorosos el silbo de los aires amorosos	13. My Beloved, the mountains, and lonely wooded valleys, strange islands, and resounding rivers, the whistling of love-stirring breezes,
14. la noche sosegada en par de los levantes del aurora la música callada la soledad sonora la cena que recrea y enamora.	14. the tranquil night at the time of the rising dawn, silent music, sounding solitude, the supper that refreshes, and deepens love.
15. Nuestro lecho florido de cuevas de leones enlazado en púrpura tendido en paz edificado de mil escudo de oro coronado.	15. Our bed is in flower, bound round with linking dens of lions, hung with purple, built up in peace, and crowned with a thousand shields of gold.
16. A zaga de tu huella los jóvenes discurren al camino al toque de centella al adobado vino, emisiones de bálsamo divino.	16. Following your footprints maidens run along the way; the touch of a spark, the spiced wine, cause flowings in them from the balsam of God.
17. En la interior bodega de mi Amado bebí, y cuando salía por toda aquesta vega ya cosa no sabía y el ganado perdí que antes seguía.	17. In the inner wine cellar I drank of my Beloved, and, when I went abroad through all this valley I no longer knew anything, and lost the herd that I was following.

18. Allí me dio su pecho
allí me enseñó ciencia muy sabrosa
y yo le di de hecho
a mí, sin dejar cosa;
allí le prometí de ser su esposa.

19. Mi alma se ha empleado
y todo mi caudal en su servicio,
ya no guardo ganado
ni ya tengo otro oficio
que ya sólo en amar es mi ejercicio.

20. Pues ya si en el ejido
de hoy más no fuere vista ni hallada,
diréis que me he perdido,
que, andando enamorada,
me hice perdidiza y fui ganada.

21. De flores y esmeraldas
en las frescas mañanas escogidas
haremos las guirnaldas
en tu amor floridas
y en un cabello mío entretejidas.

22. En solo aquel cabello
que en mi cuello volar consideraste
mirástele en mi cuello
y en él preso quedaste
y en uno de mis ojos te llagaste.

23. Cuando tú me mirabas,
su gracia en mí tus ojos imprimían:
por eso me adamabas
y en eso merecían
los míos adorar lo que en ti vían.

24. No quieras despreciarme,
que, si color moreno en mí hallaste,
ya bien puedes mirarme
después que me miraste,
que gracia y hermosura en mí
dejaste.

18. There he gave me his breast;
there he taught me a sweet and living
knowledge;
and I gave myself to him,
keeping nothing back;
there I promised to be his bride.

19. Now I occupy my soul
and all my energy in his service;
I no longer tend the herd,
nor have I any other work
now that my every act is love.

20. If, then, I am no longer
seen or found on the common,
you will say that I am lost;
that, stricken by love,
I lost myself, and was found.

21. With flowers and emeralds
chosen on cool mornings
we shall weave garlands
flowering in your love,
and bound with one hair of mine.

22. You considered
that one hair fluttering at my neck;
you gazed at it upon my neck
and it captivated you;
and one of my eyes wounded you.

23. When you looked at me
your eyes imprinted your grace in me;
for this you loved me ardently;
and thus my eyes deserved
to adore what they beheld in you.

24. Do not despise me;
for if, before, you found me dark,
now truly you can look at me
since you have looked
and left in me grace and beauty.

25. Cogednos las raposas
que está ya florecida nuestra viña,
en tanto que de rosas
hacemos una piña
y no parezca nadie en la montiña.

25. Catch us the foxes,
for our vineyard is now in flower,
while we fashion a cone of roses
intricate as the pine's;
and let no one appear on the hill.

26. Detente, cierzo muerto;
ven, austro que recuerdas los amores,
aspira por mi huerto
y corran sus olores
y pacerá el Amado entre las flores.

26. Be still, deadening north wind;
south wind, come, you that waken love,
breathe through my garden,
let its fragrance flow,
and the Beloved will feed amid the flowers.

ESPOSO

BRIDEGROOM

27. Entrado se ha la esposa
en el ameno huerto deseado
y a su sabor reposa
el cuello reclinado
sobre los dulces brazos del Amado.

27. The bride has entered
the sweet garden of her desire,
and she rests in delight,
laying her neck
on the gentle arms of her Beloved.

28. Debajo del manzano
allí conmigo fuiste desposada,
allí te di la mano
y fuiste reparada
donde tu madre fuera violada.

28. Beneath the apple tree:
there I took you for my own,
there I offered you my hand,
and restored you,
where your mother was corrupted.

29. A las aves ligeras,
leones, ciervos, gamos saltadores,
montes, valles, riberas,
aguas, aires, ardores,
y miedos de las noches veladores:

29. Swift-winged birds,
lions, stags, and leaping roes,
mountains, lowlands, and river banks,
waters, winds, and ardors,
watching fears of night:

30. por las amenas liras
y canto de sirenas os conjuro
que cesen vuestras iras
y no toquéis al muro
porque la esposa duerma más seguro.

30. By the pleasant lyres
and the siren's song, I conjure you
to cease your anger
and not touch the wall,
that the bride may sleep in deeper peace.

31. ¡Oh ninfas de Judea!,
en tanto que en las flores y rosales
el ámbar perfumea,
morá en los arrabales,
y no queráis tocar nuestros umbrales.

31. You nymphs of Judea,
while among flowers and roses
the amber spreads its perfume,
stay away, there on the outskirts:
do not so much as seek to touch our

thresholds.

CÁNTICO A

CANCIONES ENTRE EL ALMA Y *EL ESPOSO*	*SONGS BETWEEN THE SOUL* *AND THE BRIDEGROOM*
ESPOSA	BRIDE

1. ¿ Adónde te escondiste,
Amado, y me dejaste con gemido?
Como el ciervo huiste,
habiéndome herido,
salí tras ti clamando, y eras ido.

1. Where have you hidden,
Beloved, and left me moaning?
You fled like the stag
after wounding me;
I went out calling you, but you were gone.

2. Pastores los que fuerdes
allá por las majadas al otero,
si por ventura vierdes
Aquel que yo más quiero,
decilde que adolezco, peno y muero.

2. Shepherds, you who go
up through the sheepfolds to the hill,
if by chance you see
him I love most,
tell him I am sick, I suffer, and I die.

3. Buscando mis amores
iré por esos montes y riberas,
ni cogeré las flores
ni temeré las fieras
y pasaré los fuertes y fronteras.

3. Seeking my Love
I will head for the mountains and for
watersides,
I will not gather flowers,
nor fear wild beasts;
I will go beyond strong men and frontiers.

4. ¡ Oh bosques y espesuras
plantadas por la mano del Amado!
¡Oh prado de verduras
de flores esmaltado!
¡Decid se por vosotros ha pasado!

4. O woods and thickets,
planted by the hand of my Beloved!
O green meadow,
coated, bright, with flowers,
tell me, has he passed by you?

5. Mil gracias derramando
pasó por estos sotos con presura
y yéndolos mirando
con sola su figura
vestidos los dejó de hermosura.

5. Pouring out a thousand graces,
he passed these groves in haste;
and having looked at them,
with his image alone,
clothed them in beauty.

6. ¡ Ay, quién podrá sanarme?
¡ Acaba de entregarte ya de vero;

6. Ah, who has the power to heal me?
now wholly surrender yourself!

no quieras enviarme
de hoy más ya mensajero
que no saben decirme lo que quiero!

Do not send me
any more messengers,
they cannot tell me what I must hear.

7. Y todo cuantos vagan
de ti me van mil gracias refiriendo
y todo más me llagan
y déjame muriendo
un no sé qué que quedan balbuciendo.

7. All who are free
tell me a thousand graceful things of you;
all wound me more
and leave me dying
of, ah, I-don't-know-what behind their stammering.

8. Mas ¿cómo perseveras,
¡oh vid!, no viviendo donde vives
y haciendo porque mueras
las flechas que recibes
de lo que del Amado en ti concibes?

8. How do you endure
O life, not living where you live,
and being brought near death
by the arrows you receive
from that which you conceive of your Beloved?

9. ¿Por qué, pues has llagado
aqueste corazón, no le sanaste?
Y pues me le has robado,
¿por qué así le dejaste,
y no tomas el robo que robaste?

9. Why, since you wounded
this heart, don't you heal it?
And why, since you stole it from me,
do you leave it so,
and fail to carry off what you have stolen?

10. ¡Apaga mis enojos,
pues que ninguno basta a deshacellos,
y véante mis ojos,
pues eres lumbre dellos
y sólo para ti quiero tenellos!

10. Extinguish these miseries,
since no one else can stamp them out;
and may my eyes behold you,
because you are their light,
and I would open them to you alone.

11. ¡Oh cristalina fuente,
si en esos tus semblantes plateados
formases de repente
los ojos deseados
que tengo en mis entrañas dibujados!

11. O spring like crystal!
If only, on your silvered-over faces,
you would suddenly form
the eyes I have desired,
which I bear sketched deep within my heart.

12. ¡Apártalos, Amado,
que voy de vuelo!

12. Withdraw them, Beloved,
I am taking flight!

ESPOSO

BRIDEGROOM

¡Vuélvete, paloma,
que el ciervo vulnerado

Return, dove,
the wounded stag

por el otero asoma
al aire de tu vuelo, y fresco toma!

is in sight on the hill,
cooled by the breeze of your flight.

ESPOSA

BRIDE

13. Mi Amado las montañas
los valles solitarios nemorosos
las ínsulas extrañas
los ríos sonorosos
el silbo de los aires amorosos

13. My Beloved, the mountains,
and lonely wooded valleys,
strange islands,
and resounding rivers,
the whistling of love-stirring breezes,

14. la noche sosegada
en par de los levantes del aurora
la música callada
la soledad sonora
la cena que recrea y enamora.

14. the tranquil night
at the time of the rising dawn,
silent music,
sounding solitude,
the supper that refreshes, and deepens love.

15. Nuestro lecho florido
de cuevas de leones enlazado
en púrpura tendido
en paz edificado
de mil escudo de oro coronado.

15. Our bed is in flower,
bound round with linking dens of lions,
hung with purple,
built up in peace,
and crowned with a thousand shields of gold.

16. A zaga de tu huella
los jóvenes discurren al camino
al toque de centella
al adobado vino,
emisiones de bálsamo divino.

16. Following your footprints
maidens run along the way;
the touch of a spark,
the spiced wine,
cause flowings in them from the balsam of God.

17. En la interior bodega
de mi Amado bebí, y cuando salía
por toda aquesta vega
ya cosa no sabía
y el ganado perdí que antes seguía.

17. In the inner wine cellar
I drank of my Beloved, and, when I went abroad
through all this valley
I no longer knew anything,
and lost the herd that I was following.

18. Allí me dio su pecho
allí me enseñó ciencia muy sabrosa
y yo le di de hecho
a mí, sin dejar cosa;
allí le prometí de ser su esposa.

18. There he gave me his breast;
there he taught me a sweet and living knowledge; and I gave myself to him,
keeping nothing back;
there I promised to be his bride.

19. Mi alma se ha empleado

19. Now I occupy my soul

y todo mi caudal en su servicio,
ya no guardo ganado
ni ya tengo otro oficio
que ya sólo en amar es mi ejercicio.

and all my energy in his service;
I no longer tend the herd,
nor have I any other work
now that my every act is love.

20. Pues ya si en el ejido
de hoy más no fuere vista ni hallada,
diréis que me he perdido,
que, andando enamorada,
me hice perdidiza y fui ganada.

20. If, then, I am no longer
seen or found on the common,
you will say that I am lost;
that, stricken by love,
I lost myself, and was found.

21. De flores y esmeraldas
en las frescas mañanas escogidas
haremos las guirnaldas
en tu amor floridas
y en un cabello mío entretejidas.

21. With flowers and emeralds
chosen on cool mornings
we shall weave garlands
flowering in your love,
and bound with one hair of mine.

22. En solo aquel cabello
que en mi cuello volar consideraste
mirástele en mi cuello
y en él preso quedaste
y en uno de mis ojos te llagaste.

22. You considered
that one hair fluttering at my neck;
you gazed at it upon my neck
and it captivated you;
and one of my eyes wounded you.

23. Cuando tú me mirabas,
su gracia en mí tus ojos imprimían:
por eso me adamabas
y en eso merecían
los míos adorar lo que en ti vían.

23. When you looked at me
your eyes imprinted your grace in me;
for this you loved me ardently;
and thus my eyes deserved
to adore what they beheld in you.

24. No quieras despreciarme,
que, si color moreno en mí hallaste,
ya bien puedes mirarme
después que me miraste,
que gracia y hermosura en mí
dejaste.

24. Do not despise me;
for if, before, you found me dark,
now truly you can look at me
since you have looked
and left in me grace and beauty.

25. Cogednos las raposas
que está ya florecida nuestra viña,
en tanto que de rosas
hacemos una piña
y no parezca nadie en la montiña.

25. Catch us the foxes,
for our vineyard is now in flower,
while we fashion a cone of roses
intricate as the pine's;
and let no one appear on the hill.

26. Detente, cierzo muerto;
ven, austro que recuerdas los amores,

26. Be still, deadening north wind;
south wind, come, you that waken love,

aspira por mi huerto	breathe through my garden,
y corran sus olores	let its fragrance flow,
y pacerá el Amado entre las flores.	and the Beloved will feed amid the flowers.

<table>
<tr><td>ESPOSO</td><td>BRIDEGROOM</td></tr>
</table>

27. Entrado se ha la esposa	27. The bride has entered
en el ameno huerto deseado	the sweet garden of her desire,
y a su sabor reposa	and she rests in delight,
el cuello reclinado	laying her neck
sobre los dulces brazos del Amado.	on the gentle arms of her Beloved.

28. Debajo del manzano	28. Beneath the apple tree:
allí conmigo fuiste desposada,	there I took you for my own,
allí te di la mano	there I offered you my hand,
y fuiste reparada	and restored you,
donde tu madre fuera violada.	where your mother was corrupted.

29. A las aves ligeras,	29. Swift-winged birds,
leones, ciervos, gamos saltadores,	lions, stags, and leaping roes,
montes, valles, riberas,	mountains, lowlands, and river banks,
aguas, aires, ardores,	waters, winds, and ardors,
y miedos de las noches veladores:	watching fears of night:

30. por las amenas liras	30. By the pleasant lyres
y canto de sirenas os conjuro	and the siren's song, I conjure you
que cesen vuestras iras	to cease your anger
y no toquéis al muro	and not touch the wall,
porque la esposa duerma más seguro.	that the bride may sleep in deeper peace.

31. ¡Oh ninfas de Judea!,	31. You nymphs of Judea,
en tanto que en las flores y rosales	while among flowers and roses
el ámbar perfumea,	the amber spreads its perfume,
morá en los arrabales,	stay away, there on the outskirts:
y no queráis tocar nuestros umbrales.	do no so much as seek to touch our thresholds.

32. Escóndete, Carillo,	32. Hide yourself, dearest one;
y mira con tu haz a las montañas	turn your face toward the mountains,
y no quieras decillo,	and do not speak;
mas mira las compañas	but look at those companions
de la que va por ínsulas extrañas.	going with her through strange islands.

ESPOSO	BRIDEGROOM

33. La blanca palomica
al arca con el ramo se ha tornado
y ya la tortolica
al socio deseado
en las riberas verdes ha hallado.

33. The small white dove
has returned to the ark with an olive branch;
and now the turtledove
has found its longed-for mate
by the green river banks.

34. En soledad vivía
y en soledad ha puesto ya su nido
y en soledad la guía
a solas su querido
también en soledad de amor herido.

34. She lived in solitude,
and now in solitude has built her nest;
and in solitude he guides her,
he alone, who also bears
in solitude the wound of love.

ESPOSA	BRIDE

35. Gocémonos, Amado, y
vámonos a ver en tu hermosura
al monte y al collado
do mana el agua pura;
entremos más adentro en la espesura,

35. Let us rejoice, Beloved, and
let us go forth to behold ourselves in your
beauty,
to the mountain and to the hill,
to where the pure water flows,
and further, deep into the thicket.

36. y luego a las subidas
cavernas de la piedra nos iremos,
que están bien escondidas,
y allí nos entraremos
y el mosto de granadas gustaremos.

36. And then we will go on
to the high caverns in the rock
which are so well concealed;
there we shall enter
and taste the fresh juice of the pomegranates.

37. Allí me mostrarías
aquello que mi alma pretendía
y luego me darías
allí, tú, ¡vida mía!
aquello que me diste el otro día:

37. There you will show me
what my soul has been seeking,
and then you will give me,
you, my life, will give me there
what you gave me on that other day:

38. el aspirar del aire
el canto de la dulce filomena
el soto y su donaire
en la noche serena
con llama que consume y no da pena.

38. the breathing of the air,
the song of the sweet nightingale,
the grove and its living beauty
in the serene night,
with a flame that is consuming and painless.

39. Que nadie lo miraba,
Aminadab tampoco parecía
y el cerco sosegaba

39. No one looked at her,
nor did Aminadab appear;
the siege was still;

y la caballería	and the cavalry,
a vista de las aguas descendía.	at the sight of the waters, descended.

CÁNTICO B

CANCIONES ENTRE EL ALMA Y EL ESPOSO	*SONGS BETWEEN THE SOUL AND THE BRIDEGROOM*
ESPOSA	BRIDE

1. ¿ Adónde te escondiste,	1. Where have you hidden,
Amado, y me dejaste con gemido?	Beloved, and left me moaning?
Como el ciervo huiste,	You fled like the stag
habiéndome herido,	after wounding me;
salí tras ti clamando, y eras ido.	I went out calling you, but you were gone.
2. Pastores los que fuerdes	2. Shepherds, you who go
allá por las majadas al otero,	up through the sheepfolds to the hill,
si por ventura vierdes	if by chance you see
Aquel que yo más quiero,	him I love most,
decilde que adolezco, peno y muero.	tell him I am sick, I suffer, and I die.
3. Buscando mis amores	3. Seeking my Love
iré por esos montes y riberas,	I will head for the mountains and for watersides,
ni cogeré las flores	I will not gather flowers,
ni temeré las fieras	nor fear wild beasts;
y pasaré los fuertes y fronteras.	I will go beyond strong men and frontiers.
4. ¡ Oh bosques y espesuras	4. O woods and thickets,
plantadas por la mano del Amado!	planted by the hand of my Beloved!
¡Oh prado de verduras	O green meadow,
de flores esmaltado!	coated, bright, with flowers,
¡Decid se por vosotros ha pasado!	tell me, has he passed by you?
5. Mil gracias derramando	5. Pouring out a thousand graces,
pasó por estos sotos con presura	he passed these groves in haste;
y yéndolos mirando	and having looked at them,
con sola su figura	with his image alone,
vestidos los dejó de hermosura.	clothed them in beauty.
6. ¡ Ay, quién podrá sanarme?	6. Ah, who has the power to heal me?

¡ Acaba de entregarte ya de vero;
no quieras enviarme
de hoy más ya mensajero
que no saben decirme lo que quiero!

now wholly surrender yourself!
Do not send me
any more messengers,
they cannot tell me what I must hear.

7. Y todo cuantos vagan
de ti me van mil gracias refiriendo
y todo más me llagan
y déjame muriendo
un   no   sé   qué   que   quedan
balbuciendo.

7. All who are free
tell me a thousand graceful things of you;
all wound me more
and leave me dying
of, ah, I-don't-know-what behind their
stammering.

8. Mas ¿cómo perseveras,
¡oh vid!, no viviendo donde vives
y haciendo porque mueras
las flechas que recibes
de lo que del Amado en ti concibes?

8. How do you endure
O life, not living where you live,
and being brought near death
by the arrows you receive
from that which you conceive of your
Beloved?

9. ¿Por qué, pues has llagado
aqueste corazón, no le sanaste?
Y pues me le has robado,
¿por qué así le dejaste,
y no tomas el robo que robaste?

9. Why, since you wounded
this heart, don't you heal it?
And why, since you stole it from me,
do you leave it so,
and fail to carry off what you have stolen?

10. ¡Apaga mis enojos,
pues   que   ninguno   basta   a
deshacellos, y véante mis ojos,
pues eres lumbre dellos
y sólo para ti quiero tenellos!

10. Extinguish these miseries,
since no one else can stamp them out;
and may my eyes behold you,
because you are their light,
and I would open them to you alone.

11. ¡Descubre tu presencia,
y máteme tu vista y hermosura;
mira que la dolencia
de amor, que no se cura
sino con la presencia y la figura!

11. Reveal your presence,
and may the vision of your beauty be my
death; for the sickness of love
is not cured
except by your very presence and image.

12. ¡Oh cristalina fuente,
si en esos tus semblantes plateados
formases de repente
los ojos deseados
que tengo en mis entrañas dibujados!

12. O spring like crystal!
If only, on your silvered-over faces,
you would suddenly form
the eyes I have desired,
which I bear sketched deep within my heart.

13. ¡Apártalos, Amado,

13. Withdraw them, Beloved,

que voy de vuelo!	I am taking flight!

ESPOSO

BRIDEGROOM

¡Vuélvete, paloma,
que el ciervo vulnerado
por el otero asoma
al aire de tu vuelo, y fresco toma!

Return, dove,
the wounded stag
is in sight on the hill,
cooled by the breeze of your flight.

ESPOSA

BRIDE

14. Mi Amado las montañas
los valles solitarios nemorosos
las ínsulas extrañas
los ríos sonorosos
el silbo de los aires amorosos

14. My Beloved, the mountains,
and lonely wooded valleys,
strange islands,
and resounding rivers,
the whistling of love-stirring breezes,

15. la noche sosegada
en par de los levantes del aurora
la música callada
la soledad sonora
la cena que recrea y enamora.

15. the tranquil night
at the time of the rising dawn,
silent music,
sounding solitude,
the supper that refreshes, and deepens love.

16. Cazadnos las raposas,
que está ya florecida nuestra viña,
en tanto que de rosas
hacemos una piña,
y no parezca nadie en la montiña.

16. Catch us the foxes,
for our vineyard is now in flower,
while we fashion a cone of roses
intricate as the pine's;
and let no one appear on the hill.

17. Detente, cierzo muerto;
ven, austro, que recuerdas los
amores, aspira por me huerto
y corran tus olores
y pacerá el Amado entre las flores.

17. Be still, deadening north wind;
south wind, come, you that waken love,
breathe through my garden,
let its fragrance flow,
and the Beloved will feed amid the flowers.

18. ¡Oh ninfas de Judea!,
en tanto que en las flores y rosales
el ámbar perfumea,
morá en los arrabales,
y no queráis tocar nuestros umbrales.

18. You nymphs of Judea,
while among flowers and roses
the amber spreads its perfume,
stay away, there on the outskirts:
do not so much as seek to touch our
thresholds.

19. Escóndete, Carillo,
y mira con tu haz a las montañas

19. Hide yourself, dearest one;
turn your face toward the mountains,

y no quieras decillo,	and do not speak;
mas mira las compañas	but look at those companions
de la que va por ínsulas extrañas.	going with her through strange islands.

ESPOSO   BRIDEGROOM

20. A las aves ligeras,	20. Swift-winged birds,
leones, ciervos, gamos saltadores,	lions, stags, and leaping roes,
montes, valles, riberas,	mountains, lowlands, and river banks,
aguas, aires, ardores	waters, winds, and ardors,
y miedos de las noches veladores:	watching fears of night:

21. por las amenas liras	21. By the pleasant lyres
y canto de sirenas os conjuro	and the siren's song, I conjure you
que cesen vuestras iras	to cease your anger
y no toquéis al muro	and not touch the wall,
porque la esposa duerma más seguro.	that the bride may sleep in deeper peace.

22. Entrádoes ha la esposa	22. The bride has entered
en el ameno huerto deseado	the sweet garden of her desire,
y a su sabor reposa	and she rests in delight,
el cuello reclinado	laying her neck
sobre los dulces brazos del Amado.	on the gentle arms of her Beloved.

23. Debajo del manzano	23. Beneath the apple tree:
allí conmigo fuiste desposada,	there I took you for my own,
allí te di la mano	there I offered you my hand,
y fuiste reparada	and restored you
donde tu madre fuera violada.	where your mother was corrupted.

ESPOSA   BRIDE

24. Nuestro lecho florido	24. Our bed is in flower,
de cuevas de leones enlazado	bound round with linking dens of lions,
en púrpura tendido	hung with purple,
en paz edificado	built up in peace,
de mil escudo de oro coronado.	and crowned with a thousand shields of gold.

25. A zaga de tu huella	25. Following your footprints
los jóvenes discurren al camino	maidens run along the way;
al toque de centella	the touch of a spark, the spiced wine,
al adobado vino,	cause flowings in them from the balsam of
emisiones de bálsamo divino.	God.

26. En la interior bodega
de mi Amado bebí, y cuando salía
por toda aquesta vega
ya cosa no sabía
y el ganado perdí que antes seguía.

27. Allí me dio su pecho
allí me enseñó ciencia muy sabrosa
y yo le di de hecho
a mí, sin dejar cosa;
allí le prometí de ser su esposa.

28. Mi alma se ha empleado
y todo mi caudal en su servicio,
ya no guardo ganado
ni ya tengo otro oficio
que ya sólo en amar es mi ejercicio.

29. Pues ya si en el ejido
de hoy más no fuere vista ni hallada,
diréis que me he perdido,
que, andando enamorada,
me hice perdidiza y fui ganada.

30. De flores y esmeraldas
en las frescas mañanas escogidas
haremos las guirnaldas
en tu amor floridas
y en un cabello mío entretejidas.

31. En solo aquel cabello
que en mi cuello volar consideraste
mirástele en mi cuello
y en él preso quedaste
y en uno de mis ojos te llagaste.

32. Cuando tú me mirabas,
su gracia en mí tus ojos imprimían:
por eso me adamabas
y en eso merecían
los míos adorar lo que en ti vían.

26. In the inner wine cellar
I drank of my Beloved, and, when I went
abroad
through all this valley
I no longer knew anything,
and lost the herd that I was following.

27. There he gave me his breast;
there he taught me a sweet and living
knowledge; and I gave myself to him,
keeping nothing back;
there I promised to be his bride.

28. Now I occupy my soul
and all my energy in his service;
I no longer tend the herd,
nor have I any other work
now that my every act is love.

29. If, then, I am no longer
seen or found on the common,
you will say that I am lost;
that, stricken by love,
I lost myself, and was found.

30. With flowers and emeralds
chosen on cool mornings
we shall weave garlands
flowering in your love,
and bound with one hair of mine.

31. You considered
that one hair fluttering at my neck;
you gazed at it upon my neck
and it captivated you;
and one of my eyes wounded you.

32. When you looked at me
your eyes imprinted your grace in me;
for this you loved me ardently;
and thus my eyes deserved
to adore what they beheld in you.

33. No quieras despreciarme,
que, si color moreno en mí hallaste,
ya bien puedes mirarme
después que me miraste,
que gracia y hermosura en mí
dejaste.

33. Do not despise me;
for if, before, you found me dark,
now truly you can look at me
since you have looked
and left in me grace and beauty.

ESPOSO

BRIDEGROOM

34. La blanca palomica
al arca con el ramo se ha tornado
y ya la tortolica
al socio deseado
en las riberas verdes ha hallado.

34. The small white dove
has returned to the ark with an olive branch;
and now the turtledove
has found its longed-for mate
by the green river banks.

35. En soledad vivía
y en soledad ha puesto ya su nido
y en soledad la guía
a solas su querido
también en soledad de amor herido.

35. She lived in solitude,
and now in solitude has built her nest;
and in solitude he guides her,
he alone, who also bears
in solitude the wound of love.

ESPOSA

BRIDE

36. Gocémonos, Amado, y
vámonos a ver en tu hermosura
al monte y al collado
do mana el agua pura;
entremos más adentro en la espesura,

36. Let us rejoice, Beloved, and
let us go forth to behold ourselves in your
beauty,
to the mountain and to the hill,
to where the pure water flows,
and further, deep into the thicket.

37. y luego a las subidas
cavernas de la piedra nos iremos,
que están bien escondidas,
y allí nos entraremos
y el mosto de granadas gustaremos.

37. And then we will go on
to the high caverns in the rock
which are so well concealed;
there we shall enter
and taste the fresh juice of the pomegranates.

38. Allí me mostrarías
aquello que mi alma pretendía
y luego me darías
allí, tú, ¡vida mía!
aquello que me diste el otro día:

38. There you will show me
what my soul has been seeking,
and then you will give me,
you, my life, will give me there
what you gave me on that other day:

39. el aspirar del aire
el canto de la dulce filomena

39. the breathing of the air,
the song of the sweet nightingale,

el soto y su donaire
en la noche serena
con llama que consume y no da pena.

40. Que nadie lo miraba,
Aminadab tampoco parecía
y el cerco sosegaba
y la caballería
a vista de las aguas descendía.

the grove and its living beauty
in the serene night,
with a flame that is consuming and painless.

40. No one looked at her,
nor did Aminadab appear;
the siege was still;
and the cavalry,
at the sight of the waters, descended.

BIBLIOGRAPHY

A. Primary Sources

i. Spanish Editions

Cántico espiritual: Primera redacción y testó retocado, Introduction, editing and notes by Eulogio Pacho, Clásicos Olvidados 4, Madrid: Fundación Universitaria Española, 1981.

Cántico espiritual y poesías de san Juan de la Cruz según el códice de Sanlúcar de Barrameda, ed. Silverio de Santa Teresa, 2 vols., Burgos: El Monte Carmelo, 1928.

CRISÓGONO DE JESÚS SACRAMENTADO, *Vida y obras de San Juan de la Cruz*, Prologue, introductions, revisions with notes by Lucinio del SS. Sacramento, Biblioteca de Autores Cristianos 15, Section IV: Ascetica y mistica, Madrid: La Editorial Católica, 1946.

Obras del místico doctor san Juan de la Cruz, ed. Gerardo de San Juan de la Cruz, 3 vols., Toledo: J. Peláez, 1912-1914.

Obras de San Juan de la Cruz, ed. and notes Silverio de Santa Teresa, 5 vols., Biblioteca Mística Carmelitana 10-15, Burgos: El Monte Carmelo, 1929-31.

San Juan de la Cruz: Obras Completas, ed. José Vicente Rodríguez, Introduction and doctrinal notes by Federico Ruiz Salvador, 3rd edition, Madrid: Editorial de Espiritualidad, 1988.

San Juan de la Cruz: Obras Completas, ed. Eulogio Pacho, Burgos: Editorial Monte Carmelo, 1982.

ii. English Translations

The Collected Works of St. John of the Cross, trans. Kieran Kavanaugh and Otilio Rodriguez, Revisions and Introductions by Kieran Kavanaugh, Revised edition, Washington: Institute of Carmelite Studies, 1991.

398

PEERS, E. Allison, *The Complete Works of Saint John of the Cross, Doctor of the Church*, trans. and ed. E. Allison Peers from the critical edition of Silverio de Santa Teresa, 3 volumes in one, 1st edition 1935, Wheathampstead, England: Anthony Clarke, 1974.

B. Bibliographies and Reference

Concordancias de las obras y escritos del doctor de la Iglesia San Juan de la Cruz, ed. Luis de San José, Burgos: El Monte Carmelo, 1948.

PÉPIN, Fernande, *Saint Jean de la Croix: Bibliographie et état présent des travaux*, Doctoral Dissertation presented at the University of Laval, Québec, typewritten copy, January 1968.

OTTONELLO, Pier Paolo, *Bibliografia de san Juan de la Cruz*, Rome: Teresianum, 1967-1969.

The following periodical publications annually collate the bibliography in sanjuanist studies: *Carmelus* (Rome: 1954 -); *Archivum Biliographicum Carmelitanum* (Rome: 1956 -); and *Bibliographia Internationalis Spiritualitatis* (Rome: 1966 -).

C. Biographies

BRUNO DE JÉSUS-MARIE, *Saint Jean de la Croix*, with a Preface by Jacques Maritain, Revised and corrected from the 1929 edition, Paris: Plon, 1948.

CRISÓGONO DE JESÚS SACRAMENTADO, *Vida de San Juan de la Cruz*, Revised and annotated by Matía del Niño Jesús, 1st edition 1946, 11th edition, Biblioteca de Autores Cristianos 435, Madrid: Editorial Católica, 1982.

HARDY, Richard P., *Search for Nothing: The Life of St. John of the Cross*, New York: Crossroads Publishing Co., 1982.

JERÓNIMO DE SAN JOSÉ [EZQUERRA], *Historia del venerable padre Fr. Juan de la Cruz, primer descalzo carmelita, compañero y coajutor de santa Teresa de Jesús en le fundación de la Reforma*, Madrid: 1641.

JOSÉ DE JESÚS MARIA [Quiroga], *Historia de la vida y virtudes del Venerable P. Fray Juan de la Cruz Primer Religiosa de la Reformacion de los descalzos de Nuestra Senora del Carmen con Declaracion de los Grados de la vida contemplativa por donde N.S. le levanto a una rara perfección en estado de destierro. Y del singular don, que tuvo para enseñar la sabiduría divina que transforma las almas en Dios*, Brussels: Ivan de Meerbeeck, 1628.

D. Studies on the *Canciones entre el alma y el esposo*

BENOÎT-MARIE DE L'EUCHARISTIE, "Le Cantique spirituel selon Tomás Luis de Victoria," *Carmel* 59 (1990), 50-61.

CHEVALLIER, Phillipe, *Le "Cantique spirituel" de saint Jean de la Croix*, Bruges, Belgium: Desclée de Brouwer & Cie, 1930.

--------------------, "Le 'Cantique spirituel' de saint Jean de la Croix a-t-il été interpolé?" *Bulletin hispanique* 24 (1922), 307-342.

--------------------, "Le Cantique spirituel interpolé," *Vie Spirituelle* (Supplements) 14 (1926) 109-62; 15 (1927) 69-109; 22 (1930) 1-11, 80-9; 23 (1931) 29-50.

--------------------, "Deux textes du Cantique spirituel," *Vie Spirituelle* 25 (1932), 274-86.

--------------------, "La vie du 'Cantique spirituel' et l'esprit scientifique," *Études Carmelitaines* 23, no. 1 (1939), 215-236.

--------------------, *Saint Jean de la Croix: Le texte définitif du Cantique spirituel*, (Solesmes, 1951).

DUVIVIER, Roger, *Le Dynamisme existentiel dans la poésie de Jean de la Croix: Lecture du «Cántico Espiritual»*, Études de littérature étrangère et comparée, Paris: Didier, 1973.

--------------, *La genèse du «Cantique spirituel» de Saint Jean de la Croix*, Bibliothèque de la Faculté de Philosophie et Lettres de l'Université de Liège, Fasc. 189, Paris: Société d'Édition "Les Belles Lettres," 1971.

GUILLÉN, José, "La Poética en el 'Cántico espiritual'," *Revista de Espiritualidad* 1 (1942), 438-447.

HATZFELD, Helmet A. "Sobre la Prosa Sanjuanista en el 'Cántico Espiritual'," in *Estudios literarios sobre mística española*, 3rd edition, Biblioteca Románica Hispánica II, Estudios y ensayos 16, Madrid: Gredos, 1976, 306-317.

HAUSSIÉTTRE, M.A., "Du Cantique des Cantiques au Cantique Spirituel," *Carmel*

400

56 (1991), 28-45.

ICAZA, Rosa Maria, *The Stylistic Relationship Between Poetry and Prose in the Cántico espiritual of San Juan de la Cruz*, The Catholic University of America Studies in Romance Languages and Literatures 54, New York: AMS Press, 1969.

KRYNEN, Jean, *Le Cantique spirituel de saint Jean de la Croix commenté et refondu au XVIIe siècle: Un regard sur l'histoire de l'exégèse du cantique de Jaén*, Salamanca, Universidad de Salamanca, 1948.

MORALES, José L., *El Cántico espiritual de San Juan de la Cruz: su relación con el Cantar de los Cantares y otras fuentes escrituristicas y literarias*, Madrid: Editorial de Espiritualidad, 1971.

MARLAY, Peter, *On Structure and Symbol in the "Cántico Espiritual"*, Gredos: 1972.

PACHO, Eulogio, *El Cántico espiritual: Trayectoria histórica del texto*, Bibliotheca Carmelitica, Series II: Studia, vol. 7, Rome: Desclée, 1967.

-------------- [de la V. del Carmen], "La Clave exegetica del 'Cántico espiritual'," *Ephemerides Carmeliticae* 9 (1958), 307-337.

-------------, "La cuestión crítica del '*Cántico espiritual*': Nota bibliográfica," *El Monte Carmelo* 65 (1957), 309-323.

-------------, *Iniciación a S. Juan de la Cruz*, Collección Karmel 11, Burgos: Editorial Monte Carmelo, 1982.

-------------, "*El primer Cántico espiritual*" de san Juan de la Cruz: Introducción crítica y síntesis doctrinal, Doctoral Dissertation, Rome: Facultad Teológica del Colegio Internacional, o.c.d., 1957-1958.

-------------, "Lenguaje y Mensaje," in *Experiencia y pensamiento en San Juan de la Cruz*, ed. Federico Ruiz [Salvador], Madrid: Editorial de Espiritualidad, 1990, 53-81.

-------------, "Un Manuscrito famoso del 'Cántico Espiritual': Las notas del códice de Sanlúcar de Barrameda y su valor crítico," *El Monte Carmelo* 62 (1954), 155-203.

-------------, "El 'Prologo' y la hermeneutica del 'Cántico Espiritual'," *El Monte Carmelo* 66 (1958), 3-108.

------------, "La Estructura literaria del «Cántico Espiritual»," *El Monte Carmelo* 68 (1960), 383-414.

------------, "El «Cántico espiritual» retocado: Introducción a su problemática textual," *Ephemerides Carmeliticae* 27 (1976), 382-452.

------------, "Noemática e interpretación del «Cántico Espiritual»: Poesía y teología," *Teresianum* 40 (1989), 337-362.

------------, "Primeras Ediciones del Cántico Espiritual," *Ephemerides Carmeliticae* 18 (1967), 3-48.

------------, *San Juan de la Cruz y sus escritos*, Teologia y Siglo XX 10, Madrid: Ediciones Cristiandad, 1969.

------------, *San Juan de la Cruz: Temas fundamentales*, 2 vols., Burgos: Editorial Monte Carmelo, 1984.

------------, *Vértice de la poesía y de la mística: El «Cántico espiritual» de San Juan de la Cruz*, Estudios Monte Carmelo 4, Burgos: Editorial Monte Carmelo, 1983.

PÉPIN, Fernande, *Noces de Feu: Le Symbolisme nuptial du "Cántico espiritual" de saint Jean de la Croix à la lumière du "Canticum Canticorum"*, Recherches 9 Théologie, Montréal: Bellarmin, 1972.

PIKAZA, Xabier, "Introduccion al Cántico Espiritual: Anotaciones filosófico-teológicas," *Cuadernos Salmantinos de Filosofía* 18 (1991), 185-217.

TAVARD, Georges H., *Poetry and Contemplation in St. John of the Cross*, Athens: Ohio University, 1988.

THOMPSON, Colin P., *The Poet and the Mystic: A Study of the Cántico Espiritual of San Juan de la Cruz*, Oxford modern languages and literature monographs, Oxford: Oxford University Press, 1977.

E. Studies on the Poetry of Juan de la Cruz

ALONSO, Damaso, *La poesía de san Juan de la Cruz: Desde esta ladera*, Madrid: Consejo Superior de Investigaciones Científicas, Instituto Antonio de Nebrija, 1942.

------------, *Poesía Española: Ensayo de metodos y limites estilisticos*, 2nd edition, Biblioteca Romanica Hispanica II. Estudios y Ensayos, Madrid: Editorial Gredos,

402

1952.

--------------, *De Los siglos oscuros al de oro: Notas y artículos a través de 700 años de letras españolas*, 2nd edition, Biblioteca Románica Hispánica 7, Campoabierto 14, Madrid: Editorial Gredos, 1964, 271-293.

BOBES NAVES, María del Carmen, "La lírica de San Juan de la Cruz," *El Monte Carmelo* 98 (1990), 311-345.

BOUSOÑO, Carlos, "San Juan de la Cruz, poeta 'contemporáneo'," in *Teoria de la expresión poética*, 2 vols., 5th edition, Biblioteca Románica Hispánica, Madrid: Editorial Gredos, 1970, 1:280-302.

BRENAN, Gerald, *St. John of the Cross: His Life and Poetry*, Cambridge: Cambridge University Press, 1973.

DE NICOLÁS, Antonio T., *St. John of the Cross: Alchemist of the Soul*, with a Forward by Seyyed Hossein Nasr, New York: Paragon House, 1989.

DIEGO, Gerardo, "La Naturaleza y la inspiración poética en San Juan de la Cruz," *Revista de Espiritualidad* 27 (1968), 311-319.

SETIÉN, Emeterio G., "Las raíces de la poesía sanjuanista y Damaso Alonso," *El Monte Carmelo*, (April -September 1950), 149-265.

GARCÍA NIETO, José, "La Poesía de San Juan de la Cruz," *Revista de Espiritualidad* 27 (1968), 320-334.

GUILLÉN, Jorge, "The Ineffable Language of Mysticism: San Juan de la Cruz," in *Language and Poetry: Some Poets of Spain*, trans. Stephen Gilman and Ruth Whittredge, Cambridge, Mass.: Harvard University Press, 1961, 79-121.

JOSE BAYO, Marcial, "Aspecto lírico de San Juan de la Cruz," *Revista de Espiritualidad* 1 (1941-42), 300-308.

LOZOYA, Marqués de, "El Valor literario del 'Cántico espiritual' de San Juan de la Cruz," *Revista de Espiritualidad* 1 (1942), 4-9.

LUCIEN-MARIE DE ST.-JOSEPH, "Expérience mystique et expression symbolique chez saint Jean de la Croix," in *Polarité du Symbole*, Études Carmélitaines, Bruges: Desclée de Brouwer, 1960, 29-51.

MILNER, Max, *Poésie et vie mystique chez Saint Jean de la Croix*, with a Preface by Jean Baruzi, La Vigne du Carmel, Paris: Seuil, 1951.

OROZCO DIAZ, Emilio, *Poesía y mística: Introducción a la lírica de S. Juan de la Cruz*, Madrid, 1955.

F. Sanjuanist Studies - Various

Actas del Congreso Internacional Sanjuanista, 3 vols.: I Filología, II Historia, III Pensamiento, Prepared by: Centro Internacional Teresiano-Sanjuanist de Avila, Valladolid: Junta de Castilla y León, Consejería de Cultura y Turismo, 1993.

ADOLFO DE LA MADRE DE DIOS, "Estado y acto de contemplación: la contemplación adquirida, segun San Juan de la Cruz," *Revista de Espiritualidad* 8, no. 30-31 (1949), 96-126.

AHERN, Barnabas, "The Use of Scripture in the Spiritual Theology of St. John of the Cross," *Catholic Biblical Quarterly* 14 (1952), 6-17.

ARRAJ, James, *Christian Mysticism in the Light of Jungian Psychology: John of the Cross and Dr. C.G. Jung*, Chiloquin, OR: Tools for Inner Growth, 1986.

BALTHASAR, Hans Urs von, "John of the Cross," in *The Glory of the Lord III Studies in Theological Style: Lay States*, ed. John Riches, trans. from German by Andrew Louth, Francis McDonagh and Brian McNeil, San Francisco: Ignatius Press, 1984, 105-171.

BATAILLON, Marcel, *Erasme et l'Espagne: Recherches sur l'histoire spirituelle du XVIᵉ siècle*, Paris: E. Droz, 1937.

BENEDICTINE OF STANBROOK ABBEY, *Mediæval Mystical Tradition and Saint John of the Cross*, London: Burns & Oates, 1954.

BERNARD, Charles A., "L'influence de saint Jean de la Croix sur Sainte Thérèse de l'Enfant-Jésus," *Revue d'Ascétique et de Mystique* 32 (1956), 69-80.

BLANCHARD, Pierre, "Sainte Thérèse de l'Enfant-Jésus fille de saint Jean de la Croix," *L'Année Theologique* 8 (1947), 425-438.

-----------------, "Le Père de Foucauld, fils de saint Jean de la Croix," *Carmel* 1 (1959), 15-26.

BORD, André, *Mémoire et espérance chez Jean de la Croix*, with a Preface by Henri Gouhier, Bibliothèque de Spiritualité 8, Paris: Beauchesne, 1971.

BOUILLARD, Henri, "La 'sagesse mystique' selon Saint Jean de la Croix,"

404

Recherches de Science Religieuse 50 (1962), 483-529.

BRÄNDLE, Francisco de, *Biblia en San Juan de la Cruz*, Logos 39, Madrid: Editorial de Espiritualidad, 1990.

BRITO, Emilio, "Pour une logique de la Création: Hegel et Saint Jean de la Croix," *Nouvelle Revue Théologique* 106 (1984), 493-512.

CLAUDIO DE JESÚS CRUCIFICADO, "Originalidad de la doctrina mística de San Juan de la Cruz," *El Monte Carmelo* 39 (1935), 353-361; 403-407; 496-503.

COOMBS, Marie Theresa and Francis Kelly Nemeck, *O Blessed Night: Recovering From Addiction, Codependency and Attachment Based on the Insights of St. John of the Cross and Pierre Teilhard de Chardin*, New York: Alba House, 1991.

CRISÓGONO DE JESÚS SACRAMENTADO, *San Juan de la Cruz, su obra científica y su obra literaria*, 2 vols., Madrid: Editorial Mensajero de santa Teresa y de san Juan de la Cruz, 1929.

CUEVAS, Cristóbol, "La prosa sanjuanista," *El Monte Carmelo* 98 (1990), 347-377.

DE HORNEDO, Rafael M.ª, "El Humanismo de San Juan de la Cruz," *Razón y Fe* 129 (1944), 133-150.

DICKEN, E.W. Trueman, *The Crucible of Love: A Study of the Mysticism of St. Teresa of Jesus and St. John of the Cross*, New York: Sheed and Ward, 1963.

DOMINGUEZ, Carlos, *Contrafactum as Allegory*, Ph.D. Thesis, Standford University, 1983.

DONAZAR, Anselmo A., *Fray Juan de la Cruz: El hombre de las insulas extrañas*, Burgos: Editorial Monte Carmelo, 1985.

D'ORS, Eugenio, "Estilo del pensamiento de San Juan de la Cruz," *Revista de Espiritualidad* 1 (1941-42), 241-254.

EULOGIO DE SAN JUAN DE LA CRUZ, *La transformación total del alma en Dios según San Juan de la Cruz*, Extract from doctoral dissertation presented in the Faculty of Theology at the Pontifical University of Salamanca, Madrid: Editorial de Espiritualidad, 1963.

FITZGERALD, Constance, "A Discipleship of Equals: Voices from the Tradition--Teresa of Avila and John of the Cross," in *A Discipleship of Equals: Towards a Christian Feminist Spirituality*, ed. Francis A. Eigo, Villanova, PA: Villanova

University Press, 1988, 63-97.

FRANÇOIS DE SAINTE-MARIE, *Initiation à saint Jean de la Croix*, Paris: Seuil, 1944.

FUMET, Stanislaus, *Saint Jean de la Croix: Docteur de l'Eglise*, Lyon: 1942.

GARCIA, Felix, o.s.a., "San Juan de la Cruz y la Biblia," *Revista de Espiritualidad* 1 (July-December 1942), 372-388.

GARCIA MUÑOZ, Florencio, *Cristologia de San Juan de la Cruz: Sistemática y Mística*, Madrid: Universidad Pontificia de Salamanca, Fundación Universitaria Española, 1982.

GARCÍA SIMÓN, A., ed., *Introducción a la lectura de San Juan de la Cruz*, Valladolid: Junta de Castilla y León Consejería de Cultura y Turismo, 1991. Includes: Cristóbal CUEVAS, "Estudio literario," 125-201; Cristóbol CUEVAS, "La poesía de san Juan de la Cruz," 283-313;

GARRIGOU-LAGRANGE, Réginald, *Perfection chrétienne et contemplation selon saint Thomas d'Aquin et saint Jean de la Croix*, 2 vols., Paris: Editions de la Vie Spirituelle, 1923.

GAUDREAU, Marie, M., *Mysticism and Image in St. John of the Cross*, European University Studies, Series 23 Theology, Vol. 66, (Europäische Hochschulschriften. Reihe xxiii. Theologie: Band 66), Frankfurt a.M/New York: P. Lang, 1976.

GREGORIO DE JESÚS CRUCIFICADO, "Las noches sanjuanistas vividas por santa Teresa del Niño Jesús," *Ephemerides Carmeliticae* 11 (1960), 352-382.

HARDY, Richard, P., "Early Biographical Documentation on Juan de la Cruz," *Science et Esprit* 30 (1978), 313-23.

------------------, "The Hidden God and Juan de la Cruz (1542-1591)," *Ephemerides Carmeliticae* 27 (1976), 241-262.

------------------, "Liberation Theology and Saint John of the Cross: A Meeting," *Église et Théologie* 20 (1989), 259-282.

------------------, "San Juan de la Cruz (1542-1591): A Personality Sketch," *Ephemerides Carmeliticae* 29 (1978), 507-518.

------------------, "'Silencio Divino': A Sanjuanist Study," *Église et Théologie* 7 (1976), 219-233.

406

HERRERA, R.A., *Saint John of the Cross: Introductory Studies*, Madrid: Editorial de Espiritualidad, 1968.

JÉROME DE LA MÈRE DE DIEU, *La Doctrine du Carmel d'après Saint Jean de la Croix*, 2 vols., Vienne: Carmel de Vienne, 1959-1961.

JIMÉNEZ DUQUE, Baldomero, "La perfección cristiana y San Juan de la Cruz," *Revista Española de Teología* 9, no. 2 (1949), 413-443.

-----------------------, "Problemas místicos en torno a la figura de san Juan de la Cruz," *Revista Española de Teología* 1 (1941), 963-983.

KAVANAUGH, Kieran, "Spanish Sixteenth Century: Carmel and Surrounding Movements," in *Christian Spirituality III: Post Reformation and Modern*, ed. Louis Dupré and Don Saliers, World Spirituality: An Encyclopedic History of the Religious Quest 18, New York: Crossroad, 1989, 69-92.

LONGCHAMP, Max Huot de, *Lectures de Jean de la Croix: Essai d'Anthropologie Mystique*, ed. Charles Kannengiesser, with a Preface by Albert Deblaere, Théologie Historique 62, Paris: Beauchesne, 1981.

LUEVANO, Andres Rafael, *Endless Transforming Love: An Interpretation of the Mystical Doctrine of Saint John of the Cross According to the Soul's Affective Relation and Dynamic Structure*, Vacare Deo 9, Rome: Institutum Carmelitanum, 1990.

LUCIEN-MARIE DE ST. JOSEPH, *L'expérience de Dieu: Actualité du message de saint Jean de la Croix*, Paris, 1968.

MAY, Gerald, "Lightness of Soul: From Addiction Toward Love in John of the Cross," *Spiritual Life* 37 (Fall 1991), 139-147.

McCANN, Leonard A., *The Doctrine of the Void: The Doctrine of the Void as Propounded by St. John of the Cross in his Major Prose Works as Viewed in the Light of Thomistic Principles*, Rochester: Basilian Press, 1955.

MUÑOZ, Florencio Garcia, *Cristologia de San Juan de la Cruz*, Madrid: Universidad Pontificia de Salamanca, 1982.

NOVAK, P. C., *Empty Willing: Contemplative Being in the World in St. John of the Cross and Dogen*, Ph.D. Thesis, Syracuse University, 1981.

PALACIOS, Miguel Asín, *Saint John of the Cross and Islam*, trans. Howard W. Yoder and Elmer H. Douglas, New York: Vantage Press, 1981.

--------, "Un précurseur hispano-musulman de saint Jean de la Croix," *Études Carmélitaines* 1 (1932), 113-167.

PEERS, E. Allison, *Spirit of Flame: A Study of St. John of the Cross*, London: Student Christian Movement Press, 1944.

RACCAT, Marie-Antoinette, *Transcendance de dieu et relation au monde en Jean de la Croix et Dietrich Bonhoeffer*, Avrillé: Éditions du Carmel, 1974.

ROMÁN DE LA INMACULADA, "¿Es quietista la contemplación enseñada por san Juan de la Cruz?," *Revista de Espiritualidad* 8, no. 30-31 (1949), 127-155.

RUIZ SALVADOR, Federico, *Introducción a San Juan de la Cruz: El escritor, los escritos, el sistema*, Biblioteca de Autores Cristianos 279, Madrid: Editorial Católica, 1968.

RUIZ SALVADOR, Federico, *San Giovanni della Croce: iniziazione*, Rome: Teresianum, 1977.

RUIZ [SALVADOR], Federico, ed., *Experiencia y pensamiento en San Juan de la Cruz*, Madrid: Editorial de Espiritualidad, 1990.

---------------, *Vida teologal durante la purificación interior en los escritos de San Juan de la Cruz*, (Madrid: 1959).

SANDERLINE, David, "Charity According to St. John of the Cross: A Disinterested Love for Interesting Special Relationships, Including Marriage," *The Journal of Religious Ethics* 21, no. 1 (Spring 1993), 87-115.

SIMEON DE LA SAGRADA FAMILIA, "Fuentes doctrinales y literarias de San Juan de la Cruz," *El Monte Carmelo* 69 (1961), 103-9.

SIX, Jean-Francois, *Is God endangered by believers?: A critical study of the gap between religion and real faith*, Denville: Dimension Books, 1983.

VICENTE RODRIGUEZ, José, "Lectura varia sanjuanista," *Revista de Espiritualidad* 52 (1993), 285-323.

WELCH, John, *When Gods Die: An Introduction to John of the Cross*, New York: Paulist Press, 1990.

WILHELMSEN, Elizabeth, *Cognition and Communication in John of the Cross*, European University Studies, series 23 Theology, vol. 246, (Europäische Hochschulschriften. Reihe xxiii. Theologie: Band 246), Frankfurt a.M/New York:

408

P. Lang, 1985.

G. Philosophical Studies on Juan de la Cruz

BARUZI, Jean, *Saint Jean de la Croix et le problème de l'expérience mystique*, Paris: Librairie Félex Alcan, 1924.

JIMÉNEZ DUQUE, Baldomero, "Una interpretación moderna de San Juan de la Cruz," *Revista Española de Teología* 4 (1944), 315-344.

SÁNCHEZ DE MURILLO, José, "La Estructura del pensamiento de San Juan de la Cruz: Ensayo de Interpretación Fenomenologica," in *Experiencia y pensamiento en San Juan de la Cruz*, ed. Federico Ruiz [Salvador], Madrid: Editorial de Espiritualidad, 1990, 297-334.

LANGAN, E., *An Existential Analysis of St. John of the Cross*, Ph.D. Thesis, Northwestern University, Illinois, 1969.

MASSET, Pierre, "Que suis-je? Qui suis-je? Que sommes-nous? De Ricoeur à St. Jean de la Croix," *Filosofia Oggi* 57, no. 1 (January-March 1992), 31-46.

MOREL, Georges, "Nature et transformation de la volonté selon Saint Jean de la Croix," *Vie Spirituelle*, Supplement 10, (1957), 383-398.

-------------, *Le sens de l'existence selon Saint Jean de la Croix*, 3 vols., Théologie 45, 46, 47, Paris: Aubier, 1960-61.

NAZARIO DE SANTA TERESA, *Filosofia de la Mística: Análisis del Pensamiento Español*, Colección Scientia 8, Madrid: Ediciones Studium de Cultura, 1953, 118-216.

PAYNE, Steve, *John of the Cross and the Cognitive Value of Mysticism*, Norwell: Kluwer Academic Publications, 1990.

SANSON, Henri, *L'esprit humain selon saint Jean de la Croix*, Publications de la Faculté des Lettres d'Alger 22, Paris: Presses Universitaires de France, 1953.

STEIN, Edith, *The Science of the Cross: A Study of St. John of the Cross*, ed. L. Gelber and R. Leuven, trans. Hilda Graef, London: Burns & Oates, 1960.

H. Historical Studies

ADOLFO DE LA MADRE DE DIOS, "Espagne -- III. L'Age d'Or: 1. Généralités," in *Dictionnaire de Spiritualité*, vol. 4², Paris: Beauchesne: 1961, col. 1127-1146.

------------------------- and ROMÁN DE LA INMACULADA, "Espagne -- III. L'Age d'Or: 3. Déviations Spirituelles et Inquisition," in *Dictionnaire de Spiritualité*, vol. 4², Paris: Beauchesne: 1961, col. 1159-1167.

AGUIRRE, J.M., *José de Valdivielso y la poesía religiosa tradicional*, Toledo: Diputación Provincial, 1975.

ANDRÉS [MARTÍN], Melquiades, *La teología español en el siglo XVI*, 2 vols., Biblioteca de Autores Cristianos Serie maior 13 & 14, Madrid: Editorial Católica, 1976-77.

ANDRÉS [MARTÍN], Melquiades, "Pensamiento teologico y vivencia religiosa en la reforma española (1400-1600)," in *Historia de la Iglesia en Expaña III-2.° La Iglesia en la España de los siglos XV y XVI*, ed. Ricardo Garcia-Villoslada, Biblioteca de Autores Cristianos Serie maior 21, Madrid: Editorial Católica, 1980, 269-361.

ANDRÉS MARTÍN, Melquiades, "Teresa y Juan de la Cruz: Contribución al proceso de clarificación en la mística española," *Revista de Espiritualidad* 36 (1977), 481-91.

ANDRÉS MARTÍN, Melquiades, "La Teología española en el siglo XVI," *Revista Española de Teología*, 52 (1992), 129-153.

ANDRÉS MARTÍNEZ, Melquiades et al., eds., *Historia de la teologia española II Desde fines del siglo XVI hasta la actualidad*, Publicaciones de la Fundación Universitaria Española Monografias 38, Madrid: Fundación Universitaria Española, 1987.

BARUZI, Jean, "Le problème des citations scripturaires en langue latine dans l'œuvre de saint Jean de la Croix," *Bulletin hispanique* 24, no. 1, Bordeaux-Paris, (January-March, 1922), 18-40.

BELTRÁN DE HEREDIA, V., "Los alumbrados de la diócesis de Jaén," *Revista Española de Teologia* 9, no. 2 (1949), 161-222; 445-488.

BERNARD OF CLAIRVAUX, *On the Song of Songs*, trans. K. Walsh, Shannon: I.U.P., 1971.

BOUYER, Louis, "Mysticism: An Essay on the History of the Word," in *Understanding Mysticism*, ed. Richard Woods, Garden City, New York: Doubleday, 1980.

BOUYER, Louis, Dom Jean Leclercq, and Dom François Vandenbroucke, *A History of Christian Spirituality: II The Spirituality of the Middle Ages*, trans. The Benedictines of Holme Eden Abbey, Carlisle, London: Burns & Oates, 1968.

BRANDSMA, Titus, *Carmelite Mysticism: Historical Sketches*, Chicago: Carmelite Press, 1936.

BRAUDEL, Fernand, *The Mediterranean and the Mediterranean World in the Age of Phillip II*, 2 vols., trans. from french by Siân Reynolds, London: Collins, 1972.

BRUNO DE JÉSUS-MARIE, *L'Espagne mystique au 16e siècle*, Paris: 1946.

COGNET, Louis, "Mysticisme et Humanisme," in *Histoire de la Spiritualité Chrétienne III La Spiritualité Moderne*, Paris: Aubier, 1966, 39-70.

------------, "Saint Jean de la Croix," in *Histoire de la Spiritualité Chrétienne III La Spiritualité Moderne*, Paris: Aubier, 1966, 101-145.

COLOMBO, Dalmazio, "Alle origini del Cantico," in *Cantico dei Cantici*, Brescia: Editrice Queriniana, 1985, 23-37.

CRISÓGONO DE JESÚS SACRAMENTADO, *L'Ecole Mystique Carmélitaine*, trans. D. Vallois-del Real from the spanish *La escuela mística carmelitana*, (Madrid: Editorial Mensajero: 1930), Paris: Emmanuel Vitte, 1934.

Devotio moderna: Basic Writings, trans. and introduced by John Van Engen with a Preface by Heiko A. Oberman, New York: Paulist Press, 1988.

DIEGO SÁNCHEZ, Manuel, "La herencia patristica de San Juan de la Cruz," in *Experiencia y Pensamiento en San Juan de la Cruz*, ed. Federico Ruiz [Salvador], Madrid: Editorial de Espiritualidad, 1990, 83-111.

DUPRÉ, Louis and Don Saliers, eds., *Christian Spirituality III: Post-Reformation and Modern*, World Spirituality: An Encyclopedic History of the Religious Quest 18, New York: Crossroad, 1989.

ECO, Umberto, *Il problema estetico in Tommaso d'Aquino*, 2nd edition, Idee Nuove, Milano: Valeriano Bompiani, 1970, 39-68.

ENGAMMARE, Max, *Le Cantique des cantiques à la Renaissance: étude et bibliographie*, Genève: Droz, 1993.

ENRIQUE DEL SAGRADO CORAZON, "Espagne -- III. L'Age d'Or: 2. Courants Spirituels et Sources," in *Dictionnaire de Spiritualité*, vol. 4², Paris: Beauchesne: 1961, col. 1146-1159.

EVANS, Gillian Rosemary, *The Language and Logic of the Bible*, Cambridge: Cambridge University Press, 1984.

FALK, Marcia, "The *Wasf*," in *The Song of Songs*, ed. with an introduction by Harold Bloom, New York: Chelsea House Publishers, 1988, 67-78.

FIRPO, Massimo, *Tra Alumbrados e «Spirituali»: Studi su Juan de Valdes e il Valdesianesimi nella crisi religiosa del '500 Italiano*, Studi e Testi per la Storia Religiosa del Cinquecento 3, Florence: Leo S. Olschki, 1990.

FRIEDMAN, Elias, *The Latin Hermits of Mount Carmel: A Study in Carmelite Origins*, Institutum Historicum Teresianum, Studia I, Rome: Teresianum, 1979.

FROST, Bede, *Saint John of the Cross 1542-1591: An Introduction to his Philosophy, Theology and Spirituality*, London: Hodder & Stoughton, 1937.

GARCÍA SUÁREZ, German, "El pensamiento de san Juan de la Cruz en un clásico español del siglo XVII: Pedro Laserna," *Revista de Espiritualidad* 49 (1990), 599-606.

GONZÁLEZ NOVALÍN, José Luis, "La Inquisición Española," in *Historia de la Iglesia en Expaña III-2.º La Iglesia en la España de los siglos XV y XVI*, ed. Ricardo Garcia-Villoslada, Biblioteca de Autores Cristianos Serie maior 21, Madrid: Editorial Católica, 1980, 107-268.

GRANT, Robert M., *The Bible in the Church*, 4th edition (c1948), New York: Macmillan, 1960.

GRIGNON, Jacques, *Expérience mystique et contexte religio-culturel chez saint Jean de la Croix*, Louvain: Université Catholique de Louvain, 1983.

GROULT, P., *Les mystiques des Pays-Bas et la Littérature espagnole du XVI*, Louvain: 1927.

HOWE, T., *Tradition and Innovation in the Imagery of Santa Teresa and San Juan de la Cruz*, Ph.D. Thesis, Duke University, 1977.

412

----------, *Mystical Imagery: Santa Teresa de Jesus and San Juan de la Cruz*, American University Studies, Series 2: Romance Languages 76, New York: Peter Lang, 1988.

HUGHES, Philip, *The Church in the World the Church Made: From Augustine to Aquinas*, History of the Church 2, London: Sheed & Ward, 1961.

JEDIN, Hubert, *A History of the Council of Trent*, 2 vols., trans. from German by Don Ernest Graf, London: Thomas Nelson & Sons Ltd., 1957.

-------------, "Council of Trent" in *New Catholic Encyclopedia*, vol. 14, New York: McGraw-Hill, 1967, 271-278.

JIMÉNEZ DUQUE, Baldomero, "El problema mistico," *Revista Española de Teologia*, 2 (1942), 617-647.

-------------, *En torno a San Juan de la Cruz*, Colleción Remanso, Section IV, 8, Barcelona: Juan Flors, 1960.

JONES, Royston O., *The Golden Age: Prose and Poetry II The Sixteenth and Seventeenth Centuries*, A Literary History of Spain, London: E. Benn, 1971.

LEA, Henry Charles, *Chapters from the Religious History of Spain Connected With the Inquisition*, reprint of 1890 edition, Research & Source Work series 245; Selected Essay, History and Social Science 31, New York: Burt Franklin, 1967.

----------, *A History of the Inquisition of Spain*, 4 vols., New York: Macmillan, 1906-1908.

MATTER, E. Ann, *The Voice of My Beloved: The Song of Songs in Western Medieval Christianity*, Philadelphia: University of Pennsylvania Press, 1990.

MURPHY, Roland E., "The Structure of the Canticle of Canticles," *Catholic Biblical Quarterly*, 16 (1954), 381-391.

----------, *The Song of Songs: A Commentary on the Book of Canticles or the Song of Songs*, ed. S. Dean McBride, Hermeneia Commentary Series, Minneapolis: Fortress Press, 1990.

NIETO, José Constantino, *Juan de Valdes and the Origins of the Spanish and Italian Reformation*, Genève: Droz, 1970.

ORCIBAL, Jean, *Saint Jean de la Croix et les mystiques rhéno-flamands*, Présence du Carmel 6, Bruges: Desclée de Brouwer, 1966.

413

PAYNE, Steve, "The Influence of John of the Cross in the United States: A Preliminary Study," in *Carmelite Studies IV: John of the Cross*, ed. Steven Payne, Washington: I.C.S. Publications, 1992, 167-195.

PEERS, Allison, *Handbook to the Life and Times of Saint Teresa and Saint John of the Cross*, London: Burns and Oates, 1954.

----------------, "Notes on the Historical Problem of Castilian Mysticism," *Hispanic Review* 10 (1941), 18-33.

----------------, *St. John of the Cross and Other Lectures and Addresses*, London, Faber and Faber, 1946.

----------------, *Studies of the Spanish Mystics*, vol. 1, 2nd edition revised, New York: The Macmillan Co., 1951, 183-233.

POURRAT, Henri, *History of Christian Spirituality*, vol. 3, trans. from french by W.H. Mitchell, Jacques Attwater, and Donald Attwater of *La spiritualité chrétienne*, London: Burns, Oates & Washbourne, 1955.

RAITT, Jill et al., eds., *Christian Spirituality: II High Middle Ages and Reformation*, World Spirituality 17, New York: Crossroad, 1987.

ROBERT, A., "Le genre littéraire du Cantique des Cantiques," *Revue Biblique*, 52 (1943-44), 192-213.

ROMANUS RIOS, D., "The Canticle of Canticles Among the Early Discalced Carmelites," *Ephemerides Carmeliticae* 2 (1948), 305-313.

RUIZ [SALVADOR], Federico, ed., *Dios habla en la noche: Vida, palabra, ambiente de San Juan de la Cruz*, Madrid: Editorial de Espiritualidad, 1990.

SMET, Joachim, *The Carmelites: A History of the Brothers of Our Lady of Mount Carmel*, 3 vols., Darien, IL: Carmelite Spiritual Centre, 1975, 1976, 1982.

TAPIA, Ralph J., *The Alumbrados of Toledo*, Park Falls, Wisconsin: F.A. Weber & Sons, Inc., 1974.

VILNET, Jean, *Bible et mystique chex saint Jean de la Croix*, Paris: Desclée, 1949.

WALKER BYNUM, Caroline, *Jesus as Mother: Studies in the Spirituality of the High Middle Ages*, Berkeley: University of California Press, 1982.

414

I. Studies on Mysticism and Spirituality

ABHAYANANDA, Swami, *History of Mysticism: The Unchanging Testament*, Fallsburg, New York: Atma Books, 1987.

AUMANN, Jordan, Thomas Hopko, Donald Bloesch, *Christian Spirituality: East and West*, Institute of Spirituality Special Lectures 3, Chicago: Priory Press, 1968.

------, Jordan, *Christian Spirituality in the Catholic Tradition*, San Francisco: Ignatius Press, 1985.

BARUZI, Jean, *L'Intelligence Mystique*, ed. Jean-Louis Vieillard-Baron, Paris: Berg International, 1985.

Book of the Institution of the First Monks, trans. Bede Edwards, Boars Hill: Oxford, 1969.

CLAUDIO DE JESÚS CRUCIFICADO, "Aclarando posiciones acerca del 'concepto de mística sobrenatural': La naturaleza de la vida mística," *Revista Española de Teología* 9 (1949), 105-122.

BUTLER, Dom Cuthbert, *Western Mysticism*, New York: E.P. Dutton ,1924.

EWAR, Mary Anita, *A Survey of Mystical Symbolism*, London: Society For Promoting Christian Knowledge, 1933.

GRAEF, Hilda Charlotte, *The Story of Mysticism*, Garden City, New York: Doubleday, 1965.

HICK, John, "Mystical Experience as Cognition," in *Understanding Mysticism*, ed. Richard Woods, New York: Image Books, 1980, 422-448.

INGE, William Ralph, *Christian Mysticism*, 5th edition, The Bampton Lectures 1899, London: Methuen & Co., 1921.

KATSAROS, Thomas, and Nathaniel Kaplan, *The Western Mystical Tradition: An Intellectual History of Western Civilization*, 2 vols., New Haven: College & University Press, 1969.

KATZ, Steven T., "Language, Epistemology, and Mysticism," in *Mysticism and Philosophical Analysis*, ed. Steven T. Katz, New York: Oxford University Press, 1978, 22-74.

KRISTO, Jure, "The Interpretation of Religious Experience: What do Mystics

Intend When They Talk About Their Experiences?" *Journal of Religion* 62 (1982), 21-38.

LANE, Belden C. "Fierce Landscapes and the Indifference of God," *The Christian Century* 16, no. 29 (1989), 907-910.

LECLERCQ, Jean, *The Love of Learning and the Desire for God: A Study of Monastic Culture*, trans. Catharine Misrahi, 2nd edition, New York, Fordham University Press, 1974.

LOMBARDO, Domenico, "Gli stratti del testo e loro significato," in *La Regola del Carmelo oggi*, ed. Bruno Secondin, Rome: Edizioni Institutum Carmelitanum, 1983.

LOUTH, Andrew, "Patristic Mysticism and St. John of the Cross," in *The Origins of the Christian Mystical Tradition: From Plato to Denys*, Oxford: Clarendon Press, 1981, 179-190.

MALLORY, Marilyn May, *Christian Mysticism: Transcending Techniques: A Theological Reflection on the Empirical Testing of the Teaching of St. John of the Cross*, Assen: Van Gorcum, 1977.

MARITAIN, Raïssa, "Magic, Poetry, and Mysticism," in *The Situation of Poetry*, trans. Marshall Suther, New York: The Philosophical Library, 1955, 23-36.

MOORE, Peter, "Mystical Experience, Mystical Doctrine, Mystical Technique," in *Mysticism and Philosophical Analysis*, ed. Steven T. Katz, New York: Oxford University Press, 1978, 101-131.

------------, "Recent Studies of Mysticism: A Critical Survey," *Religion* (Autumn 1973), 146-156.

OTTO, Rudolph, *Mysticism East and West*, 2nd edition, New York: Macmillan Co., 1970.

PARENTE, P., "The Canticle of Canticles in Mystical Theology," *Catholic Biblical Quarterly* 6 (1944), 142-158.

ROYO MARÍN, Antonio, "El concepto de mística sobrenatural," *Revista Española de Teologia* 8 (1948), 59-79.

SHELDRAKE, Philip, *Spirituality and History: Questions of Interpretation and Method*, New York: Crossroad, 1992.

416

RAHNER, Karl, "Mysticism," in *Encyclopedia of Theology*, New York: Seabury, 1975, 1010-11.

SECONDIN, Bruno, ed., *La Regola del Carmelo: per una nuova interpretazione*, Quaderni di "Presenza del Carmelo" 5, Rome: Edizioni Institutum Carmelitanum, 1982.

STACE, Walter T., *Mysticism and Philosophy*, New York: Macmillan, 1960.

UNDERHILL, Evelyn, *Mysticism*, 1st edition 1911, New York: E.P. Dutton, 1961.

J. Paul Ricoeur and Related Studies

i) Primary Sources

RICOEUR, Paul, "Biblical Hermeneutics," *Semeia: Experimental Journal for Biblical Criticism* 4 (1975), 27-148.

------------, *The Conflict of Interpretations: Essays in Hermeneutics*, ed. Don Ihde, trans. Willis Domingo et al., Evanston: Northwestern University Press, 1974. Includes: "The Problem of Double Meaning as Hermeneutic Problem and as Semantic Problem," 62-78.

------------, "Esquisse de conclusion [at the Association catholique française pour l'étude de la Bible (A.C.F.E.B.) on 'Exégèse et herméneutique']," in *Exégèse et herméneutique*, ed. Xavier Léon-Dufour, Parole de Dieu, Paris: Seuil, 1971, 285-295.

------------, *Fallible Man*, trans. Charles A. Kelby, Chicago: Henry Regnery Co., 1965.

------------, *Freud and Philosophy: An Essay on Interpretation*, trans. Denis Savage, New Haven: Yale University Press, 1970.

------------, *From Text to Action: Essays in Hermeneutics II*, trans. Kathleen Blamey and John B. Thompson, Evanston: Northwestern University Press, 1991. Includes: "On Interpretation," 1-20; "Philosophical Hermeneutics and Biblical Hermeneutics," 89-101; "What is a Text? Explanation and Understanding," 105-124; "Explanation and Understanding," 125-143; "The Model of the Text: Meaningful Action Considered as a Text," 144-167.

------------, "Hermeneutics and the Critique of Ideology," in *The Hermeneutic Tradition: From Ast to Ricoeur*, ed. Gayle L. Ormiston and Alan d. Schrift, Albany: State University of New York Press, 1990, 298-334.

------------, *Hermeneutics and the Human Sciences*, ed., trans. and Introduction by John B. Thompson, Cambridge: Cambridge University Press, 1981. Includes: "The Hermeneutical Function of Distanciation," 131-144; "Metaphor and the Central Problem of Hermeneutics," 165-181; "Appropriation," 182-193.

------------, "The Hermeneutics of Testimony," *Anglican Theological Review* 51, no. 4 (October 1979), 435-461.

------------, *History and Truth*, trans. and Introduction by Charles A. Kelbley, Evanston: Northwestern University Press, 1965. Includes: "Objectivity and Subjectivity in History," 21-40.

------------, *Initiation à la pratique de la théologie: Tome 1 Introduction*, ed. Bernard Lauret and François Refoulé, Paris: Cerf, 1982.

------------, *Interpretation Theory: Discourse and the Surplus of Meaning*, Fort Worth: Texas Christian Press, 1974.

------------, "Naming God," *Union Seminary Quarterly Review* 34, no.4 (1979), 215-227.

------------, "Philosophical Hermeneutics and Theological Hermeneutics," *Studies in Religion* 5 (1975), 14-33.

------------, *The Philosophy of Paul Ricoeur: An Anthology of His Work*, ed. Charles Reagan and David Stewart, Boston: Beacon Press, 1978.

------------, "Philosophy and Religious Language," *Journal of Religion* 54 (1974), 71-85.

------------, *The Reality of the Historical Past*, Milwaukee: Marquette University Press, 1984.

------------, *A Ricoeur Reader: Reflection and Imagination*, ed. Mario J. Valdés, Theory/Culture 2, Toronto: University of Toronto Press, 1991. Includes: "Mimesis and Representation," 137-155; "Narrated Time," 338-354; "Between the Text and Its Readers," 390-424; "Life: A Story in Search of a Narrator," 425-437; "Poetry and Possibility," 448-462; "The Creativity of Language," 463-481.

------------, *The Rule of Metaphor: Multi-disciplinary Studies of the Creation of Meaning in Language*, trans. Robert Czerny with Cathleen McLaughlin and John Costello, Toronto: University of Toronto Press, 1977.

418

------------, *The Symbolism of Evil*, trans. Emerson Buchanan, New York: Harper and Row, 1967.

------------, "The Task of Hermeneutics" *Philosophy Today* 17 (1973), 112-128.

------------, *Time and Narrative*, vol. 1, trans. Kathleen McLaughlin and David Pellauer, Chicago: University of Chicago Press, 1984.

------------, *Time and Narrative*, vol. 2, trans. Kathleen McLaughlin and David Pellauer, Chicago: University of Chicago Press, 1985.

------------, *Time and Narrative*, vol. 3, trans. Kathleen Blamey and David Pellauer, Chicago: University of Chicago Press, 1988.

------------, "Toward a Hermeneutic of the Idea of Revelation," *Harvard Theological Review* 70, no. 1-2 (January-April 1977), 1-37.

ii) Secondary Sources

CLARK, Steven H., *Paul Ricoeur*, Critics of the Twentieth Century, London: Routledge, 1990.

DICENSO, James J., *Hermeneutics and the Disclosure of Truth: A Study in the Work of Heidegger, Gadamer, and Ricoeur*, Charlottesville: University Press of Virginia, 1990.

DORNISCH, Loretta, *Faith and Philosophy in the Writings of Paul Ricoeur*, Problems in Contemporary Philosophy 29, Lewiston, New York: Edwin Mellen Press, 1990.

GADAMER, Hans-Georg, *Truth and Method*, trans. J. Weinsheimer and D. Marshall, 2nd edition, New York: Crossroad, 1989.

GERHART, Mary, "Time and Narrative," *Journal of Religion* 69 (1989), 92-98.

------------, *The Question of Belief in Literary Criticism: An Introduction to the Hermeneutical Theory of Paul Ricoeur*, Stuttgart: Akademischer Verlag Hans-Dieter Heinz, 1979.

IHDE, Donald, "Toward the Philosophy of Language *Freud and Philosophy: An Essay On Interpretation*," *Hermeneutic Phenomenology: The Philosophy of Paul Ricoeur*, with a Foreward by Paul Ricoeur, Evanston: Northwestern University Press, 1971, 131-166.

JOHNSTON, R.E.C., *From an Author-Oriented to a Text-Oriented Hermeneutic: Implications of Paul Ricoeur's Hermeneutical Theory for the Interpretation of the New Testament*, 2 vols., Ph.D. Dissertation in Religious Studies, Katholieke Universiteit te Leuven, Faculty of Theology, 1977.

KLEMM, David E., *The Hermeneutical Theory of Paul Ricoeur: A Constructive Analysis*, Toronto: Associated University Presses, 1983.

KLEMM, David E. and Willam Schweiker, eds., *Meanings in Texts and Actions: Questioning Paul Ricoeur*, Studies in Religion and Culture, Charlottesville and London: University Press of Virginia, 1993.

LAWLOR, Leonard, "Intersection: A Reading of Ricoeur's 'Eighth Study' in *The Rule of Metaphor*" in *Imagination and Chance: The Difference Between the Thought of Ricoeur and Derrida*, New York: State University of New York Press, 1992, 29-50.

ORMISTON, Gayle L. and Alan D. Schrift, eds., *The Hermeneutic Tradition: From Ast to Ricoeur*, Albany: State University of New York Press, 1990.

PALMER, Richard E., *Hermeneutics: Interpretation Theory in Schleiermacher, Dilthey, Heidegger, and Gadamer*, Evanston: Northwestern University Press, 1969.

REAGAN, E., *Studies in the Philosophy of Paul Ricoeur*, Athens: Ohio University Press, 1979. Includes: David PELLAUER, "The Significance of the Text," 98-114.

VAN DEN HENGEL, John, *The Home of Meaning: The Hermeneutics of the Subject of Paul Ricoeur*, Washington: University Press of America, 1982.

K. Other

AURBACH, Erich, *Mimesis: The Representation of Reality in Western Literature*, trans. W.R. Trask, Princeton: Princeton University Press, 1953.

BOYD, John D., *The Function of Mimesis and its Decline*, Cambridge: Harvard University Press, 1968.

BROWN, Frank Burch, "Transfiguration: Poetic Metaphor and Theological Reflection," *The Journal of Religion* 62, no. 1 (January 1982), 39-56.

CASSIRER, E., *Philosophie des formes symboliques*, Paris: Édition de Minuit, 1972.

420

FRYE, Northrop, *Anatomy of Criticism: Four Essays*, Princeton: Princeton University Press, 1971.

GEERTZ, Clifford, *The Interpretation of Cultures: Selected Essays*, New York: Basic Books, 1973.

GREIMAS, Algirdas Julien, *Sémantique structural: Recherche de méthode*, Paris: Larousse, 1966.

GUERRIÈRE, Daniel, ed., *Phenomenology of the Truth Proper to Religion*, New York: State University of New York, 1990.

HIRSCH, Eric Donald, *The Aims of Interpretation*, Chicago: University of Chicago Press, 1976.

ISER, Wolfgang, *The Act of Reading: A Theory of Aesthetic Response*, trans. from German, Baltimore: The Johns Hopkins University Press, 1978.

-------, *Reader-Response Criticism: From Formalism to Post-Structuralism*, trans. from German, Baltimore: The Johns Hopkins University Press, 1981.

JAUSS, Hans Robert, *Toward an Aesthetic of Reception*, trans. from German by Timothy Bahti with Introduction by Paul de Man, Minneapolis: University of Minnesota Press, 1982.

JEANROND, Werner G., *Text and Interpretation as Categories of Theological Thinking*, New York: Crossroad, 1988.

KEARNEY Richard, "Ideology and Religion: A Hermeneutic Conflict," in *Phenomenology of the Truth Proper to Religion*, New York: State University of New York, 1990, 126-45.

LANGAN, Thomas, *The Meaning of Heidegger: A Critical Study of an Existential Phenomenology*, New York: Colombia University Press, 1959.

LEOCADIO GARASA, Delfin, *Los Géneros literarios*, 2nd edition, Buenos Aires: Editorial Columbia, 1971.

LÉVI-STRAUSS, Claude, *Anthropologie structurale*, Paris: Plon, 1958.

MERLEAU-PONTY, Maurice, *Phénoménologie de la perception*, Paris: Gallimard, 1945.

PREMINGER, Alex, ed., *Princeton Encyclopedia of Poetry and Poetics*, Princeton: Princeton University Press, 1974.

SCHNEIDERS, Sandra, *The Revelatory Text: Interpreting the New Testament as Sacred Scripture*, San Francisco: Harper, 1991.

SCHULTZ, Karla L., *Mimesis on the Move: Theodor W. Adorno's Concept of Imitation*, New York: Peter Lang, 1990.

SPARIOSU, Mihai, *Mimesis in Contemporary Theory*, Philadelphia and Amsterdam: John Benjamins Publishing Co., 1984.

STRELKA, Joseph P., ed., *Theories of Literary Genre*, University Park: Pennsylvania State University Press, 1978.

VEYNE, Paul, *Comment on écrit l'histoire*, Paris: Seuil, 1971.

VOGELS, Walter, *Reading and Preaching the Bible: A New Semiotic Approach*, Background Books 4, Wilmington, DE: Michael Glazier, Inc., 1986.

--------------, *Interpreting Scripture in the Third Millennium: Author - Reader - Text*, Novalis Theological Series, Ottawa: Novalis, 1993.

WELLEK, René and Austin Warren, *Theory of Interpretation*, 3rd edition, San Diego: Harcourt, Brace, Jovanich, 1977.

INDEX